THE MIDDLE EAST AND NORTH AFRICA ON FILM

GARLAND REFERENCE LIBRARY
OF THE HUMANITIES
(VOL. 159)

THE MIDDLE EAST AND NORTH AFRICA ON FILM
An Annotated Filmography

Marsha Hamilton McClintock

GARLAND PUBLISHING, INC. • NEW YORK & LONDON
1982

Library of Congress Cataloging in Publication Data

McClintock, Marsha Hamilton
  The Middle East and North Africa on film.

  (Garland reference library of the humanities ;
v. 159)
  Includes indexes.
  1. Near East—Film catalogs.   2. Africa, North—
Film catalogs.   I. Title.   II. Series.
DS44.M43   1982   011'.37   82-12114
ISBN 0-8240-9260-0

Printed on acid-free, 250-year-life paper
Manufactured in the United States of America

TO MY SISTER,
CAROL

THE MIDDLE EAST AND NORTH AFRICA ON FILM

TABLE OF CONTENTS

vii

ACKNOWLEDGMENTS

I would like to thank all those who have assisted in the preparation of the filmography. Financial assistance was provided, in part, through the Ohio State University Small Research Grants Program and the Friends of the Ohio State University Libraries. The Libraries have also provided research and travel time necessary to finish the filmography.

Special thanks to the many individuals and institutions who provided information or made their collections accessible. These include James Falk, recently of the Middle East Institute in Washington, D.C. for sharing the Institute's film files and loaning MEI intern George Smalley to view and annotate over thirty films on Israel; the staff of the Turkish Tourism Office, the Moroccan Tourism Office in New York, and Ilan Ziv of Icarus Films for allowing me to view their entire Middle East collections; Maryann Chach of the Educational Film Library Association in New York and the staff of the National Archives in Washington, D.C., Museum of Broadcasting and Donnell Film Library of the New York Public Library.

Acknowledgment must be made of the Abraham F. Rad Jewish Film Archive of the Institute of Contemporary Jewry at the Hebrew University of Jerusalem. Director Geoffrey Wigoder has graciously allowed the extensive holdings of the collection dealing with Israel and Palestine to be included in the filmography. The Library of Congress Motion Picture, Broadcasting and Recorded Sound Division has been particularly helpful and I would like to thank Emily Sieger and Barbara Humphrys, Adriane Bailey and Joseph Balian and Section Head Patrick J. Sheehan for their assistance. Pre-publication exchange of information from Ellen-Fairbanks Bodman's The World of Islam, Images and Echoes: a critical guide to films and recordings, has also improved the filmography's location and holdings coverage.

Finally I would like to recognize the assistance of Nancy Rubin, Anna Taylor, Fusun Pasinler, Kathleen Wear and Leonard Mathless and the encouragement of Frances C. Morton, Gay Henderson, Dona Straley, Nancy Heaslip and John McClintock in the five year project.

Marsha Hamilton McClintock
Columbus, Ohio
March 1982

INTRODUCTION

The Middle East and North Africa on Film: An Annotated Filmography is
a comprehensive listing of films and videotapes produced between 1903 and
January 1980. English, English sub-titled and silent films in 8, super 8,
16 and 35 mm and tapes in 1/2, 3/4 and 2 inch formats are included.
     It would be hoped that films on almost every subject would be available
for classroom or research purposes. However, this is not the case. Certain
subjects, such as nomadism and kibbutz life, are documented on film and tape
in a proportion far greater than their relative importance or population in
the Middle East or North Africa, while topics such as urbanization, law and
government, treatment of minorities or population control, though covered in
the print literature, are unrepresented in film and tape. Part of the reason
for this is the medium itself which, by nature, relies on interesting, exotic
or colorful images to capture the imagination of the viewer. Films, in
general, attempt to express ideas through images and rely secondarily on
words. Several of the better films viewed by the author have been silent or
contain a musical soundtrack without narration. Restrictions on the medium,
therefore, tend to emphasize that which is attractive and colorful or conver-
sely, offensive and repulsive to the viewing audience.
     A major factor in viewing films and videotapes, or in reading print
materials, is to understand the reason for the work's existence. Just as
writers produce literary works to present a particular viewpoint or philosophy, documentary and educational film-makers produce non-fiction works
covering art, anthropology, history, and sociology, although their motives
may not be as frequently discussed.
     Specifics to consider when criticizing documentary and educational
films and tapes include knowing the producer of a film, the date a film was
made, who is the intended audience and if possible, why the film was made.
A specific viewpoint or philosophical approach in a film can be assumed, in
part, by considering the source. The Palestine Liberation Organization
wishes to stress social, educational and political benefits it provides for
Palestinian refugees, the Ministry of Education and Culture of Israel wishes
to show benefits of travel and immigration to Israel, the Turkish Tourism
Office wishes to show the natural beauty and colorful traditions of Turkey.
Church groups promote particular religious beliefs, governments have images
they wish to project, organizations wish to raise funds and publicize projects, and individuals wish to show how capitalism, socialism, communism,
nationalism or pacifism are the only possible choice for a better future.
     Political, economic and social conditions at the time of production
greatly influence documentaries, newsreels, news broadcasts and television
presentations. Although adult viewers consider these factors when watching
television, children viewing educational films in a classroom setting should
be reminded that information found in teaching materials may be out of date,
misleading or biased.
     Knowledge of the Middle East and North Africa has never been extensive
in the English-speaking world. Understanding and interpretation of ideas

and events change radically every few years. Therefore, another factor to consider when viewing films and tapes is the date or approximate date of production. When a film or tape is placed in the context of major political and economic events of its day, its presentation and purpose become more apparent and its research value, as a reflection of current opinion, increases.

Attention should be directed not only at why a film or tape is made but also at how it is made. Restrictions of the medium itself dictate parameters for the film-maker. On the credit side is the ability to document colors, sounds, actions and nuances of expression and to lend them added meaning and context through a thoughtful, well researched narration. On the debit side is the tendency to film scenes which attract or repel rather than those which are representative but are not spectacular. Add the ability to make something seem what it is not through improper editing, poor research and inadequate writing.

All film-makers combat difficult conditions in producing films and tapes about the Middle East or North Africa. In addition to the high cost of production are political problems and difficulty in obtaining permission to film or tape on location. Language and cultural barriers are added to traditional production problems for non-local crews. The difficulty and expense of the medium should be considered as well as the changing technologies in sound, color and photography in the period between 1903 and 1980, approximately the history of film.

After considering the purpose of the film-maker and restrictions of the medium itself, a viewer might do well to approach any production with equal amounts of healthy skepticism and appreciation for what has been accomplished. It is necessary to remember, that which could only be labeled a biased piece of propaganda may also be a valuable research tool and primary resource.

The filmography is intended primarily for educators, libraries and archives, film-makers, film societies and scholars doing research in every aspect of Middle East or North African studies. Information has been gathered through on-site examination of library and archive holdings, printed catalogs and by questionnaire. Every attempt has been made to locate as many films and tapes as possible but, unfortunately, some have been missed. Additions and alterations or information on films and tapes produced after January 1980 would be greatly appreciated. Please direct correspondence to the Middle East Librarian, The Ohio State University Libraries, 1858 Neil Avenue Mall, Columbus, Ohio 43210.

Many complete collections are represented in the filmography. The Middle East and North Africa on Film contains the complete holdings acquired prior to January 1980 of the Library of Congress Motion Picture, Broadcasting and Recorded Sound Division in the area of Middle East and North African studies. These were obtained through on-site examination of the Division's massive card catalog and related print catalogs. With few exceptions, all films and tapes of the Library of Congress have been viewed by the author. Complete listings for the Museum of Broadcasting in New York and the Donnell Film Library of the New York Public Library are also listed.

Other collections have been added in their entirety from information obtained solely through printed catalogs. This category includes the Abraham F. Rad Jewish Film Archive on the Hebrew University campus in

Jerusalem and the Encyclopaedia Cinematographica Collection housed at the
University of Pennsylvania. Holdings of numerous institutions, such as the
United Nations, and literally dozens of university libraries across the
country are represented as are the collections of tourist offices,
embassies, organizations, such as the Anti-Defamation League of B'nai B'rith
and the League of Arab States, and a wide variety of private and commercial
film distributors. This information was obtained from sources including the
National Union Catalog, the NICEM catalogs, individual catalogs of universities, colleges, archives and distributors and in-house holdings lists.
Numerous films were also made available for viewing by tourist offices and
distributors.

Only a few titles represent four major collections. The holdings of
the National Archives in Washington, D.C. are extensive but ill-organized
for systematic subject searching. A few examples of U.S. Army Signal Corps.
films and the Universal Newsreel Collection are included, but these represent only a fraction of the Archives' Middle East and North African
holdings. The same is true for the ABC, CBS and NBC television networks.
Titles included produced by the networks are those held at the Library of
Congress or the Museum of Broadcasting. Close examination of the networks'
archives was, unfortunately, not feasible.

The under-utilization of film and tape resources for research can be
remedied through increased organization, documentation and description of
available films and their contents. Films and tapes are a fragile resource,
dependent on relatively few archives and university collections for their
continuing existence. Improvements in the technology of film preservation
and duplication have not made it possible or economically feasible to
transfer all unstable nitrate stock films to safety stock and repair or
reprint warped and color deteriorated prints. Early classic films and primary research materials will disappear forever unless efforts are made to
identify and preserve those which deserve preservation. This has been
accomplished in one instance with the film GRASS: A NATION'S SEARCH FOR
LIFE. This early documentary of the Bakhtiari tribe's annual migration
across the Zagros Mountains contains some of the most spectacular footage of
that much filmed trek. Many additional early films deserve the same attention and consideration.

If the reader wishes to examine the purpose behind this filmography in
order to better comprehend its philosophical orientation, then it is this;
an attempt to document, describe and locate as many films and tapes as
possible dealing with the Middle East and North Africa of use to an English-
speaking audience, in the hope that films and tapes of value for research,
education and documentation be recognized and preserved before they can no
longer be located or physically saved. For some, such as the films formerly
distributed by the embassies of Afghanistan, Iran and Libya and for
newsreels lost in the fire at the National Archives, and for many others, it
is already too late.

HOW TO USE THE FILMOGRAPHY

The filmography is divided into two main sections. The first covers general subjects such as the Arab-Israeli conflict which cannot be attributed to any one country in the Middle East and North Africa. The second section lists films and videotapes dealing with 26 Middle East and North African countries with subject sub-divisions. General subjects, countries and country sub-divisions are outlined in the Table of Contents. Use the title/series index to locate the number of a specific film or videotape or browse the Table of Contents for films by country or subject.

HOW TO READ EACH FILM OR VIDEOTAPE ENTRY

Each entry includes as much information, such as running time and date of production, as could be located for that film. Only entries followed by an asterisk * have been viewed by this author and are fully verified. All other information has been taken from the National Union Catalogs, NICEM Catalogs, major film library and archive catalogs, distributors' lists, promotional literature and filmographies in anthropology, art, and other subject areas.

TITLE
The title of each film or videotape, listed in capital letters, is the one most often used in catalogs. Alternate titles are listed in the annotation. Cross references for multi-titled films may be found in the title/series index. Spellings are those used in the film itself or in a majority of catalogs in which the film is listed. No effort has been made to cross reference British spellings in the index or provide arbitrary uniform spelling of place names.

YEAR
The year listed is the earliest known production or release date. Many catalogs list production dates decades apart for the same film leading to the assumption that one title is actually many. Every attempt has been made to indicate reprints, releases and variant dates, if known.

RUNNING TIME
Running time, or length, of each film is rounded to the nearest minute. Actual projection time may vary by several minutes. Running times listed should be used as a guide to film length.

SOUND OR SILENT
This filmography encompasses films from 1903 to 1980 and includes silent as well as sound films. Certain collections, such as the Encyclopaedia Cinematographica anthropological collection, although recently produced, are silent.

COLOR OR BLACK AND WHITE (B&W)

Some films and videotapes are released in both color and black and white editions. Color or b&w in the entry means both are available and although the distributor should be notified which print is preferred, it should be remembered that individual distributors may only have one choice available.

FILM SIZE

A most important piece of information is film size. Many older films, theatrical releases and foreign-produced documentaries were produced in 35 mm. Most educators, film societies and community groups have access only to 16 mm equipment. This should be kept in mind when ordering films. In some cities, local theaters may rent facilities to view 35 mm films. 8 or 16 or 35 mm in the entry means various film sizes are available and the distributor should be notified which is preferred.

PRODUCTION, RELEASE AND DISTRIBUTION INFORMATION

The producer, production company, or corporation responsible for the release of a film is given, if known. Production credits can only be assumed verified for entries followed by an asterisk. Distributor information is for the last known distributor. Some films may no longer be available from that source and should always be checked well in advance of a film or videocassette showing. Distributors may rotate their stock of films, remove a title from circulation, or allow another distributor to pick up a film. Updates in distributor information will be gladly accepted by the author.

SERIES AND INDENTIFICATION NUMBERS

Film and television series are listed in parenthesis after production information. Other films in a series may be located through the title/series index. Identification numbers, also in parenthesis, are given for cataloging and verification purposes. Numbers preceded by NUC indicate a National Union Catalog identification number. Those preceded by LC are Library of Congress numbers. Local accessions numbers for the Library of Congress and National Archives are listed after those locations to facilitate location of films in those collections.

LOCATIONS

As many permanent locations as are known are listed for each entry. Locations are listed in nearly full form making reference to a list of location abbreviations unnecessary. Locations are those given in college, university, library and archive catalogs. Not all locations given are in the United States; please refer to the producer and distributor index at the end of the filmography for the last known address of distributors and holding locations. It should be noted that many major holding locations, such as the Library of Congress, Abraham F. Rad Jewish Film Archive, and the Museum of Broadcasting, do not circulate films. Arrangements may be made in some cases to view films on the premises. In certain collections, copies of films and videocassettes may be purchased if this does not violate copyright. Most colleges and universities will loan films for a nominal fee for educational purposes and all locations listed allow educators or scholars the right to view films or videocassettes for research purposes. Please write or call libraries and archives for their indivi-

dual policies concerning loan, copying privileges and in-house viewing
policies. Allow sufficient time to work in major archives and film
libraries as in-house viewing facilities are often limited and booked far
in advance.

*
An asterisk means the film has been viewed by the author and all information given in the entry, except for locations, has been verified.

ANNOTATIONS
Annotations for films and videocassettes viewed by the author provide a
review of subject matter of the film, a subjective comment concerning
quality, the intended audience and condition of the print viewed.
Annotations for films not viewed are a composite of information gathered
from distributors, production companies, annotations from holding location
catalogs, and reference works. As no distributor will tell a potential
purchaser a film may be terrible or dated, these unverified annotations
should be read more carefully.

TITLE/SERIES INDEX
The title index at the back of this volume lists in alphabetical order all
titles of films and videocassettes, numbered and unnumbered series, and
titles known to be within those series. The index also includes cross
references to alternate titles. The numbered titles in the index refer to
the numbered full descriptions in the main text. Each film has only one
number and is listed only once in the main text although it may be listed
under variant forms in the index.

DISTRIBUTOR AND LOCATION INDEX
A futile attempt has been made to give the most recent address for distributors and locations listed in this filmography. Undoubtedly, some are
already out of date. Consult recent telephone directories, directory
assistance or your school or college audio-visual department for current
telephone numbers and addresses. It is recommended that film loan and
rental be done through an institution's audio-visual department, if
possible. Otherwise allow plenty of time to locate a film and distributor
before scheduling a showing.

THE FILMOGRAPHY

TRAVELOGS

1   THE ARAB MIDDLE EAST
     1955 / 16 min / sound / b&w / 16 mm
     Edward Levonian. Released by McGraw-Hill Book Co. (Lands and
     Their People series) (NUC Fi 55-248) Director-Photographers
     - J. Michael Hagopian, Edward Levonian. Locations: Iowa
     Films / Library of Congress (FBA 67) / U. of Illinois. *
         Very good, if dated, introduction to Jordan, Syria, Iraq
         and Lebanon. Begins with early Sumerian, Babylonian and
         Phoenician times and traces the contributions of the
         Romans, Jews, Christians, Arabs, Crusaders, Turks, British
         and French to the history and culture of the area.
         Profiles agriculture, city life, the impact of oil, and
         modernization on the Middle East. Includes information on
         Palestinian refugees in each of the four countries. Ends
         with a promise of future progress for the area. Intended
         for elementary-junior high school audiences. Film re-
         issued in 1970 under same title.

2   CARONIA MEDITERRANEAN CRUISE
     1962 / 30 min / sound / color / 16 mm
     Cunard Steamship Co. Formerly released to adult organiza-
     tions in the U.S. by Sterling Movies. (NUC FiA 62-1530)
         General travelog. Filmed abroad the Cunard Line ship
         Caronia, as it cruises the Mediterranean. Includes scenes
         of Bucharest, Rome, Istanbul, Yalta, Tangiers, Athens,
         Venice, Naples, Barcelona, Haifa and Lisbon. To promote
         tourism.

3   (DELHI, KASHMIR, TAJ MAHAL, KARACHI, PERSIAN GULF,
     BASRA, ALONG THE SHATT AL-ARAB)
     (c. 1930?) / 13 min / silent / b&w / 16 mm
     Source of footage unknown. Location: Library of Congress
     (FAA 4928) *
         Miscellaneous footage. Shows street scenes of various
         cities, mountains near Kashmir, tourists, various methods
         of transportation on land and water, stone-cutters and
         other craftsmen, dhows on the Gulf carrying European
         passengers and dwellings made of woven straw mats. The
         footage is interesting but of relatively low quality.
         Unspecified locations make this of use primarily for
         historic, library film footage purposes. Does contain
         good close-ups of faces but other footage is of home movie
         quality.

4   FARAWAY PLACES...IN PICTURES
1972 / 28 min / sound / color / 16 mm
Eastman Kodak Co.
> General subject travelog. Covers Turkey, Iran, Afghanistan, India, Nepal, Pakistan, Ceylon and Thailand.

5   GLIMPSES OF THE NEAR EAST
1940 / 11 min / silent / b&w / 16 mm
Eastman Kodak Co., Teaching Films Division. Released by Encyclopaedia Britannica Films. (NUC FiA 54-4130)
> Follows ancient trade routes from Europe to Asia. Shows various scenes of everyday Near Eastern life including farming, bazaars, handicraft production, madrasahs or schools, and street scenes. Signs of modernization are evident in shots of large city universities and modern architecture.

6   JACQUELINE KENNEDY'S ASIAN JOURNEY
1962 / 30 min / sound / color / 16 mm
U.S. Information Agency. Made for Hearst Metrotone News. Released for public educational use through the U.S. Office of Education in 1963. (NUC FiE 63-283) Location: Library of Congress (FEA 1340-42)
> Traces the 1962 tour of India and Pakistan by Jacqueline Kennedy and her sister, Lee Radziwill. Includes tours of the Taj Mahal, Jaipur, the Khyber Pass and Shalimar Gardens.

7   MEDITERRANEAN CRUISE
1955 / 30 min / sound / color / 16 mm
Made by John Bransby Productions. Released by Cunard Steamship Co. through Sterling Films. Kodachrome. (NUC FiA 55-391) Location: Library of Congress (FAA 2131-32)
> Highlights of a 66 day cruise of the Mediterranean. Stops include Tangiers, Athens, Larnaca, and various sites in Israel.

8   MEDITERRANEAN MEMORIES
1939 / 9 min / sound / b&w / 16 mm
20th Century-Fox Film Corp. Released for educational purposes by Teaching Film Custodians. (Magic Carpet series) (NUC FiA 52-4520)
> General travelog of various Mediterranean tourist sites. Includes Gibraltar, the Italian Riviera, Naples, Athens, and Algiers. Intended for elementary school audiences.

9   MIDDLE EAST CARAVAN
1965 / 14 min / sound / color / 16 mm
Alitalia Airlines. Made by Wilding Films. Credits: Director - Mel London, Writer - Sheryl London. (NUC FiA 67-2169)
> General travelog of the Middle East. Includes scenes of Egypt, Israel and Saudi Arabia.

10   THE MIDDLE EAST: CROSSROADS OF THREE CONTINENTS
     1955 / 14 min / sound / color or b&w / 16 mm
     Coronet Instructional Films. Credits: Educational
     Collaborator - Joseph E. Spencer. (NUC Fi 55-239)
     Locations: Brigham Young U. / Iowa Films / Kent State U. /
     Library of Congress (FBA 1086) / Syracuse U. / U. of
     Illinois / U. of Michigan / U. of Nebraska. *
         Examines three factors which have shaped the Middle
         East; geographic location between the East and West,
         scarcity of water, and discovery of oil. Shows benefits
         resulting from oil including improved housing and higher
         revenues. Includes views of Istanbul, Basra, Baghdad,
         Cairo, Tel Aviv, Jerusalem, and Tehran. Intended for
         junior-high school audiences. The film is dated, over-
         simplifies political situations and tends to be tedious.

11   THE MIDDLE EAST: A REGIONAL STUDY
     (n.d.) / ? / sound / 16 mm
     Eye Gate House.
         General overview of the Middle East. No other infor-
         mation available.

12   ODYSSEY IN ASIA
     1968 / 12 films, 25 minutes each / sound / color / 16 mm
     BBC-TV, London and Odyssey Productions. Released in the
     U.S. by Time-Life Films. (Asia series, no. 12) Credits:
     Narrator - Lowell Thomas. (LC 70-714394)
         Follows two young men on their travels from the Bosporus
         in Turkey, through Syria, Afghanistan and India to the
         Himalayas, Bangkok, Hong Kong and Japan. Shows their
         final destination of Mt. Fuji, Japan.

13   ROAD TO KATMANDU
     1979 / 58 min / sound / color / 16 mm
     Exodus Productions. *
         A group of 25 young people drive 11,000 miles by truck
         from Istanbul to Katmandu. Gives a close-up view of the
         Middle East from the road. Includes scenes of the Kurds
         in eastern Turkey, the Dasht-e-Lut in Iran, Baluchis,
         Herat, Bamian, Isfahan, Persepolis, Lahore, Kashmir,
         Delhi, Benares and Nepal. At times, narration is hard to
         hear but this detracts little from the film. Shaky pho-
         tography, a result of filming under difficult conditions,
         makes the viewer feel a part of the expedition. Useful
         for scenes of varied peoples and settings in the Middle
         East and Asia, although little background information is
         given. For senior high school to adult audiences.

14   SUDDEN SUMMER
     (n.d.) / 31 min / sound / color / 16mm
     Sterling Educational Films. Distributed by CCM Films, Inc.
         General travelog of the Middle East. Shows bazaars, rem-
         nants of Phoenician civilization and Crusader fortresses
         and palaces.

3

15　VISIT TO THE ARAB WORLD
　　(n.d.) / 20 min / sound / color / 16 mm
　　Arab Information Office, Washington, D.C.
　　　　General overview of several Arab states.　No other
　　　　information available.

16　WAC'S IN PALESTINE AND CAIRO
　　1944 / 7 min / silent / b&w / 16 mm
　　U.S. Signal Corps.　Location: National Archives (111 ADC
　　1357)
　　　　WWII footage of Palestine and Cairo.　Non-combatant
　　　　subjects.

LANGUAGE AND WRITING

17　ARABIC CALLIGRAPHY
　　1974 / 20 min / sound / color / 16 mm
　　Telmissany Brothers Productions.　Location: Ministry of
　　Information, Arab Republic of Egypt.
　　　　Describes the early development of Arabic script.
　　　　Shows various styles including Kufic, scriptive and
　　　　Diwani on Islamic reliefs and old manuscripts.　Discusses
　　　　the aesthetic aspects of proportion and style and the
　　　　relationship between Arabic calligraphy and art.

18　ARABIC X-RAY FILM
　　1962 / 15 min / sound / b&w / 16 mm
　　Haskins Laboratories.　Location: Penn. State U.
　　　　Studies standard colloquial Damascan Arabic by using x-
　　　　rays of native Arabic speakers pronouncing phrases.
　　　　Shows the relationship between phonetics and the physical
　　　　process of word formation.　Illustrates how plain and
　　　　emphatic consonants are formed.

19　KINGS WRITE TOO
　　1956 / 29 min / sound / b&w / 16 mm
　　New York University.　Released by NET Film Service.
　　(Yesterday's World)　Credits: Narrator - Casper J. Kraemer.
　　(NUC FiA 58-1474)
　　　　Discusses the correspondence of ancient Near Eastern
　　　　kings found in the Egyptian village of El-Amama, covering
　　　　such topics as politics, marriage and finance.

20　PAPYRUS
　　1957 / 10 min / sound / color / 16 mm
　　Dept. of Cinema, U. of Southern California.　(Milestone in
　　Writing series)　Credits: Narrator - Frank Baxter.　Eastman
　　color.　(NUC FiA 59-1134)
　　　　Shows techniques for making paper from the papyrus plant
　　　　used by the ancient Egyptians from instructions left by
　　　　the Roman historian Pliny.　Discusses the significance of
　　　　papyrus for ancient Egyptian civilization.　Intended for
　　　　elementary-junior high school audiences.

21   THE PEN AND THE WORLD
      1956 / 29 min / sound / b&w / 16 mm
      New York U. Released by NET Film Service. (Yesterday's
      World) Credits: Narrator - Casper J. Kraemer. (NUC FiA
      58-1617)
          Shows the writing system used by the ancient Egyptians
          around 4000 B.C. Describes how the Rosetta Stone was
          used to decipher Egyptian hieroglyphics and opened a new
          world of inscriptions carved on monuments throughout
          Egypt. Discusses how the ancients lived and thought.

ARCHEOLOGY AND ANCIENT HISTORY

22   ANCIENT CITIES OF THE EAST
      1962 / 20 min / sound / color / 16 mm
      Jackson Bailey and Carl Russell. Made by Gene Blakely.
      Released by AV-ED Films. (NUC FiA 62-1648) Location: U. of
      Illinois.
          Looks at the cities of Beirut, Damascus, Istanbul, Cairo,
          Athens and Delphi, with specific reference to Biblical
          locations. Traces early history and trade routes. Shows
          life is in some ways as it was centuries ago, while in
          other ways is very modern. Attempts to capture the fla-
          vor of the Middle East.

23   ANCIENT WORLD INHERITANCE
      1946 / 10 min / sound / color or b&w / 16 mm
      Coronet Instructional Films. Credits: Educational collabora-
      tor - Richard A. Parker. Kodachrome. (NUC FiA 53-75)
      Locations: American Museum of Natural History / Brigham
      Young U. / Kent State U.
          Describes ancient civilizations of the Mediterranean
          area. Shows how writing, organized law, agriculture,
          weaving, papermaking, and glass blowing were developed by
          the ancient Egyptians, Babylonians, Assyrians and others.
          Intended for junior-senior high school audiences. Re-
          issued in 1962 under same title.

24   THE ARCHAEOLOGIST AND HOW HE WORKS
      1965 / 19 min / sound / color / 16 mm
      International Film Bureau. Location: U. of California
      Extension Media Center.
          Follows the preparation, methodology and post-expedition
          work of an American archaeological expedition to an early
          agrarian settlement in the Tigris-Euphrates valley.
          Describes basic archaeological principles, methods, and
          findings.

25   ASCENT OF MAN, PART 2 - THE HARVEST OF THE SEASONS
      1974 / 52 min / sound / color / 16 mm or 3/4" videocassette
      BBC-TV, London. Distributed in the U.S. by Time-Life Films.
      (Ascent of Man series) Credits: Producer-Director - Adrian

Malone, Writer-Narrator - Jacob Bronowski. Locations: Kent
State U. / Museum of Broadcasting (T77:0466) / Penn. State
U. / U. of California Extension Media Center / U. of
Nebraska. *
This episode of the award winning television series
describes the relationship between sedantary agricultural
societies and nomadic tribes in ancient times. Bronowski
traces the origins of agriculture, the domestication of
animals, the formation of villages, the development of
wheat and the invention of the plow. Shot on location in
the Persian city of Sultaniyeh and in Jericho. Impressi-
vely photographed. Recreates a nomadic invasion on horseback, shows equestrian wargames and shows the yearly
migration of the Bakhtiari tribe. Literate narration and
beautiful production make the program suitable for television or classroom use. Discussion guide and Spanish
language version of the film are available for educational purposes. Highly recommended.

26   THE DESCENT OF THE HORDES
1977 / 58 min / sound / color / 16 mm
Documents Associates. (Crossroads of Civilization series)
Credits: Narrator - David Frost.
Shows the effect of the Mongol invasions. Describes the
empires built by the Mongols spreading from Korea to
Hungary. Emphasizes the pattern of ruthless conquest
followed by absorption of the invaders into the subject
peoples. Describes resulting dynasties such as the
Timurids, remembered for their contributions in the arts
and architecture.

27   DIGGING FOR THE HISTORY OF MAN. PART 1: 3000 B.C.- 600 A.D.
1970 / 40 min / sound / color / 16 mm
H.J. Hossfeld. Released by Time-Life Films. Credits: Music
- Enno Dugend. (LC 74-714466) Also issued in the series:
The History of Art.
Shows archeological excavations of Babylonian, Sumerian,
Hittite, Greek and Roman sites. Emphasizes art and
architecture.

28   DIGGING FOR THE HISTORY OF MAN. PART 2: 700 A.D.
1970 / 15 min / sound / color / 16 mm
H.J. Hossfeld. Released by Time-Life Films. (LC 78-714467)
Also issued in the series: The History of Art.
Shows archeological excavations of the ruins at a
Sassanian site, occupied in the closing days of the
Persian empire. Emphasizes architecture.

29   ECCE HOMO
1969 / 54 min / sound / color / 16 mm
NBC News in cooperation with the Radio and Television
Commission of the Southern Baptist Convention. Released by
NBC International. (Southern Baptist Hour, television

series) (LC 76-702340)
   Traces the history of man through artifacts found in
   Egypt, Greece, Jordan and Israel. Includes pieces now in
   the British Museum. Discusses the past of the human race
   and its potential.

30   HEROES OR HISTORY?
   1979 / 58 min / sound / color / 16 mm
   Documents Associates. (Crossroads of Civilization series)
   Credits: Narrator - David Frost.
      Describes the fall of the Persian empire to the armies of
      Alexander the Great. Shows the clash between Persian and
      Greek culture and the new world order established by
      Alexander.

31   ONCE CREATIVE HANDS
   (n.d.) / 22 min / sound / color / 16 mm
   Arab Information Center, New York.
      Without narration. Traces history of ancient and modern
      civilizations of the Middle East through art and arti-
      facts.

32   ORIENTAL INSTITUTE
   (n.d.) / 10 min / sound / b&w / 16 mm
   I.R. Rehm. Released by International Film Bureau. (Chicago
   Museum series) (NUC FiA 57-1065)
      Shows finds from archeological expeditions exhibited at
      the Oriental Institute of the University of Chicago.
      Included are artifacts from ancient Egypt, Babylonia,
      Persia and Palestine.

33   THE TRIUMPH OF ALEXANDER THE GREAT
   1955 / 28 min / sound / b&w / 16 mm
   CBS Television. Released by Young America Films. Reduction
   print of the 35 mm version. Distributed by McGraw-Hill.
   (You Are There, television series) Credits: Producer -
   William Dozier, Writer - Jeremy Daniel, Narrator - Walter
   Cronkite. (NUC FiA 56-149) Locations: Kent State U. / Penn.
   State U.
      A re-enactment of Alexander the Great's campaign of 324
      B.C. in which the Babylonian rebellion was suppressed.
      Describes Alexander's dream of a unified world. Intended
      for junior-senior high school audiences.

MEDIEVAL HISTORY AND ISLAMIC CIVILIZATION

34   AVICENNA
   (c. 1963) / 25 min / sound / b&w / 16 mm
   American Friends of the Middle East. Formerly distributed
   by the Embassy of Lebanon.
      Follows the life and contributions of the medieval Arab
      philosopher Ibn Sina, commonly known in the west as
      Avicenna.

35   THE BYZANTINE EMPIRE
      1959 / 14 min / sound / color or b&w / 16 mm
      Coronet Instructional Films. Credits: Educational collabora-
      tor - Crane Brinton. (NUC FiA 59-1144) Locations: Brigham
      Young U. / Indiana U. / Kent State U. / Library of Congress
      (FBA 166) / Syracuse U. / U. of Arizona. *
         Profiles the city of Istanbul, formerly called
         Constantinople, or Byzantium. Describes how the city
         served as the capital of the Eastern Roman Empire, which
         continued to flourish a thousand years after the fall of
         Rome. Shows architectural remains of the various periods
         in the city's history. Describes life, trade, arts and
         the ethnic composition of the Byzantine empire.
         Emphasizes the significance of the Greek Orthodox Church
         in the Byzantine empire but shows the fall of the city to
         the Turks in 1453 brings a new chapter to the history of
         the city. Photography, shot for the most part in Greece
         and Turkey, if of relatively low quality. Originally
         intended for junior-senior high school audiences, the
         narration is more suited to elementary school audiences.

36   GEBER, THE GREAT ARABIAN ALCHEMIST
      1975 / 33 min / sound / color / 1/2" videocassette
      Educational Communications Center, East Stroudsburg State
      College. Robert Foery and Willian Torop. No other infor-
      mation available.

37   THE GIFT OF ISLAM
      (c. 1970) / 28 min / sound / color / 16 mm
      Graham Associates. Credits: Producer - Ray Graham. Locations:
      Embassy of Libya / League of Arab States / Middle East
      Institute. *
         Spectacular visual display of art, architecture and
         crafts from Iran through the Arab countries to Turkey.
         Shows styles and technological developments in the
         medieval Middle East were adopted by European countries,
         providing a cross-fertilization of arts and thought.
         Describes the transferral of classical Greek philosophy
         and science to Europe by way of the Arab countries
         via North Africa and Spain. Shows the influence of
         Islamic civilization on the court of Sicily, on astronomy in
         India, architecture in Spain, and in mathematics, medi-
         cine, writing and education. One of the best films in
         the genre of Islamic contributions to medieval civiliza-
         tion. Beautifully filmed. Intended for high school to
         adult audiences. Recommended.

38   HISTORY AND CULTURE, PART 1
      1965 / 28 min / sound / color / 16 mm
      National Film Board of Canada. Distributed in the U.S. by
      McGraw-Hill. Locations: Boston U. / Florida State U. / Kent
      State U. / Michigan State U. / Middle East Institute / Penn.
      State U. / Syracuse U. / U. of Illinois / U. of Wisconsin /

8

U. of South Carolina.
Describes the geography and history of the Middle East
and North Africa. Covers the beginnings of Islam in the
7th century, Muhammad and his teachings, the Arab
conquests and the contribution of Islamic civilization in
art and architecture. Describes the following period of
decline and isolationism and concludes with newsreel
footage of circa 1964 personalities. Intended for senior
high school audiences.

39   ISLAM AND THE SCIENCES
1978 / 23 min / sound / color / 16 mm
Peter de Normanville. Distributed by Phoenix Films. Credits:
Director - Douglas Gordon. Location: U. of Washington.
Centered around the London Science Museum exhibit during
the 1976 World of Islam Festival in London. Traces
contributions of the Islamic world from the 7th century
to the present in the sciences, including mathematics,
geometry, art, architecture, medicine, astronomy,
geography and cartography. Discusses the transfer of
Greek and Roman knowledge to the west via the Islamic
world. Shows how Islam still influences all aspects of
life and culture in the Middle East. An interesting
topic, well covered.

40   THE LEGACY OF ISLAM
October 19, 1975 / 30 min / sound / color / 3/4" videocassette
(Lamp Unto My Feet, television series) Credits: Executive
Producer - Pamela Ilott, Producer-Narrator - Warren Wallace,
Guest Consultant - Richard Ettinghausen. Location: Museum
of Broadcasting (T78:0350)
A look at art of the Islamic world by art historian
Richard Ettinghausen. Includes examples of 16th century
weapons, lustre paintings on glass, carved wood panels,
maps and manuscript pages. Discusses the relationship
between art and Islam. Shows examples of Iranian,
Turkish, Indian and Arab art, architecture, tiles and
jewelry.

41   MIDEAST - PIONEERS OF SCIENCE
(c. 1977) / 20 min / sound / color / 16 mm
Vocational and Industrial Films, Ltd. Distributed by BFA
Educational Media. (Mideast series) Credits: Producer - John
Seabourne, Director-Writer - Richard Ashworth, Educational
Consultant - George Rentz. Location: Florida State U. /
Library of Congress (FBA 7739) / Syracuse U. / U. of
Illinois / U. of Texas at Austin / U. of Wisconsin. *
Looks at some rarely seen medieval Arabic scientific
manuscripts and explores the scientific heritage left by
Islamic and earlier Middle Eastern civilizations.
Contributions such as the 60 minute hour, air con-
ditioning, the decimal point, and other innovations in
medicine, mathematics, astronomy, geography and chemistry

are described. The transfer of Greek and Roman knowledge
through the Islamic empire is also traced. Intended for
junior-senior high school audiences.

42 THE MOSLEM WORLD: BEGINNINGS AND GROWTH
1965 / 11 min / sound / color or b&w / 16 mm
Coronet Instructional Films. Credits: Educational
Collaborator - I. James Quillen. (NUC Fi 53-299)
Locations: American Museum of Natural History (b&w print) /
Arizona State U. / Boise / Boston U. / Brigham Young U. /
Iowa Films / Kent State U. / Library of Congress (FAA 4299)
/ Oklahoma State U. / Penn. State U. / Syracuse U. / U. of
Colorado / U. of Connecticut / U. of Illinois / U. of Kansas
/ U. of Michigan.
  Re-issue of the 1953 film: THE MOHAMMEDAN WORLD:
  BEGINNINGS AND GROWTH. Shot on location in Baghdad,
  Mosul, Damascus, Cairo and Jerusalem. Traces the history
  of Islam and the Muslim world. Intended to give junior-
  senior high school students a general introduction and
  understanding of the Middle East, it instead re-inforces
  stereotype images and offers simplistic explanations of
  complex events.

43 REVIVAL: CULTURAL IMAGES OF ARAB AND ISLAMIC
CIVILIZATIONS
(n.d.) / 30 min / sound / color / 16 mm
Reflex Films, Ltd. Distributed by the League of Arab
States. No other information available.

44 RIVERS OF TIME
(c. 1962) / 26 min / sound / color / 16 mm
Iraq Petroleum Co. Made by Film Centre. Released by
Contemporary Films. Distributed by McGraw-Hill.
(McGraw-Hill Textfilms series) Credits: Producer-Writer -
Sinclair Road, Director - William Novik, Narrator - Alan
Adair. (LC 74-703657) Locations: Kent State U. / Middle
East Institute / U. of Arizona / U. of Michigan / U. of
Washington / U. of Wisconsin / Washington State U.
  Uses models and artifacts found in the Baghdad Museum to
  describe the contribution of early Mesopotamian cultures
  to the fields of writing, art and architecture.
  Describes the contributions to Iraqi and world civiliza-
  tion made during the Islamic period. Emphasis is on
  contributions adapted by the west, especially in the
  sciences.

45 SUN, SAND AND SEA
(c. 1963) / 30 min / sound / b&w / 16 mm
Contemporary Films. Distributed by McGraw-Hill.
(Crossroads of the World series)
  Reviews the cultural background of the Middle East and
  North Africa. Covers Islam, Muhammad and his teachings,
  and the contributions of Arab-Islamic civilization to the
  western world.

10

46   THE TRADITIONAL WORLD OF ISLAM: THE KNOWLEDGE
      OF THE WORLD
      1978 / 30 min / sound / color / 16 mm
      Stephen Cross. Institutional Cinema Service. Distributed
      by Exxon Corporation. (Traditional World of Islam series)
      Locations: Arizona State U. / Boston U. / Florida State U. /
      Kent State U. / Indiana U. / Los Angeles Public Library /
      Michigan Dept. of Education State Library Service / Middle
      East Institute / Minnesota Film Library Circuit / New Jersey
      State Library / Penn. State U. / Purdue / State AV Center,
      Wichita, Kansas / Syracuse U. / U. of Arizona / U. of
      California - Berkeley / U. of California - Los Angeles / U.
      of Colorado / U. of Connecticut / U. of Illinois / U. of
      Michigan / U. of Minnesota / U. of North Carolina / U. of
      Texas at Austin / U. of Wisconsin.   *
          Classic film dealing with Islamic intellectual acheive-
          ments. Well produced, visually stunning film. Covers
          Islamic thought, education and medicine from the 8th cen-
          tury to the present. Shows al-Azhar University in Cairo,
          the oldest university in the world, and early obser-
          vatories and hospitals. Looks at early Islamic medicine
          through manuscripts and traditional medicine in Pakistan
          today. Discusses the high value Islam places on reason,
          learning and the search for knowledge. Traces the
          transfer and preservation of ancient Greek and Roman
          learning in the Islamic empire before it reached Europe
          during the Renaissance. Intended for junior high school
          to adult audiences. Beautifully made. Highly recom-
          mended.

47   WE, THE ARABS
      (n.d.) / 18 min / sound / b&w / 16 mm
      Arab League. Distributed by the Arab Information Office,
      Washington, D.C.
          Discusses the contribution of Arab and Islamic civiliza-
          tion throughout history in the arts and sciences.

MODERN HISTORY - THE TWENTIETH CENTURY

48   THE ARAB WORLD'S PAST AND FUTURE
      (c. 1960?) / 47 min / sound / b&w / 16 mm
      Encyclopaedia Britannica. (Arnold Toynbee Lecture Series,
      no. 8)
          Another in the series of filmed lectures by historian
          Arnold Toynbee. Examines current problems and possibili-
          ties in the Arab world.

49   BRITISH WAR REVIEWS
      1935 / 82 min / silent / b&w / 35 mm
      British newsreel footage, revised by the U.S. Signal Corps.
      (Signal Corps. Misc. Film, no. 451) Location: National
      Archives (111M451)
          British newsreel footage from World War I. Includes sce-

nes of Palestine, Jerusalem, Turkish prisoners of war,
Allenby and the British in Mesopotamia. Reels 4,5 and 6
include footage of the Middle East campaign in WWI.

50   FOCUS ON THE MIDDLE EAST
October 28, 1970 / 14 min / sound / b&w / 16 mm
Hearst Metrotone News. (Screen News Digest, v. 13, no. 3)
(LC 72-700575) Location: Library of Congress (FBB 1487) /
U. of Wisconsin.
    Attempts to explain Soviet interest and aid to Middle
Eastern countries in light of historic Russian interest
in a warm water port. Traces Russia's ties to the region
from the time of Peter the Great in the 1700's to the
present time. Intended for junior-senior high school
audiences.

51   HISTORY AND CULTURE. PART 2
(c. 1962) / 28 min / sound / b&w / 16 mm
National Film Board of Canada. Distributed by McGraw-Hill
Book Co. (The Middle East series) Listed in some catalogs
as HISTORY AND CULTURE OF THE MIDDLE EAST,
PART 2. Locations: Boston U. / Florida State U. / Kent
State U. / Middle East Institute / Penn. State U. / Syracuse
U. / U. of Illinois / U. of South Carolina / U. of
Wisconsin.
    A continuation of the film HISTORY AND CULTURE,
PART 1 which left the Middle East in a period of isola-
tionism and decline in the post-medieval period. Begins
with the conquest of Egypt by Bonaparte in 1789 and
examines the period of British and French colonial rule.
Traces the growth of Arab nationalism before, during and
after the two world wars. Discusses the effect of the
establishment of Israel in 1948 on the Arab world.

52   HOW THE BRITISH HANDLE AMMUNITION IN THE MIDDLE EAST
1942 / 14 min / sound / b&w / 16 or 35 mm
U.S. Signal Corps. (Film Bulletin, no. 61) Location:
National Archives (111 FB 61). No other information
available.

53   IMPACT OF THE WEST
1963 / 30 min / sound / b&w / 16 mm
McGraw-Hill Textfilms. (Crossroads of the World series)
Formerly distributed by Contemporary Films.
    Covers western expansion into the Middle East from
Bonaparte's invasion of Egypt through the period of
British colonial rule to the 1960's.

54   THE MEDITERRANEAN WORLD
1961 / 23 min / sound / color or b&w / 16 mm
Made by Clifford J. Kamen and Encyclopaedia Britannica Films.
(NUC FiA 62-855) Locations: Brigham Young U. / Iowa Films /
Kent State U. / Library of Congress (FCA 3013) / Penn. State

U. / Syracuse U. / U. of Illinois.
   Examines ancient civilizations of the Middle East through
   surviving art and architecture. Shows contemporary
   Greece, Italy and Arab countries and discusses earlier
   contributions of these countries which led to the western
   European Renaissance. Profiles the building of the Suez
   Canal, which marked a substantial increase in
   Mediterranean sea trade. Describes the Middle East pri-
   marily as a source of products, a trade zone or a trouble
   spot in the eyes of western nations. Discusses the development of Arab nationalism and regional rivalries.
   Intended for junior-senior high school audiences.

55   THE MIDDLE EAST
     1959 / 25 min / sound / color / 16 mm
     International Film Foundation. Made by Julien Bryan. Credits:
     Producer-Writer - William Claiborne. (NUC FiA 66-1766)
     Locations: Boston U. / Brigham Young U. / Indiana U. / Iowa
     Films / Iowa State U. / Kent State U. / New York Public
     Donnell Film Library / New York U. / Penn. State U. /
     Portland State College / Purdue / Syracuse U. / U. of
     Arizona / U. of Colorado / U. of Connecticut / U. of
     Illinois / U. of Iowa / U. of Michigan / U. of Minnesota /
     U. of Nebraska / U. of Texas at Austin / U. of Utah / U. of
     Washington / U. of Wisconsin.
        Begins with an animated sequence which gives an over-
        view of the 5,000 year cultural heritage of the Middle
        East. Shows the rise and fall of civilizations up to
        the present day. Outlines the conflicts, poverty, lack
        of water and other problems which have shaped the area.
        Describes the Middle East as the home of the three major
        monotheistic religions, and traces the impact of reli-
        gion, oil and water on life in the Middle East.

56   THE MIDDLE EAST: AFTER CONQUERORS, CIVILIANS
     (n.d.) / ? / sound / 16 mm
     Life Education Program. Location: New York U.
        Shows the influence of Britain on the Middle East around
        the turn of the 20th century. Discusses the effect of
        tourism, trade and religious pilgrimage to holy sites.
        Profiles the rise of Arab nationalism and beginnings of
        oil exploitation.

57   THE MIDDLE EAST: BACKGROUND FOR CONFLICT
     (c. 1970?) / ? / sound / 16 mm
     Distributed by the Social Studies School Service.
        Describes the Middle East as a trouble spot due to the
        Arab-Israeli conflict and related problems.

58   THE MIDDLE EAST: EARLY ROOTS OF BITTERNESS
     1970 / ? / sound / color / 16 mm
     Life Education Program.
        Brief history of the Middle East up to the Ottoman period
        at the turn of the twentieth century.

59   THE MIDDLE EAST: A NEW STORM CENTER
      (c. 1970) / ? / sound / color / 16 mm
      Life Education Program. (Life Education Program series, no.
      75)
          Follows the period covered in THE MIDDLE EAST: EARLY
          ROOTS OF BITTERNESS. Looks at the region from the
          decline of the Ottoman empire at the end of the twentieth
          century to the creation of the state of Israel in 1948.

60   A NEW DAY IN THE MIDDLE EAST
      1956 / 25 min / sound / b&w / 16 mm
      Arab Information Office, Washington D.C.   Location: U. of
      Utah.
          Details the growth of Arab nationalism during the period
          of British and French colonial rule in the Middle East.

61   OPERATIONS IN MESOPOTAMIA, 1914 TO 1918
      (c. 1928?) / 40 min / silent / b&w / 35 mm
      U.S. Signal Corps. (Signal Corps Misc. Film, no. 483)   Location:
      National Archives (111 M 483)
          Footage of the Middle East campaign during the First
          World War.   Useful for historic and library footage film
          purposes.   A title sheet is available to describe con-
          tents of the film.

62   PROBLEMS OF THE MIDDLE EAST
      1958 / 21 min / sound / color / 16 mm
      Atlantis Productions. (Important Areas of Our World series)
      Credits: Producer-Director-Writer-Photographer - J. Michael
      Hagopian. (NUC FiA 59-348) Location: Library of Congress
      (FBA 1299)
          Shows the geographic setting of the Middle East has
          effected its history and cultures.   Traces the rise and
          fall of ancient Middle Eastern civilizations and the
          problems these cultures have bequeathed to their descen-
          dants.   Describes current problems including the treat-
          ment of minorities, the question of Israel, and problems
          in the development of agriculture, education and
          industrialization.

63   PROBLEMS OF THE MIDDLE EAST
      1967 / 22 min / sound / color / 16 mm
      Atlantis Productions. Revised version of the 1958 film of
      the same title. (LC 77-704660) Locations: Arizona State U. /
      Boston U. / Library of Congress (FBA 9491) / U. of
      California Extension Media Center / U. of Nebraska / U. of
      Washington.
          Covers much of the same material as the 1958 version.
          Uses music and art work to illustrate points.   Contains
          some factual errors.   Presents the state of Israel as
          a fulfillment of prophecy.   Intended for junior-senior
          high school classes.

64   SOVIET BUILD-UP IN THE MIDDLE EAST
      (c. 1975?) / 25 min / sound / color / 16 mm
      NBC Television. Distributed by Alden Films. Location: Gratz
      College.
         Shows the Soviet interest in the Middle East and describes
         Soviet supply of weapons to Egypt. Film was produced, or
         was meant to cover period, prior to expulsion of Soviet
         advisors from Egypt in 1972.

65   WHAT'S THE MIDDLE EAST ALL ABOUT?
      February 22, 1975 / 30 min / sound / color / 3/4" videocassette
      CBS News. (CBS News Special Report for Young People) Credits:
      Producer-Writer - Walter Lister, Director - Vern Diamond,
      Reporter - Christopher Glenn. Location: Library of
      Congress. *
         Overview of the geography and climate of the Middle East,
         followed by a profile of Israel. Describes the area as
         the birthplace of the three great monotheistic religions.
         Outlines the problems involved with early Jewish immigra-
         tion to the area culminating in the Arab-Israeli wars.
         Egypt is described, followed by a negative sketch of
         Syria. Jordan is shown as a country full of Palestinian
         refugees. Discusses the issue of terrorist activities
         within Israel, and the possible use of oil by Saudi
         Arabia for political purposes. Describes Iraq only as a
         country which has border disputes with Iran. Iran is
         shown as a country building up its arms while developing
         educational and industrial programs. Intended for an
         audience of children on television, this program is full
         of over-simplifications, misleading statements and heavy
         biases against particular Arab countries. Few issues are
         shown to be more than one-sided as in the statement
         describing the Arab-Israeli conflict as the "Arabs want
         the land where some Jews live." A slanted presentation.

POLITICS AND GOVERNMENT

66   THE ARAB WORLD'S CASE AGAINST THE WEST
      (c. 1963?) / 73 min / sound / b&w / 16 mm
      Encyclopaedia Britannica. (Arnold Toynbee Lecture Series,
      no. 9)
         One of a series of filmed lectures delivered by Arnold
         Toynbee dealing with current problems in the Middle East,
         their causes and possible solutions.

67   THE ARAB WORLD'S REACTION AGAINST WESTERN RULE
      (c. 1963?) / 79 min / sound / b&w / 16 mm
      Encyclopaedia Britannica. (Arnold Toynbee Lecture Series,
      no. 10)
         For other titles in this lecture series, check
         title/series index.

15

68   CASE STUDIES IN THE NEW NATIONALISM: THE ARAB WORLD
      1959 / 29 min / sound / b&w / 16 mm
      Metropolitan Educational Television Association, New York.
      Released by NET Film Service. (Nationalism and Colonialism
      series) (NUC FiA 61-531)
          Describes the rise of Arab nationalism in diverse settings
          from republican to monarchical Arab countries. Shows
          anti-colonial and anti-Zionist feelings have led to an
          upsurge in nationalism. Profiles Egypt under Nasser.

69   CHARLES MALIK, PART 1-4
      1960 / 4 programs, 30 min each / sound / b&w / 16 mm
      WQED, Pittsburgh. Released by National Educational
      Television and Radio Center. (Heritage series XXII) (NUC Fi
      67-466) Location: Library of Congress (FBA 4623-27) *
          Charles Malik, then President of the General Assembly of
          the United Nations and Ambassador from Lebanon, talks
          with Dr. Richard Cottam and T.F.X. Higgins in a four
          part broadcast. Part 1 includes a discussion by Malik of
          the general role of a diplomat and the relationship with
          the home government. Part 2 focuses on the problems of
          underdeveloped and newly independant nations. Part 3
          deals specifically with the advancement of Middle Eastern
          countries during the 1950's. Covers such topics as the
          effect of educating Arab students abroad, the rela-
          tionship of Islam to science and development,
          industrialization, modernization, the status of women in
          the Arab world, and the role of the intellectual class in
          Middle Eastern development. Part 4 deals with truth in
          world diplomacy, and the success and failure of the U.S.
          in transmitting its ideals to the Arab world. Material
          is too slowly paced and general to be useful for
          classroom purposes. Produced for television.

70   THE CONTEST FOR POWER
      1964 / 28 min / sound / b&w / 16 mm
      National Film Board of Canada. Distributed by McGraw-Hill,
      and by Contemporary Films. (Crossroads of the World)
      Location: Kent State U.
          Shows the diversity of political systems and types of
          government found in the Middle East, from monarchies to
          socialist states. Profiles Saudi Arabia, Egypt, Jordan,
          Iran and Iraq.

71   COWBOYS
      (c. 1973) / 25 min / sound / b&w / 16 mm
      Nefertare Films. Distributed by Icarus Films. Credits:
      Producer-Director - Sami Salamani. *
          One of the few films distributed in the U.S. by an Arab
          film-maker. Without narration. This composite of film
          clips and montage evokes the feeling of the U.S. "cowboy"
          mentality of violence and over-simplification which has
          led to U.S. crises in the Middle East and Vietnam.

Production varies in quality, not a complimentary film.
Illustrates an alternative view concerning U.S.-Arab
world relationships.

72　THE DILEMMA OF THE U.S. FOREIGN POLICY IN THE
MIDDLE EAST
1955 / 40 min / sound / b&w / 16 mm
U.S. Dept. of Defense.　Made by the U.S. Dept. of the Army.
(Order no. OC 5) (NUC FiE 56-192)
　　George B. Allen, then Asst. Secretary of State, describes
　　the Middle East and North Africa as regions significant
　　to the U.S.　Describes how their political and social
　　problems effect U.S. policy, especially in the area of
　　defense.　Ernest K.　Lindley of Newsweek Magazine serves
　　as moderator at an officer's conference, the setting of
　　Allen's speech.

73　EYE WITNESS TO HISTORY
1959-60 / 150 min / sound / b&w / 16 mm
CBS News.　Location: National Archives (No. 200.313)
　　A series of collected programs showing then President
　　Eisenhower's visits to Pakistan, Turkey, Afghanistan,
　　Iran, Tunisia, and Morocco.　Reels 2,3 and 4 show the
　　President speaking to the heads of state of these
　　countries and delivering various speeches.　Of use as
　　library film footage and for texts of speeches delivered.

74　FROM THE EARTH TO THE MOON
1977 / 43 min / sound / color / 16 mm or videocassette
5A Film Productions.　Distributed by Icarus Films.　Credits:
Producer-Director - Boubkaer Adjali.　*
　　Another in the short list of Arab films distributed in
　　the U.S.　Presents current world issues from an Arab
　　socialist viewpoint. The film-maker attempts to show how
　　nationalization of industries should be viewed not as an
　　extremist act but as a country attempting to regain
　　control of its own resources.　Other issues, including
　　oil, U.S. and Soviet relations with the Middle East,
　　distribution of wealth, power, the space program, and the
　　arms race are handled in the same way.　The taking of
　　land during the Six-Day War from Arab countries is
　　described as acceptable to western countries while
　　attempts by the inhabitants to regain it are considered
　　terrorism.　For college and adult audiences.　Good pre-
　　sentation of a frustrated, Third World intellectual's
　　view of the world and the fear that little can be done to
　　change it.

75　MEETING OF REVOLUTIONARIES (GATHAFI, NASER, NUMEIRI)
(c. 1965?) / sound / b&w / 16 mm
Embassy of Libya.　No other information available.

76　(MIDDLE EAST CONFERENCES)
1945 / 25 min / silent / b&w / 35 mm

War Department. (Bureau of Public Relations film, no. 1042)
Location: National Archives (107.1042)
   Footage of WWII conferences held in the Middle East.
   Includes coverage of Yalta and Alexandria.

77   THE MIDDLE EAST, POWDERKEG ON THE RIM OF THE
     COMMUNIST WORLD
     1952 / 28 min / sound / b&w / 16 mm
     Time, Inc. (March of Time, television series) Credits:
     Narrator - Westbrook Van Vorhees. (NUC Fi 53-180) Location:
     Library of Congress (FCA 785) *
        March of Time correspondents discuss the role of the U.S.
        in the Middle East. Views the area as a battlefield bet-
        ween Soviet and western influence. General Naguib, of
        the then recent 1952 Egyptian officer's coup, discusses
        the need to correct inequalities in land ownership and
        control corruption in Egypt. Prime Minister Mossadegh of
        Iran speaks against British involvement in Iranian oil
        production. Ayatollah Kashshani condemns western
        imperialism in Iran. A Tudeh, or Iranian communist
        party, rally is shown in Tehran. Profiles development in
        the Kuwaiti oil fields. Discusses the question of a
        divided Jerusalem in Israel followed by an interview with
        Charles Malik describing the Palestinian refugee problem
        in Lebanon. Interesting look at the state of the Middle
        East in 1952. Though originally intended for television
        audiences, this film could now be used for instructional
        as well as archival purposes. Library of Congress print
        is showing signs of deterioration.

78   THE MIDDLE EAST PROBLEM WITH DR. CHARLES MALIK
     1957 / 46 min / sound / b&w / 16 mm
     U.S. Dept. of Defense. Made by U.S. Dept. of the Army.
     (Order no. WA 5) (NUC FiE 57-120) Credits: Moderator -
     Ernest K. Lindley.
        Ernest K. Lindley of Newsweek magazine moderates a
        discussion between students at the National War College
        and Charles Malik, then Foreign Minister of Lebanon.
        Questions covered include; should the U.S. send troops
        to the Middle East to maintain stability, will Arab sta-
        tes accept Israel, what is the Soviet threat to the
        Middle East, and should the Suez Canal be placed under an
        international authority.

79   MID-EAST CRISIS -- AREA QUIET PENDING US-SUMMIT TALK
     July, 1958 / 7 min / sound / b&w / 16 mm
     Universal News. Location: National Archives (31-59-1).
        This is one short entry taken from the large Universal
        newsreel collection held at the National Archives.
        Describes events and personalities of the day. Outlines
        the state of the Middle East pending peace talks in
        1958. Useful for library footage or archival purposes.

18

80　NEW VOICES
　　(c. 1960) / 28 min / sound / b&w / 16 mm
　　National Film Board of Canada. Distributed by Contemporary
　　Films and by McGraw-Hill.
　　　　Shows the influence of Islam and Arab nationalism on
　　　　emerging African countries. Suggests African leaders
　　　　view politicians in Muslim nations and the U.N. as
　　　　examples of contemporary international leaders.

81　OUR NAVY IN THE NEAR EAST
　　(c. 1922) / 39 min / silent / b&w / 35 mm
　　Bureau of Navigation. Location: National Archives (24.24)
　　　　Documentation of the U.S. Naval presence in the Middle
　　　　East after WWI. Of use for historic and library footage
　　　　purposes.

82　PLANNING OUR FOREIGN POLICY: PROBLEMS OF THE
　　MIDDLE EAST
　　1955 / 21 min / sound / b&w / 16 mm
　　Encyclopaedia Britannica Films, in collaboration with the
　　Brookings Institution. Distributed by Iowa Films. No other
　　information available.

83　THE ROUGH ROAD TO FREEDOM
　　(c. 1960) / 30 min / sound / b&w / 16 mm
　　Distributed by Contemporary Films. (Crossroads of the World
　　series)
　　　　Shows the influence of western technology on the Middle
　　　　East and North Africa. Profiles the rising group of
　　　　young revolutionary leaders such as Bourguiba, Nasser and
　　　　Kassem, who are attempting to reorganize and modernize
　　　　their countries.

84　SUGGESTIONS FOR PEACE SETTLEMENTS IN ALGERIA
　　AND PALESTINE
　　(c. 1963?) / 75 min / sound / color / 16 mm
　　Encyclopaedia Britannica (Arnold Toynbee Lecture Series,
　　no. 12)
　　　　Another in the series of filmed lectures by Arnold
　　　　Toynbee. Discusses major problems of the Middle East and
　　　　examines possible solutions.

85　THE UPSURGE OF NATIONALISM
　　1964 / 26 min / sound / b&w / 16 mm
　　National Film Board of Canada. Released in the U.S. by
　　McGraw-Hill. (The Middle East series) (NUC FiA 66-1505)
　　Locations: Kent State U. / Middle East Institute / Ministry
　　of Education and Culture, Jerusalem / Syracuse U.
　　　　Gives a brief overview of Arab history from the 7th cen-
　　　　tury to World War I. Gives an analysis of the effects of
　　　　western domination on the area. Shows scenes of moder-
　　　　nization in Turkey, the nationalization of the Suez
　　　　Canal, and declarations of independence in Syria, Libya

and the Sudan. Discusses problems with water, energy, and technology which effect these countries. Similar in coverage to THE ROUGH ROAD TO FREEDOM, no. 83.

86   VISITORS IN SPAIN
      1957 / 12 min / sound / b&w / 35 mm
      Universal News. Location: National Archives (7617x3, 7631x9, 7691x8, 7615x5, 7646x8, 7654x7, 7615x11, 7682x11)
           Shows the state visits to Spain of several Middle Eastern leaders including King Saud, King Hussein, Premier Bourguiba, the Shah of Iran, and President Chamoun. Another Universal Newsreel of use for library footage purposes.

87   WHY PROMPT PEACE SETTLEMENTS IN ALGERIA AND PALESTINE ARE IN EVERYBODY'S INTEREST
      (c. 1963?) / 69 min / sound / b&w / 16 mm
      Encyclopaedia Britannica. (Arnold Toynbee Lecture Series, no. 11)
           Another in the series of filmed lectures by Arnold Toynbee. Deals with problems in the contemporary Middle East and possible solutions.

SOCIOLOGY AND ETHNOLOGY

88   ARAB IDENTITY: WHO ARE THE ARABS?
      1975 / 26 min / sound / color / 16 mm
      Learning Corporation of America. Made by Yorkshire Television. Distributed by Marlin Motion Pictures, Ltd. (The Arab Experience series) (LC 76-700279) Locations: Boston U. / Indiana U. / Kent State U. / Syracuse U. / U. of Minnesota / U. of Missouri / U. of South Carolina / U. of Wisconsin.
           Attempts to capture the feeling of diversity of peoples in the Arab world. Shows sophisticated city dwellers as well as desert nomads. Includes scenes of Mecca - the center of the Islamic world, modern Lebanon, poverty in Syria, and Israel. Issues covered include cultural stress resulting from modernization and secularization, western influence, and the Palestinian refugees. Intended to dispel the idea of a homogeneous Arab world for junior high school through adult audiences.

89   THE ARAB - WHO IS HE
      1973 / ? / sound / color / 16 mm
      Anti-Defamation League of B'nai B'rith. (Dateline Israel, 1973 series)
           Dr. Shimon Shamir, Director of the Shiloah Institute on Arab Studies at Tel Aviv University in Israel, discusses the life style of the average Arab man on the street.

90   CAMEL: LAST OF THE WILD
      1977 / 22 min / sound / color / 16 mm

20

Macmillan. Credits: Narrator - Lorne Greene. Location: Syracuse U.

A film for general audiences. Shows the characteristics of the camel which adapt it to desert life. The camel's hump, flexible nostrils and padded hoofs are described as adaptations to a severe climate. Discusses the use of camels by man and the relationship between nomads and the camel.

91   THE DESERT
1942 / 8 min / silent / b&w / 16 mm
Filmsets, Inc. (NUC FiA 54-3241)
Shows the life style of nomads in the Arabian, Saharan and Gobi deserts. Includes scenes of oases and Bedouin camps.

92   HEALING HANDS OF MEDICO
1968 / 14 min / sound / color / 16 mm
Care, Inc. Made by Fred Niles Communication Center. (LC 70-707864)
Describes the work of the dedicated doctors and nurses of Medico. Profiles their work in Afghanistan, Algiers, Malaysia and Tunis. Intended to show services provided by Medico worldwide.

93   JEWS IN ARAB LANDS
(c. 1970?) / ? / sound / color / 16 mm
Distributed by National Jewish Community Relations Advisory Council. No other information available.

94   LOVE THOSE ARABS
(c. 1977) / 28 min / sound / color / 16 mm
Distributed by International Films, Inc.
Film comes with a case packet for further information. Listed as being on the general theme of viewing the Arabs as a neglected ethnic group. Intended audience unknown.

95   THE MIDDLE EAST
1954 / 14 min / sound / color or b&w / 16 mm
Encyclopaedia Britannica. (NUC Fi 52-225) Credits: Educational Collaborator - Clarence W. Sorenson. Locations: Brigham Young U. / Kent State U. / Library of Congress (FBA 1085) / Syracuse U. / U. of Michigan / U. of Wisconsin.   *
Begins with a short geographic introduction to the Middle East, then follows the lives of three "average" Middle Eastern families. Mustafa and his family live in a tra-ditional village and raise sheep. The men cultivate the fields with a camel-drawn plow while the women bake bread and prepare meals. Ali the Bedouin is shown living in a tent, tending herds of sheep. The nomadic family migra-tes from one water hole to the next with their camels. Youssef lives in the city and makes his living as a merchant. Intended to show elementary-junior high school

audiences the three major life styles of the Middle East.
Simple and somewhat dated representation but a fair
introduction for lower level students.

96   MIDDLE EAST - JOURNEY INTO THE FUTURE
      1978 / 15 min / sound / color / 16 mm
      Barr Films.
          Shows the problems experienced in supporting a family in
          a small village in the Middle East. Tawfiq cannot sup-
          port his family as a farmer so he takes another job 400
          miles away in the oil fields, a sacrifice he makes for
          his growing children. Discusses the pattern of absence
          of male family members who have sought employment in
          other parts of the Arab world or Europe. Shows their
          families remaining at home.

97   MIDDLE EAST: MOSAIC OF PEOPLES
      1979 / 21 min / sound / color / 16 mm
      Coronet Films. Vladimir Bibic. (Middle East series)
      Locations: Syracuse U. / U. of Illinois.
          Traces various peoples of the Middle East from ancient
          Sumerian, Babylonian and Persian cultures to the present.
          Describes their contributions to the modern Middle East.
          Differences in religious and ethnic origins are covered
          in this well photographed overview. Intended for junior
          high school audiences.

98   MIDEAST: LAND AND PEOPLE
      1977 / 20 min / sound / color / 16 mm
      BFA Educational Media. Made by Vocational and Industrial
      Films, Ltd. (Mideast series) Credits: Producer - John
      Seabourne, Director-Writer - Richard Ashworth, Educational
      Consultant - George Rentz. Location: Florida State U. /
      Library of Congress (FBA 7736) / Syracuse U. / U. of Kansas
      / U. of Texas at Austin.
          Visually attractive look at the diversity of life and
          peoples in the Middle East from the cafes of Cairo to the
          Saudi desert. Islam is shown as the link which unifies
          Arabs, Turks and Iranians, so diverse in other aspects of
          life. The mixture of traditional and modern life, and
          the split between nomad, villager and city dweller are
          also profiled. Intended for junior high school through
          adult audiences.

99   MOSLEM FAMILY
      (1966?) / 11 min / sound / color / 16 mm
      Julien Bryan. International Film Foundation. Location:
      Library of Congress. No other information available.

100   THE MOSLEM WORLD: LANDS OF THE CAMEL
      1936 / 15 min / silent / b&w / 16 mm
      Harmon Foundation. (The Moslem World series) (NUC FiA
      54-3695) Location: National Archives (200 HF 171)

Listed in some catalogs as: LANDS OF THE CAMEL.
General, silent introduction to the Muslim world showing
scenes of nomads, bazaars, crafts, schools, mosques and
street scenes. Changes due to modernization are apparent
even in this 1930's footage.

101   (NOMADS)
      (1960?) / 20 min / silent / color / 16 mm
      Peace Corps. Location: National Archives (RG 362-74)
      Peace Corps. footage of nomads in an unnamed location.

102   PROJECT MIDDLE EAST, PART 1, THE PLACE
      (c. 1977?) / 20 min / sound / color / 3/4" videocassette or
      16 mm. New York State Education Dept. and the United
      Nations Children's Fund. Distributed by the United Nations
      and by Great Plains National ITV Library.
      Available in English, French or Italian soundtracks.
      Documents the work of UNICEF in helping children in four
      Arab countries. Scenes include an Egyptian urban health
      care center, vocational training in the Yemen, and work
      in Syria and Jordan. The changing role of women, health
      conditions, the economy and the importance of water are
      also discussed. A general introduction intended for ele-
      mentary-junior high school audiences.

103   PROJECT MIDDLE EAST, PART 2, THE PEOPLE
      (c. 1977?) / 20 min / sound / color / 16 mm
      United Nations Children's Fund. Distributed by the United
      Nations.
      Documents UNICEF programs which deal with women and
      children in the Arab Middle East. Scenes of Egypt, Syria,
      Jordan, and the Yemen are shown. Available in English, French
      and Italian soundtracks.

104   THE REFUGEES
      1957 / 8 min / sound / color / 16 mm
      United Jewish Appeal. Location: Jewish Agency Film Archive.
      Fund raising film. Uses color slides to portray the
      conditions of Jews living in Hungary, Egypt and the Arab
      countries.

105   REPORT FROM THE NEAR EAST
      1953 / 27 min / sound / color / 16 mm
      Foreign Operations Administration. Made by International
      Film Foundation. (NUC FiE 56-198)
      Documents the work of American technicians and advisors
      in Egypt, Iran and Jordan. Shows the effect their work
      has had on the life of farmers, villagers and nomads.

106   SHIP OF THE DESERT
      1933 / 5 min / silent / b&w / 16 mm
      Eastman Teaching Films. Released by Encyclopaedia
      Britannica Films. (NUC FiA 55-147) Location: Library of

23

Congress (FAA 4606)

Short film showing the camel and its relationship to the nomad. Portrays the camel as a beast of burden and a mode of transportation.

107 TALEB AND HIS LAMB
1975 / 16 min / sound / color / 16 mm
Barr Films. Made by Ami Amitai. (LC 75-703856)

Intended for juvenile audiences. Tells the story of a small Bedouin boy who cares for one of the lambs in his father's herd of sheep.

108 A TENT IS NOT ENOUGH
(c. 1974?) / 14 min / sound / b&w / 16 mm
Anti-Defamation League of B'nai B'rith. Credits: Director - Herman J. Engel, Narrator - Joseph Julian. Locations: Abraham F. Rad Jewish Film Archive / Jewish Agency Film Archive.

Produced for World Refugee Year. Shows the problems of refugees in the Arab countries and Israel created by twenty years of war. Describes some programs of international organizations to aid refugees.

109 TO BE A JEW IN ARAB LANDS
1975 / 28 or 46 min / sound / color / 16 mm
David Goldstein. Gal Productions. Distributed by Alden Films. Location: Gratz College. *

Two versions of this film are available, 28 minutes or 46 minutes in length. Also listed in some catalogs as: THE DHIMMIS: TO BE A JEW IN ARAB LANDS. Advertised as a "startling documentary". Illustrates the history of the Jews in Arab lands by showing a sad succession of discrimination, property seizure and deportation. Begins in the 7th century and continues through the Ottoman period to the twentieth century. Includes moving narrations of individuals who have suffered discrimination. Strong statement which stresses poor relations and ignores historical periods of peaceful coexistence. Serves as a bitter condemnation of the Arab and Turkish treatment of Jews.

110 THE TRADITIONAL WORLD OF ISLAM: MAN AND NATURE
1978 / 30 min / sound / color / 16 mm
Stephen Cross. Institutional Cinema Service. (Traditional World of Islam series) For more information, see no. 46.

Another in the beautifully filmed series covering varying aspects of life in the Islamic world from a Sufic, or mystical Islamic point of view. Describes the unity of Islamic culture with nature. Shows this manifested in the use of natural materials in architecture, careful water management, and use of natural energy sources. Profiles wind, water power and the complex canal systems of the Middle East. Visually pleasing,

24

intended for junior high school to adult audiences. One
of the most popular general culture series on the Middle
East. Recommended.

111   THE TRADITIONAL WORLD OF ISLAM: NOMAD AND CITY
       1978 / 30 min / sound / color / 16 mm
       Stephen Cross. Institutional Cinema Service. Distributed
       by Exxon. For more information, see no. 46. *
       Investigates the different life styles and world views of
       city and desert dwellers in the Middle East. Shows the
       nomadic North African Berbers, the Bedouin, Turkoman tri-
       bes and the Bakhtiari of Iran. Contrasts life in San'a,
       a traditional Arab city in the Yemen, and Fez in Morocco.
       Portrays the contributions of each life style and the
       tension between the two ways of life. Beautifully pho-
       tographed. Recommended.

112   WANDERERS OF THE DESERT
       1953 / 10 min / sound / color / 16 mm
       F.W. and E.S. Keller. Released by Encyclopaedia Britannica
       Films. (NUC FiA 54-413) Credits: Educational Collaborator
       - Richard Hartshorne. Distributed by Encyclopaedia
       Britannica and by the Educational Film Library. Locations:
       Kent State U. / Syracuse U.
       Profiles the life style of the desert caravaneers. Shows
       scenes of making camp, preparing food, and festivities at
       the end of the day. Also profiles the Desert Patrol,
       police who patrol the desert for illegal activities and
       smuggling.

113   WOMEN IN A CHANGING WORLD
       1975 / 48 min / sound / color / 16 mm
       Nancy Dupree and Judith Von Daler. Locations: American
       Univ. Field Staff / Indiana U. / Michigan State U. / U. of
       California at Berkeley / U. of Iowa / U. of Kansas / U. of
       Michigan / Wheelock Educational Resources.
       One of the few films dealing with women in the Middle
       East. Describes the impact of modernization on women in
       Bolivia, Northern Kenya, Afghanistan and the Hong Kong
       territory.

LAND AND WATER

114   ARID LANDS
       1960 / 27 min / sound / b&w / 16 mm
       UNESCO. Formerly distributed by Contemporary Films. (LC
       70-700323)
       Available in English, French and Spanish soundtracks.
       Looks at the problems of life in arid climates, focusing
       on Morocco, Israel and Pakistan. Discusses conversion of
       sea water to fresh for agricultural purposes, and utili-
       zation of sun and wind power for energy.

115 ASPIRATIONS
(c. 1963) / 30 min / sound / b&w / 16 mm
Contemporary Films. (Crossroads of the World series)
Shows agriculture programs in the Middle East to diversify crops and introduce new technologies to agriculture.

116 BARREN HILLS
1962 / 29 min / sound / b&w / 16 mm
Producer unknown. Location: U. of Utah.
Traces the history of agriculture and irrigation in the
Middle East.

117 BENI-ABBES, SCIENCE IN THE DESERT
1955 / 18 min / sound / color / 16 mm
Unesco. Formerly distributed by Contemporary Films.
Shows the work being done in arid zone research centers
in the Middle East.

118 DEVELOPMENT THROUGH FOOD
1967 / 27 min / sound / b&w / 16 mm
Food and Agriculture Organization of the United Nations.
Available in English and French soundtracks. Profiles
the World Food Programme Advisory Committee. Shows
assistance provided to Yugoslavia, the Sudan, Turkey,
Korea, Taiwan, India and Jordan. Covers both general
assistance and development programs as well as disaster
assistance programs.

119 LIFE IN MEDITERRANEAN LANDS
1978 / 13 min / sound / color / 16 mm
Coronet Films. Credits: Educational Collaborator - Norman
Carls. Location: Syracuse U.
Intended for junior high school audiences. Shows the
inter-relationship between the peoples and cultures of
the Mediterranean area and the climate of the region.
Discusses the effect of climate on agriculture and life
styles.

120 THE MIDDLE EAST: THE NEED FOR WATER
1967 / 16 min / sound / color / 16 mm
Jules Power Productions. Released by McGraw-Hill. (Middle
Eastern World series) (NUC FiA 67-1652) Locations:
Syracuse U. / U. of Arizona / U. of Illinois / U. of
Kansas.
The Middle East is shown as a region which must overcome
a harsh climate and lack of water. Provides general
introduction to nomads, religion, and the peoples of the
Middle East. Discusses the impact of oil revenues on
developing the economies, education, agriculture and
standard of living in oil-rich Middle Eastern countries.

121 OF TIDES AND TIMES
1979 / 27 min / sound / color / 16 mm

United Nations.
Available in English, French and Spanish soundtracks.
Shows efforts by the World Food Programme to help develop
and advance agriculture in underdeveloped areas. Scenes
include renovation of ancient cisterns in Syria,
resettlement of displaced villagers after the Aswan High
Dam was completed, and programs in Chad and Somalia to
combat severe drought in the Sahel. Shows major displace-
ment of people and starvation.

OIL AND DEVELOPMENT

122   THE ARAB WORLD: OIL, POWER, DISSENSION
       (c. 1978?) / ? / sound / color / 16 mm
       Distributed by Current Affairs Films. No other information
       available.

123   THE CHANGING MIDDLE EAST
       1975 / 25 min / sound / color / 16 mm
       International Film Foundation. (LC 76-700114) Credits:
       Producer-Writer-Director - Sam Bryan, Consultant - Mounir
       Farah, Photographers - Jullen Bryan and Sam Bryan.
       Locations: Arizona State U. / Brigham Young U. / Middle
       East Institute / Penn. State U. / U. of Arizona / U. of
       Colorado / U. of Illinois / U. of Michigan / U. of Nebraska
       / U. of Washington / U. of Wisconsin.
          Describes the Middle East as birthplace of the three
          great monotheistic religions and as a mixture of ancient
          and modern. Shows problems with lack of water and water
          projects such as the Aswan High Dam. Discusses problems
          in urban overcrowding, unemployment, poor economies, and
          the Arab-Israeli conflict. Also covers development
          resulting from oil revenues. Intended for junior-senior
          high school audiences.

124   THE ECONOMY: OIL, WATER AND ASPIRATIONS
       1962 / 24 min / sound / b&w / 16 mm
       National Film Board of Canada. Distributed in the U.S. by
       McGraw-Hill. (The Middle East series) Locations: Kent
       State U. / Syracuse U.
          Discusses social and economic reforms needed to improve
          the condition of people in the Middle East. Examines
          innovations in agricultural technology and shows the
          benefits of development and industrialization in the
          Middle East and North Africa. Intended for junior-senior
          high school audiences.

125   THE ENERGY CRISIS: OIL IN THE MIDDLE EAST
       1973 / 30 min / sound / color / 16 mm
       NBC News. (NBC White Paper, television broadcast)
       Location: U. of Illinos.
          NBC news special. Presents the problem of oil supply

from the Middle East to the U.S. With over 1/2 of the world's known oil reserves in Saudi Arabia, Iran and Kuwait, questions of U.S. policy towards those countries must be carefully examined. Discusses the U.S. commitment to Israel and the position of the Soviet Union in Middle East affairs.

126   IN ARAB LANDS: AN AGE OF CHANGE
       1979 / 28 min / sound / color / 16 mm
       Bechtel Group of Companies. Sunset Films. Distributed by
       Modern Talking Picture Service. Free.
           This well-photographed film presents the history of the
       Arabs, the origins of Islam and the contributions of
       Islamic civilization to the world of knowledge. Shot on
       location in Saudi Arabia, Kuwait, the United Arab
       Emirates and Spain. Contrasts the glories of the past
       with current develoment. Shows scenes of the transfor-
       mation of life on the Arabian peninsula as a result of
       oil, including increased industrialization and a major
       change in the standard of living. Well presented,
       detailed film. Intended for high school through adult
       audiences.

127   MIDDLE EAST: OIL AND SUDDEN WEALTH (GULF COUNTRIES)
       1979 / 21 min / sound / color / 16 mm
       Coronet Films. Location: Syracuse U.
           Describes the rapid changes taking place in the Gulf
       states as a result of the exploitation of oil and the
       resulting revenues. Current development as well as long
       term plans for the region are described. Intended for
       junior-senior high school audiences.

128   MIDEAST: ECONOMIC DEVELOPMENT
       1977 / 18 min / sound / color / 16 mm
       BFA Educational Media. Vocational and Industrial Films,
       Ltd. (Mideast series) Credits: Producer - John Seabourne,
       Director-Writer - Richard Ashworth, Educational Consultant
       - George Rentz. Locations: Brigham Young U. / Florida
       State U. / Library of Congress (FBA 7738) / Syracuse U. /
       U. of Texas at Austin / U. of Wisconsin.
           Shows the combination of modern and traditional practises
       in current economics in the Middle East. From the tradi-
       tional arts and crafts in the marketplace to the distri-
       bution of oil wealth, the changes as a result of
       modernization, industrialization and westernization are
       profiled in Saudi Arabia, the Gulf States, Egypt and
       Iran. Intended for junior high school to adult audiences.

129   OIL IN THE MIDDLE EAST
       1973-74 / 20 min / sound / color / 16 mm
       NBC Educational Enterprises. Distributed by Films, Inc.
       (Energy Crisis series) Locations: Penn. State U. / U. of
       Arizona / U. of California Extension Media Center.

Discusses the importance of Saudi Arabia, Iran and
Kuwait as oil-producing centers for the U.S., Japan and
Europe. The role of huge multi-national corporations in
the oil industry, international politics, and energy
supply are examined. Includes an interview with King
Faisal of Saudi Arabia.

130 THE OIL WEAPON
1975 / 50 min / sound / color / 16 mm
CTV Television Network. Distributed by Films, Inc.
Credits: Director - Ken Lefoli.
Shows the social and economic development in Saudi
Arabia, Kuwait and Iran as a result of oil wealth.
Describes the relations of these countries with the west.
Contains some misleading statements.

131 PROJECT MIDDLE EAST, PART 3 - THE ECONOMY
(c. 1970?) / 20 min / sound / color / 16 mm
United Nations Children's Fund.
Available in English, French and Italian soundtracks.
Shows the work being done by the United Nations to assist
children in the Middle East and the Arab countries
through improved agriculture, reclaimation of the desert
to increase food production, and mass production and
distribution of milk products.

132 STRUGGLE FOR OIL
1949 / 20 min / sound / b&w / 16 mm
J. Arthur Rank Organisation. Produced by This Modern Age.
Released in the U.S. by British Information Services, 1951.
(This Modern Age, no. 25) Credits: Producer - Sergei
Nolbandov, Associate Producer and Literary Editor - J.L.
Hodson. (NUC FiA 52-4333)
Describes the concessions awarded to British and
American oil companies in Iran and Iraq.

133 TAKE OFF
(c. 1975?) / 13 min / sound / color / 16 mm
Farm Film Foundation.
Shows the immense contrasts and changes brought about by
the influx of oil wealth to several Middle East
countries, especially Saudi Arabia.

134 THROUGH OIL LANDS OF EUROPE AND AFRICA, PART 1
(c. 1926?) / 27 min / silent / b&w / 35 mm
Bureau of Mines in cooperation with the American Oil Co.
(Pan American Petroleum and Transport Co.) Bureau of Mines
Film, no. 113) Location: National Archives (70.113)
Silent film footage of oil exploration and development
in Europe and Africa. For archival uses.

135 THROUGH OIL LANDS OF EUROPE AND AFRICA, PART 3
(c. 1926?) / 44 min / silent / b&w / 35 mm

Bureau of Mines in cooperation with the American Oil Co.
(Bureau of Mines Film, no. 115) Location: National
Archives (70.115)
   A description of oil rich areas of the world. Script is
   available for the contents of the film.

THE ARTS

136   ANCIENT ART OF BELLY DANCING
      1977 / 30 min / sound / color / 16 mm
      Phoenix Films. Location: Syracuse U.
         Traces the history of belly dancing from ancient times
         to the present. Introduces senior high school through
         adult audiences to this popular form of dance, from its
         origins in the Middle East to present day Europe and the
         U.S.

137   ARAB FOLK DANCES
      (n.d.) / 25 min / sound / color / 16 mm
      Arab Information Center, New York.
         Shows examples of different styles of Arab folk dance,
         and how each has developed. Discusses the relationship
         between different forms of dance and the environment.

138   ART OF ISLAM
      1970 / 10 min / sound / color / 16 mm
      ACI Films. Paramount Communications. (LC 70-706864)
      Locations: Boise State U. / Penn. State U. / Syracuse U. /
      U. of Illinois / U. of Utah.
         Uses examples from the Islamic Museum in Cairo to show
         the effect of Islam on traditional arts and crafts in the
         Middle East. Includes examples of calligraphic ornamen-
         tation, carved wooden panels, rugs and gold and bron-
         zework. The concept of Islamic art is investigated for
         junior high school to adult audiences.

139   ASIAN ARTS IN CRYSTAL
      (c. 1977?) / 17 min / sound / b&w / 16 mm
      USIA. Distributed by NF. (NUC FiE 57-186)
         Filmed exhibition of an art show of American crystal
         engraved with designs created by 16 artists from the
         Middle East and Southeast Asia.

140   DISCOVERING THE MUSIC OF THE MIDDLE EAST
      1968 / 20 min / sound / color / 16 mm
      Bernard Wilets. Released by Film Associates. Distributed
      by BFA Educational Media. (Discovering Music series) (NUC
      FiA 68-3180) Locations: Brigham Young U. / Kent State U. /
      Oklahoma State U. / Penn. State U. / Syracuse U. / U. of
      Arizona / U. of Colorado / U. of Illinois / U. of Kansas /
      U. of Michigan / U. of Minnesota / U. of Nebraska / U. of
      South Carolina / U. of Washington / Washington State U. *

Traces Middle Eastern music from the time of Muhammad in
the 7th century to the present day. Examines differences
between courtly and folk music and demonstrates traditional instruments including the oud, durbaki, dumbek,
qanun and santur. The influence of Middle Eastern music
on Russian and western composers is shown. Begins slowly
with the demonstration of instruments but becomes quite
enjoyable when songs and dances are performed.

141 GAMEEL GAMAL: OH BEAUTIFUL DANCER
     1975 / 24 min / sound / color / 16 mm
     Phoenix Films. Credits: Director - Gordon Inkeles.
     Traces the spread of belly dancing from the Middle East
     throughout the world. Describes the importance of
     costuming, playing of the finger cymbals and music to the
     dance. Describes the social problems faced by belly dan-
     cers in the U.S. Intended for high school to adult
     audiences.

142 ISLAMIC ART
     (n.d.) / 21 min / sound / color / 16 mm
     Embassy of Egypt. No further information available.

143 IZY BOUKIR
     1970 / 21 min / sound / color / 16 mm
     Nancy Graves. Location: New York Public Donnell Film
     Library.
     Without narration. A comic, personal view of the camel.

144 LIKE AS THE LUTE
     (1979?) / 37 min / sound / color / 16 mm
     Picture Partnership Production for the Arts Council of
     Great Britain in association with the British Council.
     Credits: Lute - Anthony Rooley. Distributed (for sale)
     from Arts Council of Great Britain. *
     Anthony Rooley and Dr. Samha el Kholy, Dean of the Cairo
     Conservatoire, discuss attempts to authentically repro-
     duce medieval music. Outlines the role of music scho-
     larship. Shows the relationship between European and
     Arab music beginning with the similarity between the Arab
     oud and the European lute. Arabic influence on
     Renaissance music and life is shown through manuscripts,
     paintings and poetry. An excellent film, though spe-
     cialized. More informative than the more general film,
     DISCOVERING THE MUSIC OF THE MIDDLE EAST, no. 140.

145 MIDDLE EASTERN MUSIC: SYSTEM, MAQAM, METER
     1973, released 1978 / 6 min / sound / color / 16 mm
     Johanna Spector.
     Khamis Ali El Fino, famous Egyptian oud player,
     demonstrates different modes on his instrument and sings
     to different meters played on the durbaki or drum.
     Without narration. Styles and meters are named in Arabic

as they are played. Intended for junior high school through adult audiences.

146   MIDEAST: ARTS, CRAFTS AND ARCHITECTURE
       1977 / 18 min / sound / color / 16 mm
       Vocational and Industrial Films, Ltd. Distributed by BFA
       Educational Media. (Mideast series) Credits: Writer -
       John Ashworth, Producer - John Seabourne, Director -
       Richard Ashworth, Educational Consultant - George Rentz.
       Locations: Library of Congress (FBA 7737) / Syracuse U. /
       U. of Colorado / U. of Illinois / U. of Minnesota / U. of
       Texas at Austin / U. of Wisconsin. *
            Looks at the variety of cultures and art forms in the
            Middle East from ancient times to the present. Begins
            with Roman and Byzantine art then focuses on Islamic art.
            Includes many examples of functional objects in wood and
            metal. Tours palaces such as the Alhambra in Spain.
            Visually pleasing film showing the attempt to make the
            functional beautiful. Lack of indentification of the
            location of specific buildings is a little confusing and
            local or national trends cannot be traced. Remains a
            good introduction to Islamic arts and crafts for junior
            high school through adult audiences.

147   SWORDS AND SCIMITARS
       1967 / 30 min / sound / b&w / 16 mm and 1" videotape
       University of Michigan TV Center. Credits: Host - Donald
       Proctor. (NUC FiA 68-287)
            Tours the 500 item collection of ancient Near Eastern
            armaments belonging to State Senator Gilbert Bursley of
            Michigan.

148   THE TRADITIONAL WORLD OF ISLAM: THE PATTERN OF BEAUTY
       1978 / 30 min / sound / color / 16 mm
       Stephen Cross. Institutional Cinema Service. Distributed
       by Exxon. For more information, see no. 46. *
            Another in the beautifully filmed series on the Islamic
            world. Traces the Islamic visual arts through architec-
            ture, decoration, painting and calligraphy in Iran,
            Turkey, India and throughout the Arab countries. The
            emphasis of the narration is on aesthetic principles
            which are interpreted from a Sufic, or mystical Islamic,
            point of view. Wonderful film, easily obtained from many
            institutions for a nominal fee. Highly recommended.

NORTH AFRICA

NOMADS

149 BACKWARD CIVILIZATION: THE BERBERS OF NORTH AFRICA
1937 / 21 min / sound / b&w / 16 mm
John A. Haeseler. Released by Erpi Picture Consultants
(later, Encyclopaedia Britannica Films) Credits:
Educational Collaborator - Ellsworth Huntington.
Distributed by Encyclopaedia Britannica Educational Corp.
(NUC FiA 54-4063) Locations: Syracuse U. / U. of Nebraska.
Describes the separation of the Berbers from the
mainstream of North African life, their unique customs
and daily life style. Intended for elementary through
high school audiences. Contains much dated, non-
objective material which makes it unsuitable for current
educational purposes.

150 BEDOUINS OF THE SAHARA
(1930?) / 8 min / silent / b&w / 16 mm
Producer unknown. Location: Library of Congress (FAA 3334)
*
Includes a display of varying facial types found among
Bedouin Arabs, scenes of transportation by camel, and
migrations to find pasturage for camels and sheep. Shows
people doing a variety of tasks including churning
butter and milking sheep. Shows women spinning and
weaving and men preparing coffee. Footage, which is in
relatively good condition considering its age, appears to
be spliced from other sources. Of interest historically,
most footage of performance of daily tasks can be found
elsewhere in better condition.

151 BERBER DANCES
1947-50 / 12 min / sound / b&w / 16 mm
Centre cinematographique Marocain, Rabat. Distributed by
Radim Films. Longer version in German only, entitled
BERBER-TANZE.
Contains Berber songs and dances including a town dance
with orchestra, war dance of the Taskeuine, and guedra
dance of the shepherds. Four additional songs and dances are included in the longer German version available
from Encyclopaedia Cinematographica, Nonnenstieg 72, 34
Gottingen, West Germany.

152 CAMEL TRANSPORTATION AND COMMERCE IN THE DESERT
1970 / 3 min / silent / color / super 8 mm film loop
Doubleday Multimedia. (North Africa series) (LC 73-708015)

Documents how camels are used for transportation in
North Africa.

153   DESERT CARAVAN
      1971 / 13 min / sound / color / 16 mm
      NBC News. Released by NBC Educational Enterprises.
      Distributed by Films, Inc. (LC 72-700082) Locations:
      Syracuse U. / U. of Illinois.
          An NBC News documentary adapted for classroom use for
          elementary through high school audiences. Traces a 12
          year old nomad boy's first caravan trip. Follows the
          1000 mile trek across the Sahara desert with some men of
          his tribe. Their destination is a distant market where
          they will trade salt for food before returning home. A
          nicely filmed production which evokes an image
          of Tuareg life.

154   FACE OF THE SAHARA
      (n.d.) / 22 min / sound / color / 16 mm
      Sterling Educational Films.
          Shows the radical change in the lifestyle of the Tuaregs
          as drought and modernization in communications and
          transportation render their nomadic, trading life style
          obsolete.

155   FAMILY LIFE OF DESERT NOMADS
      1968 / 4 min / silent / color / super 8 mm film loop, also
      in standard 8 mm. Walt Disney Productions. Released by
      International Communication Films. (North Africa series)
      (LC 70-703199)
          A 4 minute excerpt from the 1958 film, BLUE MEN OF
          MOROCCO - TRIBAL LIFE ON THE SAHARA. Footage shows
          Tuaregs setting up camp for a short period of time
          before moving on to a camel market. Shows the rela-
          tionship between the harsh climate and nomadism.

156   HOW THE DESERT PEOPLE LIVE
      (1938?) / 12 min / sound / b&w / 16 mm
      Knowledge Builders. (NUC FiA 55-580)
          Shows life among desert nomads in the Sahara, Turkistan
          and the Gobi deserts. Includes scenes of a caravan in a
          sandstorm.

157   KABYLIA
      1949 / 10 min / sound / b&w / 16 or 35 mm
      Les Actualites francaises, Paris. Released in the U.S. by
      A.F. Films. Distributed by Radim Films and by Film Images.
          Kabylia, between the Sahara desert and the
          Mediterranean, is the home of the Kabyles or Berbers of
          North Africa. Their traditional life style and the
          effects of modernization are shown.

158   LIFE IN THE SAHARA
      1932 / 16 min / silent / b&w / 16 mm

Eastman Teaching Films (Eastman Classroom Films series)
Location: Library of Congress (FAA 5072) *
Sub-titled. Shows scenes of nomads with sheep, women making bread and grinding salt, the way to market in a caravan, and stopping at an oasis where faces of men and women are shown. Shows trading of animals for food in the bazaar. Quality of the film is good considering its age, but most of the footage can be found elsewhere in newer, color films. For historical purposes only.

159   LIFE IN THE SAHARA
1952 / 15 min / sound / color / 16 mm
Encyclopaedia Britannica Educational Corp. Credits: Educational Collaborator - Clarence W. Sorensen. Kodachrome. (NUC Fi 53-268) Locations: Brigham Young U. / Kent State U. / Library of Congress / Penn. State U. / Syracuse U. / U. of Illinois / U. of Nebraska.
Also listed as released in 1953. Documents life in the Sahara desert for nomad tribesmen. Shows activities such as grinding salt, life at an oasis, and a trip to market. The importance of the camel to nomad life is described.

160   LIFE OF NOMAD PEOPLE (DESERT DWELLERS)
1949 / 11 min / sound / b&w / 16 mm
Coronet Instructional Films. (Desert Dwellers series) Credits: Educational Collaborator - W.R. McConnell. Kodachrome. (NUC FiA 52-2112) Locations: Kent State U. / U. of Illinois / U. of Kansas / U. of Nebraska.
Intended for junior-senior high school audiences. Follows two young children of an Algerian nomad tribe in the Sahara as they go about their chores, helping to pitch the tents, tend sheep, weave cloth and grind flour. Shows how nomadic life is the only alternative to a desert environment.

161   MAKING AND FUNCTIONING OF A DECORATIVE LOCK (TUAREG, NORTH AFRICA, HOGGAR MOUNTAINS)
1953, released 1957 / 13 min / silent / b& w / 16 mm
Encyclopaedia Cinematographica. (Ency. Cinematographica, no. E 126) Distributed by Pennsylvania State University.
A short ethnographic film documenting the production of a lock using traditional methods by a Tuareg tribesman.

162   PLACES PEOPLE LIVE: DESERT PEOPLE
1970 / 13 min / sound / color / 16 mm
William Claiborn. Released by Sterling Educational Films. (Places People Live series) Location: U. of Illinois.
Listed in some catalogs as DESERT PEOPLE. Compares the life style of the Tuaregs of the Sahara desert with the Rajputs of the Rajastan Desert in India. Shows how these two groups have adapted to a desert environment.

163   SAHARA
1969 / 62 min / sound / color / 16 mm

NBC Broadcasting Inc. Released by Films, Inc. Locations:
Syracuse U. / U. of Iowa. *
A two part film, sometimes listed as being only 50 minutes in length. Follows the progress of a 1000 mile
caravan trip across the desert made by nomads to trade
salt at a market town for food and other supplies.
Intended for junior high school to adult audiences.
Well filmed, an excerpt from this was made into a
separate film, DESERT CARAVAN, no. 153.

164 SAHARA - LA CARAVANE DU SEL
1969 / 52 min / sound / color / 16 mm
NBC. Released by NBC Enterprises. Distributed by Films,
Inc. Credits: Narrator - Charles Boyer,
Director-Photographer -Tom Priestly, Producer-Writer - Lou
Hazam. (LC 74-706100) Locations: Kent State U. / Library
of Congress (FDA 683) / Syracuse U. / U. of Arizona / U. of
Illinois / U. of Iowa / U. of Michigan / U. of Minnesota /
U. of Washington. *
Despite the French sub-title, this is an English
language film. Beautifully photographed. One of the
best viewed films on the subject of North African nomads.
Relates the same story as many of the others listed
but with better production and narration. Follows the
cycle of salt as it is mined, made into cone shaped
blocks, and moved in camel trains to market. The caravan
begins with about 25 men and 300 camels, with Tuaregs as
the caravaneers. Shows the making of camp and preparation of food each night. Averaging 25 miles per day, one
trip per year, they cover 1000 miles round trip in one
caravan. Describes the traits of the camel for desert
travel at length. A spectacular scene of the caravan
encountering a sand storm finishes this lengthy but
excellently produced film.

165 TOUAREG
1948 / 12 min / sound / b&w / 16 or 35 mm
Les Actualites francaises, Paris. Released in the U.S. by
A.F. Films. (NUC FiA 52-702)
Shows the Tuareg of the Sahara desert and how life is
dominated by the need to secure food and water for themselves and their animals. Includes information on
marriage customs.

166 TOUREG
1949 / 14 min / sound / b&w / 16 mm
Julian Roffman. Distributed by Film Images. Credits:
Director - A. Mahuzifr. Location: New York Public Donnell
Film Library.
Brief enthnographic film depicting the traditional
life of the Tuaregs of the Hoggar Mountains of North
Africa.

167   TUAREG
      1940 / 14 min / sound / b&w / 16 mm
      Distributed by Radim Films. No other information available.

NORTH AFRICA - FILMS PRODUCED BETWEEN 1910-1949

168   AFRICA - LAND OF CONTRAST
      1934 / 10 min / sound / b&w / 16 mm
      Metro-Goldwyn-Mayer. Released for educational purposes by
      Teaching Film Custodians, 1939. (James A. FitzPatrick's
      Traveltalks series) (NUC FiA 52-4981)
          Presents a portrait of Africa in a travelog from Algeria
          to Capetown. Scenes of North Africa include El Kantara,
          a camel caravan and nomads. Originally released in
          theaters as a short subject.

169   AFRICA - PRELUDE TO VICTORY
      1942 / 18 min / sound / b&w / 35 mm
      Time, Inc. (March of Time, vol. 9, no. 4) Location:
      National Archives (200 MT 9.4)
          Newsreel footage of the North African campaign in WWII.
          Includes scenes of Algeria and Tunis.

170   (AFRICAN DESERTS)
      (1930?) / 11 min / silent / b&w / 16 mm
      Source unknown. Location: Library of Congress (FAA 2958) *
          Short, silent film showing typical activities of nomad
          life. Includes scenes of herding sheep, women making
          bread, grinding grain, crushing salt, and spinning.
          Shows a camel caravan as it heads for market where goats
          and donkeys are sold. Men and women gather in separate
          groups to talk. A muezzin calls men to prayer. After
          the market, nomads leave the oasis for the desert.
          Little information is given on what is being viewed. The
          photography is not exceptional and the quality of the
          film is poor due to age. For historical purposes only.

171   AN AFRICAN VILLAGE - NORTH AFRICA
      (1911?) / 3 min / silent / b&w / 16 mm
      Pathe freres, France. Released in the U.S. by George Kleine.
      Location: Library of Congress (FLA 1358) *
          Strange collection of staged scenes supposedly showing
          typical North African life. Filmed in a humorously arti-
          ficial manner, scenes include a mother and child playing
          with a kitten, a man winding a turban, a caravan, men
          riding and shooting, and a very odd scene labelled
          "Attacking a Courier", showing a lone British officer
          being "attacked" by an Arab. In good condition con-
          sidering age. An early attempt at travelog/ethnographic
          filming.

172   ALLIED OFFENSIVE IN NORTH AFRICA
      1943 / 16 min / sound / b&w / 35mm

Signal Corps. (Film Bulletin, no. 51) Location: National
Archives (lll FB 51) No other information available.

173   AT THE FRONT IN NORTH AFRICA WITH THE U.S. ARMY
1943 / 41 min / sound / color / 35 mm
(Misc. Film, no. 1001) Location: National Archives (lll M
1001)
> Footage of the U.S. Army during WWII in Algeria and
> Tunisia.

174   AXIS SABOTEURS - NORTH AFRICA
1945 / 8 min / sound / b&w / 16 mm
(Combat Film Report, no. 403) Location: National Archives
(18 C 403)
> Footage of two captured Arab saboteurs during WWII in
> North Africa.

175   BOMBERS OVER NORTH AFRICA
1944 / 21 min / sound / b&w / 35 mm
Army Air Forces (Combat Film Report, no. 320A) Location:
National Archives (18 C 320A)
> Footage of bombed out Tunisian ports during WWII.

176   DESERT VICTORY
1943 / 60 min / sound / b&w / 16 mm
British Ministry of Information, London. Produced by
British Service Film Units. Released in the U.S. by
British Information Services. United World Film, Inc.
Distributed by Radim Films, by Contemporary Films and
McGraw-Hill. (NUC FiA 52-861) Credits: Producers - David
MacDonald, Roy Boulting, Commentary - J.L. Hodson, Music -
William Alwyn. Locations: Library of Congress (FBA 2544-45)
/ National Archives (111 M 1002) / U. of California. *
> This remarkable film has little to do with North Africa
> except as a battleground, a setting for the Allied vic-
> tory at El Alamein in 1942. Following Rommel's advance
> on Tobruk, the British fall back to El Alamein with its
> natural defenses. In vividly photographed battle
> footage, the intricacies of the battle and strategies of
> both armies are explained. Of special interest are sce-
> nes of the destroyed Benghazi harbor and the surrender
> of Tripoli by the Italians. Nothing is said of the indi-
> genous populations in this film. Several cameramen died
> while obtaining footage for this classic documentary,
> shown in theaters during the war. Highly recommended.
> Print held in the National Archives is the 35 mm version
> released to theaters in the U.S. by 20th Century-Fox.

177   NORTH AFRICA
1942 / 8 min / silent / b&w / 16 mm
Filmsets, Inc. (NUC FiA 54-3239)
> General film showing people of the North African country-
> side. Includes scenes of nomads living in the Sahara and
> Libyan deserts.

178   NORTH AFRICA IN WARTIME
       (c. 1941) / 6 min / silent / b&w / 16 mm
       Producer unknown. German Collection. Location: Library of
       Congress (MID 2656) *
            Use for research and historical purposes. Shows German
            troops and equipment moving down the street of an uniden-
            tified North African town amid large crowds. A guard
            unit of local mounted troops escorts dignitaries in an
            auto while a military band and local troops parade.
            Quality of the film is fair considering age. Lack of
            identification makes this film of less use.

NORTH AFRICA - FILMS PRODUCED BETWEEN 1950-1959

179   AFRICA: NORTH AFRICA
       1956 / 29 min / sound / b&w / 16 mm
       WTTW, Chicago Television Station. Released by NET Film
       Service (America Looks Abroad series) (NUC FiA 58-1216)
       Credits: Moderator - Carter Davidson.
            Introduces the geography, people and culture of the Arab
            North African countries. Discusses the importance of this
            area to the U.S.   Looks at Arab nationalism and its effects.

180   THE AIR FORCE STORY - NORTH AFRICA
       1953 / 14 min / sound / b&w / 16 mm
       U.S. Dept. of Defense, Dept. of the Air Force.
            Describes the Allied invasion of North Africa from
            November 1942 to May 1943, and the attempt to drive back
            Rommel's Afrika Corps. Follows the campaign from El
            Alamein to Tunis.

181   BATTLE OF NORTH AFRICA, PART 1
       1960 / 28 min / sound / b&w / 16 mm
       Dept. of the Army.
            First of a two part series showing military campaigns in
            Africa during WWII.

182   BATTLE OF NORTH AFRICA, PART 2
       1960 / 28 min / sound / b&w / 16 mm
       Dept. of the Army.
            Second in the series, on Allied North African campaigns
            during WWII. Covers the period between the sinking of
            the fleet at Oran in June 1940 to the battle of El
            Alamein.

183   CONSTRUCTION OF THE NORTH AFRICAN BASES
       1956 / 13 min / sound / color / 16 mm
       U.S. Army Engineers. U.S. Office of Education. (NUC FiE
       56-181)
            Profiles the work undertaken by the U.S. Army Corps. of
            Engineers in constructing army bases in the Middle East.

Shows bases in Morocco, Tripoli, Iran and Saudi Arabia.
Explains reasons for construction of the bases and how
they serve U.S. interests.

184   THE DESERT NORTH AFRICA 1940-1943
       1953 / 56 min / sound / color / 16 mm
       Heritage Visual Sales, Ltd. Distributed by Iowa Films.
       (The World at War series, #8) Location: U. of Illinois.
            Intended for senior high school to adult audiences.
            Covers the Allied campaigns in North Africa to drive back
            Rommel, culminating in the battle of El Alamein.

185   MEDITERRANEAN AFRICA
       1952 / 12 min / sound / color or b&w / 16 mm
       Encyclopaedia Britannica Films in cooperation with Clifford
       J. Kamen Productions. (NUC Fi 53-183) Credits:
       Educational Collaborator - Clarence W. Sorensen.
       Kodachrome. Locations: Brigham Young U. / Iowa Films /
       Kent State U. / Library of Congress (FAA 4253) / Syracuse
       U. / U. of Illinois / U. of Michigan / U. of Nebraska.
            For junior to senior high school audiences. Introduces
            the geography, climate and peoples of the North African
            countries bordering the Mediterranean. Shows how the
            climate of the region has influenced its history, and its
            location has made it a crossroads of trade and invading
            armies. Shows evidence of the mixture of several peoples
            and civilizations in North Africa today.

186   NORTH AFRICA KALEIDOSCOPE
       1955 / 15 min / sound / color / 16 mm
       Africa Film Foundation (White Fathers) Made by Hervey F.
       Armington. Released by White Fathers Film Distribution
       Center. (NUC FiA 57-839)
            Introduces the Berber and Arab North Africans, shows the
            area in which they live, and gives a brief history of
            North Africa. Suggestions for techniques used in con-
            verting Muslims and doing missionary work in Islamic
            countries are discussed. A training and information
            film for missionary groups.

187   NORTH OF THE SAHARA
       1954 / 20 min / sound / color / 35 mm
       Vitaphone Corp. (A Warner Bros. short subject) (NUC Fi
       55-513) Credits: Director-Photographer - Andre De La
       Varre, Writer - Owen Crump, Narrator - Marvin Miller.
       Technicolor. Location: Library of Congress (FEA 926, FEA
       1698)
            General travelog covering typical sights found in
            Kairowan, Algiers, Tunis, Casablanca and Marrakesh.

188   REPORT FROM AFRICA, PART 2.
       1956 / 60 min / sound / b&w / 16 mm or 3/4" videocassette
       CBS Television. Released by McGraw-Hill. Distributed by

Contemporary Films. (See It Now, television series) (NUC
FiA 58-856) Credits: Co-producers - Edward R. Murrow,
Fred W. Friendly. Locations: Kent State U. / Library of
Congress (FCA 1123-24) / Museum of Broadcasting.
   This 16 mm print is a reduction of the 35 mm print
   broadcast on the See It Now television series. Part 1
   deals with Sub-Saharan Africa. Part 2 describes the
   then current situations in Algeria, Libya, Morocco,
   Egypt, the Sudan and Ethiopia, with interviews of six
   African leaders. Topics covered include the relationship between the newly independent countries and
   former and current colonial powers, Algeria's revolution, and Nasser's effect on Egypt. A good look at the
   political situation circa 1956 and an interesting view
   of American attitudes towards newly emerging nations.

189   REPORT FROM AFRICA - SUDAN, ETHIOPIA, EGYPT
      1957 / 21 min / sound / b&w / 16 mm
      CBS Television. (See It Now television series) Credits:
      Reporter - Edward R. Murrow.
         Excerpt from REPORT FROM AFRICA, PART 2, no. 188.
         Covers only the situations in Egypt, Ethiopia and the
         Sudan. A shorter version intended for classroom
         instructional use.

190   THE SEVEN BROTHERS OF THIBAR
      1954 / 33 min / sound / color or b&w / 16 mm
      Africa Film Foundation (White Fathers) Made by Hervey F.
      Armington. Released by White Fathers Film Distribution
      Center. (NUC FiA 57-1055)
         Describes the missionary work undertaken by seven mem-
         bers of the White Fathers in North Africa, working with
         the local population in agricultural as well as reli-
         gious programs.

191   TWO AFRICAS
      1953 / 15 min / sound / color or b&w / 16 mm
      Africa Film Foundation (White Fathers) Made by Hervey F.
      Armington. Released by White Fathers Distribution Center.
      (NUC FiA 57-1053)
         Compares areas in Africa where Christianity has taken
         hold and where it has not. Sub-Saharan Black Africa has
         been much more receptive to Christian conversion than
         North Africa where strong Muslim traditions make
         missionary work difficult. These two spheres of reli-
         gious influence make up the Two Africas of the title. A
         film for missionary groups.

NORTH AFRICA - FILMS PRODUCED BETWEEN 1960-1969

192   AFRICA
      Sept. 10, 1967 / 4 parts, each 60 min / sound / color / 3/4"

41

videocassette. ABC Television. Credits: Exec. producer -
James Fleming, Narrator - Gregory Peck. Location: Museum of
Broadcasting (no. T77:0080)
A 4 hour special broadcast showing "the people and land
that are Africa today". Part 1 covers Tanzania, Botswana
and the bushmen of the Kalahari Desert. A profile of
Ethiopia covers its history and architecture as well as a
look at Haile Selassie. Part 2 shows Nigeria, Ghana,
Liberia, Tanzania and includes interviews with President
Nasser of Egypt and Boumediene of Algeria. Part 3 looks
at the west coast of Africa, including Kenya and the
Congo. Part 4 covers South Africa, Angola and Rhodesia.
An examination, for the most part, not of the history of
these areas, but of the current social and political
problems experienced by each.

193   AFRICA: AN INTRODUCTION
1967 / 17 min / sound / color / 16 mm
Wayne Mitchell. Released by Film Associates of California.
Distributed by BFA Educational Films. (NUC FiA 68-381)
Locations: U. of Illinois / U. of Kansas / U. of Michigan /
U. of Nebraska.
For junior-senior high school audiences. Introduction
to the geography, life styles and climates of Africa from
Egypt across North Africa to South Africa. In the north
are scenes of nomad life, oasis farming, and city scenes
in Cairo. Diversity of peoples is stressed.

194   AFRICAN CONTINENT: NORTHERN REGION
1962 / 14 min / sound / color or b&w / 16 mm
Coronet Instructional Films. (NUC FiA 62-1386) Locations:
Boston U. / Florida State U. / Indiana U. / Iowa Films /
Kent State U. / Michigan State U. / Syracuse U. / U. of
Illinois / U. of Iowa / U. of Kansas / U. of Michigan / U.
of Minnesota / U. of Nebraska / U. of Wisconsin.
Intended for junior-senior high school audiences. Shows
three major influences on North African life are lack of
water, its strong Arab culture and heritage, and the
European and colonial presence.

195   AFRICANS ALL
1963 / 23 min / sound / color / 16 mm
International Film Foundation. (NUC FiA 66-185) Location:
Penn. State U. / Syracuse U. / U. of Wisconsin.
Elementary to junior high school level film combining
live action footage and Phillip Stapp's animation to show
the diversity of African life. Attempts to dispel
misconceptions about the "dark continent". Covers Africa
from Cairo, Algiers, Khartoum, south to the Masai and
South Africa. Looks at city, nomad and tribal life and
shows differences in culture, peoples and music.

196   ANCIENT KINGDOMS IN NORTH EAST AFRICA
1969 / 30 min / sound / b&w / 16 mm

WCBS TV and Columbia University. Released by Holt, Rinehart and Winston, Inc. (Black Heritage: A History of Afro-America Series, Section 3: Where Did They Come From?) (LC 77-704033) Credits: Educational Collaborator - Joseph E. Harris.

Intended for junior high school through adult audiences. Attempts to show the history of Africa and its relationship to slavery. The ancient kingdoms of the Nile Valley and Ethiopia are profiled and the present day relationship between African nations and Afro-Americans is discussed.

197   CONTINENT OF AFRICA
1966 / 15 min / sound / color / 16 mm
(Africa series) Locations: U. of Illinois / U. of Nebraska.

Shows how each of the four major regions of Africa is highly influenced by its geography and climate. Dry North Africa, western Africa with its large forests, the highlands of the east coast and the industrialized areas of South Africa are profiled.

198   LIFE IN AN OASIS (NORTH AFRICA)
1962 / 11 min / sound / color or b&w / 16 mm
Coronet Instructional Films. (NUC FiA 62-600) Credits: Educational Collaborator - Earl B. Shaw. Locations: Kent State U. / Syracuse U. / U. of Illinois / U. of Kansas / U. of Michigan / U. of Nebraska.

For junior high school audiences. Shows life in an oasis settlement. The oasis, whether natural or man-made, is based on digging or drilling wells to provide water for agriculture, construction of mud-brick houses and for human consumption. Shows new techniques in agriculture including chemical fertilizers and attempts being made to hold back endless sand from the oasis agricultural area.

199   THE NEW NORTH AFRICA
1964 / 16 min / sound / color / 16 mm
Stanton Films. Distributed by Doubleday. (NUC FiA 65-1822) Credits: Producer-Director - Thomas Stanton, Narrator - Ed Stoddard. Eastmancolor. Location: Embassy of Tunisia.

General introduction for junior high school audiences to the newly independent North African countries. Tunisia is shown in greatest depth. Profiles the geography, climate, people, government and leaders of that nation. Stresses its modernity and shows scenes of city and university life.

200   NORTH AFRICA
1960 / 20 min / sound / b&w / 16 mm
U.S. Dept. of Defense. (LC 75-701184)

General view of Morocco, Algeria, Tunisia, and Libya. Includes information on their social and political problems and their relationships to the U.S.

201   NORTHERN AFRICA: WATER AND MAN
       1966 / 16 min / sound / color / 16 mm
       ACI Productions. Released by McGraw-Hill. (Africa series)
       (NUC FiA 67-108) (Also part of the Water and Man series)
       Credits: Advisors - Clyde F. Kohn, Graham W. Irwin.
       Locations: Kent State U. / Library of Congress (FBA 6183) /
       Syracuse U. / U. of Illinois / U. of Nebraska.
            For junior-senior high school audiences. Shows how North
            Africa has been slow to develop as a result of water
            shortage. Discusses how industrialization and major
            irrigation projects will overcome this problem.
            Discusses the implications of oil exploitation in North
            Africa.

202   OASIS OF THE SAHARA
       1965 / 8 min / sound / color or b&w / 16 mm
       Authentic Pictures. Made by Chris Hansen. Released by
       McGraw-Hill. (NUC FiA 66-1258) Locations: Kent State U. /
       Library of Congress (FAA 5905) / Syracuse U. / U. of
       Illinois.
            For junior high school audiences. Shows how life in the
            Sahara is totally dependent on water found at oases or
            brought through underground tunnels from wells. The date
            tree, adapted to desert conditions, is especially impor-
            tant to oasis agriculture. Looks at ancient rock pain-
            tings in Saharan caves which show the region was not
            always a desert but once had a much gentler climate.

203   SAHARA STORY
       (c. 1963?) / 20 min / sound / b&w / 16 mm
       Producer unknown.
            Looks at the Sahara Desert and the technological advan-
            ces which are combatting it. Includes scenes of
            construction of new highways, irrigation projects, and
            exploitation of mineral resources such as oil and coal.

204   WAR IN THE DESERT
       1961 / 11 min / sound / b&w / 16 mm
       Twentieth Century-Fox Films. Released by Blackhawk Films.
       Location: U. of Illinois.
            Quentin Reynolds, war correspondent for Collier's maga-
            zine, narrates this film made up of newsreel footage.
            Shows the Italian conquest of North Africa from the
            Ethiopian campaign to the movement of Italian settler
            families to Libya.

NORTH AFRICA - FILMS PRODUCED BETWEEN 1970-1979

205   AFRICA: HISTORICAL HERITAGE
       1971 / 9 min / sound / color / 16 mm
       Encyclopaedia Britannica. (LC 72-715520) Location: U. of
       Texas at Austin.

Archeological evidence of ancient civilizations in Egypt
and the Sudan are explored. Shows the advanced state of
several ancient African kingdoms which disappeared before
or during the period of European colonization.

206   ANCIENT AFRICANS
      1970 / 27 min / sound / color / 16 mm
      Julien Bryan Productions. Distributed by International Film
      Foundation. (LC 70-710865) Locations: Brigham Young U. /
      Indiana U. / Kent State U. / Penn. State U. / Syracuse U. / U. of
      Arizona / U. of California / U. of Illinois / U. of Iowa /
      U. of Kansas / U. of Michigan / U. of Minnesota / U. of
      Nebraska / U. of North Carolina / U. of Texas at Austin / U.
      of Wisconsin / Washington State U.
          Combines location photography with Phillip Stapp's ani-
          mation. Covers African civilizations from pre-historic
          times to the 16th century. Describes ancient trade
          routes, artifacts, and ancient kingdoms as well as the
          influence of Islam on African life. Egyptian, Sudanese,
          Ethiopian and sub-Saharan civilizations are covered.
          Intended for junior high school to adult audiences.

207   EVERYDAY LIFE IN A ROMAN PROVINCE
      (n.d.) / 12 min / sound / color / 16 mm
      Paramount Communications.
          Shows the style of life lived in a Roman provincial town
          in North Africa through location photography of North
          African Roman ruins. Narration is composed of historical
          Roman correspondence.

208   LIVESTOCK BREEDING IN NORTH AFRICA
      (c. 1970) / 4 min / silent / color / 8mm
      Associated Instructional Materials.
          Short film showing North African livestock.

209   OASIS AND CASBAH ON THE SAHARA
      (c. 1970) / 4 min / silent / color / 8 mm
      Associated Instructional Materials. No other information
      available.

210   TWO DESERTS: SAHARA AND SONORA
      1970 / 17 min / sound / color / 16 mm
      Learning Corp. of America. Locations: Kent State U. / U. of
      Illinois.
          Similar conditions can be found in these two former sea
          beds thousands of miles apart. Shows the attempts by
          North Americans to change the Sonora desert in contrast
          to the efforts by African desert dwellers to adapt to
          their environment. Intended for junior-senior high
          school audiences.

45

INTER-RELIGIOUS RELATIONS

211   ABC PRESENTS DEAN PIKE
      (n.d.) / 25 min / sound / b&w / 16 mm
      ABC Television.   Distributed by Middle East Institute, and
      American Friends of the Middle East.
          The Rev. Dean Pike speaks with Shaykh al-Bitar of Syria,
          and Dr. Abd al-Hakim of Pakistan, about the relationship
          between Islam and the Judeo-Christian tradition.   Common
          elements of the three religions are discussed.

212   CONVERSATION WITH ARCHBISHOP GEORGE APPLETON
      (n.d.) / 30 min / sound / color / 16 mm
      Anti-Defamation League of B'nai B'rith.   Distributed by Alden
      Films.   (Dateline Israel series) Location: Gratz College.
          Arnold Forster discusses the status of Jerusalem as a
          holy city for the three great monotheistic religions;
          Judaism, Christianity and Islam, with Archbishop George
          Appleton, an Anglican churchman living in Jerusalem.   The
          relationship between the three religious communities in
          Israel is also discussed.

213   DREW PEARSON REPORTS ON RELIGIONS IN ISRAEL
      1957 / 16 min / sound / b&w / 16 or 35 mm
      Orb Films.   Released by Orb Films and United Israel Appeal.
      (NUC FiA 64-574) Credits: Producer-Director - Baruch
      Dienar, Camera - Rolf N. Kneller.   Location: Abraham F. Rad
      Jewish Film Archive.
          Listed in some catalogs as: DREW PEARSON REPORTING ON
          RELIGION IN ISRAEL.   Describes Israel as the "birthplace
          of religion", where all may worship as they choose.

214   FOUR RELIGIONS, PART 2 - ISLAM AND CHRISTIANITY
      1960 / 30 min / sound / b&w / 16 mm
      National Film Board of Canada and James Beveridge.   Released
      in the U.S. in 1961 by McGraw-Hill.   (NUC FiA 67-1362)
      Credits: Narrator - Arnold Toynbee.   Locations: Boston U.
      / Indiana U. / Kent State U. / Syracuse U. / U. of Arizona /
      U. of Illinois / U. of Minnesota / U. of Wisconsin.
          Introduces the basic tenets of Islam, the youngest of the
          three large monotheistic religions, along with its rela-
          tionship to Christianity.   Both religions' borrowings
          from Judaism are discussed.   Intended for senior high
          school audiences.

215   ISRAEL: COVENANT AND CONFLICT
      1969 / 28 min / sound / b&w / 16 mm
      Anti-Defamation League of B'nai B'rith.
          Television studio interview by Mitchell Krauss with the
          Rev. Edward H. Flammery and Dr. Franklin H. Littell, who

speak persuasively on behalf of Israel. Topics covered include Jerusalem, Christianity in Israel, phophecy, and Israel's relations with Arab refugees. Of use mostly for church groups.

216　ISRAEL - PAST AND PRESENT
(n.d.) / 30 min / sound / color / 16 mm
Distributed by Alden Films. Location: Gratz College.
Depicts places in Israel of special interest to Christians because of Biblical references. Intended to help Jewish audiences understand the significance of Israel to Christians, and for Christian church groups.

217　MAJOR RELIGIONS OF THE WORLD: DEVELOPMENT AND RITUALS
1954 / 20 min / sound / color or b&w / 16 mm
Encyclopaedia Britannica Educational Corp. Locations: Brigham Young U. / Kent State U. / Ministry of Education and Culture, Jerusalem / Penn. State U. / Syracuse U. / U. of Arizona / U. of Illinois / U. of Kansas / U. of Kansas / U. of Michigan / U. of Nebraska / U. of Washington.
An overview of five of the major world religions: Hinduism, Buddhism, Judaism, Christianity and Islam. Discusses the basic tenets and beliefs of each faith. Shows the borrowing and building of ideas from one religion to another. Intended for junior high school to adult audiences to give basic information and promote tolerance of other faiths.

218　THE MOSLEM WORLD: CHRISTIANITY FACES ISLAM
1936 / 15 min / silent / b&w / 16 mm
Harmon Foundation. (The Moslem World, part 3) (NUC FiA 54-3697) Locations: Library of Congress (FAA 6046) / National Archives (200 HF 173) *
In fair to poor condition considering age. Describes how Muslims are less likely converts to Christianity due to strong unifying ties of language and common beliefs and practises. Has some grave errors concerning Islam. Suggests missionary work should be coupled with medical and agricultural missions if it is to be accepted by local Muslim populations. Discusses the problems of western influence, including spread of ideas such as nationalism, commercialism and militarism. Mostly of historical interest, this was originally intended for church groups.

219　PEOPLE OF THE BOOK
(n.d.) / 41 min / sound / color / 16 mm or videocassette
McGraw-Hill Films.
One of several films by this title. Shows the similarities between Judaism, Christianity and Islam. Discusses the lack of tolerance of each other, especially during the periods of the Crusades and the Inquisition.

47

220　PEOPLE OF THE BOOK
1976 / 45 min / sound / color / 16 mm
Granada Television. Bamber Gascoigne. (The Christians,
Part 5) Locations: U. of California / U. of Washington.
Part 5 of a 13 part series called "The Christians", and
possibly another version of no. 219. Portrays the relationship between Christians and Muslims from the 7th
through 15th centuries, with a commentary by Bamber
Gascoigne.

221　A PEOPLE REBORN
1977 / 28 min / sound / color / 16 mm
Gerald Struber. Distributed by Gospel Films. Available
from the Consulate General of Israel and from Alden Films.
Describes the meaning of Israel to evangelical
Protestants, as the Rev. Billy Zeoli tours places in
Israel of interest to Christians. Discusses the Israeli
Jew as a fulfillment of Biblical prophecy. Intended for
church groups and ecumenical programs. Includes inter-
views with Christians living in Israel.

222　RELIGION IN ISRAEL
(n.d.) / 16 min / sound / b&w / 16 mm
Orb Films. Baruch Dienar. Credits: Photographer - Rolf
Kneller, Narrator - Drew Pearson. Locations: Abraham F. Rad
Jewish Film Archive / Jewish Agency Film Archive.
A look at Judaism, Christianity and Islam in Israel.
Possibly the same as item 213.

THE CRUSADES

223　THE CRUSADES
1935 / 29 min / sound / 16 mm
Paramount News Service. Edited by Teaching Film Custodians.
Locations: Indiana U. / U. of Illinois.
Abridged version of the Paramount feature film of the
same title edited for classroom purposes. Presents the
story of Richard the Lion-Heart's trip from England to
the Holy Land, and the battles for Acre and Jerusalem.
Intended for junior high school audiences.

224　THE CRUSADES
1948 / 30 min / sound / b&w / 16 mm
Teaching Films, Inc. Teaching Film Custodians. (NUC FiA
52-4918) Credits: Director - Cecil B. DeMille, Screenplay -
Harold Lamb, Waldemar Young, Dudley Nichols. Locations:
Colorado State U. / Indiana U. / Oklahoma State U. / Oregon
State System of Higher Education / U. of Colorado / U. of
Illinois, Champaign / U. of Oklahoma / U. of Nebraska / U.
of Utah.
Re-issue of the 1935 classroom film, in turn abridged
from the feature film of the same name (see no. 223).

48

Prepared for school use by the Audio-Visual Committee of the National Council for Social Studies. Approaches its subject matter through the eyes of its director, Cecil B. DeMille, whose attempts to reproduce historical events have seldom been hampered by a desire for authenticity.

225 CRUSADES
1969 / 16 min / sound / color / 16 mm
Centron Corporation. Locations: Arizona State U. / Kent State U. / Library of Congress (FBA 9460) / Oklahoma State U. / Purdue / Syracuse U. / U. of Connecticut / U. of Idaho / U. of Illinois / U. of Kansas / U. of Washington.
Intended to provide the visual setting of the Crusades for junior-senior high school audiences. Uses line drawings of the 19th century French artist Gustave Dore, with an historical narrative, to describe the eight Crusades. The progress and eventual outcome of each Crusade is discussed from the viewpoint of the Christian European knights.

226 THE CRUSADES: SAINTS AND SINNERS
1969 / 25 min / sound / color / 16 mm
Learning Corp. of America. Filmed by International Film Associates, Inc. (Western Civilization:: Majesty and Madness series) Credits: Producer-Director - Victor Vicas, Writer - Linda Gottlieb. Locations: Boston U. / Florida State U. / Indiana U. / Kent State U. / Library of Congress (FCA 5928) / New York U. / Penn. State U. / Syracuse U. / U. of Connecticut / U. of Illinois / U. of Michigan / U. of Minnesota / U. of Missouri / U. of Nebraska / U. of South Carolina / U. of Texas / U. of Wisconsin. *
Uses actors and locations to re-enact events from the Crusades during the period 1095-1291. Intended for junior-senior high school audiences. Covers the capture and re-capture of Jerusalem, the Seljuk Turks opposing the Byzantine Empire, the financing of the Crusades and the preparation leading to the actual journey from western Europe to the Holy Land. Internal dissention and disease plague the European forces, leading to acts of slaughter of Muslim and Jewish civilians. Of interest due to its emphasis on religious intolerance on the part of the European knights, this film is unfortunately very poorly produced, using a feeble script, poor actors and terrible sets and costumes. It is also poorly dubbed. The narration in part saves the film by attempting to view the Crusades from both the European and Eastern perspectives.

227 THE CRUSADES (1095-1291)
1969 / 16 min / sound / color / 16 mm
Centron Educational Films. Location: U. of Illinois.
Also listed in sources as: THE CRUSADES (1095-1272). Another issue of no. 225. Covers the eight Crusades as illustrated by the engravings of Gustave Dore.

228   THE MEDIEVAL CRUSADES
      1956 / 27 min / sound / color / 16 mm
      Encyclopaedia Britannica. Locations: U. of Illinois / U. of
      Michigan.
          Photographed on location in France, Asia Minor and
          Palestine. Traces one family through the period of the
          Crusades. In the form of a narrated letter, events
          leading to the call by the Pope for a Holy War are
          described. Animated maps chart the progress of the
          European knights and the outcome and effect of the
          Crusades are discussed.

229   MEDIEVAL TIMES: THE CRUSADES
      1965 / 14 min / sound / color or b&w / 16 mm
      Coronet Instructional Films. (NUC FiA 65-1040) Credits:
      Educational Collaborator - James L. Cate. Locations:
      Syracuse U. / U. of Illinois / U. of Michigan.
          Shot on location. Attempts to show the divisive nature
          of the Crusades on European society. For over 200 years,
          the attempt to recapture the Holy Land caused great
          changes in European life and thought.

BIBLICAL, JUDEO-CHRISTIAN HISTORY

230   ARCHAEOLOGY PROVES THE BIBLE
      1968 / 30 min / sound / color / 16 mm
      DBSA. Dawn Film Service.
          Professor Yigael Yadin of the Hebrew University describes
          archaeological evidence uncovered which proves the
          historical nature of certain passages from the Bible.

231   THE BIBLE: A LITERARY HERITAGE
      1970 / 27 min / sound / color / 16 mm
      Learning Corp. of America. Filmed by International Film
      Associates. (Western Civilization: Majesty and Madness
      series) Location: U. of Illinois.
          Explores the diversity of styles found in different
          passages of the Bible, from tribal history to the Sermon
          on the Mount. Narrated by Donald Pleasance, filmed on
          location in Israel.

232   THE BOOK AND THE IDOL
      (c. 1963?) / 15 min / sound / color / 16 mm
      Alden Films. Samuel Elfert. Locations: Israel Office of
      Information / Ministry of Tourism, Jerusalem.
          Filmed exhibition held at the Metropolitan Museum of
          Art in New York, entitled "From the Land of the Bible".
          Traces the conflict between paganism and monotheism in
          ancient Israel.

233   THE INHERITANCE
      1965 / 2 films, 30 min each / sound / color or b&w / 16 mm

Radio and Television Commission, Southern Baptist
Convention, and the National Broadcasting Co. (The Southern
Baptist Hour, television series) (LC 70-711034/5) Credits:
Producer-Director - Martin Hoade, Writer - Philip Scharper,
Narrator - Alexander Scourby.
 An archaeological view of the Bible, showing the begin-
 nings of Christianity in Egypt, Iraq, Jordan, Iran and
 Israel. Looks at the place of prophecy in the Bible.

234   LAND OF THE BIBLE
      1958 / 20 min / sound / color / 16 mm
      Air France. (NUC FiA 59-744)
       Travelog view of holy places mentioned in the Old and
       New Testaments found in modern day Israel and Lebanon.

JUDAISM - GENERAL

235   AS LONG AS I LIVE
      1960 / 17 min / sound / color / 16 mm
      Keren Hayesod, Jerusalem. Released in the U.S. by United
      Israel Appeal. Distributed by Alden Films. (NUC FiA
      64-568) Credits: Producer - Lazar Dunner, Director -Edgar
      Hirshbein. Locations: Jewish Agency Film Archive, Jerusalem
      / Keren Hayesod, Jerusalem.
       Explores the place of Judaism in the state of Israel.
       Shows the balance of secularism and religion. Orthodox
       Jewish life is profiled in the cities, army, on the kib-
       butz and in various ethnic communities. Scenes of a
       Hassidic wedding and other celebrations are shown.

236   CHASID
      1970 / 18 min / sound / b&w / 16 mm
      Dept. of Radio-Television-Film, Temple University. Made by
      Jonathan Greene. (LC 79-712769)
       Explains the meaning and way of life of the Chasidic
       Jews.

237   DEAD SEA SCROLLS
      (n.d.) / 90 min / silent / b&w / 16 mm
      Location: Abraham F. Rad Jewish Film Archive.
       Profiles the excavations of Professors Yadin and Bar-Adon,
       which led to the discovery of the Dead Sea Scrolls.

238   GOSSAMER THREAD
      1972 / 28 min / sound / color / 16 mm
      Productions Unlimited. Released by Macmillan Films.
      Distributed by Alden Films. (LC 73-700481)
       Traces the history of Judaism through architecture and
       the building of synagogues from early Babylonian times to
       the medieval Spanish period.

239   GRANT US PEACE
      (c. 1976?) / 29 min / sound / color / 16 mm

Jewish Chautauqua Society.
Stresses the importance of peace in Judaism and suggests
this principle could be applied to modern world problems.

240 IN THE PATH OF PRAYER
(n.d.) / 24 min / sound / color / 16 mm
Distributed by Alden Films.
The story of the Jewish presence in Israel, from ancient
times throughout history, is viewed through architecture
of synagogues. Examines artistic motifs which show the
close attachment to Jerusalem. Scenes from Masada,
Qumran, Barom, Kfar Nahum, Koravim, Bet Alfa, Tiberias,
Safad and Jerusalem are shown.

241 IT WAS THE CUSTOM (MINHAG HAYA BEYISRAEL)
1969 / 16 min / sound / b&w / 16 mm
Yitzhak Krymolovski. Distributed by Alden Films. Credits:
Director-Writer - Nathan Gross. Locations: Gratz College /
Jewish Agency Film Archive / Ministry of Education and
Culture, Jerusalem.
Available in English or Hebrew soundtracks. Based on the
work of David Davidowitz of the Tel Aviv Museum for
Jewish Folklore and Ethnography. Shows the diversity of
customs and religious observances found in the different
Jewish ethnic groups who have immigrated to Israel. Not
all countries and groups are represented, but the film
attempts to show the great diversity of peoples found in
Israel today.

242 JEWISH HOLY PLACES IN THE LAND OF ISRAEL
(n.d.) / 20 min / sound / color / 16 mm
Distributed by Alden Films.
Scenes of Israel show the importance of the land to Jews
due to religious and historical connotations. Includes
scenes of the Wailing Wall, the Mount of Olives, tombs
and synagogues, and the site of the Sanhedrin in
Tiberias.

243 JEWS AND THEIR WORSHIP
(c. 1976?) / 30 min / sound / b&w / 16 mm
Anti-Defamation League of B'nai B'rith. Location: Middle
East Institute.
Shows the basic religious observances practised by Jews.
Describes the historic evolution of prayer and the place
of the synogogue in Jewish life.

244 JUDAISM, PART 1
1955 / 30 min / sound / b&w / 16 mm
KETC-TV, St. Louis. Released by NET Film Service.
(Religions of Man series, no. 12) (NUC FiA 58-1465)
Credits: Educational Collaborator - Dr. Huston Smith.
Locations: Kent State U. / Indiana U. / Syracuse U.
Intended for a senior high school to adult audience.

Traces the basic beliefs of Jewish philosophy, including
the rights and responsibilities of Jews, the concept of a
chosen people, the place of justice and truth in Judaism,
and the meaning of suffering.

245   JUDAISM, PART 2
      1955 / 30 min / sound / b&w / 16 mm
      KETC-TV, St. Louis. Released by NET Film Service.
      (Religions of Man series, no. 13) . (NUC FiA 58-1466)
      Locations: See no. 244.
          Dr. Huston Smith of Washington University continues to
          describe Jewish traditions with the meaning of the Ten
          Commandments, the basis of Jewish law. The division of
          law between ritualistic and ethical spheres is examined.

246   JUDAISM
      1968 / 17 min / sound / color / 16 mm and super 8mm cartridge
      Lew Ayres. Released by International Communication Films.
      (Religions of the Eastern World series) (LC 70-703278)
      Locations: Syracuse U. / U. of Illinois.
          For junior-senior high school audiences. Examines the
          development of Orthodox, Conservative and Reform Judaism,
          and the manner in which they are practised in the U. S.
          Historical development of law from the Torah, Talmud and
          ritual, the concept of one God and religious literature
          are profiled.

247   JUDAISM
      1973 / 28 min / sound / color / 16 mm
      Films Incorporated. (World Religions series)
          For junior-senior high school audiences. Traces the
          history of Judaism. Introduces the concept of monotheism
          and describes Jewish ceremonies and observances.

248   JUDAISM: THE CHOSEN PEOPLE
      1977 / 51 min / sound / color / 16 mm and videocassette
      BBC-TV. Distributed in the U.S. by Time-Life. (The Long Search
      series, no. 7) Credits: Narrator - Ronald Eyre. Locations:
      Penn. State U. / U. of Illinois / U. of Michigan.
          The definition of what and who is a Jew is examined.
          Elie Wiesel in New York, a rabbi in Jerusalem, and others
          describe what it means to be a Jew. Scenes of the
          Wailing Wall, synagogues, the Museum of the Holocaust,
          and other sites develop a feeling for the history and
          traditions of Jewish life. Part of a well produced
          series on religions of the world. Very good introduction
          to Jewish life and traditions.

249   JUDAISM - ORTHODOX, CONSERVATIVE, REFORM
      (c. 1976?) / 30 min / sound / b&w / 16 mm
      Anti-Defamation League of B'nai B'rith.
          Describes the three major branches of Judaism and the
          ways in which they differ in religious observances.

250   THE LAW AND THE PROPHETS
      1965 / 52 min / sound / color / 16 mm
      NBC Television. Distributed by McGraw-Hill. Locations:
      Kent State U. / Syracuse U.
         For senior high school to adult audiences. Describes
      the history of the Jewish people. Begins with the
      Biblical account of creation and continues through the
      time of the prophets and patriarchs to the destruction of
      the Kingdom. Traces both ancient Jewish religious and
      political life.

251   LET THY CAMP BE HOLY
      1966 / ? / sound / 16 mm
      S. Soriano. Location: Israel Film Studios, Herzliyah.
         Available in English and Hebrew soundtracks. Explores
      the presence and meaning of Judaism in the Israeli army.

252   A PEOPLE CHOSEN: WHO IS A JEW?
      1973 / 56 min / sound / color / 16 mm
      Krosney Productions. Distributed by Phoenix Films, and by
      Alden Films. Locations: Gratz College / Kent State U.
         For senior high school to college audiences. Examines
      the question of who is a Jew. Interviews with Israeli
      citizens, Israeli Arabs, and public figures such as Abba
      Eban, Rabbi Goren, Yiagal Alon, and David Ben-Gurion
      cover the diversity of peoples and customs found among
      Jews in Israel today. Also looks at the relationship
      between the state and religion in Israel.

253   QUMRAN AND THE DEAD SEA SCROLLS
      1972 / 25 min / sound / color / 16 mm
      Locations: U. of Kansas / U. of Wisconsin. No other infor-
      mation available.

254   THE SCHOOL
      1944 / 16 min / sound / b&w / 16 mm
      Religious Films, London. Released in the U.S. by United
      World Films, 1946. (Two Thousand Years Ago series) (NUC
      FiA 52-546) Credits: Director - Mary Field, Educational
      Committee of the Christian Cinema.
         Describes life of a Jewish family in Palestine in Biblical
      times. Shows a boy attending the synagogue school and a
      girl helping with household work.

JUDAISM - HOLIDAYS AND RELIGIOUS OBSERVANCES

255   BAR MITZVA BOYS
      1962 / 20 min / sound / c olor / 16 mm
      Israel Motion Picture Studios. Credits: Director - Y. Roden,
      Writer - A. Potashnik. Location: Prime Minister's Office,
      Information Dept., Jerusalem.
         Traces the story of young boys who come to Israel from

Canada to celebrate their Bar Mitzva. Not to be confused
with a feature of the same title.

256   THE FEAST OF LIGHTS - CHANUKHA
        (c. 1960?) / 16 min / sound / color / 16 mm
        Israel Motion Picture Studios, Herzliyah. (Holidays in
        Israel series) Credits: Director - F. Steinhardt, Producer-
        Writer - Y. Brandstatter, Photographer - B. Korecki.
        Location: Library of Congress (FAA 6127) *
            Obtained through the P.L. 480 Israel program. Also
            listed in some catalogs as: HANUKA OR HOLIDAYS
            IN ISRAEL, and THE FEAST OF LIGHTS, CHANUKHA.
            Well produced film depicting the origins of the festival
            of Hanukha in 168 B.C. with Antiochus and the Maccabees
            fighting for Jerusalem. Present day observances in
            Israel are shown ranging from a cheerful exchange of pre-
            sents and lighting of candles in the home to a more
            somber observance in an army camp. Good introduction for
            non-Jews. General film suitable for junior high school
            to adult audiences.

257   FEAST OF THE FIRST FRUITS (CHAG HABIKKURIM)
        (n.d.) / 10 min / sound / color / 16 mm
        Location: Abraham F. Rad Jewish Film Archive.
            Shows the celebration of Shavu'ot performed at Kibbutz
            Gan Shmuel in Israel.

258   HANUKKAH
        (c. 1960?) / 15 min / sound / color / 16 mm
        Distributed by Alden Films. (Holidays in Israel series)
            Re-issue or possibly the same film as no. 256. Traces
            the history of the festival of Hanukkah.

259   HOLIDAYS
        (n.d.) / 3 min / silent / b&w / 16 mm
        Location: Abraham F. Rad Jewish Film Archive.
            Short, silent film. Shows scenes of holidays as they
            are celebrated in Israel. Includes the cutting of the
            Omer on a kibbutz at Pesach, the pilgrimage to Mt. Zion
            on Shavu'ot and Christmas celebrations in Jerusalem and
            Nazareth.

260   JEWISH DIETARY LAWS
        1968 / 7 min / sound / color / 16 mm
        Lew Ayres. (Religions of the World series) (LC 76-703277)
            Intended for junior high school to college audiences.
            Explains the origins of Jewish dietary laws in the Old
            Testament and in rabbinical writings. Describes how meat
            and wine should be prepared.

261   KIBBUTZ SUCCOTH CELEBRATION
        1969 / 4 min / silent / color / super 8 mm cartridge
        Eye Gate House. (Living in Israel series) (LC 74-703717)

Shows the harvest festival of Succoth celebrated on a kibbutz in Israel.

262   PASSOVER
(c. 1960?) / 14 min / sound / color / 16 mm
Distributed by Alden Films. (Holidays in Israel series)
Locations: Abraham F. Rad Jewish Film Archive / Gratz College.
Describes basic historic origins of the Passover holiday and describes the way in which Passover is celebrated in Israel today, from a seder in a home to a kibbutz celebration. The "festival of spring" aspect of the holiday is shown with footage of natural scenes shot during Passover. Shows pilgrimages undertaken during the holiday.

263   PURIM
(c. 1960?) / 15 min / sound / color / 16 mm
Distributed by Alden Films. (Holidays in Israel series)
Location: Gratz College.
Shows how Purim is celebrated in Israel. Includes scenes of children in costume, customs of different ethnic communities, the reading of the Megilah, the Mishloach Manot, and sequences of the Ad Lo Yadah parade. Closes with a pantomime recounting events in the Book of Esther performed by children.

264   THE SEVENTH DAY (YOM SHEKULO TOV)
1966 / 13 min / sound / b&w / 16 mm
H. Krymolovsky for Nehora. Distributed by Alden Films.
Credits: Director-Writer - Nathan Gross. Locations: Abraham F. Rad Jewish Film Archive / Histadrut - General Federation of Jewish Labor / Ministry of Education and Culture, Jerusalem / Nehora, Jerusalem.
Available in English and Hebrew soundtracks. Shows public and domestic preparations for the Shabbat in towns and villages. Features illustrations from the "Jewish Family Album" by Moritz Oppenheim, showing Sabbath observances.

265   SHAVU'OT
(c. 1970?) / 11 min / sound / color / 16 mm
Keren Hayesod, Jerusalem. Distributed by Alden Films.
(Holidays in Israel series) Locations: Abraham F. Rad Jewish Film Archive / Gratz College / Ministry of Education and Culture, Jerusalem.
Listed in some catalogs as: SHAVUOTH (FEAST OF WEEKS). Describes the origins of the holiday in the giving of the Ten Commandments and the harvest. A Bikurim ceremony, the celebration of the first fruits, is shown on a kibbutz in Israel. Includes scenes of sheep shearing and folk dancing by the Imbal Troupe.

266   SUCCOTH
       (c. 1960?) / 15 min / sound / color / 16 mm
       Distributed by Alden Films. (Holidays in Israel series)
       Location: Gratz College.
          Shows celebration of the Succoth holiday in Israel.

267   THE SYNOGOGUE
       1944 / 22 min / sound / b&w / 16 mm
       Religious Films, London. Released in the U.S. by United
       World Films, 1946. (Two Thousand Years Ago series) (NUC
       FiA 52548) Credits: Director - Mary Field, The Education
       Committee of the Christian Cinema.
          Describes life in Jewish Palestine in ancient times.
          Re-enacts observance of the Passover meal in Jerusalem,
          a Sabbath service, singing of the Psalms, and attendance
          at the synagogue. Describes Jewish customs and observan-
          ces for young audiences.

CHRISTIANITY

268   AND THIS IS WHERE IT ALL BEGAN
       1969 / 28 min / sound / color / 16 mm
       K-L-M Royal Dutch Airlines. Made by De La Varre Visual
       Public Relations. Released by Tribune. Distributed by
       Alden Films. (LC 70-711526) Location: Gratz College.
          Uses narration from the New Testament and music from the
          Max Bruch Violin Concerto. Depicts events from the life,
          teachings and death of Jesus of Nazareth. Discusses how
          and where Christian traditions began.

269   BLESSED FOOTSTEPS ON THE EGYPTIAN EARTH
       (c. 1978?) / ? / sound / 16 mm
       Saad Nadim for the Egyptian National Center for Documentary
       Films. Location: Library of Congress.
          Filmed on location in Egypt. Depicts the flight of the
          Holy Family down the Nile into Egypt. Shows Coptic
          monasteries from the Nile Delta to Dayr al-Miharrak in
          Upper Egypt, near the town of Manfalut.

270   CHRIST IS BORN
       1966 / 54 min / sound / color / 16 mm
       Learning Corp. of America. (Saga of Western Man series)
       Location: U. of Illinois.
          Uses narration from the Old and New Testament read by
          John Huston. Traces the history of the Jewish people
          from the time of Abraham through Roman rule to the birth
          of Jesus. Filmed on location.

271   CHRISTIANITY IN WORLD HISTORY
       1969 / 14 min / sound / color / 16 mm
       Coronet Instructional Films. Location: Syracuse U.
          Intended for senior high school to adult audiences. Tra-

ces the history of Christianity from its early spread in the Roman empire to the division of the eastern and western churches in 1054 A.D. Emphasizes the role of Christianity as a political as well as religious force. Stresses its role in the development of modern Europe. Filmed on location in Italy, Turkey and Israel.

272   HOPE FOR LIFE
1978 / 36 min / sound / color / 16 mm
Church World Service. National Council of Churches. Distributed by the United Methodist Film Service, Nashville. Of special interest to church groups. Examines the different ministries and missions in the Middle East to spread Christianity. Filmed in Egypt, Lebanon, the West Bank and Gaza. Local Arab Christians describe the meaning of their religion and their traditions.

273   IN THE YEAR OF OUR LORD
(c. 1958?) / 80 min / sound / color / 16 mm
Louis de Rochemont Associates. Credits: Narrator - Father Eric Weymeersch. (NUC FiA 58-1109)
Filmed on location in Israel, Jordan, Lebanon and Syria. Depicts life as it was lived in Biblical times. Shows some of the customs and traditions which are still observed today in the Middle East.

274   ISRAEL, THE HOLY LAND (CATHOLIC) (YISRAEL, ERETZ KEDOSHA)
1965 / 22 min / sound / color / 16 or 35 mm
Israfilm, Ltd., Tel Aviv. Released in the U.S. by American Educational Films. Distributed by Alden Films. Credits: Directors - Y. Ephrati, P. Perry. Locations: Gratz College / Prime Minister's Office, Information Dept., Jerusalem / Syracuse U.
Available in English, French, Spanish, German and Italian soundtracks. Tours the holy Christian sites of Israel accompanied by Baroque music. Follows the path of Jesus from the Sea of Galilee to Bethlehem, finally to Jerusalem and the Via Dolorosa. Intended for junior high school to adult audiences.

275   ISRAEL - HOLY PLACES
1968 / 22 min / sound / color / 16 or 35 mm
Location: Abraham F. Rad Jewish Film Archive.
Available in English, German, French, Spanish and Italian soundtracks. Shows sites holy to Christians. Possibly the same film or a re-issue of no. 274.

276   ISRAEL, LAND OF THE BIBLE (YISRAEL, ERETZ HATANACH)
1966 / 15 min / sound / color / 16 or 35 mm
Israfilm Ltd., Tel Aviv. Credits: Directors - Y. Ephrati, P. Perry. Locations: Abraham F. Rad Jewish Film Archive / Prime Minister's Office, Information Dept., Jerusalem.

Available in English and French soundtracks. Shows sites
of special interest to Protestants in Israel.

277   LAND OF HOPE AND PRAYER
      (c. 1970?) / 15 min / sound / color / 16 mm
      The Anglo-Saxon Community in Israel. Distributed by Alden
      Films. Locations: Abraham F. Rad Jewish Film Archive /
      Ministry of Tourism, Jerusalem.
          Available in English and French soundtracks. Follows a
          group of Baptist pilgrims on their tour through Israel
          visiting various holy sites.

278   MID-EAST PROFILE
      1958 / 29 min / sound / color or b&w / 16 mm
      Joint Commission on Missionary Education. Made by Film
      Productions International. Released by Broadcasting and
      Film Commission. (NUC FiA 58-1180) Credits: Producer -
      Lloyd Young, Director - Douglas Cox. Location: Religious
      Film Library.
          Filmed on location in the Middle East. Asks how
          Christians can best solve the political and social
          problems of the area through missionary work. Discusses
          how to most effectively convert the (then) 100 million
          Muslims in the Middle East.

279   THE WAKING MIDDLE EAST
      1956 / 31 min / sound / color / 16 mm
      Bob Jones University. Made and released by Unusual Films.
      (NUC FiA 59-116) Credits: Director - Katherine Stenholm.
      Location: Library of Congress (FCA 1559)
          Filmed on location in Egypt, Syria, Lebanon, Jordan and
          Israel. Dr. Bob Jones, Jr. discusses the Middle East
          situation from a religious viewpoint and relates the
          current problems of the area to Biblical prophecy.

280   WHERE JESUS LIVED
      1950 / 15 min / sound / color / 16 mm
      Brigham Young University.
          Travelog of Israel showing holy spots related to the life
          and teachings of Jesus.

ISLAM

281   THE AGA KHAN
      1970 / 54 min / sound / b&w / 16 mm
      Drew Associates and Time-Life. Released by Time-Life Films.
      (The Living Camera series, no. 13) (LC 74-714659)
          Profiles the Aga Khan, hereditary religious leader of
          Shi'i Muslims. Describes how his practises differ from
          those of his father and grandfather.

282   ALAHU AKBAR - FAITH OF FOUR HUNDRED MILLION
      1969 / 10 min / sound / color / 16 mm

ACI Productions. Distributed by Paramount Communications.
(LC 76-706863) Locations: Boise State U. / Syracuse U. / U.
of Illinois.
> For junior high school to adult audiences. Outlines the
> basic beliefs of Islam and emphasizes the relationship
> between the daily life of the Muslim and the activities
> of the mosque. Describes the mosque as the center of
> worship, education and social gatherings. Outlines some
> of the rituals and responsibilities of Muslims, espe-
> cially as practised in Egypt. Also listed as being
> released in 1970.

283 DANSEURS DE DIEU
1978 / 10 min / sound / color / 16 mm
Marc Mopty. Location: Turkish Tourism Office, New York. *
> Excellently photographed short film. Shows a dervish
> group contemplating with song and their famous whirling
> dance. Uses minimal narration. Shows a portrait of
> Rumi, founder of the Mevlevi dervish order, on the wall
> behind the whirling dervishes. For junior high school to
> adult audiences. A very beautiful film but provides
> little information. In English despite French title.

284 THE HOLY QUR'AN (KORAN)
1978 / 18 min / sound / color / 16 mm
Frances Cockburn. Distributed by Phoenix Films. Credits:
Director-Writer - David Thompson.
> Intended to introduce junior high school through adult
> audiences to the meaning of the Qur'an for Muslims.
> Shows exquisite calligraphy and ornamentation found in
> texts of the Muslim holy book, written down in the 1st
> century of Islam. Shows 15th and 16th century
> calligraphic examples from the Mamluke period in Syria
> and Egypt and present day Qur'ans.

285 THE HOWLING DERVISHES
1968 / 25 min / sound / color / 16 mm
BBC-TV, London and Odyssey Productions. Released in the
U.S. by Time-Life Films. (Asia series, no. 11) (LC
77-714393) Credits: Narrator - Lowell Thomas.
> Shows members of the Turksih Rufa'i dervish order, an
> outlawed religious group famous for their spinning ritual
> dances.

286 IN THE NAME OF ALLAH
1969 / 76 min / sound / b&w / 16 mm
Roger Graef. Granada Television, London. Released in the
U.S. by National Educational Television and Radio Center,
Indiana University Audio-Visual Center. (LC 74-711456)
Credits: Narrator - James Mason. Locations: Indiana U. /
Purdue / U. of California / U. of Michigan / U. of Texas at
Austin / U. of Washington.
> Intended for senior high school to adult audiences. Tra-

ces Islamic rituals and ceremonies practised in Fez,
Morocco. Looks at the Qur'an, teachings of Muhammad, and
the relationship between religion and the material world.
Looks at a Moroccan Islamic community performing wed-
dings, circumcisions and other rituals and observances.

287   ISLAM, PART 1
1955 / 30 min / sound / b&w / 16 mm
KETC-TV, St. Louis. Released by NET Film Service. (The
Religions of Man series, no. 10) (NUC FiA 58-1460)
Locations: Brigham Young U. / Indiana U. / Kent State U. /
Syracuse U. / U. of Arizona / U. of California.
     Listed in some catalogs as: THE STRAIGHT PATH.
     The first of a two part series of filmed lectures by Dr.
     Huston Smith on Islam. Topics covered include jihad,
     polygamy, stereotypes of Islam, tolerance in Islam, and
     the meaning of the straight path for Muslims. The two
     lectures should be viewed together although they are a
     little tedious with no extra visual material but maps.
     Intended for college and adult audiences.

288   ISLAM, PART 2
1955 / 30 min / sound / b&w / 16 mm
KETC-TV, St. Louis. Released by NET Film Service. (The
Religions of Man series, no. 11) (NUC FiA 58-1461)
Locations: See no. 287.
     Second part of the filmed lecture series by Dr. Huston
     Smith of Washington University. Topics covered include
     the five pillars of the Islamic faith and how they relate
     to the daily life of a Muslim. Part 2 is listed in some
     catalogs under the title: THE FIVE PILLARS.

289   ISLAM
1962 / 19 min / sound / color or b&w / 16 mm
National Film Board of Canada. Released in the U.S. by
McGraw-Hill. Distributed by Contemporary Films. (Great
Religions series) (NUC FiA 63-1176) Credits: Producer -
James Beveridge, Director-Writer - David Millar. Locations:
Kent State U. / Middle East Institute / Penn. State U. /
Syracuse U. / U. of California / U. of Illinois / U. of
Nebraska / U. of Texas at Austin / U. of Washington.
     Intended for senior high school to adult audiences.
     Describes Islam from the time of Muhammad at Mecca to the
     present day. Traditions and concepts, such as submission
     to God, the pilgrimage to Mecca and tithing, are
     discussed. Looks at the universality of Islam. Well
     photographed.

290   ISLAM
1968 / 16 min / sound / color / 16 mm or super 8 mm cartridge
Lew Ayres. Released by International Communication Films.
(Religions of the Eastern World series) (LC 79-703275)
Locations: Boston U. / Syracuse U. / U. of Arizona.

For junior-senior high school audiences. Re-edited version of the 1956 film: PILLARS OF ALLAH. Describes the beginning of Islam, the life of Muhammad, the revelations of the Qur'an, and the five pillars, or obligations, of Islam.

291   ISLAM
1972 / 28 min / sound / color / 16 mm
Ontario Educational Communications Authority. Distributed by Films Incorporated. (World Religions series) Location: Penn. State U.
For junior high school to adult audiences. Describes the basic tenets of Islam and shows the ways in which Canadian Muslims function in a non-Muslim society. Describes Islam as the last of the three major monotheistic religions, following and building on Judaism and Christianity. Shot on location in Egypt and Arabia.

292   ISLAM
1975 / 34 min / sound / color / 16 mm
RAI-Texture Films. Location: New York Public Donnell Film Library.
Tells the story of Islam from the time of the prophet Muhammad in the 7th century to the present. Shows the influence of Islam on the Middle East today.

293   ISLAM
1976 / 17 min / sound / color / 16 mm
Lew Ayres. Doubleday Multimedia. (Altars of the World series) (LC 76-700605)
Possibly the same film as no. 290. Explains the rituals and teachings of Islam. Describes the growth of Islam and the meaning of the five pillars, or obligations, Muslims should perform.

294   ISLAM: THE GREAT RELIGION
1962 / 20 min / sound / color / 16 mm
Brigham Young University.
Describes the religious and cultural aspects of Islam and the relationship of Islam to political life.

295   ISLAM IN EGYPT
1931 / 15 min / silent / b&w / 16 or 35 mm
Harmon Foundation, Inc. (Comparative Religions series)
(NUC FiA 54-3712) Locations: Library of Congress (FAA 6012) / National Archives (200 HF 78) *
Probably intended for Christian church groups. Describes the way of life in the Middle East at the time of Muhammad. Discusses the effect of the spread of Islam on the area. Concepts covered include the idea of one God, daily prayers, the quibla and mihrab. Scenes of Coptic congregations in Egypt, and al-Azhar University in Cairo, the center of Islamic learning, are shown. The caravan

taking the black cloth to Mecca to cover the Ka'aba is
also seen. Explains restricted rights of women as one of
the more offensive aspects of Islam as far as Christians
are concerned.

296   ISLAM, PROPHET AND THE PEOPLE
       1975 / 34 min / sound / color / 16 mm or super 8 mm or
       videocassette. RAI-Texture Films. Released in the U.S by
       Texture Films. (LC 75-704188) Credits: Producer-Director -
       Folco Quilici, Writer-Editor - Sonya Friedman. Locations:
       Brigham Young U. / Kansas State U. / Purdue / U. of Michigan / U.
       of Washington.
           Intended for junior high school to adult audiences.
           Describes the life of Muhammad and the spread of Islam
           from the Middle East to Indonesia, Africa, the Soviet
           Union, North and South America and India. Gives an
           explanation of the basic tenets of Islam and a brief
           history of the Islamic world.

297   ISLAM: THERE IS NO GOD BUT GOD
       1977 / 55 min / sound / color / 16 mm or videocassette
       BBC-TV. Released in the U.S. by Time-Life Multimedia. (The
       Long Search, television series, no. 5) Credits: Producer -
       Peter Montagnon, Narrator - Ronald Eyre. Locations: Florida
       State U. / Penn. State U. / U. of California / U. of
       Illinois / U. of Michigan / Washington State U. *
           Excellent film, first broadcast as part of a television
           series. Traces the Islamic experience in Egypt today.
           Shows the history and basic beliefs in Islam and proof of
           Islamic influence in Egypt. Al-Azhar University in Cairo
           is shown as well as scenes of a marriage ceremony and the
           pilgrimage to Mecca. Sincere attempt to present Islam to
           western adult audiences as a meaningful belief system and
           a major force in the world today. One of the better
           films available dealing with Islam.

298   THE ISLAMIC CENTER IN WASHINGTON, D.C.
       (n.d.) / 15 min / sound / b&w / 16 mm
       Blue Nile Productions. Distributed by the Middle East
       Institute.
           Not strictly within the definition of this filmography
           but of related interest. Gives the history of the
           mosque and Islamic cultural center in Washington, D.C.
           formed in 1953 as a center for Islamic studies and educa-
           tion. Scenes of the Center include a tour of the
           grounds, Muslims at prayer and religious observances.

299   MIDEAST: ISLAM - THE UNIFYING FORCE
       1977 / 17 min / sound / color / 16 mm
       CBS, Inc. Produced by Vocational and Industrial Films.
       Distributed by BFA Educational Media. (Mideast series)
       Credits: Producer - John Seabourne, Director - Richard
       Ashworth, Educational Collaborator - George Rentz.

Locations: Florida State U. / Library of Congress (FBA 7473) / Syracuse U. / U. of Texas at Austin. For junior high school to adult audiences. Provides an introduction to Islam, Muhammad's prophetic role, and the meaning of the Qur'an for Muslims. Shows the massive yearly pilgrimage to Mecca. General introduction to Islam.

300 THE MOSLEM WORLD: OUT OF THE DESERT
1936 / 15 min / silent / b&w / 16 mm
Harmon Foundation, Inc. (The Moslem World series) (NUC FiA 54-3696) Locations: Library of Congress (FAA 6045) / National Archives (200 HF 172).
General introduction to Islam. Describes the teachings of Muhammad and describes the problems which have arisen when Islam and Christianity have opposed each other.

301 O DEAR SAVIOR
1978 / 22 min / sound / color / 16 mm
National Iran Radio/Television. P. Kimiavi.
A film by Parviz Kimiavi intended to introduce non-Muslims to the Shi'i sect of Islam. Shows daily activities at the Shrine of Imam Reza in Mashad, Iran. Includes prayers, lamentations for Husayn and other Shi'i martyrs. One of the few films which shows practises and beliefs of the Shi'i Muslims. Location of extant copies unknown.

302 RAMADAN
(c. 1960?) / 20 min / sound / b&w / 16 mm
Described by the French American Cultural Services. No other information available.
Detailed description of the way in which the month long Fast of Ramadan is practised in Tunisia.

303 THE SHADOW OF GOD ON EARTH
1977 / 58 min / sound / color / 16 mm
Documents Associates, Inc. (Crossroad of Civilization) Credits: Narrator - David Frost.
Also listed as released in 1979. Deals with the Shi'i branch of Islam in Iran. Discusses the political and ideological split from traditional Sunni Islam. Also shows a calligrapher and director of restoration at the Imam Reza shrine in Mashad who discusses devotions and their relationship to art. The differences between Shi'i and Sunni Islam are not adequately described for the beginner but this remains one of the few films dealing with Shi'i Islam.

304 THE SUFI WAY
1971 / 28 min / sound / color / 16 mm
Hartley Productions. (LC 72-700758) Credits: Writers: Huston Smith, Elda Hartley and Irving Hartley. Locations: Arizona State U. / Brigham Young U. / Florida State U. /

64

Iowa Films / Middle East Institute / Purdue / Syracuse U. /
U. of California / U. of Illinois / U. of Iowa / U. of
Michigan / U. of Minnesota / U. of Washington.
Listed in some catalogs as: ISLAMIC MYSTICISM: THE
SUFI WAY. Intended for college and adult audiences.
Describes the basic tenets of Sufi or mystical Islam, and
how it varies from traditional Sunni Islam. Well pho-
tographed on location in North Africa, Turkey, and the
Middle East. Includes scenes of sites from Islamic
history, mosques and monuments. Shows whirling dervish
dances in Turkey and the practise of Sufi rituals in
North Africa. Well produced introduction.

305   THE TRADITIONAL WORLD OF ISLAM: THE INNER LIFE
1978 / 28 min / sound / color / 16 mm
Stephen Cross. Institutional Cinema Service. (The
Traditional World of Islam series) For complete locations,
see no. 46. *
Classic film dealing with Islamic Sufism. Well produced,
visually stunning film in the series covering Islamic
thought and civilization. The Inner Life or the mystical
branch of Islam, is viewed through architecture, poetry
and art in Egypt, Morocco and Iran. A Sufi devotion in
India proves the widespread geographic influence of
Sufism. Examples of Sufi influence in music and the arts
demonstrate its impact on all areas of life and
expression in the medieval Islamic world and the modern
Middle East. Intended for senior high school to adult
audiences. Highly recommended film.

306   THE TRADITIONAL WORLD OF ISLAM: UNITY
1978 / 30 min / sound / color / 16 mm
Stephen Cross. Institutional Cinema Service. (Traditional
World of Islam series) For complete locations, see no. 46.
*
A Sufic interpretation of the meaning of unity in Islam.
Shows unity and universality in Islam are the reasons
behind its spread to 1/7th of the world's population.
Concepts covered include equality before God, responsibilities of Muslims for hajj (pilgrimage) and prayer,
and the search for knowledge. Excellent footage of the
pilgrimage to Mecca seen from the air. Well photographed
introduction to Islam. Intended for senior high school
to adult audiences. Highly recommended.

307   THE WASHINGTON MOSQUE
1957 / 16 min / sound / color / 16 mm
U.S. Information Agency. Made by Craven Films Corp.
Released for public educational use in the U.S. by the U.S.
Office of Education, 1958. (NUC FiE 58-313)
Not strictly within the confines of this filmography, but
of related interest. Short introduction to the mosque
established in Washington, D.C. in 1953 to serve as a
center for Islamic cultural and religious activities.

308   ZOROASTRIANISM
       1968 / 15 min / sound / color / 16 mm and super 8 mm cartridge
       Lew Ayres. Released by International Communication Films.
       (LC 71-703281)
           Adapted from the 1956 film entitled: THE FLAME OF
           ZOROASTER. Shows ceremonies of initiation, weddings and
           funerals according to Zoroastrian customs as practised in
           Bombay, India.

309   ZOROASTRIANISM AND THE PARSIS
       1976 / 7 min / sound / color / 16 mm
       Lew Ayres. Location: U. of Iowa.
           Shorter version of no. 308. Shows scenes of a wedding
           and a male puberty rite as practised by Parsis in Bombay,
           India. Dualism and the symbolism of fire are discussed in
           this very short introduction to Zoroastrianism.

THE ARAB-ISRAELI CONFLICT

GENERAL FILMS

310 ADVOCATES, PART 1 AND 2
(n.d.) / 45 min / sound / b&w / 16 mm
Arab Information Office, Washington. Credits: Moderator -
Roger Fisher.
Interviews with Arab leaders concerning the Arab-Israeli
conflict.

311 AMERICAN STUDENTS VIEW THE MIDDLE EAST
1970 / 28 min / sound / b&w / 16 mm
Anti-Defamation League of B'nai B'rith. (LC 79-707432)
Intended for junior high school to adult audiences.
Interview by news analyst David Schoenbrun of five
college students from the U.S. Topics include a com-
parison of U.S. and Israeli youth, the Arab-Israeli
conflict, U.S. foreign policy in the Middle East and
Soviet involvement in the area. Presents positive
aspects of Israel.

312 ANTI-TERRORIST DEMONSTRATIONS
(n.d. pre-1950?) / 10 min / silent / b&w / 16 mm
Location: Abraham F. Rad Jewish Film Archive.
Israelis stage a protest demonstration against acts of
terrorism by Arabs.

313 ARAB BOYCOTT
1973 / ? / sound / color / 16 mm
Anti-Defamation League of B'nai B'rith. (Dateline Israel
series)
Israeli economist Yuval Elizur discusses the purpose and
effect of the Arab boycott of Israel.

314 THE ARAB-ISRAELI CONFLICT
1974 / 20 min / sound / color or b&w / 16 mm
Atlantis Productions, Inc. (LC 74-702814) Credits: Producer-
Writer - J. Michael Hagopian. Locations: Boston U. /
Library of Congress (FBB 2593) / New York U. / U. of
Illinois / U. of Washington. *
An introduction to the Arab-Israeli conflict intended for
junior high school to adult audiences. Uses well
selected WWI and WWII footage in its presentation.
Begins with history of the Jews at the time of Abraham
and ends with the 1973 War. Attempts to describe the
territorial conflicts and refugee problems involved in
the conflict. Solutions offered tend to be simplistic.
Pro-Israeli presentation makes this less suitable for

general classroom purposes. Generally a good introduction to a very difficult subject.

315   ARAB-ISRAELI DIALOGUE
1973 / 40 min / sound / color or b&w / 16 mm
Impact Films. Distributed by Icarus Films and by Impact
Films. Credits: Director - Lionel Rogosin.   *
Palestinian poet Rasheed Hussein and Israeli writer Amos
Kenan debate the Arab-Israeli conflict. Both insist on
a peaceful solution but recognize that individual
friendship and peaceful coexistence on a local level can
not solve the massive territorial, political and social
problems which now exist. A filmed discussion, a little
slow in sections, but even-handed. Shot on location in
Israel.

316   ARABS AND JEWS: THE CRISIS
(n.d.) / ? / sound / color / 16 mm
Schloat Productions. Cited in the Jewish Media Service
Bulletin. No other information available.

317   BEYOND THE MIRAGE
1970 / 25 min / sound / color / 16 mm
Jewish Chautauqua Society. Distributed by Alden Films. (LC
70-715446) Credits: Narrator - Lorne Greene. Locations:
Brigham Young U. / Gratz College.
Filmed on location in Israel by a Jewish production company in a cinema verite style. Asks whether Jews and
Arabs can live and work together. Topics covered
include the aspirations of both groups, their comparative
social conditions, and the effect of the Arab refugee
problem on solutions for peace. Looks at how both Arabs
and Jews in Israel feel about their work, life and
future.

318   A COMMON HOUSE
1968 / 14 min / sound / color / 16 mm
U. Yoresh, Jerusalem. Released in the U.S. by Mirimar Films
Library, 1969. (LC 72-703169) Locations: Gratz College /
Hadassah Film Library.
Originally entitled: TWENTY YEARS. Animated Israeli
film for juvenile audiences. Presents the Arab-Israeli
conflict in parable form. Shows a new boy moving into an
apartment building where all the neighbors are inexpli-
cably hostile. Oversimplified, even for children.
Presents the Israeli impression of the position of Israel
in the Middle East. Does not address the causes of the
Arab-Israeli conflict. Nevertheless, generally con-
sidered a charming film due to the animation.

319   DREW PEARSON REPORTS
(c. 1960?) / 60 min / sound / b&w / 35 mm
Baruch Dienar. Location: Jewish Agency, Jerusalem.

Roving reporter Drew Pearson interviews Israelis concerning the idea of peace.

320   EGYPT-ISRAEL
       March 13, 1956 / 90 min / sound / b&w / 16 mm
       CBS-TV. Jefferson Production, Inc. Distributed by
       McGraw-Hill, and by Contemporary Films. (See It Now,
       television series) (NUC Fi 56-289) Credits: Producer-
       Editors - Edward R. Murrow, Fred W. Friendly. Locations:
       Indiana U. / Library of Congress (FCA 2430-32) / New York U.
       / U. of Iowa.   *
          Lengthy and detailed presentation of the history of the
          Arab-Israeli conflict. Attempts to provide both sides
          of the issue and usually suceeds. Looks predominantly at
          the situation in Egypt and Israel in 1956. CBS
          correspondents interview major political figures on loca-
          tion, covering issues including Arab refugees, the
          creation of Israel, diversion of Jordan River water to
          Israel, and social and political differences between
          Egypt and Israel. Originally for television audiences,
          now of use for classroom and research purposes.
          Recommended.

321   ISRAEL - THE RIGHT TO BE
       (c. 1975) / 52 min / sound / color / 16 mm
       Dore Schary. Distributed by Alden Films. Locations:
       Anti-Defamation League of B'nai B'rith / Gratz College.
          Intended mainly for religious groups. Counters the claim
          that Israel has no right to exist. Discusses many justi-
          fications for the existence of Israel as a state and
          attempts to produce a sympathic view of the country while
          promoting tourism and immigration.

322   A JUST PEACE IN THE MIDDLE EAST - HOW CAN IT BE
       ACHEIVED?
       1970 / 60 min / sound / color / 16 mm
       Distributed by the Middle East Institute.
          I.L. Kenan of the American-Israeli Public Affairs
          Committee and editor of the Near East Report, Allen
          Pollock of American Professors for Peace in the Middle
          East, Rabbi Elmer Berger of the American Jewish
          Alternatives to Zionism and the American Council of
          Judaism and Christopher Mayhew, British Member of
          Parliament participate in a discussion of the
          Arab-Israeli conflict and discuss the possibility of
          peace.

323   MAN IN THE BLUE HELMET
       (c. 1960?) / 25 min / sound / b&w / 16 mm
       Distributed by Contemporary Films. Credits: Narrator -
       Alistair Cooke.
          Documents the UN peace-keeping missions to the Gaza Strip
          and the Congo.

324 MIDDLE EAST
January 8, 1975 / 29 min / sound / color / 3/4" videocassette
Worldwide Church of God (Garner Ted Armstrong, television
program no. 633) Location: Library of Congress. *
Intended for Christian television audiences. An example
of anti-Arab diatribe. Arabs are referred to as
"greasy", "ferret-faced", and "with table cloths on their
heads". Intended to show how Biblical prophecy fortells
a nuclear war in the Middle East, it becomes a per-
sonalized history lesson by Garner Ted Armstrong on the
Middle East conflict. For research purposes. Good
example of how public opinion is molded against Arab
countries and Muslims. Example of Christian interpretation of the Middle East crisis. Would probably offend
many Israelis and would certainly offend all Arabs.

325 THE MIDDLE EAST: CRADLE OF CRISIS
1958 / 10 min / sound / b&w / 16 mm
Location: U. of Colorado. No other information available.
Describes the Middle East conflict. Looks at potential
crisis in the future.

326 MIDDLE EAST - THE SEARCH FOR PEACE
(c. 1970?) / 60 min / sound / color / 16 mm or 1/2"
videocassette (Bill Moyer's International Journal, no.
108, television series) No other information available.

327 POINT OF VIEW: A CONVERSATION ON THE MIDDLE EAST, 1974-75
1975 / 28 min / sound / b&w / 16 mm
Anti-Defamation League of B'nai B'rith.
Intended for high school to adult audiences. Writer
James Michener and playwright Dore Schary discuss the
history and current political situation in the Middle
East. Includes dicussion of the ongoing military
conflict.

328 PROSPECTS FOR PEACE: AN ARAB VIEW
(c. 1973?) / 90 min / sound / color / 16 mm
Robert S. Hirschfield. Distributed by Hunter College.
Robert S. Hirschfield, political scientist at Hunter
College, interviews Anwar Nuseibeh, former Jordanian
Minister of Defense, concerning the viewpoint of the
Palestinian Arabs on the Arab-Israeli conflict. Looks at
the possiblility of a peaceful solution to the terri-
torial and political problems of the area.

329 PROSPECTS FOR PEACE: ISRAELI VIEWS
(c. 1973?) / 60 min / sound / color / 16 mm
Robert S. Hirschfield. Distributed by Hunter College.
Robert S. Hirschfield, political scientist at Hunter
College, interviews Shmuel Tamir, of the Israeli Knesset,
General Mati Peled, and Shlomo Avineri of Hebrew
University concerning the possibilities of a peaceful

solution to the Arab-Israeli conflict. Filmed in
Jerusalem.

330   SADAT IN ISRAEL, PART 1, 2 AND 3
       November 20, 1977 / 3 programs, 60 min. each / sound / color
       / 3/4" videocassette. CBS News. (CBS News Special Report)
       Location: Museum of Broadcasting (T77:0589/0590/0591)
            Three hour-long special news broadcasts covering Anwar
            Sadat's historic visit to Jerusalem. Menachim Begin is
            shown greeting Sadat and discusses the meaning of Israel
            as the Jewish national homeland. Sadat speaks on the
            possibility of peace and the rights of the Palestinians.
            Very useful historic and documentary footage.

331   TWENTY-YEAR'S WAR (MILCHEMET ESRIM HASHANA)
       1968 / ? / sound / color / 16 mm
       Michael Shvili and Y. Got. Location: Israel Ministry of
       Trade and Commerce.
            Examination of twenty years of conflict between Israel
            and surrounding Arab countries. Produced by an Israeli
            film crew.

332   THE VISIT OF ANWAR SADAT TO JERUSALEM
       (c. 1977) / ? / sound / color / 16 mm
       Distributed by TRC Productions. (Israel Report series) No
       other information available.

333   WHOSE HOME THIS HOLY LAND?
       1969 / 53 min / sound / color / 16 mm
       Avco Broadcasting Corp. Released by Avco Embassy Pictures.
       (LC 79-705718).
            General introduction to the Arab-Israeli conflict. Looks
            at the origins of the conflict and the effect it has had
            on the peoples of the region.

ARAB-ISRAELI CONFLICT BY WAR - 1948

334   MIDDLE EAST
       1952 / 25 min / sound / b&w / 16 mm
       March of Time. Location: Iowa Films / Iowa State U.
            A 1952 broadcast in the March of Time television series.
            Describes the status quo in the Middle East. Intended
            for adult television audiences.

335   NASSER VS. BEN-GURION
       1964 / 25 min / sound / b&w / 16 mm
       Wolper Productions. Released by Public Media Inc.
       Distributed by Films Incorporated. (Men in Crisis series)
       (LC 74-706746) Credits: Narrator - Edmund O'Brien.
            Describes the situation in 1948 which led to the birth of
            Israel and the first Arab-Israeli war. Pro-Israeli
            presentation which interprets the conflict as one between
            Israel's Ben-Gurion and Egypt's Nasser.

71

336   PARAMOUNT NEWS (NOVEMBER 10)
       1948 / 8 min / sound / b&w / 35 mm
       Paramount Pictures. (Paramount News, vol. 8, no. 22)
       Location: National Archives (200PN8.22)
            Newsreel footage of Israeli, Arab and UN troops in the
            Negev in 1948. Of use for historic or library footage
            purposes.

337   SHA'AR HAGAI
       1965 / 13 min / sound / b&w / 16 or 35 mm
       Chevra Le Omanut Ha Kolno'a Ltd. Credits: Director-Writer-
       Photographer - A. Greenburg. Locations: Film Dept.
       Histadrut, Tel Aviv / Israel Ministry of Education and
       Culture, Jerusalem / Prime Minister's Office, Information
       Dept., Jerusalem.
            Available in English, Hebrew and French soundtracks.
            Short Israeli documentary made up of footage of the
            aftermath of the battle of Sha'ar HaGai, during the
            Israeli War of Independence. Shows disabled equipment
            and scenes of destruction.

338   THIRTY-FIVE LIVES FOR FREEDOM
       (c. 1950?) / 13 min / sound / b&w / 16 mm
       Detla Films, Holland. Credits: Drawings by Eppo Doove.
       Location: Israel Film Archives.
            Commemorates the "Battle of the Thirty-five" during the
            1948 Israeli War of Independence, near Kfar Etzion.

ARAB-ISRAELI CONFLICT BY WAR - 1956

339   AFTER THE BATTLE
       1957 / 10 min / sound / b&w / 35 mm
       Israel Motion Picture Studios. Location: Israel Film Studios,
       Ltd., Herzliyah.
            Short Israeli film shot after the 1956 War in the Sinai.

340   DREW PEARSON REPORTS ON WAR AND PEACE IN ISRAEL
       1958 / 23 min / sound / b&w / 35 mm
       Location: Abraham F. Rad Jewish Film Archive.
            Listed in some catalogs as: DREW PEARSON REPORTING
            ON WAR AND PEACE IN ISRAEL. Documents the situation
            within Israel after the 1956 War.

341   OPERATION KADESH
       1956-57 / 15 min / sound / b&w / 16 mm
       Location: Abraham F. Rad Jewish Film Archive.
            Shows the situation in the Sinai during the 1956 War.
            Footage by Israeli cameramen.

342   PLEASE ANSWER MY LETTER (ANA ANU LEMICHTAVI)
       1957 / 17 min / sound / b&w / 16 or 35 mm
       Israel Motion Picture Studios. Locations: Israel Film

Studios, Ltd. / Jewish Agency, Jerusalem.
Intended to gather support for Israel's position during
the 1956 War. In the form of an open letter to the
United Nations. Describes military actions against Israel
before the war and stories by Jewish refugees from Egypt.
Shows Abba Eban at the U.N.

343   THE SINAI CAMPAIGN
1956 / 12 min / sound / b&w / 16 mm
Berkey Pathe Humphries. Location: Prime Minister's Office,
Information Dept., Jerusalem.
   Available in English, Hebrew, French, Spanish and German
soundtracks. Records scenes of battles during the Sinai
campaign. Shows the taking of the Egyptian destroyer
"Ibrahim El-Awal" by Israeli forces.

344   WAR AND PEACE IN ISRAEL
(c. 1957) / 15 min / sound / b&w / 16 mm
Baruch Dienar. Orb Films. Locations: The Jewish Agency
Film Archive, Jerusalem / Keren Hayesod, Jerusalem.
   Interview with Israeli Prime Minister Ben-Gurion con-
cerning his interpretation of the reasons for the 1956
War. Probably the same film as: DREW PEARSON
REPORTS ON WAR AND PEACE IN ISRAEL, no. 340.

ARAB-ISRAELI CONFLICT BY WAR - 1967

345   CARICATURES (CARICATUROT)
1968 / 10 min / sound / b&w / 16 or 35 mm
Yoram Gross Films, Ltd. Locations: Natan Gross / Prime
Minister's Office, Information Dept., Jerusalem.
   Review of the Six-Day War seen in the world press through
political and editorial caricatures. An Israeli film
available in English, French and Spanish soundtracks.

346   EXODUS '67
(c. 1967) / 18 min / sound / b&w / 16 mm
Embassy of Jordan. Distributed by the Middle East
Institute, and by the League of Arab States.
   View of the effects of the 1967 War on Jordan. King
Hussein of Jordan speaks at the U.N. about the enormous
refugee problem caused by the war. A review of Israeli
army actions against Arab civilians follows. One of the
few films available dealing with the 1967 War from an
Arab viewpoint.

347   GO THROUGH THE GATES
1968 / 12 min / sound / color / 16 mm
Distributed by Alden Films. Location: Jewish National Fund,
Jerusalem.
   Available in English, Hebrew, French, Spanish and German
soundtracks. Footage by Israeli cameramen. Shows the

Six Day War in the Golan Heights, settlements on the Gaza
Strip and the Old City of Jerusalem.

348   HOW ISRAEL WON THE WAR
       1967 / 56 min / sound / b&w / 16 mm
       CBS News. (NUC Fi 67-2344) Credits: Producers - Gene
       DePoris, Palmer Williams, Reporter - Mike Wallace, Military
       Advisor - S.L.A. Marshall. Locations: Library of Congress
       (FBA 4897) / Ministry for Foreign Affairs, Jerusalem. *
       Well produced analysis of the tactics, strategies and
       weapons used by Egypt and Israel during the 1967 War.
       Those interviewed include Brig. General Mehdat Fahmy,
       Ahmed Abd el-Naby, and Major General Salat Yacout of
       Egypt and Brig. General Avraham Yoffe, Mordechai Gur,
       Moshe Dayan, and Itzhak Rabin of Israel. Interviews are
       informative although Mike Wallace is embarassingly biased
       in favor of the Israeli victory. Produced for television
       audiences, and of use for library footage and historic
       purposes. Would also be useful for classroom study of
       the 1967 War. Emphasis is placed on Israeli strategy.
       Little is presented of the Egyptian campaigns.

349   ISRAEL TODAY
       1967 / 16 min / sound / color / 16 mm
       Distributed by Alden Films.
       Describes the situation in Israel after the Six Day War.
       Looks at the question of how to deal with the newly cap-
       tured Arab territories.

350   ISRAEL, VICTORY OR ELSE
       1967 / 68 min / sound / color / 16 mm
       NBC News. (NUC Fi 68-689) Credits: Producer - George F.
       Murray, Director - Gerald Polikoff, Narrators - John
       Chancellor, Dean Brelis. Locations: Library of Congress
       (FBA 5025-5027) / Ministry of Foreign Affairs, Jerusalem. *
       An NBC News special broadcast using 1967 war footage to
       describe the victory of Israeli forces over Egypt. Well
       presented production when dealing with the campaigns and
       strategy but biased in favor of Israel when sketching
       national characteristics of the Israeli and Egyptian
       peoples and armies. Includes lengthy discussions of the
       Sinai, West Bank and Golan Heights campaigns. Looks at
       increasing Arab refugee problem. Of use for historic and
       research purposes. Though well produced, biases may make
       it offensive to all but pro-Israeli audiences.

351   (ISRAELI-ARAB WAR, JUNE 1967, NO. 1)
       1967 / 5 min / silent / b&w / 16 mm
       Geva Films, Tel Aviv. (NUC Fi 67-512) Location: Library of
       Congress (FAA 5934) *
       Silent, grainy footage shot by Israeli cameramen during
       the 1967 War. Shows tank-mounted missiles firing at
       targets. Of use for library footage purposes.

352   (ISRAELI-ARAB WAR, JUNE 1967, NO. 2)
      1967 / 5 min / silent / b&w / 16 mm
      Geva Films, Tel Aviv.   (NUC Fi 67-546)   Location: Library of
      Congress (FAA 5935)   *
          Of varying quality.   Footage shot by Israeli soldiers
          during the 1967 War.   Shows the invasion of Quneitra,
          footage of Israeli military personnel, and Levi Eshkol
          visiting settlements.

353   (ISRAELI-ARAB WAR, JUNE 1967, NO. 3)
      1967 / 5 min / silent / b&w / 16 mm
      Geva Films, Tel Aviv.   (NUC Fi 67-866)   Location: Library of
      Congress (FAA 5936)   *
          More scenes of the 1967 War shot by Israeli soldiers.
          Includes footage of Itzhak Rabin, Chief of Staff, touring
          the West Bank area, and victory celebrations by the
          Israeli army.   For library footage purposes.

354   JEWISH NATIONAL FUND NEWSREEL, NO. 11
      (c. 1967) / 7 min / sound / color / 16 mm
      Jewish National Fund.
          Describes the Six Day War from Israel's point of view.
          Includes some Egyptian newsreel footage.

355   THE LIGHTNING WAR IN THE MIDDLE EAST
      1967 / 16 min / sound / b&w / 16 mm
      Hearst Metrotone News.   (Screen News Digest, vol. 10, no. 1)
      (NUC FiA 68-1654)   Location: Penn. State U.
          Originally intended for theater newsreel audiences, later
          used for adult classroom audiences.   Describes the
          background conflicts which led to the eventual outbreak
          of the 1967 War.

356   MIDDLE EAST PERSPECTIVE: CAN PEACE BREAK OUT?
      August 23, 1967 / 60 min / sound / b&w / 16 mm
      CBS News.   (CBS News Special Report)   Credits: Correspondent
      - Mike Wallace.   Location: Library of Congress (FAA 9033-34)
      *
          Follow-up program to the broadcast five weeks earlier
          (see no. 348).   Shows the closing of the Suez Canal, the
          destruction of the wall dividing Jerusalem, and the state
          of no peace and no war.   Israelis are interviewed con-
          cerning the granting of Israeli citizenship to
          Palestinians.   King Hussein of Jordan speaks about refu-
          gees.   Ahmad Shukairy of the PLO describes Israeli bruta-
          lity and Abba Eban discusses the Soviet Union's interest
          in the Arab countries.   Though peace is not a reality at
          this time, the weak economies of Egypt and Jordan are
          seen as potential aids to a peace settlement with Israel.
          Tries to present multiple sides to the situation in the
          Middle East in 1967, but retains a pro-Israeli orien-
          tation.

357 MIDDLE EAST PERSPECTIVE: THE CORRESPONDENT'S REPORT
June 13, 1967 / 30 min / sound / color or b&w / 16 mm
CBS News. (CBS News Special Report) Credits:
Correspondents - Charles Collingwood, Peter Kalischer,
Hughes Rudd, Winston Burdett and Morley Safer. Location:
Library of Congress (FBA 8955) *
Self-analysis of the way the CBS News team covered the
1967 War. Filmed in London beyond both Israeli and
Egyptian censorship. Correspondents discuss their
problems covering the war and the impressions they formed
which could not be placed in earlier programs (see nos.
348 and 356). Describes Ismailia as an Egyptian gra-
veyard, the determination of the Israeli troops, the near
collapse of the Egyptian economy, Soviet arms sale
problems, and the Arab refugees. Though lauding each
other for their non-biased reporting, it is clear that
two correspondent's held under house-arrest in Egypt
during the fighting were understandably anti-Egyptian
government in their reporting. A valuable look at the
way international news is gathered and presented to the
American public.

358 NAPALM VICTIMS
(c. 1968?) / 15 min / sound / b&w / 16 mm
Egyptian Ministry of Education. Distributed by the Arab
Information Office, Washington.
Attempts to present the horror of the 1967 War from the
Arab point of view by showing victims of Israeli napalm
attacks.

359 PRICE OF PEACE
(c. 1968?) / 10 min / sound / b&w / 16 mm
Location: Abraham F. Rad Jewish Film Archive.
Shot during and after the Six Day War. Describes the
effects of the short war on Israel.

360 THE SIX-DAY WAR
(c. 1967) / 30 min / sound / b&w / 16 mm
Warner Brothers. No other information available.

361 SIX-DAY WAR COMMENTARY
(c. 1967) / 8 min / sound / color or b&w / 16 mm
Location: Abraham F. Rad Jewish Film Archive.
Uses maps and captured Egyptian newsreel footage.
Israeli General Chaim Herzog describes the Six Day War's
strategy and outcome.

362 THE SIX DAYS
1968 / 90 min / sound / b&w / 16 mm
Y. Ephrati. Location: Israel Ministry of Trade and
Commerce, Information Dept.
Available in English and Hebrew soundtracks. Listed in
some catalogs as running 110 minutes. Gives a detailed

description of the strategies and campaigns of the 1967
War from the Israeli viewpoint.

363 SIX DAYS IN JUNE
1967 / 13 min / sound / b&w / 16 or 35 mm
Israel Motion Picture Studios, Herzliyah. Distributed by
Alden Films. Locations: Gratz College / Keren Hayesod,
Jerusalem / Prime Minister's Office, Information Dept.,
Jerusalem.
     Intended to justifiy, not glorify, the 1967 War. Uses
     Israeli and Egyptian newsreel footage to show the build-
     up of hostilities which led to the outbreak of war.
     Describes the campaigns and the taking of divided
     Jerusalem. An Israeli film available in English, Hebrew,
     French and Spanish soundtracks.

364 SIX DAYS TO ETERNITY
1967 / 90 min / sound / b&w / 16 mm
Michael Shvili. Israel Motion Picture Studios, Herzliyah.
Distributed by Israfilm, Ltd.
     Includes footage shot during the Six Day War edited with
     Arab newsreel footage. An Israeli post war documentary.

365 STANDING BY
1968 / 55 min / sound / b&w / 16 mm
Jewish Agency Film Archives. Credits: Arnan Tzafrir.
     Shows groups of Jewish vounteers who traveled to Israel
     from around the world in May of 1967 to assist Israel
     should there be a war. Includes scenes of volunteers
     arriving, their life on a kibbutz, working on projects,
     and eventually returning home.

366 THREE HOURS IN JUNE
1967 / 90 min / sound / 16 mm
Israel Air Force. Location: Israel Ministry of Trade and
Commerce.
     Documents the role of the Israeli Air Force in the
     fighting during the 1967 War.

367 A VERY SERIOUS MATTER
1968 / 8 min / sound / b&w / 16 mm
Location: Abraham F. Rad Jewish Film Archive.
     Political and editorial cartoons illustrate the way in
     which the world press presented the 1967 War to the
     public.

368 WAR IN THE MIDDLE EAST
June 5, 1967 / 60 min / sound / color / 2" videocassette
CBS News. (CBS News Special Report) Location: Library of
Congress. No other information available.

ARAB-ISRAELI CONFLICT BY WAR - 1973

369   ARAB ARMED FORCES
      1973 / 15 min / sound / b&w / 16 mm
      Government of Egypt. Distributed by the Arab Information
      Center, San Francisco.
          Uses Egyptian newsreels shot during the 1973 War.
          Presents the conflict from the Arab point of view.

370   THE LAST WAR
      (c. 1973) / 18 min / sound / color / 16 mm
      Herb Krosney. Distributed by the New Jewish Media Project.
          Interviews with Israelis made after the 1973 War emphasize
          the desire that this be the last war Israel need ever
          fight.

371   LETTER FROM THE FRONT
      (c. 1973) / 21 min / sound / color / 16 mm
      Distributed by Alden Films.
          In the format of a letter written to his family. One
          Israeli soldier's involvement in the Yom Kippur War is
          described. The problem of a ceasefire which doesn't
          solve anything, the desire not to be killed in war, and
          the waste of the continuing conflict are issues covered.

372   THE MIDDLE EAST: PEACE OR ELSE
      November 19, 1973 / 90 min / sound / color / 16 mm
      NBC News. Credits: Narrator - Edwin C. Newman. Location:
      Abraham F. Rad Jewish Film Archive.
          Interviews with prominent Arab and Israeli leaders con-
          cerning the Yom Kippur War. Shows scenes of military and
          diplomatic campaigns. An NBC News Special Report.

373   ROVING REPORT
      (c. 1973) / 26 min / sound / color / 16 mm
      U.P.I.T.N., London. Location: Abraham F. Rad Jewish Film
      Archive.
          The Anglo-American news consortium, U.P.I.T.N. outlines
          the history and effects of the 1973 War.

374   SOLDIERS IN SINAI: A PEACEKEEPING STORY
      1975 / 27 min / sound / color / 16 mm
      United Nations. Distributed by United Nations Films.
          Documents the work of the U.N. peace-keeping mission to
          the Sinai following the 1973 War. Shows their attempt to
          keep fighting from breaking out while diplomatic solu-
          tions are underway.

375   UNITED NATIONS EMERGENCY
      1973 / 27 min / sound / color / 16 mm
      United Nations. Distributed by United Nations Films.
          Describes the efforts of the U.N. peace-keeping mission.
          Shows U.N. troops moving into the Suez Canal area
          following the U.N. Security Council vote for a peace-
          keeping force while the Geneva Peace Talks are underway.

376   WAR ON YOM KIPPUR
       1974 / 30 min / sound / color / 16 mm
       Distributed by Alden Films. Locations: Abraham F. Rad
       Jewish Film Archive / Gratz College.
          Available in English, French and German soundtracks.
          Listed in some catalogs as: YOM KIPPUR WAR.
          Attempts to produce a feeling for the waste and destruc-
          tion of war. Israeli Kol Nidre walks through Jerusalem
          narrating a chronology of 1973 War events. Uses newsreel
          footage of fighting.

377   YOM KIPPUR WAR NEWSFILM
       1973 / 50 min / sound / color / 16 mm
       Location: Abraham F. Rad Jewish Film Archive.
          Uses international newsreel footage. Documents the major
          campaigns of the 1973 War.

BORDERS AND THE OCCUPIED TERRITORIES

378   BORDER AHEAD (GVUL LEFANECHA)
       1962 / 18 min / sound / 35 mm
       Grifit-Mukadi. Israel Film Studios, Ltd.
          Available in English, Hebrew and French soundtracks.
          Discusses the security of Israel's borders. Originally
          an Israeli Army information film.

379   BOUNDARIES AGAINST WAR
       1975 / 28 min / sound / color / 16 mm
       Anti-Defamation League of B'nai B'rith. (Dateline Israel
       series) Location: Gratz College.
          Intended for senior high school to adult audiences.
          Filmed interview by Arnold Forster of Chaim Herzog,
          former Head of Israel Military Intelligence and
          Ambassador to the U.N. Topics covered include Israel's
          official position concerning the occupied territories,
          the concept of secure and recognizable borders, and
          defensible boundaries. Scenes of the 1973 War are inter-
          cut with the interview.

380   DANGER, BORDER AHEAD
       1963 / 20 min / sound / color / 16 mm
       Jewish National Fund Newsreel. Distributed by Alden Films.
       Location: Jewish National Fund, Jerusalem.
          Available in English, Hebrew, French, Spanish and German
          soundtracks. Discusses the need to strengthen Israeli
          borders.

381   A DAY IN JUNE: DISENGAGEMENT IN THE GOLAN
       1975 / 27 min / sound / color / 16 mm
       United Nations. Distributed by United Nations Films.
          Chronicles the dispatch of 1200 men from the United
          Nations Disengagement Observer Force (UNDOF) to the Golan

Heights to maintain peace between Israel and Syria.
Discusses differences between this mission and the force
sent to the Sinai. Looks at problems with displaced per-
sons in the Golan.

382   DEADLOCK ENDS - ISRAELIS TO QUIT EGYPTIAN TERRITORY
      February 1957 / 8 min / sound / b&w / 35 mm
      Universal News. Location: National Archives (30-20-1)
      Universal newsreel footage. Shows captured Egyptian
      territory returned by the Israeli army following the 1956
      War.

383   FRONTIER
      1954 / 11 min / sound / b&w / 16 mm
      Location: Abraham F. Rad Jewish Film Archive.
      Actor Robert Mitchum appeals for funds and support for
      Israel. Includes a description of Israel's security
      problems in 1954.

384   THE GOLAN HEIGHTS
      1975 / 12 min / sound / color / 16 mm
      Location: Abraham F. Rad Jewish Film Archive.
      Analysis of the importance of the Golan Heights to Israel
      due to its strategic location. Produced to gain support
      for annexation of occupied Arab territories by Israel.

385   INSIDE OCCUPIED TERRITORIES
      (c. 1974?) / 20 min / sound / color / 16 mm
      Arab Information Office, Washington. No other information
      available.

386   KUNEITRA, DEATH OF A CITY
      (c. 1974?) / 22 min / sound / color / 16 mm
      Lane End Production Co. Distributed by the League of Arab
      States / Arab Information Center, San Francisco / Arab
      Information Center, Washington. / National Association of
      Arab Americans.
            Listed in some catalogs as: QUNEITRA: DEATH OF A CITY.
      Describes the destruction of the provincial captial of
      the Syrian Golan Heights by the Israeli Army when Israel
      was required to return the city as agreed upon in a 1974
      disengagement treaty. Shows Quneitra being dynamited and
      bulldozed before return to the Syrians.

387   THE LONG BORDER (HAGVUL HA'AROCH)
      1967 / 15 min / sound / b&w / 16 or 35 mm
      Alfred Steinhardt. Locations: Film Dept. Histadrut, Tel
      Aviv / Israel Film Studios, Herzliyah / Jewish Agency Film
      Archive, Jerusalem / Keren Hayesod, Jerusalem / Prime
      Minister's Office, Information Dept., Jerusalem.
            Listed in some catalogs as: THE LONG FRONTIER.
      Available in English, Hebrew and French soundtracks. An
      Israeli film dealing with problems resulting from its

80

950 km. border with various Arab countries. Precautions
and army outposts along the Israeli border are shown.
Filmed before the 1973 War.

388   ON THE BORDER (BASPHAR)
       1968 / 12 min / sound / b&w / 16 or 35 mm
       Castel Films, Ltd. Y. Ephrati. Location: Prime Minister's
       Office, Information Dept., Jerusalem.
            An English language Israeli film also available with
            Hebrew or French sub-titles. Describes how despite
            Israeli war-time victories, the activities of al-Fatah
            continue to harass Israeli border settlements, making
            life unsafe.

389   REPORT FROM GAZA
       1971 / 10 min / sound / b&w / 16 mm
       Gaza Solidarity Committee. Distributed by the League of Arab
       States.
            Includes clandestinely shot footage from inside the Gaza
            Strip. Documents the destruction of parts of Gaza by
            Israel since its capture during the 1967 War. Presents
            the Israeli occupation of Arab territories from the Arab
            point of view.

390   SHARM EL SHEIKH
       1971 / 10 min / sound / color / 16 mm
       D. Goldstein, for the Ministry of Foreign Affairs, Israel.
            Available in English, French and Spanish soundtracks.
            Describes the military importance to Israel of Sharm el
            Sheikh, an area at the southern tip of the Sinai
            Peninsula captured from Egypt in the 1967 War. Intended
            to gather support for continued Israeli occupation of the
            captured territories.

391   SINAI
       1973 / 36 min / sound / color / 16 mm
       NBC News. Released by NBC Educational Enterprises.
       Distributed by Films Incorporated. (LC 74-701334) Credits:
       Narrator - John Dancy.
            NBC news broadcast. Describes the effects of Israel's
            capture of the Sinai Peninsula during the 1967 War. Oil
            reserves, minerals, added territories and increased Arab
            population are among the acquisitions for Israel, as well
            as the historic importance of the area. Filmed before
            the negotiations which returned portions of the Sinai to
            Egypt. This broadcast favors continued occupation of the
            Sinai by Israel.

392   SINAI - BETWEEN WAR AND PEACE
       1973 / 16 min / sound / color / 16 mm
       Location: Abraham F. Rad Jewish Film Archive.
            Describes the historic position and strategic importance
            of the Sinai peninsula to Israel as demonstrated by the

81

1948, 1956, and 1967 Wars. An Israeli film which propo-
ses the Sinai should be taken from Egypt.

393   SINAI FIELD MISSION
       (c. 1978) / 127 min / sound / b&w / 16 mm
       Zipporah Films. Frederick Wiseman.
           Possibly a feature film. Deals with an American sur-
       veillance base in the Sinai.

394   TENSION EASES IN EGYPT-ISRAEL BORDER DISPUTE
       February 1957 / 13 min / sound / b&w / 35 mm
       Universal News. Location: National Archives. (30-19-1)
       Newsreel footage. No other information available.

395   TO LIVE OUT OF RANGE
       1971 / 22 min / sound / color / 16 mm
       Locations: Abraham F. Rad Jewish Film Archive / Gratz
       College.
           Traces the history of Arab and Israeli hostilities from
       the early days of Zionism to the 1967 War. Intended to
       form opinion in favor of Israel's annexation of the
       occupied territories, for security reasons. Shot before
       the negotiations which returned part of the Sinai to
       Egypt.

EFFECTS OF CONFLICT ON ADULTS

396   ABRAHAM AND ISAAC
       1977 / 35 min / sound / b&w / 16 mm or videocassette
       Ilan Ziv. Distributed by Icarus Films. *
           Anti-war film by a young Israeli film-maker. Traces the
       connection between the story of Abraham sacrificing his
       son Isaac with the desire of parents, conditioned by the
       horrors of the Holocaust, to send their sons to repeated
       wars instead of looking for a diplomatic solution. Shot
       on location in Israel. Includes scenes of the Musuem of
       the Holocaust, Masada, and a war museum where the film
       develops a strong personal statement concerning the role
       of militarism in Israeli life and education. Follows
       personal reminiscenes of the film-maker in talks with his
       younger brother and of his own experiences during the
       October War. A moving presentation of a seldom heard
       viewpoint. Intended for college and adult audiences.
       In sharp contrast to the majority of Arab-Israeli war
       films which recount endless injustices suffered by both
       sides. Well produced. Highly recommended.

397   BLACKOUT
       1974 / 55 min / sound / color / 16 mm
       Michel Katz and Richard S. Kramisen. Sunrise Films.
           Uses a folk-rock soundtrack geared to younger audiences.

Describes the state of the Israeli home front awaiting
news from the field during the Yom Kippur War. Includes
scenes of students on a kibbutz, city dwellers and
soldiers on the front.

398   ISRAEL: AFTERMATH OF WAR
      1974 / 15 min / sound / color / 16 mm
      Distributed by Alden Films. Location: Abraham F. Rad Jewish
      Film Archive.
         Shows the Israeli home front awaiting news of the
         fighting during the 1973 War.

399   ISRAEL REVISITED
      1974 / 42 min / sound / color / 16 mm
      Location: Abraham F. Rad Jewish Film Archive.
         Looks at the "typical" Israeli before and after the 1973
         War. Shows changes in the life and mood of the country.

400   LIFE TODAY IN THE MIDDLE EAST
      1956 / 29 min / sound / b&w / 16 mm
      New York Herald Tribune. Released by NET Film Serivce. (The
      World We Want series: 1956) (NUC FiA 58-1493)
         Helen Hiet Waller and members of the New York Herald
         Tribune Forum discuss the effect of the 1956 War on
         Israel, Jordan and Lebanon. Includes discussion of the
         stress of military training on Israeli youth and economic
         problems of the Arab countries weakened by war.

401   A MESSAGE OF LIFE
      1974 / 26 min / sound / color / 16 mm
      Distributed by Alden Films. Location: Abraham F. Rad Jewish
      Film Archive.
         Shows stress experienced by Israelis during the 1973 War
         while waiting for word from the front. Describes the
         effect of the war on the average Israeli. Includes sce-
         nes of a celebration of the Simchat Torah, and Soviet
         Jews immigrating to Israel.

402   A PEOPLE LIKE ANY OTHER
      1973 / 30 min / sound / color / 16 mm
      Association Films, Inc. Sponsored by the Consul General of
      Israel in Chicago. Distributed by Alden Films, and by the
      Jewish Media Service. Location: Gratz College.
         For high school to adult audiences. Contains an inter-
         view by Martin Agronsky of Israeli writer Amos Oz, poli-
         tician Aryeh Eliav, and a cross section of Israelis
         concerning the state of Israel after the 1973 War.
         Topics covered include the war economy, social problems,
         the question of security, return of the occupied terri-
         tories and relations with Arab countries.

403   SHALOM TO ZVI
      1973 / 16 min / sound / color / 16 mm

Daneli International Films.
Shot on location. Shows an American couple flying to
Israel to be with family during the 1973 War, inter-cut
with war footage and scenes of Jerusalem. Attempts to
bring home the meaning of war and its impact on Israel to
American Jews.

404   THIRD DAY OF THE WAR
1973 / 14 min / sound / color / 16 mm
Distributed by Alden Films. Location: Abraham F. Rad Jewish
Film Archive.
Filmed on the third day of the 1973 War. Shows the sup-
port of Jews worldwide who travelled to Israel to help
run essential services, give blood and raise funds for
Israel during the short war.

405   A TIME BETWEEN
1974 / 27 min / sound / color / 16 mm
Distributed by Alden Films. Location: Abraham F. Rad Jewish
Film Archive.
Presented from the viewpoint of an Israeli soldier in the
reserves. Describes the uncertain mood created in Israel
as a result of mixed success in military actions during
the 1973 War.

406   THE WILL TO DO
1974 / 25 min / sound / color / 16 mm
Location: Abraham F. Rad Jewish Film Archive.
Available in English, Hebrew and Spanish soundtracks.
Focuses on the lingering effects of the 1973 War in
Israel. Describes the problem of war widows, injured
soldiers in need of care, the position of the Civil
Guard, and stress of the war on the Israeli economy.

407   WOMEN, CHILDREN AND WAR
1975 / 15 min / sound / color / 16 mm
United Jewish Appeal. Distributed by Alden Films.
Intended for high school to adult audiences. Looks at
tension caused by waiting for news from the front during
the 1973 War in Israel. Includes interviews with wives
and mothers of soldiers on the effect of war on average
citizens.

EFFECT OF CONFLICT ON CHILDREN

408   AS CHILDREN SAW IT
(c. 1968?) / 15 min / sound / color / 16 mm
Distributed by Alden Films.
The effects of the Six Day War of 1967 on Israeli
children is shown in their drawings and in a discussion
of their feelings about the war.

409   CHILDREN IN SHELTERS
      1969 / 13 min / sound / b&w / 16 mm
      Distributed by Alden Films. Location: Abraham F. Rad Jewish
      Film Archives.
          Children living on a kibbutz are shown sleeping in
          shelters to protect them from possible border attack.
          Shows the effect of this type of life on the children
          through their paintings and description of their lives.

410   REFLECTIONS OF THUNDER
      1970 / 13 min / sound / color / 16 or 35 mm
      Location: Abraham F. Rad Jewish Film Archive.
          Available in English, Hebrew and Spanish soundtracks.
          Shows pictures drawn by Israeli border settlement
          children. Depicts the effect of war on their lives.

411   TO CHANGE THE PICTURE
      1974 / 12 min / sound / color / 16 mm
      Distributed by Alden Films. Location: Abraham F. Rad Jewish
      Film Archive.
          Fund-raising film. Stresses emotional, pyschological and
          physical hardships experienced by Israeli youth at kin-
          dergarten to university level due to the Yom Kippur War.
          Asks for support of the United Jewish Appeal.

THE PALESTINIANS

HISTORY OF THE STRUGGLE FOR PALESTINE

412   ARAB DISTURBANCES AND FIRES
      1929 / 10 min / silent / b&w / 35 mm
      Location: Abraham F. Rad Jewish Film Archive.
      Footage of fires during the 1929 Arab Palestinian riots.

413   ARAB GROUP RECEPTION FOR MR. ARAFAT AT THE U.N.
      (n.d.) / 20 min / sound / color / 16 mm
      Distributed by League of Arab States. No other information
      available.

414   ARAFAT: SPEECH AT THE U.N.
      (n.d.) / 90 min / sound / b&w / 16 mm
      Distributed by the League of Arab States. No other infor-
      mation available.

415   COUNT BERNADOTTE ASSASSINATED
      1961 / 4 min / sound / b&w / 16 mm
      Filmrites Associates. Released by Official Films. (Greatest
      Headlines of the Century series) (NUC Fi 62-1071) Credits:
      Producer - Sherm Grinberg, Narrator - Tom Hudson, Writer -
      Allan Lurie. Location: Library of Congress (FAA 3718) *
      Short newsreel. Follows the career of Count Folk-
      Bernadotte, head of Sweden's Red Cross and international
      negotiator in Palestine. Bernadotte suggests a partition
      of Palestine found unacceptable to both Jews and
      Palestinians. Soon after, three members of the Jewish
      Stern Gang assassinate Bernadotte on Sept. 17, 1948.
      Well made, short library footage presentation.

416   DAY OF THE LAND
      1977 / 40 min / sound / color / 16 mm
      Palestine Liberation Organization Office, New York. (Free)
      Shows annual Day of the Land celebrations. West Bank
      Palestinian mayors give speeches and Israeli occupation
      forces clash with marchers and demonstrators.

417   EQUAL TIME
      (n.d) / 30 min / sound / b&w / 16 mm
      Arab Information Office, Washington. No other information
      available.

418   FOCUS ON ISRAEL AND THE PALESTINIANS
      1977 / 59 min / sound / color / 3/4" videocassette.
      Producer unknown. Location: Penn. State U.

For college and adult audiences. Discusses possible
solutions to the Arab-Israeli conflict including those
presented by major Arab countries. Covers arguments for
and against an independent Palestinian state and the role
of the U.S. and Soviet Union in the conflict.

419 THE KEY
1975 / 30 min / sound / color / 16 mm
Samed Productions. Distributed by Icarus Films, by the
League of Arab States, and by the Palestine Liberation
Organization Office (free). *
  One of the few films produced by Palestinians available
  in the U.S. Begins with an historical view of the
  conflict for Palestine. Includes interviews with
  Palestinians in refugee camps and throughout the world.
  A personal statement, very moving. Best production
  screened of the Palestinian viewpoint. Recommended.

420 PALESTINE
1963 / 16 min / sound / b&w / 16 mm
American Friends of the Middle East. Location: Syracuse U.
  Review of the problems and issues involved in the contest
  for what was once Palestine. Looks at the current
  situation of the Palestinian people.

421 PALESTINE OCCUPIED
(n.d.) / 2 parts totalling 100 min / sound / color / 16 mm
Paul-Louis Soullier. Formerly available from the League of
Arab States.
  Available in English and French soundtracks. Documents
  the transformation of Palestinians from farmers and tradespeople to refugees. Describes the development of the
  Palestinian resistance movement. Part 2 deals with the
  development of the al-Fatah. Presented from an Arab
  viewpoint.

422 PALESTINE: PROMISES, REBELLION, ABDICATION
1978 / 3 programs, each 90 min / sound / color / 16 mm
BBC-Thames Television. *
  Lengthy, well produced British series tracing the history
  of the Middle East from WWI to the creation of Israel in
  1948. Traces the decline of the Ottoman Empire and the
  British Mandate period in Palestine. Given from Arab,
  Israeli and British viewpoints. Uses archival film
  footage, eye witness reports and interviews to show the
  post-WWI British commitment to rule Palestine, growth of
  the Zionist movement, Palestinian resistance to Zionism,
  and the 1922, 1929 and 1936 Arab riots. Following WWII
  and the European Holocaust, Jewish immigration to
  Palestine brings the conflict to a climax. U.S.
  involvement, the U.N. partition plan and Britain's
  "abdication" of responsibility in Palestine lead to the
  withdrawal of troops, the 1948 War and the creation of a

state of Israel. Shows resulting Palestinian refugee
problem and continuing Arab-Israeli conflict. This
massive, ambitious series is the most in-depth study of
events leading to the creation of Israel and the
Palestinian, Arab-Israeli conflict. Excellently produced. Intended for television audiences, but suitable
for high school and college instructional purposes.
Recommended.

423   THE PALESTINIAN PEOPLE DO HAVE RIGHTS
      1979 / 53 min / sound / color / 16 mm
      United Nations. Distributed by United Nations Films, by
      the Palestinian Liberation Organization Office, New York
      (free), and by Icarus Films. *
         Reviews the history of the Palestinian problem.
         Shows what life is like for Palestinians in different
         walks of life, from refugees to prosperous business
         people. Ends with an explanation of the U.N. Committee
         on the Exercise of the Inalienable Rights of the
         Palestinian People and what that group is doing to find
         solutions to the refugee problem. Available in English,
         Arabic, French and Spanish soundtracks. Well produced
         statement of the refugee problem and its history from the
         Arab viewpoint. Recommended.

424   THE PALESTINIANS
      June 15, 1974 / 48 min / sound / color / 16 mm
      CBS News. (CBS Reports) Credits: Producer-Director-Writer -
      Howard Stringer, Correspondent - Bill McLaughlin,
      Photographer - John Peters. Location: Library of Congress
      (FBB 2506-07) *
         Correspondent Bill McLaughlin interviews middle class
         Palestinians, PLO members and Yassir Arafat. Topics
         covered include how far will the PLO go to achieve its
         goals, history of the struggle for Palestine, the refugee
         problem, various partition and peace solutions and what
         Palestinians really want. Profiles Palestinians living
         in Israel and occupied territories. McLaughlin stresses
         the idea of a Palestinian state on the West Bank as a
         solution to the conflict. Well presented, with less bias
         than usual for a network news broadcast. Intended for
         television audiences, useful for library footage.

425   REVOLUTION UNTIL VICTORY
      1973 / 52 min / sound / b&w / 16 mm
      Cine News. Distributed by San Francisco Newsreel, by Third
      World Newsreel, New York, and by Tricontinental.
         Available in English and Spanish soundtracks. Examines
         the Palestinian conflict. Shows early Zionist settlers,
         Arab strikes of the 1930-40's, and the establishment of
         Israel in 1948, from an Arab point of view. Uses archi-
         val footage of Jews in Europe during WWII. Shot on loca-
         tion in Palestinian refugee camps. Looks at social and

military programs of the Palestine Liberation
Organization. Includes an interview with Yassir Arafat.
Discusses role of U.S. in Middle East conflict and use of
oil in politics.

426   SUMMER OF '77: THE WEST BANK
August 12, 1977 / 60 min / sound / color / 3/4" videocassette
CBS, Inc. (CBS Reports) Location: Library of Congress (VBA
2412) *
Bill Moyers travels to Israel and the West Bank to show
current conditions only reinforce violence and discourage
a meaningful Middle East peace. Discusses terrorist
activities, treatment of Arab mayors, desecration of
Muslim and Jewish holy sites, Bible students carrying
guns, Arab refugees, and Israeli settlements on occupied
Arab land. Suggests peace is not being pursued.
Includes interviews with Menachim Begin, Azor Weizman and
others. Tries to show complexity of issues involved in
the Arab-Israeli conflict and suggests issues may have
two "right" sides. Intended for television audiences.

427   THE TRUE STORY OF PALESTINE
1962 / 90 min / sound / b&w / 35 mm
Israel Motion Picture Studios, Herzliyah. Locations:
Ministry of Trade and Commerce, Jerusalem / Israel Film
Studios, Ltd.
Uses footage from the Carmel Film Archives. Presents
history of Palestine prior to the creation of Israel from
an Israeli point of view.

428   WE ARE THE PALESTINIAN PEOPLE
1973 / 52 min / sound / b&w / 16 mm
Cine News. Distributed by Tricontinental Films. Locations:
U. of California Extension Media Center / U. of California
at Berkeley.
Made by an American film crew, including Jewish
Americans. A history of the struggle for Palestine.
Shows the Holocaust during WWII, immigration of Jews to
Palestine, Arab resistance to British and Zionist
encrouchments, and the creation of Israel. Reviews the
Arab-Israeli wars and beginnings of an Arab resistance
movement which resulted in the Palestine Liberation
Organization. Includes interview with Yasir Arafat.
Shows military and social programs of the PLO. Attempts
to create sympathy for the Palestinians and their
historical dilemma.

INTERVIEWS AND BIOGRAPHIES

429   ARAB POINT OF VIEW
1970 / 40 min / sound / b&w / 16 mm
Arab Information Office, Washington.

Problems faced by Palestinians are discussed by the
Councilor of the Kuwait Mission to the U.N.

430   PALESTINE IN TURMOIL
       (c. 1977?) / 28 min / sound / b&w / 16 mm
       Distributed by the Embassy of Kuwait.
       Dr. John Davis, President of the American Near East
       Refugee Aid Organization, moderates a panel discussion
       featuring Dr. Fayez Sayegh of the Kuwaiti Embassy and
       three American journalists on the topic of the
       Palestinians. Possibly shorter version of no. 429.

431   YASSAR ARAFAT: PROFILE OF A HERO
       1975 / 29 min / sound / color / 3/4" videocassette
       Worldwide Church of God. (Garner Ted Armstrong, program no.
       641) Location: Library of Congress. *
       Intended for conservative Christian television audiences.
       Features a commentary on Yassar Arafat and the PLO, cen-
       tering on his address to the U.N. General Assembly on
       Palestinian rights. Military and terrorist activities of
       the Palestine Liberation Organization and its branches
       are stressed. Garner Ted Armstrong advocates turning to
       Biblical prophecy and creation of a world government to
       solve problems like the Middle East. This program does
       nothing to present the problems of the Palestinians or
       enlighten viewers concerning the needs of Israelis.
       Intended to stress terrorist image of the PLO and to con-
       tinue non-recognition of that body.

REFUGEES AND THE PALESTINIAN DIASPORA

432   AFTERMATH
       (c. 1969) / 46 min / sound / color / 16 mm
       United Nations/UNRWA. Distributed by Associated Films.
       Location: Embassy of Libya.
       Documents the aftermath of the 1967 War. Shows
       Palestinian refugees moving across the Allenby bridge
       into Jordan. Discusses settlement of refugees in camps
       and efforts to assist refugees with schools and social
       programs. Describes both government and voluntary orga-
       nization efforts to assist displaced Palestinians.

433   THE ARAB REFUGEES
       1967 / 25 min / sound / b&w / 16 mm
       United Nations/UNWRA and U.N. Educational T.V. Distributed
       by United Nations Films, and by the League of Arab States.
       Shows the problems faced by Palestinian refugees.
       Discusses the increase of refugees as a result of the
       1967 War. Profiles life in a refugee camp and describes
       U.N. efforts to provide education and health care
       programs despite shortage of funds.

434   ARAB REFUGEES (WHO ARE WE?)
       (n.d.) / 8 min / sound / b&w / 16 mm
       Distributed by the Embassy of Egypt. No other information
       available.

435   BLOWN BY THE WIND
       (c. 1968) / 25 min / sound / color / 16 mm
       Jack Madro. Distributed by the League of Arab States, and
       by the Arab Information Center, Dallas.
           Uses minimal narration. Tells the story of Palestinian
           refugees in camps. Shows children's painting of the 1967
           War and their images of a Palestine they have never seen.

436   CLEVELAND FRIENDSHIP CLOTHING CARAVAN
       (c. 1960?) / 8 min / sound / b&w / 16 mm
       American Middle East Relief Association.
           Shows the Cleveland Chapter of the American Middle East
           Relief Association sending clothes to needy Palestinian
           refugees. Shot before the 1967 War.

437   THE HOLY LAND: RUIN OR RECONCILIATION
       (n.d.) / 20 min / sound / color / 16 mm
       United Presbyterian Film Distribution, Dept. of Supporting
       Services.
           Reviews the Palestinian refugee problem.

438   ISRAEL GOVERNMENT ALLOWS REFUGEES TO RETURN
       (c. 1967?) / 10 min / sound / b&w / 16 mm
       Location: Abraham F. Rad Jewish Film Archive.
           Newsreel footage. Shows Palestinians returning to their
           West Bank homes after fleeing to the East Bank during the
           1967 War. Looks at their land now under Israeli occupa-
           tion.

439   THE PALESTINE RIGHT
       (n.d.) / 18 min / sound / b&w / 16 mm
       Distributed by the Embassy of Jordan. No other information
       available.

440   THE PALESTINIAN
       1977 / 180 min / sound / color / 16 mm
       The Workers League. Vanessa Redgrave Productions.
       Distributed by Workers League, and by the Palestine
       Information Office, Washington. Credits: Producer - Vanessa
       Redgrave, Director - Roy Battersby. *
           Ambitious project with mixed results. Overly long.
           Shows what life is like in refugee camps and in
           resistance groups. Includes interviews with Yasir
           Arafat, Lebanese Phalangists, and individual
           Palestinians. Shows military and social programs of the
           PLO and a border skirmish. Discusses the role of
           Palestinians in the Lebanese civil war. Technically well
           produced but suffers from a bad script, poor editing and

simplistic presentation. Nonetheless contains some
excellent footage and moving passages despite the intru-
sive presence of Vanessa Redgrave. Of interest mainly to
audiences already sympathetic to the Palestinian plight.
Supposedly a shorter version is also available.

441   PALESTINIAN REFUGEES IN LEBANON
(c. 1974) / 40 min / sound / color / 16 mm
Roger Pic. Distributed by Icarus Films. *
Listed in some catalogs under the original French title:
LES REFUGEES DES LA PALESTINE. Uses English
narration. Traces a family of Palestinian refugees in
Lebanon. 300,000 refugees in an original Lebanese population of 3 million have greatly influenced current
affairs, the economy and politics of Lebanon. Shows
Palestinian camps with their separate industries, services, schools and culture. Describes the strain these
create on the Lebanese economy and delicate political
system. Filmed before the Lebanese civil war. Documents
conditions which led to the breakdown of the Lebanese
system under the strain of the refugees' presence. Well
presented. Recommended.

442   SANDS OF SORROW
1950 / 29 min / sound / b&w / 16 mm
Pathe News. Originally distributed by the American Middle
East Relief Association. Location: National Archives
(59.166)
Describes the life of Palestinian Arabs who became refugees following the 1948 Israeli War of Independence.

443   SOME OF THE PALESTINIANS
1976 / 56 min / sound / color / 16 mm
United Nations Relief and Works Agency for Palestine
Refugees in the Near East (UNWRA). Distributed by United
Nations Films.
Available in English, Arabic, French and German
soundtracks. Shows UNWRA efforts to provide education
and vocational training for three generations of
Palestinians made homeless by war. Shows a camp doctor
in Syria, a Lebanese refugee camp after an Israeli air
attack, and a refugee farmer in Jordan.

PALESTINIAN CHILDREN

444   CHILDREN OF PALESTINE
1979 / 35 min / sound / color / 16 mm or videocassette
Monica Maurer and Samir Nimer. Palestine Cinema Institution
and the Red Crescent. Distributed by Icarus Films, and by
the Palestine Liberation Organization Office, New York. *
Emotional film. Presents the plight of Palestinian
refugee children in camps with poor health facilities and

little chance for schooling or employment. Physical
damage resulting from Israeli air raids is shown on young
burn victims in a hospital. Shows children being fitted
with artificial limbs. The Lebanese civil war and
Israeli raids in Lebanon are shown to be a major cause of
death and disease coupled with breakdown of health care
and agriculture. Strongly stated. Intended to shock
audiences by showing the effect of war on children. Of
most interest to audiences sympathetic to the Palestinian
plight.

445   PEACE IS MORE THAN A DREAM
      (c. 1974) / 27 min / sound / color / 16 mm
      UNWRA. Distributed by Association-Sterling Films. (free)
          Examines children growing up in refugee camps near
          Damascus and Amman through their drawings and paintings.
          Shows expressions of fear and hope for the future.

446   YOUR FRIEND, OMAR
      1963 / 25 min / sound / b&w / 16 mm
      UNWRA. Released by Association Films. Distributed by the
      Middle East Institute. (NUC FiA 64-534)
          Follows one Palestinian refugee boy made homeless by the
          1948 War. Shows high unemployment rate among refugees
          and efforts of UNWRA in a vocational training center near
          Jerusalem. Includes scenes of Palestinian camp life in
          Jordan.

POLITICAL/MILITARY ORGANIZATIONS

447   AL FATEH
      (c. 1971) / 80 min / sound / b&w / 16 mm
      Unitele Film. English version produced by Black Star
      Productions, Detroit. Distributed by San Francisco
      Newsreel, and by Third World Newsreel.
          Describes resistance of Palestinians to losing their
          homeland and the political/military solutions of Al
          Fateh. Shows Al Fateh meetings in refugee camps, social
          services, and combat training. Includes interviews with
          Yasir Arafat, Palestinian professional people and El
          Fateh soldiers. Explains the aims and hopes of the orga-
          nization.

448   LAND OF THE FATHERS
      (c. 1975) / 35 min / sound / color / 16 mm
      No production information available.
          Discusses the political and military programs of the
          Palestine Liberation Organization.

449   THE PALESTINIANS AND THE PLO
      (n.d.) / 30 min / sound / color / 16 mm
      Anti-Defamation League of B'nai B'rith. (Dateline Israel

series) Distributed by Alden Films. Location: Gratz
College.
Arnold Forster interviews Joseph Tekoa concerning the
Palestinians and the PLO. An Israeli viewpoint.

450   THE RUSSIAN CONNECTION
(c. 1978) / 50 min / sound / color / 16 mm
Herbert Krosney. Distributed by Phoenix Films. *
Television broadcast. Expose shows the connection between the PLO and the Soviet Union using Soviet arms sales
to the PLO as proof. Intended to persuade American
audiences the PLO is a Soviet puppet organization.

EDUCATION

451   HEAD START FOR OMAR
1971 / 27 min / sound / color / 16 mm
United Nations Relief and Works Agency for Palestine
Refugees in the Near East. Distributed by United Nations
Films, by Association-Sterling Films, and by the Middle East
Institute.
Follow up to YOUR FRIEND, OMAR, no. 446. Shows refugees
like Omar from the 1948 War have been joined by hundreds
of thousands of refugees from later wars. Follows Omar
at school near Jericho and in training at the Kalandria
Vocational Centre. Shows him studying to be a radio
operator and obtaining a job in Qatar on the Persian
Gulf. Describes how Omar must wait for a settlement to
the Arab-Israeli conflict before he can return to his
homeland. Available in English, Arabic, French and
Spanish soundtracks.

452   MIRACLE IN THE HOLY LAND
(c. 1975?) / 21 min / sound / color / 16 mm
Distributed by the Middle East Institute.
Tells the story of Musa Alamy, former lawyer and
Palestinian refugee, who now devotes his life to training
refugee boys to become craftsmen and farmers. An epilo-
gue was added to the film ten years later in the mid-70's.
Shows what has happened to the refugee camp where Alamy
taught.

453   THREE "R's" IN THE SAND
1955 / 20 min / sound / b&w / 16 mm
UNWRA. Distributed by Contemporary Films.
Filmed by students at UNWRA Visual Information Services.
Shows education programs available to Palestinian refugee
children.

454   TO BECOME A MAN
(c. 1970) / 27 min / sound / b&w / 16 mm
UNWRA. Distributed by Association-Sterling Films.

Shows technical training provided by UNWRA. Focuses on the story of two teenage Palestinian boys who receive vocational education through this UN program.

INTERNATIONAL COOPERATION AND ASSISTANCE

455   AMERICAN AID TO ARAB REFUGEES
      (c. 1960?) / 6 min / sound / b&w / 16 mm
      American Middle East Relief Association.
          Describes the work of the American Middle East Relief
          Association in aiding Palestinian refugees. See also no.
          436 for the work of this organization.

456   FOUNTAIN OF JABALIA
      1958 / 15 min / sound / b&w / 16 mm
      United Nations. Distributed by Contemporary Films. (NUC FiA
      60-665) Credits: Narrator - Alistair Cooke.
          Describes problems in Palestinian refugee camps formed
          after the 1948 Arab-Israeli war. Discusses the need for
          long-term educational and social programs as well as
          daily relief efforts.

457   JOURNEY TO UNDERSTANDING
      (c. 1970) / 27 min / b&w / 16 mm
      UNWRA. Distributed by Association-Sterling Films.
          Hugh Downs tours refugee camps where 1/2 million young
          people are receiving UNRWA schooling and vocational edu-
          cation.

458   PALESTINE RED CRESCENT
      1979 / 45 min / sound / color / 16 mm
      Distributed by the Palestine Liberation Organization Office,
      New York. (free)
          Shows humanitarian activities in Lebanon by the Red
          Crescent, the Middle Eastern equivalent of the Red Cross.

459   TOMORROW BEGINS TODAY
      (c. 1963?) / 15 min / sound / color / 16 mm
      UNRWA. Distributed by Association Films, by the Middle East
      Institute and by the American Friends of the Middle East.
          Shows the plight of Palestinian refugees of the 1948 War.
          Examines what is being done by the United Nations Relief
          and Works Agency to provide basic health services, food
          and shelter for immediate relief and education and
          training programs for long-range assistance.

HISTORY FROM BIBLICAL TIMES. SIGNIFICANCE OF JERUSALEM
IN JUDAISM, CHRISTIANITY AND ISLAM

460   HEZEKIAH'S WATER TUNNEL
1963 / 28 min / sound / color / 16 mm
Griffon Graphics. Made and released by Rarig's. (The Marks
of Man, series no. 1) Credits: Director-Writers - Jay Kulp,
James H. Lawless, Narrator - Dr. Frank Baxter, Educational
Collaborator - Siegfried H. Horn. Locations: Brigham Young
U. / Library of Congress (FBA 3286) / New York Public
Donnell Film Library / Penn. State U. / U. of Illinois. *
Shot on location in Jerusalem and Istanbul. Shows recent
archeological excavations in Jerusalem of the water tun-
nel system used by King Hezekiah to withstand the
Assyrian siege of 701 B.C. Shows how the tunnel was
built and quotes Biblical references to the Jerusalem
water transport system. Intended for junior high school
through adult audiences.

461   JERUSALEM
1971 / 5 min / sound / color / 16 mm
Ken Rudolph. Distributed by Pyramid Films. (LC 74-712358)
Credits: Producer - David Adams, Editor - Ken Rudolph.
Uses over 800 still photographs and short film clips.
Impressionistic short film. Traces the history of
Jerusalem from the time of King David to the 1967 War.

462   JERUSALEM AND ITS CONTRIBUTIONS
1970 / 17 min / sound / color / 16 mm
Atlantis Productions. J. Michael Hagopian. (LC 75-705591)
Locations: Library of Congress (FBB 1070) *
Listed in some sources as: JERUSALEM AND HER
CONTRIBUTIONS. Intended for elementary-junior high
school audiences. Describes how an Israeli boy regards
the city. Discusses the importance of Jerusalem to
Christians and Muslims as well as Jews.

463   JERUSALEM - CENTER OF MANY WORLDS
1969 / 29 min / sound / color / 16 mm
Atlantis Productions. J. Michael Hagopian. (LC 78-702425)
Locations: Boston U. / Brigham Young U. / Indiana U. /
Library of Congress (FBB 0250) / New York U. / U. of Arizona
/ U. of Illinois / U. of Michigan / U. of South Carolina /
U. of Washington. *
Historical presentation of Jerusalem from the time of
King David through the Roman destruction to the Christian
and Muslim periods. Shows sites such as the Dome of the
Rock and the Wailing Wall. Intended for senior high
school to adult audiences. Well photographed.

464   JERUSALEM - CITY OF DAVID
       1971 / 21 min / sound / color / 16 mm
       Jim Morgan. Anti-Defamation League of B'nai B'rith.
       Distributed by Alden Films. Location: Gratz College.
           Jim Morgan of WPVI-TV in Philadelphia goes to Israel to
           interview Dr. Douglas Young, President of the American
           Institute for Holy Land Studies. Discusses the dif-
           ference in occupation of Jerusalem under the pre-1967
           Jordanian administration and the post-1967 Israeli admi-
           nistration. The Mufti of Jerusalem, Brig. General Uzi
           Narkiss and others are interviewed. Argues the city
           should remain under Israeli rule.

465   JERUSALEM, DAVID'S CITY
       1967 / 13 min / sound / b&w / 16 mm
       Capital Films, Jerusalem. Credits: Director - A. Be'eri,
       Photographer - F. Czaznik. Locations: Abraham F. Rad Jewish
       Film Archive / Prime Minister's Office, Information Dept.,
       Jerusalem.
           Shows the city after the 1967 War united under Israeli
           rule. Scenes of old and new Jerusalem show the signifi-
           cance of the city to Jews, Christians and Muslims.

466   JERUSALEM THE GOLDEN
       1967 / 7 min / sound / b&w / 16 mm
       Location: Abraham F. Rad Jewish Film Archive.
           Stresses freedom to practise all religions and visit
           shrines is protected in Jerusalem under the Israeli admi-
           nistration since unification in 1967.

467   JERUSALEM, THE HOLY CITY
       1934 / 10 min / sound / b&w / 16 mm
       Warner Brothers. Released for educational purposes by
       Teaching Film Custodians, 1939. (Musical World Journeys
       series) (NUC FiA 52-4642) Credits: Producer - E.M. Newman,
       Editor - Bert Frank.
           Scenes of Jerusalem and the surrounding countryside ori-
           ginally taken from a Warner Bros. travelog. Includes
           scenes of religious observances in Jerusalem, shepherds
           on the hillsides, the Dead Sea, a Bedouin girl, an Easter
           procession, the Wailing Wall and Arab Muslims.

468   JERUSALEM: HOLY CITY
       1951 / 10 min / sound / color or b&w / 16 mm
       F.W. von Keller. Released by Encyclopaedia Britannica Films.
       (NUC FiA 53-1039) Credits: Educational Collaborator -
       Casper J. Kraemer, Jr. Technicolor. Locations: American
       Museum of Natural History / Kent State U. / Syracuse U. / U.
       of Illinois.
           Available in English and French soundtracks. Listed in
           some catalogs with a release date of 1955. Shows sites
           in Jerusalem of historical or Biblical interest.
           Describes the influence of Jewish, Christian and Islamic
           traditions on the city.

97

469 JERUSALEM, JERUSALEM
1977 / 27 min / sound / color / 16 mm
Distributed by Consulate General of Israel, and by Alden
Films.
Traces the 4000 year history of Jerusalem from the time
of Abraham, David and Solomon through the Roman period,
the Crusaders, the Ottoman empire, the creation of Israel
and the 1967 War. Shows Jerusalem unified under Israeli
control following the 1967 War.

470 JERUSALEM LIVES
1975 / 52 min / sound / color / 16 mm
Charles Guggenheim. Distributed by Alden Films. Location:
Gratz College.
For senior high school to adult audiences. Shows the
city of Jerusalem through the eyes of an Israeli, an
Arab, a priest, an archeologist and a minister. Each
shows different aspects of the city.

471 JERUSALEM QUARTET
1978 / 4 films, 29 min each / sound / color / 16 mm
Zev Kedem. Jerusalem Film Corp., Maryland.
Series of four films investigating different quarters of
the city of Jerusalem. The Jewish, Muslim, Armenian and
Christian quarters, and life in each, are shown.

472 JERUSALEM, THE SACRED CITY
1960 / 14 min / sound / color or b&w / 16 mm
FAMF. (Land of the Bible series)
For junior high school and religious groups. Follows a
boy on a tour of Jerusalem as he describes sites of
significance to Christians. Relates events in the Bible
dealing with Jerusalem.

473 JORDAN: THE CRADLE OF RELIGIONS
1963 / 20 min / sound / color / 16 mm
American Friends of the Middle East. Formerly distributed
by the Permanent Mission of Jordan to the U.N.
Shot on location when Jerusalem was under Jordanian administration. Shows sites of interest to Christians in
Jerusalem and describes the Holy Places in the city.

474 OF JERUSALEM STONE
1974 / 30 min / sound / color / 16 mm
Distributed by Alden Films. Location: Gratz College.
Shows the Old City of Jerusalem. Describes its history
at the time of the second Temple using archeological finds
in the old Jewish Quarter.

475 OUR CITY JERUSALEM
1968 / 14 min / sound / color / 16 mm
Yona Zarecki. Locations: Abraham F. Rad Jewish Film Archive
/ Israel Film Studios, Herzliyah.

View of the city of Jerusalem. Explains its significance
to Jews and Christians. Shows modern memorials to
Israeli dead and historic sites on a scale model of the
ancient city.

476   THREE RELIGIONS IN JERUSALEM - JUDAISM, CHRISTIANITY, ISLAM
1969 / 4 min / silent / color / super 8 mm film loop in
cartridge.   Eye Gate House.   (Living in Israel series) (LC
74-703720)
Shows the three major monotheistic religions found in
Jerusalem and the significance of the city to each of
them.

TWENTIETH CENTURY HISTORY OF JERUSALEM

477   EL AQSA MOSQUE FIRE
1969 / 5 min / sound / b&w / 16 mm
Location: Abraham F. Rad Jewish Film Archives.
Available in English, French and Spanish soundtracks.
Short film shows firemen fighting the El Aqsa Mosque fire
despite crowd interference.   Jerusalem mayor Teddy Kollek
gives his view of the incident.

478   (HERD OF SHEEP ON THE ROAD TO JERUSALEM)
June, 1903 / silent / b&w / 16 mm
Thomas Edison.   Location: Library of Congress Paper Print
Collection (FLA 3422)
A flock of sheep with eight shepherds in Palestinian dress
proceed down a road in this early Edison film.   For
historic purpose only.   Footage is unfortunately in poor
condition.

479   I WAS BORN IN JERUSALEM
(c. 1979) / ? / sound / 16 mm
Yehoran Gaon.   MD Productions.   Available from the JWB
Lecture Bureau, New York.   No other information available.

480   IMPACT OF JERUSALEM
1971 / 26 min / sound / color / 16 mm
Pictura Film Distributors.   (Charles Blair's A Better World
series) Location: Brigham Young U.
For high school to adult audiences.   Listed in some catalogs as released in 1973.   Examines David Ben-Gurion's
role in shaping the state of Israel.   Teddy Kolleck,
mayor of Jerusalem, is interviewed.   Presents Israel as a
place where Arabs, Christians and Jews are learning to
live together.

481   JERUSALEM IN THE '20's
(c. 1920) / 5 min / silent / b&w / 16 mm
Location: Abraham F. Rad Jewish Film Archive.
Shows various scenes of life in Jerusalem during the early
days of the British mandate.

482 (JERUSALEM'S BUSIEST STREET SHOWING MT. ZION)
     June, 1903 / 1 min / silent / b&w / 16 mm
     Thomas Edison. Location: Library of Congress Paper Print
     Collection (FLA 4674)
          Early Edison film. Shows a Jerusalem street scene with a
          camel-drawn carriage. Photographed by A.C. Abadie for
          Edison. Useful for historic purposes. One of the series
          of short film clips shot by Abadie in 1903 to show the
          exotic Middle East. Library of Congress print is in fair
          condition.

483 (A JEWISH DANCE AT JERUSALEM)
     June, 1903 / 1 min / silent / b&w / 16 mm
     Thomas Edison. Location: Library of Congress Paper Print
     Collection (FLA 3707)
          A line dance by men in Jewish dress is performed in the
          street while on-lookers offer comment and stare at the
          camera. Another in the series of short films by Adabie
          for Edison documenting the Middle East. For historic
          purposes. Library of Congress print is in fair condition.

484 (SOWING AND HARVESTING WHEAT IN JERUSALEM
     (n.d.) / ? / b&w / silent / 16 mm
     Harmon. Location: National Archives (200HF438) No other
     information available.

THE ARAB-ISRAELI CONFLICT AND INTERNATIONALIZATION
     OF JERUSALEM

485 ALL THE NIGHTS TO COME
     (n.d.) / 15 min / sound / color / 16 mm
     Distributed by Alden Films.
          Israeli poet Yehuda Amichai looks at Jerusalem at dif-
          ferent times of the day and speaks out against war.
          Scenes of smiling babies and young lovers alternate with
          WWII footage and war ruins.

486 AND ON THE SEVENTH DAY
     (c. 1967) / 27 min / sound / color / 16 mm
     Distributed by Alden Films.
          Shows Jerusalem after the Six Day War through the eyes of
          three people. An Israeli soldier who fought for the
          city, a Jewish woman born in the Old City able to return
          after many years, and an American Jewish war volunteer
          watch the religious observances of Jews, Christians and
          Muslims in the city.

487 DIVIDED CITY: JERUSALEM
     1978 / 60 min / sound / color / 16 mm
     BBC-TV and WNET Television. Credits: Narrator - Richard
     Kershaw. *
          Examines the conflicting views of the Arab and Jewish

population in Jerusalem and the media's impact on that
balance. Shows the building boom in Jerusalem and Arabs
being removed from their homes for urban renewal. Of
primary interest is differing Arabic and Hebrew television news broadcasts. Arabic language news in Israel is
censored to prevent unrest in the Arab populace. This
has created a distrust of Israeli newscasts since different coverage on Jordanian and Lebanese TV can be
received by Arabs in Israel. Director of Jordanian television is interviewed concerning his viewing public which
is about 1/2 Palestinian. Interesting, well produced
program covering a specialized topic.

488   JERUSALEM MARKET BOMBED
      1968 / 8 min / sound / b&w / 16 mm
      Location: Abraham F. Rad Jewish Film Archive.
          After a bomb explodes in Mahane Yehuda, killing 12 and
          wounding 55 people, a curfew is imposed on East Jerusalem.
          Prime Minister Levi Eshkol addresses the nation con-
          cerning the incident.

489   UNITED NATIONS NEWSREEL NO. 1
      (n.d.) / 15 min / sound / b&w / 16 mm
      United Nations Films. Location: Ministry of Education and
      Culture, Jerusalem.
          Describes several U.N. projects including the plan for
          internationalization of Jerusalem, U.N. health programs
          and assistance for developing countries.

490   A WALL IN JERUSALEM
      1969 / 91 min / sound / b&w / 16 or 35 mm
      Parafrance, Paris. Released in the U.S. by EYR Programs.
      Distributed by Alden Films, and by JWB Lecture Bureau, and by
      Budget Films. (LC 72-700786) Credits: Director - Frederic
      Rossif, Writer - Joseph Kessel, Narrator - Richard Burton.
      Locations: Gratz College / U. of Michigan / U. of Washington.
          Listed in some catalogs with a release date of 1971.
          Follows history of Zionism from its beginnings in the
          1890's to 1968. Looks at the Ottoman and British periods
          and the struggle for a Jewish homeland after WWII. For
          high school to adult audiences. Covers history of
          Palestine and Israel from the Jewish viewpoint.

URBAN RE-DEVELOPMENT

491   THE INNOCENT DOOR
      1973 / 29 min / sound / color / 16 mm
      Canada Ministry of State for Urban Affairs, Ottawa, and the
      National Film Board of Canada. (LC 75-701881) Credits:
      Producers - Wolf Koenig, Peter Raymont, Director - Ken
      McCready, Photographers - Pierre Letarte, Andreas Poulsson.
          Shows Jerusalem as it appeared in 1973 and in scale

models as it will appear in the future. Shows Israeli
architect Moishe Safdie's plans to rebuild certain sections of the city. Does not discuss the controversy of
these plans.

492   JERUSALEM IN DANGER
       1971 / 20 min / sound / color / 16 mm
       Icon Films. Distributed by the League of Arab States.
       From the Arab viewpoint. Presents the controversy over
       the urban re-development of Jerusalem, a city with reli-
       gious significance to Jews, Christians and Muslims.
       Expresses fear that Israeli development will turn the
       city from a religious and historical center into a Middle
       Eastern "Los Angeles" with sprawling suburbs and high-
       rise apartment complexes.

493   JERUSALEM IN THE YEAR 2000: THE FUTURE OF THE PAST
       (c. 1970) / 24 min / sound / color / 16 mm
       Documents Associates. (Towards the Year 2000 series)
       Examines the problems of urban development in Jerusalem.
       Discusses the religious and historic significance of the
       ancient city and the needs of visitors and residents.
       Looks at controversy over preservation of historic areas
       and urban development. Shows the discovery of a ruined
       site while digging a parking lot.

494   JERUSALEM: PROPHETS AND PARATROOPERS
       1973 / 30 min / sound / color / 16 mm
       Howard Tiro, The Film Co. Distributed by the Embassy of the
       State of Kuwait, by the Middle East Institute, and by the
       League of Arab States.
       Presents the complex case of Jerusalem, sacred to three
       religions. Traces changes in the Old City of Jerusalem
       since annexation by Israel after the 1967 War. Presents
       arguments for putting Jerusalem under international
       control. Attempts to present the issue of Jerusalem and
       internationalization from multiple viewpoints.

495   THE REBUILDING OF JERUSALEM
       1973 / ? / sound / color / 16 mm
       Anti-Defamation League of B'nai B'rith. (Dateline Israel
       series)
       Features an interview with mayor Teddy Kolleck of
       Jerusalem who describes plans for the city in the future.
       Stresses his desire to make the city as beautiful as
       possible.

496   STAIRWAY TO JERUSALEM
       1961 / 18 min / sound / color / 16 mm
       Locations: Abraham F. Rad Jewish Film Archive / Jewish
       National Fund, Jerusalem.
       Available in English, Hebrew, Spanish and German
       soundtrack. Israeli-produced film. Shows development
       projects underway in the Jerusalem area.

497   TIME DIMENSION
      1967 / 23 min / sound / b&w / 16 mm
      Location: Abraham F. Rad Jewish Film Archive.
        With musical background. Israeli-produced film. Shows
        Jerusalem over the last 100 years through old pho-
        tographs. Looks at urban decay and urban development
        programs and reconstruction designed to combat the
        effects of time on the city.

TRAVELOGS AND SCENES OF THE CITY

498   AL-QUDS - JERUSALEM
      (n.d.) / 18 min / sound / b&w / 16 mm
      Distributed by the Arab Information Office, Washington. No
      other information available.

499   AMONG SACRED STONES
      1974 / 7 min / sound / color / 16 mm
      Sol Rubin. Distributed by Arthur Mokin Productions.
        With musical soundtrack. Shows the Wailing Wall in
        Jerusalem and Jews at worship. Short, personal film
        intended for junior high school to adult audiences.
        Recipient of a 1974 Cannes Film Festival award.

500   ARCHBISHOP SPELLMAN IN JERUSALEM
      1944 / 40 min / silent / b&w / 16 mm
      U.S. Signal Corps. Location: National Archives (18CS117-2)
      No other information available.

501   AS THE MOUNTAINS ROUND JERUSALEM
      (n.d.) / 13 min / sound / color / 16 mm
      Distributed by Alden Films.
        Describes Jerusalem as an historic, economic and reli-
        gious center for centuries. Scenes include the Seven
        Gates of the city, King Herod's tomb, the Mount of
        Olives, Rachel's tomb, and other religious and historic
        sites.

502   CAMPUS IN JERUSALEM
      1960 / 17 min / sound / b&w / 16 mm
      Copyright: Israel Defense Forces. Locations: Israel Film
      Studios, Herzliyah / Abraham F. Rad Jewish Film Archive.
        Travelog of the Hebrew University in Jerusalem.

503   DAMASCUS AND JERUSALEM
      1936 / 10 min / sound / b&w / 16 mm
      (Screen Traveler series) Distributed by the Catholic Film
      Center. Location: U. of Colorado.
        Listed in catalogs as: ISRAEL, DAMASCUS AND
        JERUSALEM and as DAMASCUS AND PALESTINE. These many
        actually be more than one film. Each is listed as a tra-
        velog of the cities of Jerusalem and Damascus.

103

504   A DAY IN JERUSALEM
       (n.d.) / 28 min / sound / b&w / 16 mm
       Distributed by Alden Films.
       Tour of Jerusalem from the Old City, the Western Wall,
       monasteries and mosques to the modern parts of the city.
       Includes scenes of the Knesset (Israeli Parliament
       building), Hebrew University and the Israel Museum.

505   ELIE WIESEL'S JERUSALEM
       (n.d.) / 50 min / sound / color / 16 mm
       Distributed by Learning Corp. of America. No other infor-
       mation available.

506   IN JERUSALEM (BIYERUSHALAYIM)
       1963 / 33 min / sound / color / 16 or 35 mm
       Berkey Pathe Humphries. Credits: Directors - D. Perlov, Y.
       Malchin. Locations: Abraham F. Rad Jewish Film Archive /
       Prime Minister's Office, Information Dept., Jerusalem.
       Available in English, Hebrew, French and Spanish
       soundtracks. Israeli film. Evokes impressions of
       Jerusalem on the Sabbath. Shows scenes of different eth-
       nic communities, Me'a She'arim, and the new Jerusalem.

507   IN SEARCH OF A CITY: JERUSALEM
       (c. 1968) / 24 min / sound / color / 16 mm
       Distributed by Alden Films.
       Israelis and visitors make pilgrimages to sacred spots in
       the Old City in Jerusalem. Shows the 5000 year history
       of the city through its architecture.

508   JERUSALEM
       (n.d.) / 50 min / sound / color / 16 mm
       Learning Corp. of America.
       Personal view of Jerusalem by Israeli Elie Wiesel.
       Probably the same film as no. 505.

509   JERUSALEM
       1956 / 14 min / sound / b&w / 16 mm
       McGraw-Hill Textfilms.
       For junior high school to adult audiences. Shows the
       religious, social and economic significance of Jerusalem
       to the surrounding countryside. The beauty of the city
       and the life style of its people are examined.

510   JERUSALEM
       1965 / 5 min / sound / 35 mm
       Roll Films. Location: Israel Film Studios, Herzliyah.
       Travelog of the city and its sites.

511   JERUSALEM
       (c. 1970?) / 10 min / sound / b&w / 16 mm
       (This is Jerusalem series) Credits: Photographers - Zvi
       Voscovic, Larry Frish. Locations: Abraham F. Rad Jewish

Film Archive / Jewish Agency Film Archive.
Explores the religious, social and economic significance
of Jerusalem.

512   JERUSALEM (YERUSHALAYIM)
       (c. 1970?) / 20 min / sound / color / 16 mm
       Information Office, Prime Minister's Office, Jerusalem.
       Location: Ministry of Education and Culture, Jerusalem.
           Available in English and Hebrew soundtracks. Israeli
           film. Shows various sections of the city, bringing the
           Torah scrolls to Jerusalem, some non-Jewish sites and
           Me'a She'arim.

513   JERUSALEM - AND THE HILLS AROUND HER
       (YERUSHALA'IM HARIM SAVIV LA)
       1970 / 13 min / sound / color / 35 mm
       Roll Films. Israel Film Service. Locations: Abraham F. Rad
       Jewish Film Archive / Prime Minister's Office, Information
       Dept., Jerusalem.
           Available in English and Hebrew soundtracks. Listed in
           some catalogs as JERUSALEM: SURROUNDED BY HILLS.
           Shows various roads leading to the city. Discusses the
           place of Jerusalem as a spiritual and economic center
           from ancient times to the present.

514   JERUSALEM AND THE MOUNTAINS AROUND IT
       1971 / 20 min / sound / color / 16 mm
       Producer unknown. Location: Gratz College.
           Shows the city of Jerusalem as a regional center of
           history and tradition. May be the same as no. 513.

515   JERUSALEM, CITY OF PEACE
       (c. 1940?) / 10 min / sound / b&w / 16 mm
       Bray Studios Inc. (NUC FiA 55-437)
           A silent version of this film is also available. Shows
           city of Jerusalem, Mount of Olives, Zionist settlements
           and the life style of its people. Appears to have been
           produced during the British mandate period.

516   JERUSALEM, HERE WE COME
       1967 / 17 min / sound / color / 16mm
       Rank Organization, Denham. Released by A. Krymoloneski-
       Schreiber Productions, Tel Aviv. Distributed by Alden
       Films. Locations: Abraham F. Rad Jewish Film Archive /
       Library of Congress (FBA 5444) / Ministry of Tourism,
       Jerusalem. *
           Shows the revival of the ancient pilgrimage to Jerusalem
           undertaken yearly in a festival procession by young
           and old Israelis. Shows the four day march to Jerusalem.

517   JERUSALEM IS MINE
       (n.d.) / 13 min / sound / color / 16 mm
       Distributed by Alden Films.

Short portraits of Israelis living in Jerusalem.
Describes their hopes and aspirations and tours sites in
the modern parts of the city.

518   JERUSALEM, MY CITY
       1951 / 15 min / sound / b&w / 16 mm
       United Israel Appeal. Made by Palestine Films. (NUC FiA
       54-1209) Credits: Producer-Director - Victor Vicas, Writer
       - Michael Elkins.
            Available in English, Hebrew and Spanish soundtracks.
            Follows a tour of the modern city of Jerusalem. Narrated
            by a blind Israeli veteran of the 1948 Israeli War of
            Independence. Stresses significance of Jerusalem to Jews
            and Israelis.

519   JERUSALEM PEACE
       1977 / 58 min / sound / color / 16 mm
       Benjamin Productions. Distributed by Phoenix Films.
       Location: Kent State U.
            Intended for senior high school to adult audiences. Pre-
            sents Jerusalem as an allegory for the Middle East
            problem. Shows a city divided between Israeli and
            Palestinian inhabitants, holy to three religions, and a
            center of religious and historic traditions. Follows an
            archeologist who describes the life of Muslim and
            Christian Arabs and Jews living in Jerusalem.

520   JERUSALEM SCENES
       (n.d.) / 10 min / silent / b&w / 16 mm
       Location: Abraham F. Rad Jewish Film Archive.
            Travelog. Includes scenes of the Old City, holy sites,
            Yad Vashem and Mea Shearim.

521   JERUSALEM SONG
       (n.d.) / 18 min / sound / color / 16 mm
       Embassy of Jordan. Sub-titled in English. No other infor-
       mation available.

522   NEVEIM STREET
       (c. 1970?) / 58 min / sound / color / 16 mm
       Amnon Rubinstein. Distributed by Icarus Films.
            Traces one street in Jerusalem from the Nablus Gate in
            the Old City to the Western entrance. Shows the inhabi-
            tants of the street including a Christian scholar from
            Sweden, an old Palestinian, a Jewish doctor who remembers
            the Ottoman period and others. A microcosm of the city.

523   OLD CITY OF JERUSALEM - A VISIT TO THE MARKET
       1969 / 4 min / silent / color / super 8 mm film loop in
       cartridge. Eye Gate House. (Living in Israel series) (LC
       74-703718)
            Follows a young boy during his visit to the market in the
            Old City.

524   TO TOUCH A CITY: JERUSALEM
       1978 / 18 min / sound / color / 16 mm
       Israel Film Service. Distributed by Jewish Media
       Service, JWB. Credits: Director - Dan Wolman.
           Without narration. Evokes a feeling for the ancient
           and modern city of Jerusalem. Looks at individuals and
           buildings which make up the city.

525   WITH HITCHCOCK IN JERUSALEM
       (IM HITCHCOCK BI'YERUSHALAYIM)
       1967 / 16 min / sound / color / 16 mm
       Producer unknown. Locations: Abraham F. Rad Jewish Film
       Archive / Prime Minister's Office, Information Dept.,
       Jerusalem. Credits: Photographer - M. Ya'acovlovitz.
           Produced before the Six-Day War in 1967. Follows Alfred
           Hitchcock on his visit to Jerusalem.

JERUSALEM IN THE ARTS

526   GENII OF THE GLASS
       1978 / 30 min / sound / color / 16 mm
       Robert Haber. Distributed by Phoenix Films. Location: New
       York Public Donnell Film Library.
           Portrait of Muhamid Gzazz, the last traditional Arab
           glassblower living and working in Jerusalem. Presents
           his opinions and knowledge of the local community of
           Arab craftsmen.

527   JERUSALEM: IMAGE AND ART
       (n.d.) / 25 min / sound / color / 16 mm
       Distributed by Alden Films. No other information available.

528   JERUSALEM IN THE ARTS
       (n.d.) / ? / sound / color / 16 mm
       Israel Film Services, Jerusalem. No other information
       available.

529   JERUSALEM THROUGH ART
       1972 / 25 min / sound / color / 16 mm
       Locations: Abraham F. Rad Jewish Film Archive / Gratz
       College.
           Available in English, Hebrew, Spanish and French
           soundtracks. Uses examples in art and mosaics to show
           Jerusalem and its symbols produced by Jews, Christians
           and Muslims throughout the ages. Includes examples of
           art dealing with modern Jerusalem.

530   JOURNEY TO JERUSALEM
       1968 / 84 min / sound / color / 16 mm
       Michael Mindlin. Released by Audio Brandon. CCM. (LC
       72-703153) Location: Abraham F. Rad Jewish Film Archive.
           Filmed three weeks after the Six-Day War. Follows the

trip of conductor Leonard Bernstein and violinist Isaac Stern to Israel for the Mt. Scopus Concert commemorating the reunification of Jerusalem. Shows scenes of the city including the Wailing Wall, schools and military installations. Intended for junior high school to adult audiences.

AFGHANISTAN

AFGHANISTAN - HISTORY

531 ANNUAL JESHAN CELEBRATION
     1975 / 4 min / silent / color / super 8 mm film loop in
     cartridge. Grise, Inc. Made by Arthur C. Twomey. Released
     by Sound Book Press Society. (Afghanistan: The Land and the
     People, series no. 5) (LC 75-701137) *
         Includes scenes of a military parade and national dances
         performed on Jeshan, the Afghan celebration of national
         independence.

532 BLAZING TRAILS IN AFGHANISTAN
     1956 / 29 min / sound / b&w / 16 mm
     New York University. Released by NET Film Service.
     (Yesterday's World series) (NUC FiA 58-1271) Credits:
     Educational Collaborator - Dr. Casper J. Kraemer.
         Describes recent explorations by the American Museum of
         Natural History in Afghanistan, Baluchistan and the Indus
         Valley.

533 THE GIANT BUDDHAS OF AFGHANISTAN
     1963 / 4 min / silent / color / 8 mm
     International Communications Foundation. (South Asia:
     Afghanistan series) (NUC FiA 63-1490) Credits: Writer-
     Cinematographer - L. Van Mourick.
         Shows scenes of the 2000 year old giant Buddhas of
         central Afghanistan and their surrounding frescoes.
         Illustrates the influence of Indian and Far Eastern
         culture on the area.

534 THE NEW OPIUM ROUTE
     1973 / 54 min / sound / color / 16 mm or videocassette
     Catherine and Marianne Lamour. Distributed by Icarus Films.
     *
         Shows the semi-autonomous Pashtus living in the Khyber
         Pass on the border between Afghanistan and Pakistan.
         Argues the area's economy has become geared to opium and
         arms production. Shows how local craftsmen fashion small
         arms and cannons from original pieces. Follows a group
         of French film-makers as they purchase 5 tons of opium
         for $9 million to show the route by which drugs are
         smuggled across Afghanistan to Iran, Baluchistan, to the
         Gulf or Abu Dhabi for transport by ship to Europe or
         America. Shows how an area poor in agriculture can

thrive on illegal activities in scenes few anthropologists or ethnologists would cover. Uses an expose attitude. The French crew's commentary is at times both naive and irritating but this is an interesting film made under difficult conditions. Useful for examination of illegal activities in the Middle East.

AFGHANISTAN - NOMAD AND TRIBAL LIFE

535   AFGHAN NOMADS: THE MALDAR
1974 / 20 min / sound / color / 16 mm
American Universities Field Staff Production. (Faces of Change series, no. 5)   Credits: Filmmakers - David Hancock, Herbert DiGioia, Cultural Advisors - Louis and Nancy Dupree, Producer -Norman Miller, with Toryali Shafaq, Afghan Films and the National Film School of Great Britain. Locations: Indiana U. / Kansas State U. / Purdue / Syracuse U. / U. of California / U. of Illinois / U. of Kansas / U. of Wisconsin / Wheelock Educational Resources. *
Excellent ethnographic film. Shows the annual migration of the Maldar to Aq Kupruk from the foothills of the Hindu Kush, about 250 miles. Shows the interaction between nomadic Maldar and townspeople. Maldar men discuss the difficulties of the migration, getting land, the government, education for their children and ideas on wealth. Intended for junior high school to adult audiences. Beautifully photographed. Recommended.

536   BUZKASHI: THE NATIONAL GAME
1968 / 8 min / sound / color / 16 mm
Julien Bryan. Distributed by International Film Foundation. (Mountain Peoples of Asia series) Locations: Kent State U. / Penn. State U. / Syracuse U. / U. of Washington.
At a Jeshan, or annual independence day celebration, Afghan tribesmen on horseback honor the King by riding in a game of Buzkashi. In the formerly illegal game, a rider attempts to obtain and keep a ball made of animal skin. Shows great riding skill and endurance required of both rider and horse.

537   BUZKASHI - THE NATIONAL GAME
1975 / 4 min / silent / color / super 8 mm film loop in cartridge. Grise Inc. Made by Arthur C. Twomey. Released by Sound Book Press Society. (Afghanistan: The Land and the People series, no. 6) (LC 75-701138)
Shows a game of Buzkashi in which skilled horsemen try to carry a calf skin ball across a goal line.

538   EQUESTRIAN GAME "BUZKASI" (AFGHANISTAN)
1963, released 1965 / 12 min / silent / color / 16 mm
Encyclopaedia Cinematographica. (Ency. Cinematographica no. E 750) Distributed by Pennsylvania State University.

One of a long series of silent ethnographic films. Shows
a game of Buzkashi, the Afghan national game.

539 ISTALA MASHI - MAY YOU NEVER BE TIRED
1960 / 10 min / sound / b&w / 16 mm
UNICEF. Released by Association Films. (NUC FiA 60-3464)
Credits: Director - P.K. Barni, Narrator-Editor -
Cummins-Betts.
Filmed on location. Shows work of UNICEF and World
Health Organization dusting migrating nomadic tribes with
DDT to prevent possible spread of typhus during annual
migrations. Discusses annual migration from Afghanistan
to Pakistan to find winter pasturage for herds of sheep
and camels.

540 KUCHI HERDERS
1975 / 4 min / silent / color / 8 mm film loop in cartridge
Grise Inc. Made by Arthur C. Twomey. Released by Sound Book
Press Society. (Afghanistan: The Land and the People
series, no. 15) (LC 75-701147)
Shows Kuchi herders who provide links between isolated
Afghan villages while tending their flocks.

541 NOMADS OF BADAKHSHAN
1975 / 27 min / sound / color / 16 mm
Judith and Stanley Hallet. Distributed by Film Images.
Locations: Middle East Institute / Ohio State U. / U. of
Washington. *
For junior high school to adult audiences. Follows one
group of wealthy north Afghan nomads. Shows their annual
migration to grazing lands for herds of livestock. Shows
the uneasy interaction between villagers and nomads and
the difficulties of nomadic life. Includes sequences on
lack of medical care and high infant mortality. Well
photographed, excellently produced ethnographic film.
Recommended.

542 PASTORAL NOMADS
1972 / 60 min / sound / color / 16 mm
National Film Board of Canada. (LC 74-701215) Credits:
Producer - George Pearson, Director - Bill Brind.
Examines the way of life of nomad tribes in Afghanistan.

543 SHEARING YAKS
1972 / 10 min / sound / color / 16 mm
Julien Bryan. Distributed by International Film Foundation.
(Mountain Peoples of Central Asia series) (LC 73-702415)
Credits: Director-Photographer - Hermann Schlenker.
Location: Penn. State U.
Shows Tajik villagers of Afghanistan shearing yaks,
pounding the wool and spinning the hair into yarn. Uses
no narration. Possibly the same film as: GATHERING AND
SHEARING YAKS (TADZHIK, AFGHANISTAN).

111

Silent Encyclopaedia Cinematographica film on the same
subject (no. E 679) also available from Penn. State
University.

AFGHANISTAN - VILLAGE LIFE

544 AFGHAN VILLAGE
1974 / 44 min / sound / color / 16 mm
American University Field Staff. Produced with the coopera-
tion of Toryali Shafaq, Afghan Films and the Govt. of
Afghanistan. (Faces of Change series, no. 1) Credits:
Producer - Norman Miller, Cultural Advisors - Louis and
Nancy Dupree. Locations: Indiana U. / Kansas State U. /
Middle East Institute / Purdue / Syracuse / U. of California
Extension Media Center / U. of Illinois / U. of Kansas / U.
of Wisconsin / Wheelock Educational Resources. *
Excellent ethnographic film. Shows life in the village
of Aq Kapruk in northern Afghanistan. Scenes include the
bazaar, working in the fields and with livestock, working
on an irrigation project, and the annual Jeshan independence day celebration. Finishes with a game of buzkashi
played on horseback in a river. Well filmed with a minimum of narration. Intended for junior high school to
adult audiences. One of the few films which shows Afghan
village life as opposed to more exotic but vanishing
nomads. Recommended.

545 BASKET PLAITING (TADZHIK, AFGHANISTAN, BADAKHSHAN)
1963, released 1965 / 16 min / silent / b&w / 16 mm
Encyclopaedia Cinematographica. Distributed by Pennsylvania
State U. (Ency. Cinematographica no. E 746)
Silent ethnographic film. Shows baskets being woven from
reeds.

546 BRIDGE BUILDING
1968 / 10 min / sound / b&w / 16 mm
International Film Foundation. (Mountain Peoples of Central
Asia series) Locations: Kent State U. / Penn. State U. / U.
of Illinois.
For junior high school to adult audiences. Shows Tajik
of northeastern Afghanistan in the village of Kultook
rebuilding a bridge, their only road to other villages.
The bridge is repaired yearly after spring rains. Uses
no narration. Listed in some catalogs as: TAJIK
PEOPLE - BRIDGE BUILDING. Probably one of the
Encyclopaedia Cinematographica films re-released with a
musical soundtrack.

547 CONSTRUCTION OF THORN-HEDGE FENCES (TADZHIK,
AFGHANISTAN, BADAKHSHAN)
1963, released 1964 / 9 min / silent / b&w / 16 mm
Encyclopaedia Cinematographica. Distributed by Pennsylvania

State U. (Ency. Cinematographica no. E 709)
Another in the series of silent ethnographic films.
Shows how fences are constructed using thorn bushes.

548 CUTTING WHEAT (TADZHIK, AFGHANISTAN, BADAKHSHAN)
1963, released 1964 / 4 min / silent / color / 16 mm
Encyclopaedia Cinematographica. Distributed by Pennsylvania
State University (Ency. Cinematographica no. E 712)
Another in the series of silent ethnographic films.
Shows a wheat harvest in Afghanistan.

549 FORGING A HORSESHOE, HORSESHOEING (TADZHIK,
AFGHANISTAN, BADAKHSHAN)
1963, released 1964 / 10 min / silent / b&w / 16 mm
Encyclopaedia Cinematographica. Distributed by Pennsylvania
State University. (Ency. Cinematographica no. E 681)
Another in the series of silent ethnographic films.
Shows how Tajik of Afghanistan make horseshoes using tra-
ditional tools.

550 GRINDING WHEAT (TAJIK, AFGHANISTAN)
(n.d.) / 7 min / silent / b&w / 16 mm
International Film Foundation.
Another in the series of silent ethnographic films
depicting a single action collected in the Encyclopaedia
Cinematographica series. Shows wheat being ground.

551 HERAT TILE MAKERS: CHARIKAR GRAPE HARVEST
1975 / 4 min / sound / color / super 8 mm film loop in
cartridge. Grise Inc. Made by Arthur C. Twomey. Released
by Sound Book Press Society. (Afghanistan: The Land and the
People series, no. 11) (LC 75-701143)
Shows tile makers in the city of Herat working on mosaics
for a Mosque. An unrelated piece of footage shows the
Charikar grape harvest.

552 HIGHLAND VILLAGE: THE BAMIAN VALLEY
1975 / 4 min / silent / color / super 8 mm film loop in
cartridge Grise, Inc. Made by Arthur C. Twomey. Released
by Sound Book Press Society. (Afghanistan: The Land and the
People series, no. 2) (LC 75-701134)
Shows the mountainous central area of Afghanistan and the
lifestyle of its inhabitants.

553 MAKING A PELLET BOW (TADZHIK, AFGHANISTAN,
BADAKHSHAN)
1963, released 1965 / 16 min / silent / b&w / 16 mm
Encyclopaedia Cinematographica. Distributed by Pennsylvania
State University. (Ency. Cinematographica no. E 745)
Another in the series of silent ethnographic films.
Shows bow manufacturing techniques.

554 MAKING BLACK EXPLOSIVE POWDER (TADZHIK,
AFGHANISTAN, BADAKHSHAN)

1963, released 1965 / 15 min / silent / b&w / 16 mm
Encyclopaedia Cinematographica. Distributed by Pennsylvania
State University. (Ency. Cinematographica no. E 744)
Another in the series of silent ethnographic films.
Shows techniques used for making gunpowder.

555 MAKING BOOTS (TADZHIK, AFGHANISTAN, BADAKHSHAN)
1963, released 1965 / 15 min / silent / b&w / 16 mm
Encyclopaedia Cinematographica. Distributed by Pennsylvania
State University. (Ency. Cinematographica no. E 742)
Another in the series of silent ethnographic films.
Shows how boots are constructed by the Tadzhik of
Afghanistan.

556 MAKING GUNPOWDER (TAJIK, AFGHANISTAN)
(n.d.) / 10 min / silent / b&w / 16 mm
International Film Foundation. (Mountain Peoples of Central
Asia series)
Another in a series of films distributed by International
Film Foundation originally from the Encyclopaedia
Cinematographica collection, a large group of silent eth-
nographic films highlighting a single typical activity or
action for study.

557 MOCK COMBAT (PASHTUN, AFGHANISTAN, BADAKHSHAN)
1963, released 1964 / 4 min / silent / color / 16 mm
Encyclopaedia Cinematographica. Distributed by Pennsylvania
State University. (Ency. Cinematographica no. E 686)
Another in a series of silent ethnographic films. Shows
Pashtun of Afghanistan engaging in mock battle.

558 MOULDING AND CASTING OF IRON (TADZHIK, AFGHANISTAN,
BADAKHSHAN)
1963, released 1965 / 38 min / silent / b&w / 16 mm
Encyclopaedia Cinematographica. Distributed by Pennsylvania
State University. (Ency. Cinematographica no. E 748)
Another in a series of silent ethnographic films. Shows
iron working techniques used by the Tajik of Afghanistan.

559 NEW GIRL IN TOWN
1962 / 28 min / sound / b&w / 16 mm
United Nations Films.
Despite the many films dealing with nomad life in
Afghanistan, the majority of Afghanis live in small
farming villages. Shows the results of a 1954 rural
improvement program supported by the Afghani government
with assistance of the UN. Follows a girl who becomes
the first trained public health nurse in Afghanistan.

560 POTTERY MAKING (TAJIK, AFGHANISTAN)
(n.d.) / 15 min / silent / b&w / 16 mm
International Film Foundation.
Another in the series of silent single activity ethnographic films. Shows traditional clay working tech-

114

niques for pottery construction used by the Tajik of
Afghanistan.

561   POTTERY: MAKING VESSELS (TADZHIK,
      AFGHANISTAN, BADAKHSHAN)
      1963, released 1965 / 32 min / silent / b&w / 16 mm
      Encyclopaedia Cinematographica. Distributed by Pennsylvania
      State University. (Ency. Cinematographica no. E 747)
          Another in a series of silent ethnographic films. Shows
      additional footage of pottery making techniques.

562   SHEEP SHEARING AND MAKING OF FELT (PASHTUN,
      AFGHANISTAN, BADAKHSHAN)
      1963, released 1964 / 18 min / silent / color / 16 mm
      Encyclopaedia Cinematographica. Distributed by Pennsylvania
      State University. (Ency. Cinematographica no. E 683)
          Shows shearing of sheep, gathering of the wool and washing,
      pounding and rolling of wool to make felt for carpets
      and other uses.

563   SLAUGHTERING A SHEEP (PASHTUN, AFGHANISTAN, BADAKHSHAN)
      1963, released 1964 / 6 min / silent / color / 16 mm
      Encyclopaedia Cinematographica. Distributed by Pennsylvania
      State University. (Ency. Cinematographica no. E 682)
          Another in a series of silent ethnographic films. Shows
      traditional methods for slaughtering a sheep and meat
      preparation.

564   STONES OF EDEN
      1964 / 25 min / sound / color / 16 mm
      William A. Furman. Released by Contemporary Films.
      Distributed by McGraw-Hill. (NUC FiA 66-545 rev) Credits:
      Writers - William Furman, Mel Carlson, Music - Henry Alto.
      Locations: Indiana U. / Middle East Institute / U. of
      Michigan / U. of Washington.
          Story of harsh realities of farm life in Dessab, a
      village in central Afghanistan. Hasan, a poor wheat
      farmer using traditional tools, must deal with uncertain
      weather and the death of one of his two oxen. His son's
      education must be postponed indefinitely due to this set
      back in the family's fortunes.

565   TANNING AN IBEX HIDE (TADZHIK, AFGHANISTAN, BADAKHSHAN)
      1963, released 965 / 18 min / silent / b&w / 16 mm
      Encyclopeadia Cinematographica. Distributed by Pennsylvania
      State University. (Ency. Cinematographica no. E 741)
          Another in a series of silent ethnographic films. Shows
      traditional skin processing techniques used by the Tajik
      of Afghanistan.

566   WINNING OF CHARCOAL (TADZHIK, AFGHANISTAN, BADAKHSHAN)
      1963, released 1965 / 12 min / silent / b&w / 16 mm
      Encyclopaedia Cinematographica. Distributed by Pennsylvania

State University. (Ency. Cinematographica no. E 743)
Another in a series of silent ethnographic films. Shows
preparation of charcoal by the Tajik of Afghanistan.

AFGHANISTAN   -   WOMEN AND CHILDREN

567   AFGHAN WOMEN
1974 / 17 min / sound / color / 16 mm
American Universities Field Staff Productions. (Faces of
Change series, no. 4) (Credits: Filmmakers - Josephine
Powell, Nancy Hatch Dupree, Producer - Norman Miller, Editor
- Bridgett Reiss. Locations: American Universities Field
Staff, Hanover, New Hampshire / Australian News and
Information Bureau, New York / Indiana U. / Kansas State U.
/ Library of Congress (FBB 3942) / Michigan State U. /
Middle East Institute / Syracuse U. / U. of California Media
Extension Service / U. of Illinois / U. of Kansas / U. of
Wisconsin / Wheelock Educational Resources. *
    Excellently produced film. Deals specifically with the
    daily lives of women in Aq Kupruk, a village in northern
    Afghanistan. Daily activities such as making bread are
    interspersed with preparations for the wedding of a young
    girl. Activities include embroidering, spinning, making
    a felt rug and washing. Women discuss marriage, death,
    children and their lives. One of the few films on women
    in the Middle East or North Africa. Narration is very
    informative and enjoyable. Recommended.

568   BAKING OVEN BREAD (TAJIK, AFGHANISTAN)
1966 / 11 min / silent / b&w / 16 mm
International Film Foundation. Julien Bryan Productions.
(Mountain Peoples of Central Asia series). Locations:
Indiana U. / Penn. State U. / U. of Illinois / U. of
Washington.
    Silent ethnographic film with musical background. Shows
    preparation and baking of bread by a Tajik woman.
    Another in the series of Encyclopaedia Cinematographica
    films (no. E 715) held by Pennsylvania State University.

569   BAKING UNLEAVENED BREAD (PUSHTU, AFGHANISTAN)
1968 / 10 min / silent / color / 16 mm
International Film Foundation. Location: Syracuse U.
    Probably a re-release of the 1963 Encyclopaedia
    Cinematographica film (no. E 685) entitled: BREAD
    BAKING (PASHTUN, AFGHANISTAN, BADAKHSHAN),
    distributed by Pennsylvania State University.

570   BOY'S GAME (PUSHTU, AFGHANISTAN)
(n.d.) / 5 min / silent / color / 16 mm
Julien Bryan. Distributed by International Film Foundation.
(Mountain Peoples of Central Asia) Location: Penn. State U.
    Short, silent ethnographic film. Possibly from the
    Encyclopaedia Cinematographica collection.

571 FLUFFING AND SPINNING YAK WOOL (TADZHIK, AFGHANISTAN,
     BADAKHSHAN)
     1963, released 1964 / 5 min / silent / b&w / 16 mm
     Encyclopaedia Cinematographica. Distributed by Pennsylvania
     State University. (Ency. Cinematographica no. E 680)
          Another in a series of silent ethnographic films. Shows
          preparation of yak wool into thread.

572 MAKING FELT RUGS (PUSHTO, AFGHANISTAN)
     (n.d.) / 9 min / silent / b&w / 16 mm
     International Film Foundation. (Mountain Peoples of Central
     Asia series)
          Shows how wool is washed, rolled and pounded into felt to
          make rugs.

573 NAIM AND JABAR
     1974 / 43 min / sound / color / 16 mm
     American Universities Field Staff. Produced with the
     cooperation of Toryali Shafaq, Afghan Films, and the
     National Film School of Great Britain. (Faces of Change
     series, no. 2) Credits: Directors - David Hancock, Herbert
     DiGioia. Locations: Library of Congress (FBB 3282) / New
     York Public Donnell Film Library / Purdue / Syracuse / U. of
     California Extension Media Center / U. of Illinois / U. of
     Kansas / Wheelock Educational Resources. *
          Follows the lives of two boys in rural Afghanistan.
          Shows the importance of education in their hopes for
          advancement. Fifteen year old Jabar has completed one
          year of secondary school. Naim, 14 years old,
          laboriously applies for admission but is not accepted.
          Discusses the lifestyle of the two boys and their rela-
          tionship with their families and school. At times film
          may appear staged. Very useful for instructional pur-
          poses in junior-senior high school. For junior high to
          adult audiences.

574 WOMEN OF AFGHANISTAN
     1975 / 4 min / silent / color / super 8 mm film loop in
     cartridge. Grise, Inc. Made by Arthur C. Twomey. Released
     by Sound Book Press Society. (Afghanistan: The Land and the
     People series, no. 14) (LC 75-701146)
          Short, silent ethnographic film. Shows the changing
          role of women in modern Afghanistan.

AFGHANISTAN - TRAVELOGS AND REGIONAL STUDIES

575 AFGHAN TREASURE: BAMIYAN
     1959 / 21 min / sound / color / 16 mm
     Kabul Film Unit. Released in the U.S. by the Royal Afghan
     Embassy. (NUC FiA 64-1364) Credits: Director - Kurt Wenzel.
          Travelog of the Bamiyan River Valley of Afghanistan.
          Shows ruins from pre-historic, Greek, Hindu, Buddhist,

117

Central Asian and Islamic periods. Examines the diversity of peoples who have passed through the area. Shows recent changes as a result of development and modernization.

576 AFGHANISTAN
1972 / 15 min / sound / color / 16 mm
ACI Films. Distributed by Paramount Communications. (LC 75-704408) Locations: Boise State U. / Syracuse U. / U. of Illinois / U. of Michigan.
Intended for junior high school to adult audiences. Without narration. Shows beauty of the Afghan countryside and the daily activities and work of the Afghani people. Shows life in Kabul, the capital city, remote farming villages, a game of buzkashi played on horseback and scenes of architecture and art. Well filmed with Afghani musical soundtrack.

577 AFGHANISTAN: EMERGING FROM ISOLATION
1968 / 20 min / sound / color / 16 mm
McGraw-Hill Book Co. Made by Authentic Pictures. (The Oriental World series) (NUC FiA 68-640) Credits: Advisors - Robert R. Drummond, Dorothy W. Drummond, Clyde F. Kohn. Locations: Kent State U. / Library of Congress (FBA 6558) / U. of Illinois. *
Travelog. Shows diverse lifestyles in Afghanistan. Follows several university students on visits to their home regions. Ranges from nomads to the capital city of Kabul. Other students represent Pul-i-Khumri, a rice and cotton region, Mayar-i-Sharif, a domed city with Turkoman and Mongol ruins, Herat near Iran, a corn growing and rug weaving center, and Kandahar in the south, a fruit producing region. Shows geography and diversity of Afghanistan in a loose travelog style. Suitable for junior-senior high school audiences. Color deteriorated in Library of Congress print.

578 AFGHANISTAN: LAND OF BEAUTY AND HOSPITALITY
(n.d.) / 41 min / sound / color / 16 mm
Location: Middle East Institute.
Shows historical sites of Afghanistan, nomad and city life, national dances and crafts. General introduction to the country.

579 ASSIGNMENT IN AFGHANISTAN
1968 / 27 min / sound / color / 16 mm
International Labor Organization. Distributed by United Nations Films.
Available in English and French soundtracks. Shows dependence of the people of Afghanistan on agriculture and livestock production. Describes the 15 million inhabitants living in villages or cities. Profiles assistance and development programs of the International Organization of Labor and the Afghani government.

118

580   BAMIAN
       (c. 1960?) / 20 min / sound / color / 16 mm
       Formerly distributed by the Embassy of Afghanistan.
       Travelog of Bamian, a village north of Kabul, one of the
       most important centers of Buddhism in Asia. Bamian is
       the location of the largest statue of the Buddha. Shows
       the statue carved in the side of a cliff outside the
       village.

581   BASIC FACTS: AFGHANISTAN
       1964 / ? / sound / color / 16 mm
       American Friends of the Middle East.
       Introduction to geography, communications, social trends
       and major events in the history of Afghanistan.

582   CITY LIFE IN AFGHANISTAN
       1963 / 4 min / silent / color / 8 mm
       International Communications Foundation. (South Asia:
       Afghanistan series) (NUC FiA 63-1486) Credits: Writer - L.
       Van Mourick, Cinematographers - Noble Trenham, L. Van
       Mourick, Jr.
       Examines life in urban Afghanistan. Shows Kabul, the
       capital, and Herat near the Iranian border.

583   KABUL: THE CAPITAL
       1975 / 4 min / silent / color / supr 8 mm film loop in
       cartridge. Grise, Inc. Made by Arthur C. Twomey. Released
       by Sound Book Press Society. (Afghanistan: The Land and the
       People series, no. 4) (LC 75-701136)
       Travelog contrasting modern and traditional areas of
       Kabul. Shows the Bala Hissar Fort and Jada-i Maiwand
       Avenue.

584   LAND OF THE AFGHANS
       1954 / 16 min / sound / color / 16 mm
       Mavro Productions. Released by University of Utah. (NUC FiA
       64-1365) Credits: Producer-Directors - Ruth Cade, Arthur
       Rosenblum, Photographer - Baron Hans de Meiss.
       General survey of modern Afghanistan. Shows traditional
       farming, handicrafts and culture. Profiles current
       modernization. Shows festivals and dances.

585   LIVESTOCK MARKET: KABUL
       1975 / 4 min / silent / color / super 8 mm film loop in
       cartridge. Grise, Inc. Made by Arthur C. Twomey. Released
       by Sound Book Press Society. (Afghanistan: The Land and the
       People series, no. 8) (LC 75-701140)
       Shows shepherds in a livestock market in Kabul, the capi-
       tal of Afghanistan. Includes scenes of herds and
       bargaining for animals.

586   THE PAINTED TRUCK
       1972 / 28 min / sound / color / 16 mm

119

Judith Hallet, Stanley Hallet and Sebastian C. Schroeder.
Released by Film Images/Radim Films. (LC 73-702756)
Locations: Kansas State U. / Middle East Institute / New
York Public Donnell Film Library / U. of Arizona. *
Follows trip over the 12,700 foot Hajigak Pass in the
Hindu Kush from Qabul to Bamian undertaken by a group of
Afghani caravaneers in a truck covered with folk decora-
tions. Shows the mechanic working to keep the truck
running over the rugged terrain. Shows the loads of
livestock, produce and people the truck carries on its
journey. Interesting, pleasant ethnographic film. Shows
geography of Afghanistan and transformation of camel
caravan trade routes to truck transportation.

587   TRANSPORTATION: THE SALANG PASS AND KABUL
      1975 / 4 min / silent / color / super 8 mm film loop in
      cartridge. Grise, Inc. Made by Arthur C. Twomey. Released
      by Sound Book Press Society. (Afghanistan: The Land and the
      People series, no. 10) (LC 75-701142)
      Shows rugged terrain of Afghanistan and explains the
      importance of roads and truck transportation in linking
      isolated cities and villages.

AFGHANISTAN - WATER AND LAND USE

588   AFGHANISTAN: HEART OF ASIA, PART 1
      1976 / 17 min / sound / color / 16 mm
      Vision Habitat. Distributed by United Nations Films, or
      through United Nations Audio-Visual Information Centre on
      Human Settlements, Vancouver, British Columbia (Canada).
      Available in English, Arabic, French and Spanish
      soundtracks. Covers projects underway to encourage
      Afghan nomads to settle in permanent housing and turn to
      truck transportation for their livelihood. Former
      nomads, who have preferred to move to cities for
      industrial jobs, are also encouraged to resettle in agri-
      cultural settlements to control housing and employment
      shortages in cities. Looks at settlement of nomads as a
      desired pattern.

589   AFGHANISTAN: HEART OF ASIA, PART 2
      1976 / 21 min / sound / color / 16 mm
      Vision Habitat. Distributed by United Nations Films.
      Available in English, Arabic, French and Spanish
      soundtracks. Second film in the series. Shows problems
      of agriculture in an arid, mountainous country. Examines
      water systems and irrigation methods, community coopera-
      tion, mechanization, soil surveys and diversification of
      crops. Shows the Helmand River Valley citrus groves in a
      formerly arid region.

590   HELMAND VALLEY
      (c. 1960?) / 20 min / sound / color / 16 mm

Formerly distributed by the Embassy of Afghanistan.
Examines the progress of the Helman Valley irrigation
project, intended to produce acreage for citrus farming.

AFGHANISTAN - AGRICULTURE

591 AFGHANISTAN MOVES AHEAD
1952 / 10 min / sound / b&w / 16 mm
United Nations. Distributed by Contemporary Films. (NUC
FiA 60-667)
Shows the work of the United Nations Technical Assistance
Program in introducing new technologies in agriculture
and industry.

592 AFGHANISTAN: WHEAT CYCLE
1975 / 16 min / sound / color / 16 mm
American University Field Staff. (Faces of Change series, #3)
Locations: Indiana U. / Syracuse U. / U. of California
Extension Media Center / U. of Kentucky / Wheelock
Educational Resources.
Uses no narration. Shows the process of reaping,
threshing, winnowing and milling wheat in Aq Kupruk in
Northern Afghanistan. Impressionistic, pastoral film.
Louis and Nancy Dupree served as cultural advisors.
Intended for junior high school to adult audiences.

593 CASTING IRON PLOW SHARES
1972 / 11 min / sound / b&w / 16 mm
Julien Bryan. Distributed by International Film Foundation.
(Mountain Peoples of Central Asia series) Location: Penn.
State U.
Uses a background of natural sounds. Shows people of the
Tajik tribe of northern Afghanistan casting plow shares.

594 FIELD IRRIGATION (TADZHIK, AFGHANISTAN, BADAKHSHAN)
1963, released 1964 / 11 min / silent / b&w / 16 mm
Encyclopaedia Cinematographica. Distributed by Pennsylvania
State University. (Ency. Cinematographica, no. E 711)
Another in the series of silent ethnographic films high-
lighting a single, typical activity. Shows field
irrigation techniques used by the Tajik of northern
Afghanistan.

595 MILLING GRAIN (TADZHIK, AFGHANISTAN, BADAKHSHAN)
1963, released 1964 / 6 min / silent / b&w / 16 mm
Encyclopaedia Cinematographica. Distributed by Pennsylvania
State University. (Ency. Cinematographica, no. E 714)
Silent ethnographic film. Shows technique of milling
grain used by the Tajik of northern Afghanistan.

596 PLOUGHING WITH A BODY ARD (HAZARA, AFGHANISTAN, BAMIAN)
1959, released 1962 / 2 min / silent / b&w / 16 mm

Encyclopaedia Cinematographica. Distributed by Pennsylvania State University. (Ency. Cinematographica, no. E 245) Short, silent ethnographic film. Shows plowing techniques used in the high Bamian Valley of Afghanistan.

597 PRIMITIVE AGRICULTURE: THE BAMIAN VALLEY
1975 / 4 min / silent / color / super 8 mm film loop in cartridge. Grise, Inc. Made by Arthur C. Twomey. Released by Sound Book Press Society. (Afghanistan: The Land and the People series, no. 1) (LC 75-701133)
Shows traditional agriculture in the Bamian Valley of Afghanistan. Includes scenes of plowing with a bent tree root, hand sowing and harvesting, and winnowing of grain.

598 SPRING CULTIVATION OF FIELDS (TADZHIK, AFGHANISTAN, BADAKHSHAN)
1963, released 1964 / 12 min / silent / b&w / 16 mm
Encyclopaedia Cinematographica. Distributed by Pennsylvania State University. (Ency. Cinematographica, no. E 710)
Shows traditional methods of agriculture practised in northern Afghanistan among the Tajik.

599 THRESHING AND WINNOWING WHEAT (TADZHIK, AFGHANISTAN, BADAKHSHAN)
1963, released 1964 / 24 min / silent / b&w / 16 mm
Encyclopaedia Cinematographica. Distributed by Pennsylvania State University. (Ency. Cinematographica, no. E 713)
Shows traditional methods used to thresh and winnow wheat practised by the Tajik in northern Afghanistan.

600 THRESHING WHEAT (TAJIK, AFGHANISTAN)
(n.d.) / 9 min / silent / b&w / 16 mm
International Film Foundation.
Possibly an edited version of no. 599 of the Encyclopaedia Cinematographica series. Shows threshing of wheat by Tajik in northern Afghanistan.

601 WATER-DRIVEN RICE POUNDER (PASHTUN, AFGHANISTAN, BADAKHSHAN)
1963, released 1965 / 5 min / silent / b&w / 16 mm
Encyclopaedia Cinematographica. Distributed by Pennsylvania State University. (Ency. Cinematographica, no. E 749)
Shows traditional methods of pounding the hull from rice using a water powered device. Filmed in Northern Afghanistan among the Pashtun.

AFGHANISTAN - EDUCATION

602 KABUL FAMILY: A DAY AT ELEMENTARY SCHOOL
1975 / 4 min / silent / color / super 8 mm film loop in cartridge. Grise, Inc. Made by Arthur C. Twomey. Released by Sound Book Press Society. (Afghanistan: The Land and the

People series, no. 7) (LC 75-701139)
Follows a young Afghani boy as he goes to school and
works in the family garden.

603 TRANSITION GENERATION: A THIRD WORLD PROBLEM
1977 / 20 min / sound / color / 16 mm
Alexander Von Wetter. Distributed by International Film
Foundation. Location: Middle East Institute.
Intended for junior high school to adult audiences. Traces problems faced by western-oriented Afghani students
who must reconcile traditional society with modernization
and westernization. Shows students differ in their
backgrounds and social classes and perceive the problem
in different ways. Topics covered include the position
of women in cities and villages, poverty in the country,
the place of the extended family and family ties, educ-
tion, and lack of jobs for restless, educated young
people.

AFGHANISTAN - THE ARTS

604 CINEMA
1973 / 2 min / sound / color / 16 mm
Sebastian Schroeder. Distributed by Film Images/Radim Films.
Location: New York Public Donnell Film Library.
Short film. Shows an Afghani street vendor who has
devised a motion picture projector using the sun as a
light source. He hand cranks a short film for the amusement of a crowd.

605 FOUR MEN'S DANCES (TADZHIK, AFGHANISTAN, BADAKHSHAN)
1963, released 1964 / 14 min / silent / b&w / 16 mm
Encyclopaedia Cinematographica. Distributed by Pennsylvania
State University. (Ency. Cinematographica, no. E 718)
Possibly the same film as: VIER MANNERTANZE (FOUR
MEN'S DANCES). Silent ethnographic film. Shows Tajik
men from northern Afghanistan performing traditional dan-
ces.

606 MEN'S DANCE (PASHTUN, AFGHANISTAN, BADAKHSHAN)
1963, released 1964 / 13 min / silent / b&w / 16 mm
Encyclopaedia Cinematographica. Distributed by Pennsylvania
State University. (Ency. Cinematographica, no. E 717)
Possibly the same films as: MANNERTANZ (MEN'S DANCES) and
MEN'S DANCE. MEN'S DANCE is also listed in some sources
as a 1968 film produced by Julien Bryan and distributed
by the International Film Foundation as part of the
Mountain Peoples of Central Asia series. Shows tradi-
tional dances of the Pashtun.

607 MEN'S DANCE WITH THE PANTOMIMIC INTERLUDE (PASHTUN,
BADAKHSHAN, AFGHANISTAN)

123

1963, released 1965 / 10 min / silent / color / 16 mm
Encyclopaedia Cinematographica. Distributed by Pennsylvania
State University. (Ency. Cinematographica, no. E 766)
  Listed in some catalogs as: MANNERTANZ UND
  PANTOMIMISCHES ZWISCHENSPIEL. Silent ethnographic
  film. Shows a traditional dance with a pantomime of mock
  combat.

608   THE RUGMAKERS OF MAZAR-I-SHARIF
      1975 / 4 min / silent / color / super 8 mm film loop in
      cartridge. Grise, Inc. Made by Arthur C. Twomey. Released
      by Sound Book Press Society. (Afghanistan: The Land and the
      People series, no. 12) (LC 75-701144)
        Shows traditional Bokhara rugs produced in the weaving
        center of Mazar-i-Sharif in Afghanistan.

609   WEAVING A CARPET (PASHTUN, AFGHANISTAN, BADAKHSHAN)
      1963, released 1964 / 20 min / silent / color / 16 mm
      Encyclopaedia Cinematographica. Distributed by Pennsylvania
      State University. (Ency. Cinematographica, no. E 684)
        Silent ethnographic film. Shows techniques of rug
        weaving used by the Pashtun of Afghanistan.

610   WEAVING A RUG (TADZHIK, AFGHANISTAN, BADAKHSHAN)
      1963, released 1964 / 34 min / silent / b&w / 16 mm
      Encyclopaedia Cinematographica. Distributed by Pennsylvania
      State University. (Ency. Cinematographica, no. E 719)
        Shows traditional rug weaving techniques and designs used
        by the Tajik of northern Afghanistan.

611   WEAVING CLOTH (PUSHTO, AFGHANISTAN)
      (n.d.) / 9 min / silent / b&w / 16 mm
      International Film Foundation. (Mountain Peoples of Central
      Asia series)
        Possibly an Encyclopaedia Cinematographica film re-
        released by International Film Foundation. Shows tech-
        niques of cloth weaving used by Pushto women in
        Afghanistan.

ALGERIA - HISTORY

612 ALGERIA
1962 / 28 min / sound / b&w / 16 mm
National Film Board of Canada. Released in the U.S. by
McGraw-Hill Book Co., 1964. Distributed by Contemporary
Films. (Crossroads of the World: A Study of North Africa
and the Middle East series) (NUC FiA 66-1776) Credits:
Producer-Narrator -James Beveridge, Researcher - Margaret
Ellis. Locations: Florida State U. / New York Public
Donnell Film Library / Syracuse U. / U. of Illinois / U. of
South Carolina.
    Intended for junior high school to college audiences.
Traces history of the European presence in Algeria up to
the signing of the French-Algerian agreement and the
independence of Algeria. Presents the position of the
French and Algerians in the conflict. Discusses the
larger issue of emerging Arab nationalism.

613 ALGERIA: BIRTH OF A NATION
1962 / 9 min / sound / b&w / 16 mm
Producer unknown. Location: U. of Colorado.
    Traces the history of Algeria from ancient times to inde-
pendence from French colonial rule.

614 ALGERIA: THE IMPOSSIBLE INDEPENDENCE
1976 / 43 min / sound / color / 16 mm or videocassette
Gordian Troller and Marie Claude Deffarge. Distributed by
Icarus Films.
    Argues that former colonial countries retain great depen-
dence on Europe as a result of shifts in the economy and
work force during colonial years. Problems produced
during the colonial period in Algeria include growing
unemployment, migration to the cities, dependence on
sophisticated technology and highly skilled labor, ero-
sion of the agricultural basis of the economy and the
emergence of a technocratic class. Argues that
industrialization/modernization programs only deepen
Third World dependence on the West. Intended for college
and adult audiences. Useful for starting discussion on
the effect of colonization and modernization on Middle
Eastern countries.

615 ALGERIA ON ITS OWN
1962 / 28 min / sound / b&w / 16 mm
CBS News. (Eyewitness, television series) (NUC Fi 67-2182)
Credits: Producers - Leslie Midgley, John Sharnik, Director
- Ted Marvel, Reporter - Charles Collingwood, Robert
Kleiman. Location: Library of Congress (FCA 2491). *
    Eyewitness CBS News broadcast. Discusses the effect of
independence on Algeria's one million French inhabitants.

Shows the emerging leadership of Ben Yousef Ben Kedda
and Vice President Ben Bella, the organization of a
national army and the establishment of a civil government
following years of warfare with France. Discusses the
stress and effect of the war on France, the fall of
the 4th Republic and the return of Charles DeGaulle.
Profiles French Algerians who either return to France or
stay in the new Algerian nation.

616   ALGERIA: TEN YEARS LATER
      (c. 1972) / 60 min / sound / color / 16 mm
      Independent Television Corp.
          Traces the outcome of independence for Algeria ten
      years after the revolution. Shows changes experienced by
      the 10th largest country In the world.

617   ALGERIA - WHAT PRICE FREEDOM
      1964 / 54 min / sound / b&w / 16 mm
      NET.
          Intended for high school to adult audiences. Traces the
      Algerian struggle for independence beginning in 1954.
      Profiles a Europeanized Algerian family and shows the
      balance between traditional and westernized patterns in
      modernization, literacy and the status of women.

618   FOCUS ON ALGERIA
      1962 / 10 min / sound / b&w / 16 mm
      Producer unknown. Location: Seattle Public Schools. No
      other information available.

619   OLD SOLDIERS NEVER DIE
      1969 / 31 min / sound / color / 16 mm
      BBC-TV, London. (The Glory That Remains series, no. 9)
      Location: U. of Illinois.
          Robert Erskine examines life for the typical Roman
      soldier in a provincial city in Algeria under the Emperor
      Trajan, circa 100 A.D. Re-creates life of the Third
      Legion of the Roman Army stationed in North Africa.

620   REPORT FROM AFRICA - ALGERIA
      1957 / 15 min / b&w / sound / 16 mm
      CBS-TV. (See It Now, television series)
          Looks at social and political problems in Algeria during
      its struggle for independence from France. Current
      affairs broadcast intended for television audiences.

621   TASSILI-N-AJJER - SAHARA ROCK PAINTINGS 4000-2000 B.C.
      1970 / 16 min / sound / color / 16 mm
      Les Edition cinegraphiques, France. Released in the U.S. by
      Time-Life Films. From the Anthony Roland collection of
      films on art. (The History of Art. Program 1: Man Revealed
      - Origins of Great Cultures 4000 B.C. - 600 A.D. series)
      (LC 74-714529) Credits: Director - Jean Dominique Lajoux,

Music - Maurice Le Roux.
  Award winning film. Documents rock paintings found near
  Tassili-n-Ajjer in the Eastern Sahara desert painted
  some time between 4000 and 2000 B.C. Vivid colors and
  bold scenes of human and animal life have been preserved
  by dry desert conditions. Describes how desert developed
  after the original rock paintings were made, giving evidence of climactic change in the Sahara.

ALGERIA - SOCIOLOGY AND ETHNOLOGY

622   BERBER COUNTRY
      1958 / 16 min / sound / b&w / 16 mm
      Churchill-Wexler Film Productions. (NUC FiA 62-807)
      Location: Syracuse U.
        Profiles the semi-nomadic Berber tribes of Algeria.
        Shows how harsh climate of the area effects their way of
        life and survival.

623   THE CONSTANTINE PLAN
      1961 / 15 min / sound / b&w / 16 mm
      Caisse d'equipement de l'Algerie, Algiers. Released in the
      U.S. by Sterling Movies. (NUC FiA 62-1537)
        Describes the efforts of the French in Algeria to raise
        the standard of living, develop industry and agriculture
        and build new housing despite the continuing fight for
        Algerian independence from France. Intended to show
        benefit of French presence in the area.

624   DES PIERRES QUI LIENT LES HOMMES
      (c. 1960?) / 15 min / sound / color / 16 mm
      Formerly available from the French American Culture Service.
        Looks at housing problems in Algiers, Oran, Constantine
        and Bone in Algeria. Describes what is being done to
        build new apartments, "emergency cities" and relieve
        housing shortages.

625   THE INHERITANCE
      1963 / 35 min / sound / b&w / 16 mm
      Mithras Films. Distributed by Third World Film. Credits:
      Producer - Maurice Hatton, Director - John Irvin.
        Filmed after the withdrawal of the French following
        Algerian independence. Profiles the inheritance of
        war and need for medical and technical services formerly
        provided by the French.

626   NOMADIC TRIBES IN THE EL-KANTARA GORGES (ALGERIA)
      (c. 1910?) / 3 min / silent / color / 16 mm
      Pathe freres, France. Originally released in 35mm, hand
      tinted. In the Douglas Fleming-Lynn Moore Film Collection,
      Library of Congress. (FLA 491) (NUC Fi 68-541)
        Early film showing scenes of nomads in Algeria.

627   SHAAMBA ARABS: PREPARATIONS FOR A FESTIVAL,
       SLAUGHTERING SHEEP AND CUSCUS PREPARATION
       1953 / 10 min / silent / color / 16 mm
       Encyclopaedia Cinematographica. Distributed by Pennsylvania
       State U. (Ency. Cinematographica no E 158)
           Filmed in the El-Golea oasis in Algeria. Shows ritual
           slaughter of a lamb, women preparing the lamb on a spit,
           and celebration of a festival. Lack of soundtrack makes
           this of use primarily for ethnological and archival
           footage purposes.

628   STRANGERS TO HOPE
       1962 / 25 min / sound / b&w / 16 mm
       American Friends Service Committee. (NUC FiA 64-1456)
       Credits: Photographers - Edith Worth, Robert Worth.
           Shows missionary and relief work performed in Algeria by
           Quaker missionaries.

ALGERIA - TRAVELOGS AND REGIONAL STUDIES

629   ALGERIA, HOME OF THE SHEIKH
       (n.d.) / 20 min / silent or sound / b&w / 16 mm
       Bray Studios. (NUC FiA 55-467, silent / FiA 55-468 sound)
           General travelog of Algeria. Shows the town of Bou-Saada
           and profiles traditional Algerian sheikhs or tribal
           leaders.

630   ALGERIA: THE NEW MEN
       1970 / 27 min / sound / color / 16 mm
       United Nations. Distributed by United Nations Films.
           Available in English, French and Arabic soundtracks.
           Examines Algeria's 14 million inhabitants, half under
           twenty years of age. Limited arable land means Algeria
           is faced with problem of how to find food and water for
           its population. Shows the United Nations programs in the
           area.

631   ALGERIAN SAHARA
       1976 / 30 min / sound / color / 16 mm
       Films, Inc. (Africa File series) Credits: Director - John
       Labow. Locations: Syracuse U. / U. of Illinois. *
           French film, overdubbed in English. Follows history of
           Algeria from prehistory times. Shows early period when
           the climate supported more wildlife and inhabitants of
           hunting and fishing cultures painted rock and cave pic-
           tures of their relatively lush surroundings. Following
           the desertification of the region, water became too
           scarce for agriculture and nomadic society developed.
           The French colonial period is covered briefly. List of
           programs and development projects undertaken by the
           Algerian government since independence includes settling
           of nomads, pushing back the Sahara desert and stressing

advances in agriculture. Very optimistic view of Algeria
today and its potential for the future.

632   CONSTANTINE
        (c. 1930) / 11 min / silent / b&w / 16 mm
        U.S. Office of Strategic Services, Pictorial Records Section.
        (LC 76-701587) Location: Library of Congress (FAA 68)   *
        Shows the city of Constantine, founded by the Romans.
        Tours the viaduct, gorge, markets, streets, hot springs
        at Hammam Meskoutine, with its interesting rock and
        mineral formations, the Hippone mosaics and Phoenician
        wall of 700 B.C. General, early travelog of Algeria.
        Much of the footage is of jerky, home movie quality. Of
        use for library footage purposes.

633   DESERT FANTASY
        1955 / 15 min / sound / color / 35 mm
        Twentieth Century-Fox Film Corp. (NUC Fi 55-1030) Credits:
        Producer - Edmund Reek, Director - Fred Fesneau, Narrator -
        Ed Stokes. Location: Library of Congress (FEA 330)   *
        Travelog of Algeria including scenes of the Sahara,
        Algiers, city of Gardia, the Tuaregs or Blue Men, and a
        war dance. Relates all images to the Arabian Nights
        stories and uses a patronizing narration to entertain
        without giving much information. Intended as a theatri-
        cal short subject. Library of Congress print is
        experiencing color deterioration.

634   THE EARTH'S BLOOD
        (c. 1960?) / 18 min / sound / color / 16 mm
        Formerly available from the French American Cultural Service.
        Shows programs intended to convert the Algerian desert
        into arable land through irrigation. Filmed before
        Algerian independence.

635   JOURNEY TO NOWHERE
        1956 / 30 min / sound / color or b&w / 16 mm
        Africa Film Foundation. Made by Francis E. Blake. Released
        by White Fathers Film Distribution Center. (NUC FiA 57-845)
        Travelog from Algiers to Timbuctoo. Shows the Sahara
        desert, the Niger River Valley and the people of these
        regions. Filmed by missionaries.

636   UNVEILING ALGERIA
        1940 / 10 min / sound / b&w / 16 mm
        Columbia Pictures, Corp. Released for educational purposes
        by Teaching Film Custodians, 1941. (Columbia Tour series)
        (FiA 52-4663) Credits: Producer - Andre De La Varre.
        Originally a theatrical short subject, re-released for
        junior-senior high school audiences. Shows traditional
        Algiers and modern changes resulting from French
        influence on the city.

BAHRAIN

637   MYSTERY OF THE MOUNDS
       (c. 1960?) / 30 min / sound / color / 16 mm
       Sterling Movies. Location: Middle East Institute.
       Shows archeological explorations underway in Bahrain.

638   PEARL OF THE GULF
       1959 / 29 min / sound / color / 16 or 35 mm
       California Texas Oil Corp. Made by Greenpark Productions,
       London, in association with Film Producers Guild. (Caltex
       International Public Relations series) Distributed by
       Sterling Movies. (NUC FiA 61-1024) Credits: Director -
       Humphrey Swingler, Photographer - Arthur Lavis.
          Reviews the change in life in Bahrain following the
       discovery and exploitation of oil resources. Shows the
       Bahrain Petroleum Company Refinery, scenes of life of
       Bahrain Island, archeological excavations, and
       Bab-El-Bahrain.

CYPRUS - HISTORY AND DEVELOPMENT

639 THE APOSTOLIC CHURCH OF CYPRUS
1961 / 15 min / sound / color / 16 mm
Office of Education, Cyprus. Made and released by Davis
Productions. (NUC FiA 61-964) Credits: Narrator - Stavrous
Syrimis. Kodachrome.
Uses frescoes and mosaics to trace history of the church
in Cyprus from the time of St. Paul and Barnabas to the
present. Includes scenes of Archbishop Makarios. Listed
in some catalogs as: CYPRUS: THE APOSTOLIC CHURCH.

640 CYPRUS IS AN ISLAND
1946 / 34 min / sound / b&w / 16 mm
British Ministry of Information. Produced by Greenpark
Productions, in association with Film Producer's Guild,
London. Released in the U.S. by British Information
Services, 1946. (NUC FiA 52-4192) Credits: Producer-
Director - Ralph Keene, Writer - Laurie Lee, Narrator -
Valentine Dyall.
General travelog of Cyprus. Traces its history from
ancient Greek times to the present. Shows modernization
of agriculture and forestry on the island.

641 CYPRUS, THE NEW REPUBLIC
1962 / 19 min / sound / color / 16 mm
Dept. of Commerce and Industry, Cyprus. Made and released by
Davis Productions. (NUC FiA 61-1044) Kodachrome.
History of Cyprus from Neolithic ruins to ancient Greek
times to the present. Shows modern Cyprus, Archbishop
Makarios and Dr. Kuchuk.

642 ISLAND OF APHRODITE
(c. 1975?) / 40 min / sound / color / 16 mm
Embassy of Cyprus.
General film. Introduces the history, culture and modern
life of Cyprus.

643 REPORT ON CYPRUS
1955 / 11 min / sound / b&w / 16 mm
British Central Office of Information, London. Made by
Leander Films. Released in the U.S. by British Information
Services. (NUC FiA 56-1028) Credits: Producer-Editor -
Joan Duff, Narrator - Colin Wills.
General travelog of Cyprus. Shows developments in agri-
culture, health and communications since the turn of the
century. Stresses the British view of Cyprus as a stra-
tegic location for the defense of the Middle East.

131

644 BITTER FRUIT
(c. 1975) / 27 min / sound / color / 16 mm
Embassy of Cyprus.
Looks at life in Cyprus for Greek Cypriots before and
after the Turkish invasion of July 1974. Describes
problems experienced by Greek Cypriots who became refugees.

645 CYPRUS - HOT-BED OF VIOLENCE
1961 / 4 min / sound / b&w / 16 mm
Filmrite Associates. Released by Official Films. (Greatest
Headlines of the Century series) (NUC Fi 62-1869) Credits:
Producer - Sherm Grinberg, Narrator - Tom Hudson, Writer -
Allan Lurie. Location: Library of Congress (FAA 3720) *
Short newsreel synopsis of the problem of Cyprus. Begins
with the desire of Greek Cypriots to unite Cyprus with
Greece in the 1930's. British, using the island as a
base for troops and planes, face riots and violence from
Cypriots supporting self-determination. Shows the role
of Archbishop Makarios as the leader of the independence
movement. Explanation of events is necessarily shallow
in this brief film. Turkish Cypriots are not mentioned.

646 EXPULSION
(c. 1975?) / ? / sound / b&w / 16 mm
Embassy of Cyprus.
Examines the expulsion of Greek Cypriots from Karpassia
in the north of Cyprus after the Turkish invasion.
Filmed from a Greek Cypriot viewpoint.

647 IT WAS AN ISLAND
(c. 1975) / 28 min / sound / b&w / 16 mm
Embassy of Cyprus.
Without narration. Tells the story of the Turkish inva-
sion of Cyprus in 1974 and 1975. Supports the Greek
Cypriot point of view.

648 LADDER TO PEACE
1969 / 29 min / sound / color / 16 mm
United Nations. Released by Contemporary Films/McGraw Hill.
(International Zone series) (LC 70-702056)
Shows efforts being made by the United Nations to assist
Cyprus in peace keeping programs and in development.
Covers the peace talks underway between Greece and Turkey
to solve Greco-Turkish Cypriot violence, programs to
divert needed fresh water from flowing into the sea, and
development of new industries and technologies.

649 OF THOSE WHO ARE LOST
1977 / 50 min / sound / color / 16 mm or videocassette
Eric Durschmied. Distributed by Icarus Films. *

Deals with human rather than political issues. Moving
film. Shows the misery created for both Turkish and
Greek Cypriots as a result of civil war and partial
peace. Shows demonstrators in Nicosia demanding news of
missing relatives and friends. Shows peace negotiations
and mourning families. Many of the 197,000 refugees
created from the war are in camps or prisoners. 3000 are
missing. Intended for college and adult audiences. Well
produced film intended to show there is no end to human
suffering or pain in a civil war. Covers both Greek and
Turkish Cypriot problems.

650   OPERATION ATTILA
      (c. 1974) / 25 min / sound / b&w / 16 mm
      Embassy of Cyprus.
      Describes the Turkish invasion of Cyprus in July-August
      1974 from the Greek Cypriot point of view.

651   YOU ARE WELCOME, SIRS, TO CYPRUS
      1965 / 21 min / sound / color / 16 or 35 mm
      National Film Board of Canada. (NUC FiA 65-1774) Credits:
      Producer-Director - Richard Gilbert, Commentary - J. Reeve.
      Told from the point of view of Canadian United Nations
      peace-keeping forces in Cyprus. Covers the struggle bet-
      ween Turkish and Greek Cypriots. Includes interviews
      with Archbishop Makarios representing Greek Cypriots and
      Dr. Kutchuk representing the Turkish point of view.

CYPRUS - THE LAND AND THE PEOPLE

652   LAND OF CYPRUS
      1951 / 10 min / sound / b&w / 16 mm
      British Colonial Office. Produced by Anglo-Scottish Pictures.
      Released in the U.S. by British Information Services. (NUC
      FiA   52-838)
      Describes the efforts of the British colonial administra-
      tion in Cyprus to combat soil erosion and fresh water
      loss.

653   LIFE CHANGES
      1970 / 43 min / sound / b&w / 16 mm
      London School of Economics. Location: U. of California
      Extension Media Center.
      Ethnographic study of four village families in Cyprus.
      Shows how life has changed for them over the last fifty
      years. Looks at the small farming economy, size of fami-
      lies, education, and other factors. Analyzes the changes
      in western Cyprian life.

EGYPT

EGYPT - ARCHEOLOGY

654 ANCIENT EGYPT (REVISED)
1977 / 11 min / sound / color / 16 mm
Producer unknown. Location: U. of Illinois.
Shows techniques used by archeologists to reconstruct the
Pyramid Age, Middle Kingdom and New Kingdom periods of
ancient Egyptian history. Shows monuments, the Sphinx,
pyramids and tombs. Describes advances made by the
ancient Egyptians in writing, mathematics, architecture,
art, agriculture, government and religion.

655 ANCIENT EGYPT: DIGGING UP HER RICH PAST
1971 / 51 min / sound / color / 16 mm
Time-Life Multimedia.
Also available in Spanish soundtrack. Traces the history
of interest in Egypt and Egyptological studies from the
time of Bonaparte's invasion of Egypt in 1798 to the present. Explains how the Rosetta Stone made it possible to
interpret ancient heirogylphics and uncode records of
every aspect of ancient Egyptian life and thought.

656 ANCIENT NILE CIVILIZATION
1966 / 4 min / silent / color / 8 mm film loop or super 8 mm
Gateway Film Productions. Released in the U.S. by
International Communication Films. Distributed by Double
Day Multimedia. (North Africa series) (LC 76-700512)
Shows ancient Egyptian ruins. Includes scenes of the
pyramids, temples and statues.

657 ARCHAEOLOGICAL DISCOVERIES
1955 / 290 meters / sound / b&w / 16 or 35 mm
Saad Nadim. Location: Ministry of Culture and National
Guidance, Egypt.
Shows excavation of the sun boats buried beside the Great
Pyramid at Giza. Explains boats were used to ferry souls
of the dead. Shows political figures visiting the site.

658 CAIRO TO KARNAK
(n.d.) / 11 min / sound / b&w / 16 mm
Producer unknown. Location: U. of Kansas.
Examines the ruins of the temple complex at Karnak.
Describes the significance of various structures and
temples built by the ancient Egyptians. Explains the
detrimental effect of the annual flooding of the Nile
River on the ruined temple city.

659 CHAMPOLLION: EGYPTIAN HIEROGLYPHICS DECIPHERED
1977 / 33 min / sound / color / 16 mm
Magic Films Production. Made by Jean Vidal in collaboration

134

with Julien Pappe. Distributed by International Film Bureau.
Intended for senior high school to adult audiences. Traces the story of Jean-Francois Champollion, who deciphered Egyptian hieroglyphic writings. The Rosetta Stone, with passages in hieroglyphics, Coptic and Greek, made it possible to unlock the vast body of inscriptions left by the ancient Egyptians. Second part of the film traces Champollion's travels throughout Egypt from Abu Simbel to Karnak and the Valley of the Kings.

660   EGYPT: LAND OF MEMORIES
(n.d.) / 25 min / sound / color / 16 mm
Formerly distributed through the UAR Tourist Office (Egyptian Tourism Office).
Shows ruins, sites of ancient Egyptian civilization, and surviving antiquities.

661   EGYPT THE ETERNAL
1950 / 34 min / sound / color / 16 mm
Rosicrucian Order (AMORC). (NUC FiA 56-181) Credits: Photographer - James R. Whitcomb.
Traces ancient Egyptian life through remaining ruins, temples, and tombs. Looks at contemporary life along the Nile River Valley. Made by the Rosicrucian Order.

662   EGYPT YESTERDAY
1957 / 12 min / sound / color / 16 mm
Classroom Film Distributors. Location: U. of Illinois.
Travelog of famous ancient Egyptian ruins including the Sphinx and temple of Rameses II. Shows tombs and objects left by the ancients. Examines problem of shifting sands covering the ruins.

663   EGYPT'S PYRAMIDS, HOUSES OF ETERNITY
1978 / 22 min / sound / color / 16 mm or videocassette
National Geographic Society. (LC 78-700737) Location: Library of Congress.
Describes the architectural evolution of Egyptian pyramids from the earliest surviving pyramid at Saqqara, to Dahshur, Meidum and the Great Pyramid at Giza.

664   IN SEARCH OF THE MUMMY'S CURSE
1976 / 24 min / sound / color / 16 mm
Producer unknown. Location: U. of Minnesota.
Recounts the opening of Tutankhamon's tomb in 1922 by Howard Carter. Describes problems which plagued the expedition leading to stories of a curse and the theory of a bacteriological disease spread from the tombs. Possibly one of the IN SEARCH OF television series programs.

665   MYSTERIES OF THE GREAT PYRAMID
1977 / 50 min / sound / color / 16 mm

135

David Wolper Productions. Distributed by Films Inc. Credits:
Director-Writer - William Kronick, Narrator - Omar Sharif.
Locations: Kent State U. / New York Public Donnell Film
Library. *
   Intended for junior high school to adult audiences. Examines the history and purpose of the Great Pyramid at
   Giza. Looks at ancient Egyptian culture through
   remaining artifacts. Discusses current popular ideas
   of the pyramids concerning construction and "pyramid
   power". Uses footage from a 1955 feature film to suggest
   how the pyramids were constructed. Gives equal time and
   examination to unproven and "crank" theories concerning
   the pyramids as it does to accepted Egyptian history.

666   THE MYSTERY OF NEFERTITI
      1975 / 46 min / sound / color / 16 mm or videocassette
      British Broadcasting Corp. Released in the U.S. by Indiana
      University Audio-Visual Center. (LC 75-703968) Credits:
      Director - Paul Jordan. Locations: U. of California
      Extension Media Center / Indiana U.
         Traces a six-year project by archeologists using com-
         puters to reconstruct the 3,500 year old temple of
         Nefertiti. Shows analysis of thousands of carved stones
         at Karnak. Explains techniques and discoveries con-
         cerning ancient Egyptian life at the time of the reli-
         gious reformer Akhenatan and his wife, Nefertiti.

EGYPT - PRESERVATION OF ANTIQUITIES

667   ABOU SIMBEL
      1968 / 28 min / sound / color / 16 mm
      UNESCO. Released by the National Film Board of Canada. (LC
      72-706941)
         Intended for high school to adult audiences. Traces the
         enormous effort expended to move the two temples of Abu
         Simbel and reconstruct them at a safe location.
         Describes need to move the temples following the creation
         of Lake Nasser behind the Aswan High Dam.

668   THE EGYPTOLOGISTS
      1965 / 45 min / sound / color / 16 mm
      Oriental Institute, University of Chicago. Made by Cameras
      International Productions. Distributed by Encyclopaedia
      Britannica Educational Corp. (NUC FiA 66-395)
         Intended for high school to adult audiences. Documents
         the work of the Oriental Institute Egyptologists in Luxor
         and Karnak and in the northern Sudan. Well photographed.

669   THE EGYPTOLOGISTS
      1967 / 24 min / sound / b&w or color / 16 mm
      Oriental Institute, University of Chicago. Made by Cameras
      International Productions. Distributed by Encyclopaedia

Britannica Educational Corp. (NUC FiA 68-482) Credits: Narrator - Charlton Heston. Locations: New York Public Donnell Film Library / Penn. State U. / Syracuse U. / U. of Kansas / U. of Texas at Austin.
Edited version of the 1965 film, see no. 668. Intended for senior high school to adult audiences. Documents the work of the Oriental Institute to study and preserve antiquities before flooding by the Aswan High Dam project created Lake Nasser at Abu Simbel.

670 THE EGYPTOLOGISTS
1967 / 38 min / sound / color / 16 mm
Oriental Institute, University of Chicago. Distributed by Encyclopaedia Britannica Educational Corp. (NUC FiA 68-2134) Location: U. of California Extension Media Center.
Another version of nos. 668 and 669, narrated by Charlton Heston.

671 HISTORY'S HERITAGE
1969 / 29 min / sound / b&w / 16 mm
United Nations Films.
Shows the work being done by UNESCO to help countries preserve their national and cultural heritage. Documents work at Abu Simbel and other ancient temples in Egypt and the Sudan and work to restore damage caused by the 1966 Italian floods in Florence and Venice.

672 NUBIA 64
(c. 1964) / 40 min / sound / color / 16 mm
Institute Geographique National. The Roland Collection.
Shows work being undertaken to save the massive stone statues of Ramses II and the temples at Abu Simbel from Lake Nasser. An award winning film.

673 PHILAE IN THE SAVING
1975 / 14 min / sound / color / 16 mm
UNESCO. Distributed by United Nations Films.
Available in English, Arabic, French, Russian and Spanish soundtracks. Documents international salvage work sponsored by UNESCO to dismantle and move the temples at Philae to the island of Agilkia, safe from the Nile.

674 THE RACE TO SAVE ABU SIMBEL
1966 / 7 min / sound / color / 16 mm
Reader's Digest. Made and released by Vavin. (NUC FiA 68-1617)
Documents efforts to save the temple and statues at Abu Simbel. Shows statues being dismantled and moved to higher ground where the flooding Nile River will not touch them.

675 RESCUE IN NUBIA
1966 / 27 min / sound / b&w / 16 mm

United Nations Films.
Available in English and Arabic soundtracks. Documents
the saving of the temple and statues at Abu Simbel.
Shows other monuments in Nubia which would otherwise have
been submerged in 200 feet of water as a result of the
Aswan High Dam project. Describes UNESCO's part in the
salvage program.

676   SUBMERGED GLORY - A STUDY IN STONE
       1962 / 28 min / sound / b&w / 16 mm
       United Nations. Released by Contemporary Films.
       (International Zone series) (NUC FiA 64-1089) Credits:
       Producer - Alistair Cooke, Director - Frank Jacoby.
       Traces remains carved in stone of ancient civilizations
       such as the Mayans, Aztecs, Greeks, Romans, Arabs,
       Indians, Cambodians and Egyptians. Shows the statues
       and temple at Abu Simbel threatened by water as a result
       of the Aswan High Dam. Outlines efforts needed to save
       these monuments. Narrated by Alistair Cooke.

677   THE TREASURES OF ABU SIMBEL
       1964 / 3 min / sound / b&w / 16 mm
       Hearst Metrotone News. (Screen News Digest, v 6, no. 10)
       (NUC FiA 68-2083)
       Short newsreel. Shows how and why the statues at Abu
       Simbel are being saved from the rising Nile River.

678   THE WORLD SAVES ABU SIMBEL
       1969 / 28 min / sound / color / 16 mm
       UNESCO. Distributed by Contemporary Films, and by
       McGraw-Hill. (LC 74-704157) Credits: Producer - Herbert
       Meyer-Franck, Animation - Rudi Mann. Location: Middle East
       Institute.
       Shows the significance of the temple and statues at Abu
       Simbel. Shows how monuments were moved and reconstructed
       on safe ground before the Aswan High Dam project created
       Lake Nasser.

EGYPT - PHARAONIC HISTORY

679   ANCIENT CIVILIZATIONS: EGYPT
       1974 / 4 min / silent / color / super 8 mm film loop in
       cartridge. Coronet Instructional Media. (LC 74-701512)
       Profiles the development of agriculture and writing in
       ancient Egypt.

680   ANCIENT EGYPT
       1952 / 10 min / sound / color / 16 mm
       Coronet Instructional Media. Distributed by Modern Film
       Rentals. (NUC Fi 52-260) Credits: Educational Collaborator
       - Richard A. Parker. Locations: American Museum of Natural
       History / Brigham Young U. / Kent State U. / Library of

Congress (FAA 3259) / U. of Arizona / U. of Illinois / U. of
Iowa / U. of Kansas / U. of Nebraska / U. of Texas at Austin
/ U. of Washington / U. of Wisconsin. *
Traces the development of ancient Egyptian civilization
and describes its contribution to agriculture, writing,
and mathematics. Includes scenes of the Great Pyramid at
Giza and describes building techniques used. Shows grain
measurements and tax records in hieroglyphics. Intended
for junior-senior high school audiences. Good introduction to ancient Egyptian civilization.

681   ANCIENT EGYPT
1971 / 27 min / sound / color / 16 mm
Brian Brake for Time-Life Films. Distributed by Time-Life.
Locations: New York Public Donnell Film Library / U. of
California Extension Media Center / U. of Illinois / U. of
Michigan.
Shows ancient Egyptian life and culture through art and
architecture. Reviews the study of Egypt and
Egyptological research from the time of Bonaparte's invasion of Egypt to the present. Describes the deciphering
of hieroglyphics using the Rosetta Stone. Stresses the
significance of the vast body of inscriptions translated
which record ancient Egyptian life and culture.

682   ANCIENT EGYPT: THE LAND OF AMUN RA
1969 / 19 min / sound / color / 16 mm
Coleman Film Enterprises. Released by RMI Film Productions.
(LC 71-710233) Credits: Producer-Narrator - Walter M. Burks.
Intended for high school to adult audiences. Revised
version of the 1967 film: LAND OF THE GOD PHARAOHS.
Traces the history of ancient Egypt from 2900 B.C. to the
18th dynasty. Shows monuments, tombs, and artifacts of
the ancient Egyptians. Filmed on location.

683   ANCIENT EGYPT: THE SUN AND THE RIVER
1971 / 58 min / sound / color / 16 mm
Brian Blake. Distributed by Time-Life Films. Locations: U.
of Illinois / U. of Michigan.
Traces the history and culture of ancient Egypt through
ancient artifacts and architecture. Follows the development of Egyptology and the deciphering of Egyptian
hieroglyphics using the Rosetta Stone. Uses a restored
harp and trumpet to perform ancient music.

684   THE ANCIENT EGYPTIAN
1963 / 26 min / sound / color / 16 mm
Julien Bryan. Distributed by International Film Foundation.
(NUC FiA 64-651) Credits: Director-Writer - LeRoy
Leatherman, Consultants - John Wilson, Zaki Saad, Animation
- Philip Stapp. Locations: Brigham Young U. / Indiana U. /
Iowa Films / Iowa State U. / Kent State U. / Library of
Congress (FCA 4214) / Penn. State U. / Syracuse U. / U. of

139

Arizona / U. of California Extension Media Center / U. of
Illinois / U. of Michigan / U. of Nebraska / U. of Texas at
Austin. *
    Intended for junior high school to adult audiences.
    Traces the history of Egypt and Egyptology from 2700 B.C.
    to the Roman period. Shows how western understanding of
    Egyptian history has expanded with the study of hiero-
    glyphics, monuments and artifacts. Uses animation and
    Egyptian art to create a feeling for the life, religion
    and culture of ancient Egypt. Discusses the monuments
    threatened by flooding as a result of the Aswan High Dam
    project. Sound quality is poor on Library of Congress
    print. Good general film.

685   ANCIENT EGYPTIAN IMAGES
       (c. 1970?) / 13 min / sound / b&w / 16 mm
       Brandon. Location: Syracuse U.
           Traces the rise and fall of ancient Egyptian culture
           through Egyptian statuary in the Louvre Museum in Paris.

686   THE ANCIENT WORLD: EGYPT (PARTS 1 AND 2)
       1955 / 66 min / sound / color / 16 mm
       Archeological Institute of America, Harmon Foundation and the
       Egyptian Government. Released by New York University Film
       Library. (Ancient World series) (NUC FiA 65-1306) Credits:
       Producer - Ray Garner, Narrator - Michael Kane. Ektachrome.
       Locations: Brigham Young U. / National Archives (200HF354) /
       U. of Washington.
           Traces the history of ancient Egypt from prehistory to
           the Ptolemies. Uses the step pyramid at Sakkara and
           other monuments, tombs, paintings and artifacts to
           illustrate the various kingdoms and periods in Egyptian
           history and culture.

687   EGYPT: CRADLE OF CIVILIZATION
       1961 / 11 min / color or b&w / 16 mm
       Encyclopaedia Britannica Films. (NUC FiA 62-1423) Credits:
       Collaborators - John A. Wilson, Mohamed Awad, Producer -
       William F. Deneen. Locations: Brigham Young U. / Iowa Films
       / Kent State U. / Library of Congress (FBA 3085) / Syracuse
       U. / U. of California Media Extension Center / U. of
       Illinois / U. of Iowa / U. of Nebraska. *
           Intended for elementary to junior high school audiences.
           Traces contributions of the ancient Egyptians in art,
           architecture, agriculture, writing and religion through
           analysis of artifacts and monuments in Thebes and Karnak.
           Shows daily activities of the ancients. Color deteriora-
           tion is evident in Library of Congress print.

688   EGYPT: GIFT OF THE NILE
       1973, released 1977 / 29 min / sound / color / 16 mm
       John Seabourne. Distributed by Centron Films. (People and
       Places of Antiquity series) Locations: Syracuse U. / U. of

Illinois / U. of Kansas.
Follows the history of ancient Egypt through the Old,
Middle and New Kingdoms by examining artifacts, monuments
and pyramids. Traces the growth and decline of divine
monarchy during the Middle Kingdom and its revival in the
New Kingdom as seen in art and architecture.

689 THE GOOD LIFE ON THE NILE
1956 / 29 min / sound / b&w / 16 mm
New York University. Released by NET Film Service.
(Yesterday's World series) (NUC FiA 58-1416) Credits: Dr.
Casper J. Kraemer.
Reconstructs a trip down the Nile as it would have been
experienced by a nobleman of the XIth dynasty around 2000
B.C. Examines history and culture of ancient Egypt.

690 THE HERETIC KING
1956 / 29 min / sound / b&w / 16 mm
New York University. Released by NET Film Service.
(Yesterday's World series) (NUC FiA 58-1424) Credits: Dr.
Casper J. Kraemer.
Casper J. Kraemer discusses the reign of Akhnaton.
Covers religious, artistic and governmental changes that
occured during his life around 1400 B.C. Stresses the
introduction of monotheistic religion into ancient Egypt
under Akhnaton.

691 HYMN TO ATON
1978 / 15 min / sound / color / 16 mm
Miguel Aleman Velasco. Distributed by Phoenix Films.
Credits: Director - Nadine Markova, Introduction - Eartha
Kitt, Narrator - John Huston. *
Intended for high school to adult audiences. Follows the
introduction of monotheism to ancient Egypt under
Akhnaton, also called Amenhotep IV, from 1375 to 1357
B.C. Shows the radical changes involved in turning from
multiple gods to the one God Aton. Describes dissention
caused by the new religion. Recites the "Hymn to Aton",
the beautiful prayer to a single God, precursor to the
Judeo-Christian God. Well produced.

692 IN THE BEGINNING
1975 / 58 min / sound / color / 16 mm
Reader's Digest Association. Released by Pyramid Films.
(LC 75-704030) Credits: Narrator - Sir Kenneth Clark.
Locations: Kent State U. / New York Public Donnell Film
Library.
Intended for junior high school to adult audiences. Sir
Kenneth Clark travels through Egypt and the Nile Valley
discussing the life, culture and history of the ancient
Egyptians. Describes the "first great home of civilized
man".

693　THE LAND OF THE GOD PHARAOHS
　　1967 / 29 min / sound / color / 16 mm
　　Coleman Film Enterprises.　Released by RMI Film Productions.
　　(LC 72-710236)　Credits: Producer-Narrator - Walter M. Burks.
　　Traces the history of ancient Egypt from its unification
　　under King Menes around 2000 B.C. to the 18th dynasty.
　　Shows monuments, ruins, tombs, and temples at Sakkarah,
　　Giza, Luxor, Karnak and the Valley of the Kings and
　　Queens.　Traces history through architectural remains.

694　LIFE IN ANCIENT EGYPT
　　1962 / 29 min / sound / color / 16 mm
　　Gateway Film Productions, London.　Released in the U.S. by
　　United World Films.　(NUC FiA 63-882)　Credits: Prepared by
　　Clyde F.　Kohn.　Locations: U. of Illinois / U. of Kansas.
　　Traces the history of ancient Egypt during the New
　　Kingdom from 1580 to 1090 B.C. using models,
　　hieroglyphics and reproductions of wall paintings from
　　ancient Egyptian tombs.

695　LIFE IN THE TOMB
　　1956 / 29 min / sound / b&w / 16 mm
　　New York University.　Released by NET Film Service.
　　(Yesterday's World series) (NUC FiA 58-1491)　Credits:
　　Narrator - Dr. Casper J. Kraemer.
　　Studies ancient Egyptian beliefs in afterlife as seen in
　　wall paintings on ancient tombs.　Examines paintings and
　　symbols in tomb of King Rekh-mi-re.

696　A MATTER OF DEATH AND LIFE (EGYPT)
　　1969 / 31 min / sound / color / 16 mm
　　BBC-TV.　Released in the U.S. by Time-Life Films.　(The
　　Glory That Remains series, no. 10)　(LC 79-710732)　Credits:
　　Writer-Narrator - Robert Erskine.　Location: U. of Illinois.
　　Archeologist Robert Erskine reconstructs ancient Egyptian
　　daily life and civilization through paintings and arti-
　　facts.　Examines the personal side of ancient Egyptian
　　culture and discusses belief in life and the afterlife.

697　MYTH OF THE PHARAOHS
　　1970 / 13 min / sound / color / 16 mm
　　Felix Bodrossy.　ACI Films.　Distributed by Paramount
　　Communications, and by Modern Film Rentals.　Locations:
　　Brigham Young U. / Kent State U. / Syracuse U. / U. of
　　Illinois / U. of Kansas.　*
　　Intended for junior-senior high school audiences.　Uses
　　animation in the style of ancient Egyptian tomb paintings
　　to introduce the main concepts of Egyptian mythology,
　　beliefs in life, death and judgement, and ideas of good
　　and bad.　Traces the life of a "typical" Pharaoh from
　　birth to death and judgement in the afterlife.　Novel
　　idea and presentation.　Of interest mostly to younger
　　audiences.

698   THE PHARAONIC LADY
       (n.d.) / 10 min / sound / b&w / 16 mm
       Embassy of Egypt. No other information available.

699   RA - THE SOUL
       1979 / 27 min / sound / 16 or 35 mm
       Nagui Riad. Distributed by Horusfilm, Cairo.
           Shot on location at Luxor, Dendera, Abydos, Beni Hassan,
           Mallawi, Giza, Sakkara and Alexandria. Describes the
           daily life of ordinary men and women in ancient Egypt.
           Topics include their beliefs, relationship with the Nile
           River, theories on death and building of the pyramids.

700   THE SIX FACES OF PHARAOH
       1954 / 13 min / sound / color / 16 mm
       (New York University. Released by NET Film Service?)
       (Yesterday's World series)
           Traces the life and accomplishments of six ancient
           Egyptian pharaohs. Shows the role the Nile River has
           played in shaping Egypt's history. Includes shots of
           Khufu's Great Pyramid, tombs, temples and mummies.

701   THE THOUSAND YEAR WALK (EGYPT)
       1969 / 30 min / sound / color / 16 mm
       BBC-TV. Released in the U.S. by Time-Life Films. (The
       Glory That Remains series, no. 11) (LC 70-710735) Credits:
       Writer-Narrator - Robert Erskine. Location: U. of Illinois.
           Shot on location at the temple of Karnak. Robert Erskine
           traces a thousand years in the history of ancient Egypt
           recorded on the carved relief walls of the temple
           complex.

702   THUNDER OF THE KINGS
       (n.d.) / 60 min / sound / color / 16 mm
       Egyptian Government Tourist Office, New York.
           Intended for junior high school audiences. Views ancient
           Egyptian life through the eyes of a modern Egyptian boy.

703   THE UNLUCKY TRAVELER
       1956 / 29 min / sound / b&w / 16 mm
       New York University. Released by NET Film Service.
       (Yesterday's World series) (NUC FiA 58-1760) Credits: Dr.
       Casper J. Kraemer.
           Traces the deterioration of law and order in the remote
           reaches of the ancient Egyptian empire. Recounts the
           record of an Egyptian envoy to Syria written in 1200 B.C.
           Relates difficulties suffered by ancient travelers.
           Creates a human view of ancient Egyptian culture.

704   WOMAN'S WORK IS NEVER DONE
       1956 / 29 min / sound / b&w / 16 mm
       New York University. Released by NET Film Service.
       (Yesterday's World series) (NUC FiA 58-1813) Credits: Dr.

Casper J. Kraemer.
Shows what life might have been like for ancient Egyptian
women by examining household utensils, ornaments, cosme-
tics, and artifacts.

EGYPT - TUTANKHAMEN

705 CURSED TOMB OPENED
1960 / 4 min / sound / b&w / 16 mm
Filmrite Associates. Released by Official Films. (Greatest
Headlines of the Century series) (NUC Fi 62-1807) Credits:
Producer - Sherm Grinberg, Narrator - Tom Hudson, Writer -
Allan Lurie. Location: Library of Congress (FAA 3719) *
Short newsreel reconstruction of the February 16, 1922
opening of King Tutankhamen's tomb by Howard Carter.
Lists problems and illnesses faced by members of the
expedition which brought about the legend of a curse on
the tomb. Uses excellent footage, but has mediocre
narration.

706 OF TIME, TOMBS AND TREASURE: THE TREASURES OF
TUTANKHAMUN
1977 / 27 min / sound / color / 16 mm
Exxon/Esso Film. Distributed by Modern Talking Pictures.
Location: Middle East Institute.
For junior high school to adult audiences. Dramatizes
the opening of King Tutankhamun's tomb. Views artifacts
from the tomb in Egypt, London and Washington, D.C.
Discusses Egyptian society at the time of Tutankhamun and
Akhenaten. Describes the significance of the tomb and
its contents. Hosted by J. Carter Brown of the National
Gallery of Art.

707 TREASURES OF TUTANKHAMUN
1977 / 5 min / sound / color / 16 mm
The Extension Service, National Gallery of Art. Distributed
by the National Gallery of Art, Washington, D.C.
Produced during the 1976-77 exhibition held at the
National Gallery. Shows some of the individual objects
of gold and alabaster found in the tomb of Tutankhamun.

708 TUT: THE BOY KING
July 27, 1977 / 52 min / sound / color / 3/4" videocassette
NBC. Distributed by Films Inc. Credits: Executive Producer
- George A. Heinemann, Producer-Director - Sid Smith,
Narrator - Orson Wells. Location: Kent State U. / Museum of
Broadcasting (T77:0301). *
Filmed at the National Gallery exhibition of 1976-77.
Recreates the life of Tutankhamun by closely examining 55
objects from the tomb discovered by Howard Carter.
Beautifully displayed and photographed. Intended for
junior high school to adult audiences. Originally broad-
cast on television during the traveling Tut exhibit.

709   THE TUT PHENOMENON
       1978 / 60 min / sound / color / 16 mm
       WNET. Distributed by WNET-TV, New York. (Skyline, televi-
       sion series) Credits: Host - Kitty Carlisle, Producer -
       Peggy Daniel.
           Kitty Carlisle speaks with Thomas Hoving, former director
           of the Metropolitan Museum of Art, and Philippe de
           Montebello, his successor, concerning the exhibit of
           objects from Tutankhamun's tomb. Seven galleries of
           Egyptian art were redone for the exhibit. Shows the
           reconstructed 2000 year old Temple of Dendur, the only
           complete Egyptian temple in the western hemisphere. Also
           shows footage of the 1922 expedition led by Howard Carter
           which discovered the tomb of Tutankhamun.

710   TUTAKHAMUN: THE IMMORTAL PHARAOH
       1962 / 12 min / sound / color / 16 mm
       University of Houston. Made and released by KUHT Film
       Productions. Distributed by Paramount Communications.
       (NUC FiA 64-803) Locations: Brigham Young U. / Kent State
       U. / Penn. State U. / U. of Houston / U. of Illinois / U. of
       Kansas / U. of Nebraska.
           For junior high school to adult audiences. Traces the
           discovery of Tutankhamun's tomb in 1922 and its signifi-
           cance. Shows beautiful objects found in the tomb and
           describes their function.

EGYPT   -   GENERAL HISTORY FROM PHARAONIC TO MODERN TIMES

711   EGYPT AND THE NILE
       1954 / 16 min / sound / color or b&w / 16 mm
       Encyclopaedia Britannica Films. (NUC Fi 55-99) Credits:
       Producer - Donald G. Hoffman, Collaborator - Clarence W.
       Sorensen. Locations: American Friends of the Middle East /
       Brigham Young U. / Iowa Films / Penn. State U. / Syracuse U.
       / U. of Illinois / U. of Iowa.
           Intended for elementary to high school audiences.
           Describes the relationship between Egyptians and the Nile
           River from ancient times to the present. Emphasizes the
           river's importance to life, agriculture and civilization
           in Egypt. Includes scenes of ancient temples in upper
           and lower Egypt and the Delta.

712   EGYPT: LAND OF THE NILE
       1962 / 17 min / sound / color / 16 mm
       Dudley Pictures Corp. Released by United World Films. (Our
       World of the Sixties series) (NUC FiA 66-1761) Credits:
       Director - Carl Dudley, Writer - Herman Boxer. Location:
       American Friends of the Middle East.
           Traces the general history of Egypt from ancient times to
           the present. Shows the importance of the Nile River to
           all aspects of life in Egypt.

713 FORTY CENTURIES
1957 / 11 min / sound / b&w / 16 mm
Pictura Films Corp.
Traces the history of Egypt through postage stamps.

714 MAKING OF MODERN EGYPT
1963 / 10 min / sound / color / 16 mm
Precedent Films. Released by Sterling Educational Films.
Distributed by Didactic Films. Credits: Producers - George
and Sherry Zabriskie.
Intended for junior high school to adult audiences.
Suggests life in Egypt has changed little in 5000 years.
Looks at the plan for the Aswan High Dam project and
discusses progress in the field of education and women's
rights.

715 MODERN EGYPT
1967 / 11 min / sound / color / 16 mm
C-B Films. Released by AV-ED Films. (LC 78-701200)
Credits: Director - Joe Burnham, Writer - Elizabeth Hayter.
Briefly summarizes ancient Egyptian contributions to
western civilization. Shows the importance of Egypt today
in the Arab world. Profiles Egyptian government, education, industry, agriculture and regional influence.

716 NILE - THE CREATOR
1965 / 26 min / sound / color / 16 or 35 mm
Anthony Gilkison Associates. (Caltex International Public
Relations Series) (NUC FiA 66-1525) Credits: Director -
Laurie Hardie Brown. Locations: League of Arab States /
Middle East Institute.
Short history of Egypt from ancient times to the present.
Shows statues of Ramses II at Abu Simbel, the Pyramids,
Luxor, and the cities of Cairo and Alexandria. Includes
scenes of mosques and Coptic churches. Plans for Egypt's
future in industry, land reclamation and education are
reviewed.

717 UNVEILING EGYPT
1978 / 26 min / sound / color / 16 mm
Utah State Board of Education. Locations: Utah State Board
of Education / U. of Texas / U. of Utah. *
Produced through the summer program at the American
University of Cairo. Traces Egyptian life and culture in
four segments. THIS IS CAIRO, THIS IS EGYPT
gives a brief historical background and information on
current government. LAND OF MINARETS gives an
overview of religion in Egypt. THE NILE GIVES LIFE
deals with agriculture and geography. STONE IS
FOREVER looks at Egyptian arts in stone from ancient
times to modern sculpture. Useful teaching tool although
slow at times. Of interest to junior-senior high school
audiences.

146

718   JOURNEY THROUGH A BOOK: DESCRIPTION OF EGYPT
      1972 / 20 min / sound / 16 mm
      Telmissany Brothers Production.   Location: Arab Republic of
      Egypt, Ministry of Information.
          View of Egyptian history from Pharaonic times to the
          French invasion shown through illustrations from
          Description de l'Egypte, a 37 volume work collected by
          146 scientists and artists attached to Bonaparte's
          Egyptian Campaign from 1798-1801.

719   THE STORY OF MODERN EGYPT
      1969 / 20 min / sound / b&w / 16 mm or videocassette
      BBC-TV, London.   Released in the U.S. by Time-Life Films.
      (World History from 1917 to the Present, no. 15.   Unit 5:
      New Nations) (LC 75-714765)
          Available in English and Spanish soundtracks.   Tells the
          story of British rule in Egypt, the 1922 accession of
          King Faud, the emergence of Arab nationalism and the rise
          of Gamal Abdul Nasser.   Discusses the nationalization of
          the Suez Canal in 1954, the British-French invasion of
          Egypt, and the 1967 Arab-Israeli War.   Intended for high
          school to adult audiences.   Covers over 100 years of
          modern Egyptian history.   One of the few films which
          looks at 18th century Egyptian history.

EGYPT - THE TWENTIETH CENTURY

720   EGYPT, A COUNTRY IN TRANSITION
      1961 / 10 min / sound / color / 16 mm
      International Film Bureau, in cooperation with American
      Friends of the Middle East.   Released by IFB.   (NUC FiA
      65-377)   Credits: Consultant - John A. Wilson.   Location:
      Syracuse U.
          Listed in some catalogs as released in 1962 or 1963.
          Intended for junior high school to adult audiences.
          Contrasts traditional and modern aspects of Egyptian
          life.   Shows how new technologies and industries exist
          alongside ancient methods in agriculture, manufacturing
          and education.   Stresses the dependence of Egypt on the
          Nile.   Looks at the structure of society, including the
          status of women and different ethnic and racial groups.

721   EGYPT - THE ECONOMIC FACTOR
      1976 / 15 min / sound / color / 16 mm
      Hollywood Associates.   (LC 76-702797)
          Stresses the importance and centrality of Egypt in
          today's Arab business and economic world.   Released
          before the Arab world boycott of Egypt.

722   EGYPT: THE STRUGGLE FOR STABILITY
      1975 / 28 min / sound / color / 16 mm

Anthony Thomas. Made by Yorkshire Television. Distributed by Learning Corp. of America. (The Arab Experience series) Locations: Boston U. / Kent State U. / Middle East Institute / New York Public Donnell Film Library / Oklahoma State U. / Syracuse U. / U. of Kansas / U. of Minnesota / U. of Missouri / U. of Washington. *

Intended for junior high school to adult audiences. Looks at poverty and contrasts found in modern Egypt. An Arab country without oil wealth, heavily overpopulated Egypt is nonetheless a center within the Arab world. Gives brief history of Egypt and looks at people and places in modern Egypt. Interesting study, valuable for classroom use. Describes major problems facing Egypt and solutions which are being attempted.

723   EGYPT TODAY: UNITED ARAB REPUBLIC
       1968 / 17 min / sound / color / 16 mm
       Paul Hoefler Productions. Released by Bailey-Film
       Associates. (LC 72-702926) Credits: Writer-Photographer -
       Jackson Winter. Locations: Penn. State U. / Syracuse U.
       Listed in some catalogs as released in 1969. Intended
       for elementary to senior high school audiences. Looks at
       contrasts in traditional and modern Egypt. Shows income
       from cotton, tourism and the Suez Canal. Profiles the
       Aswan High Dam. Shows modernization in agriculture and
       industry alongside ancient methods in farming and manu-
       facturing practised by the majority of Egyptians.

724   EL ALAMEIN
       1942 / 9 min / silent / b&w / 16 mm
       War Dept. Official Film, Giorno 257. Location: Library of
       Congress (FAA 9100) *
       Possibly captured Italian footage. Shows supplies being
       stored, troops marching, convoys, trenches, bunkers dis-
       guised as haystacks, blankets being distributed, men
       baking bread, and medals being awarded. Includes scenes
       of Egyptian and North African beach fortifications,
       airplane and anti-aircraft gun sequences, tank and gun
       battles, destroyed aircraft in the desert, and footage
       from the air. Of use for archival and library footage
       purposes. Minimal identification of scenes.

725   FIGHT FOR EGYPT
       (c. 1944) / ? / sound / b&w / 16 mm
       Distributed by Iowa Films. Location: Iowa State.
       Scenes of tank and aerial battles in North Africa during
       WWII.

726   HISTORY 1917-67: THE STORY OF MODERN EGYPT.
       1970 / 21 min / sound / b&w / 16 mm
       Producer unknown. (History Makers series) Location: U. of
       Illinois.
       Probably the same film as no. 719. Tells the story of

Egypt from the British occupation up to the 1967
Arab-Israeli War. Looks at British colonial period
followed by growth in Arab nationalism.

727   MEMOIRS OF AN ENGINEER
       (n.d.) / 18 min / sound / b&w / 16 mm
       Distributed by the Embassy of Egypt. No other information
       available.

728   MIDDLE EAST: LEADERSHIP AND IDENTITY (EGYPT)
       1979 / 28 min / sound / color / 16 mm
       Coronet. (Middle East series) Locations: Library of
       Congress / Syracuse U.
          One of a four part series dealing with modern Egypt by
          Coronet. Intended for junior-senior high school audien-
          ces. Looks at contrast between urban and village
          dwellers in Egypt today, problems of overpopulation, and
          government responses to these and other problems.
          Discusses Egypt's plans for the future.

729   MODERN EGYPT
       1965 / 18 min / sound / color or b&w / 16 mm
       Audio Productions. Released by McGraw-Hill. (NUC FiA
       66-1284) Locations: Kent State U. / Library of Congress
       (FBA 4433) / Syracuse U. / U. of Kansas / U. of Nebraska.
          Intended for junior high school to adult audiences.
          Looks at problems and opportunities faced by Egypt today
          in modernization and development. Covers urban vs.
          village life, dependence of agriculture on the Nile
          River, the dry climate, industry, education and housing.

730   MOVIETONE NEWS
       1963 / 7 min / sound / b&w / 35 mm
       Twentieth Century-Fox. (Movietone News, Vol. 46, no. 33)
       Location: National Archives (200MN46-33)
          Short newsreel released theatrically. Covers Egypt and
          its position in the Middle East.

731   WAR PICTORIAL NEWS, No. 210 (May 14)
       1945 / 10 min / sound / b&w / 35 mm
       British Newsreel. Location: National Archives (208WP210)
          Short British newsreel. Shows Greek and Yugoslav
          displaced persons in the Sinai following WWII. For
          library footage purposes.

EGYPT - THE SUEZ CANAL

732   CRISIS AT SUEZ
       1962 / 30 min / sound / b&w / 16 mm
       CBS News. (The Twentieth Century, television series) (NUC
       Fi 64-107) Credits: Producer - Isaac Kleinerman, Writer -
       Frank Kearns, Reporter - Walter Cronkite. Location: Library

of Congress (FCA 3649).
Traces events which led to the 1956 War. Shows Nasser's nationalization of the Suez Canal, attempts to gain international control of the Canal followed by the combined British-French-Israeli invasion of Egypt. Looks at the U.N. emergency peace-keeping force sent to the area.

733   CRISIS OVER THE SUEZ, OCTOBER 30, 1956
1956 / 4 min / sound / b&w / 16 mm
Richard B. Morros, Inc. in association with Hearst Metrotone News, Inc. (Almanac Newsreel) Location: Library of Congress (FAA 3180) *
Brief newsreel. Reports events of the 1956 War over the Suez Canal. Shows Nasser's nationalization of the Canal, the French-British-Israeli invasion of Egypt, and the U.N.'s efforts to keep peace. About 32 British and French dead are reported as opposed to 2000 Egyptians. Does not cover effects or implications of the war.

734   MIDDLE EAST: TROUBLE AT SUEZ
(n.d.) / 7 min / sound / 16 mm
Warner Brothers. Location: U. of Colorado.
Short newsreel. Covers the conflict following the nationalization of the Suez Canal.

735   SUEZ
1939 / 6 min / sound / b&w / 16 mm
Luce. (Italian Collection) Location: Library of Congress (FAA 8976) No other information available.

736   SUEZ
1956 / 13 min / sound / color or b&w / 16 mm
International Film Foundation. Released by McGraw-Hill. (NUC FiA 57-291) Credits: Producer - Julien Bryan. Locations: Kent State U. / Library of Congress (FBA 4382) / New York U. *
Intended for junior high school to college audiences. Shows plans for a canal at Suez dating back to Pharaonic times. Shows boats being brought through the Canal and expresses concern over access to the Canal after nationalization by Egypt. Library of Congress print has experienced color deterioration. Slowly paced and too out of date for teaching purposes.

737   SUEZ
1956 / 55 min / sound / b&w / 16 mm
CBS Television. Released by McGraw-Hill. (See It Now, television series) (NUC Fi 57-49) Credits: Producer-Editors - Edward R. Murrow, Fred W. Friendly. Locations: Kent State U. / Library of Congress (FCA 1323-24) / Syracuse U.
Originally intended for television audiences and later released for classroom purposes. Traces history of the

Suez Canal to the time of its nationalization by Nasser
in 1956. Discusses implications of nationalization for
trade by western nations. Includes interviews with
President Nasser and British Foreign Minister Lloyd concerning the Canal.

738   SUEZ BOILS OVER
       1960 / 3 min / sound / b&w / 16 mm
       Filmrite Associates. Released by Official Films. (Greatest
       Headlines of the Century series) (NUC Fi 62-1836) Credits:
       Producer - Sherm Grinberg, Narrator - Tom Hudson, Writer -
       Allan Lurie. Location: Library of Congress (FAA 3882)
           Short newsreel presentation. Shows nationalization of
       the Suez Canal followed by invasion of Egypt by
       French-British-Israeli forces. Presented with an
       anti-Egyptian point of view.

739   THE SUEZ CANAL
       1955 / 18 min / sound / color / 16 mm
       Louis de Rochemont Associates. Released by Louis de
       Rochemont Associates Film Library. (Our Times: Of Men,
       Ideas and Events Which Distinguish Today from Yesterday and
       Tomorrow series, no. 1) (NUC FiA 56-1145) Credits:
       Animators - Halas and Batchelor. Location: U. of Utah.
           Uses animation and location photography. Gives the
       history of the Suez Canal from original plans during
       Pharaonic times to the Canal finished by de Lessups in
       1869. Explains importance of the Canal to shipping and
       trade.

740   THE SUEZ CANAL
       1965 / 11 min / sound / color or b&w / 16 mm
       Gateway Educational Films, London. Released in the U.S. by
       Coronet Instructional Films. (NUC FiA 67-934) Locations:
       Iowa Films / Kent State U. / Library of Congress (FAA 6141)
       /Syracuse U. / U. of Illinois, Champaign / U. of Iowa / U.
       of Nebraska. *
           Traces the history of a canal across Suez from Pharaonic
       times to the Canal completed by de Lessups in 1869.
       Follows the ship STRATHEDEN through the Canal. Includes
       statistical information but no political comment. For
       elementary to high school audiences.

741   THE SUEZ CANAL
       1966 / 4 min / silent / color / standard or super 8 mm loop
       in cartridge. Gateway Film Productions, London. Released
       in the U.S. by International Communication Films. (North
       Africa series) (LC 70-700513)
           Uses animation and location photography. Shows how the
       Suez Canal saves time in shipping and trade by avoiding
       rounding the southern tip of Africa. Gives a short
       history of the importance of the Canal.

742   THE SUEZ CANAL - GATEWAY TO WORLD TRADE
1962 / 11 min / sound / color or b&w / 16 mm
Encyclopaedia Britannica Films. (NUC FiA 62-1366) Credits:
Collaborator - Mahmoud Younes, Producer - William F. Deneen.
Locations: Library of Congress (FBA 3924) / U. of Iowa / U.
of Nebraska / U. of Texas at Austin. *
Uses engravings and location photography to explain the
need for a canal to shorten trade routes from the Far
East and India to Europe and the west. Shows how the
Suez Canal is maintained. Follows ship REZA PAHLAVI
through the canal. Explains the role of the Canal
Authority. Library of Congress print experiencing color
deterioration. For elementary to high school audiences.
Slow-paced at times.

743   SUEZ CRISIS (1956)
1971 / 4 min / silent / b&w / super 8 mm film loop in
cartridge. Thorne Films. (8mm Documents Project, no. 387)
(LC 72-701425) Credits: Producer - Dennis Grogan.
Location: Library of Congress.
Short documentary. Follows events up to and during the
Suez Crisis of 1956.

744   VITAL WATERWAY - THE SUEZ CANAL
1975 / 13 min / sound / b&w / 16 mm
Hearst Metrotone News. (Screen News Digest, vol. 18, issue
3) Location: Library of Congress (FBA 2181) *
Uses engravings and line drawings to show the building of
the Suez Canal. Describes history of the conflict over
the Canal and its nationalization in 1956. Traces the
periods of the Canal opening and closing as a result of
war. Describes how the Canal is now too narrow to handle
supertankers. Plays down the role of the Canal in modern
shipping. Quality is poor for being a recent film. For
high school to college audiences. Lets many biases show,
such as calling the Egyptian army "the enemy".

EGYPT - INTERVIEWS

745   HUSSEIN SELIM
August 10, 1958 / 30 min / sound / b&w / 16 mm
NBC Television. (Meet the Press, television series)
Location: Library of Congress (FRA 6921-22)
Contains interview with Hussein Selim, Egyptian Delegate
to the U.N. and commentator on world events for Egyptian
Broadcasting.

746   MUHAMMAD KAMIL 'ABD AL-RAHIM
November 25, 1951 / 28 min / sound / b&w / 16 mm
NBC Television. (Meet the Press, television series) (LC
79-701447) Credits: Discussants - Martha Rountree, John
Henry, John Hightower, John O'Donnell, Lawrence Spivak.

Location: Library of Congress (FBA 5573)   *
Interview with Egypt's ambassador. Topics covered
include Egypt's alliances with Britain, Iran, and the
U.S., the question of ownership of the Suez Canal, the
role of Egypt in the 1948 Arab-Israeli War, Egyptian
history in the 20th century and the growth of nationalism
in Egypt. Very good description of Egyptian history
and current affairs from 1900-1950. Also a good example
of discussants talking at cross purposes from the subject
interviewed. Intended for television audiences. Useful
for library footage and research purposes.

747 SADAT
June 18, 1974 / 30 min / sound / b&w / 16 mm
CBS News. (CBS News Special Report, television series)
Credits: Executive Producer - Russ Bensley, Director - Joel
Banow. Location: Library of Congress (FCA 7601) *
Also called: CRONKITE INTERVIEWS SADAT in some sources.
Moderately informative interview with Anwar Sadat in
Alexandria. Topics covered include President Nixon's
visit to Egypt, U.S.- Egyptian relations, economic aid,
the Palestinian problem and its relation to all Middle
East questions, arms and arms control in the Middle East,
the relationship between Egypt and the Soviet Union, and
the question of what should happen in Egypt should Sadat
not run again for President.

EGYPT - BIOGRAPHIES

748 FAROUK FLEES
1960 / 4 min / sound / b&w / 16 mm
Filmrite Associates. Released by Official Films. (Greatest
Headlines of the Century series) (NUC Fi 62-1851) Credits:
Producer - Sherm Grinberg, Narrator - Tom Hudson, Writer -
Allan Lurie. Location: Library of Congress (FAA 3744) *
Short newsreel. Outlines life of King Farouk. Shows
his accession to the throne of Egypt in 1936, with a new
wife and high public opinion, to his downfall on July 23,
1952. Covers the officer's coup which forced Farouk to
flee Egypt and go into permanent exile. Traces the
steady deterioration of public trust in Farouk over a
twenty year period. Good use of library footage.

749 FAROUK: LAST OF THE PHARAOHS
1977 / 50 min / sound / color / 16 mm
Peter Batty. (The Real World, television series)
Traces the life of King Farouk of Egypt from his
accession to the throne at age 16 to the Egyptian revolution of 1952 when he was deposed. Shows his decline in
participation in governing Egypt after WWII and his repu-
tation for greed and avarice. Continues to his death in
1965 at age 45. British-made production. Uses newsreel
footage and interviews.

750 LIFE OF YOUSSEF KAMEL
(n.d.) / 22 min / sound / b&w / 16 mm
Embassy of Egypt. No other information available.

751 SADAT: AN ACTION BIOGRAPHY
1975 / 52 min / sound / color / 16 mm
Aetna Life and Casulty.
Traces the life of Anwar Sadat from his childhood in an
Egyptian village to the presidency. Also looks at the
modernization of Egypt during the same period of time.

EGYPT - MINORITIES

752 BEDOUINS OF SINAI
1974 / 41 min / sound / color / 16 mm
Location: Abraham F. Rad Jewish Film Archive.
Available in English and Hebrew soundtracks. Traces the
nomadic life of the Sinai Bedouin during different
seasons of the year.

753 COPTIC DECORATION
1975 / 30 min / sound / color / 16 mm
Telmissany Brothers Production. Credits: Producer - Adel
Tahir. Locations: Arab Republic of Egypt, Ministry of
Information / Egyptian Embassy. *
Shows Coptic, or Egyptian Christian, decoration from the
1st century A.D. to the present. Scenes include artifacts found in the Coptic Museum, churches and
monasteries of Cairo, and the Valley of Natroun. Tours
the mountains near the Red Sea and rural areas of
southern Egypt. Slowly paced, but an interesting topic.

754 THE COPT'S MUSEUM
(n.d.) / 12 min / sound / 16 mm
Embassy of Egypt. No other information available.

755 A PROPHECY REALIZED
(n.d.) / 20 min / sound / color / 16 mm
Location: Egyptian Government Tourist Office, New York.
Looks at Coptic Egypt. Filmed on location at a Coptic
monastery in the Egyptian desert.

EGYPT - WOMEN AND CHILDREN

756 DEATH LAMENT (TOTENKLAGE)
1967 / 2 min / silent / b&w / 16 mm
Institut fur Musikwissenschaft, Leipzig. UNESCO Films on
Traditional Music and Dance.
Short, silent documentary. Shows Egyptian women working
in the fields while singing.

757   (EGYPTIAN BOYS IN SWIMMING RACE)
       June 1903 / 1 min / silent / b&w / 16 mm
       Thomas Edison. Library of Congress Paper Print Collection.
       Location: Library of Congress (FLA 3632)   *
       Useful for historical purposes. Short film made by A.C.
       Abadie in Luxor. Shows young boys jumping into the
       water, swimming towards the camera, and jumping onto the
       shore, hands outstretched for their reward for racing.

758   THE EGYPTIAN WOMAN IN FIFTY YEARS
       (c. 1979) / ? / sound / 16 mm
       Saad Nadim for the Egyptian National Center for Documentary
       Films. Location: Library of Congress.
       Documents the story of the modern Egyptian woman from the
       national revolution of 1919 to the present. Told by
       Sayza Nabarawi, a leader in the Egyptian women's move-
       ment.

759   MAKING BASKETS FROM PALM LEAF VEINS (FELLAHIN,
       NORTH AFRICA, UPPER EGYPT)
       1963, released 1964 / 8 min / silent / color / 16 m
       Encyclopaedia Cinematographica. (Ency. Cinematographica,
       no. E 687) Distributed by Pennsylvania State University.
       Another in the series of silent ethnographic films
       following one typical activity. Shows village women of
       southern Egypt making baskets.

760   WHERE IS MY FREEDOM?
       (c. 1975?) / 75 min / sound / color / 16 mm
       Laila Abou Saif. Distributed by Icarus Films. *
       In Arabic with English sub-titles. A portrait of nine
       modern Egyptian women. Shows their personal struggles
       and triumphs in overcoming bias and discrimination at the
       workplace, in the courts, and in traditional Egyptian
       society. Follows a pharmacist, a French language
       teacher, a painter, a lawyer, a flower exporter and a
       social worker. Traces the history of the women's move-
       ment in Egypt and the areas in which Egyptian women need
       to focus their efforts for future advancement. Film is
       poorly edited and too long but covers a little known sub-
       ject. The content of the film is sincere and troubling.
       Gives a good idea of the amount of legal reform necessary
       in Egypt to provide women with equal rights. Despite
       poor technical quality and length, this should be of spe-
       cial interest to women's groups. Recommended for college
       level study of modern Egypt and Egyptian women.

EGYPT   -   VILLAGE LIFE

761   EGYPT - SABHA DISCOVERS THE PAST
       1967 / 20 min / sound / color / 16 mm
       Universal Education and Visual Arts. (NUC FiA 67-5896)

155

Credits: Consultants - Durward Pruden, Helen B. Warrin.
Locations: Syracuse U. / U. of Illinois.
Intended for junior-senior high school audiences.
Follows a 15 year old girl whose Bedouin family has
decided to settle in an Egyptian village and turn to
agriculture as a way of life. Shows Sabha working on an
archaeological dig. Discusses the historical significance of the artifacts found.

762   AN EGYPTIAN VILLAGE
1960 / 18 min / sound / color or b&w / 16 mm
Goudsou's Productions, Canada. Released in the U.S. by Film
Associates. (NUC FiA 60-611) Locations: Boston U. / Kent
State U. / Syracuse U. / U. of Iowa / U. of Michigan / U. of
Minnesota / U. of Missouri / U. of South Carolina / U. of
Utah / U. of Washington.
Shows traditional life style of the Egyptian villager.
Typical life of a small village farmer includes religious
observance in the mosque and in religious schools, family
life and minimal contact with the urban, modern world.

763   EGYPTIAN VILLAGERS
1969 / 14 min / sound / color / 16 mm
Public Media, Inc. Released by Films Incorporated. (Man
and His World series) (LC 76-704763) Locations: Kent State
U. / Library of Congress (FBB 1965) / Middle East Institute
/ Penn. State U. / U. of Illinois / U. of Michigan / U. of
Minnesota / U. of Nebraska. *
Edited version of the film made by Institut fur Film und
Bild, Munich. In English. Intended for junior high to
adult audiences. Follows Mustapha and his family in an
Egyptian village of around 3000 people. Shows what it is
like to live in a small farming village near the Nile.
Covers farming methods used, education and health
programs for the villagers and looks at local craftsmen
and tradespeople. Good general introduction to village
life. Widely used for teaching purposes.

764   FELLAHIN, MAKING BASKETS FROM PLAITED BANDS
1962 / 5 min / silent / color / 16 mm
Encyclopaedia Cinematographica. Distributed by Pennsylvania
State University. (Ency. Cinematographica, no. E 504)
Filmed at the El Kharga oasis in Egypt. Records the
traditional craft of making baskets with palm leaves.

765   GUEZIRET ELDAHAB: AN EGYPTIAN VILLAGE
1960 / 18 min / sound / color / 16 mm
Goudsou Films. Distributed by Film Associates. Location:
Kent State U.
Shows Egyptian village life as it was lived by around 2/3
of the population of Egypt in the 1960's. Scenes include
preparation of meals, arrangements for a wedding, working
in the fields and meeting with other villagers. Intended
for junior-senior high school audiences.

766   (SHEARING A DONKEY IN EGYPT)
       June 1903 / 1 min / silent / b&w / 16 mm
       Thomas Edison. Library of Congress Paper Print Collection.
       Location: Library of Congress (FLA 4873) *
          In good condition for its age. Short film by A.C. Abadie
          for Thomas Edison. Shows about ten men shearing a donkey
          with great abandon using a variety of specialized tools
          and knives. For historic and documentary purposes.

EGYPT - URBAN LIFE

767   EGYPT TODAY
       1957 / 13 min / sound / color / 16 mm
       Classroom Film Distributors.
          Contrasts Egypt's past and present in urban centers such
          as Cairo.

768   THE IMPACT OF AGRESSION ON THE ARAB LABORERS
       (n.d.) / 15 min / sound / b&w / 16 mm
       Embassy of Egypt. No other information available.

769   A MODERN EGYPTIAN FAMILY
       1977 / 17 min / sound / b&w / 16 mm
       Julien Bryan. Distributed by International Film Foundation.
       Location: Middle East Institute. *
          Shows modern Egyptian middle class life. Observes the
          family reunion of the Allam family. The family includes
          an oil engineer, a farmer, an architect, and a construc-
          tion engineer. Traces major events in Egyptian life in
          the last thirty years through members of the family.
          Includes segments on the Aswan High Dam project, the
          Arab-Israeli wars, re-opening of the Suez Canal, oil
          exploration in the Red Sea and urban problems. Good look
          at urban middle class life. Intended for junior high to
          adult audience and for teaching purposes.

770   MUD HORSE
       (c. 1974) / 10 min / sound / b&w / 16 mm
       Atiyat el Abnoudi. Distributed by Icarus Films. *
          Shows work at a brick factory on the Nile where people
          and horses mix mud for bricks. A statement on the con-
          dition of workers in Egypt. Despite poor technical
          quality, this is a thought provoking look at an ignored
          group, the urban working poor.

EGYPT - DRUG PROBLEM

771   DOPE FIENDS: WHAT THEY ARE AND HOW THEY END
       1931 / 10 min / silent / b&w / 35 mm
       Central Narcotics Bureau of Egypt. Location: National
       Archives (170.3, Narcotics, Bureau of. RI2960)
          One in a series of early anti-drug films from Egypt.

772   DOPE IN EGYPT
       1931 / 11 min / silent / b&w / 35 mm
       Central Narcotics Bureau of Egypt. Location: National
       Archives (170.5)
          Early Egyptian anti-drug film.

773   THE DRUG EVIL IN EGYPT
       1931 / 47 min / silent / b&w / 35 mm
       Central Narcotics Bureau of Egypt. Location: National
       Archives (170.4)
          Longest film in the series of early silent anti-drug
          films from Egypt.

EGYPT - STREET ENTERTAINERS

774   (EGYPTIAN FAKIR WITH DANCING MONKEY)
       June 1903 / 1 1/2 min / silent / b&w / 16 mm
       Thomas Edison. Library of Congress Paper Print Collection.
       Location: Library of Congress (FLA 4599) *
          In good condition for its age. Another short film by
          A.C. Abadie for Thomas Edison. Shows a costumed monkey
          dancing and twirling a baton to the beat of a drum played
          by a street entertainer in Egypt. They have a mock
          battle with sticks. For historic or documentary pur-
          poses.

775   SAD SONG FOR TOUHA
       1972 / 12 min / sound / b&w / 16 mm
       Atiyat el-Abnoudi. Distributed by Icarus Films. *
          In Arabic with English sub-titles. Briefly follows a
          group of street performers in Egypt. Includes scenes of
          a carnival, shadow puppeteers, street performances,
          children being trained as acrobats, people dancing and
          juggling fire. Filmed to a poem. Shows the small-time
          glory and weariness of the street performers. Relatively
          poor technical quality but good content. For college and
          adult audiences.

EGYPT - TRAVELOGS PRODUCED BEFORE 1952

776   AROUND THE WORLD ON THE U.S. ARMY TRANSPORT
       CABLESHIP "DELLWOOD"
       1930 / 88 min / silent / b&w / 35 mm
       Signal Corps. (Signal Corps. Misc. Film, no. 797) Location:
       National Archives (111M797)
          Follows the cableship "Dellwood" around the world. Reel
          3 covers a stopover in Egypt. Reel 4 includes passing
          through the Suez Canal.

777   CLEOPATRA'S PLAYGROUND
       1951 / 9 min / sound / b&w / 35 mm

RKO Pathe. (Screenliner series, no. 12) Credits: Producer -
Burton Benjamin, Director - Hamilton Wright, Narrator - Peter
Roberts. Location: Library of Congress (FEA 247) *
General travelog of Egypt originally intended as a
theatrical short subject. Includes scenes of the
University of Cairo, the pyramid at Sakkarah, Tounis
excavations undertaken by the French and Egyptian governments, Luxor and Karnak. Shows work being done to restore
ancient sites and discover new sites for excavation.
Nothing to do with Cleopatra, this film has a tendency to
be overly cute. Has good footage of restoration work.

778   EGYPT
(c. 1928) / 8 min / silent / b&w / 16 mm
Producer unknown. Location: Library of Congress (FAA 3535)
*
General travelog. Contains excellent silent footage of
craftsmen working with hand tools, metalsmiths, potters,
a village market in the Delta, a camel market, farming
with a wooden plow and scenes of farm animals. Shows
sites in Luxor and ancient Egyptian monuments. For
historic and library footage purposes.

779   EGYPT
1951 / 9 min / sound / b&w or color / 16 or 35 mm
Dudley Pictures Corp. Released by Republic Pictures.
Distributed by International Film Foundation. (This World
of Ours series) (NUC Fi 52-943) Credits: Producer - Carl
Dudley. Color by Trucolor. Location: Library of Congress
(FAA 3533) *
General travelog of Egypt. Shows modern life in Cairo,
street scenes, men praying, and crafts at the bazaar.
Also includes scenes of the Suez Canal, Karnak, Luxor, the
pyramids and other ancient monuments. Of little value
for research or instruction.

780   EGYPT, FATHER NILE
(c. 1950?) / 10 min / sound or silent / b&w / 16 mm
Bray Studios, Inc. New York. Location: Library of Congress
(NUC FiA 55-435)
Shows scenes of life along the Nile and in the Delta.
Includes scenes of Cairo, fishermen and farmers and a
trip on a Nile steamer. Tours ancient monuments
including the Sphinx and the Pyramids.

781   EGYPT - KINGDOM OF THE NILE
1934, released for educational purposes 1939 / 10 min /
sound / b&w / 16 mm. Metro-Goldwyn-Mayer. Released for
educational purposes by Teaching Film Custodians. (James A.
FitzPatricks's Traveltalks series) (NUC FiA 52-4992)
Locations: Indiana U. / Iowa Films / U. of Iowa.
Originally a theatrical short subject. General travelog.
Includes scenes of Tutankhamun's tomb, the Pyramids and

Sphinx, Valley of the Kings in Luxor, and ruins and monuments. Ruins are shown in contrast to present day Egypt represented by farmers, craftsmen and urban Cairenes. Intended for elementary to college audiences.

782   EGYPT: LAND OF THE PYRAMIDS
(c. 1930) / 9 min / silent / b&w / 16 mm
Metro-Goldwyn-Mayer. (James A. FitzPatrick's Traveltalks series) (LC 72-703852) Credits: Photographer - Hubert S. Dawley. Location: Library of Congress (FAA 3534) *
Originally a theatrical short subject. Travelog includes street scenes, dhows on the Nile, farmers, veiled and unveiled women at a market, a camel and animal market, and a party of European tourists on camelback going to the Pyramids. Includes some excellent street footage documenting Egyptian urban life in the 1930's. Library of Congress print is somewhat scratched and warped.

783   EGYPT SPEAKS
1951 / 10 min / sound / color / 35 mm
Metro-Goldwyn-Mayer. (People on Parade series) Credits: Producer-Director - James A. FitzPatrick, Photographer - Howard Nelson. Location: Library of Congress (FEA 374) *
Shows pre-revolutionary Egypt in a glossy travelog. Includes scenes of Alexandria, a soccer game, women in professions and public life, village life of the fellahin and a segment on British-trained Egyptian police. Soundtrack includes the famous Wheat Song. Outdated but interesting footage.

784   AN EGYPTIAN ADVENTURE
1928 / 12 min / silent / b&w / 16 mm
Four Star Films. Credits: Producers - L.C. de Rochemont, Jack Glenn. Location: Library of Congress (FAA 7845) *
One in a series (including IN THE STEPS OF GENGHIS KHAN) of travelogs of eastern life. Follows a group of American sailors on leave in various ports. Shows scenes of Cairo and famous Egyptian tourist sights. Uses flip, uninformative titles but includes some fascinating, if bizarre, footage. Shows sailors doing a Charleston on top of the Great Pyramid to the music of a portable phonograph. Portrays Egyptians as dishonest and cunning and tourists as gullible buffoons. The story line is foolish but contains some unique footage.

785   (EGYPTIAN MARKET SCENE)
June 1903 / 1 1/2 min / silent / b&w / 16 mm
Thomas Edison. Library of Congress Paper Print Collection. Location: Library of Congress (FLA 4600) *
In fair condition for its age. Shot by A.C. Abadie for Thomas Edison. Shows a crowded market with women carrying produce. Men in turbans carry and sell goods. For historic and documentary purposes.

160

786   LAND OF THE PYRAMIDS
       1951 / 7 min / sound / b&w / 16 mm
       Castle Films. (The World Parade series) (NUC Fi 52-1206
       rev.) Locations: Library of Congress (FAA 4136) / U. of
       Illinois.
           General travelog showing scenes of Cairo and the Egyptian
       desert. Includes scenes of mummies and an excavation.

787   (PANORAMIC VIEW OF AN EGYPTIAN CATTLE MARKET)
       June 1903 / 2 min / silent / b&w / 16 mm
       Thomas Edison. Library of Congress Paper Print Collection.
       Location: Library of Congress (FLA 4796)   *
           In fair condition for its age. Another in the series of
       short films made by A.C. Abadie for Thomas Edison. Made
       up of a 360 degree pan of the people and buildings in an
       Egyptian livestock market. Includes scenes of open sheds
       full of cattle, and men bargaining, smoking and talking.
       For historic and documentary purposes.

EGYPT - TRAVELOGS PRODUCED AFTER 1952

788   ASSIGNMENT EGYPT
       1961 / 9 min / sound / color / 35 mm
       Twentieth Century-Fox Film Corp. (Movietone Adventure
       series) (NUC Fi 67-1448) Credits: Producer - Edmund Reek,
       Director - Jack Kuhne, Writer - Joe Wills. Location: Library
       of Congress (FEA 70)   *
           Originally a theatrical short subject. General travelog
       showing Cairo, Alexandria, Suez and Abu Simbel. Looks at
       many famous Egyptian sites including the Muhammad Ali
       Mosque, the University of Cairo, the then incomplete
       Aswan High Dam, and ancient monuments.

789   EGYPT - LAND OF ANTIQUITY
       1969 / 17 min / sound / color / 16 mm
       Paul Hoefler Productions. Released by Bailey-Film
       Associates. (LC 79-702925) Credits: Writer-Photographer -
       Jackson Winter. Locations: Iowa Films / Syracuse U. / U. of
       Iowa.
           Intended for junior-senior high school audiences. Trave-
       log of Egypt. Focuses on the wealth of antiquities found
       in Egypt. Includes scenes of Karnak, Luxor, the Pyramids
       at Giza, granite quarries in Nubia in southern Egypt and
       the giant statues of Ramses II at Abu Simbel.

790   EGYPT, LAND OF TIME
       (n.d.) / 25 min / sound / color / 16 mm
       Producer unknown. Location: Middle East Institute.
           Shows monuments of ancient Egypt found in Cairo, Luxor
       and Alexandria. Also looks at churches, mosques and
       bazaars. Shows village life and industrial development.
       Includes information on modern education.

791   EGYPT - THE NEW HORIZON
       1976, released 1977 / 14 min / sound / color / 16 mm
       Michael Carr. The Hollywood Associates, Inc. Credits:
       Producer - Michael Carr, Director - Peter Sturken.
       Intended for high school to adult audiences. Looks
       briefly at Egypt's ancient past, the modern life of
       Egypt and plans for future development and modernization.

792   LAND OF THE NILE
       1955 / 9 min / sound / color / 35 mm
       Twentieth Century-Fox Film Corp. (NUC Fi 55-777) Credits:
       Producer - Otto Lang, Director - Robert Snody, Narrator -
       Hugh Marlowe. Cinemascope.
       Originally a theatrical short subject. Travelog includes
       scenes of Cairo, the Pyramids at Giza, the Sphinx and
       Luxor.

793   LAND OF THE NILE
       1963 / 17 min / sound / color / 16 mm
       Universal Education and Visual Arts.
       Intended for junior-senior high school audiences. Looks
       at ancient Egyptian monuments and contrasts them with
       modern Egyptian villages and cities. General travelog of
       Egypt.

794   THE LAND OF THE PHARAOH
       1967 / 29 min / sound / color / 16 mm
       RMI Educational Films. No other information available.

795   OUT OF THE DESERT
       1956 / 19 min / sound / color / 35 mm
       Vitaphone Corp. (A Warner Brothers Short Subject) (NUC Fi
       57-611) Credits: Producer - Cedric Francis, Director-
       Photographer-Writer - Jackson Winter. Location: Library of
       Congress (FEA 963-64)
       Contrasts modern Cairo with scenes of ancient Egypt.
       Theatrically released travelog.

796   OUT OF THE DESERT
       1963 / 25 min / sound / color / 16 mm
       American Friends of the Middle East. Distributed by the
       Egyptian Tourist Office.
       Travelog showing scenes of ancient and modern Egypt.

797   THIS IS EGYPT
       (c. 1960?) / 25 min / sound / color / 16 mm
       Egyptian Tourist Office.
       To encourage tourism. General travelog covering many
       famous Egyptian tourist sites.

798   TREASURES OF THE NILE
       1963 / 11 min / sound / color / 35 mm
       Twentieth Century-Fox Film Corp. Location: Library of

Congress (FEA 2530)   No other information available on this
theatrical short subject.

799   THE WORLD OF TWA - EGYPT
      (c. 1970?) / 25 min / sound / color / 16 mm
      TWA. Distributed by Association-Sterling Films.
      To promote tourism and airline travel. Shows scenes of
      famous tourist sites in Egypt including the Sphinx,
      Valley of the Kings, Tutankhamun's tomb, Alexandria, the
      Aswan Dam and the Suez Canal.

EGYPT - TRAVELOGS - BY CITY

800   ALEXANDRIA
      1963 / 15 min / sound / color / 16 mm
      Egyptian Tourist Office.
      Shows some of the tourist attractions and famous resort
      areas of Egypt including Alexandria.

801   CAIRO
      (n.d.) / 4 min / silent / b&w or color / 16 or 8 mm
      World in Color Productions, New York. (World in Color
      Travel Series) (NUC FiA 54-3894) Kodachrome.
      Short general travelog showing scenes of Cairo.

802   CAIRO SKYLINE
      (n.d.) / 10 min / sound / 16 mm
      Embassy of Egypt. No other information available.

803   COLORFUL CAIRO
      (c. 1960?) / 10 min / sound / b&w / 16 mm
      Nu-Art Films.
      Travelog of Cairo. Presents Cairo as heir to contribu-
      tions of several great civilizations.

804   (GOING TO MARKET, LUXOR, EGYPT)
      June 1903 / 49 seconds / silent / b&w / 16 mm
      Thomas Edison. Library of Congress Paper Print Collection.
      Location: Library of Congress (FLA 3429) *
      In fair to poor condition. Another in the series of
      short films made by A.C. Abadie for Thomas Edison. Shows
      a group of people in a market. Animals pass in front of
      the camera in a crowded market scene. For documentary
      and historic purposes.

805   (MARKET SCENE IN OLD CAIRO, EGYPT)
      March 28, 1903 / 55 seconds / silent / b&w / 16 mm
      Thomas Edison. Library of Congress Paper Print Collection.
      Location: Library of Congress (FLA 3543) *
      In good condition for its age. Short film made by A.C.
      Abadie for Thomas Edison. Shows a crowded market area
      with massive walls and buildings of the city in the
      background.

163

806   (QUAINT SPOTS IN CAIRO, EGYPT)
       1913 / 9 min / silent / b&w / 35 mm
       Thomas Edison. Kleine Collection. Location: Library of
       Congress (FLA 2999) *
           Scenes from Cairo. Includes a street bazaar, dhows on
           the Nile, children drinking from a fountain, vegetable
           and bread markets, a letter-writer in the street, the
           camel market, and a side-walk cafe. In a busy street
           scene a trolley car and camel-riding musicians lead a
           procession through the streets. Shows several different
           modes of transportation including a two camel chair,
           carts, and carriages. Very good piece of footage for
           documentary and library footage purposes.

807   STREETS OF CAIRO
       (n.d.) / 10 min / sound or silent / b&w / 16 mm
       Bray Studios, Inc. New York. (NUC FiA 55-436)
           General travelog of Cairo. Shows mosques, bazaars, and
           street scenes. Looks at people and places in Cairo.

808   (TOURISTS STARTING ON DONKEYS FOR THE PYRAMIDS
       OF SAKKARAH, EGYPT)
       June, 1903 / 1 min / silent / b&w / 16 mm
       Thomas Edison. Library of Congress Paper Print Collection.
       Location: Library of Congress (FLA 3552) *
           In fair condition for its age. Another of the films made
           by A.C. Abadie for Thomas Edison. Shows European men and
           women coming onto shore from a Nile River boat and
           mounting donkeys led by Egyptians. Tourists start off to
           go sightseeing at the pyramid at Sakkarah. The pyramid
           is not shown. An Egyptian guide is wearing a Cook's
           Tours shirt.

EGYPT - LAND RECLAMATION

809   DESERT RECLAMATION
       (n.d.) / 10 min / sound / 16 mm
       Embassy of Egypt. No other information available.

810   STORY OF THE DESERT
       1938 / 40 min / sound / b&w / 16 mm
       Knowledge Builders. (NUC FiA 55-602)
           Shows reclamation efforts being made in Egypt. Describes
           the struggle to reclaim land from the desert. Includes
           scenes of nomadic tribes on the Sahara.

811   YELLOW AND GREEN
       1976 / 22 min / sound / color / 16 mm
       Vision Habitat. Distributed by United Nations Films.
           Available in English, Arabic, French and Spanish
           soundtracks. Discusses desert reclamation and irrigation
           projects in Egypt. Shows how areas are chosen, prepared

for planting and irrigated. Describes which crops and
animals are used on this type of land. Shows new settlements and discusses their architecture and social structure.

EGYPT - THE NILE RIVER

812   FATHER NILE
      (n.d.) / 11 min / sound / b&w / 16 mm
      Bray Studios, Inc. New York.
      Shows life on the Nile River and in the Delta. Includes
      scenes of dhows and ships on the Nile.

813   (FORDING THE NILE RIVER ON DONKEYS)
      June, 1903 / 2 min / silent / b&w / 16 mm
      Thomas Edison. Library of Congress Paper Print Collection.
      Location: Library of Congress (FLA 4630)   *
         In good condition for its age. Another in the series of
      short films made by A.C. Abadie for Thomas Edison. Shows
      about a dozen reluctant donkeys being driven across a
      ford by men and boys. For documentary and historical
      purposes.

814   LIFE IN THE NILE VALLEY
      1952 / 11 min / sound / color or b&w / 16 mm
      Coronet Instructional Films. (NUC Fi 52-258) Credits:
      Educational Collaborator - John H. Garland. Locations:
      Brigham Young U. / Syracuse U. / U. of Illinois / U. of
      Nebraska.
         Listed in some catalogs with a release date of 1954.
      Shows agricultural life style of the majority of Egyptian
      villagers living in the Nile River Valley. Looks at
      irrigation, transportation and flood control. Describes
      the structure of the Egyptian village family. Intended
      for junior-senior high school audiences.

815   THE NILE IN EGYPT
      1966 / 10 min / sound / color or b&w / 16 mm
      Gateway Educational Films, London. Released in the U.S. by
      Coronet Instructional Films. (NUC FiA 66-1754) Locations:
      Kent State U. / Library of Congress (FAA 6317) / Syracuse U.
      / U. of Illinois / U. of Iowa.
         Intended for elementary to junior high school audiences.
      Shows the dependence of Egypt and Egyptian farmers on the
      water of the Nile River. Shows traditional and modern
      methods of irrigation and flood control of the Nile
      water.

816   NILE RIVER VALLEY AND THE PEOPLE OF THE LOWER RIVER
      1951 / 17 min / sound / color or b&w / 16 mm
      Academy Films. (NUC FiA 53-189) Credits: Producer - James
      A. Larsen, Photographer - J. Michael Hagopian. Kodachrome.

165

Locations: Educational Film Library / Syracuse U. / U. of
Illinois / U. of Texas at Austin.
Looks at the Nile River and its role in Egyptian life.
Shows dependence of Egyptians on the Nile for water.
Outlines irrigation projects. Shows monuments and cities
left by the ancient Egyptians including Karnak, Luxor,
the Sphinx, and Pyramids at Giza. Scenes of modern urban
life include shots of Cairo.

817   THE NILE VALLEY AND ITS PEOPLE
       1962 / 15 min / sound / color or b&w / 16 mm
       Encyclopaedia Britannica Films. (NUC FiA 62-1365) Credits:
       Collaborator - Douglas D. Crary. Locations: Iowa Films /
       Library of Congress (FBA 3572) / U. of Illinois / U. of Iowa.
       Intended for elementary to junior high school audiences.
       Traces the Nile River from its source at Lake Victoria to
       the Mediterranean. Shows the dependence of the people of
       Egypt, the Sudan and Uganda on its waters for irrigation
       and transportation. Looks at different water control
       methods from the water wheel to the Aswan High Dam.

818   THE NILE: WORLD'S LARGEST RIVER
       1973 / ? / sound / 16 mm
       Denoyer-Geppert Audio-Visual.
       Shows early civilizations along the Nile River, their
       dependence on the river, and their effect on world civi-
       lization.

819   RIVER NILE
       1962 / 34 min / sound / color / 16 mm
       Lou Hazam. NBC News. Distributed by McGraw-Hill. (NUC FiA
       67-1398) Credits: Director - Ray Garner, Narrator - James
       Mason. Locations: Kent State U. / Middle East Institute /
       New York Public Donnell Film Library / Syracuse U. / U. of
       California Extension Media Center / U. of Illinois / U. of
       Nebraska. *
       Traces history of the search for the source of the Nile
       River and looks at the people along its 4000 mile course.
       Looks at the history of civilizations along the Nile.
       Includes scenes of the Pyramids at Giza and the Aswan
       High Dam. Shorter version of no. 820. Intended for
       classroom instruction.

820   RIVER NILE
       October 28, 1962 / 52 min / sound / color / 16 mm or 3/4"
       videocassette. NBC News. (NUC FiA 63-591) Credits:
       Producer-Writer - Lou Hazam, Director - Ray Garner,
       Consultant - Henry G. Fisher, Narrator - James Mason.
       Locations: Kent State U. / Museum of Broadcasting (T790081)
       / New York Public Donnell Film Library / Syracuse U. *
       Award-winning television broadcast. Traces the history
       and course of the Nile River from Lake Victoria to the
       Mediterranean. Discusses the people, past and present,

who have lived along the banks of the Nile. Includes
scenes of Abu Simbel, the Aswan High Dam, the Pyramids,
and Sphinx. Shows villagers, fishermen and urban
dwellers, all of whom are dependent on the Nile for life.
Very well produced. A little long for classroom use.
Full version of no. 819.

821   SEARCH FOR THE NILE
1974 / six episodes, 52 min each / sound / color / 16 mm or
videocassette. BBC-TV. Distributed in the U.S. by Time-Life
Films. (LC 73-701098) Locations: New York Public Donnell
Film Library / U. of Illinois.
    Also available in Spanish soundtrack. Six part series
dramatizes the search for the origin of the Nile River by
British explorers in the 19th century. Continues to look
at African exploration of the same period. Well re-
enacted accounts. Part 1. is entitled THE DREAM OF
THE WANDERER. Traces explorers Burton and Speke in their
race to find the source of the Nile River. Other series
titles are listed separately below.

822   THE SEARCH FOR THE NILE. PART 2. DISCOVERY AND
BETRAYAL
1972 / 52 min / sound / color / 16 mm
BBC-TV. Distributed in the U.S. by Time-Life Films.
Available in videocassette and in Spanish language
soundtrack. For complete series entry, see no. 821.
Part 2 follows Burton and Speke from Zanzibar in 1856 to
Tanzania where Burton remains ill with fever. Speke
discovers Lake Victoria and returns to England with news
of his discovery. Burton feels betrayed by Speke's
actions and claims.

823   THE SEARCH FOR THE NILE. PART 3. THE SECRET
FOUNTAIN.
1972 / 52 min / sound / color / 16 mm
BBC-TV. Distributed in the U.S. by Time-Life Films.
Available in videocassette and in Spanish soundtrack.
For complete series entry, see no. 821. Speke continues
his exploration of the Nile for the Royal Geographical
Society and discovers Ripon Falls where the Nile leaves
Lake Victoria. Others, including Dr. Livingstone and
Samuel Baker, continue to explore the Nile's origin.

824   SEARCH FOR THE NILE. PART 4. THE GREAT DEBATE.
1972 / 52 min / sound / color / 16 mm
BBC-TV. Released in the U.S. by Time-Life Films.
Available in videocassette and in Spanish soundtrack.
For complete series entry, see no. 821. The Bakers continue the search for the source of the Nile in 1864,
discovering Murchison Falls and Lake Albert. Livingstone
debates Speke's claims of Lake Victoria as the source. A
public debate on the river is planned. Speke is later
found dead under mysterious circumstances.

825   SEARCH FOR THE NILE. PART 5. FIND LIVINGSTONE.
       1972 / 52 min / sound / color / 16 mm
       BBC-TV. Released in the U.S. by Time-Life Films.
       Available in videocassette and in Spanish soundtrack.
       For complete series entry, see no. 821. Dr. Livingstone
       continues to explore Africa but sends no word back to
       England. The New York Herald sends reporter Henry
       Stanley to find him. Stanley succeeds in 1871 in finding
       Livingstone who later becomes ill and dies. Stanley
       carries Livingstone's papers and body 1500 miles to the
       coast.

826   THE SEARCH FOR THE NILE. PART 6. CONQUEST AND
       DEATH.
       1972 / 52 min / sound / color / 16 mm
       BBC-TV. Released in the U.S. by Time-Life Films.
       Available in videocassette and in Spanish soundtrack.
       For complete series entry, see no. 821. Stanley con-
       tinues Livingstone's exploration work in Africa,
       including further investigation of Lake Victoria.

827   SOURCE AND COURSE OF THE NILE
       1970 / 3 min / silent / b&w / super 8 mm film loop in
       cartridge. Doubleday Multimedia. (North Africa series)
       (LC 74-708018)
       Uses animation and location footage to trace the Nile
       River from its source, through the Sudan, north to Egypt.

EGYPT - ASWAN HIGH DAM

828   ASWAN DAM
       1965 / 9 min / sound / b&w / 16 mm
       Location: U. of Colorado.
       Discusses the effect of the Aswan High Dam on Egypt.

829   ASWAN: HIGH DAM ON THE NILE
       1973 / ? / sound / 16 mm
       Denoyer-Geppert Audio-Visuals.
       Shows scenes of the building of the Aswan High Dam.

830   FOCUS ON THE ASWAN DAM - HARNESSING THE NILE
       1964 / 9 min / sound / b&w / 16 mm
       Hearst Metrotone News. (Screen News Digest, vol. 7, no. 5)
       (NUC FiA 68-2092)
       Shows the buildings of the High Dam at Aswan and
       discusses the implications of the Dam for the Nile River
       and the people of Egypt.

831   MAN CHANGES THE NILE
       1969 / 13 min / sound / color / 16 mm
       Public Media, Inc. Distributed by Films, Inc. (Man and His
       World Series) (LC 76-705480) Credits: Production -

Institut fur Film und Bild. Adaptation by Visual Education
Centre. Locations: Kent State U. / Library of Congress (FBB
1960) / Penn. State U. / U. of Illinois / U. of Nebraska. *
Uses animation to show the course of the Nile River.
Shows the smaller dams at Aswan built around the turn of
the century and the building of the Aswan High Dam.
Good aerial footage of the Dam, the Nile Valley and
fields, shows how dependent life is on Nile River water.
Footage was shot before the completion of the High Dam.
Describes the flooding cycle of the river well but is
somewhat dated. Intended for junior-high school audiences.

832   THE MEN AT THE WATERS EDGE
1965 / 28 min / sound / b&w / 16 mm
United Nations Films.
Available in English and French soundtracks. Looks at
the massive relocation of 100,000 Egyptian villagers made
necessary when the Aswan High Dam project created Lake
Nasser. Describes how thousands of acres will be flooded
above the dam. Follows one family from their partially
submerged home to their new home. Discusses differences
in life before and after the dam.

833   NILE DESERT CROPS
1972 / 3 min / silent / color / super 8 mm film loop in
cartridge. Institut fur Film und Bild, Munich. Edited and
released in the U.S. by Films Incorporated. (Man and His
World series) (LC 72-701556)
Shows how dependent the Egyptian farmer is on the waters
of the Nile River for agriculture and irrigation.
Discusses significance of the Aswan High Dam project for
farmers. Looks at potential spread of cultivatable land
into formerly desert regions.

EGYPT - AGRICULTURE

834   COTTON IN EGYPT
1969 / 13 min / sound / color / 16 mm
Public Media, Inc. Released by Films Incorporated. Edited
version of film made by Institut fur Film und Bild, Munich.
(Man and His World series) (LC 70-704759)
Explains the importance of cotton to the Egyptian economy.
Describes the method by which cotton is grown and har-
vested, how the fibers are separated, and the cotton is
baled and exported. Looks at the Cotton Exchange in
Alexandria.

835   EGYPT VILLAGE IRRIGATION
1966 / 4 min / silent / color / super or standard 8 mm
Gateway Film Productions, London. Released in the U.S. by
International Communication Films. Distributed by Walt

169

Disney Productions, and by Doubleday Multimedia. (North
Africa series) (LC 71-700519)
   Listed in some catalogs as released in 1964. Shows irrigation of crops in Egypt using the water lever, water
   wheel and tube devices for water transport. Covers irrigation methods in other countries as well.

836   FARMERS OF THE NILE VALLEY
      (c. 1963) / 18 min / sound / b&w / 16 mm
      United World Films. Distributed by Didactic Films, Ltd.
      (Your World Neighbors series) (NUC FiA 63-909) Credits:
      Educational Collaborator - Clyde F. Kohn.
         Intended for junior high school to college audiences.
         Profiles the farming community at Garawan, north of
         Cairo. Shows standard traditional methods of irrigation
         and cultivation of fields. Discusses life style of rural
         families.

837   THE GREEN SANDS
      (n.d.) / 8 min / sound / 16 mm
      Embassy of Egypt. No other information available.

838   HARVESTING AND THRESHING BARLEY (FELLAHIN,
      NORTH AFRICA, UPPER EGYPT)
      1963, released 1964 / 17 min / silent / color / 16 mm
      Encyclopaedia Cinematographica. Distributed by Pennsylvania
      State University. (Ency. Cinematographica no. E 688)
         Another in a series of silent ethnographic films
         depicting traditional activities. Shows Egyptian farmers
         harvesting crops of barley.

839   LIFE AROUND THE WORLD: AFRICA - NILE FARMER
      1972 / 4 min / silent / color / super 8 mm film loop in
      cartridge. Coronet Instructional Materials. (LC 72-702493)
         Shows scenes of villagers farming along the Nile River in
         Egypt.

840   (PRIMITIVE IRRIGATION IN EGYPT)
      June 1903 / 57 seconds / silent / b&w / 16 mm
      Thomas Edison. Library of Congress Paper Print Collection.
      Location: Library of Congress (FLA 3592)   *
         Another of the series of films made by A.C. Abadie for
         Thomas Edison. Shows several traditional methods for
         drawing water used in Egypt including a rope and bucket
         counterweighted with stones and an ox-powered water
         wheel. For documentary and historic purposes. Library
         of Congress print is in poor condition due to age.

841   SUGAR IN EGYPT
      1969 / 13 min / sound / color / 16 mm
      Public Media, Inc. Released by Films Incorporated. Edited
      version of the film made by Institut fur Film und Bild,
      Munich. (Man and His World series) (Man at Work series)

(LC 77-705467) Locations: Kent State U. / Library of
Congress (FBB 1935) / Penn. State U. / U. of Illinois / U.
of Nebraska.
Intended for junior high school to college audiences.
Profiles the Egyptian sugar industry. Shows efforts
being made to change cultivation of sugar from small
farms to larger, modernized sugar plantations. Contrasts
traditional hand processing and machine farming of sugar.

842   TOWARDS BETTER NUTRITION
1955 / 12 min / sound / b&w / 35 mm
Ministry of Agriculture. Distributed by Ministry of Culture
and National Guidance, Egypt. Credits: Producer - Saad
Nadim.
Documents the work of the Egyptian Ministry of
Agriculture in its attempt to introduce new technologies,
diversify crops and increase production. Looks at rice,
fish, milk farming and animal husbandry.

843   WATER-RAISING WORKS (FELLAHIN, NORTH AFRICA, EGYPT)
1957, released 1962 / 4 min / silent / b&w / 16 mm
Encyclopaedia Cinematographica. Distributed by Pennsylvania
State University. (Ency. Cinematographica no. E 117)
Another in the series of silent ethnographic films
featuring a traditional activity. Looks at irrigation
and traditional methods of transporting water used in
Egypt.

EGYPT - EDUCATION, MEDICINE

844   ALONG THE NILE
1956 / 29 min / sound / b&w / 16 mm
Dept. of Cinema, University of Southern California.
Released by NET Film Service. (The Written Word) (NUC FiA
60-698) Credits: Host - Dr. Frank Baxter.
Intended for elementary-junior high school audiences.
Describes history of ancient Egyptian writing and education. Shows development of picture symbols into
hieroglyphics, demotic and Coptic writing. Shows how
papyrus was used to produce paper.

845   EDUCATION IN EGYPT
(n.d.) / 8 min / sound / 16 mm
Embassy of Egypt.
Describes educational opportunities and programs in Egypt
sponsored by the Egyptian government.

846   OPERATION BEHEIRA
1965 / 10 min / sound / b&w / 16 mm
World Health Organization. Distributed by United Nations
Films.
Available in English and French soundtracks. Describes

171

the work of the World Health Organization in its attempts
to control schistosomiasis in Beheira, Egypt. Shows
health education programs and preventive measures used to
control the snails that transmit schistosomiasis.

EGYPT - THE ARTS

847   ARABESQUE
      1974 / 20 min / sound / color / 16 mm
      Telmissany Brothers Production. Distributed by the Ministry
      of Information, Egypt.
         Documents Arab Islamic decorative arts. Examples include
         architectural ornamentation, minarets, domes, woodwork,
         marble inlay, mother-of-pearl inlay and stained glass
         work. Filmed on location in Egypt in various ruins,
         ancient palaces and modern buildings.

848   ART STUDIO IN THE VILLAGE
      1973 / 30 min / sound / color / 16 mm
      Telmissany Brothers Productions. Distributed by the
      Ministry of Information, Egypt, and the Egyptian Government
      Tourist Office, New York.
         Documents the work of Dr. Ramses Wissa Wassef in making
         carpets, tapestries and weavings. Shows education of
         children in his village of Harrania, Egypt, in these
         crafts.

849   AS I WANDER
      (n.d.) / 40 min / sound / color / 16 mm
      Distributed by the Egyptian Government Tourist Office, New
      York.
         Documents the various arts and crafts produced and sold
         in the Khan el Khalili market quarter of Cairo. Includes
         traditional crafts, such as wood working, metal working,
         sewing and embroidery, stained glass work and pottery.

850   FOLK DANCE (BAMBOUTIA)
      (n.d.) / 5 min / sound / 16 mm
      Embassy of Egypt. No other information available.

851   MOKHTAR THE SCULPTOR
      1957 / 14 min / sound / b&w / 35 mm
      Wali-el-Din Sameh. Distributed by the Ministry of Culture
      and National Guidance, Egypt.
         Documents the life and works of monumental sculptor
         Mokhtar of Egypt.

852   NAGUI THE ARTIST
      1957 / 12 min / sound / color / 35 mm
      Ihsan Farghal. Distributed by the Ministry of Culture and
      National Guidance, Egypt.
         Depicts the life and works of renowned Egyptian painter
         Nagui.

ETHIOPIA - HISTORY

853 ETHIOPIA - AFRICA'S ANCIENT KINGDOM
1962 / 17 min / sound / color / 16 mm
Paul Hoefler Productions. Distributed by BFA Educational
Services. (Far Places Series) (NUC FiA 62-1302)
Locations: Brigham Young U. / Indiana U. / Oregon State
System of Higher Education / U. of Arizona / U. of
California / U. of Illinois / U. of Kentucky / U. of
Minnesota / U. of Utah / U. of Washington.
General look at the history of Ethiopia. Describes how
the country is cut off due to poor communications and
transportation. Traces the development of the Coptic
religion and Amharic language in Ethiopia. Discusses the
long tradition of hereditary monarchs and the various
tribal groups who make up the population of Ethiopia.
Profiles Haile Selassie and shows scenes of traditional
and modern Ethiopia.

854 ETHIOPIA: CULTURES IN CHANGE
1971 / 20 min / sound / color / 16 mm
National Geographic Society. Released by Films Incorporated.
(LC 77-715390) Location: Syracuse U.
Shorter version of ETHIOPIA: THE HIDDEN EMPIRE,
no. 856. For junior-senior high school audiences.
Traces the history, geography and livelihood of the people
of Ethiopia. Shows Christian, Muslim and Jewish communities and their ways of life.

855 ETHIOPIA: EMPIRE ON THE MOUNTAIN
1965 / 20 min / sound / color / 16 mm
Sterling Educational Films. Made by G. Franco Romagnoli and
Robert J. Giuliana. (NUC FiA 66-551) Location: Syracuse U.
Intended for elementary to senior high school audiences.
Describes geography and history of Ethiopia. Shows the
traditional way of life followed by most of its people.
Discusses the role played by the monarchy and Coptic
Church in Ethiopian life.

856 ETHIOPIA: THE HIDDEN EMPIRE
1970 / 50 min / sound / color / 16 mm
Metromedia Producers Corp. National Geographic Society. (A
National Geographic Society Special, television series) (LC
76-710943) Credits: Producer-Director - N.H. Cominois,
Writers - Jack Kaufman, N.H. Cominois, Photographer - Andre
Gunn. Locations: Brigham Young U. / Florida State U. / Kent

State U. / Library of Congress (FDA 935) / Penn. State U. /
Syracuse U. / U. of Arizona / U. of Florida / U. of Illinois
/ U. of Iowa / U. of Kansas / U. of Michigan / U. of
Nebraska / U. of South Carolina / U. of Washington / U. of
Wisconsin. *
Originally broadcast as a National Geographic Society
Special. Beautifully photographed documentary presen-
tation. One of the single best introductions to
Ethiopia. Covers geography, history of Christian, Muslim
and European influence on Ethiopia, traditional and
modern cities and ways of life. Shows Falasha Jews and
other minorities. Traces the history of the Italian invasion and domination preceding and during WWII. Profiles
emperor Haile Selassie and shows his close ties to the
Ethiopian Orthodox Church. Visually stunning film with
beautiful background music. An excellent look at
Ethiopia before the revolution. Recommended.

857 MAN IN ETHIOPIA
1967 / 26 min / sound / color / 16 mm
Independent Film Producers Company. Location: U. of
Illinois.
Looks at traditional and modern Ethiopia from villages to
life in the capital city of Addis Ababa. Covers
Judeo-Christian traditions in Ethiopia. Looks at
archeological evidence which may point to the Ethiopian
highlands as the location of earliest man.

858 THE SECURITY COUNCIL IN AFRICA
1972 / 16 min / sound / color / 16 mm
United Nations.
Available in English and French soundtracks. Documents
the meeting of the U.N. Security Council in Addis Ababa
in 1972 to discuss the position of African nations and
the U.N. on South Africa. Marked the first time the
Council had met outside of New York in twenty years.
Includes address of Haile Selassie, Emperor of Ethiopia
to the Council.

ETHIOPIA - ITALIAN INVASION AND WORLD WAR II

859 ETHIOPIA: 50 YEARS OF HISTORY
1955 / 20 min / silent / b&w / 16 mm
George Rony Collection. Distributed by Educational Film
Enterprises, Inc. Credits: Producer-Narrator - George Rony,
Technical Advisor - Rudy Behlmer. Location: Library of
Congress (FBB 3635) *
Difficult to follow due to lack of narration or sub-
titles. Shows scenes of desert, village and urban
life in Ethiopia, Haile Selassie, Mussolini, the Italian
invasion of Ethiopia, warships, the evacuation of
Europeans from Ethiopia, and destruction following the

174

invasion. Follows the work of Selassie in England and
the U.S. and his attempts to collect guns and support to
recapture Ethiopia from the Italians. Useful as a source
of library footage.

860 (ETHIOPIA, WAR IN AFRICA)
(c. 1936-1955) / 30 min / silent / b&w / 16 mm
George Rony. Educational Films. Location: Library of
Congress (FBB 3697-98) *
Difficult to follow due to lack of soundtrack or titles.
Contains some excellent footage, useful for library
footage films or documentary purposes. Contains scenes
of Haile Selassie, Ethiopian tribesmen, Addis Ababa and
the Ethiopian countryside. Reel 2 contains crowds with
"We Reject Partition" signs, Christians and Muslims,
tanks entering Addis Ababa, and Selassie in America
gathering support to fight the Italians. Then switches
back to Italian war footage and Mussolini. Difficult to
ascertain the location or meaning of some pieces of film.
Scenes are not in any chronological order. Some footage
is repeated and scenes from different decades and places
are spliced together.

861 ITALIAN CONQUEST OF ETHIOPIA
1967 / 5 min / silent / b&w / standard or super 8 mm
Thorne Films. (8 mm Documents Project, no. 133) (NUC FiA
67-5456) Credits: Producer - Dale C. Willard.
Scenes include Mussolini delivering a speech from his
balcony, Italian troops entering Ethiopia, Ethiopian
troops resisting the invasion, the surrender of Ethiopia
to the Italians and Mussolini celebrating the victory.

862 ITALY INVADES ETHIOPIA
1960 / 3 min / sound / b&w / 16 mm
Filmrite Associates. Released by Official Films. (Greatest
Headlines of the Century series) Credits: Producer - Sherm
Grinberg, Narrator - Tom Hudson, Writers - Allan Lurie, Ray
Parker. Location: Library of Congress (FAA 3786) *
Uses newsreel footage. Recreates the October 3, 1935
Italian invasion of Ethiopia as a result of an incident
along the Eritrean border. Haile Selassie gathers tribesmen to resist Italian tanks. Shows scenes of destruction and Selassie at the League of Nations calling for
action to aid Ethiopia. On May 5, 1936, Addis Ababa
falls. Selassie travels to Palestine looking for support. Good footage. Well edited presentation of the
Italian invasion.

863 THE LIGHT OF ETHIOPIA
1956 / 25 min / sound / b&w / 16 mm
Educational Film Enterprises. (Fifty Years of History
series) (NUC Fi A 56-954) Credits - Producer-Writer and
Narrator - George Rony.

175

Documents the Italian invasion of Ethiopia and work by
Haile Selassie to gather world support to confront Italy
and recapture Ethiopia.

864   MUSSOLINI VS. SELASSIE
       1964 / 25 min / sound / b&w / 16 mm
       Wolper Productions. Released by Public Media, Inc. (Men in
       Crisis series) (LC 70-706745) Credits: Narrator - Edmond
       O'Brien.
           Shows the struggle of Emperor Haile Selassie to resist
           the Italian invasion of Ethiopia in 1936. Includes sce-
           nes of air raids on Adowa and Addis Ababa.

865   RETURN OF AN EMPEROR: THE STORY OF ETHIOPIA
       (c. 1944-45) / 9 min / sound / b&w / 16 mm
       African Film Production, Ltd. Ministry of Information,
       London. Credits: Director-Photographer - Guy Johnson,
       Narrator - Wensley Pithey. Locations: Library of Congress
       (FAA 524) / U. of Missouri, Columbia. *
           Quick run through Ethiopian history from the 1920's to
           the period following WWII, presented from a British
           viewpoint. Uses Beethoven as musical background. Shows
           scenes of Selassie at the League of Nations, Italy
           invading Ethiopia, Selassie taking refuge in England, the
           five year struggle to retake Addis Ababa from the
           Italians, and the final relocation of all Ethiopian
           Italian nationals after the war. Newsreel presentation.
           Of use for library footage and documentary purposes.

866   WAR NEARS END IN ABYSSINIA
       1935 / 6 min / sound / b&w / 35 mm
       Paramount News. (Signal Corp. Misc. Film, no. 503)
       Location: National Archives (111M503)
           Paramount newsreel. Gives a contemporary view of the
           Italian invasion of Ethiopia.

ETHIOPIA   -   INTERVIEWS AND BIOGRAPHIES

867   HAILE SELASSIE
       October 6, 1963 / 28 min / sound / b&w / 16 mm
       NBC Television. (Meet the Press, television series)
       Location: Library of Congress (FRA 7437-39)
           Moderated panel discussion featuring Ethiopian Emperor
           Haile Selassie.

868   LION OF JUDAH: HAILE SELASSIE
       1972 / 50 min / sound / color / 16 mm
       BBC-TV, London. Released in the U.S. by Time-Life Films.
       (LC 73-700665)
           Traces events in the life of Ethiopian Emperor Haile
           Selassie and indirectly traces the history of Ethiopia
           from the 1920's to the 1970's.

869 ETHIOPIAN DANCES
1965 / 24 min / sound / b&w / 16 mm
Hungarian Academy of Sciences, Folk Music Research Group.
Distributed by the Folk Music Research Group, Hungarian
Academy of Science, Roosevelter 9, Budapest.
Filmed on location in Dessie, Hayk, Kuaram, Makale,
Aksum, Enda Selassie, Lekemti, Harar and Dire Dawa.
Documents folk music and dances of Ethiopia. Includes
Tigrean flute and drum dances, Somalian umbrella dance,
Amhara neck and shoulder dance, Galla couple line dance,
Amhara group dance, Galla hunter dance and war and sword
dances.

870 FALASHAS
1974 / 28 min / sound / color / 16 mm
Meyer Levin. Distributed by the New Jewish Media Project,
New York.
Documents the Falasha Jewish community of Ethiopia.

871 MINING OF IRON (DIME, NORTH-EAST AFRICA, SOUTH
ETHIOPIA)
1927, released 1961 / 8 min / silent / b&w / 16 mm
Encyclopaedia Cinematographica. Distributed by Pennsylvania
State University. (Ency. Cinematographica no. E 388)
Another in the series of silent ethnographic films
depicting a single traditional activity. Shows ore
mining operations in Ethiopia.

872 MOURNING CELEBRATIONS (SALA, NORTH-EAST AFRICA,
SOUTH ETHIOPIA)
1951, released 1959 / 6 min / silent / b&w / 16 mm
Encyclopaedia Cinematographica. Distributed by Pennsylvania
State University. (Ency. Cinematographica no. E 266)
Another in the series of silent ethnographic films
depicting a traditional activity. Shows Ethiopian
mourning customs.

873 MOURNING CELEBRATIONS AND BURIAL OF A WOMAN
(SHANGAMA, NORTH-EAST AFRICA, SOUTH ETHIOPIA)
1951, released 1959 / 9 min / silent / b&w / 16 mm
Encyclopaedia Cinematographica. Distributed by Pennsylvania
State University. (Ency. Cinematographica no. E 267)
Silent ethnographic film. Depicts traditional Ethiopian
burial and mourning customs.

874 OBSEQUIES FOR A HIGH DIGNITARY AND FOR TWO
WOMEN OF HIS RELATIONSHIP (SIDAMO, NORTH-EAST
AFRICA, SOUTH ETHIOPIA)
1955, released 1960 / 13 min / silent / color / 16 mm
Encyclopaedia Cinematographica. Distributed by Pennsylvania
State University. (Ency. Cinematographica no. E 257)

Silent ethnographic film. Documents relationship between dignitaries and common people in Ethiopia.

875   ON THE ETHIOPIAN FRONTIER
(c. 1911-15) / 4 min / silent / b&w / 16 mm
Pathe, Kleine Collection. Location: Library of Congress
(FLA 1697) *
Footage shows men roasting meat over a fire, tribesmen dancing and a dead hippo being picked over by birds. A European shoots a bird which is then eaten by a crocodile. Men are shown fishing with spears. Miscellaneous footage of little use even as historical or library footage.

876   PROCESSING HIDES AND SKINS (DARASSA AND SIDAMO, NORTH-EAST AFRICA, SOUTH ETHIOPIA)
1955, released 1960 / 17 min / silent / b&w / 16 mm
Encyclopaedia Cinematographica. Distributed by Pennsylvania State University. (Ency. Cinematographica no. E 256)
Another in the series of silent ethnographic films portraying a single traditional activity. Shows method for processing hides.

877   RIVERS OF SAND
1974 / 83 min / sound / color / 16 mm
Robert Gardner. Released by Phoenix Films. (LC 74-703498)
Locations: Kent State U. / New York Public Donnell Film Library / Penn. State U. / Syracuse U. / U. of California at Berkeley / U. of Illinois.
Intended for senior high school to adult audiences. Documents traditional male-oriented life of the Hamar of southwestern Ethiopia. Discusses the role of men and women, burial customs, and the hunting and agricultural basis of society. Includes scenes of animals being slaughtered.

878   THE SILENT SKY
(n.d.) / 8 min / sound / color / 16 mm
United Nations Children's Fund. Distributed by United Nations Films.
Available in English and French soundtracks. Shows drought and famine in Ethiopia. Describes U.N. programs to assist victims of the drought. Depicts conditions along the border of Somalia and Kenya.

879   SOMALIA
1968 / 26 min / sound / color / 16 mm
AV-ED Production. (LC 72-701204)
Despite the title, supposedly deals with the geography, customs, religions and traditional way of life in Ethiopia.

880   TEENAGERS OF THE WORLD: ETHIOPIA
(n.d.) / 27 min / sound / color / 16 mm

178

United Nations Children's Fund. Distributed by United
Nations Films.
Available in English and French soundtracks. Shows work
done by UNICEF to train young Ethiopians in various tra-
des and skills. Shows how training projects relate to
modernization, development and future planning.

881   TWO BOYS OF ETHIOPIA
1970 / 20 min / sound / color / 16 mm
Encyclopaedia Britannica Educational Corp. Made by Visual
Education Centre. (The African Scene series) (LC 77-712321)
Locations: Kent State U. / Library of Congress (FBB 0183).
For elementary-junior high school audiences. Contrasts
the life of a young boy from Addis Ababa, the capital of
Ethiopia, with a young mountain boy who must share tasks
and responsibilities with adults in his village.

ETHIOPIA - TRAVELOGS AND REGIONAL STUDIES

882   ADDIS ABABA - PAN AFRICAN CENTER
1970 / 4 min / silent / color / super 8 mm film loop
Ealing Corporation. (Africa series) (LC 70-706777)
Shows life in Addis Ababa. Contrast new modern buildings
and apartments to the slums on the outskirts of the city.

883   BIRTHDAY FOR ERITREA
1953 / 10 min / sound / b&w / 16 mm
United Nations Dept. of Public Information. (NUC FiA
62-1277)
Describes the status of Eritrea as a new nation federated
to Ethiopia, according to a U.N. agreement. Shows the
people, geography and social and economic problems of
the new nation.

884   (ETHIOPIA)
(n.d.) / 2 rolls / sound / 16 mm
Peace Corps. Location: National Archives (RG 362-31) No
other information available.

885   ETHIOPIA
1968 / 26 min / sound / color / 16 mm
AV-ED Films. Made by Helene Fischer. (LC 76-701193)
General look at Ethiopia. Covers geography, economy,
customs and ethnic and tribal composition of the nation.

886   ETHIOPIA: THE LION AND THE CROSS, PARTS 1-2
1963 / 54 min / sound / b&w / 16 mm
CBS News. (The Twentieth Century, television series) (NUC
Fi 67-152) Credits: Producer - Isaac Kleinerman,
Director-Writer - Harry Rasby, Narrator - Walter Cronkite.
Location: Library of Congress (FCA 3653-54)
Television news program. Looks at poverty and living

179

conditions in Ethiopia. Includes interviews with Emperor
Haile Selassie, Peace Corps. workers and students.
Highlights efforts being made in Ethiopia to modernize
the country.

887   ETHIOPIA: NEW FRONTIER OF TRAVEL
      (n.d.) / 26 min / sound / color / 16 mm
      Location: U. of Illinois.
            General travelog of Ethiopia. Tours the modern capital
            city of Addis Ababa and shows wild game found in the back
            country. Shows tribal and city life and programs sup-
            ported by Haile Selassie to modernize Ethiopia.

888   ETHIOPIA 9
      (n.d.) / 14 min / sound / 16 mm
      Association Films. Location: Library of Congress.
            Describes problems of disease and health care in
            Ethiopia. Describes what is being done to curb epidemic
            diseases. Looks at lack of hospitals and doctors in pre-
            sent health programs.

889   ETHIOPIAN MOSAIC
      1967 / 10 min / sound / color / 16 or 35 mm
      National Film Board of Canada. Distributed by the
      International Film Bureau. (NUC FiA 68-1240) Credits:
      Producer - Hugh O'Connor, Photographer - David Mayerovitch.
      Locations: New York Public Donnell Film Library / Syracuse
      U. / U. of Illinois.
            Available in English and French soundtracks. Presents a
            montage of images of modern and traditional Ethiopia.
            Uses no narration. Intended for junior high school to
            adult audiences.

890   THE OLD AFRICA AND THE NEW: ETHIOPIA AND BOTSWANA
      1968 / 17 min / sound / color / 16 mm
      ABC. Released by McGraw-Hill. (ABC News Presentation)
      (NUC FiA 68-314) Locations: Indiana U. / U. of Illinois.
            Traces the problems faced by all African nations.
            Contrasts the particular problems associated with newly
            independent nations, like Botswana, to those faced by tra-
            ditional governments such as Ethiopia.

ETHIOPIA - AGRICULTURE

891   CULTIVATION OF THE LAND (SHANGAMA, NORTH-EAST
      AFRICA, SOUTH ETHIOPIA)
      1951, released 1959 / 9 min / silent / b&w / 16 mm
      Encyclopaedia Cinematographica. Distributed by Pennsylvania
      State University. (Ency. Cinematographica no. E 265)
            Another in the series of silent ethnographic films
            depicting one typical traditional activity. Shows
            Ethiopian farming methods.

180

892   LAND OF THE QUEEN OF SHEBA
1971 / 27 min / sound / color / 16 mm
Food and Agriculture Organization of the United Nations.
Distributed by United Nations Films.
Narrated by Peter Ustinov. Looks at traditional
Ethiopian agriculture and animal husbandry. Follows traditional and modern methods being used to manage herds
and fields. Describes problem of protecting wildlife
areas containing rare animal species.

MUSLIM AND MUGHAL INDIA

MUGHAL HISTORY

893   AKBAR
      1967 / 23 min / sound / color / 16 mm
      Bhownagary. Distributed by the Embassy of India.
      Intended for high school to adult audiences. Traces the
      life and religious beliefs of the Mughal Emperor Akhbar.
      Uses illustrations and miniature paintings of the 16th
      century.

894   THE DELHI WAY
      1964 / 45 min / sound / color / 16 mm
      James Ivory. Credits: Director-Writer-Photographer - James
      Ivory, Music - Vilayat Khan.
      Uses old film footage, paintings and photographs to
      reproduce a picture of the city of Delhi during the
      Mughal and British periods.

895   THE GREAT MOGUL
      1969 / 30 min / sound / color / 16 mm
      BBC-TV. Released in the U.S. by Time-Life Films. (The
      Glory That Remains series) (LC 76-714488) Credits:
      Writer-Narrator - Robert Erskine.
      Shows the deserted city of Fathepur-Sikri built by
      Akhbar, the third Mughal emperor. Describes how the city
      was abandoned due to lack of a safe water supply. Also
      shows port of Agra and the Taj Mahal.

896   INDIA - ARTS AND ARTISANS
      1964 / 17 min / sound / color / 16 mm
      Producer unknown. Location: U. of Illinois.
      Shows various regions of India and describes the types of
      arts and crafts each is noted for producing. Looks at
      architecture, textiles, woodcarving, lacquer work, rugs,
      metal work, enamaling, and jewelry making. Shows scenes
      of the Taj Mahal.

897   INDIA'S HINDI AND MOSLEM HERITAGE
      1963 / 4 min / silent / color / 8 mm
      International Communications Foundation. (South Asia: India
      series) (NUC FiA 63-1493) Credits: Writer - L. Van Mourick.
      Traces stages in Indian architecture from ancient Hindu
      buildings to later Mughal sites. Shows the Taj Mahal
      and ancient Hindu temples.

898   INDIA'S HISTORY: MOGUL EMPIRE TO EUROPEAN
      COLONIZATION

1956 / 11 min / sound / color or b&w / 16 mm
Coronet Instructional Films. (Part 3 of the India's History
series) (NUC Fi 56-199) Credits: Educational Collaborator -
Merrill R. Goodall. Locations: Boston U. / Florida State U. /
Indiana U. / Kent State U. / Library of Congress (FAA 4024)
/ Syracuse U. / U. of Arizona / U. of California at Los
Angeles / U. of Colorado / U. of Illinois / U. of Kansas /
U. of Minnesota / U. of Nebraska / U. of North Carolina / U.
of Washington. *
    Intended for junior high school to college audiences.
    Traces Indian history from 1200 to 1760. Looks at the
    influences introduced by Muslim rulers of India including
    monotheism and new styles of art and architecture.
    Traces major historical events leading to the decline of
    the Mughal rulers. Describes early exploration of India
    by the Portuguese, English and French. Covers a great
    deal of time in a short film with fair results.

899   JAIPUR
      1958 / 28 min / sound / color / 16 mm
      Government of India Films Division. Ministry of Information
      and Broadcasting, Bombay. (NUC Fi 67-2325) Credits:
      Producer - Ezra Mir, Director - Shanti Varma. Location:
      Library of Congress (FBA 4749)
          General travelog of the city of Jaipur built by Jai Singh
          II in 1728. Shows the port of Amber, the Sheesh Mahal,
          the observatory and Hawa Mahal. Includes scenes of local
          festivals and handicrafts.

900   LAND OF THE TAJ MAHAL
      1952 / 8 min / sound / color / 35 mm
      Loew's Inc. (James A. FitzPatrick's Traveltalks series)
      (NUC Fi 52-1192) Credits: Producer-Narrator - James A.
      FitzPatrick, Music - Joseph Nussbaum. Technicolor.
          Theatrically released travelog. Tours Bombay, Delhi
          and Agra. Includes scenes of the Taj Mahal, Hindu
          temples, theaters in Delhi, folk dances and scenes of
          everyday life.

901   MAGNIFICENT MEMORY
      1956 / 10 min / sound / b&w / 16 mm
      D.R.D. Productions and Film Group of India. Released in the
      U.S. by Information Service of India. Distributed by the
      Embassy of India. (NUC FiA 58-122)
          Shows the court of the Mughal emperor Shah Jahan.
          Includes a presentation of the kathak dance of northern
          India.

902   MIRZA GHALIB
      1969 / 20 min / sound / b&w / 16 mm
      Distributed by the Embassy of India.
          Biography of Mirza Asad Allah Khan Ghalib, an early 19th
          century writer who produced works in both Persian and

183

Urdu. Segments from his works are read behind photographs, engravings and live footage to evoke an image of his times.

903 THE MOGHULS
     (n.d.) / 10 min / sound / 16 mm
     Distributed by the Embassy of India. No other information available.

904 THE PINK CITY
     1969 / 30 min / sound / color / 16 mm
     BBC-TV. Released in the U.S. by Time-Life Films. (The Glory That Remains series, no. 7) (LC 70-714489) Credits: Writer-Narrator - Robert Erskine. Location: U. of Illinois. Looks at history, architecture and art of Jaipur during the reigns of Man Singh, Jai Singh and Sawai Jai Singh, its three most famous rulers. Includes scenes of the observatory as well as palaces and gardens.

905 RAJASTAN: PART 1 JAIPUR
     1951 / 11 min / sound / b&w / 16 mm
     Government of India Films Division, Ministry of Information and Broadcasting, Bombay. Released in the U.S. by Information Service of India. (NUC FiA 58-142)
        Travelog of Jaipur, capital city of Rajastan. Shows the observatory of Jai Singh built in 1727. Includes scenes of the Hawa Mahal, Heera Mandir and Jantar Mantar.

906 RAJASTAN: PART 2 MEMORIES OF MEWAR
     1950 / 10 min / sound / b&w / 16 mm
     Government of India Films Division, Ministry of Information and Broadcasting, Bombay. Released in the U.S. by Information Service of India. (NUC FiA 58-128) Location: Library of Congress (FAA 6131)
        Travelog of Udaipur, the capital of Mewar. Includes scenes of the Jagmandar Palace, Jagdish Mandir, and Maharaja's palace and gardens.

907 RAJASTAN: LAND OF THE CAMEL
     1951 / 11 min / sound / b&w / 16 mm
     Government of India Films Division, Ministry of Information and Broadcasting, Bombay. Released in the U.S. by Information Service of India. (NUC FiA 58-144)
        Shows Rajastan on the northwestern frontier of India. Includes scenes of temples, palaces and the Bikaner Camel Corps.

908 THE SWORD AND THE FLUTE
     1959 / 22 min / sound / color / 16 mm
     James Ivory. Released by Film Images. Distributed by Radim Films. (NUC FiA 59-522) Credits: Narrator - James Ivory, Music - Ravi Shankar. Locations: New York Public Donnell Film Library / Oklahoma State U. / U. of California at Los

Angeles / U. of Connecticut / U. of Iowa / U. of Minnesota /
U. of Missouri / U. of Utah / U. of Washington / U. of
Wisconsin. *
Uses 16th to 18th century Mughal miniatures to recreate
the courtly life of the Turkoman Muslim emperor Akhbar.
Describes the ascetic life of Indian mystics and Hindu
influence on Muslim art. Beautifully filmed.
Accentuated by a Ravi Shankar score. One of the most
stylish films on the history of art and life of Mughal
India. Intended for junior high school to adult audien-
ces.

909   TAJ MAHAL
(n.d.) / 14 min / sound / color / 16 mm
Distributed by the Embassy of India.
Shows the detailed stone inlay work and beautiful gardens
of the Taj Mahal, built by Shah Jahan as a memorial to
Mumtaz Mahal.

910   TAJ MAHAL
1948 / 20 min / sound / color / 16 mm
Romantic Travel Films, Franklin Sahu Films Production, India.
Released in the U.S. by Information Service of India. (NUC
FiA 58-37)
Shows the beauty and detail of the Taj Mahal built bet-
ween 1630-1648 by Shah Jahan in memory of Mumtaz Mahal.

911   (UDAIPUR AND JAIPUR)
(1930?) / 10 min / silent / b&w / 16 mm
Producer unknown. (LC 73-704292) Location: Library of
Congress (FAA 4415)
Sub-titled travelog. Shows palaces, gardens and natural
sites of Udaipur and Jaipur in northwest India.

912   UDAIPUR: CITY OF LAKES
1961 / 13 min / sound / color / 16 mm
Government of India Films Division, Ministry of Information
and Broadcasting, Bombay. (NUC Fi 67-2330) Credits:
Producer - Ezra Mir, Director-Writer - P.R.S. Pillay.
Location: Library of Congress (FAA 5927)
Shows scenes of the lakes, palaces, temples and gardens
of the city of Udaipur in the state of Rajastan.

MUSLIM AND MUGHAL INDIA   -   MUSLIM LIFE IN INDIA TODAY

913   CENTERS OF ISLAMIC STUDIES
(n.d.) / 25 min / sound / color / 16 mm
Information Service of India.
Shows opportunities for Muslim education in India and
various Muslim educational institutions.

914   INDIAN MUSLIMS AND THEIR RELIGIOUS OBSERVANCE
1971 / 25 min / sound / color or b&w / 16 mm

Ashis Muckherjee. Distributed by the Information Service of India.
Depicts the mixture of Muslim and Hindu traditions in India. Shows shrines at which both Muslims and Hindus worship. Includes scenes of Muslim festivals in India, the Islamic University, Taj Mahal and a Muslim wedding.

915   JAMA MASJID STREET JOURNAL
1979 / 20 min / sound / b&w / 16 mm or videocassette
Mira Nair. Distributed by Icarus Films. *
Uses a minimum of narration. Shows life in the Muslim minority community in India. Focuses on the community near the Jama Masjid or Great Mosque in the old city of Delhi. Shows interaction between people in the community and between the community and the film-maker.

916   JAMIA MILLIA ISLAMIA
(n.d.) / 12 min / sound / b&w / 16 mm
Information Service of India. Distributed by the Embassy of India.
Shows the National Muslim University at Okhla near New Delhi. Describes the functions and activities of the university and its role as a Muslim center of learning in the Hindu state.

917   MUSLIM FESTIVALS IN INDIA
(n.d.) / 12 min / sound / color / 16 mm
Information Service of India. Distributed by the Embassy of India.
Listed in some catalogs as: MUSLIM FESTIVALS IN SECULAR INDIA. Shows two Muslim festivals which are national holidays in India, Id-ul-Fitr and Id-uz-Zuha. Shows celebration of these two festivals by thousands of Indian Muslims at the Jama Masjid or Great Mosque in Delhi.

918   RANA
1977 / 19 min / sound / color / 16 mm
Wombat, Films Australia. (Our Asian Neighbors series)
Locations: U. of Illinois / U. of Washington.
A 21 year old Muslim college student in India discusses traditional family life and customs practised by Muslims in Delhi. Includes segments on purdah, the extended household, arranged marriages and women's place in society.

IRAN

IRAN - ARCHEOLOGY

919   THE BROKEN COLUMN
       1969 / 15 min / sound / color / 16 mm
       Iran Information and Tourism Center. Formerly distributed
       by the Embassy of Iran.
          Shows 2500 year old ruins at the city of Persepolis built
       by the Archaemenids, rulers of the early Iranian empire.

920   HOLY PIT (ANCIENT IRANIAN ATHLETIC RITUALS)
       (n.d.) / 20 min / sound / color / 16 mm
       Formerly distributed by the Embassy of Iran. No other infor-
       mation available.

921   MUSEUM OF ANTHROPOLOGY
       (c. 1960?) / 10 min / sound / 16 mm
       Formerly distributed by the Embassy of Iran. No other infor-
       mation available.

922   SEARCH IN THE PAST
       (c. 1960?) / 17 min / sound / color / 16 mm
       Formerly distributed by the Embassy of Iran.
          Exams the ancient ruins of Persepolis, former capital of
       the Archaemenid Iranian empire.

IRAN - HISTORY OF ANCIENT PERSIA

923   ANCIENT CIVILIZATIONS: PERSIA
       1974 / 4 min / silent / color / super 8 mm film loop in
       cartridge. Coronet Instructional Media. (LC 74-701518)
          Silent with captions. Follows the growth, decline and
       final days of the Persian Empire. Covers the conquest of
       the empire by Alexander the Great.

924   ANCIENT PERSIA
       1964 / 11 min / sound / color or b&w / 16 mm
       Coronet Instructional Films. (NUC FiA 64-1035) Credits:
       Collaborator - Pinhas P. Delougaz. Locations: Iowa Films /
       Kent State U. / Library of Congress (FAA 5334) / Oklahoma
       State U. / Syracuse U. / U. of Illinois, Champaign / U. of
       Iowa / U. of Kansas / U. of Michigan / U. of Missouri,
       Columbia. *
          Traces the history of the ancient Persian empire and the
       great capital of Persepolis from 600-331 B.C. Shows the
       destruction of the Persian state by Alexander the Great.
       Covers religion, politics, agriculture, architecture and

187

the writing system of the ancient Persians. Intended for junior-senior high school audiences.

925   GUARDIANS OF THE SACRED FLAME
1979 / 58 min / sound / color / 16 mm
Documents Associates, Inc. (Crossroads of Civilization series) Credits: Narrator - David Frost.
Traces the decline of Greek and Roman influence in the East. Describes the rise of the Sassanian empire and growth of the Zoroastrian religion in Iran. Discusses the contributions of the Sassanian empire in the arts and government. Includes a discussion on absolute kingship.

926   ORIGINS AND EVIDENCE
1979 / 58 min / sound / color / 16 mm
Documents Associates, Inc. (Crossroads of Civilization series) Credits: Narrator - David Frost.
Traces the lives of Cyrus and Darius, leaders who changed ancient tribal monarchies into a vast Persian empire.

927   THE PAST IN PERSIA
1956 / 29 min / sound / b&w / 16 mm
New York University. Released by NET Film Service. (Yesterday's World series) (NUC FiA 58-1612) Credits: Host - Dr. Casper J. Kraemer.
Describes the Persian empire under Darius and its destruction by Alexander the Great. Reconstructs life in the ancient Persian empire through art and gold artifacts.

928   THE SUDDEN EMPIRE
1969 / 30 min / sound / color / 16 mm
BBC-TV, London. Released in the U.S. by Time-Life Films. (The Glory That Remains series, no. 1) (LC 78-714483) Credits: Writer-Narrator - Robert Erskine. Location: U. of Illinois.
Shot on location in the ruined capital city of Persepolis. Traces the rise and fall of the Archaemenid empire. Looks at cross influences with other civilizations such as the Assyrians, Egyptians, Babylonians and Greeks. Describes the final defeat of the Archaemenids at the hands of Alexander the Great.

IRAN - HISTORY FROM ANCIENT TIMES TO THE PRESENT

929   THE GREAT SOPHY
1969 / 29 min / sound / color / 16 mm
BBC-TV, London. Released in the U.S. by Time-Life Films. (The Glory That Remains series, no. 3) Location: U. of Illinois.
Recreates the world of the Great Sophy or great Sufi, ruler of the Safavid Persian empire. Shows magnificent

188

16th century architecture of the city of Isfahan.
Includes scenes of the Great Mosque, Khajou Bridge, and
Chehil Sutun.

930   INVADERS AND CONVERTS
1969 / 30 min / sound / color / 16 mm
BBC-TV, London. Released in the U.S. by Time-Life Films.
(The Glory That Remains series, no. 2) (LC 71-714484)
Credits: Writer-Narrator - Robert Erskine. Location: U. of
Illinois.
Intended for high school to adult audiences. Shows how
Iran has been used as a path for conquering Mongol hordes
from the 6th to 16th centuries. Also shows examples of
the most exquisite Persian art, architecture, and
painting of the same period. Includes scenes of the holy
city of Mashad.

931   IRAN FROM ACHAMENIAN TO PAHLAVI ERA
(n.d.) / 19 min / sound / 16 mm
Formerly distributed by the Embassy of Iran. No other information available.

932   IRAN: LANDMARKS IN THE DESERT
1973 / 52 min / sound / color / 16 mm
Chatsworth Films. Centron. (People and Places of Antiquity
series) Credits: Producer - John Seabourne, Anthony Quayle.
Locations: Syracuse U. / U. of Arizona / U. of Illinois / U.
of Kansas.
Also available in a 28 minute version. Intended for
junior high school to adult audiences. Traces the
history of civilization on the Iranian plateau. Begins
with the ancient Persian empire based at Persepolis and
continues through the Sassanian period, the rise of
Islam, the Mongol invasion and Timurid dynasty. Uses
art, artifacts and architecture to outline historical
periods. Shows how Persian carpets are produced.

933   LEGACY OF CYRUS THE GREAT
1962 / 54 min / sound / color / 16 mm
U.S. Information Agency. Released for educational use in
the U.S. through U.S. Office of Education. Formerly distributed by the Embassy of Iran. (NUC FiE 63-124)
Traces the history and development of Iranian civilization from the time of Cyrus the Great to the 1960's.
Describes U.S. financial and technical aid to modernize
Iran.

IRAN - THE TWENTIETH CENTURY

934   CRISIS IN IRAN
1951 / 18 min / sound / b&w / 16 mm
Time, Inc. Released by McGraw-Hill Book Co. A Forum Film.

189

(March of Time series) (NUC FiA 52-2561)
Current events summary of Iran in 1951. Discusses the
oil situation, economic and political instability, social
and religious attitudes and the importance of Iran to the
U.S. due to its strategic location.

935   IRAN: BRITTLE ALLY
1959 / 54 min / sound / b&w / 16 mm
CBS News. (CBS Reports, television series) (NUC Fi 67-744)
Credits: Producers - William K. McClure, Winston Burdett,
Reporters - Edward R. Murrow, Winston Burdett. Location:
Library of Congress (FCA 210-11)
    Looks at conditions in Iran. Portrays Iran as a country
    with extremes of wealth and poverty. Profiles programs
    by the Shah of Iran to bring about agrarian reform and
    promote literacy and health care. Discusses the proxi-
    mity of the Soviet Union and discusses Soviet-Iranian
    relations.

936   IRAN IN TURMOIL
1960 / 4 min / sound / b&w / 16 mm
Filmrites Associates, Inc. Distributed by Official Films.
(Greatest Headlines of the Century series) (NUC Fi 62-1904)
Credits: Producer - Sherm Grinberg, Narrator - Tom Hudson,
Writer - Allan Lurie. Location: Library of Congress (FAA
3783) *
    Newsreel presentation of the period from 1951-March 3,
    1953 in Iran. Traces Anglo-Iranian Oil Company's efforts
    to retain control of the Iranian oil industry despite
    nationalization by Prime Minister Mossadegh. Outlines
    the power struggle between Mossadegh and the Shah, the
    role of the World Court and the U.N. in the conflict, and
    the overthrow of Mossadegh. Describes how Iran returned
    to favorable European oil concessions after the return of
    the Shah. Good use of library footage.

937   IRAN TODAY
1974 / 25 min / sound / color / 16 mm
NBC. Distributed by Films Incorporated. Location: Syracuse
U.
    Intended for junior high school to adult audiences.
    Shows the effect of oil wealth and modernization on Iran.
    Looks at the build up of arms in Iran, the "Shah People
    Revolution", government education programs, industriali-
    zation and new health care and legal programs. Promotes
    a positive picture of Iran's modernization.

938   THE PREDATORS
1979 / 58 min / sound / color / 16 mm
Documents Associates. (Crossroads of Civilization series)
Credits: Narrator - David Frost.
    Argues exploration and exploitation of oil resources in
    Iran have profited the western world at Iran's expense.

Looks at British, Russian and Qajar exploitation of
Iranian resources over the last century. Describes the
bitterness in Iran as a result of these experiences.
Portrays the Shah of Iran as an ambitious ruler in the
same category as Ataturk of Turkey. Uses early film
footage and interviews. Filmed on location.

939   UPRISING IN IRAN AGAINST PREMIER, AUGUST 16, 1953
       1960 / 4 min / sound / b&w / 16 mm
       Richard B. Morros, Inc. in association with Hearst Metrotone
       News.   Distributed by Official Films. (Almanac Newsreel
       series) Location: Library of Congress (FAA 3105) *
       Short newsreel production. Traces the overthrow of Shah
       Mohammed Reza Pahlavi by "red-backed" premier Mossadegh.
       Shows the wave of anti-American, anti-British sentiment
       which swept Iran in 1953. Russian desire for Iranian oil
       is seen as a major factor in the overthrow of the Shah.
       Follows return of the Shah to power and the resulting
       western-Iranian oil contracts, new welfare programs and
       taxes on large landholders. Pro-Shah viewpoint. Good
       use of library footage.

IRAN - SHAH MOHAMMED REZA PAHLAVI

940   CORONATION
       (n.d.) / 20 min / sound / 16 mm
       Formerly distributed by the Embassy of Iran.
       Filmed review of the coronation ceremonies of Shah
       Mohammed Reza Pahlavi.

941   CORONATION OF HIS MAJESTY
       (n.d.) / 90 min / sound / b&w / 16 mm
       Formerly distributed by the Embassy of Iran. No other infor-
       mation available.

942   THE DAY OF THE SHAH AND THE PEOPLE
       (n.d.) / 8 min / sound / b&w / 16 mm
       Formerly distributed by the Embassy of Iran. No other infor-
       mation available.

943   ETERNAL FLAME
       1972 / 60 min / sound / color / 16 mm
       Formerly distributed by the Iran Information and Tourism
       Center.
       Shows celebration and ceremonies of the 2,500 year anni-
       versary of Iranian history held in 1972. Shows foreign
       dignitaries being welcomed and the festivies held to
       honor the founding of the Persian Empire under Cyrus the
       Great at Persepolis 2500 years earlier.

944   FLAME OF PERSIA
       1972 / 55 min / sound / color / 16 mm

191

National Iran Radio/TV. Made by MacDonald Hastings.
Credits: Narrator - Orson Wells. Location: U. of North
Carolina.
Documentary coverage of the 2500 anniversary celebration
in 1972 of the founding of the Persian Empire under Cyrus
the Great. Shows pomp and opulence of events and the new
sports arena built for the occassion. Describes efforts
to harken back to Zoroastrian, not Islamic themes, in
history. Shows scenes of the events at Persepolis in
October, 1971.

945   SHAH OF IRAN LEAVING UNITED STATES
       1949 / 631 ft. / silent / b&w / 16 mm ?
       Signal Corps. Location: National Archives (111 ADC 7774-2)
       No other information available.

946   STATE VISIT OF THE SHAH OF IRAN
       (n.d.) / 25 min / sound / b&w / 16 mm
       Formerly distributed by the Embassy of Malaysia. No other
       information available.

947   THE TEMPTATION OF POWER
       1976, released in the U.S. 1979 / 43 min / sound / 16 mm
       Gordien Troeller, Claude Deffarge and Francois Partant.
       Distributed by Icarus Films.
            Intended for high school to adult audiences. Outlines
            economic problems under Shah Mohammed Reza Pahlavi
            including the collapse of agriculture, reliance on
            imported foodstuffs, importation of a large arsenal of
            military and police weaponry, and the opulent life style
            of the Shah. Looks at erosion of traditional life styles
            and emphasis on westernization and modernization brought
            about by oil wealth. Covers the separation of wealth,
            foreign-owned industry and the discontent of large
            segments of the population including the middle class,
            religious mullahs, nomads, and the peasantry. Filmed
            while the Shah was still in power. Good inventory of the
            problems which led to the overthrow of the Shah.

948   WHITE REVOLUTION
       (n.d.) / 8 min / sound / b&w / 16 mm
       Formerly distributed by the Embassy of Iran. No other infor-
       mation available.

IRAN - THE REVOLUTION

949   BLOODY SEPTEMBER
       1978 / 50 min / sound / b&w / 16 mm
       Producer unknown.
            Filmed while the Shah was still in power. Documents mass
            demonstrations in Tehran on September 4 and 7, 1978.
            Shows the September 8, 1978 demonstration, called Bloody

Friday, in which government troops opened fire on demonstrators. Purpose of film is to show extreme brutality of the Shah's regime.

950 ISLAM
January 17, 1980 / 90 min / sound / color / 3/4"
videocassette. WTBS News, Atlanta. (WTBS News Special)
Credits: Panel Discussants - Gene Griesman, L. Dean Brown,
William C. Crawford, Rouhollah K. Ramazani, Nouha
Alheljeloun. Location: Middle East Institute.
Panel discussion on Iran after the revolution. Topics
covered include the role of Islam in Iranian politics and
U.S. interests in the Middle East and Iran.

951 WALLS
1979 / 39 min / sound / b&w / 16 mm
Alishiva Azizian. Distributed by Azizian, 139 E. 30th St.,
New York, NY.
Shows fight for supremecy of influence between wealthy,
modern secular society in Iran, financed by oil wealth and
centered in Tehran, with traditional religious society
centered in cities such as Yezd. Shows the attempts of
both camps to gain support for their way of life.
Differences in viewpoint and beliefs are illustrated by
architectural examples.

IRAN - INTERVIEWS

952 AYATOLLAH KHOMEINI
December 1, 1978 / 30 min / sound / color / 3/4"
videocassette. WNET-TV. (MacNeil/Lehrer Report, television
series) Credits: Producer - Jo Franklin, Director - Duke
Struck. Location: Museum of Broadcasting. *
Filmed in Pontchartrain, France before the fall of the
Shah. James MacNeil, aided by translator Ibrahim Yazdi,
speaks with Ayatollah Khomeini on Iranian strikes and
demonstrations, the possibilty of open war with the Shah,
whether a compromise is possible, if a Khomeini-led
government would break ties with Israel and stop shipments of oil to Israel, and what U.S.-Iranian relations
would be under a Khomeini-led government. Very
interesting, if slow, interview.

953 HIS IMPERIAL MAJESTY MOHAMMED REZA PAHLAVI,
SHAHANSHAH OF IRAN
October 26, 1969 / 30 min / sound / b&w / 16 mm
NBC News. (Meet the Press, television series) Credits:
Director - Max Schindler, Discussants - Lawrence Spivak,
John Chancellor, John Hightower, Marquis Childs, Stewart
Hensley. Location: Library of Congress (FBB 3812) *
Meet the Press interview. The Shah discusses the
Palestinian problem, Iranian views of the Soviet Union,

193

the role of the U.S. in supporting the Shah, Iran's need
for military equipment, modernization and industrialization programs, trade relations with Israel, and religious
beliefs of the people. The Shah stresses oil wealth in
Iran is used for development not lost to corrupt officials as in other countries. Of research value. Good
source of library footage. Brings up many points which
would later be used against the Shah during the revolution. Library of Congress print is a Kinephoto copy of
the original broadcast with commercials intact.

954   INTERVIEW WITH THE SHAH OF IRAN
       April 6, 1977 / 60 min / sound / color / 3/4" videocassette
       ABC-TV. (Barbara Walters Special) Location: Museum of
       Broadcasting (T77:0100)
              One of a series of interviews between Barabara Walters
              and the Shah of Iran. Includes comments by the Empress
              Farah.

955   MOHAMMED REZA PAHLAVI
       May 18, 1975 / 30 min / sound / color / 3/4" videocassette
       NBC-TV. (Meet the Press, television series) Location:
       Library of Congress (VBA 2010)
              One of several occassions in which the Shah of Iran
              appeared on the Meet the Press program during visits to
              the U.S. Panel discussants cover a variety of questions
              concerning Iran, the Shah's policies and the role of the
              U.S. in the Middle East and Iran in particular.

956   MOHAMMED REZA PAHLAVI, SHAH OF IRAN
       July 29, 1973 / 30 min / sound / color / 2" videotape
       NBC-TV. (Meet the Press, television series) Location:
       Library of Congress (VDA 0356)
              Another in the series of Meet the Press interviews with
              the Shah concerning U.S.- Iranian policies and current
              events.

957   THE SHAH OF IRAN
       May 18, 1975 / 30 min / sound / color / 3/4" videocassette
       NBC-TV. (Meet the Press, television series) Credits:
       Discussants - Lawrence Spivak, Bill Monroe, Robert Keatley,
       Joseph Kraft, Carl T. Rowan. Location: Library of Congress
       (VBA 2010) *
              Concerned mainly with current oil prices. Interview with
              the Shah including original commercials. Excellent pre-
              sentation of the Shah's policies and viewpoints on human
              rights, current public figures, oil, and his vision of
              Iran's future. Good source of library footage. Topics
              include possible depletion of oil resources in the Middle
              East, pricing of oil, inflation, the need for a strong
              Iranian military presence and foreign aid from oil-rich
              countries to poor Third World nations. The Shah also
              discusses things for which he would like to be remem-

bered and answers questions about political prisoners, alleged torture, terrorism, Communists in Iran, change to a one party government system and social programs in Iran. Very good interview covering many topics of importance.

IRAN - NOMADS AND TRIBES

958   BAKHTIARI MIGRATION
       1973 / 52 min / sound / color / 16 mm
       Anthony-David Productions, London. Released in the U.S. by
       Films Incorporated. (LC 74-702551) Credits: Directors -
       Anthony Howarth, David Koff. Locations: Brigham Young U. /
       Iowa Films / Penn. State U. / U. of Iowa / U. of Washington.
       *
       Shows the largest annual migration in the world is the
       Bakhtiar tribal migration of 500,000 people, their
       possessions and livestock across mountains and rivers in
       the Zagros range of southern Iran. Documents the annual
       migration from winter to summer pasturage. The 200 mile,
       five week migration has been filmed by many documentary
       film-makers. This particular film covers the route
       followed by the Bakhtiar for the last 2500 years.
       Intended for senior high school to adult audiences.

959   BAKTIARI MIGRATION
       1974 / 27 min / sound / color / 16 mm
       Anthony-David Productions. Released in the U.S. by Films
       Incorporated. (LC 74-702552)
       Edited version of no. 958. Follows the annual migration
       of the Bakhiari tribe with their large herds of goats,
       sheep, camels and cows from winter to summer pasturage.
       Shows the hazards in crossing mountains and fording
       rivers during the 200 mile, five week migration.

960   BURNING POPPIES (BAKHTIARI TRIBE MIGRATION)
       (n.d.) / 25 min / sound / color / 16 mm
       Formerly distributed by the Embassy of Iran.
       Well filmed documentary. Covers the annual migration of
       the Bakhtiari tribe to obtain pasturage for their herds.

961   GRASS: A NATION'S BATTLE FOR LIFE
       1925 / 62 or 45 min / silent / b&w / 16 mm
       Famous Players-Lasky Corp. Distributed by Film Classics
       Exchange. In the American Film Institute Collection,
       Library of Congress. (LC 76-709593) Credits: Photographer -
       Ernest Schoedsack, Producer - Merian C. Cooper, with Ernest
       Schoedsack and Marguerite Harrison. Locations: 62 minute
       version - Film Classics Exchange / U. of California; 45
       minute version - Film Classics Exchange / Middle East
       Institute / U. of California Extension Media Center / U. of
       Utah. *

195

The earliest, and perhaps most spectacular, film of the Bakhtiar annual migration. Made by Merian C. Cooper who later made the feature film KING KONG. Silent with sub-titles. Follows in detail the 48 day migration of people and animals across the Zagros Mountains and the Karun River to find pasturage. Longer version shows the hazar-dous crossing of the snow covered mountains by barefoot nomads. Classic documentary film production. Still con-sidered a landmark film of the Bakhtiari despite simplistic film titles due to the quality and difficulty of camera work. Usually listed in catalogs simply as GRASS. Revised version with soundtrack and narration is now available. Recommended.

962   IRAN ON THE MOVE
       (n.d.) / 17 min / sound / color / 16 mm
       Humphries Film Labs, produced in cooperation with the Iran
       Oil Companies. Location: Middle East Institute.
            Looks at tribal migrations in Iran including those of
       the Bakhtiari, Kurds, Qashqai and other tribes. Shows
       efforts underway to provide education for children of
       nomadic groups.

963   LAND OF THE BAKHTIYARIS
       1969 / 20 min / sound / color / 16 mm
       Formerly distributed by the Iran Information and Tourism
       Center.
            Shows manners and customs of the nomadic Bakhtiari tribe
       and their traditional pattern of annual migration.

964   A NATION'S SEARCH FOR GRASS
       1938 / 10 min / sound? / b&w / 16 mm
       Distributed by Knowledge Builders. Location: U. of
       California Extension Media Center.
            Shorter version of no. 961. Shows scenes of the annual
       migration of the Bakhtiari tribe from winter to summer
       pasturage for their extensive herds.

965   NOMADS OF IRAN
       1976 / 13 min / sound / color / 16 mm
       Russell Wulff. Distributed by Paramount Communications.
            Intended for elementary to high school audiences. Looks
       at the Qashqai tribe of the Zagros Mountains, their self-
       reliant way of life, migration for pasturage and tradi-
       tional arts.

966   PEOPLE OF THE WIND
       1978 / 127 or 90 min / sound / color / 16 mm
       Elizabeth F. Rogers Production. Distributed by
       Tricontinental Film Service. Credits: Producers - Anthony
       Howarth, David Koff, Narrator - James Mason. *
            One of the best films on nomads of the Middle East.
       Beautifully photographed, well produced feature length

film. Looks at the Bakhtiari of western Iran, their annual migration and relations between people and groups within the tribe. Follows Jafar Qoli who must decide when the migration should begin and must lead the tribe safely across rivers and mountains to summer pasturage. Some women and older nomads now cross the mountains by road while the tribe herds animals on the 4-6 week migration. Discusses the pressure on nomads today to be sedentary. Excellent quality production. Makes nomadic life understandable to western audiences. Intended for high school to adult audiences. Edited 90 minute version is also available. Recommended.

967 TRIBES OF IRAN
(n.d.) / ? / sound / color / 16 mm
Humphries Film Labs. No other information available.

968 TWO GRASSLANDS: TEXAS AND IRAN
1971 / 21 min / sound / color / 16 mm
International Cinemedia Center, Montreal. Released in the U.S. by Learning Corp. of America. (Comparative Geography series) (LC 76-710028) Credits: Consultants - Trevor Lloyd, Philip C. Salzman. Locations: Kent State U. / Library of Congress (FBB 3369) / U. of Illinois.
   For general audiences. Compares similar conditions, vegetation and rainfall in the Edwards plateau of Texas and the steppes of Iran. Looks at the life of the inhabitants of the two areas, the relationship between people and the land, technology used to make use of the land and differences between Texas ranchers and Qashqai herdsmen.

969 WOVEN GARDENS (QASHQAI OF IRAN)
1975 / 52 min / sound / color / 16 mm
BBC-TV. Released by Time-Life Films. (Tribal Eye series, no. 7) Credits: Director - David Collison, Camera - Walt Crosby, Narrator - David Attenborough. Locations: New York Public Donnell Film Library / Ohio State U. / Penn. State U. / U. of California Extension Media Center / U. of Washington. *
   Excellent production. Looks at the Persian carpet industry in Iran. Shows traditional patterns and methods of hand-weaving used by tribal Qashqai women. Also looks at nomadic life and how it has contributed to the production of Persian carpets. Includes scenes of a wedding, dancing, sheep raising, processing of wool, dyeing wool, and village schools for rug-making. Shows closeups of beautiful carpet designs.

IRAN - MINORITIES AND WOMEN

970 BAKING FLAT BREAD (PERSIANS, IRAN, TEHRAN)
1959, released 1962 / 4 min / silent / b&w / 16 mm

Encyclopaedia Cinematographica. Distributed by Pennsylvania State University. (Ency. Cinematographica no. E 252) Another in the series of silent ethnographic films documenting a traditional activity. Shows urban women baking bread using traditional methods.

971   COURTSHIP
1961 / 16 min / sound / 16 mm
National Film Board of Canada. Distributed in the U.S. by McGraw-Hill. Location: New York Public Donnell Film Library. Compares courtship and marriage customs in Sicily, India, Iran and Canada.

972   DIPPING WELL (PERSIANS, IRAN, HAMADAN)
1959, released 1962 / 2 min / silent / b&w / 16 mm
Encyclopaedia Cinematographica. Distributed by Pennsylvania State University. (Ency. Cinematographica no. E 251) Another in the series of silent ethnographic films depicting a single activity.

973   THE IRANIAN WOMEN
(c. 1960?) / 19 min / sound / 16 mm
Formerly distributed by the Embassy of Iran. No other information available.

974   MAKING OF A MAN
(n.d.) / 29 min / sound / color / 16 mm
Distributed by Alden Films. Location: Abraham F. Rad Jewish Film Archive.
    Details Jewish ghetto life in Iran before the revolution. Follows attempts by a young boy to obtain schooling and better himself while maintaining his Jewish identity.

975   MISSION TO SHIRAZ
(n.d.) / 12 min / sound / b&w / 16 mm
ORT. Location: Abraham F. Rad Jewish Film Archive.
    An Iranian student trained at the Central ORT Teacher's Institute in Anieres, Switzerland discusses programs sponsored by ORT to work with Jews in Tehran and Shiraz.

976   WEDDING IN A PERSIAN VILLAGE
1962 / 11 min / sound / color / 16 mm
Monsour Ali Faridi. Made by Dept. of Television, Motion Pictures, and Radio. Released by New York University Film Library. (LC 76-706445) Credits: Narrators - Donald J. Pringle, Lee Osborne. Location: Library of Congress (FAB 138) / New York Public Donnell Film Library / New York University.
    Shows a traditional village wedding in Karvenah in northwest Iran. Scenes include dancing, the wedding feast, preparation of the bride, the wedding procession and traditional music.

IRAN - THE ARMED FORCES

977   ASSIGNMENT - IRAN
       1965 / 29 min / sound / b&w / 16 mm
       U.S. Dept. of the Army. Released by National Audiovisual
       Center. (Big Picture series) (LC 74-706031)
           Shows training received by U.S. Army personnel before
           being sent to Iran. Preparations include guerilla warfare
           instruction, language, history and culture training.

978   CONVOY, HAMADAN TO KAZVIN, IRAN
       1944 / 909 ft / silent / b&w / 16mm ?
       Signal Corps. Location: National Archives (111 ADC 677) No
       other information available.

979   CONVOY ROUTE IRAN TO RUSSIA
       1944 / 997 ft / silent / b&w / 16 mm ?
       Signal Corps. Location: National Archives (111 ADC 1237-38,
       1245) No other information available.

980   THE IRANIAN ARMY
       1963 / 17 min / sound / color / 16 mm
       American Friends of the Middle East. Formerly distributed
       by the Embassy of Iran.
           Shows training and equipment of the Iranian Army.

981   THE SELLING OF THE F-14
       August 27, 1976 / 60 min / sound / color / 3/4" videocassette
       CBS News. Credits: Producer-Director-Writer - Jay L.
       McMullen, Reporters - Jay L. McMullen, Bill McLaughlin.
       Location: Museum of Broadcasting (T77:0091)
           Discusses the $2 billion sale of F-14 Tomcat fighters to
           Iran. Motives behind the sale are debated as well as
           the effect of the planes on the balance of power in the
           Middle East. Includes an interview with the Shah of
           Iran. Profiles American workers in Iran.

IRAN - TRAVELOGS AND REGIONAL STUDIES -
         PRODUCTION DATE UNKNOWN

982   BRIDGE OF VICTORY (TRANS-IRANIAN RAILWAY)
       (c. 1960?) / 20 min / sound / b&w / 16 mm
       Formerly distributed by the Embassy of Iran. No other infor-
       mation available.

983   IRAN
       (c. 1960?) / 14 min / sound / b&w / 16 mm
       Peace Corps. Location: National Archives (RG 362-158) No
       other information available.

984   IRAN
       (n.d.) / 30 min / sound / b&w / 16 mm

Formerly distributed by the Embassy of Iran. No other information available.

985 IRAN (PERSIA)
(n.d.) / 824 ft / silent / b&w / 16 mm ?
Signal Corps. Location: National Archives (111 ADC 905-2)
No other information available.

986 IRAN'S NATURE
(c. 1960?) / 18 min / sound / 16 mm
Formerly distributed by the Embassy of Iran. No other information available.

987 LIFE
(c. 1960?) / 20 min / sound / 16 mm
Formerly distributed by the Embassy of Iran. No other information available.

988 NORTHERN IRAN
(c. 1960?) / 20 min / sound / color / 16 mm
Formerly distributed by the Embassy of Iran. No other information available.

989 SEVEN SPLENDOURS OF PERSIA
(c. 1965?) / 18 min / sound / color / 16 mm
Distributed by Macmillan Films.
General travelog of Iran. Contrasts the remains of ancient Persian civilization with the modern capital city of Tehran.

990 SKIING
(c. 1960?) / 6 min / sound / color / 16 mm
Formerly distributed by the Embassy of Iran.
Shows opportunities for skiing on the mountainous slopes in Iran. To promote tourism.

IRAN - TRAVELOGS AND REGIONAL STUDIES - 1950-1979

991 CROWN JEWELS OF IRAN
1966 / 10 min / sound / color / 16 mm
Formerly distributed by the Iran Information and Tourism Center.
Contrast wealth and poverty in Iran by comparing scenes of rural Iran and the "treasures of the Kings", the Iranian crown jewels.

992 FISHING IN THE CASPIAN SEA
(c. 1960) / 17 min / sound / b&w / 16 mm
Formerly distributed by the Embassy of Iran.
Discusses sturgeon fishing and the caviar industry in the Caspain Sea area. Describes caviar as a significant export for Iran.

993   IRAN
1972 / 15 min / sound / color / 16 mm
Claude Lelouch. Distributed by Pyramid Films. Locations:
Boston U. / Kent State U. / Penn. State U. / Syracuse U. /
U. of Illinois / U. of Washington. *
Intended for junior high school to adult audiences. Fast
paced impressionistic view of Iran made up of hundreds of
brief clips without narration. Looks at people, sports,
education, business, industry, architecture, geography
and the arts. Beautiful little film. Of less use for
instructional purposes due to lack of narration and identification of what is shown. Well produced.

994   IRAN - BETWEEN TWO WORLDS
1954 / 14 min / sound / color or b&w / 16 mm
Kenneth Richter. Released by Encyclopaedia Britannica Films.
(NUC FiA 54-731) Credits: Collaborator - William S. Haas.
Locations: Educational Film Library / Kent State U. /
Library of Congress (FBA 932) / U. of Illinois.
Shows contrasts in Iran. Looks at westernized, modern
urban areas such as Tehran and rural areas and villages
where life has changed little in 2000 years.

995   SIGHTS OF IRAN
1974 / 20 min / sound / color / 16 mm
Formerly distributed by the Iran Information and Tourism
Center.
General travelog of Iran. Shows varied geography of the
country, the change of seasons seen in the countryside,
and ancient monuments, architecture and arts of Iran.

996   STRATEGIC IRAN
1952 / 14 min / sound / b&w / 16 or 35 mm
U.S. Dept. of Defense. Made by U.S. Dept. of the Army.
(Order no. AFIF 27) (NUC FiE 53-656)
Looks at Iran's geography, government, culture, economics
and political problems. Emphasizes the importance of
Iran to the U.S. because of oil resources. Made for U.S.
Army personnel.

IRAN - TRAVELOGS AND REGIONAL STUDIES - BY CITY

997   ESFAHAN
(c. 1958?) / 20 min / sound / color / 16 mm
Audio-Visual Service of the Fine Arts Administration, Govt.
of Iran.
Shows in detail the famous mosques of the city of
Isfahan. Shows beautiful architectural details of the
buildings.

998   HALF THE WORLD
1977 / 58 min / sound / color / 16 mm

201

Paradine. Distributed by Documents Associates. (Crossroads of Civilization series) Credits: Narrator - David Frost, Collaborators - John Gurney, Oleg Grabar.
Shows the jewel-like city of Isfahan built by Shah Abbas. Recreates 16th and 17th century Safavid life through the architecture and art of Isfahan.

999 ISFAHAN
1963 / 17 min / sound / color / 16 mm
American Friends of the Middle East. Formerly distributed by the Embassy of Iran.
Shows Isfahan, the capital of Safavid Iran at the end of the 15th century, famous for its beautiful architecture.

1000 ISFAHAN OF SHAH ABBAS
1975 / 30 min / sound / color / 16 mm
Fogg Fine Arts Films, Harvard University. (Films for the Humanities series) Credits: Collaborator - Oleg Grabar.
Locations: Fogg Museum / Penn. State U. / U. of Michigan / U. of Washington.
Shows in detail the architectural beauty of the city of Isfahan, capital of the Safavid Persian dynasty, built by Shah Abbas. Also looks at the arts and crafts of the period including calligraphy, painting, metalwork, weaving and ceramics. Focuses on the Royal Square of Isfahan.

1001 SHAHYAD MONUMENT
1973 / 20 min / sound / color / 16 mm
Formerly distributed by the Iran Information and Tourism Center.
Shows the monumental arch gateway built as an entrance to the city of Tehran in commemoration of the 2500 anniversary of the founding of the Persian Empire under Cyrus the Great. Built by Shah Mohammed Reza Pahlavi, the arch contains museums and visual displays.

1002 SKYLINE OF SHIRAZ
(n.d.) / 20 min / sound / color / 16 mm
Producer unknown. Location: Middle East Institute.
Shows the ancient and modern city of Shiraz. Includes scenes of the ruins of Persepolis, tombs and monuments, modern hospital facilities, the Pahlavi University, and bazaars filled with crafts and produce. Short segments cover oil, industrialization, and the nomadic tribes.

1003 TEHERAN
(c. 1960?) / 17 min / sound / color / 16 mm
American Friends of the Middle East. Formerly distributed by the Embassy of Iran.
General travelog of the city of Tehran, capital of Iran. Shows combination of ancient and modern styles and ways of life.

1004   TEHRAN TODAY
        (n.d.) / 15 min / sound / b&w / 16 mm
        Formerly distributed by the Embassy of Iran. No other infor-
        mation available.

IRAN   - INDUSTRY AND OIL

1005   IRAN: THE STRUGGLE TO INDUSTRIALIZE
        1967 / 17 min / sound / color / 16 mm
        Jules Power Productions. Released by McGraw-Hill. (Middle
        Eastern World series) (NUC FiA 67-1695) Locations: Kent
        State U. / Syracuse U. / U. of Illinois.
            Intended for junior-senior high school audiences.
            Follows a 14 year old Iranian boy who travels from his
            village to the city. Shows differences between Iranian
            rural and urban life. Looks at modernization funded by
            oil revenues and the importance of oil and irrigation to
            the economy of Iran. Describes Iran's dependence on
            western nations in its struggle to industrialize.

1006   IRAN'S INDUSTRIAL PROGRESS
        (n.d.) / 17 min / sound / 16 mm
        Formerly distributed by the Embassy of Iran. No other infor-
        mation available.

1007   OIL FOR THE 20TH CENTURY
        (n.d.) / 30 min / sound / b&w / 16 mm
        Jack Howells Productions. Distributed by British Petroleum
        Company.
            Traces the history of the Anglo-Persian Oil Company from
            the early 20th century to the present. Looks at the
            first exploration for oil in Iran and the growing demand
            for oil 50 years later. Uses old film footage to trace
            history of oil in Iran.

1008   OIL, THE STORY OF IRAN
        1952 / 13 min / sound / b&w / 16 mm
        Anglo-Iranian Oil Co. Made and released by Sterling Films.
        (NUC FiA 54-207)
            Edited version of OIL FOR THE 20TH CENTURY, no.
            1007, and ANGLO-IRANIAN OIL DISPUTE. Looks at
            political and economic implications of the oil industry
            in Iran.

1009   PERSIAN WORKERS AT TRUCK ASSEMBLY PLANT
        "LITTLE DETROIT", ANDIMESHK, IRAN
        1944 / 25 min / silent / b&w / 16 mm
        Signal Corps. Location: National Archives (111 ADC 1515-16)
        No other information available.

1010   PROJECT CHAM
        (n.d.) / 50 min / sound / color / 16 mm

Producer unknown. Location: Middle East Institute.
Traces the history of oil exploration and exploitation in
Iran. Follows oil industry up to building of the world's
largest crude oil export terminal on Kharg Island.

1011   RIG 20
1951 / 15 min / sound / b&w / 16 mm
Verity Films. Distributed by British Petroleum Co.
Shows the struggle to put out a fire on Rig 20, an oil
drilling rig at Naft Safid in May 1951. Efforts to
extinguish the fire and the dramatic blaze from the rig
were filmed by a British Petroleum cameraman. Winner of
a 1952 Venice Film Festival prize.

1012   STORY OF IRAN
1952 / 43 min / sound / b&w / 35 mm
Stratford Pictures Corp. (NUC Fi 52-2270) Location:
Library of Congress (FEA 1273-76)
Traces the origins and growth of the Anglo-Iranian Oil
Company. Shows difficulties experienced by the company
in importing materials, digging wells, and transporting
oil to the Abadan refinery.

1013   WAVE, CORAL AND ROCK
(n.d.) / 45 min / sound / color / 16 mm
Producer unknown. Distributed by Middle East Institute.
Describes the work of the Iranian Oil Consortium to link
the Gachsaran oil fields in the Zagros Mountains to the
loading terminal on Kharg Island. Profiles the export of
oil from Iran.

IRAN - EDUCATION

1014   ASHRAF NURSING SCHOOL
(n.d.) / 10 min / sound / b&w / 16 mm
Producer unknown. Location: U. of Utah.
Shows the modern hospital and nursing school facilities
at the Ashraf Nursing School.

1015   DEVELOPMENT CORPS OF IRAN
(n.d.) / 20 min / sound / b&w / 16 mm
Formerly distributed by the Embassy of Iran. No other information available.

1016   FACTS FROM FAECES
1966 / 33 min / sound / color / 16 mm
Food and Agriculture Organizaion of the United Nations.
Distributed by United Nations Films.
Describes efforts of the Razi Institute of Iran to study
internal parasites among sheep and goats. Shows diseases
have cost herders about $40 million annually in lost pro-
duction. Explains sampling techniques for faeces, tech-

niques for locating eggs and larvae and examination of
animals in the field and during autopsies. Dosing techniques using anthelmin are also shown. Specialized film
for adult audiences dealing in animal husbandry and animal research.

1017   IRAN'S TRAINING FOR SOCIAL WORKERS
        (n.d.) / 12 min / sound / color / 16 mm
        United Nations.
            Shows training received by future social workers at the
            Teheran School of Social Work. Describes how program was
            developed with assistance of the United Nations.

1018   LIBRARIES
        (n.d.) / 22 min / sound / 16 mm
        Formerly distributed by the Embassy of Iran. No other infor-
        mation available.

1019   LITERACY CORPS
        (n.d) / 10 min / sound / b&w / 16 mm
        Formerly distributed by the Embassy of Iran.
            Looks at efforts being made by the government to promote
            literacy in Iran. Describes programs in rural areas and
            among nomads.

1020   NEAR EAST ADVENTURE
        1956 / 24 min / sound / color / 16 mm
        Near East Foundation. Made by Peggy and Pierre Streit.
        Released by Thomas Craven Film Corp. (NUC FiA 64-1007)
            Describes efforts being made by private groups such as
            the Near East Foundation to offer technical assistance
            programs to developing countries. Shows work being done
            in Iran to help rural poor fight poverty and disease.

1021   THE NEAR EAST FOUNDATION IN IRAN
        (c. 1960) / 20 min / sound / color or b&w / 16 mm
        The Near East Foundation.
            Describes assistance programs being offered to Iran by
            the Near East Foundation.

1022   WORLD ORIENTALISTS CONGRESS IN IRAN
        (n.d.) / 15 min / sound / b&w / 16 mm
        Formerly distributed by the Embassy of Iran. No other infor-
        mation available.

IRAN - THE ARTS - ARCHITECTURE

1023   ALI QAPU PALACE OF ISFAHAN
        1969 / 30 min / sound / color / 16 mm
        Formerly distributed by the Iran Information and Tourism
        Center.
            Describes the Ali Qapu Palace in Isfahan according to a

16th century traveler's account. Includes a study of the palace's floor plan.

1024 CHEHELSOTON PALACE OF ISFAHAN
1969 / 30 min / sound / color / 16 mm
Formerly distributed by the Iran Information and Tourism Center.
A study of the floor plan and architectural detail of the Chehelsoton Palace in Isfahan. Includes details of carved woodwork.

1025 HASHT BEHEST PALACE OF ISFAHAN
1969 / 15 min / sound / color / 16 mm
Formerly distributed by the Iran Information and Tourism Center.
Looks at restoration work underway at the Hasht Behest Palace in Isfahan. Includes details of architectural design of the palace.

IRAN - THE ARTS - PAINTING

1026 THE ART OF THE BOOK: PERSIAN MINIATURES FROM THE SHAHNAMEH
1975 / 55 min / sound / color / 16 mm
Fogg Art Museum and National Iranian Radio-TV. Distributed by Tomlin Films. Credits: Script - Oleg Grabar.
Profiles three centuries of Mongol, Timurid and Safavid manuscripts and art. Gives detailed look at illuminated copies of the Shahnameh, the Iranian national epic. Narration consists of selected stories from the epic. Miniatures shown are beautifully photographed and the commentary is very good. Interesting film despite lack of live action footage.

1027 BOASTING
1974 / 10 min / sound / color / 16 mm
Producer unknown. Location: Kent State U. / U. of Illinois.
Short animated film without narration done in the style of Persian miniature art. Illustrates a parable about two dwindling armies who boast their way through a series of encounters. Eventually two surviving combatants learn to live in peace. Example of modern Iranian art using medieval models.

1028 THE PRESENCE OF PERSIA: IRANIAN ART IN AMERICA
1976 / 55 min / sound / color / 16 mm
Fogg Art Museum and Iranian National Television.
Distributed by Tomlin Films. Credits: Script - Oleg Grabar.
Shows Iranian art on display in American museums. Includes examples from the Walter Museum of Baltimore, New York Metropolitan Museum, Cleveland Museum of Art, Cincinnati Museum, and the Textile Museum in Washington,

D.C. Includes additional location footage shot in Iran.
Narrated by art historian Oleg Grabar. Intended for art
history classes.

1029 THE SEVEN WIVES OF BAHRAM GUR
1961 / 19 min / sound / color / 16 mm
Indiana University, Audio-Visual Center. (Art of the Orient
series) (NUC FiA 61-288) Locations: Indiana U. / Library
of Congress (FBA 1402) / U. of Michigan / U. of Washington.
Uses miniature paintings from the New York Metropolitan
Museum of Art and New York Public Library to tell the
story of Bahram Gur according to the 12th century Persian
poet Nizami. Follows Bahram Gur's childhood, his studies, accession to the throne and unsuccessful courtship
of Fitna. His unhappy life with seven wives and final
reconciliation with Fitna are told in a courtly, stylized
manner.

1030 TALES FROM A BOOK OF KINGS
1973 / 26 min / sound / color / 16 mm
Metropolitan Museum of Art. Distibuted by Time-Life
Multimedia. Credits: Supervisor - Richard Ettinghausen.
Locations: Middle East Institute / Ohio State U. / U. of
Washington. *
Presents excerpts from the story of the Shahname, or Book
of Kings, the Iranian national epic. Follows Iran's
history from the near-mythical time of the ancient
Persian empire to the 7th century A.D. Beautifully
filmed, a feast for the eyes. Interesting despite lack
of live action footage.

IRAN - TRADITIONAL CRAFTS

1031 ART OF THE PERSIAN CARPET
1975 / 13 min / sound / color / 16 mm
Paul Shaper. Released by Centron Educational Films. (LC
75-703620) Locations: Arizona State U. / Kent State U. /
Syracuse U. / U. of Illinois / U. of Kansas / Wayne State U.
*
Intended for high school to adult audiences. Traces the
art of Persian carpet weaving. Shows raising of sheep
for wool, dyeing of wool, spinning and finally weaving
the design with a cartoon as a pattern guide. Shows different types of looms and weaving patterns. Discusses
the historical background of different patterns made in
various regions or by nomadic tribes. Shows bright
colored Fars and Qashqai tribal rugs. The finished products are clipped, washed and dried before sale in the
rug markets. Interesting subject, well photographed.
Might be viewed in conjunction with WOVEN GARDENS,
no. 969.

207

1032   CERAMICS
1970 / 5 min / sound / color / 16 mm
Formerly distributed by the Iran Information and Tourism
Center.
Traces history of ceramic art in Iran from examples found
in the archaeological Museum in Tehran to modern ceramic
and glass pieces. Emphasizes new patterns and designs
have been influenced by ancient ones.

1033   EXHIBITION OF CERAMIC AND GLASS WORK
(n.d.) / 5 min / sound / 16 mm
Formerly distributed by the Embassy of Iran. No other information available.

1034   EXHIBITION OF INLAY JEWELRY
(n.d.) / 5 min / sound / 16 mm
Formerly distributed by the Embassy of Iran. No other information available.

1035   IRANIAN WOMEN'S CLOTHES
1972 / 20 min / sound / color / 16 mm
Formerly distributed by the Iran Information and Tourism
Center.
Historical look at changes in Iranian women's clothes
during different periods. Costumes are modeled in
buildings of that period.

1036   KHATAM (INLAID WORK)
(c. 1958?) / 15 min / sound / color / 16 mm
Audio-Visual Service of the Fine Arts Administration, Govt.
of Iran. Formerly distributed by the Embassy of Iran.
Also listed in embassy publications under the titles:
KHATMA and KHAATAM. Looks at the traditional
Iranian craft of wooden inlay or mosaic applied to fur-
niture and musical instruments as ornamentation.

1037   PERSIAN CARPETS
1966 / 10 min / sound / color / 16 mm
Formerly distributed by the Iran Information and Tourism
Center.
Traces the production of Persian carpets. Shows how wool
is gathered and dyed and how carpets are woven. Looks at
rugs being clipped and washed before going to the rug
market. Profiles traditional nomadic methods of rug
weaving.

1038   POTTERS ART
1969 / 10 min / sound / color / 16 mm
Formerly distributed by the Iran Information and Tourism
Center.
Looks at pre-Islamic and Islamic pottery designs in Iran.
Traces the influence of traditional and ancient patterns
on modern potters.

1039   STRINGS OF WOOL
        (n.d.) / 8 min / sound / 16 mm
        Formerly distributed by the Embassy of Iran.
        Short film. Looks at the beauty of traditional Persian
        carpets of Iran.

1040   WOOD CARVING
        (n.d.) / 10 min / sound / b&w / 16 mm
        Formerly distributed by the Embassy of Iran.
        One in a series of films portraying traditional Iranian
        crafts. Looks at craftsmen working with wood in contem-
        porary Iran.

IRAN - DANCE AND MUSIC

1041   BOJNURD FOLK DANCES
        1970 / 10 min / sound / color / 16 mm
        Formerly distributed by the Iran Information and Tourism
        Center.
        Shows men and women of the city of Bojnurd performing
        traditional regional folk dances.

1042   KHOROSAN FOLK DANCES
        1969 / 15 min / sound / color / 16 mm.
        Producer unknown.
        Shows folk dances from the province of Khorosan in Iran.

1043   SHUSHA
        1973 / 27 min / sound / color / 16 mm
        Anthony Howarth and David Koff. Distributed by Films
        Incorporated.
        Persian folk singer Shusha Guppy sings songs about Iran
        against a backdrop of the Zagros Mountains.

1044   TORBATJAM FOLK DANCE
        (n.d.) / 8 min / sound / 16 mm
        Formerly distributed by the Embassy of Iran.
        Another in a series of short films showing Iranian folk
        dances of various cities and regions.

1045   TORKAMN FOLK DANCE
        (n.d.) / 5 min / sound / 16 mm
        Formerly distributed by the Embassy of Iran.
        Another in a series of short films showing Iranian folk
        dances of various cities and regions.

1046   WEDDING DANCE
        (n.d.) / 17 min / sound / 16 mm
        Formerly distributed by the Embassy of Iran. No other infor-
        mation available.

IRAQ - ARCHEOLOGY AND ANCIENT HISTORY

1047 ANCIENT CIVILIZATIONS: MESOPOTAMIA
1974 / 4 min / silent / color / super 8 mm film loop in
cartridge. Coronet Instructional Media. (LC 74-701513)
General, short introduction to ancient peoples who have
inhabited the Tigris-Euphrates River Valley. Describes
some of their accomplishments in writing and astronomy.
Includes discussion of the Semites, Sumerians and
Assyrians.

1048 ANCIENT MESOPOTAMIA
1953 / 11 min / sound / color or b&w / 16 mm
Coronet Instructional Films. (NUC Fi 53-202) Credits:
Educational Collaborator - Richard A. Parker. Locations:
Brigham Young U. / Iowa Films / Kent State U. / Library of
Congress (FAA 6291) / Penn. State U. / Syracuse U. / U. of
Arizona / U. of Illinois / U. of Iowa / U. of Kansas / U. of
Nebraska / U. of Texas at Austin / U. of Washington. *
Brief, much simplified history of Mesopotamia from 3500
B.C. to the Greek and Roman periods. Looks at contact
between Mesopotamian and other ancient civilizations
through trade and empire building. Discusses contribu-
tions of the Sumarians, Egyptians, Akkadians, Amorites,
Kassites, Assyrians and Chaldeans in writing, agriculture, law, war and the sciences. Covers a great deal
of area in a short period of time. Intended for junior-
senior high school audiences.

1049 ARCHAEOLOGY IN MESOPOTAMIA
1964 / 17 min / sound / color / 16 mm
Educational Services Inc. (Social Studies Program series)
(Fi A 65-353) Credits: Producer - Quentin Brown,
Photographers - Wheaton Galentine, Abraham Morochnik, Jesse
L. Paley. Location: Penn. State U.
Dr. Robert Adams describes the archeological significance
of tells or mounds in Mesopotamia. Shows excavation of a
tell uncovering pottery shards and artifacts. Describes
how archeologists map, catalog and preserve pieces found.

1050 BETWEEN THE RIVERS
1956 / 29 min / sound / b&w / 16 mm
Dept. of Cinema, University of Southern California.
Released by NET Film Service. (The Written Word series)
(NUC FiA 60-696) Credits: Host - Dr. Frank Baxter.
Describes early writing and cuneiform used in the Tigris
and Euphrates River Valley area by various ancient civi-
lizations.

1051   FROM UR TO NINEVAH
        1968 / 18 min / sound / color / 16 mm
        Pierre Levie, Belgium. Released in the U.S. by Radim Films
        for Film Images. (NUC FiA 68-3063)
        Reconstructs Sumerian life using artifacts found in
        temples, ruins and ziggurats. Includes information found
        on carved stone steles.

1052   IRAQ: STAIRWAY TO THE GODS
        1973 / 27 min / sound / color / 16 mm
        Centron. Chatsworth Film Distributors, Ltd. (People and
        Places of Antiquity series) Credits: Narrator - Anthony
        Quayle. Locations: Syracuse U. / U. of Illinois / U. of
        Kansas.
        Also available in 52 minute version listed in some cata-
        logs as STAIRWAY TO THE GODS. Looks at
        civilization in Ninevah, last of the Assyrian capital
        cities. Shows development of cuneiform writing. Briefly
        covers the history of Mesopotamia under Sargon, Hammurabi
        and the Persians. Describes how the massive Assyrian
        Winged Bull was moved from Iraq to the British Museum in
        London in recent times.

1053   THE MISSING CITY GATES
        (n.d.) / 29 min / sound / b&w / 16 mm
        Location: Indiana U.
        Describes the excavations at Nimrud in Iraq. Shows the
        bronze gates from Balavat near Nimrud now in the British
        Museum.

IRAQ - THE LAND AND PEOPLE

1054   AGELESS IRAQ
        1961 / 21 min / sound / color / 16 mm
        Location: Washington State U.
        General film. Covers Iraq's geography, history and
        efforts to modernize.

1055   BELADUNA 7
        1955 / 13 min / sound / color / 16 mm
        Iraq Petroleum Company, London. Distributed by Film Centre.
        Shows scenes of traditional Iraqi life and music.
        Includes scenes of harvesting of the orange crop, making
        an 'oud, a lute-like instrument, and traditional songs.

1056   BUILDING A HUT OF REEDS WITH A GABLE ROOF
        (MA'DAN ARABS, WEST ASIA, SOUTH IRAQ)
        1955, released 1958 / 11 min / silent / b&w / 16 mm
        Encyclopaedia Cinematographica. Distributed by Pennsylvania
        State University. (Ency. Cinematographica no. E 153)
        Another in the series of silent ethnographic films
        showing a traditional activity. Shows construction of
        houses made of reeds by marsh dwellers in southern Iraq.

211

1057   BUILDING A TUNNEL-SHAPED HUT OF REEDS
(MA'DAN ARABS, WEST ASIA, SOUTH IRAQ)
1955, released 1958 / 10 min / silent / b&w / 16 mm
Encyclopaedia Cinematographica. Distributed by Pennsylvania
State University. (Ency. Cinematographica no. E 154)
Another in the series of silent ethnographic films
showing a traditional activity. Shows methods used
to construct houses from reeds in marsh areas of Iraq.

1058   DATE CULTURE IN IRAQ
1929 / 26 min / silent / b&w / 35 mm
Dept. of Agriculture. Credits: Photographer - Roy W. Nixon.
Location: National Archives (33.357)
Silent film. Shows methods used to cultivate and harvest
dates in Iraq.

1059   DESERT - BAGHDAD
(c. 1928) / 12 min / silent / b&w / 16 mm
Source unknown. Location: Library of Congress (FAA 4948)   *
Shows various scenes in Iraq including officials at
Baghdad airport, a sword dance, Europeans and Iraqis
using various forms of transportation, a wedding party
traveling through the city, homes, mosques, street scenes,
craftspeople, and panoramas of Baghdad. Good source of
footage. Includes some unusual shots but nothing is
identified. Some segments are out of focus, quality
varies. For research and library footage purposes only.

1060   GARDEN OF EDEN
1945 / 11 min / sound / b&w / 16 mm
British Ministry of Information, London. Released in the
U.S. by British Information Services. (NUC FiA 52-866)
Credits: Producer - Charles Martin, Director-Cameraman -
Frank Hurley, Commentator - Rex Keating.
Shows life along the Euphrates River as viewed by a
British entertainment riverboat showing films during
WWII. Not to be confused with a feature film of the same
name.

1061   LAND AND WATER IN IRAQ
1964 / 14 min / sound / color / 16 mm
Educational Services. Produced by the University of Chicago.
(Social Studies Program series) (NUC FiA 65-356) Credits:
Producer - Quentin Brown, Photographers - Wheaton Galentine,
Abraham Morochnik, Jesse L. Paley. Location: Middle East
Institute.
Shows life in the Tigris-Euphrates River Valley today.
Looks at the reliance of Iraq on water from these rivers
for irrigation and navigation and problems caused by
flooding and marsh lands around the rivers. Discusses
high salt content of the ground water. Shows life has
changed little among the villagers and nomads of the
southern swamp areas of Iraq.

1062   MAKING REED MATS (MA'DAN ARABS,
        WEST ASIA, SOUTH IRAQ)
        1955, released 1958 / 10 min / silent / b&w / 16 mm
        Encyclopaedia Cinematographica. Distributed by Pennsylvania
        State University. (Ency. Cinematographica no. E 152)
        Another in the series of silent ethnographic films
        showing a traditional activity. Shows methods of weaving
        reeds into mats used by the marsh Arabs of southern Iraq.

1063   MISCHIEF IN THE LAND
        (n.d.) / 25 min / sound / b&w / 16 mm
        Location: Middle East Institute.
        Outlines the role of Communists in Iraq from the end of
        the monarchy through the rise and fall of Qassim to the
        time of President Aref. Shows interviews with government
        officials. Includes some information on agriculture and
        the Iraqi oil industry.

1064   SIGN LANGUAGE (MA'DAN ARABS, WEST ASIA,
        SOUTH IRAQ)
        1955, released 1958 / 6 min / silent / b&w / 16 mm
        Encyclopaedia Cinematographica. Distributed by Pennsylvania
        State University. (Ency. Cinematographica no. E 182)
        Another in the series of silent ethnographic films
        showing a traditional activity. Shows sign language used
        among the marsh Arabs of southern Iraq.

1065   SILENCE IS KILLING
        1974 / 18 min / sound / color / 16 mm
        Location: Abraham F. Rad Jewish Film Archive.
        Two Iraqi Jewish refugees describe how their husbands
        were arrested and executed.

1066   THE THIRD RIVER
        1952 / 28 min / sound / b&w / 16 mm
        Iraq Petroleum Co., London. Made by Film Centre Ltd.
        Released in the U.S. by British Information Services. (NUC
        FiA 57-83) Credits: Music - Elisabeth Lutyens.
        Profiles the third river in Iraq, the oil pipeline
        crossing the country which moves around 200 million tons
        of oil per year.

1067   VESTING THE METROPOLITAN OF MOSSUL WITH THE
        LITURGICAL GARMENT (CHRISTIAN CHURCHES, SYRIAN
        ORTHODOX CHRISTIANS (JACOBITES) IRAQ)
        1971 / 6 min / silent / color / 16 mm
        Encyclopaedia Cinematographica. Distributed by Pennsylvania
        State University. (Ency. Cinematographica no. E 1941)
        Another in the series of silent ethnographic films
        depicting a traditional activity. Shows a ceremony of
        the Syrian Orthodox Church in Iraq.

ISRAEL
INCLUDING PALESTINE UNTIL 1948

ISRAEL - ARCHEOLOGY

1068 ANCIENT PALESTINE
1968 / 14 min / sound / color or b&w / 16 mm
Coronet Instructional Films. Distributed by Modern Film
Rentals. Credits: Collaborator - Robert E. Cooley. (NUC
FiA 68-1794) Locations: Kent State U. / Library of Congress
(FBA 6487) / Syracuse U. / U. of Illinois / U. of Kansas /
U. of Nebraska. *
Intended for junior high school to adult audiences.
Traces history of Palestine from ancient times to 50
B.C. Describes effect the arid climate has had on the
civilizations of Palestine. Shows artifacts in the
Palestine Archeological Museum which trace contributions
of the Canaanites, Hebrews, Phoenicians, Assyrians,
Greeks, Romans, Byzantines and Muslims to Palestinian
civilization.

1069 BE'ER SHEVA FOUR
1972 / 56 min / sound / color / 16 mm
Ira Meishich. Distributed by the University of California
Media Extension Center.
Documents excavations at Be'er Sheva in the Negev region
of southern Israel. Uses artifacts, maps and Biblical
references to recreate the history of the site from early
Bronze Age to the Roman period.

1070 THE BIG DIG
1973 / 54 min / sound / color / 16 mm
Televisual Productions. Released by Encyclopaedia
Britannica Educational Corp. (LC 75-701995) Locations:
Brigham Young U. / U. of California Extension Media Center.
Examines methods used during an archeological excavation
of the ancient mound at Tel Gezar. Looks at field work
by archeologists, anthropologists and volunteer students
at the site. Shows artifacts found. Describes significance of the mound, a city occupied for over 140 generations.

1071 THE BOOK AND THE SPADE
1966 / 29 min / sound / color / 16 mm
University Museum of the University of Pennsylvania. Made
by Glenn Bernard Film Productions. (NUC FiA 67-316)
Looks at sites of archeological significance in the
Jordan Valley. Includes the Dead Sea area, Jericho,

Gideon and Samaria. Examines the excavations at Tell es Sa'idiyeh in Gilead.

1072 ECHOES OF MASADA
(n.d.) / 30 min / sound / color / 16 mm
Nathan Cohen. Distributed by Telema-First Tier Films, Inc. Credits: Narrator - Eli Wallach.
Uses passages from the historian Josephus to recreate events at Masada. Describes the group of Jewish Zealots who held the mountain fortress against Roman troops for three years before committing mass suicide.

1073 EXCAVATIONS AT HAZOR
(n.d.) / 22 min / silent / color / 16 mm
Location: Abraham F. Rad Jewish Film Archive.
Examines the excavations at Hazor under the supervision of Israeli archeologist Yigael Yadin.

1074 GHOST TOWN IN THE NEGEV
1956 / 29 min / sound / b&w / 16 mm
New York University. Released by NET Film Service. (Yesterday's World series) (NUC FiA 58-1412) Credits: Host - Dr. Casper J. Kraemer.
Looks at excavation of the village of Nesson in the Negev. Shows how the site was rediscovered after 2000 years with information found in a deciphered papyrus record.

1075 IN SEARCH OF HISTORY
1961 / 25 min / sound / color / 16 mm
Distributed by Alden Films. Location: Abraham F. Rad Jewish Film Archive.
Available in English and Spanish soundtracks. Traces the work of Yigael Yadin in the Judean hills. Looks at evidence of the Jewish rebellion by Bar Kokhba against the Romans. Shows finds being examined in the Givat Ram laboratories.

1076 IN THE FOOTSTEPS OF THE PAST (BE'IKVOT HE'AVAR)
1962 / 26 min / sound / color / 16 mm
Pioneer Films. Location: Prime Minister's Office, Information Dept., Jerusalem.
Looks at archeological evidence which led to the discovery of the Bar-Kochba scrolls in the Judean desert.

1077 IN THE MIRROR OF TIME - HISTORICAL SITES IN ISRAEL (BIREI HAZMAN - ATARIM HISTORI'YIM BEYISRAEL)
1966 / 25 min / sound / color / 16 or 35 mm
Producer unknown. Credits: Director-Photographer - G. Passis, Script - E. Kenan. Location: Histadrut - General Federation of Jewish Labor, Tel Aviv / Prime Minister's Office, Information Dept., Jerusalem.
General look at various archeologically significant

215

sites in Israel. Traces the history of the Canaanites, the twelve tribes of Israel, Solomon, the destruction of the First Temple, and the return to Zion. Considers Roman sites in Beit She'an and Ashkelon and looks at Masada as a symbol of Jewish freedom. Available in English, Hebrew and French soundtracks.

1078   LAST STAND
1974 / 20 min / sound / color / 16 mm and videocassette
National Instructional Television Center. Made by WETA-TV.
(A Matter of Fact series) (LC 74-703196) Credits: Director
- Hyman Field, Writer-Narrator - John Robbins,
Cinematographer - George Koutsoukos. Location: U. of
Illinois.
      Not to be confused with a film by the same name dealing
with the U.S. Civil War. Tells the story of the Zealots
at Masada who held a mountain fortress against the Romans
in the first century A.D. Reviews several books on the
topic including: THE RIDER AND HIS HORSE
by Erik Hougaard, THE ZEALOTS OF MASADA: THE STORY
OF A DIG by Moshe Pearlman, REVOLT IN JUDEA: THE
ROAD TO MASADA by Alfred Tamaren and HEROD'S
FOREST AND THE ZEALOT'S LAST STAND by Yigael Yadin.

1079   MASADA
1967 / 30 min / sound / b&w / 16 mm
Jewish Theological Seminary of America and NBC. Released by
National Academy for Adult Jewish Services. (Eternal
Light, television series) (LC 72-700964) Credits: Writer -
Hugh Nissenson.
      Edwin Newman interviews archeologist Yigael Yadin con-
cerning the significance of excavations at the mountain
fortress of Masada. Discusses the meaning of the last
Jewish outpost held against the Romans.

1080   MASSADA
1969 / 12 min / sound / color / 35 mm
Yitzhak Harvest. Israel Film Service. Distributed by Alden
Films. Locations: Abraham F. Rad Jewish Film Archive /
Gratz College / Jewish Agency, Jerusalem / Prime Minister's
Office, Information Dept, Jerusalem.
      Available in English, Hebrew and French soundtracks.
Examines work supervised by archeologist Yigael Yadin to
restore the site of the ancient fortress of Masada.
Looks at the historical significance of the site.

1081   RETURN TO MASADA
(n.d.) / 25 min / sound / b&w / 16 mm
Producer unknown. Location: Gratz College.
      Yigael Yadin discusses historical facets of the excava-
tions at Masada. Shows reconstruction of the site, unco-
vered mosaics and views of the excavation.

1082   SEA DIVER
        1969 / 27 min / sound / color / 16 mm
        Televenture. Location: Syracuse U.
        Intended for junior high school to adult audiences.
        Looks at archeological excavations off Israel in the Sea
        of Galilee and Mediterranean. Exploration of Herod's
        Harbor and other sites uncovers pots, coins and arti-
        facts. Shows techniques used to retrieve objects from
        the sea.

1083   THE TEMPLE
        (n.d.) / 30 min / sound / color / 16 mm
        Producer unknown.
        Looks at excavations underway at a temple in Israel.

1084   TRACING MT. SINAI
        1975 / 42 min / sound / color / 16 mm
        Distributed by Alden Films. Location: Abraham F. Rad Jewish
        Film Archive.
        Traces attempts to locate the exact position of Mt. Sinai
        using traditional Biblical accounts of its location.

1085   WRITTEN IN STONE (NICHTAV BA'EVEN)
        1970 / 20 min / sound / color / 16 mm
        Capital Films. Locations: Abraham F. Rad Jewish Film
        Archive / Jewish Agency, Jerusalem / Prime Minister's
        Office, Information Dept., Jerusalem.
        Available in English, Hebrew, French and Spanish
        soundtracks. Looks at various sites of archeological
        and Jewish historical interest in Israel.

ISRAEL - STAMPS AND COINS

1086   BRIDGE OF STAMPS
        1969 / 12 min / sound / color / 16 or 35 mm
        Producer unknown. Location: Abraham F. Rad Jewish Film
        Archive.
        Available in English, Hebrew, German, French and Spanish
        soundtracks. Looks at Israeli stamps depicting a variety
        of subjects.

1087   HISTORY OF COINS IN ISRAEL
        1972 / 25 min / sound / color / 16 mm
        Producer unknown. Location: Abraham F. Rad Jewish Film
        Archive.
        Available in English and Hebrew soundtracks. Traces
        coins used in Israel throughout history.

1088   ISRAEL STAMPS
        1969 / 13 min / sound / color / 16 or 35 mm
        Shesh Vesheva Films, Israel Film Service. Locations: Jewish
        Agency, Jerusalem / Prime Minister's Office, Information

Dept, Jerusalem.
Available in English, Hebrew, German, French and Spanish
soundtracks.   Looks at stamps printed in Israel. For
the serious collector. Produced in cooperation with the
Israel Philately Society.

1089   A SELECTION OF STAMPS
(c. 1965?) / 12 min / sound / color / 16 or 35 mm
Yoram Gross Films. Location: Prime Minister's Office,
Information Dept., Jerusalem.
Available in English, Hebrew, French, Spanish and German
soundtracks. Looks at Israeli stamps issued over a five
year period dealing with landscapes and landscape art.

1090   A STAMP IS BORN
1959 / 13 min / sound / color / 16 mm
Israel Philatelic Services of the State of Israel,
Jerusalem. Made by Keren Hayesod. Released in the U.S. by
Israel Office of Information. Distributed by Alden Films.
(NUC FiA 64-879) Credits: Producer-Photographer - Rolph N.
Kneller, Narrator - Theodore Bikel. Locations: Abraham F.
Rad Jewish Film Archive / Keren Hayesod, Jerusalem.
Traces subjects covered by Israeli stamps including
archeological excavations, landscapes, and historical
events and sites.

1091   STAMPS TELL STORIES (BULIM MESAPRIM)
1964 / 12 min / sound / color / 16 or 35 mm
Yoram Gross Films. Location: Ministry of Education and
Culture, Jerusalem / Prime Minister's Office, Information
Dept., Jerusalem.
Looks at stamps issued in Israel. Shows footage of sce-
nes and objects portrayed on Israeli stamps.

1092   THE STORY OF STAMPS
(n.d.) / 10 min / sound / color / 16 mm
Distributed by Alden Films.
Recreates the history of Israel through stamps.

1093   SYMBOLS IN A CIRCLE (SMALIM BEMA'AGAL)
1966 / 13 min / sound / color / 16 or 35 mm
A. Membush Films. Location: Prime Minister's Office,
Information Dept., Jerusalem.
Available in English, Hebrew or French soundtracks.
Looks at symbols shared by ancient and modern Israeli
coins. Includes the palm tree, anchor, urn and can-
delabra in coin art. Shows ties of Israel to history,
the land and tradition. Winner at the International
Television Film Festival, 1966.

1094   WITHIN THE CIRCLE
(n.d.) / 12 min / sound / color / 16 mm
Producer unknown. Distributed by Alden Films.

Looks at excavation of ancient coins. Shows use of ancient motifs on modern Israeli coins.

ISRAEL - ANCIENT TO MODERN HISTORY

1095   ANCIENT CIVILIZATIONS: PALESTINE
       1974 / 4 min / sound / color / super 8 mm film loop in
       cartridge. Coronet Instructional Media. (LC 74-701515)
       Traces history of the Canaanites, Hebrews and Assyrians
       in ancient Palestine and the kingdom of Israel.

1096   THE ANCIENT SEA
       1960-61 / 20 min / sound / color / 16 mm
       I.G.T.C. Location: Ministry of Tourism, Jerusalem.
       Available in English and French soundtracks. Looks at
       historical sites on the Jordan River, Tiberias and near
       the Sea of Galilee.

1097   THE DAY'S WORK
       1944 / 21 min / sound / b&w / 16 mm
       Religious Films, London. Released in the U.S. by United
       World Films, 1946. (Two Thousand Years Ago series) (NUC FiA
       52-545) Credits: Director - Mary Field with the help of the
       Education Committee of the Christian Cinema.
       Reconstructs the life of workers in Palestine in Biblical
       times. Shows how people lived, the evening meal with the
       family, nightly devotions and various occupations.

1098   DRY BONES
       1970 / 30 min / sound / color / 16 mm
       Shira Linzi. Location: Jewish Agency, Jerusalem.
       Traces the story of ancient Israel using narration from
       the Book of Prophets.

1099   THE HOLY LAND - FROM ABRAHAM TO ALLENBY
       (n.d.) / ? / 16 mm
       Location: National Archives (200 HF 114) No other infor-
       mation available.

1100   THE HOME
       1944 / 19 min / sound / b&w / 16 mm
       Locations: Indiana U. / Seattle Public Library.
       Portrays life of a carpenter and his family in ancient
       Palestine.

1101   ISRAEL
       1959 / 40 min / sound / color / 35 mm
       Warner Brothers. Sponsored by the Israel Bond Organization
       and the State of Israel. Credits: Narrator - Edward G.
       Robinson, Writer-Producer - Leon Uris. Cinemascope.
       Location: Library of Congress (FGB 4793-94) *
       Theatrically produced. Used for fund-raising purposes.

Traces the history of Israel from Biblical times to the present. Shows archeological excavations. Promotes Israel as the hope of Jews everywhere.

1102   ISRAEL
1964 / 27 min / sound / color / 16 mm
International Film Foundation. Locations: Brigham Young U. / Gratz College / Iowa Films / Penn. State U. / Syracuse U. / U. of Kansas.
Intended for junior high school to adult audiences. Gives an overview of 4000 years of Jewish history from the time of the Patriarchs to the creation of the state of Israel in 1948. Uses animation by Philip Stapp, newsreel footage and on-location shots to show ancient and modern Israel.

1103   ISRAEL: EXODUS TO INDEPENDENCE
1972 / 29 min / sound / b&w / 16 or 8 mm
Metromedia Producers Corp. Released by Films Incorporated. (LC 73-700465)
Edited version of the 1965 film: LET MY PEOPLE GO. Traces oppression and persecution of Jews in Europe from the Middle Ages to Nazi Germany. Describes the movement to return to Palestine. Looks at the creation of the state of Israel and its significance for Jews. Intended for junior high school to adult audiences.

1104   ISRAEL: HISTORY, LAND AND PEOPLE
1978 / 18 min / sound / color / 16 mm
CBS. Released by Encyclopaedia Britannica Films. Distributed by BFA Educational Media. Location: Library of Congress / Syracuse U.
For junior high school to adult audiences. Traces the history of Jews from Biblical times to the creation of the state of Israel. Shows growth of Israeli agriculture, industry and population due to immigration. Also considers problems with border conflicts, Palestinian Arabs and minorities within Israel.

1105   ISRAEL IN HISTORY AND PROPHECY
1967 / 30 min / sound / color / 16 mm
Dawn Film Service.
Discusses the establishment of the state of Israel in relation to Biblical prophecy.

1106   ISRAEL - ITS HISTORY AND PEOPLE
1974 / 17 min / sound / color / 16 mm
Atlantis Productions. Credits: Writer-Producer - J. Michael Hagopian. Location: Library of Congress (FBB 2591) *
Revised version of film entitled: ISRAEL - NATION OF DESTINY. Traces exodus of the Jews, formation of ancient Israel and the history of Roman Palestine. In the modern period, examines the growth of the Zionist

movement, the Holocaust and immigration to Israel after
WWII. Looks at modern Israel and problems facing the
nation including the Palestinians and the Arab-Israeli
wars.

1107   ISRAEL: A SEARCH FOR FAITH
        1977 / 58 min / sound / color / 16 or super 8 mm
        Reader's Digest. Distributed by Pyramid Films and by Alden
        Films. (James Michener's World, no. 101, television series)
        Credits: Producer - Albert Waller.
            Also released in edited 26 minute version. Asks why the
        home of three great religions should be centered in such
        a small area of the world. James Michener looks at
        Jerusalem, Mt. Sinai, Galilee and Masada and discusses
        the significance of these sites to modern Muslims,
        Christians and Jews.

1108   ISRAEL: THE STORY OF THE JEWISH PEOPLE
        1965 / 31 min / sound / color / 16 mm
        Julien Bryan. Distributed by International Film Foundation.
        (NUC FiA 66-737) Credits: Historical Consultants - Lloyd
        Gartner, Samuel Terrien, Animator - Philip Stapp,
        Writer-Producer - Walter J. Carroll. Locations: Kent State
        U. / Library of Congress (FCA 5467) / U. of Illinois / U. of
        Texas at Austin. *
            Traces the story of the Jewish people from the Old
        Testament through periods of persecution in Europe to the
        establishment of the state of Israel. Looks at Israeli
        agriculture, immigration of Jews from eastern countries,
        traditions shared by Jews and the problem of admi-
        nistering Jerusalem. Discusses the Arab-Israeli
        conflict. Uses animated sequences, newsreel and live
        footage. Intended for junior high school to adult
        audiences.

1109   LAND OF THE BOOK
        1967 / 28 min / sound / color / 16 mm
        Ray Garner. Released by AV-ED Films. (LC 78-701199)
        Location: U. of Illinois.
            Traces the history of ancient Israel from the time of
        Abraham to the fall of Masada. Uses passages from the
        Bible, Talmud, the historian Josephus and the Dead Sea
        scrolls.

1110   LET MY PEOPLE GO
        1965 / 54 min / sound / b&w / 16 mm
        David Wolper. Metromedia Producers Corp. Distributed by
        Films Incorporated and by Alden Films. Credits: Narrator -
        Richard Basehart, Director - Marshall Flaum. Locations:
        Gratz College / New York Public Donnell Film Library / U. of
        Illinois / U. of Michigan / U. of Nebraska.
            Produced in part from footage from the following films:
        MEMORANDUM ON A VICTORY, A FREE PEOPLE, EDGE

221

OF DANGER, LOOK HOMEWARD WANDERER, THE
DEFENDERS, HOME COMING, TRANSITION, ISRAEL
IN ACTION, and ISRAEL REBORN. Looks at the
persecution of Jews in Europe, the beginning of the
Zionist movement and increase in immigration of Jews to
Palestine. Shows immigration followed by Arab unrest.
Describes the withdrawal of British troops and the War of
Independence which led to the state of Israel.

1111   PICTORIAL GEOGRAPHY
        1950 / 15 min / sound / color / 16 mm
        Location: Brigham Young U.
        Brief look at the geographical importance of Palestine
        in history.

1112   THE RETURN
        1971 / 30 min / sound / color / 16 mm
        Nathan Cohen. Distributed by Telema-First Tier Films, and by
        Pyramid Films. Credits: Narrator - Hal Lindsay.
        Christian film. Deals with the fulfillment of Biblical
        prophecy with the return of Jews to Israel after 19 cen-
        turies. Discusses the implication of this prophecy for
        the future.

1113   THE SIEGE OF THE ROCK (ISRAEL)
        1969 / 30 min / sound / color / 16 mm
        BBC-TV, London. Released in the U.S. by Time-Life Films.
        (The Glory That Remains series, no. 8) (LC 70-710387)
        Credits: Producer - Geoffrey Baines, Writer-Narrator -
        Robert Erskine. Location: U. of Illinois.
        Retells the story of the siege of the Jewish Zealots at
        the mountain stronghold of Masada. Describes how the
        remnants of the Jewish force committed mass suicide
        rather than surrender to Roman troops.

1114   TERRA SANCTA: A FILM OF ISRAEL
        1968 / 31 min / sound / color / 16 mm
        Distributed by International Film Bureau. Location: Middle
        East Institute / Syracuse U.
        Narrated by a Yemeni Israeli Jew. Looks at Israel in
        history and today as a haven for Jews from around the
        world. Includes scenes of Israeli cities. Stresses
        urban centers are seen as the hope for the future.
        Discusses problems of assimilation of immigrants from
        around the world. Shows sites of significance to Jews,
        Christians and Muslims in Israel.

1115   THE TRAVELLERS
        1944 / 22 min / sound / b&w / 16 mm
        Religious Films, London. Released in the U.S. by United
        World Films. (Two Thousand Years Ago series) (NUC FiA
        52-547) Credits: Director - Mary Field with the help of the
        Education Committee of the Christian Cinema.

222

Recreates the life of a traveler in Palestine in Biblical
times. Shows observance of the Sabbath at an inn.

1116   TREASURES FROM THE LAND OF THE BIBLE
        1956 / 29 min / sound / b&w / 16 mm
        New York University. Released by NET Film Service.
        (Yesterday's Worlds series) (NUC FiA 58-1738) Credits:
        Host - Dr. Casper J. Kraemer.
        Discussion of the discovery and significance of the Dead
        Sea scrolls. Traces the history of Palestine from
        earliest recorded times. Includes examples of
        Palestinian art.

1117   WHERE TIME IS TIMELESS
        1966 / 25 min / sound / color / 16 or 35 mm
        Producer unknown. Location: Abraham F. Rad Jewish Film
        Archive.
        Available in English, Hebrew and French soundtracks.
        Traces history of Palestine since Canaanite times through
        archeological sites and artifacts.

ISRAEL - WORLD WAR I TO THE PRESENT

1118   THE DEATH OF ABRAHAM LEIB
        1964 / 13 min / sound / b&w / 16 or 35 mm
        Berkey Pathe Humphries. Locations: Abraham F. Rad Jewish
        Film Archive / Histadrut - General Federation of Jewish
        Labor, Tel Aviv / Prime Minister's Office, Information
        Dept., Jerusalem.
        Available in English and Hebrew soundtracks. Listed in
        some catalogs as: DEATH OF ABRAHAM LEV and
        MOTO SHEL AVRAHAM LEV. Uses old photographs
        to tell the story of early Jewish settlers in Palestine.
        Shows the founders of the moshavim, a type of communal
        settlement, the beginning of Tel Aviv and early Jewish
        laborers in Israel.

1119   (FROM DREAM TO REALITY)
        (n.d.) / 60 min / silent / b&w / 16 mm
        Educational Film Enterprises. George Rony. (George Rony
        Collection, no 132) Location: Library of Congress (FCA
        7894-95)   *
        Excellent source of footage. Silent film. Contains sce-
        nes of people, places and events which figured in the
        creation of the state of Israel. Includes footage from
        the 1930's to '50's covering treatment of Jews in Europe
        during WWII, British Parliamentary meetings, scenes of
        Jerusalem, the Arab-Israeli conflicts, the War of
        Independence and development plans of the new state.
        Useful for research purposes.

1120   GENESIS 1882: A FAMILY PORTRAIT
        (c. 1975?) / ? / sound / color / 16 mm

Audio-Visual Dept. Anti-Defamation League of B'nai B'rith.
No other information available.

1121 THE ISSUE IS PEACE
1976 / 30 min / sound / color / 16 mm
Association Films. Sponsored by the Consulate General of
Israel in Chicago. Distributed by Alden Films. Location:
Middle East Institute.
Uses newsreels and animation. Emphasizes desire for
peace on the part of Israel from its creation to the pre-
sent. Looks at mistreatment of Jews in Europe and the
need for a Jewish homeland. Presents the surrounding
Arab countries as terrorists, unreasonable and war-like.
Contains some omissions and inaccuracies.

1122 MIRACLE OF SURVIVAL
(n.d.) / 85 min / sound / b&w / 16 or 35 mm
Maurice Rabinoff Associates.
Traces the history of Israel and Jewish life. Covers
a seventy year period from Russian pograms to the Six Day
War.

1123 PALESTINE
1945 / 15 min / sound / b&w / 16 mm
Time-Life-Fortune. (The March of Time, Forum Edition,
series) Locations: Gratz College / Jewish Agency Film
Archive.
Uses documentary footage from 1917 to 1945 to cover the
background of the creation of an Israeli state.
Describes the Balfour Declaration, refugee camps, the
work of Weizmann, and the creation of the Hadassah
Hospital. Covers the dilemma of Palestine as seen in
1945. Tries to cover both the Jewish and Arab points of
view. Contains good historical footage.

1124 PALESTINE
1947-48 / 8 min / silent / b&w / 16 mm
Location: Abraham F. Rad Jewish Film Archive.
Shows the U.N. Special Commission on Palestine visiting
Jerusalem and the settlement of Beit Ha'arava near the
Dead Sea.

1125 PALESTINE: PATH TO TRAGEDY
(n.d.) / 20 min / sound / b&w / 16 mm
Distributed by the Arab Information Center, New York.
Uses archival footage from the British Museum to show the
occupation of Palestine under the British followed by the
creation of an Israeli state. Describes the loss of land
from various Arab states to Israel during the 1967 War.
From the Arab point of view.

1126 PALESTINE PROBLEM
1945 / 17 min / sound / b&w / 35 mm

Time, Inc. (March of Time, vol. 12, no. 1) Location:
National Archives (200 MT .12.1)
March of Time newsreel. Covers the situation in
Palestine in 1945.

1127 PROMISED LAND, TROUBLED LAND
1973 / 14 min / sound / b&w / 16 mm
Hearst Metrotone News. (Screen News Digest, v. 16, no. 4)
(LC 74-701523) Location: Library of Congress FBB 2938) *
Uses archival footage to show history of Palestine under
Ottoman rule, the turbulent British Mandate period and
the creation of Israel. Includes scenes of the 1956,
1967 and 1973 wars and peace talks. Discusses problem of
Arabs living in Israel. Offers little prospect for
peace.

1128 SHALOM (PARTS 1 AND 2)
1972 / 74 min / sound / color / 16 mm
Macmillan. Location: Syracuse U.
Intended for junior high school to adult audiences.
Covers history of Israel from early 19th century Jewish
settlers through the creation of the state to the pre-
sent. Shows scenes of Jerusalem, Haifa, Bethlehem, Tel
Aviv and Gaza. Describes kibbutz life and discusses the
conflict between Israel and the Arab states. Narrated by
Robert Vaughn.

1129 SOUTH WINDOW
1958 / 26 min / sound / color / 16 mm
National Committee for Labour, Israel.
Looks at the struggle of early Jewish pioneers in
Palestine.

1130 THE TWICE-PROMISED LAND
1964 / 53 min / sound / b&w / 16 mm
Hearst Metrotone News. Released by B.C.G. Films.
(Perspective on Greatness, television series) (NUC Fi
67-919) Credits: Producer-Director - Robert Foster, Writer
- John O'Toole, Host - Rod Serling. Location: Library of
Congress (FBA 3667-68)
Traces history of Palestine from the Balfour Declaration
in 1917 to the creation of the state of Israel in 1948.
Covers the resulting series of Arab-Israeli wars.

1131 TWO MINUTES
(n.d.) / 2 min / sound / color / 16 mm
Producer unknown. Location: Gratz College.
A collage of photographs with musical background and no
narration. Traces history of Israel from the time of
Herzl to after the Six Day War. Of most use to those
already familiar with major events in Israel's history.

1132 THE YEARS OF DECISION
1962 / 30 min / sound / b&w / 16 mm

Lazar Dunner. Locations: Histadrut - General Federation of
Jewish Labor, Tel Aviv / Jewish Agency Film Archive,
Jerusalem / Keren Hayesod, Jerusalem / Ministry of Education
and Culture, Jerusalem.
Available in English and Hebrew soundtracks. Traces
history of the Zionist movement from Herzl through the
first Aliyot, or migration. Shows the impact of World
War I and the creation of an Israeli state. Covers the
mass immigration of Jews from Iraq, nicknamed "Operation
Ali Baba".

1133   YEARS OF DESTINY
        1961 / 27 min / sound / b&w / 16 mm
        Keren Hayesod, Jerusalem. Lazar Dunner. Released in the
        U.S. by United Israel Appeal. Distributed by Alden Films.
        (NUC FiA 64-581) Credits: Writer - Marc Siegel, Narrator -
        Alexander Scourby. Location: Abraham F. Rad Jewish Film
        Archive.
        Traces the history of Zionism from the time of Herzl to
        the 1960's. Includes scenes of WWI, Turkish rule,
        creation of the state of Israel and the immigration of
        Jews from Iraq. May be the same film as no. 1132.

1134   THE ZIONIST COMMITTEE FROM PALESTINE - 1938
        1938 / ? / b&w / 8 mm
        Mordechai Bentov. Location: Central Zionist Archives.
        Shows members of the Zionist Committee from Palestine
        attending the Zionist Committee meetings in London in
        1938.

ISRAEL   -   1948 TO THE PRESENT

1135   AGE OF ACHIEVEMENT
        1953 / 30 min / sound / b&w / 16 mm
        National Committee for Labor, Israel. (NUC FiA 55-986)
        Credits: Producer - David Zeitani, Writer - Nahum Guttman.
        Looks at early Jewish settlers in Palestine who laid the
        foundation for the state of Israel. Traces Histadrut
        (Federation of Jewish Labor) activities in various
        cities and discusses contributions of Histadrut to
        Israeli life.

1136   AS ISRAEL IS 30 - WE ARE ONE
        (c. 1978) / 12 min / sound / 16 mm
        Distributed by Alden Films. No other information available.

1137   AT WAR WITH THE EXPERTS: THE CONFLICTS OF HARRY
        S. TRUMAN
        1964 / 25 min / sound / b&w / 16 mm
        Location: Abraham F. Rad Jewish Film Archive.
        Former President Truman discusses his decision to help in
        the establishment of the state of Israel. Includes

historical footage of abuse of Jews in Europe, relocation
camps for Jews in Cyprus and early Jewish settlement in
Palestine.

1138   BARON EDMUND DE ROTHSCHILD'S REMAINS BROUGHT
        TO ISRAEL
        1954-55 / ? / sound / b&w / 16 mm
        Israel Motion Picture Studios, Herzliyah.
        Newsreel. Shows transfer to Israel of the remains of
        Baron de Rothschild for burial. Depicts the Baron as a
        major financial and political force behind the Jewish
        state.

1139   BIRTHDAY OF A PROPHECY
        1948 / 25 min / sound / color / 16 mm
        Irving Jacoby. Affiliated Film Production. Locations:
        Abraham F. Rad Jewish Film Archive / Jewish Agency Film
        Archive / Keren Hayesod, Jerusalem.
        Looks at the creation of the state of Israel through the
        eyes of a Polish Jewish immigrant, a Jewish Agency worker
        and an American Jewish fund-raiser.

1140   BUILDING A NATION: ISRAEL
        1950 / 20 min / sound / b&w / 16 mm
        United World Films. Produced by Louis de Rochemont
        Associates. (The Earth and Its People series) (NUC FiA
        52-348) Credits: Director-Photographer - Victor Vicas,
        Consultants - Clyde F. Kohn, W.A. Atwood. Locations:
        Indiana U. / Library of Congress (FCA 171) / Syracuse U. /
        U. of Illinois. *
        Intended for junior-senior high school audiences. Looks
        at efforts of the new state of Israel to develop agri-
        culture, transportation and the cities. Portrays Arabs
        incorrectly as nomads living in tents not as villagers
        and urban dwellers. Describes progress Israel is making
        in development. Discusses problems facing Israel inclu-
        ding lack of water and mass immigration of Jews from
        around the world.

1141   CHILDREN OF THE EXODUS
        (c. 1970?) / 28 min / sound / color / 16 mm
        United Jewish Appeal. Distributed by Alden Films. Credits:
        Narrator - Zero Mostel. Locations: Abraham F. Rad Jewish
        Film Archive / Gratz College.
        Listed in some catalogs as: CHILDREN OF EXODUS.
        Traces some of the people who traveled on the original
        ship made famous by the feature film EXODUS. They are
        shown living in Israel today and working in a variety
        of professions. Follows a youth director, a farmer, a
        kibbutz manager and a diamond cutter. Uses still pho-
        tographs and interviews to recreate the incident of the
        ship Exodus in 1947.

1142 THE DAY HAS COME
1951 / 45 min / sound / b&w / 16 mm
Victor Vicas Productions. United Israel Campaign and the
Information Dept. of the Jewish Agency. (NUC FiA 54-1200)
Credits: Producer-Director - Samuel J. Schweig, Writer -
Michael Elkins. Locations: Abraham F. Rad Jewish Film
Archive / Histadrut - General Federation of Jewish Labor,
Tel Aviv / Keren Hayesod, Jerusalem / Library of Congress
(FBA 4909-10) *
Looks closely at the Israeli War of Independence of 1948.
Shows the creation of the state of Israel, problems in
assimilating large numbers of Jewish immigrants from
around the world and the continued Arab-Israeli conflict.

1143 DAY OF INDEPENDENCE
1952 / 20 min / sound / b&w / 16 mm
United Israel Appeal. (NUC FiA 54-1202) Credits: Producer -
Samuel J. Schweig, Director - Victor Vicas.
Looks at the creation of the state of Israel and the
implications of a Jewish state for Jews around the world.

1144 DECLARATION OF INDEPENDENCE (MEGILLAT HA'ATZMA'UT)
1958 / 17 min / sound / b&w / 16 or 35 mm
Berkey Pathe Humphries. Locations: Histadrut - General
Federation of Jewish Labor, Tel Aviv / Jewish Agency,
Jerusalem / Ministry of Education and Culture, Jerusalem /
Prime Minister's Office, Information Dept., Jerusalem.
Available in English and Hebrew soundtracks. Looks at
the U.N. vote on Israel and the establishment of the
state. Uses a series of photographs to show David
Ben-Gurion reading the Declaration of Independence at the
Israel Museum in Tel Aviv.

1145 EIGHT YEARS OF ISRAEL INDEPENDENCE
(c. 1956) / 18 min / sound / b&w / 16 mm
Samuel Elfert. Location: Jewish Agency Film Archive,
Jerusalem.
Summary of Israel's history since independence. Includes
scenes of discovery of oil, discovery of the Dead Sea
Scrolls and industrial and agricultural development.
Looks at absorption of Jewish immigrants from other
countries.

1146 FIFTH ANNIVERSARY OF THE STATE OF ISRAEL
1953 / 7 min / sound / b&w / 16 mm
Location: Abraham F. Rad Jewish Film Archive.
Looks at the celebration of Israeli Independence Day in
1953.

1147 HERUT NEWSREELS
1948-49 / ? / b&w / 8 mm
Jabotinsky Institute in Israel.
Newsreel footage shot at the time of the creation of

Israel. Includes scenes of a reception for Menachem
Begin at the New York airport and reception given by the
Mayor of New York in 1948. Shows the Waldorf Astoria
meeting in New York in 1949 when the American Committee
for a Free Palestine was disbanded.

1148 ISRAEL
1961 / 11 min / sound / color / 16 mm
Jackson Bailey and Carl Russell. Released by AV-ED Films.
Distributed by Alden Films. (NUC FiA 62-1657)
For junior to senior high school audiences. Outlines the
history of the establishment of an Israeli state.
Describes progress in agriculture, industry and develop-
ment. Looks at immigration of Jews from other countries.

1149 ISRAEL IN ACTION
1948 / 10 min / sound / b&w / 16 mm
United Palestine Appeal. Made by Palestine Films. (NUC FiA
54-1207 rev) Location: Abraham F. Rad Jewish Film Archive /
Jewish Agency Film Archive, Jerusalem / Keren Hayesod, Jerusalem
/ Ministry of Education and Culture, Jerusalem.
Uses newsreel footage to show the political and military
birth of Israel. Includes coverage of the Israeli War of
Independence.

1150 ISRAEL IN THE FAMILY OF NATIONS
1958 / 17 min / sound / b&w / 16 mm
Orb Films. Released by United Israel Appeal. Distributed by
Alden Films. (NUC FiA 64-579) Credits: Producer - Baruch
Dienar.
Short diplomatic history of Israel. Includes scenes of
the vote to include Israel in the U.N., Ben-Gurion's
visit to New York, Golda Meir's visit to Ghana, and Moshe
Dayan in Paris.

1151 ISRAEL IS LABOR
1949 / 10 min / sound / b&w / 16 mm
United Electrical, Radio and Machine Workers of America.
Made by Union Films. (LC 73-704371) Credits:
Reporter-Photographer - Arthur Gaeth. Location: Library of
Congress (FAA 4115) *
Compares U.S. and Israeli traditions in gaining indepen-
dence from the British. Discusses labor unions in
Israel, kibbutz life and statistical information on
unions. Presents Israel as a haven for organized labor
and stresses Arab and Israeli harmony in the work place.

1152 ISRAEL: MIDDLE EAST NEIGHBOR
1962 / 16 min / sound / color / 16 mm
Bailey Films. Distributed by BFA Educational Media and by
Alden Films. (NUC FiA 63-645) Credits: Photographer - Ed
Lark. Eastman color. Locations: Iowa Films / Kent State U.
/ Syracuse U. / U. of Illinois / U. of Iowa.

Intended for junior high school to adult audiences.
Looks at progress made by Israel in industry and agriculture. Discusses the place of Arabs in Israel today.

1153   ISRAEL, A NATION
        1960 / 4 min / sound / b&w / 16 mm
        Filmrite Associates. Released by Official Films. (Greatest
        Headlines of the Century series) (NUC Fi 62-2171) Credits:
        Producer - Sherm Grinberg, Narrator - Tom Hudson, Writers -
        Allan Lurie, Ray Parker. Location: Library of Congress (FAA
        3784) *
           Good source of archival footage. Traces the establish-
           ment of the state of Israel. Describes plans for par-
           tition, Arab riots, British administrative problems,
           heavy illegal immigration of Jews from war-torn Europe,
           British withdrawal and the Declaration of Independence
           read by David Ben-Gurion. Good summary of the creation
           of Israel.

1154   ISRAEL - A NATION IS BORN
        1963 / 17 min / sound / color or b&w / 16 mm
        Dudley Pictures Corp. Released by United World Films. (Our
        World of the Sixties series) (NUC FiA 64-832) Locations:
        Penn. State U. / Syracuse U. / U. of Illinois / U. of
        Wisconsin.
           For elementary to junior high school audiences. Shows
           the geography of Israel and discusses progress made in
           agriculture and industrialization. Describes how Jews
           immigrate to Israel looking for a better life.

1155   ISRAEL - A NATION IS BORN
        1970 / 4 min / silent / b&w / 8 and super 8 mm film loops
        Anargyros Film Library. (Highlights in World History series)
        (LC 75-707474)
           Looks at the creation of the state of Israel following the
           British Mandate. Covers the first Arab-Israeli War, also
           called the Israeli War of Independence.

1156   ISRAEL...NATION OF DESTINY
        1971 / 28 min / sound / color / 16 mm
        Atlantis Productions. J. Michael Hagopian. (LC 75-715466)
        Locations: Gratz College / Library of Congress (FBB 1740) /
        Syracuse U. *
           Uses footage gathered from a variety of other films.
           Traces history of Israel, progress made in the fields of
           agriculture and industry and the Arab-Israeli wars. Very
           emotional narration. Presents a pro-Israeli viewpoint.

1157   ISRAEL 1948
        1948 / 30 min / silent / color / 16 mm
        Location: Abraham F. Rad Jewish Film Archive.
        Documents the creation of the state of Israel in 1948.

1158   ISRAEL REBORN
        1948 / 10 min / sound / b&w / 16 mm
        United Palestine Appeal. Made by Palestine Films. (NUC FiA
        54-1208 rev)
            Newsreel coverage of the establishment of the state of
        Israel, the declaration of independence, arrival of new
        immigrants, the first Arab-Israeli War, the U.N. debate
        and recognition of Israel by the U.S.

1159   ISRAEL REBORN
        1948 / 25 min / sound / b&w / 16 mm
        Palestine Films. Location: Abraham F. Rad Jewish Film
        Archive / Jewish Agency Film Archive, Jerusalem / Keren
        Hayesod, Jerusalem / Ministry of Education and Culture,
        Jerusalem.
            In-depth account of the creation of the state of Israel.
        May be a longer version of no. 1158.

1160   ISRAEL, THEODORE HERZL: THE JEWISH STATE
        (n.d.) / 30 min / silent / b&w / 16 mm
        George Rony Production. (George Rony Collection, no. 133)
        Location: Library of Congress (FRA 6152) holds a negative of
        the film. No other information available.

1161   ISRAELI INDEPENDENCE
        1971 / 4 min / silent / b&w / super 8 mm film loop in
        cartridge. Thorne Films. (8 mm Documents Project series,
        no. 378) (LC 72-701416) Credits: Producer - Dale Willard.
        Location: Library of Congress. No other information
        available.

1162   MAY 14TH, 1948
        (c. 1949) / 15 min / sound / b&w / 16 mm
        Location: Abraham F. Rad Jewish Film Archive.
            Shows the establishment of the state of Israel and the
        defeat of Arab armies in the Israeli War of Independence,
        the first Arab-Israeli War.

1163   NEW PIONEERS (CHALUTZIM CHADASHIM)
        1958 / 10 min / sound / 35 mm
        Baruch Dienar. Israel Film Studios, Herzliyah.
            Shows new pioneers and immigrants helping in Israel's
        development circa 1958.

1164   NEWSFOCUS/ISRAEL: AN INTERNATIONAL PRESS PERSPECTIVE
        (n.d.) / 28 min / sound / b&w / 16 mm
        Anti-Defamation League of B'nai B'rith.
            Looks at possible threats to Israel as a result of inter-
        national political and economic interests. Discusses the
        problem of supply of oil, shipping needs through the
        Suez Canal and the Soviet presence in the Mediterranean.

1165   NO OTHER CHOICE
        1968 / 27 min / sound / b&w / 16 mm

Location: Abraham F. Rad Jewish Film Archive.
Available in English, Hebrew and Spanish soundtracks.
Presents progress and development seen in Israel over a
twenty year period. Uses animated still photographs.
Stresses progress despite three wars.

1166   THE NOBEL PRIZE, 1978, PART 2
December 21, 1978 / 30 min / sound / color / 3/4"
videocassette. PBS. Production of WQED Pittsburgh.
Credits: Producer-Writer - David H. Vowell, Executive
Producer - Jay Michaels. Location: Museum of Broadcasting
(T79:0075)
Television special. Deals with the awarding of the Nobel
Prize to Anwar Sadat of Egypt and Menachem Begin of
Israel. Both speak about peace followed by short
biographies. Sadat is seen in Jerusalem putting a wreath
on the Israeli tomb of the unknown soldier and at the
Knesset. Sadat and Begin are shown addressing the
Knesset. Representatives of the two winners receive the
peace medals. Other winners of the Noble prize for 1978
are also profiled in the remaining 20 minutes of this
broadcast.

1167   ON THE BRINK OF PEACE
(c. 1979?) / 30 min / sound / color / 16 mm
United Jewish Appeal. Credits: Narrator - Eli Wallach.
Discusses the Arab-Israeli conflict and possible solutions. Intended for junior-senior high school audiences.

1168   OUR ROAD TO LIFE
(c. 1958) / 18 min / sound / b&w / 16 mm
Baruch Dienar. Location: Abraham F. Rad Jewish Film Archive
/ Jewish Agency Film Archive, Jerusalem.
Review of the first ten years of Israel's existence pre-
sented by the Israel Tenth Anniversary World Committee.

1169   PEACE - WHEN THERE IS NO PEACE
1956-57 / 10 min / sound / b&w / 16 mm
Israel Motion Pictures for the Israel Defense Forces.
Location: Abraham F. Rad Jewish Film Archive.
Describes the Israeli War of Independence, early Jewish
immigration, agricultural and industrial acheivements and
training of the armed forces during the first ten years
of Israeli statehood.

1170   PORTRAIT OF A DECADE
(c. 1958) / 28 min / sound / color / 16 mm
Location: Abraham F. Rad Jewish Film Archive.
Describes cultural, social and economic developments in
Israel in the first ten years of statehood.

1171   STATE IN ACTION
(c. 1950) / 18 min / sound / color / 16 mm

Location: Abraham F. Rad Jewish Film Archive.
Documents the changeover to Israeli control of government
institutions, currency, stamp production, law courts, land
development, maritime services, and railways after
declaration of the state of Israel.

1172 A STATE IS BORN
1967 / 20 min / sound / color / 16 mm
Jewish National Fund.
Describes the formation of Israel and the events leading
to the founding of the Jewish state in 1948.

1173 TOWARDS THE THIRD DECADE
1968 / 20 min / sound / color / 16 mm
Location: Jewish National Fund, Jerusalem.
Newsreel. Outlines programs for land development and
formation of settlements during the first twenty years of
Israeli statehood.

1174 A TRIBUTE TO ISRAEL
(C. 1950) / 9 min / sound / b&w / 16 mm
Location: Abraham F. Rad Jewish Film Archive.
Outlines events leading up to the formation of Israel.
Describes some of the early accomplishments of Israel.

ISRAEL - CONTEMPORARY VIEWS OF ISRAEL - 1948-1959

1175 DREW PEARSON REPORTS ON THE HOLY LAND
1957 / 60 min / sound / b&w / 16 or 35 mm
Orb Films. Released by Orb Films and United Israel Appeal.
(NUC FiA 64-572) Credits: Producer-Director - Baruch Dienar,
Cameraman - Rolf N. Kneller. Location: Abraham F. Rad
Jewish Film Archive.
Drew Pearson interviews farmers, housewives, fishermen
and clergymen in Israel about accomplishments in science,
education, agriculture and religion. Stresses coopera-
tion between Arabs and Jews. Includes statement by
Ben-Gurion concerning official Israeli policy toward the
Arab states.

1176 FILM MAGAZINE, NOVEMBER 1956
1956 / 15 min / sound / b&w / 16 mm
The Jewish Agency. Location: The Jewish Agency Film Archive,
Jerusalem.
Numbers 1176-1207 list newsreels produced by the Jewish
Agency. With English, Hebrew, French and Spanish
soundtracks. Covers a variety of current interest
topics. Others in the series produced in the 1960's are
listed in a later section. November 1956 covers a U.J.A.
visit to Urim, capture of the Egyptian ship "Ibrahim
el-Awal", Golda Meir receiving Japanese and Indian
correspondents and footage from the Sinai campaign of the
1956 War.

1177   FILM MAGAZINE, DECEMBER 1956
       1956 / 15 min / sound / b&w / 16 mm
       The Jewish Agency. See no. 1176 for full information.
       Includes scenes of Hanukkah celebrations, evacuation of
       troops from Sinai, immigration of Egyptian and Hungarian
       Jews, Dimona in the Negev, students helping in border
       settlements, launching of the ship "Theodore Herzl" and
       archeological excavations at Hatzor.

1178   FILM MAGAZINE, JANUARY 1957
       1957 / 15 min / sound / b&w / 16 mm
       The Jewish Agency. See no. 1176 for more information.
       Includes scenes of discussions on immigration, an attack
       on Tel Mond, Pierre Medes visiting the Prime Minister,
       a tour of a steel plant, immigrants from Egypt and
       Hungary, a profile of life on the Gaza Strip, mobile post
       office unit in the Negev, orange picking, Christmas
       celebrations, and St. Catherine's Monastery in the Sinai.

1179   FILM MAGAZINE, FEBRUARY 1957
       1957 / 15 min / sound / b&w / 16 mm
       The Jewish Agency. See no. 1176 for more information.
       Includes scenes of fishing in Gaza, arrival of
       immigrants, planting of forests, Jerusalem, Israel's navy
       and army, excavations at archeological sites, Marc
       Chagall in Israel, sports events and Israel's stand
       against Egypt.

1180   FILM MAGAZINE, MARCH 1957
       1957 / 15 min / sound / b&w / 16 mm
       The Jewish Agency. See no. 1176 for more information.
       Includes scenes of Israeli troop withdrawal, WIZO's 13th
       Congress, housing for immigrants, a new health clinic in
       Nazareth, the olives in season, Eilat, Mane Katz exhibi-
       tion and the carnival at Purim.

1181   FILM MAGAZINE, APRIL 1957
       1957 / 15 min / sound / b&w / 16 mm
       The Jewish Agency. See no. 1176 for more information.
       Includes scenes of Jews leaving Egypt, forests planted
       outside Jerusalem, Ben-Gurion receiving an honorary doc-
       torate, women in Israel, the port at Eilat, Jewish youth
       leaders in Israel, industrial accomplishments, the annual
       march to Jerusalem, and Maronite and Druze celebrations.

1182   FILM MAGAZINE, MAY 1957
       1957 / 15 min / sound / b&w / 16 mm
       The Jewish Agency. See no. 1176 for more information.
       Includes scenes of a jubilee in Israel, harvest in the
       Negev, a student's carnival and Independence Day celebra-
       tions.

1183   FILM MAGAZINE, JUNE 1957
       1957 / 15 min / sound / b&w / 16 mm

The Jewish Agency. See no. 1176 for more information.
Includes scenes of the land, a children's village, Lag
Ba'Omer at Meron, army training, the Haifa Technical
Institute and new fashions.

1184   FILM MAGAZINE, AUGUST 1957
        1957 / 15 min / sound / b&w / 16 mm
        The Jewish Agency. See no. 1176 for more information.
        Includes scenes of delegations, the Congress for Judaism,
        Tira, a Home and Garden exhibition, finding homes for new
        immigrants, and a profile of naval cadets.

1185   FILM MAGAZINE, SEPTEMBER 1957
        1957 / 15 min / sound / b&w / 16 mm
        The Jewish Agency. See no. 1176 for more information.
        Includes scenes of children going to school, the Nazareth
        Seminary, a police parade, paratroopers, the International
        Atomic Conference, International Stamp Exhibition, the
        grape harvest, and the fifth Maccabiah.

1186   FILM MAGAZINE, OCTOBER 1957
        1957 / 15 min / sound / b&w / 16 mm
        The Jewish Agency. See no. 1176 for more information.
        Includes scenes of Eilat Hospital, chess games, Druze
        soldiers, sailing, the "Family of Man" exhibition, a new
        concert hall, the Armoured Corps. manoeuvres, tobacco
        growing and a day at the zoo.

1187   FILM MAGAZINE, NOVEMBER 1957
        1957 / 15 min / sound / b&w / 16 mm
        The Jewish Agency. See no. 1176 for more information.
        Includes scenes of the swearing in of the President,
        planting of forests, life-guards on duty, cotton fields,
        excavations at Hatzor and a profile of the reclamation
        project at the Huleh swamp.

1188   FILM MAGAZINE, DECEMBER 1957
        1957 / 15 min / sound / b&w / 16 mm
        The Jewish Agency. See no. 1176 for more information.
        Includes a summary of the major events of the year 1957.

1189   FILM MAGAZINE, JANUARY 1958
        1958 / 15 min / sound / b&w / 16 mm
        The Jewish Agency. See no. 1176 for more information.
        Includes scenes of celebration of Hanukkah, industry,
        members of the Brazilian Parliament visit the Galilee, a
        meeting of veteran settlers at Nahalal, Yotvata in the
        Negev and a profile of new naval officers.

1190   FILM MAGAZINE, FEBRUARY 1958
        1958 / 15 min / sound / b&w / 16 mm
        The Jewish Agency. See no. 1176 for more information.
        Includes scenes of spring in Israel, visit of diplomats

from Indonesia, Haifa oil refineries, visitors from Ghana in Jerusalem, and the Chief of Staff inspects officer cadets.

1191 FILM MAGAZINE, APRIL 1958
1958 / 15 min / sound / b&w / 16 mm
The Jewish Agency. See no. 1176 for more information. Includes scenes of celebration of Purim, the march to Jerusalem, Rehovot School of Agriculture, Arabs visiting the Negev and a profile on tourism.

1192 FILM MAGAZINE, MAY 1958
1958 / 15 min / sound / b&w / 16 mm
The Jewish Agency. See no. 1176 for more information. Newsreel devoted to the celebration of Israel's tenth anniversary.

1193 FILM MAGAZINE, JUNE 1958
1958 / 15 min / sound / b&w / 16 mm
The Jewish Agency. See no. 1176 for more information. Includes scenes of visitors to Israel for the 10th Anniversary celebrations, a profile of the Arab community, the new campus of Hebrew University, youth villages and children at a party for the President.

1194 FILM MAGAZINE, JULY 1958
1958 / 15 min / sound / b&w / 16 mm
The Jewish Agency. See no. 1176 for more information. Includes scenes on Safed, growing sugar beets, and a youth "takeover" of Haifa for one day.

1195 FILM MAGAZINE, AUGUST 1958
1958 / 15 min / sound / b&w / 16 mm
The Jewish Agency. See no. 1176 for more information. Includes scenes of a Bible quiz, the Congress of Jewish Youth, Air Force Day, the port at Haifa, and antiquities at Athlit and Caesarea.

1196 FILM MAGAZINE, OCTOBER 1958
1958 / 15 min / sound / b&w / 16 mm
The Jewish Agency. See no. 1176 for more information. Includes scenes of the President receiving visitors, the Acre exhibition, a kibbutz exhibition, crossing the Kinneret, terracing on the hillsides, industry in Jerusalem and a profile of a new industrial crop.

1197 FILM MAGAZINE, DECEMBER 1958
1958 / 15 min / sound / b&w / 16 mm
The Jewish Agency. See no. 1176 for more information. Contains a profile of projects designed to bring life to the Negev Desert region.

1198 FILM MAGAZINE, JANUARY 1959
1959 / 15 min / sound / b&w / 16 mm

The Jewish Agency. See no. 1176 for more information. Includes scenes of arrival of immigrants, locusts, the orange crop, and study groups from Asia and Africa.

1199   FILM MAGAZINE, FEBRUARY 1959
1959 / 15 min / sound / b&w / 16 mm
The Jewish Agency. See no. 1176 for more information. Includes scenes of Joseph Sprinzak's funeral, the Bible and Israeli stamps, a look at milk production and housing for immigrants.

1200   FILM MAGAZINE, MARCH 1959
1959 / 15 min / sound / b&w / 16 mm
The Jewish Agency. See no. 1176 for more information. Includes scenes of the Tel Aviv Jubilee, new rural centers, Shalom Aleichem Centenary, and a profile on winter resorts such as Tiberias.

1201   FILM MAGAZINE, APRIL 1959
1959 / 15 min / sound / b&w / 16 mm
The Jewish Agency. See no. 1176 for more information. Profiles immigrants coming to Israel in 1959.

1202   FILM MAGAZINE, MAY 1959
1959 / 15 min / sound / b&w / 16 mm
The Jewish Agency. See no. 1176 for more information. Includes scenes of celebration of Purim, youth Aliyah programs, the annual march to Jerusalem, Burmese visitors, the International Farmer's Congress, a new museum in Tel Aviv, and Israel's first royal visitor.

1203   FILM MAGAZINE, JULY 1959
1959 / 15 min / sound / b&w / 16 mm
The Jewish Agency. See no. 1176 for more information. Includes scenes of Independence Day celebrations for 1959, a B'nai B'rith Convention, Lag Ba'Omer, Sachne, and a look at the Glass Pavilion.

1204   FILM MAGAZINE, AUGUST 1959
1959 / 15 min / sound / b&w / 16 mm
The Jewish Agency. See no. 1176 for more information. Includes scenes of the Knesset, Tel Aviv, Lydda International Airport, and the Wingate Institute.

1205   FILM MAGAZINE, SEPTEMBER 1959
1959 / 15 min / sound / b&w / 16 mm
The Jewish Agency. See no. 1176 for more information. Includes scenes of the 25th anniversary of Chaim Nachman Bialik, the national water project, a profile of summer institutes and the Tel Aviv exhibition.

1206   FILM MAGAZINE, OCTOBER 1959
1959 / 15 min / sound / b&w / 16 mm

The Jewish Agency. See no. 1176 for more information. Includes scenes of the International Harp Contest, industry in developing area and a look at the city of Caesarea.

1207 FILM MAGAZINE, NOVEMBER 1959
1959 / 15 min / sound / b&w / 16 mm
The Jewish Agency. See no. 1176 for more information. Includes scenes of the celebration of Succoth, Israel's first subway, ceramics from Beersheva and a profile of Israeli football.

1208 INDEPENDENCE DAY 1951
1951 / 19 min / sound / b&w / 16 or 35 mm
Schweig-Vicas Production. Locations: Abraham F. Rad Jewish Film Archive / Keren Hayesod, Jerusalem.
Shows celebration of Israel's third anniversary in 1951.

1209 INDEPENDENCE DAY 1953
1953 / 8 min / sound / b&w / 16 mm
Berkey Pathe Humphries. Locations: Abraham F. Rad Jewish Film Archive / Keren Hayesod, Jerusalem.
Shows scenes of Israeli Independence Day celebrations in 1953.

1210 INSIDE ISRAEL
1954 / 16 min / sound / b&w / 16 mm
Location: Abraham F. Rad Jewish Film Archive.
South African newsreel. Shows border security measures used in Jewish settlements and in Jerusalem, Lag Ba'Omer celebrations at Meron, the commemoration of the 50th anniversary of Theodore Herzl's death and a look at oriental folkdances.

1211 ISRAEL - 1950'S
(c. 1959?) / 10 min / sound / color / 16 mm
Location: Abraham F. Rad Jewish Film Archive.
Includes general scenes of life in Israel throughout the 1950's.

1212 ISRAEL 1955-56
1956 / 18 min / sound / b&w / 16 mm
Location: Abraham F. Rad Jewish Film Archive.
Looks at Israel's progress since statehood. Shows scenes of the oil industry at Heletz, the Dead Sea Scrolls, Ben-Gurion returning from retirement, a profile of industrial and agricultural growth and work to help new immigrants integrate into Israeli life.

1213 ISRAEL 1957
1957 / 25 min / sound / b&w / 16 mm
Samuel Elfert. Locations: Abraham F. Rad Jewish Film Archive / Jewish Agency Film Archive, Jerusalem.

Review of the major political, economic and cultural
events of 1957. Includes scenes of the Industrial Fair,
archeological discoveries at historical sites, the
Eilat-Halfa pipeline, programs to plant trees, sports in
Israel, the Children's Ambassador, the anniversary of the
Philharmonic Orchestra, Abba Ebban's speech at the U.N.
and scenes of Ben-Gurion and Golda Meir addressing the
Knesset.

1214   ISRAEL MIRROR
       1956 / 12 min / sound / b&w / 16 mm
       Location: Abraham F. Rad Jewish Film Archive.
       South African newsreel for 1956. Shows Golda Meir at
       home, laying of the foundation stone at the new Ashkelon
       Hospital, a cattle show, the Ulpan at Sdot Yam, a youth
       rally, an air-raid drill, the Israeli navy, and a foot-
       ball match between Israel and the USSR.

1215   ISRAEL MY COUNTRY
       1959 / 17 min / sound / color / 16 mm
       United Israel Appeal. (NUC FiA 59-773) Credits:
       Producer-Director-Photographer - Lazar Dunnar, Script -
       Harold Steinberg. Location: Abraham F. Rad Jewish Film
       Archive.
       Available in English, French and Spanish soundtracks.
       Looks at Israel through the eyes of a young newspaperman
       from Jerusalem. Includes scenes of people at work and
       play, city streets, factories, a Bedouin market at
       Beersheba, Independence Day celebrations, the Trade Fair
       Exhibition and a profile of the city of Eilat.

1216   MIRACLE - YEAR FIVE
       1953 / 30 min / sound / b&w / 16 mm
       Mende Brown. Locations: Abraham F. Rad Jewish Film Archive /
       Jewish Agency Film Archive, Jerusalem / Keren Hayesod,
       Jerusalem.
       Reviews the economic, technical, industrial and cultural
       progress of Israel in the first five years of statehood.

1217   NEWSREELS (YARCHONIM)
       1956-61 / 3-7 min / sound / b&w / 16 or 35 mm
       Israel Film Service in conjunction with the Jewish Agency
       and the Foreign Ministry of Israel. Location: Prime
       Minister's Office, Information Dept., Jerusalem.
       Available in English, Hebrew, French, Spanish, German and
       Portuguese soundtracks. Collection of 53 newsreels.
       Documents life in Israel, Judaism and Zionism, the
       Israeli army and police, government, communications,
       agriculture, archeology, art, health, culture and youth
       education, religion, business and industry, immigration,
       sports and minority groups. A different newsreel collec-
       tion than nos. 1176 to 1207 with different running times
       and titles.

1218   TA'ARUCHAT HAMERED (THE REBELLION EXHIBITION)
        1958 / ? / sound / b&w / 16 mm
        Herut Brit-Hatzohar, World Directorate. Location: Jabotinsky
        Institute, Tel Aviv.
        Documents the Rebellion Exhibition held at Metzudat Ze'ev
        in Tel Aviv between December 18, 1958 and May 13, 1959.

1219   TWENTY-FOURTH ZIONIST CONGRESS
        1956 / 2 min / silent / b&w / 16 mm
        Location: Abraham F. Rad Jewish Film Archive.
        Brief footage of the 24th Zionist Congress at Biryanei
        Hauma, Jerusalem.

ISRAEL - CONTEMPORARY VIEWS OF ISRAEL IN THE 1960'S

1220   AFTER THE MIRACLE
        1967 / 60 min / sound / b&w / 16 mm
        NET. (Intertel series) Location: Indiana University.
        Intended for high school to adult audiences. Looks at
        life in Israel. Includes scenes of preparation for war,
        the place of religion in the government, lack of
        integration between western and oriental Jews, develop-
        ment of agriculture and industry, and the question of the
        Arab minority in Israel.

1221   CELEBRATING ISRAEL'S TWENTIETH ANNIVERSARY
        1968 / 10 min / sound / color / 16 mm
        Distributed by Alden Films. Location: Abraham F. Rad Jewish
        Film Archive.
        Listed in some catalogs as: CELEBRATION - ISRAEL'S
        20TH INDEPENDENCE DAY. Shows Independence Day
        celebrations including singing, dancing, fireworks and a
        military parade in Jerusalem.

1222   CHILDREN OF ISRAEL
        1967 / 13 min / sound / color / 16 mm
        Julien Bryan. International Film Foundation. (How We Live
        series) (LC 70-707525) Credits: Editor - Yehuda Yaniv,
        Music - Stephen M. Gould, Photographers - Ray Garner, Julien
        Bryan. Locations: Kent State U. / Library of Congress (FBA
        1380) / U. of Illinois / U. of Michigan. *
        General interest film with no narration. Shows Israeli
        children in a variety of settings, at home, work, play,
        on a kibbutz, in the synagogue, at meals and on the
        phone. Gives a view of the daily life of a child in
        Israel.

1223   DISCOVERY GOES TO ISRAEL
        1969 / 21 min / sound / color / 16 mm
        American Broadcasting Co., Made by Daniel Wilson. Released
        by International Film Bureau. (Discovery, ABC television
        series) (LC 76-707268) Credits: Producer - Jules Power,

Hostess -Virginia Gibson, Writer-Director - Gene Feldman.
Locations: Library of Congress (FBA 9435) / Middle East
Institute / Syracuse U. *
Intended for young television audiences. Looks at an
Arab village family and at an Israeli family in Haifa.
Compares and contrasts their lives, cultures and tradi-
tions. Promotes the idea of Arab-Israeli coexistence and
cooperation but does mention conflicts by the end of the
program. General, well-presented view of life in Israel
for children.

1224   FILM MAGAZINE, JANUARY 1960
        1960 / 15 min / sound / b&w / 16 mm
        The Jewish Agency. See no. 1176 for more information.
        Includes scenes of Baka El Gharbiya, an Arab village, a
        profile of students in Israel, celebrations at Christmas,
        and fishing in the Red Sea.

1225   FILM MAGAZINE, FEBRUARY 1960
        1960 / 15 min / sound / b&w / 16 mm
        The Jewish Agency. See no. 1176 for more information.
        Includes scenes of Beit Brodetsky, a kindergarten in
        Jaffa and a profile of home industries in Israel and
        Avdat.

1226   FILM MAGAZINE, APRIL 1960
        1960 / 15 min / sound / b&w / 16 mm
        The Jewish Agency. See no. 1176 for more information.
        Includes scenes of Ben-Gurion's visit to the U.S., Habad
        village and Givat Chaim.

1227   FILM MAGAZINE, MAY 1960
        1960 / 15 min / sound / b&w / 16 mm
        The Jewish Agency. See no. 1176 for more information.
        Includes scenes of planting of forests, the annual march
        to Jerusalem, and a profile of artist Zahara Schatz.

1228   FILM MAGAZINE, JUNE 1960
        1960 / 15 min / sound / b&w / 16 mm
        The Jewish Agency. See no. 1176 for more information.
        Includes scenes of a housing seminar, a profile of
        industry at Kibbutz Afikim and a look at the Yarkon
        River.

1229   FILM MAGAZINE, JULY 1960
        1960 / 15 min / sound / b&w / 16 mm
        The Jewish Agency. See no. 1176 for more information.
        Looks at the Herzl Centenary in Israel, celebration of
        the hundredth birthday of Theordore Herzl, leader of the
        Zionist movement.

1230   FILM MAGAZINE, OCTOBER 1960
        1960 / 15 min / sound / b&w / 16 mm

241

The Jewish Agency. See no. 1176 for more information.
Includes a profile of sabras, a look at the fur industry
and a tour of the central bus station.

1231   FILM MAGAZINE, DECEMBER 1960
        1960 / 15 min / sound / b&w / 16 mm
        The Jewish Agency. See no. 1176 for more information.
        Includes scenes of the Kiryat Gat Youth Center, a profile
        of Israel Inland Airline - Arkia, and a look at the
        Nachal Entertainment Group.

1232   FILM MAGAZINE, JANUARY 1961
        1961 / 15 min / sound / b&w / 16 mm
        The Jewish Agency. See no. 1176 for more information.
        Documents sections of the 25th Zionist Congress.

1233   FILM MAGAZINE, MARCH 1961
        1961 / 15 min / sound / b&w / 16 mm
        The Jewish Agency. See no. 1176 for more information.
        Includes scenes of the Beersheva Hospital, a profile of
        the diamond industry in Israel and an ancient Haggodot.

1234   FILM MAGAZINE, APRIL 1961
        1961 / 15 min / sound / b&w / 16 mm
        The Jewish Agency. See no. 1176 for more information.
        Includes scenes of Phoenician glass works and a profile
        of Beit Golomb on the Dead Sea.

1235   FILM MAGAZINE, MAY 1961
        1961 / 15 min / sound / b&w / 16 mm
        The Jewish Agency. See no. 1176 for more information.
        Looks at Independence Day, 1961 and a profile of the
        Nachal settlement corps.

1236   FILM MAGAZINE, SEPTEMBER 1961
        1961 / 15 min / sound / b&w / 16 mm
        The Jewish Agency. See no. 1176 for more information.
        Profiles the town of Ashdod.

1237   FILM MAGAZINE, OCTOBER 1961
        1961 / 15 min / sound / b&w / 16 mm
        The Jewish Agency. See no. 1176 for more information.
        Includes a look at celebrations on Rosh Hashanah, Ramat
        Gan Park in Israel and a look at fishermen in Jaffa.

1238   FILM MAGAZINE, NOVEMBER 1961
        1961 / 15 min / sound / b&w / 16 mm
        The Jewish Agency. See no. 1176 for more information.
        Includes a look at the ancient resort of Caesarea, a pro-
        file of the Police College, and a look at the exhibition
        grounds.

1239   FILM MAGAZINE, JANUARY 1962
        1962 / 15 min / sound / b&w / 16 mm

The Jewish Agency. See no. 1176 for more information.
Includes a profile of the family Ulpan at Netanyah and a
look at an old age home.

1240   FILM MAGAZINE, FEBRUARY 1962
       1962 / 15 min / sound / b&w / 16 mm
       The Jewish Agency. See no. 1176 for more information.
       Includes scenes of celebrations in Israel for
       Tanganyika's independence, a look at the ORT Center in
       Netanyah and a profile of the new Cameri (Chamber)
       Theater.

1241   FILM MAGAZINE, MARCH 1962
       1962 / 15 min / sound / b&w / 16 mm
       The Jewish Agency. See no. 1176 for more information.
       Includes a look at cobblers in Jaffa, immigration to
       Israel and a profile of the Haifa Maritime Museum.

1242   FROM MONDAY TO THE POLLS
       1966 / 1339 ft. / sound / color / 16 mm
       Yanin-Hiresh. Israel Film Studios, Herzliyah.
       Documents the 1966 Israeli elections. Includes inter-
       views with Prime Minister Levi Eshkol.

1243   INDEPENDENCE DAY 1960
       1960 / ? / sound / b&w / 16 mm
       Berkey Pathe Humphries. Location: Keren Hayesod, Jerusalem.
       Documents the Independence Day celebrations in Israel in
       1960.

1244   INDEPENDENCE DAY 1962 (YOMAN YOM HA'ATZMA'UT 1962)
       1962 / 10 min / sound / b&w / 16 or 35 mm
       Israel Motion Picture Studios. Locations: Israel Film
       Studios, Herzliyah / Prime Minister's Office, Information
       Dept., Jerusalem.
       Newsreel available in English, Hebrew and French
       soundtracks. Documents the 1962 Independence Day
       celebrations in Israel.

1245   INDEPENDENCE DAY 1965 (YOMAN YOM HA'ATZMA'UT 1965)
       1965 / 11 min / sound / b&w / 16 or 35 mm
       Israel Motion Picture Studios. Distributed by Alden Films.
       Locations: Abraham F. Rad Jewish Film Archive / Israel Motion
       Picture Studios, Herzliyah / Prime Minister's Office,
       Information Dept., Jerusalem.
       Newsreel available in English, Hebrew, French, Spanish
       and Arabic soundtracks. Documents the 1965 Israel
       Independence Day celebrations.

1246   INDEPENDENCE DAY 1968 (YOMAN YOM HA'ATZMA'UT 1968)
       1968 / 11 min / sound / b&w / 16 or 35 mm
       Israel Motion Picture Studios. Locations: Abraham F. Rad
       Jewish Film Archive / Prime Minister's Office, Information

Dept., Jerusalem.
Newsreel available in English, Hebrew, French and Spanish
soundtracks. Documents the 1968 Israel Independence Day
celebrations.

1247   ISRAEL, SEVENTEEN YEARS OF INDEPENDENCE (YISRAEL,
17 SHNOT ATZMA'UT)
1965 / 22 min / sound / b&w / 16 mm
Berkey Pathe Humphries. A Film Service Production.
Locations: Abraham F. Rad Jewish Film Archive / Ministry of
Education and Culture, Jerusalem / Prime Minister's Office,
Information Dept., Jerusalem.
Uses archival film and newsreels. Traces accomplishments
of Israel in the fields of education, defense, settlement
programs, agriculture, industry and immigration during
the first seventeen years of statehood.

1248   ISRAEL THROUGH JAPANESE EYES
1964 / 40 min / silent / b&w / 16 mm
Location: Abraham F. Rad Jewish Film Archive.
Produced by Japanese film-makers. Looks at development
and progress in Israel.

1249   ISRAEL TODAY
1965 / 25 min / sound / color / 16 mm
Martin Murray. Released by Rothschild Film Corp. (NUC FiA
68-1499)
Intended for high school to adult audiences. Looks at
technical advancements made in Israel since statehood in
1948. Includes a look at industrial development, religious sites, history and geography of Israel.

1250   ISRAEL'S FOURTEENTH INDEPENDENCE DAY
1962 / ? / sound / b&w / 16 mm
Israel Motion Picture Studios. Location: Keren Hayesod,
Jerusalem.
Newsreel. Shows Israel's 14th Independence Day celebra-
tions.

1251   ISRAEL'S SEVENTEENTH INDEPENDENCE DAY PARADE 1965
1965 / ? / sound / color / 16 mm
Berkey Pathe Humphries. Distributed by Alden Films.
Location: Keren Hayesod, Jerusalem.
Shows the celebrations on Israel's 17th Independence Day
including the annual parade.

1252   ISRAEL'S THIRTEENTH ANNIVERSARY
1961 / 12 min / sound / b&w / 16 mm
Location: Abraham F. Rad Jewish Film Archive.
Available in English and Hebrew soundtracks. Documents
Independence Day celebrations in 1961.

1253   MANY SIDES OF THE COIN (FINANCIAL WORK)
1964 / 11 min / sound / color / 16 mm

Yoram Gross Films. Location: Prime Minister's Office,
Information Dept., Jerusalem.
Available in English and Hebrew soundtracks. Profiles
banking and finance in Israel since statehood. Shows the
Bank of Israel, its monetary policies for economic stability, and a humorous explanation of the devaluation of
currency.

1254   MESSAGE FROM MR. DAVID BEN-GURION
1962 / 7 min / sound / b&w / 16 mm
Berkey Pathe Humphries. Credits: Producer - Rolf Kneller.
Location: Keren Hayesod, Jerusalem.
Ben-Gurion speaks about Israel's progress in absorbing
new immigrants, the development of agriculture, industry
and afforestation and the work done to cultivate the
Negev Desert.

1255   NEWSREELS 1962
1962 / ? / silent / color / 16 mm
Berkey Pathe Humphries. Location: Ministry of Tourism,
Jerusalem.
Includes stock newsreel footage of the Independence Day
parade and celebrations in 1962. Shows various cities
including Eilat, Jerusalem, Tel Aviv, Haifa and Galilee.

1256   POLICE (MISHTARA)
1962 / 875 ft. / sound / 16 mm
Shreiber. Israel Film Studios, Herzliyah.
Available in English, Hebrew and French soundtracks.
Describes the Israeli police system.

1257   PORTRAITS OF ISRAEL
1967 / 15 min / sound / color / 16 mm
Jewish National Fund.
Describes cultural, social and economic development in
Israel.

1258   SEVENTEENTH INDEPENDENCE DAY 1965
1965 / ? / sound / b&w / 16 mm
Israel Motion Picture Studios. Locations: Abraham F. Rad
Jewish Film Archive / Keren Hayesod, Jerusalem.
Documents activities during the 17th Independence Day
celebrations in 1965.

1259   TARGET PEACE
(c. 1968?) / 15 min / sound / b&w / 16 mm
Location: Gratz College.
Intended for high school to adult audiences. Looks at
life in Israel after the Six Day War. Discusses the need
for a state of military preparedness and civilian mobili-
zation to assist in absorption of immigrants, admi-
nistering occupied Arab territories, and fighting Arab
resistance.

1260   THIRD SIDE OF THE COIN (DESCRIPTION OF A STRUGGLE)
        1963 / ? / sound / color / 16 mm
        Van Leer Productions. Location: Ministry of Trade and
        Commerce, Jerusalem.
        Describes the contrast between the ideals which led to
        the founding of the modern state of Israel and the
        compromises required of the state to handle everyday
        problems.

1261   TWENTIETH INDEPENDENCE DAY PARADE
        1968 / ? / sound / b&w / 16 mm
        Israel Film Studios, Herzliyah. Location: Keren Hayesod,
        Jerusalem.
        Documents the activities of the 20th Independence Day
        celebrations including the annual parade.

1262   THE TWENTY-FIFTH ZIONIST CONGRESS IN JERUSALEM
        1960 / 20 min / sound / b&w / 16 mm
        Israel Motion Picture Studios. (Israel Film Magazine, no.
        43) (NUC Fi 68-730) Locations: Abraham F. Rad Jewish Film
        Archive / Jewish Agency Film Archive, Jerusalem / Library of
        Congress (FBA 5036)
        Describes the activities of the World Conference of
        Zionists. Includes surveys of goals and future aims of
        the organization.

ISRAEL - CONTEMPORARY VIEWS OF ISRAEL IN THE 1970'S

1263   A DREAM LIVES ON
        1974 / 11 min / sound / color / 16 mm
        Distributed by Educators Progress Service. Location:
        Consulate General of Israel.
        Documents the visit of Martin Luther King, Sr. to Israel.
        King speaks about universal brotherhood, visits the Yad
        Yashem Memorial to Jewish victims of the Holocaust and
        tours Jerusalem, Nazareth and other cities.

1264   HOLY LAND
        1973 / 60 min / sound / color / 16 mm
        NBC News. Produced in association with the National Council
        of Churches. Credits: Director - Joseph Vadala, Writer -
        Philip Scharper. Location: Library of Congress (FDA 2984)
        *
        Television news special filmed before the 1973 War but
        broadcast after the war. Describes the efforts of indi-
        vidual Christians, Muslims and Jews in Israel to bring
        about peaceful co-existence and harmony for all three
        religions. Includes interviews with Russian Jewish
        emigres, Anglican churchmen, Arab Palestinians, farmers,
        judges and teachers each working to promote humanitarian
        ideals.

1265   ISRAEL AFTER TWENTY-FIVE YEARS
        1973 / ? / sound / color / 16 mm
        Anti-Defamation League of B'nai B'rith. (Dateline Israel,
        1973 series)
            Interview with Prime Minister Golda Meir. Discusses
            the meaning of the 25th anniversary of the state of
            Israel.

1266   ISRAEL REPORT
        (c. 1970) / 20 min. each / sound / color / 16 mm
        Distributed by TRC Productions. Location: Gratz College.
            Twenty part, fast-paced film magazine covering current
            activities in Israel each with an historical episode.
            Intended for general audiences to provide current aware-
            ness of Israel and historical background of the state.
            The following are contents summaries for the 20 known
            segments. 1. Allenby Bridge, Western Wall, Hadassah
            Hospital, Mt. Scopus, Israel Museum, Yom Kippur War,
            Israeli Festival with the Panovs. 2. UN General
            Assembly, November 29, 1947 , Dr. Josef Borman, open
            heart surgeon, Lake Kinneret, kibbutz life, Rabbi Adin
            Steinsalz, the Jerusalem March. 3. Early immigration,
            the Bedouins, life detector at Weizmann Institute,
            Hanukkah lamps, Mayor Teddy Kollek. 4. Interviews with
            two alleged terrorists, Sassoon collection in Israel,
            Boy's Town in Jerusalem, illegal settlements on the West
            Bank, Isaac Stern at the Jerusalem Music Center. 5.
            Bezalel Art School, three Christian ministers discuss
            Israel, wheat growing discoveries at the Weizmann
            Institute, underwater exploration of the Red Sea, Eliezer
            Ben Yehuda. 6. Prof. Yshayahu Leibowitz, Nes Ammim, a
            Christian kibbutz, ghettos fighter's kibbutz, kibbutz
            Givat Brenner, Purim celebrations. 7. Theodore Herzl,
            movie making in Israel, visitors from Japan, skiing on
            Mt. Hermon. 8. Abba Eban, ancient coins, Georgian dan-
            cers, Chaim Weizmann. 9. Jerusalem Festival with Habimah
            National Theatre, Israel Commedia dell'Arte, Arthur
            Rubenstein, Danny Kaye and others. 10. Schooling for
            blind children in Nazareth, ancient Jericho, Asian
            Olympic Football (soccer) Qualifying Match, Russian
            scientists in Israel, Bat-Dor dancers. 11. Jewish Agency
            Assembly, L.A. Mayor Memorial Institute for Islamic Art,
            Rabbi Pappenheim on Orthodox Judaism, flamenco dancers,
            Jerusalem. 12. Jerusalem, Folklore Festival, the Western
            Wall, Air Force Day, the Lebanese. 13. Moshe Safdie, Ohr
            Somayach Yeshiva, inflation in Israel, Habimah National
            Theatre, David Ben-Gurion. 14. Joseph Tekoah, Sephardic
            synagogues, ancient inscriptions, fashion week in Israel,
            kibbutzim. 15. The Jewish Museum, Old City of Jerusalem,
            the diamond industry, 3,000 United Jewish Appeal donors
            in Israel, an Israeli doctor and an Arab boy. 16. Keren
            Hayesod community centers, Yeshivat Hagolan, "O
            Jerusalem" tour, Canadian Pelatron complex, Israeli movie

247

making of film "Entebbe Rescue", Golda Meir. 17. WIZO
mothercraft training center, sun painting, laser beam
surgery, Avdat, Bat-Dor dancers. 18. Maccabi basketball
team, solving water shortage, Sisters of Nazareth in
Akko, Yaacov Kirschen political cartoons, Tel Aviv Wax
Museum. 19. K'far Etzion, a Bar Mitzvah, volunteers of
WIZO, Vietnamese refugees, Weizmann Institute's
International Student Program, the marina at Tel Aviv.
20. WIZO teaching skills to Druze, children's painting
competition, aging, Tel Akko, Jerusalem.

1267   THE ISRAELI EXPERIENCE
       (c. 1978?) / ? / sound / 16 mm
       Israel Government Tourist Office, New York.
       Looks at life in Israel. Produced for the 30th anniver-
       sary celebrations.

1268   ISRAEL'S 25TH ANNIVERSARY PARADE
       1973 / 30 min / sound / color / 16 mm
       United Jewish Appeal.
       Shows Israel Independence Day celebrations including the
       annual parade.

1269   ISRAVISION - ISRAEL VIDEO MAGAZINE
       (n.d.) / 15 min / sound / color / 3/4" videocassette
       Elul Productions, Tel Aviv.
       A cassette video magazine offered on an annual subscrip-
       tion basis from Elul. Contents of the magazine and dates
       of production are unknown.

1270   JUST ANOTHER DAY
       1971 / 27 min / sound / color / 16 mm
       United Israel Appeal. Distributed by Alden Films. (LC
       72-702945) Location: Abraham F. Rad Jewish Film Archive.
       Available in English, Hebrew, Spanish and German
       soundtracks. Looks at daily life in Israel and how
       threat of border disturbances and war are an ever present
       worry. Intended for college and adult audiences.

1271   PROFILES OF ISRAEL
       1976 / 11 min / sound / color / 16 mm
       Distributed by Alden Films. Location: Gratz College.
       Looks at the activities of the Histadrut, the General
       Federation of Jewish Labor. Discusses industry in
       Israel, health and recreation in the Dead Sea area, agri-
       culture at a Moshav and social welfare programs for the
       poor and old.

1272   PROMISED LANDS
       1973 / 55 or 87 min / sound / color / 16 mm
       Susan Sontag. Distributed by New Yorker Films. Location:
       New York Public Donnell Film Library. *
       Without narration. Presents feeling and texture of life

248

in Israel with wit and understanding. Originally banned
in Israel. Includes scenes on the effect of war on the
countryside, interviews with Israeli soldiers, a look at
anti-Jewish statements in Arab textbooks of the 1960's,
life in Israel before and after the Six Day War, a
discussion of Arab-Israeli strife since the 1920's, Arab
fears of an Israeli takeover of their land, a scene at a
pyschiatric hospital of treatment for an Israeli soldier
effected by the war, and interviews dealing with the
meaning of being a Jew, Zionism, the Holocaust and survival. Although the 87 minute version runs too long at
times, this is one of the best films at the college and
adult level dealing with life in Israel today. Made by
film-maker and author Susan Sontag. Looks at Israeli
life with all the problems and fears presented. Allows
the viewer a better understanding of life in Israel.
Attempts to look into the realities of Israeli life.
Recommended.

1273   30 YEARS OF ISRAEL
        (c. 1978) / ? / sound / 16 mm
        Produced in cooperation with Maxwell House Coffee.
        Distributed by Joseph Jacobs Organization. No other infor-
        mation available.

1274   THIS GATE IS OPEN
        (c. 1978?) / 27 min / sound / color / 16 mm
        Producer unknown. Formerly distributed by Alden Films.
        Stresses peaceful cooperation and goodwill between Israel
        and Arab countries, particularily Lebanon. Discusses the
        unification of Jerusalem under Israeli rule and the con-
        cept of open relations with Arab neighbors. Filmed
        before the hostilities between Israel and Lebanon.

1275   TWENTY-FIFTH ANNIVERSARY OF YOUTH ALIYAH
        (c. 1973?) / 26 min / sound / b&w / 16 mm
        Location: Abraham F. Rad Jewish Film Archive.
        Discusses the history of Youth Aliyah over the last
        twenty-five years. Outlines Aliyah programs in immigra-
        tion and settlement.

1276   27TH ANNIVERSARY OF THE STATE OF ISRAEL
        1975 / 15 min / sound / b&w / 16 mm
        Location: Abraham F. Rad Jewish Film Archive.
        Uses newsreel footage to trace major events in Israel's
        history from statehood in 1948 until 1975.

1277   VISTAS OF ISRAEL, NO. 1
        1957 / 14 min / sound / b&w / 16 mm
        Israel Office of Information. Distributed by Alden Films.
        Credits: Producer - Samuel Elfert, Narrator - J. Julian.
        Locations: Abraham F. Rad Jewish Film Archive / Jewish
        Agency Film Archive, Jerusalem / Library of Congress (FiA

64-877, 881-883)
Profiles a traffic policeman's life in Tel Aviv and shows
road construction underway through the Negev to Elath and
the Red Sea. Contains two segments entitled: CITY ON
WHEELS and THE ROAD BUILDERS.

1278   VISTAS OF ISRAEL, NO. 2
1957 / 14 min / sound / b&w / 16 mm
Israel Office of Information. See no. 1277 for more information.
Includes three segments. ON THE TOWN follows Druze
soldiers on leave in Tel Aviv, entertaining themselves
with traditional dances and by observing Israeli
industrial plants. OLIVES OF JUDEA profiles the olive
industry. DOOR TO THE FUTURE looks at construction
of the Yarkon-Negev pipeline running from the Yarkon
River to Nir Yitzchak.

1279   VISTAS OF ISRAEL, NO. 3
1957 / 14 min / sound / b&w / 16 mm
Israel Office of Information. See no. 1277 for more information.
Includes three segments. HELETZ looks at the discovery
of oil in Israel and combined American-Israeli efforts to
obtain oil. BIBLICAL ZOO visits the Jerusalem zoo which
specializes in Biblically significant animals. GOLD IN
THE TREES looks at the orange industry.

1280   VISTAS OF ISRAEL, NO. 4
1957 / 14 min / sound / b&w / 16 mm
Israel Office of Information. See no. 1277 for more information.
Includes three segments. MACCABIAH looks at the sports
festival by that name. PATTERNS OF LIVING profiles
Israeli home industries. HOUSE OF FAITH looks at the
laying of the cornerstone of the Church of the
Annunciation in Nazareth. Includes scenes of Christian
spots in Nazareth.

1281   YOU AND WE
1970 / 27 min / sound / color / 16 mm
Distributed by Alden Films. Location: Abraham F. Rad Jewish
Film Archive.
Available in English and Spanish soundtracks. Looks at
successes and failures in trying to integrate Diaspora
Jews and Israeli Jews into a partnership economically and
culturally. Looks at industry and agriculture in Israel
and problems in housing and education resulting from
absorption of immigrants.

ISRAEL   -   INTERVIEWS

1282   BEN-GURION ON THE BIBLE
        April 22, 1967 / 26 min / sound / b&w / 16 mm
        CBS News. (CBS News Special Report, television series)
        Credits: Producer - Gene De Poris. Location: Library of
        Congress (FBA 9109) *
            Alexander Kendrick interviews Ben-Gurion concerning his
            research on the Bible. Topics covered include the image
            of God, history of the Bible, the meaning of a "chosen
            people", the Bible as a universal text, Biblical
            prophecy, and interpretation of the Bible. Ben-Gurion
            uses examples from Israeli politics and personal
            experience. Illustrates how Ben-Gurion's Biblical
            interpretations have influenced his personal philosophy
            and his policies as a statesman.

1283   A CONVERSATION WITH ABBA EBBAN
        (c. 1973) / 27 min / sound / color / 16 mm
        Anti-Defamation League of B'nai B'rith. (Dateline Israel
        series)
            Interview with Abba Ebban by Arnold Foster. Topics
            covered include the significance of the U.N., Israel's
            relations with other countries, and the impact of a
            Jewish state on a non-Jewish world.

1284   A CONVERSATION WITH GOLDA MEIR
        1973 / 27 min / sound / color / 16 mm
        Anti-Defamation League of B'nai B'rith. (Dateline Israel
        series)
            Arnold Foster interviews Golda Meir concerning Israel as
            a home for Christians and Muslims as well as Jews.
            Discusses early work of Golda Meir in helping establish a
            Jewish state, and her opinions concerning the future sta-
            tus of Israel.

1285   A CONVERSATION WITH YIGAEL YADIN
        1962 / 30 min / sound / b&w / 16 mm
        Jewish Theological Seminary of America, and NBC. Released
        by National Academy for Adult Jewish Studies. (Eternal
        Light, television series) (NUC FiA 64-1107) Credits:
        Interviewer - Martin Agronsky.
            Interview with former Commander-in-Chief of the Israeli
            Army and Professor of Archeology at the Hebrew
            University. Yigael Yadin discusses the Dead Sea Scrolls
            and recent archeological excavations. Yadin makes com-
            parisons between tactical problems faced by an army in
            ancient and modern Israel.

1286   DAVID BEN-GURION
        1958 / 29 min / sound / b&w / 16 mm
        NBC. Released by Encyclopaedia Britannica Films. (The
        Wisdom Series) (NUC FiA 58-634) Locations: Michigan State
        U. / Oregon State System of Higher Education / U. of
        Illinois, Champaign.

Interview at Ben-Gurion's home in Tel Aviv. Ben-Gurion discusses his childhood in Poland, his immigration to Palestine, early Jewish settlers and the eventual establishment of the state of Israel. He comments on his own studies in philosophy, religion and government.

1287   DAVID BEN-GURION, PRIME MINISTER OF ISRAEL
        April 19, 1958 / 30 min / sound / b&w / 16 mm
        CBS. (Face the Nation, television series) Credits:
        Moderator - Stuart Novins, Interviewers - Seth King, Winston
        Burdette. Location: Library of Congress (FBA 3123) *
        Made at the time of Israel's tenth anniversary of state-
        hood. Ben-Gurion is interviewed in Jerusalem concerning
        the Arab refugee problem, the possibility of peace with
        the Arab states, the role of the U.S. in peace nego-
        tiations, Israeli expansion and security interests, eco-
        nomy and trade, and the history of Russian Jewry and
        Zionism.

1288   GOLDA MEIR INTERVIEW
        1975 / 18 min / sound / color / 16 mm
        WNET Television. (Robert MacNeil Report, television series)
        Location: Gratz College.
        Golda Meir discusses the idea of negotiation, the P.L.O.,
        return of captured Arab territories, and general problems
        in Arab-Israeli negotiations and relations.

1289   LINE OF LIFE (WITH GOLDA MEIR)
        (n.d.) / 20 min / sound / color / 16 mm
        Producer unknown. Distributed by Alden Films.
        Interview covers the general accomplishments of Israel
        in the last thirty years and problems yet to be solved.

1290   ROBERT FROST IN ISRAEL
        1961 / 17 min / sound / b&w / 16 mm
        Location: Abraham F. Rad Jewish Film Archive.
        Chet Huntley reports on Robert Frost's visit to Israel.
        Includes Frost's impression of the country and shows
        Frost lecturing at the Hebrew University.

1291   SWORD OR PLOWSHARE, PART 2. HER EXCELLENCY,
        MRS. GOLDA MEIR
        September 21, 1969 / 43 min / sound / color / 16 mm
        CBS News. (CBS News Religious Special, television series)
        Credits: Writer-Producer - Pamela Ilott, Correspondent -
        Frank Kearns. Location: Library of Congress (FBB 2497) *
        Frank Kearns interviews Golda Meir concerning the meaning
        of being a Jew, treatment of Jews behind the Iron
        Curtain, sabras or native-born Israelis, loyalties of
        Jews in America, administration of the holy places of
        Jerusalem by Israel, the possibility of peace, the role
        of King Hussein in the 1967 War, and the question of
        Soviet involvement in the Middle East.

1292 BEN-GURION
1962 / 25 min / sound / b&w / 16 mm
Wolper Productions. Released by McGraw-Hill, Official Films.
(Biography, television series) Credits: Series Producer -
Jack Haley Jr., Producer-Writer-Director - Alan Landsburg,
Narrator -Mike Wallace. (NUC FiA 63-1029) Locations: Kent
State U. / Library of Congress (FCA 2116) / Syracuse U. / U.
of Illinois / U. of Kansas / U. of New Hampshire. *
   Looks at the establishment of Israel and Ben-Gurion's
part in it. Begins in Poland in 1886 with David Green,
later called Ben-Gurion, becoming a Zionist organizer.
Discusses his immigration to Palestine, WWI years in New
York and his return to Palestine, first as an organizer
and later as Prime Minister. Outlines history of the
formation of Israel with events in Ben-Gurion's life.
Library of Congress print has experienced some damage due
to age.

1293 BEN-GURION
1967 / 20 min / sound / 35 mm
Alex Ben Dor. Israel Film Studios.
   Available in English and Hebrew soundtracks. Traces the
early life and political career of David Ben-Gurion,
first Prime Minister of Israel.

1294 BEN-GURION, BUILDER OF A NATION
1956 / 21 min / sound / b&w / 16 mm
Baruch Dienar. Released by United Israel Appeal. (NUC FiA
64-569) Location: Abraham F. Rad Jewish Film Archive /
Jewish Agency Film Archive, Jerusalem.
   Based on an interview with Drew Pearson at Sdeh Boker.
Looks at major events in Israel's first ten years and the
role played by Ben-Gurion during that time.

1295 BINYAMIN ZE'EV HERZL, PROPHET OF THE JEWISH
STATE, 100TH ANNIVERSARY OF HIS BIRTH (1860-1960)
1960 / 13 min / sound / color / 16 or 35 mm
Berkey Pathe Humphries. Location: Prime Minister's Office,
Information Dept., Jerusalem.
   Available in English, Hebrew, French, Spanish and German
soundtracks. Traces major events in the life of Herzl.
Looks at memorials to Herzl in Israel.

1296 CALL OF THE HOLY LAND
1960 / 19 min / sound / b&w / 35 mm
Twentieth Century-Fox Film Corporation. (NUC Fi 62-39)
Credits: Narrators - Arnold Moss, Anne Revere, Associate
Producer -Dorothy Silverstone. Location: Library of
Congress (FEA 206-207) *
   Biography of Henrietta Szold, founder of the Hadassah
medical organization. Commemorates her birth in 1860.

Traces her early shock at disease and health conditions
in Palestine seen while on a visit to religious sites.
Traces Szold's immigration to Palestine in 1918 and
work in education and health care for the Jewish community. Outlines her work in youth Aliyah programs to
bring Jewish children to Palestine from Germany to avoid
persecution. Profiles work of the youth Aliyah movement
and youth centers.

1297   DAVID BEN-GURION (1886-1973)
        (c. 1974) / 29 min / sound / color / 16 mm
        Distributed by Alden Films. Locations: Abraham F. Rad
        Jewish Film Archive / Gratz College.
        Uses still photographs to trace the life of Israel's
        first Prime Minister. Intertwines the history of Zionism
        and Israel during the period of Ben-Gurion's life.

1298   GOLDA MEIR OF ISRAEL
        1973 / 52 min / sound / color / 16 mm
        Time-Life Films. Made by BBC-TV. Released by Time-Life
        Films. (LC 73-701681) Location: U. of Michigan.
        Uses interviews and newsreel footage to trace the career
        of Golda Meir as a proponent of statehood for Israel and
        as Prime Minister.

1299   HENRIETTA SZOLD
        1946 / 28 min / sound / b&w / 16 mm
        Hazel Greenwald. Location: Central Zionist Archives.
        Available in English and Hebrew soundtracks. Traces the
        life and work of Henrietta Szold, founder of Hadassah and
        an early supporter of health care and education in
        Palestine for the Jewish community.

1300   HERZL
        1967 / 53 min / sound / color / 16 or 35 mm
        Y. Ephrati. Locations: Abraham F. Rad Jewish Film Archive /
        Jewish Agency, Jerusalem / Prime Minister's Office,
        Information Dept, Jerusalem.
        Uses still photographs to trace the life and work of
        Theodore Herzl and the Zionist movement.

1301   HERZL - FATHER OF THE JEWISH STATE
        1960 / 15 min / sound / color / 16 mm
        Locations: Abraham F. Rad Jewish Film Archive / Jewish
        Agency Film Archive, Jerusalem.
        Celebration the 100th anniversary of Herzl's birth.
        Looks at his early life and the formation of the World
        Zionist Organization. Shows the meeting of the First
        Zionist Congress, Herzl's trip to Palestine, publication
        of "Old-New Land" and Herzl's re-burial.

1302   I REMEMBER CHAIM WEIZMANN
        1975 / 20 min / sound / color / 16 mm

Location: Abraham F. Rad Jewish Film Archive.
Meyer Weisgal, Ezer Weizmann and Abba Eban discuss
Israel's first President.

1303   OLD YOUNG MAN
(n.d.) / 15 min / sound / color / 16 mm
Location: Abraham F. Rad Jewish Film Archive.
Ben-Gurion is shown in his office and on the kibbutz of
Sde Boker.

1304   OUT OF THE WILDERNESS
(c. 1970?) / 20 min / sound / color / 16 mm
Edith Sorel. Distributed by Alden Films. Location: Gratz
College / Ministry for Foreign Affairs, Jerusalem.
Available in English and Hebrew soundtracks. Profiles
the life of General Abraham Yaffe. Traces Yaffe's life,
thirty year army career and his retirement to manage the
Nature Reserves.

1305   RABIN: AN ACTION BIOGRAPHY
1976 / 52 min / sound / color / 16 mm
ABC TV. Aetna Life and Casualty Film Library.
Traces the life and career of Israeli Prime Minister
Yitzhak Rabin. Focuses on Rabin's views concerning the
possibility of peace in the Middle East.

1306   VISION OF CHAIM WEIZMANN
1964 / 21 min / sound / b&w / 16 mm
Lazar Dunner. Distributed by Alden Films. Locations:
Abraham F. Rad Jewish Film Archive / Keren Hayesod,
Jerusalem.
Uses still photographs to trace the life of Israel's
first President. Also covers history of Zionism and the
formation of the state of Israel.

ISRAEL - IMMIGRATION AND ABSORPTION OF IMMIGRANTS

1307   ABSORPTION
(n.d.) / 23 min / sound / b&w / 16 mm
Distributed by Alden Films.
Traces the absorption of English speaking immigrants into
Israel. Describes problems in intergrating immigrants
into Israeli life. Shows the dedicated people who assist
immigrants with government programs.

1308   ARAD
1963 / 12 min / sound / color / 16 or 35 mm
Yitzhak Harvest. Location: Prime Minister's Office,
Information Dept., Jerusalem.
Available in English, Hebrew and Spanish soundtracks.
Looks at the first year program and preparations to
absorb settlers and immigrants at Arad.

255

1309   A CHASIDIC TALE
        (c. 1970?) / 31 min / sound / color / 16 mm
        United Synagogue Audio Visual Aids. Location: Ministry of
        Education and Culture, Jerusalem.
        Follows twin sisters as they immigrate to a youth
        village. Looks at difficulties and problems of absorp-
        tion and integration into Israeli life.

1310   A DAY OF DELIVERANCE
        1958 / 24 mn / sound / b&w / 16 mm
        Joint Distribution Committee (American Jewish) (NUC FiA
        63-1088) Credits: Producer - Paul Falkenberg, Script -
        Raphael Levy, Narrator - Martin Gabel. Location: Abraham F.
        Rad Jewish Film Archive.
        Looks at the work of the Joint Distribution Committee to
        aid displaced European Jews during the British Mandate
        period in Palestine. Traces the program after 1948 to
        airlift Yemenite Jews from Aden to Israel. Shows help
        given to Jews immigrating from Arab countries.

1311   THE DAYS WORK
        1957 / 16 min / sound / b&w / 16 mm
        Berkey Pathe Humphries. Locations: Abraham F. Rad Jewish
        Film Archive / Keren Hayesod, Jerusalem / Ministry of
        Education and Culture, Jerusalem.
        Looks at some of the problems Israel faces in absorbing
        immigrants and providing them with work and housing.
        Profiles agriculture, industrial development and natural
        resources in Israel.

1312   DEMONSTRATIONS AGAINST BEVIN
        1947 / 10 min / silent / b&w / 16 mm
        Location: Abraham F. Rad Jewish Film Archive.
        Jews in Palestine demonstrate against British Foreign
        Minister Ernest Bevin's refusal to allow open Jewish
        immigration to Palestine.

1313   DREAMS DEMAND STRUGGLE
        1972 / 14 min / sound / color / 16 mm
        United Jewish Appeal. Distributed by Alden Films. Location:
        Abraham F. Rad Jewish Film Archive / Gratz College.
        Listed in some catalogs as: A DREAM DEMANDS
        STRUGGLE. Fund raiser. Discusses the absorption of
        refugees from the Soviet Union and Arab countries. Looks
        at the successful Migdal HaEmek community and the failed
        Netivot refugee town near Ashkelon. Discusses massive
        social and economic problems in absorption of immigrants.
        Requests funds for assistance.

1314   FACES OF FREEDOM
        1959 / 15 min / sound / color / 16 mm
        Lazar Dunner. Locations: Abraham F. Rad Jewish Film Archive /
        Jewish Agency Film Archive / Keren Hayesod, Jerusalem.

256

Traces the absorption of four different immigrant families into Israel life and the different types of problems
faced by each. Includes scenes of Purim celebrations.

1315   FOOTHOLD IN THE DESERT - FIRST DAYS
        1962 / 15 min / sound / b&w / 16 mm
        David Mark. Location: Abraham F. Rad Jewish Film Archive.
        Available in English, French and Spanish soundtracks.
        Listed in some catalogs as: FIRST DAYS / YAMIM
        RISHONIM. Follows settlement and absorption of new
        immigrants into the desert community of Dimona.

1316   THE GAP
        1966 / 27 min / sound / b&w / 16 mm
        Nachman Zerwanitzer, A. Steinberg, Herzliyah and Rank
        Laboratories. Locations: Jewish Agency Film Archive / Keren
        Hayesod, Jerusalem.
        Outlines requirements in housing, employment, education
        and medical care needed for the large number of Jewish
        immigrants arriving in Israel.

1317   HOMECOMING
        1949 / 20 min / sound / b&w / 16 mm
        Joseph Krumgold, Norman Lourie (Palestine Films Ltd)
        Locations: Abraham F. Rad Jewish Film Archive / Jewish
        Agency Film Archive / Keren Hayesod, Jerusalem.
        Newsreel. Shows the opening of Israel to Jewish
        immigrants after the creation of the state in 1948.

1318   I AM A ZIONIST
        (c. 1970?) / 41 min / sound / color / 16 mm
        Distributed by Alden Films.
        Looks at the different types of Jews who immigrate to
        Israel from around the world. Traces immigrants from the
        Soviet Union, U.S., Yemen, Morocco, Poland and from Czech
        concentration camps following WWII. Suggests nationalism
        and pride are the factors which bring these immigrants
        together despite differences in socio-economic and
        cultural traditions.

1319   I CAME TO BEERSHEBA
        (c. 1970?) / 29 min / sound / color / 16 mm
        Stephen Scharff. Locations: Abraham F. Rad Jewish Film
        Archive / Central Zionist Archives, Jerusalem.
        Listed in some catalogs as: I CAME TO BE'ER SHEVA.
        Looks at the youth Aliyah Center in Be'er Sheva and shows
        the settlement of children in Israel.

1320   THE JOURNEY
        1951 / 20 min / sound / b&w / 16 mm
        John Ferno. Locations: Abraham F. Rad Jewish Film Archive /
        Jewish Agency Film Archive / Keren Hayesod, Jerusalem.
        Henry Morgenthau, Jr., Honorary Chairman of the United

Jewish Appeal, discusses the resettlement of immigrants in Israel. Shows his visit to Tel Shachar, a village named in his honor. Makes an appeal for financial support of these programs.

1321   A LAND OF THEIR OWN
(c. 1960?) / 20 min / sound / color / 16 mm
Central Zionist Archives, Jerusalem.
Looks at the work of the Youth Aliyah movement. Follows children as they arrive in Israel from other countries. Shows their care, training and resettlement.

1322   MEETING A CHALLENGE
1974 / 32 min / sound / color / 16 mm
Distributed by Alden Films. Location: Abraham F. Rad Jewish Film Archive.
Looks at the absorption of immigrants to Israel from affluent western countries. Filmed at Kibbutz Adamit and Tefizot Yeshiva. Looks at the immigrants' adjustment to life in Israel. Immigrants discuss their careers and work in the arts, sciences and social services, their feelings about Israel and about the people living in Israel.

1323   MEETING IN ISRAEL (PEGISHA BE'YISRAEL)
1958 / 20 min / sound / b&w / 16 or 35 mm
Israel Motion Picture Studios, Herzliyah. Locations: Israel Film Studios, Herzliyah / Jewish Agency Film Archive, Jerusalem / Keren Hayesod, Jerusalem.
Traces four new arrivals in Israel as they tour Ashkelon, Tel Aviv, Jerusalem, the Sanhedria, Nazareth, Capernaum, Kibbutz Yagur and Caesarea.

1324   MIDDLE EAST: BUILDING A DREAM (ISRAEL)
1979 / 21 min / sound / color / 16 mm
Coronet Instructional Media. Locations: Library of Congress / Syracuse U.
Later edition of the film: ISRAEL: THE LAND AND THE PEOPLE. Intended for intermediate to senior high school audiences. Looks at work accomplished by Jewish immigrants to Israel in reclamation of the desert, building urban areas, and in agriculture. Shows integration of Jews with diverse backgrounds and languages into one country.

1325   MISCELLANEOUS
(c. 1950?) / 8 min / silent / color / 16 mm
Israel Film Archives. Credits: Photographer - W. Van Leer.
Footage of new immigrants, Ma'abarot (transit camps) and villages where immigrants settle.

1326   NEURIM - VILLAGE OF HOPE
(c. 1970?) / 18 min / sound / color / 16 mm

Hadassah. Location: Hadassah Film Library.
Outlines care given to immigrant children by Youth Aliyah
to help them adjust to life in Israel.

1327   A NEW LIFE
(n.d.) / 20 min / sound / b&w / 16 mm
Producer unknown. Credits: Narrator - Henry Fonda.
Location: Gratz College.
Looks at the difference between immigration to Israel at
the present and 15 years ago. Describes new programs for
helping immigrants to adjust to Israeli life. Includes
interviews with early immigrants and a description of
their work.

1328   NEW ROOTS
(n.d.) / 20 min / sound / color / 16 mm
Location: Abraham F. Rad Jewish Film Archive.
Looks at the problem of absorption and integration of
immigrants recently arrived in Israel.

1329   THE NEWCOMERS
(c. 1970?) / 40 min / sound / color / 16 mm
Israel Ringel, Roll Films. Distributed by Alden Films.
Locations: Abraham F. Rad Jewish Film Archive / Jewish
Agency Film Archive.
Looks at the absorption and integration problems of
English speaking immigrants from England, Canada, the
United States and South Africa. Discusses why they came
to Israel, how they arranged their work and private lives
during the transition and how the Jewish Agency assisted
them.

1330   NOBODY RUNS AWAY
1956 / 21 min / sound / b&w / 16 mm
Producer unknown. Credits: Director - Joseph Parker.
Narrator - Joseph Cotton. Locations: Abraham F. Rad Jewish
Film Archive / Jewish Agency Film Archive.
Looks at the open-door policy Israel maintains concerning
immigration of Jews from around the world, despite
problems immigration causes with the economy and integration of diverse peoples. A fund raising film intended
for American audiences.

1331   NOW THEIR HOME IS ISRAEL
1972 / 27 min / sound / color / 16 mm
Hadassah. Made by the Center for Mass Communication. (LC
72-702319) Location: Hadassah Film Library.
Follows a young immigrant girl at Kiryat Y'arim.
Describes her new life in Israel and assistance offered
by the Youth Aliyah program to help new immigrants.

1332   ONE OF MANY
(n.d.) / 15 min / sound / b&w / 16 mm

259

Location: Abraham F. Rad Jewish Film Archive.
Looks at the programs of the World International Zionist
Organization in immigrant camps in Israel.

1333   POURQUOI L'ISRAEL
        (c. 1973) / 3 1/4 hours / sound / color / 16 mm
        Distributed by Alden Films.
        In French with English sub-titles. Looks at integration
        of Sephardic or Eastern Jews into the life of Israel.
        Describes the problems of building a nation out of
        diverse communities and integrating immigrants into the
        economic and political life of their new country.

1334   A SACRED TRUST
        (c. 1978?) / ? / sound / color / 16 mm
        Hadassah. Location: Hadassah Film Library.
        Brief history of the Youth Aliyah or immigration move-
        ment from its beginnings in Germany, through the period
        of mass immigration of Oriental Jews, to the present.
        Looks at Youth Aliyah programs and the problems and
        progress of the state of Israel during that period.

1335   SECRET JOURNEY
        1962 / 20 min / sound / 16 mm
        Central Information Office of the Government of Israel.
        Credits: Producer - Paul Falkenberg, Photographers - Emil
        Knebel, Rolf Kneller, Narrator - Rabbi H.A. Friedman.
        Looks at immigration to Israel during 1962.

1336   SHED NO. 12
        1965 / 27 min / sound / color / 16 mm
        Location: Abraham F. Rad Jewish Film Archive.
        Available in English, Spanish and French soundtracks.
        Explains difficulties encountered by new immigrants to
        Israel. Shows a customs shed in Haifa where new
        immigrants are assisted by several special programs
        intended to help in their integration into Israeli life.
        Includes language classes to assist in learning a new
        language, Hebrew.

1337   THE THIRD TEMPLE
        1965 / 30 min / sound / color / 16 or 35 mm
        Jewish National Fund. Distributed by Alden Films.
        Available in English and French soundtracks. Newsreel.
        Compares the story of the "wandering Jew" with immigra-
        tion to Israel today. Shows Yemenite, Kochin and
        European Jews immigrating to Israel. Uses a background
        narration of Biblical quotations.

1338   TRANSITION
        1954 / 15 min / sound / b&w / 16 mm
        Keren Hayesod. Made by American Film Producers. Released
        in the U.S. by United Israel Appeal. (NUC FiA 54-1215)

260

Credits: Writer-Director - Michael Elkins, Narrator -
George Bryan, Photographer - Jacob Jonilovich. Location:
Abraham F. Rad Jewish Film Archive.
Looks at transit camps for new immigrants to Israel.
Describes the daily life of new immigrants.

1339   TWENTY FIVE YEARS OF ALIYAH
(n.d.) / 18 min / sound / color / 16 mm
Distributed by Alden Films.
Looks at the history of immigration to Israel from the
1930's until Israeli statehood. Shows footage of
European concentration camps and illegal immigration to
Palestine during the British Mandate period. Describes
the importance of Israel to Jews around the world.

1340   U.J.A. REPORT FROM ISRAEL
(c. 1960?) / 10 min / sound / b&w / 16 mm
Credits: Producer - Paul Falkenberg, Narrator - Albert Grobe.
Locations: Abraham F. Rad Jewish Film Archive / Jewish Agency
Film Archive, Jerusalem / Keren Hayesod, Jerusalem.
Looks at the immigrant tent city of Pardess Hannah.
Presents a picture of immigration to Israel today and
appeals for funds to support more programs. United
Jewish Appeal fund raising film.

1341   UPWARD ROAD
1967 / 30 min / sound / color / 16 mm
Hadassah. Locations: Abraham F. Rad Jewish Film Archive /
Hadassah Film Library.
Looks at special programs offered through Youth Aliyah to
help immigrant and underprivileged children adjust to
life in Israel. Reviews activities at day centers, youth
villages and special training seminars for youth leaders.

1342   WHERE ALL MAY COME
1957 / 10 min / sound / b&w / 16 mm
Location: Jewish Agency Film Archive.
Fund raising message directed to American Jewish audiences by Prime Minister David Ben-Gurion.

1343   WHICH IS ON THE GATE (ASHER AL HASHA'AR)
(c. 1965?) / 18 min / sound / b&w / 16 mm
Nehora Heichal Shlomo. Locations: Histadrut - General
Federation of Jewish Labor, Tel Aviv / Ministry of Education
and Culture, Jerusalem.
Looks at the 700th anniversary celebration of the aliyah
or immigration of Ramban C. Nachmanides to Israel.
Describes his work and life as an interpreter of the
Scriptures.

ISRAEL - IMMIGRATION FROM EUROPE

1344   AND STILL THEY COME
        1962 / 27 min / sound / color / 16 mm
        Hadassah, the Women's Zionist Organization of America. (NUC
        FiA 63-473) Credits: Director - Hazel Greenwald,
        Photographer - Fred Csasznik. Locations: Abraham F. Rad
        Jewish Film Archive / Hadassah Film Library / Library of
        Congress (FBA 2774). *
            Shot at Ramat Hadassah Szold, Yemin Orde and other Youth
            Aliyah villages in Israel. Looks at programs in
            language, vocational training, education and health care
            for young immigrants to Israel. Includes a profile of
            Yehuda Bacon, Israeli artist, who was helped by Youth
            Aliyah after WWII. Stresses the cultural, emotional and
            social deprivation of children assisted by Youth Aliyah.
            Useful for fund raising purposes.

1345   AUFBRUCH DER JUGEND
        (c. 1935) / 15 min / silent / b&w / 16 mm
        Location: Abraham F. Rad Jewish Film Archive.
            Youth Aliyah programs to assist emigrating German youth
            in the 1930's are shown. On their arrival at the port of
            Haifa, Jewish German children are greeted by Henrietta
            Szold and Hans Beyth and taken to Ein Harod.

1346   B'RIHA - FLIGHT TO SECURITY
        (c. 1970?) / 30 min / sound / 16 mm
        Arthur Zegart.
            Looks at B'riha Organization of Jewish Volunteers who
            helped smuggle Jews out of Europe and into Israel
            following WWII.

1347   THE CAMEL AND I
        1955 / 30 min / sound / color / 16 mm
        National Academy for Adult Jewish Studies.
            Looks at adjustment problems faced by European immigrants
            to Israel.

1348   A FREE PEOPLE
        1958 / 25 min / sound / b&w / 16 mm
        Keren Hayesod, Jerusalem. Made by Michael Elkins. Released
        in the U.S. by United Israel Appeal. Distributed by Alden
        Films. (NUC FiA 64-578) Location: Abraham F. Rad Jewish
        Film Archive.
            History of Jewish immigration to Palestine from Germany
            and Hungary after WWII. Shows increased immigration to
            Israel after the creation of the Jewish state. Uses
            footage of early illegal and later immigration from the
            Yemen and Egypt to show growth of the population of
            Israel through immigration.

1349   INSIGHTS
        1970 / 26 min / sound / b&w / 16 mm
        Ze'ev Rothman. Location: Jewish Agency Film Archive,

Jerusalem.
Looks at absorption of immigrants from Britain into
Israel.

1350   IT IS NO DREAM
(n.d.) / 6 min / sound / color / 16 mm
Distributed by Alden Films.
Looks at Soviet Jewish immigrants to Israel. Shows
absorption into Israeli society and problems of adjustment.

1351   JONATHAN AND TALLI (YONATAN VE TALLI)
(c. 1965?) / 40 min / sound / b&w / 35 mm
Israel Motion Picture Studios. Location: Israel Film
Studios, Herzliyah / Jewish Agency Film Archive.
Traces the dilemma of a woman survivor of a European con-
centration camp who finds her two children settled in
Israel with two different families.

1352   THE LONGEST WAVE
(n.d.) / 25 min / sound / color / 16 mm
Distributed by Alden Films. Location: Abraham F. Rad Jewish
Film Archive.
Shows Soviet Jewish immigrants in Beersheva learning a
new language and trying to find work and housing in
competitive Israeli society. Discusses adjustment to a
new way of life in Israel.

1353   LOOK HOMEWARD WANDERER
1947 / 20 min / sound / b&w / 16 mm
U.P.A. New York. Credits: Narrator - Marta Mannes.
Locations: Abraham F. Rad Jewish Film Archive / Central
Zionist Film Archives / Jewish Agency Film Archive / Keren
Hayesod, Jerusalem.
Shows European Jewish immigration to Palestine on the eve
of the establishment of the state of Israel.

1354   RACHEL SHALL BE THY NAME
(c. 1970?) / 14 min / sound / color / 16 mm
Stephen Scharff. Locations: Abraham F. Rad Jewish Film
Archive / Central Zionist Archives, Jerusalem.
Follows Ilana, a Hungarian Jewish girl in Israel, and the
programs available to assist her. Looks at Hadassah-
sponsored Seligsberg School and Brandeis Vocational High
School in Jerusalem. Shows programs to assist young
adults with learning a trade.

1355   THE RETURN
(c. 1970?) / 23 min / sound / color / 16 mm
Distributed by Alden Films. Location: Abraham F. Rad Jewish
Film Archive.
Made by a crew of Soviet Jewish film-makers. Profiles
the Soviet immigrant experience in Israel and problems of
adjustment to Israeli life.

1356   ROAD TO TOMORROW
       1958 / 20 min / sound / color / 16 mm
       Location: Abraham F. Rad Jewish Film Archive.
       Shows the Working Women's Council in Israel, sister group
       to Pioneer Women, assisting Polish immigrant families
       with their adjustment to life in Israel.

1357   THE SECOND CHANCE
       1958 / 40 min / sound / b&w / 16 mm
       Location: Abraham F. Rad Jewish Film Archive.
       Looks at Polish Jewish immigration to Israel.

1358   THEY FIND A HOME
       1941 / 15 min / sound / b&w / 16 mm
       J. Gal-Ezer. Locations: Abraham F. Rad Jewish Film Archive /
       Jewish Agency Film Archive.
       Covers the 1933 crisis in Germany which led to immigra-
       tion of German Jews to Palestine. Follows the integra-
       tion and accomplishments of German Jews in Israel during
       the period 1936-1940.

1359   A TIME TO REJOICE
       1972 / 14 min / sound / color / 16 mm
       United Jewish Appeal. Distributed by Alden Films.
       Locations: Abraham F. Rad Jewish Film Archive / Gratz
       College.
       Shows absorption of Soviet Jews in the village of Beth
       Shemesh. Intended for fund raising purposes.

1360   TOMORROW IS A WONDERFUL DAY
       (n.d.) / 50 min / sound / b&w / 16 mm
       Hadassah. Locations: Abraham F. Rad Jewish Film Archive /
       Keren Hayesod, Jerusalem / Ministry of Education and
       Culture, Jerusalem.
       Follows a German Jewish boy who immigrates to Israel with
       the help of Youth Aliyah.

ISRAEL - IMMIGRATION FROM MIDDLE EASTERN COUNTRIES

1361   AIRLIFT OF YEMENITE JEWS
       1949 / 8 min / silent / b&w / 16 mm
       Location: Abraham F. Rad Jewish Film Archive.
       Looks at "Operation Magic Carpet", the airlift of
       Yemenite Jews from Aden to Israel.

1362   THE ARAB JEWS
       1976 / 30 min / sound / color / 16 mm
       Verite Film Productions, Canada. Distributed by Phoenix
       Films. Credits: Producer - Lyla Lebane, Director-Writer -
       Mark Dolgoy. Location: Jewish Media Service.
       Made by a Canadian Jewish crew. Argues that the suf-
       fering of Jews in Arab countries like Iraq and Syria

264

counterbalances the suffering of Arab Palestinian refugees. Includes interviews with Jewish immigrants from
Arab countries.

1363   EXODUS "57"
1957 / 13 min / sound / b&w / 16 mm
United Jewish Appeal. CRT Productions. Credits: Narrator -
Robert Preston. Locations: Abraham F. Rad Jewish Film
Archive / Jewish Agency Film Archive / Keren Hayesod,
Jerusalem.
        Listed in some catalogs as: EXODUS 1957. Fund raising
        film. Describes the immigration of Jews to Israel from
        Egypt and from countries behind the Iron Curtain.

1364   FLIGHT TO FREEDOM
1949 / 20 min / sound / b&w / 16 mm
William Zimmerman, Metro-Goldwyn-Mayer. Credits: Director -
Michael Elkins, Narrator - Sam Jaffe. Locations: Abraham F.
Rad Jewish Film Archive / Jewish Agency Film Archive / Keren
Hayesod, Jerusalem.
        Profiles "Operation Magic Carpet", the airlift of
        Yemenite Jews to Israel in 1949. Includes Yemenite musi-
        cal soundtrack.

1365   HOME AT LAST
(c. 1970?) / 15 min / sound / color / 16 mm
Lazar Dunner. Distributed by Alden Films. Locations:
Abraham F. Rad Jewish Film Archive / Jewish Agency Film
Archive.
        Looks at resettlement of Jews from Arab countries in the
        Lachish region of Israel.

1366   ISRAEL IN CRISIS
1956 / 6 min / sound / color / 16 mm
Producer unknown. Locations: Abraham F. Rad Jewish Film
Archive / Jewish Agency Film Archive / Keren Hayesod,
Jerusalem.
        Uses slides to trace immigration of Jews from Arab
        countries like Morocco and Tunisia to Israel.

1367   IT IS GOOD TO BE ALIVE
1958 / 28 min / sound / color / 16 mm
Hazel Greenwald. Hadassah. Locations: Central Zionist
Archives, Jerusalem / Ministry of Education and Culture,
Jerusalem.
        Looks at assistance offered by the Anne Frank Havens
        Program to Jewish immigrant children from Tehran, Iran.
        Promotes support for Youth Aliyah programs such as the
        youth village at Kfar Vitkin.

1368   THE LACHISH STORY
1955 / 35 min / sound / b&w / 16 mm
Paul Tyras for Keren Hayesod. Israel Motion Picture

265

Studios. Credits: Director - Baruch Dienar. Locations:
Abraham F. Rad Jewish Film Archive / Jewish Agency Film
Archive / Keren Hayesod, Jerusalem.
Available in English and Spanish soundtracks. Also
available in a 35 mm, 60 minute version. Looks at the
immigration of a group of Moroccan Jews by boat to
Israel. Shows their integration into Israeli life in the
Lachish region.

1369　MIMOUNA
1970 / 13 min / sound / color / 16 or 35 mm
Location: Abraham F. Rad Jewish Film Archive.
Available in English, French and Hebrew soundtracks.
Looks at traditional festivities of the Moroccan Jewish
community in Israel.

1370　MY BROTHER AND I
1950 / 20 min / sound or silent / color / 16 mm
Hadassah. (NUC FiA 62-917) Credits: Producer-Photographer
- Ben Oyserman, Writers - Norman Borisoff, Mina Brownstone.
Locations: Abraham F. Rad Jewish Film Archive / Central
Zionist Archives, Jerusalem / Ministry of Education and
Culture, Jerusalem.
Looks at the absorption of two Jewish brothers from
Morocco into an Israeli youth village and the changes
brought about by their new life.

1371　THE OATH
(n.d.) / 27 min / sound / color / 16 mm
Distributed by Alden Films. Location: Abraham F. Rad Jewish
Film Archive.
Available in English, Hebrew, Spanish, French and German
soundtracks. Examines condition of Jews in the Soviet
Union and Arab countries. Uses footage from French tele-
vision and the Syrian government to profile life in the
Jewish quarters of various countries. Describes life in
Israel for new immigrants. Discusses problem of
absorbing new immigrants and concerns about social ine-
quality in Israel.

1372　SPELL OF ISRAEL
(n.d.) / 40 min / sound / color or b&w / 16 mm
Location: Abraham F. Rad Jewish Film Archive.
Evangelist Oral Roberts interviews Yemenite Jews in
Israel. Includes newsreel footage of "Operation Magic
Carpet", the airlift of Jews from Yemen to Israel.

1373　TEN DAYS - AND 500 YEARS
1965 / 14 min / silent / b&w / 16 mm
Location: Abraham F. Rad Jewish Film Archive.
Two Jewish families from a village in southern Morocco
are moved to Kfar Yeruham in Israel. Contrasts village
life in Morocco and their new life.

266

1374 TENT CITY
1951 / 33 min / sound / b&w / 16 mm
United Israel Appeal. Made by Israel Motion Picture Studios.
(NUC FiA 54-1214) Credits: Wrlter-Producer - Baruch Dienar,
Director - Leopold Lahola. Location: Abraham F. Rad Jewish
Film Archive.
Reenacts the immigration of a family of Jews from Baghdad
to Israel. Describes programs available to immigrants to
assist in their integration into Israeli life.

1375 TO SAVE ONE LIFE
(n.d.) / 28 min / sound / color / 16 mm
Hadassah. Location: Abraham F. Rad Jewish Film Archive /
Ministry of Education and Culture, Jerusalem.
Follows two Jewish orphans during their emigration from
Yemen to Israel.

1376 YEMENITE IMMIGRANTS
(n.d.) / 5 min / silent / b&w / 16 mm
Location: Abraham F. Rad Jewish Film Archives.
Short look at immigration of Yemenite Jews to Israel.
Includes discussion of vandalized cemetaries and synogo-
gues in the Yemen.

ISRAEL - IMMIGRATION FROM THE AMERICAS

1377 BUILDING A FUTURE
(c. 1970?) / 25 min / sound / color / 16 mm
Credits: Producer - Henry Roth, Supervisor - Miriam Ranan.
Locations: Abraham F. Rad Jewish Film Archive / Jewish
Agency Film Archive.
Looks at immigrants from South America, their life on a
kibbutz in Israel and education at youth centers.

1378 A LETTER TO DEBORAH
1947 / 9 min / sound / b&w / 16 mm
Location: Abraham F. Rad Jewish Film Archive.
An American immigrant to Palestine describes the work of
the Rassco Rural and Suburban Settlement Corporation
which assisted him in purchasing land for agricultural
purposes. A promotional film.

1379 THIS YEAR IN JERUSALEM
(c. 1976?) / 25 min / sound / color / 16 mm
Distributed by Alden Films. (People, Places and Things
series)
Special interest news report by Geraldo Rivera on
Americans who have emigrated to Israel despite problems
of inflation and political and military unrest. Looks at
the 28th annual Independence Day celebration and parade
in Jerusalem. Includes interviews with former New
Yorkers living in Kibbutz Adamit, an agricultural settlement.

267

ISRAEL - ASSISTANCE TO ISRAEL

1380 AM YISRAEL CHAI - THE PEOPLE OF ISRAEL LIVE
1959 / 28 min / sound / color or b&w / 16 mm
Hadassah. (NUC FiA 65-307) Credits: Producer - Hazel
Greenwald, Writer - Stanford Sobel.
Looks at contributions of Hadassah to Israeli life.
Includes short biography of Henrietta Szold, founder of
Hadassah. Shows Hadassah's work in health, research,
land reclamation and afforestation, child rescue and
rehabilitation and vocational training.

1381 AMERICAN-ISRAEL CULTURAL FOUNDATION (KEREN TARBUT
AMERICA-YISRA'EL)
1966 / 22 min / sound / color / 16 mm
Roll Films Ltd. Credits: Director - A. Eldar, Writer - B.
Hyams. Location: Prime Minister's Office, Information
Dept., Jerusalem.
Profiles the work of the American-Israel Cultural
Foundation in Israel to support programs to encourage
young artists. Describes programs to support music
libraries and other cultural institutions.

1382 AS ALWAYS, HADASSAH
(c. 1973?) / 26 min / sound / color / 16 mm
Hadassah. Location: Hadassah Film Library.
Shows HMO footage of the Hadassah Hospital and its personnel during the Yom Kippur war.

1383 B'NAI B'RITH'S ISRAEL
1966 / 33 mm / sound / color / 16 mm
B'nai B'rith Commission on Israel. Made by Academy Film
Productions. (NUC FiA 67-315)
Looks at accomplishments of the Israel Commission of
B'nai B'rith in supporting children's homes, libraries,
agricultural settlements and additional settlements in
Israel as reported during the Triennial Convention in
1965.

1384 CHANGING THE LAND
1970 / 18 min / sound / color / 16 mm
Jewish National Fund. Locations: Abraham F. Rad Jewish Film
Archive / Hadassah Film Library / Jewish National Fund.
Available in English, Hebrew, French, Spanish and German
soundtracks. Looks at programs in land reclamation,
afforestation, swamp drainage and road building supported
by the Jewish National Fund.

1385 DEEDS AND DREAMS
(n.d.) / 12 min / sound / color / 16 mm
Location: Abraham F. Rad Jewish Film Archive.
Looks at Hadassah programs for advanced child welfare and
medical aid in Israel.

1386   THE DREAM AND THE DEED
        1971 / 20 min / sound / color / 16 mm
        Hadassah. Made by Aegis Productions. (LC 71-713227)
        Credits: Narrator - Oscar Brand. Location: Hadassah Film
        Library.
            Traces the work of Hadassah from its founding by
            Henrietta Szold to present programs. Profiles the Mount
            Scopus Hospital and the Hadassah-Hebrew University
            Medical Center in Ein Kerem. Outlines Hadassah medical
            support during the Six-Day War.

1387   FOR THE GOOD OF ALL
        (c. 1975?) / 28 min / sound / color / 16 mm
        Hadassah. Location: Hadassah Film Library.
            Shows how Hadassah's medical work is performed "for the
            good of all", and how it benefits Israel and its people.

1388   HADASSIM
        (n.d.) / 20 min / sound / color / 16 mm
        Jewish National Fund. Location: Abraham F. Rad Jewish Film
        Archive / Jewish National Fund, Jerusalem.
            Looks at the Hadassim youth institutions near Natanya and
            Tel Aviv.

1389   HIGHLIGHTS OF THE 1970 ISRAELI DAY PARADE
        1970 / 20 min / sound / color / 16 mm
        Martin Levinson. Martin's Media. Location: Library of
        Congress (FBA 9581) *
            Covers the Israeli Independence Day parade held in New
            York City in 1970. Groups participating in the parade
            include B'nai B'rith, National Council of Young Israel,
            Mizrachi Women, and the Association of Jewish Court
            Attaches among many others. Intended to build goodwill
            of Americans towards Israel. Has some technical flaws
            including a poor soundtrack.

1390   INVESTMENT AND DEVELOPMENT IN ISRAEL (HASHKA'OT
        UFITU'ACH BEYISRA'EL)
        (c. 1970?) / 35 min / sound / color / 16 mm
        Producer unknown. Location: Prime Minister's Office,
        Information Dept., Jerusalem.
            Available in English, Hebrew and French soundtracks.
            Describes various industrial, agricultural and scientific
            projects and institutions developed through investment
            from outside Israel.

1391   JEWISH NATIONAL FUND NEWSREEL 01
        (n.d) / 7 min / sound / color / 16 mm
        Jewish National Fund.
            Looks at the Modin and Biranit regions of Israel. Shows
            building and dedication of new settlements supported by
            the Jewish National Fund.

269

1392   JEWISH NATIONAL FUND NEWSREEL 02
        (n.d.) / 7 min / sound / color / 16 mm
        Jewish National Fund.
        Shows the 1960 agreement signing ceremony between the
        Jewish National Fund and the Israeli government. Looks
        at projects supported by the Fund including those for the
        Lake Huleh area, the Netua settlement and construction of
        the John F. Kennedy Memorial.

1393   JEWISH NATIONAL FUND NEWSREEL 03
        (n.d.) / 7 min / sound / color / 16 mm
        Jewish National Fund.
        Profiles efforts of the Jewish National Fund to find jobs
        for the unemployed during the 1966 recession in Israel.

1394   JEWISH NATIONAL FUND NEWSREEL 04
        (n.d.) / 7 min / sound / color / 16 mm
        Jewish National Fund.
        Looks at the John F. Kennedy Memorial dedication, a bar
        mitzvah held in a Jewish National Fund-supported forest,
        and the border settlement of Tzur-nalhan.

1395   JEWISH NATIONAL FUND NEWSREEL 05
        (n.d.) / 7 min / sound / color / 16 mm
        Jewish National Fund.
        Looks at JNF supported projects including Yatir in the
        Negev Desert and an afforestation project where one
        million trees are being planted.

1396   JEWISH NATIONAL FUND NEWSREEL 06
        (n.d.) / 7 min / sound / color / 16 mm
        Jewish National Fund.
        Looks at JNF supported projects in Jerusalem, Ramallah
        and the Canadian Centennial Forest. Shows Beth Shean and
        a JNF road building project along the Jordan River.

1397   JEWISH NATIONAL FUND NEWSREEL 07
        (n.d.) / 7 min / sound / color / 16 mm
        Jewish National Fund.
        Shows the B'nai B'rith convention of 1966, the dedication
        of the Martyr's Forest, the settlement of Maale Hagilboa
        and tells the story of Herzl's cyprus tree.

1398   JEWISH NATIONAL FUND NEWSREEL 08
        (n.d.) / 7 min / sound / color / 16 mm
        Jewish National Fund.
        Looks at Keren Kayemeth supported work in irrigation and
        dam building at Adorayim in southern Israel.

1399   JEWISH NATIONAL FUND NEWSREEL 09
        (n.d.) / 7 min / sound / color / 16 mm
        Jewish National Fund.
        Shows the dedication of the Rubinstein Forest, the exca-

vation at Tel Dan, the Paul Schutzer Woods and Beth
Eshel.

1400   JEWISH NATIONAL FUND NEWSREEL 10
        (n.d.) / 7 min / sound / color / 16 mm
        Jewish National Fund.
        Profiles the 70th anniversary of the Jewish National Fund
        on August 26, 1971 held on Mt. Herzl. Includes speeches
        by JNF and Israeli government officials, including Golda
        Meir.

1401   JORDAN VALLEY
        (n.d.) / 8 min / silent / color / 16 mm
        Location: Abraham F. Rad Jewish Film Archive.
        Looks at Jewish National Fund projects in the Jordan
        Valley.

1402   JOURNEY TO TOMORROW
        1953 / 12 min / sound / b&w / 16 mm
        Producer unknown. Locations: Abraham F. Rad Jewish Film
        Archive / Jewish Agency Film Archive.
        Looks at U.J.A. and Joint Distribution Committee sponsored
        projects in Paris, Morocco and Israel. Fund raising film
        for the Jewish Agency.

1403   LETTER FROM ISRAEL
        (c. 1970?) / 15 min / sound / b&w / 16 mm
        Hadassah. Credits: Producer - Hazel Greenwald, Director -
        Stephen Scharff. Locations: Abraham F. Rad Jewish Film
        Archive / Central Zionist Archives, Jerusalem.
        The President of Hadassah reads a letter from a nurse at
        the Mt. Scopus Hadassah Hospital describing their work.
        Includes footage of the Israeli War of Independence and
        Jerusalem. A fund raising film.

1404   MAKE DEEP THEIR ROOTS
        1970 / 20 min / sound / color / 16 mm
        Jewish National Fund.
        Available in English, Hebrew, French, Spanish and German
        soundtracks. Looks at Jewish National Fund activities in
        Israel and throughout the world.

1405   A NEW MORNING
        1953 / 28 min / sound / color / 16 mm
        Hadassah. Credits: Producer - Hazel Greenwald. (NUC FiA
        65-302) Locations: Abraham F. Rad Jewish Film Archive /
        Central Zionist Archives, Jerusalem.
        Brief travelog of Israel emphasizing Hadassah sponsored
        projects in hospitals, clinics, health stations, schools,
        and Youth Aliyah child rehabilitation settlements.

1406   A NEW YEAR'S CARD FROM ISRAEL
        1966 / 27 min / sound / color / 16 mm

271

Hadassah, the Women's Zionist Organization of America. Made
by Lazar Dunner. (NUC FiA 67-517) Location: Hadassah Film
Library.
Profiles training and vocational education programs supported by Hadassah in Israel. Describes how trained
industrial and agricultural workers aid the economy of
Israel.

1407 ON A DAY LIKE THIS
(n.d.) / 22 min / sound / color / 16 mm
Location: Abraham F. Rad Jewish Film Archive.
Looks at Jewish National Fund supported projects in
Israel. Includes scenes of clearing land for new settlements, planting trees, water collection projects and
building security roads.

1408 THE PEOPLE OF ISRAEL LIVE
(n.d.) / 28 min / sound / color / 16 mm
Hadassah. Credits: Producer - Hazel Greenwald. Locations:
Abraham F. Rad Jewish Film Archive / Central Zionist Archives,
Jerusalem.
Looks at Hadassah sponsored projects including medical
services, youth villages and vocational education
programs.

1409 PEOPLE OF PEACE (AM SHALOM)
1950 / 10 min / sound / b&w / 16 mm
Hadassah. Credits: Producer - Hazel Greenwald. Locations:
Abraham F. Rad Jewish Film Archive / Central Zionist Archives,
Jerusalem.
Covers projects supported by Hadassah during the first
two years of Israeli statehood. Shows how these projects
"help a people of peace build a peaceful tomorrow".

1410 RIGHT HAND OF THE STATE
(n.d.) / 15 min / sound / color / 16 mm
Location: Abraham F. Rad Jewish Film Archive.
Shows Jewish National Fund projects in land settlement
and reafforestation in Israel.

1411 THE STORY OF THE JEWISH NATIONAL FUND
1966 / 18 min / sound / b&w / 16 mm
Jewish National Fund.
Available in English, Hebrew, French, Spanish and German
soundtracks. Gives history and development of the Jewish
National Fund. Shows JNF leaders, projects and
accomplishments.

1412 STRANGE HOLIDAY
1963 / 22 min / sound / color / 16 mm
Location: Abraham F. Rad Jewish Film Archive.
Looks at the World International Zionist Organization's
work in Kiryat Gat as seen through the eyes of a
sociology student visiting family members there.

1413   TEN YEARS HELP
        1962 / 32 min / sound / color / 16 mm
        Israel Film Studios, Herzliyah. Credits: Director - P.
        Steinhardt. Location: Prime Minister's Office, Information
        Dept., Jerusalem.
            Looks at American technical assistance to Israel over a
            ten year period.

1414   VERDICT ON SURVIVAL
        1971 / 10 min / sound / color / 16 mm
        United Jewish Welfare Fund. Made by Robert Story
        Productions. Released by Jewish Federation - Council of
        Greater Los Angeles. (LC 73-715452)
            Fund raising film made by the United Jewish Welfare
            Fund. Stresses the threat to Jews worldwide resulting
            from Soviet intervention in the Middle East. Looks at
            problems faced by Jews in Los Angeles, Israel and in
            various countries.

1415   A WAY TO GROW
        1965 / 27 min / sound / b&w / 16 mm
        Hadassah, the Women's Zionist Organization of America. (NUC
        FiA 66-675)
            Traces the history of Hadassah in Israel and the U.S.
            over the last fifty years.

1416   WHAT'S NEW AT HADASSAH?
        1969 / 27 min / sound / color / 16 mm
        Hadassah, the Women's Zionist Organization of America. Made
        by Wim Van Leer Production Co. (LC 71-705018) Location:
        Israel Film Archives, Haifa.
            Looks at Hadassah supported medical programs in Israel
            including the Hadassah-Hebrew University Medical Center
            in Jerusalem. Shows programs for wounded soldiers and
            new equipment being used to treat patients.

ISRAEL - INTERNATIONAL COOPERATION AND SEMINARS

1417   AFRICAN AND ASIAN STUDENTS MEET IN ISRAEL - SEMINARS
        1960 / 28 min / sound / b&w / 16 mm
        Israel Motion Picture Studios, Tel Aviv. Released in the
        U.S. by Israel Office of Information. (NUC FiA 64-884)
        Credits: Director-Writer - Nathan Gross.
            Looks at seminars held in Israel for Asian and African
            students to share skills and promote cultural exchanges.

1418   AFRO-ASIAN STUDENTS IN ISRAEL
        1961 / 20 min / sound / b&w / 16 or 35 mm
        Nathan Gross, for the Foreign Ministry.
            Available in English and French soundtracks. Outlines
            seminars, coursework, international meetings and exhibi-
            tions for Asian and African students in Israel. Includes

273

scenes of Burmese soldiers training in Israel. Profiles
Israeli women.

1419   THE BRIDGE TO FRIENDSHIP (GESHER LAYEDIDUT)
1968 / 13 min / sound / b&w / 16 or 35 mm
Berkey Pathe Humphries, for the Histadrut. Distributed by
Alden Films. Credits: Director - Nathan Gross, Photographer
- Hayim Schreiber. Locations: Abraham F. Rad Jewish Film
Archive / Histadrut Film Dept.
       Shows the Afro-Asian seminar on cooperation held at Beir
Sefer le Pe'ilei Hahistadrut, the school for Histadrut
officials in Israel.

1420   CO-OP (AFRO-ASIAN SEMINARS)
1961 / 15 min / sound / b&w / 16 mm or 35 mm
Nathan Gross, Israel Film Studios. Distributed by Alden
Films. Location: Abraham F. Rad Jewish Film Archives.
       Available in English, French and Spanish soundtracks.
Documents the Afro-Asian seminar of 1961.

1421   INDEPENDENCE DAY (ZAMBIA)
1964 / 450 ft. / sound / b&w / 16 or 35 mm
Israel Film Studios, Herzliyah.
       Shows the celebration of Zambia's Independence Day in
Jerusalem in 1964.

1422   SEMINARS IN ISRAEL
(n.d.) / 28 min / sound / b&w / 16 mm
Distributed by Alden Films.
       Looks at an Afro-Asian student seminar in Israel.

1423   TOOLS AND THE MAN (DES OUTILS ET DES HOMMES)
1972 / 15 min / sound / b&w / 16 mm
Dept. for International Cooperation of the Israel Ministry
for Foreign Affairs in cooperation with the ORT, Israel.
Locations: Abraham F. Rad Jewish Film Archive / Jewish
Agency Film Archive, Jerusalem.
       Profiles a program to train teachers from African
countries at the Israel Centre for Instructors from
Developing Countries.

ISRAEL - ARABS IN ISRAEL

1424   ARABS OF ISRAEL
1969 / 4 min / silent / color / super 8 mm film loop in
cartridge. Eye Gate House. (Living in Israel series) (LC
74-703708)
       Looks at the Christian and Muslim Arab population of
Israel.

1425   THE ARABS OF ISRAEL: AS THEY SEE IT
(n.d.) / 28 min / sound / color / 16 mm

Anti-Defamation League of B'nai B'rith. Distributed by
Alden Films. (Dateline Israel series) Location: Gratz
College.
Arnold Forster interviews four Israeli Arabs concerning
their feelings about being Arab and living in Israel.
Includes interviews with a Bedouin doctor discussing
medical care, a lawyer outlining civil rights, a professor speaking on education, and a college student
discussing his future. Made by a Jewish production company.

1426   THE ARABS OF ISRAEL: IN THEIR OPINION
(n.d.) / 30 min / sound / color / 16 mm
Anti-Defamation League of B'nai B'rith. Distributed by
Alden Films. (Dateline Israel series) Location:
Audio-Visual Dept, Anti-Defamation League of B'nai B'rith.
Further interviews by Arnold Forster concerning the
feeling of Israeli Arabs and integration of Arabs into
Israeli society. Includes interviews with Arab intellec-
tual Shukhry Araf and a student at the Hebrew University
concerning their feelings as Arabs in Israel. Made by a
Jewish production company.

1427   COMPARATIVE GEOGRAPHY: A CHANGING CULTURE
1971 / 17 min / sound / color / 16 mm
BFA Educational Media. Location: Syracuse U.
Intended for intermediate to junior high school audiences.
Follows a nomadic Bedouin family as they are settled by
the Israeli government in permanent housing. Considers
the change in life style this entails for the vanishing
nomadic Bedouin.

1428   DOCTOR IN THE DESERT
1966 / 13 min / sound / b&w / 16 mm
Emanu'el Porat. Israel Film Studios, Herzliyah.
Distributed by Alden Films. Location: Abraham F. Rad Jewish
Film Archive.
Available in English and Hebrew soundtracks. Looks at
medical services available to the Bedouin of the Negev.
Shows a central clinic in Beersheba and programs for
child care. Profiles the enrollment of the first Bedouin
medical student in Israel.

1429   SON OF SULAM
1960 / 15 min / sound / 35 mm
Israel Motion Picture Studios.
General look at the Bedouin Arabs of Israel.

1430   TO LIVE IN FREEDOM
1973 / 54 min / sound / color / 16 mm
Simon Louvish. Distributed by Third World Newsreel.
Credits: Producers - Simon Louvish, Kostas Chronopoulos,
Jorge Tsoucarossa, Antonia Caccia, Anna Rozen, Uri Davis,

275

Rakhelta Tsehlana.
Produced by an Israeli crew but supporting an Arab point
of view. Looks at discrimination against Palestinian
Arabs in Israel as well as discrimination against
Oriental Jews by European Jews. Shows job and legal
restrictions against Arabs and traces the history of the
struggle for Palestine and Zionism in Europe. Includes
footage from early films promoting Jewish immigration to
Israel at the expense of the Arab population. Relatively
few films cover this viewpoint.

ISRAEL - THE DRUZE AND CHRISTIANS IN ISRAEL

1431   BET JANN
        1966 / 13 min / sound / b&w / 35 mm
        Shmuel Imberman and Kibbutz Dan, Hod Hasharon.
        Available in English or Hebrew soundtracks. Looks at the
        Druze community at Bet Jann, Mount Merron in Israel.
        Includes scenes of a wedding. Records folk melodies as
        well as wedding music of the Druze.

1432   DRUZIM (THE DRUZE)
        (c. 1960?) / 15 min / silent / b&w / 16 mm
        W. Van Leer. Location: Israel Film Archives, Haifa.
        Looks at a Druze village in Israel during the Nebi Shueib
        or Jethro festivities.

1433   THE PEOPLE OF NES AMMIM
        (c. 1979) / 60 min / sound / color / 16 mm or 3/4"
        videocassette. PBS. WNET-Channel 13. (Bill Moyer's
        Journal, television series) Distributed by WNET, New York.
        Looks at a non-Arab Christian community in Northern
        Israel. Investigates their feelings about the country
        and anti-semitism.

ISRAEL - THE KIBBUTZ

1434   COLLECTIVE ADVENTURE
        1939 / 29 min / sound / b&w / 16 or 35 mm
        Location: Abraham F. Rad Jewish Film Archive.
        Profiles life at Kibbutz Negba, settled by early Jewish
        pioneers in one day.

1435   COMMUNITY LIFE IN ISRAEL: THE KIBBUTZ
        1968 / 4 min / silent / color / super 8 mm film loop
        Ealing Corporation. (How Man Lives series) (NUC FiA
        67-5731) Credits: Writer - Ray Garner.
        Short look at kibbutz life. Shows men and women working
        in the fields, children in communal day centers and eve-
        nings when children and parents spend time together.

1436   COOPERATION - DRIVING FORCE OF ISRAEL
        (n.d.) / 24 min / sound / b&w / 16 mm
        Location: Abraham F. Rad Jewish Film Archive.
        Looks at cooperation in Israel on kibbutzim including Or
        Haner, Sde Boker and Degania. Shows moshav collective
        settlements like Kfar Vitkin, Cochav and Nir Banim and
        commercial cooperatives such as Tnuva, Hamashbir, Egged
        and Solel Boneh. Describes the significance of these
        cooperative ventures for Israeli life.

1437   A DAY IN DEGANIA
        1940 / 15 min / sound / color / 16 mm
        United Palestine Appeal. (NUC FiA 54-1201) Credits:
        Producer - Lazar Dunner, Narrator - Maurice Samuel.
        Technicolor. Location: Abraham F. Rad Jewish Film
        Archive.
        Profiles Degania, the first Jewish cooperative settlement
        established in Palestine. Looks at the responsibilities
        and duties of the members of the colony. Asks for finan-
        cial support for the settlement.

1438   DEGANIA
        1960 / 12 min / sound / color / 16 mm
        Location: Abraham F. Rad Jewish Film Archive.
        Looks at the 50th anniversary celebration of the founding
        of Degania, the oldest Jewish cooperative settlement in
        Israel.

1439   A DIFFERENT PATH: THE KIBBUTZ - SEARCH FOR A NEW SOCIETY
        1973 / 28 min / sound / color / 16 mm
        EMC Corporation. Distributed by Alden Films. (LC 75-700184)
        Credits: Producer - Bastian Wimmer. Locations: Gratz
        College / Penn. State U. / U. of California Extension Media
        Center.
        Intended for senior high school to adult audiences.
        Looks at the kibbutz as a social experiment. Shot on
        location. Uses archival footage to show the history of
        several kibbutzim in Israel. Outlines the challenges,
        pressures and satisfactions of communal life and social
        values. Listed in some catalogs as: A DIFFERENT PATH.

1440   THE END OF THE ROAD
        1971 / 13 min / sound / color / 16 or 35 mm
        Location: Abraham F. Rad Jewish Film Archive.
        Available in English and Hebrew soundtracks. Profiles
        the border kibbutz of Misgav Am.

1441   FAMILY LIFE: A KIBBUTZ
        1970 / 15 min / sound / color / 16 mm
        Yehuda Tarmu. Released by BFA Educational Media. (LC
        70-711159) Locations: Syracuse U. / U. of Illinois.
        Intended for intermediate to junior high school audien-
        ces. Explores the collective nature of kibbutz life.

Discusses work, education, recreation and the bonds
created by shared experience and the ties of family life.

1442   THE FRONTIER
        (n.d.) / 15 min / sound / b&w / 16 mm
        Distributed by Alden Films. Location: Abraham F. Rad Jewish
        Film Archive.
            Looks at life in the border kibbutz of Beit Shean.
            Describes stress of border bombardments and the need to
            protect children in underground shelters during breaks in
            the ceasefire.

1443   GALILEE REBORN
        (n.d.) / 6 min / sound / b&w / 16 mm
        Location: Abraham F. Rad Jewish Film Archive.
            Profiles the kibbutz of Sasa. Describes Jewish National
            Fund projects in land reclamation in northern Israel.

1444   GVUL (BORDER)
        1966 / 13 min / silent / b&w / 16 mm
        Ulpanei Kibbutz Dan. Locations: Histadrut - General
        Federation of Jewish Labor, Tel Aviv / Ministry of Education
        and Culture, Jerusalem.
            Profiles life at Kibbutz Dan in the Upper Galilee area.
            Describes dangers and damage experienced as a result of
            Syrian shelling before the Six Day War. Outlines daily
            life on the kibbutz.

1445   HAGIT - A 17 YEAR OLD ON A KIBBUTZ
        1973 / 22 min / sound / color / 16 mm
        Education Development Center. (Exploring Human Nature
        series) (LC 73-702035)
            Follows a kibbutz teenager as she works in an orange
            grove. She discusses life, her family, sex, work and
            marriage.

1446   HERITAGE
        1953 / 28 min / sound / color / 16 mm
        Location: Abraham F. Rad Jewish Film Archive.
            Looks at hostilities between Arab settlements and Jewish
            kibbutzim during the Israeli War of Independence. Pre-
            sents a post-war image of cooperation between Arab and
            Jewish communities in Israel.

1447   HOME IN THE DESERT
        1960 / 20 min / sound / b&w / 16 mm
        Credits: Director - Emil Knebel. Locations: Abraham F. Rad
        Jewish Film Archive / Jewish Agency Film Archive / Keren
        Hayesod.
            Available in English, French and Spanish soundtracks.
            Shows the 10th anniversary celebration of the border kib-
            butz of Ein Hashlosha.

1448   THE IMMORTAL ROAD
        1950 / 18 min / sound / color / 16 mm
        Producer unknown. Locations: Abraham F. Rad Jewish Film
        Archlve / Jewlsh Agency Film Archive, Jerusalem / Keren
        Hayesod, Jerusalem.
        Profiles the settlement of Kibbutz Dalia founded by
        Itzhak Ochberg from its origins until the Israeli War of
        Independence in 1948.

1449   ISRAEL - 20TH CENTURY MIRACLE
        1974 / 60 min / sound / color / 16 mm
        Bob Bailey Studios, Inc. Distributed by Alden Films, and
        Association Films. Locations: Brigham Young U. / Gratz
        College / Library of Congress (FDA 2981) *
        Well produced look at Israeli agricultural advances.
        Looks at kibbutzim, or communal settlements and moshav,
        cooperatives which are privately owned and run. Profiles
        technological advances in grafting, new crop management
        and automation. Explores problems in obtaining water and
        general desert agriculture. Good film for audiences
        interested in dry area or Israeli agriculture.

1450   ISRAELI KIBBUTZ
        1973 / 20 min / sound / color / 16 mm or videocassette
        Institut fur Film und Bild. Distributed by Films, Inc.
        (LC 74-702563)
        Intended for junior high school to college audiences.
        Examines the way of life followed in over 300 kibbutzim
        in Israel. Describes why young people work in the kib-
        butz environment and the strength of the kibbutz in sup-
        porting the Israeli economy and protecting borders.

1451   JUBILEE AND A DAY (KINNERET)
        1964 / 13 min / sound / b&w / 16 or 35 mm
        Israel Film Studios. Locations: Histadrut - General
        Federation of Jewish Labor, Tel Aviv / Ministry of Education
        and Culture, Jerusalem / Prime Minister's Office,
        Information Dept., Jerusalem.
        Looks at anniversary celebrations at Kibbutz Kinneret.
        Traces daily activities on the kibbutz and the history of
        kibbutz life in Israel.

1452   A KIBBUTZ
        (n.d.) / 28 min / sound / color / 16 mm
        Producer unknown. Distributed by Alden Films.
        Looks at Kibbutz Hazorea, established by European Jewish
        immigrants 45 years ago, totalling 700 people at the time
        this film was made. Questions whether kibbutz life will
        appeal to the younger generation in Israel and looks at
        Kibbutz Eilot, a settlement formed by a second generation
        of kibbutz dwellers.

1453   KIBBUTZ (HA-KIBBUTZ)
        1961-63 / 43 min / sound / b&w / 16 or 35 mm

Israel Motion Picture Studios. Credits: Producers - Eliezer
Deutsch, Morton Parker. Locations: Jewish Agency Film
Archive, Jerusalem / Keren Hayesod, Jerusalem / Prime
Minister's Office, Information Dept., Jerusalem.
Available in English, Hebrew, French and Spanish
soundtracks. Shows life in Kibbutz Ma'ayan Zvi and
Kibbutz Ma'agan Micha'el. Shows children's halls, dining
rooms, work, cultural activities and youth programs.

1454   A KIBBUTZ
        1963 / 20 min / sound / b&w / 16 mm
        Israel Motion Picture Studios. Distributed by Alden Films.
        Locations: Abraham F. Rad Jewish Film Archive / Library of
        Congress (2 copies, FBA 5032, 5033) *
            Idealized view of life on Kibbutz Ma'ayan Zvi and Ma'agan
            Michael showing the "ideal community" life on the kib-
            butz. Shows weekly meeting, children with their parents
            in the evenings and at nurseries during the day, and a
            play being rehearsed. Follows the discussion of a couple
            who are thinking of leaving the kibbutz for a more pri-
            vate life.

1455   THE KIBBUTZ
        1965 / 28 min / sound / color / 16 mm
        Orthogenic School. University of Chicago. Made by Cameras
        International Productions. (NUC FiA 66-449) Locations:
        Brigham Young U. / New York Public Donnell Film Library.
            Looks at kibbutz Ramat Yohanan. Describes the communal
            raising of children, equality of men and women, life in a
            collective society and work. Traces the history of the
            kibbutz community.

1456   KIBBUTZ DAIRY
        1969 / 4 min / silent / color / super 8 mm film loop in
        cartridge. Eye Gate House. (Living in Israel series) (LC
        74-703710)
            Looks at automated dairy farming on a kibbutz.

1457   KIBBUTZ DAPHNA
        1968 / 26 min / sound / color / 16 mm
        Ray Garner. Released by AV-ED Films. Distributed by Alden
        Films. Credits: Producer-Director - Ray Garner, Writer -
        Virginia Garner. (LC 74-701198) Locations: Consulate
        General of Israel / Gratz College / U. of Illinois.
            Intended for high school to adult audiences. Shows the
            50 year old agricultural settlement of Kibbutz Daphna in
            the northern Galilee region of Israel. Outlines communal
            life and shared values of the 700 inhabitants of the kib-
            butz.

1458   KIBBUTZ FAMILY WITH YOUNG CHILD
        1969 / 4 min / silent / color / super 8 mm film loop in
        cartridge. Eye Gate House. (Living in Israel series)

(LC 74-703713)
Traces the daily activities of a family in a kibbutz.

1459   KIBBUTZ IRRIGATED FIELDS AND DATE GROVES
       1969 / 4 min / silent / color / super 8 mm film loop in
       cartridge. Eye Gate House (Living in Israel series)
       (LC 74-703714)
       Looks at irrigation methods used in a kibbutz date grove.

1460   KIBBUTZ KFAR MENACHEM: CROSSROADS
       1974 / 26 min / sound / color / 16 mm
       Encyclopaedia Britannica Films. Made by Lawrence Levy.
       (LC 74-703522) Location: U. of Texas at Austin.
       Intended for junior-senior high school audiences. Exami-
       nes life on Kibbutz Kfar Menachem. Looks at the problems
       of communal living as well as the economic advantages and
       satisfactions of kibbutz life. Includes interviews with
       kibbutz members.

1461   KIBBUTZ KITCHEN AND DINING HALL
       1969 / 4 min / silent / color / super 8 mm film loop in
       cartridge. Eye Gate House. (Living in Israel series) (LC
       74-703715)
       Looks at the communal dining area and food preparation
       area of a kibbutz.

1462   THE KIBBUTZ - A SELF-CONTAINED COMMUNITY
       1969 / 4 min / silent / color / super 8 mm film loop in
       cartridge. Eye Gate House. (Living in Israel series) (LC
       74-703712)
       Explores some of the service departments in a kibbutz.
       Shows how the settlement can provide most services for
       its members.

1463   MAY PEACE BEGIN WITH ME
       1973 / 29 min / sound / color / 16 mm
       Guggenheim Productions. Distributed by Films, Incorporated
       and by Alden Films. Locations: Abraham F. Rad Jewish Film
       Archive / Gratz College.
       Intended for junior-senior high school audiences. Looks
       at four young people on a kibbutz in the Golan, their
       background and work. Traces immigration of Jews from
       Europe, Asia and Africa to Israel. Explains the ambiva-
       lent feeling of young kibbutz dwellers concerning peace
       and whether Israelis should be the ones to initiate any
       peace proposals.

1464   NEVER AGAIN TO BE DENIED
       (n.d.) / 20 min / sound / b&w / 16 mm
       United Jewish Appeal. Distributed by Alden Films.
       Locations: Abraham F. Rad Jewish Film Archive / Gratz
       College.
       Intended for general audiences for fund raising purposes.

Looks at a border kibbutz and the dangers faced from
Jordanian shelling. Looks at daily work and routines,
children in shelters, soldiers in the fields and shows
how border settlers must live in armed camps.

1465   A PROMISE TO MASADA
        1961 / 17 min / sound / color / 16 mm
        Acinex, Paris. Released in the U.S. by Film Images. (NUC
        FiA 62-886) Credits: Director - Nicole Stephane,
        Commentator - Meyer Levin.
            Looks at the agricultural settlement of Kibbutz Ein Gedi
            and a chemical factory at the Dead Sea, both near the
            ancient fortress of Masada.

1466   THIS IS OUR FARM
        (c. 1967) / 11 min / sound / color / 16 mm
        Jewish Agency for Israel. Distributed by Alden Films.
        Locations: Abraham F. Rad Jewish Film Archive / Histadrut -
        General Federation of Jewish Labor, Tel Aviv / Jewish Agency
        Film Archive / Library of Congress (FAA 6126)
            Available in English, Hebrew, French and Spanish
            soundtracks.   Shows the agricultural settlement of
            Kibbutz Gan Shmuel. Explores the life of children and
            looks at kibbutz fields and livestock.

1467   TO GATHER AND GROW
        January 9, 1977 / 28 min / sound / color / 16 mm
        CBS-TV. (Look Up and Live, television series)
            Profiles the religious settlement of Kibbutz Lavi.

1468   THE WOMEN OF NEVE UR
        1971 / 29 min / sound / b&w / 16 mm
        North German Television. Distributed by Alden Films, and by
        the Anti-Defamation League of B'nai B'rith. Location: Gratz
        College.
            Looks at the life of the women at a kibbutz in the Jordan
            River Valley at Neve Ur. Traces their daily work, child
            care and continued agricultural work despite cross border
            shelling following the Six Day War.

ISRAEL - KIBBUTZ CHILD CARE

1469   A BOY NAMED AMI
        (c. 1970?) / 28 min / sound / color / 16 mm
        Distributed by Alden Films. Locations: Abraham F. Rad
        Jewish Film Archives / Central Zionist Archives, Jerusalem
        / Hadassah Film Library.
            Looks at the integration of a young boy into the life of
            the fishing kibbutz of Ma'agan Michael as a result of his
            membership in a Youth Aliyah group.

1470   THE CHILDREN OF BET ALPHA
        1973 / 29 min / sound / color / 16 mm

Krosney Productions. Released by Phoenix Films. (LC
74-701563) Credits: Producer - Herb Krosney, Director - Tue
Ritzau. Locations: Kent State U. / U. of Illinois.
Looks at child rearing practises at Kibbutz Bet Alpha.
Traces programs for infants, 3, 7 and 10 year olds and
shows collective education classes in keeping with the
collective nature of kibbutz life. Intended for senior
high school to adult audiences.

1471   CHILDREN OF THE KIBBUTZ
1972 / 15 min / sound / color / 16 mm
Yaniv Productions. Made by Yehuda Yaniv. Released by ACI
Films. Distributed by Paramount Communications. (LC
73-701419) Locations: Gratz College / Syracuse U. / U. of
Illinois.
Shows the communal life of children on an agricultural
kibbutz. Children are taught, fed and work together and
spend evenings free with their parents. Intended to
introduce general audiences to kibbutz life. This won a
1973 film award.

1472   DAY CARE FOR A KIBBUTZ TODDLER
1973 / 22 min / sound / color / 16 mm
Institute for Child Mental Health. Made by Ethnography,
Inc. Released by New York University Film Library.
Distributed by Campus Film Distributors, University of
California Extension Media Center. (LC 74-701431) Credits:
Producer-Directors - L. Joseph Stone, Jeannette G. Stone.
Locations: Penn. State U. / U. of California Extension
Media Center / U. of Michigan.
Looks at the care provided by "care-givers" for infants
in a kibbutz. Examines this type of communal day care
system and discusses its applicability to other countries.

1473   INFANT DEVELOPMENT IN THE KIBBUTZ
1973 / 27 min / sound / color / 16 mm
Institute for Child Mental Health. Made by Ethnography, Inc.
Released by New York University Film Library. Distributed by
Campus Film Distributors, University of California Extension
Media Center. (LC 74-701432) Credits: Producer-Directors -
L. Joseph Stone, Jeannette G. Stone.
Documents a kibbutz "baby house" where newborn infants
are kept for up to 21 months for working parents. Looks
at the close relationships between children and between
the children and their "care-giver". Discusses concerns
with institutionalization of child care, socialization of
children and the possibility of stress.

1474   ISRAELI BOY: LIFE ON A KIBBUTZ
1973 / 17 min / sound / color / 16 mm
Encyclopaedia Britannica. (LC 73-700657) Credits:
Collaborator - Nathaniel Stampfer, Producer-Director - Ruth
Ariella Broyde. Distributed by Alden Films. Locations:

283

Brigham Young U. / Consulate General of Israel / Gratz
College / Kent State U. / Library of Congress (FBB 1758) /
New York Public Donnell Film Library / Syracuse U. / U. of
California Extension Media Center. *
Intended for elementary to high school audiences.
Follows the life of a young boy working on a kibbutz
which grows and cans fruit. Shows his work, communal
meals, Sabbath observation, a visit to Tel Aviv and
Jerusalem and general scenes of kibbutz life. An
excellent introduction to kibbutz life for children.
Well made.

1475   KIBBUTZ SCHOOL CHILDREN
1969 / 4 min / silent / color / super 8 mm film loop in
cartridge. Eye Gate House. (Living in Israel series) (LC
74-703716)
Brief look at school children living on a kibbutz and
attending a communal school.

1476   REARING KIBBUTZ BABIES
1973 / 27 min / sound / color / 16 mm
Institute for Child Mental Health. Made by Ethnography, Inc.
Released by New York University Film Library. Distributed by
Campus Film Distributors, University of California Extension
Media Center. (LC 74-701433) Credits: Producer-Directors -
L. Joseph Stone, Jeannette G. Stone. Location: Penn. State
U.
Looks at communal child rearing practises in a kibbutz by
following the daily routine of Hannah, a "care-giver" in
a baby house. In the afternoons, she visits her own
children in another communal day care area. Examines the
relationship between infants, parents and day care workers.

1477   YOUNG CHILDREN ON THE KIBBUTZ
1973 / 28 min / sound / b&w / 16 mm
Education Development Center. (Exploring Childhood series)
(LC 73-702071)
Looks at communal child rearing practises on a kibbutz.
Focuses on a group of 4 year olds being taught, fed and
living in an area separate from their parents.

ISRAEL - THE MOSHAV

1478   THE MOSHAV: ISRAEL'S MIDDLE WAY
1970 / 29 min / sound / color / 16 mm
ABC Merchandising. Released by McGraw-Hill. Distributed by
Alden Films. (Directions series) (LC 78-711875)
Locations: Abraham F. Rad Jewish Film Archive / Brigham
Young U. / Gratz College / U. of Illinois.
Bill Beutel of ABC News narrates this look at Ta'amach, a
communally owned agricultural settlement, or moshav,
populated by Jews formerly from the Atlas Mountains of

Morocco. Looks at their small individual farms and communal farming area and life on the moshav.

1479 RAMOT ME'IR (UN AN APRES)
1971 / 11 min / sound / b&w / 16 mm
Willi Feffer. Locations: Abraham F. Rad Jewish Film Archive /
Jewish Agency Film Archive, Jerusalem.
Available in English, Hebrew, Spanish and French
soundtracks. Looks at the 1st anniversary of Ramot
Me'ir, a communally owned agricultural settlement. Life
on the moshav is shown. Includes interviews with new
Jewish immigrants from France.

1480 TA'ANACHIM (REGION OF TANACH)
1970 / 22 min / sound / color / 16 mm
Studio 16 Films. Produced by Israel Film Service. Credits:
Director-Writer - Arnan Tzaphrir. Locations: Gratz College /
Jewish Agency Film Archive, Jerusalem / Ministry for Foreign
Affairs, Jerusalem / Prime Minister's Office, Information
Dept., Jerusalem.
Available in English, Hebrew, French and Spanish
soundtracks. Shows a group of new moshavim, or communal
settlements in the Jordan Valley. Looks at the problem
of absorption of European and Oriental Jews to moshav
life. Includes interviews with moshav members. Profiles
Moroccan Jewish settlers in Ta'anach.

1481 A VILLAGE CALLED NETUA
(n.d.) / 16 min / sound / color / 16 mm
Producer unknown. Location: Abraham F. Rad Jewish Film
Archive.
Available in English and French soundtracks. Looks at
Netua, a moshav on the Lebanese border. Stresses the
importance of the Jewish National Fund in aiding this
settlement.

ISRAEL - DEVELOPMENT TOWNS AND NEW SETTLEMENTS

1482 ADULAM
(c. 1970?) / 20 min / sound / color / 16 mm
Producer unknown. Locations: Abraham F. Rad Jewish Film
Archive / Histadrut - General Federation of Jewish Labor,
Tel Aviv / Jewish National Fund, Jerusalem.
Available in English, Hebrew and Spanish soundtracks.
Looks at the agricultural settlement of Adulam.
Discusses some of the problems and the aims of the
settlement. Listed in some catalogs as: ADULLAM.

1483 ARAVA IS MY HOME
(c. 1975?) / 25 min / sound / color / 16 mm
Hadassah. Location: Hadassah Film Library.
Profiles the struggles and accomplishments of early
Jewish settlers in the Arava area.

285

1484   ASHDOD: JULY 1961
        1967 / 15 min / sound / b&w / 16 mm
        Geva Films, Ltd., Tel Aviv. (Israel Film Magazine series)
        Locations: Library of Congress (FBA 5034) / Prime Minister's
        Office, Information Dept., Jerusalem. *
        Available in English, Hebrew, French, Spanish, German and
        Portuguese soundtracks. Looks at development plans for
        the new settlement of Ashdod. Describes programs for new
        housing, streets, a port and city buildings. Shows new
        immigrants for the city being assisted by the Jewish
        Agency. Discusses the energy and frustrations involved
        in developing a new settlement. Intended for general
        audiences. Library of Congress print in fair condition.

1485   BALLAD OF KIRIAT SHMONA
        (c. 1974) / 18 min / sound / color / 16 mm
        Producer unknown. Distributed by Alden Films.
        Profiles the city of Kiriat Shmona settled by 18,000
        Jewish immigrants from Morocco, the Yemen, and Romania
        with new arrivals from Russia and western countries. A
        border skirmish kills 18 people. The anger and frustra-
        tion of the settlers is shown.

1486   BLACK ROCKS OF CHORAZIM
        (n.d.) / 14 min / sound / color / 16 mm
        Producer unknown. Location: Abraham F. Rad Jewish Film
        Archive.
        Shows a new Nachal settlement founded on the ancient site
        of Chorazim. Produced on location in Israel.

1487   BORDER OUTPOSTS
        1965 / 14 min / sound / color / 16 mm
        Newsreel footage. Locations: Abraham F. Rad Jewish Film
        Archive / Jewish National Fund, Jerusalem.
        Available in English, Hebrew, French, Spanish and German
        soundtracks. Newsreel footage of five Nachal border
        settlements.

1488   BUILT IN A DAY
        1938 / 15 min / silent / b&w / 35 mm
        Producer unknown. Location: Abraham F. Rad Jewish Film
        Archive.
        Shows the construction of the Tirat Zvi settlement in
        Palestine. Built in one day to provide security against
        surrounding Arab Palestinian farmers.

1489   THE DEFENDERS
        1956-57 / 15 min / sound / b&w / 16 mm
        Producer unknown. Locations: Abraham F. Rad Jewish Film
        Archive / Central Zionist Film Archive.
        Shows how the border settlement of Nahal Oz is both an
        agricultural settlement and a para-military defense post.

1490 DIMONA
1962 / 10 min / sound / b&w / 16 mm
Producer unknown. Location: Abraham F. Rad Jewish Film
Archive.
The development town of Dimona in the central Negev
region is shown.

1491 ECHAD LEME'AH, 1:100 (ONE TO A HUNDRED)
1967 / 12 min / sound / color / 16 or 35 mm
Yoram Gross Films Ltd. Locations: Histadrut - General
Federation of Jewish Labor, Tel Aviv / Prime Minister's
Office, Information Dept., Jerusalem.
In Hebrew with English sub-titles. Looks at the National
Housing Construction program. Shows how buildings are
planned in models on the scale of 1:100. Includes infor-
mation on materials and tools used in construction and
shows a completion ceremony for a residential area.

1492 THE EDGE OF DANGER
1955 / 20 min / sound / b&w / 16 mm
Keren Hayesod, Jerusalem. Made by Michael Elkins. Released
in the U.S. by United Israel Appeal. (NUC FiA 64-576)
Credits: Producer-Director-Writer - Michael Elkins,
Photographer - Rolf N. Kneller. Locations: Abraham F. Rad
Jewish Film Archive / Central Zionist Film Archive / Jewish
Agency Film Archive, Jerusalem / Ministry of Education and
Culture, Jerusalem.
Available in English and French soundtracks. Shows the
border settlements of Gezer and Netiv Halamed. Shows how
residents are constantly worried about Arab infiltration.
Profiles special police and guard units assigned to pro-
tect border settlements.

1493 GATEWAY TO PARADISE
(n.d.) / 20 min / sound / color / 16 mm
Producer unknown. Location: Abraham F. Rad Jewish Film
Archive.
Available in English and Spanish soundtracks. Shows
Jewish settlements created soon after the Six Day War in
the Israeli-occupied Golan Heights.

1494 HOUSE IN THE DESERT
1947 / 30 min / sound / b&w / 16 mm
United Palestine Appeal. Made by Palestine Films. (NUC FiA
54-1206) Credits: Producer - Norman Lourie with Joseph
Krumgold, Director - Ben Oyserman. Locations: Israel Film
Archives, Haifa / Jewish Agency Film Archive, Jerusalem /
Rothschild Centre, Haifa.
Looks at the settlement of Beit Ha'arava, or House in the
Desert. Shows difficulties overcome by this agricultural
settlement in the Dead Sea area.

1495 KFAR GILADI
(n.d.) / 7 min / silent / color / 16 mm

Producer unknown. Location: Abraham F. Rad Jewish Film
Archive.
Shows the Jewish National Fund sponsored settlement of
Kfar Giladi.

1496   KORAZIM
1962 / 14 min / sound / color / 16 mm
Jewish National Fund.
Available in English, Hebrew, French, Spanish and German
soundtracks. Israeli newsreel profiles a settlement outpost on the Syrian border.

1497   MEMORANDUM ON A VICTORY
1948 / 12 min / sound / b&w / 16 mm
United Palestine Appeal. Released by United Jewish Appeal.
(NUC FiA 54-1211) Credits: Producer - Joseph Krumgold,
Writer -Norman Borisoff. Locations: Abraham F. Rad Jewish
Film Archive / Central Zionist Film Archive.
Looks at the settlement of Negba. Israeli film made
before statehood. Shows Jewish settlers at Negba
fighting and working to bring other Jewish immigrants to
Palestine.

1498   MITZPEH RAMON (BETWEEN BEERSHEBA AND EILAT)
1958 / 15 min / sound / b&w / 16 mm
Producer unknown. Location: Abraham F. Rad Jewish Film
Archive.
Available in English and Hebrew soundtracks. Examines
the first year of the development town of Mitzpeh Ramon.

1499   THE NACHAL ARE COMING (HANADA'IM BA'IM)
(c. 1970?) / 13 min / sound / color / 16 or 35 mm
Roll Studios, Tel Aviv. Credits: Producer - Y. Ephrati.
Locations: Histadrut - General Federation of Jewish Labor /
Prime Minister's Office, Information Dept., Jerusalem.
Available in English, Hebrew, French and Spanish
soundtracks. Shows the Nachal, para-military agri-
cultural settlers establishing settlements in border
areas. Includes a performance by the Nachal Variety
Ensemble.

1500   NACHAL: FIGHTING PIONEER UNIT
1968 / 14 min / sound / color / 16 mm
Producer unknown. Distributed by Alden Films. Locations:
Abraham F. Rad Jewish Film Archive / Gratz College.
Available in English, Hebrew, French and Spanish
soundtracks. Listed in some catalogs as NAHAL: FIGHTING
PIONEER YOUTH. The Nachal, part of the Citizen's Army of
Israel, are shown on border settlements, working,
fighting, entertaining themselves and building more
settlements.

1501   THE SKYLARK OF THE GALILEE
1975 / 20 min / sound / color / 16 mm

Hadassah. Distributed by the Jewish National Fund, New York.
Listed in some catalogs as: SKYLARK OF GALILEE. Looks
at an agricultural settlement on the border of Lebanon.
Shows how the settlers must worry about border skir-
mishes and work with rocky terrain. Profiles assistance
of the Jewish National Fund to the settlement.

1502   THEY CAME TO STAY
        1974 / 10 min / sound / color / 16 mm
        Producer unknown. Distributed by Alden Films. Location:
        Abraham F. Rad Jewish Film Archive.
            Looks at the effect of Arab Palestinian raids on the two
        border settlements of Kiriat Shmona and Ma'alot in
        April-May, 1974. Shows destruction of property and loss
        of lives has strengthened the spirit of the Jewish
        settlers.

1503   UNPAVED ROAD
        (n.d.) / 28 min / sound / color / 16 mm
        Film Division, Dept. of Information for OLIM, Jerusalem.
        Distributed by Israel Film Service.
            Available in English, French and Spanish soundtracks.
        Profiles the settlement of Kiryat Shmona. Describes the
        raid on the settlement in 1974.

ISRAEL - THE ISRAELI

1504   AN ISRAELI FAMILY
        1978 / 20 min / sound / color / 16 mm
        International Film Foundation. Credits: Director - Yehuda
        Yaniv.
            Looks at the Spector family living in a small town in
        central Israel. Shows the father spending one month each
        year in the army reserves. The mother takes turns
        guarding her daughter's school against raids. Shows
        family routines, a trip to Jerusalem, singing folk songs
        and participating in traditional festivals. General film
        introducing the European Israeli to intermediate and
        junior high school audiences.

1505   THE ISRAELI - WHO IS HE?
        1973 / ? / sound / color / 16 mm
        Anti-Defamation League of B'nai B'rith. (Dateline Israel,
        1973 series)
            Dr. Amnon Rubenstein, Professor of Constitutional Law and
        Dean of Tel Aviv University's School of Law, describes
        the typical Israeli man on the street.

1506   THE ISRAELIS
        1973 / 36 min / sound / color / 16 mm
        CBS News. Distributed by Carousel Films, and by Alden Films.
        (LC 74-701330) Locations: Iowa Films / U. of California

Extension Media Center / U. of Iowa.
Narrated by Israeli journalist and author Amos Elon.
Attempts to show the nature and feeling of the diverse
people who make up Israel. Describes the fear of exter-
mination brought about by the Holocaust, shows children
studying Masada, military parades and civilian life.
Profiles the 300,000 Christian and Muslim Palestinian
Arabs in Israel and how they live with Israelis.
Originally broadcast on television. Intended for junior
high school to adult audiences.

1507   THE ISRAELIS
1973 / 50 min / sound / b&w / 16 mm
CBS News. Released by Carousel Films. Distributed by Alden
Films. (CBS News Special, television broadcast) (LC
74-701330) Credits: Narrator - Amos Elon, Producer-Director
- Isaac Kleinerman, Writers - Amos Elon, Perry Wolff.
Locations: Library of Congress (FCA 7596-97) / U. of Arizona
/ U. of California / U. of Connecticut / U. of Iowa / U. of
Minnesota. *
        Originally broadcast two weeks after the 1973 War.
        Attempts to describe the Israeli national character.
        Shows the multi-racial, multi-national population of
        Israel and the large Arab population increased by one
        million Arabs in the occupied territories after the 1967
        War. Follows the regular daily activities which make up
        Israeli life. Elon explains the strong civilian spirit,
        "shared sense of purpose and a national fear" which per-
        vade life in Israel. Well produced program on a dif-
        ficult topic. Recommended.

1508   THE PEOPLE OF THE BOOK
1959 / 30 min / sound / b&w / 16 mm
Jewish Theological Seminary of America and NBC. Made by
NBC. Released by the National Academy for Adult Jewish
Studies. (Eternal Light, television series) (NUC FiA
64-1122)
        Shows the diverse peoples and professions found in
        Israel. Profiles David Ben-Gurion, engineers at the
        Institute of Technology at Haifa, Druse children with a
        Christian Arab teacher, Jewish orphans, and a variety of
        children and adults in different walks of life. Intended
        to introduce the people of Israel to an American televi-
        sion audience.

1509   THE SAMARITANS: PEOPLE OF THE SACRED MOUNTAIN
(c. 1972) / 30 min / sound / color / 16 mm
Johanna Spector. Distributed by Icarus Films. Credits:
Director - Dan Wolman. *
        Shows remaining Samaritan communities in Israel. Looks
        at Biblical and historical Samaritan life. Shows the
        Hebrew sect in Nablus, an Arab city. Shows how prayers,
        ceremonies, education of children and marriage is closely

kept within the Samaritan community along traditional
lines. The only film located dealing specifically with
the Samaritans. Well produced, valuable study of a
disappearing people.

1510   WE ARE ARAB JEWS IN ISRAEL
       1977 / 120 min / sound / color / 16 mm
       Igaal Niddam. Distributed by New Yorker Films.
       In French with English sub-titles. Looks at Israel's
       Oriental, eastern or Sephardic Jews. Although a
       majority, the Sephardic Jews of Israel have little
       social, military or political power in Israeli life and
       are termed second-class citizens in their own country.
       Made by a Sephardic film-maker. Argues the Sephardic
       community should be given more opportunity to participate
       in foreign policy decisions, especially in the
       Arab-Israeli arena, since many formerly lived in Arab
       countries and understand the problems those countries
       face better than current European Jewish leaders.
       Includes interviews with Moshe Dayan, Sephardic Jews and
       Arabs. Interesting proposal although a lengthy film.

ISRAEL - CHILDREN, WOMEN AND THE ELDERLY

1511   CONNECTIONS
       (c. 1978) / 28 min / sound / color / 16 mm
       Hadassah. Location: Hadassah Film Library.
       Shows eight teenage children in a youth village in
       Israel. Describes the services and purpose of the Youth
       Aliyah movement.

1512   GROWING UP IN ISRAEL
       (c. 1975?) / 15 min / sound / color / 16 mm
       Hadassah. Location: Hadassah Film Library.
       Shows the work of Hadassah in helping Israeli children
       grow in a healthy environment.

1513   OLD PEOPLE'S HOME (BEIT ZEKENIM)
       1964 / 8 min / sound / b&w / 16 or 35 mm
       Israel Film Studios, Herzliyah. Credits: Director - D.
       Perlov, Photographer - M. Yokovlevitz. Location: Prime
       Minister's Office, Information Dept., Jerusalem.
       Available in English, Hebrew, French, Spanish and German
       soundtracks. Profiles the "malben" Old People's Home.
       Shows the people living in the home, the atmosphere and a
       theatrical performance at the home.

1514   A PROMISE SHARED: WOMEN IN ISRAELI SOCIETY
       (c. 1974) / 25 min / sound / color / 16 mm
       WOSU-TV, Columbus, Ohio. Distributed by Anti-Defamation
       League of B'nai B'rith.
       Looks at legal and social status of women in Israel.

291

Compares women's movements in the U.S. and Israel and
shows women in the professions, on a kibbutz, and in
various walks of Israeli life.

1515 RENDEZVOUS WITH YOUTH
(c. 1960?) / 20 min / sound / color / 16 mm
Producer unknown. Location: Abraham F. Rad Jewish Film
Archive.
Shows how love of the land is instilled in Israeli youth
at an early age. Shows kindergarten classes, festivals
and field trips by students to historic sites where they
are taught Jewish history.

1516 SABRAS OF ISRAEL
1969 / 28 min / sound / color / 16 mm
Raya Productions. (LC 77-705006)
Shows Arab and Jewish children in Israel growing up,
working, playing and attending school.

1517 SNAPS
1970 / 20 min / sound / color / 16 mm
David Kedem and Yigal Durstein. Distributed by Alden Films.
Locations: Abraham F. Rad Jewish Film Archive / Jewish
Agency, Jerusalem.
Looks at youth in Israel and their way of life in 1970.

1518 SOCIAL WORK IN TEL AVIV
(n.d.) / 25 min / sound / b&w / 16 mm
Producer unknown. Location: Abraham F. Rad Jewish Film
Archive.
Shows social work activity in poor areas of Tel Aviv and
work with delinquent youth.

1519 TWO CLIMATES OF CHILDHOOD IN ISRAEL
1973 / 26 min / sound / color / 16 mm
Marianne Marschak. Released by New York University Film
Library. Sponsored by Foundation for Research in
Psychoanalysis, Los Angeles. (Kibbutz Care and Family
Care series) (LC 73-700395)
Compares the child raising techniques for a child on a
kibbutz with a child raised by its own parents.
Contrasts the typical days of each child.

1520 A VERY SPECIAL VILLAGE
1957 / 30 min / sound / b&w / 16 mm
Jewish Theological Seminary of America and NBC. Made by
NBC. Released by National Academy for Adult Jewish Studies.
(Frontiers of Faith, television series) (LC FiA 64-1133)
Credits: Script - Will Lorin.
Looks at social welfare programs for Jewish elderly in
Israel. Profiles Shaar Menashe, a village comprised of
people over 65.

1521   THE VOICE OF YOUTH
       1976 / 28 min / sound / color / 16 mm
       Anti-Defamation League of B'nai B'rith. Distributed by
       Alden Films. Locations: Consulate General of Israel /
       Gratz College.
       Israeli teenagers between the ages of 13 and 17 are
       interviewed by Arnold Forster concerning their views on
       Israel, Judaism, Arabs and Jerusalem. Shows the teena-
       gers at their studies and hobbies.

1522   WOMEN OF ISRAEL
       (c. 1969?) / 20 min / sound / b&w / 16 mm
       Robert Varrall. Locations: Jewish Agency Film Archive,
       Jerusalem / Ministry of Tourism, Jerusalem.
       Looks at the role of women in the development of Israel.

ISRAEL - THE ARMED FORCES

1523   ARMY PARADE, 1965 (MITZAD ZAHAL, 1965)
       1965 / 12 min / sound / color / 16 mm
       Berkey Pathe Humphries. Location: Prime Minister's Office,
       Information Dept., Jerusalem.
       Available in English, Hebrew and French soundtracks.
       Looks at Independence Day celebrations in 1965 including
       the opening festivities at Jerusalem University Stadium
       and the Army Parade in Tel Aviv on the next day.

1524   CHEN (WOMEN'S AUXILIARY CORPS)
       1970 / 15 min / sound / color / 16 or 35 mm
       Raz Films. Produced by Israel Film Service in cooperation
       with the Military Spokesman's Office. Distributed by
       Alden Films. Location: Abraham F. Rad Jewish Film Archive
       / Gratz College / Jewish Agency, Jerusalem / Prime
       Minister's Office, Information Dept., Jerusalem.
       Available in English, Hebrew and French soundtracks.
       Profiles the duties and service performed by the Women's
       Army Corps during their national military service. Shows
       women soldiers training, parading, and relaxing.
       Intended for high school to adult Israeli audiences.

1525   CITIZEN ARMY
       (c. 1970?) / 15 min / sound / color / 16 mm
       Israel Defense Forces. Distributed by Alden Films.
       Location: Jewish National Fund, Jerusalem.
       Looks at the Israel Defense Forces on manoeuvres and
       during an Independence Day parade.

1526   DAY OF CELEBRATION (BE'YOM CHAG)
       1968 / 13 min / sound / color / 16 or 35 mm
       Roll Films. Locations: Ministry of Education and Culture,
       Jerusalem / Prime Minister's Office, Information Dept.,
       Jerusalem.

293

Available in English, Hebrew, French and Spanish
soundtracks. Shows the 1968 Independence Day Army parade
through Jerusalem.

1527   FROM PIPER CUB TO JET
        1955 / 12 min / sound / b&w / 16 mm
        Producer unknown. Location: Abraham F. Rad Jewish Film
        Archive.
        Eight years after independence the Israel Air Force is
        shown to have made great strides in modernization,
        training and equipment.

1528   THE HEART OF A NATION OF SOLDIERS (LEV HA'AM IM
        CHA'YALAV)
        1964 / 14 min / sound / color / 16 or 35 mm
        Israel Film Studios. Location: Prime Minister's Office,
        Information Dept., Jerusalem.
        In Hebrew with English sub-titles. Looks at the Soldier's
        Welfare Committee and the services it provides on the
        front lines and in army camps.

1529   THE HEIGHT OF 40,000 FEET (HAGOVAH 40,000 REGEL)
        1961 / 15 min / sound / color / 16 or 35 mm
        Berkey Pathe Humphries. Locations: Histadrut - General
        Federation of Jewish Labor / Ministry of Education and
        Culture, Jerusalem / Prime Minister's Office, Information
        Dept., Jerusalem.
        Available in English, Hebrew, French and Spanish
        soundtracks. Profiles the Israel Air Force and shows its
        constant readiness on the ground and in the air.

1530   IF ONLY WE HAD LOVE
        1975 / 22 min / sound / color / 16 mm
        Producer unknown. Distributed by Alden Films, and by
        United Jewish Appeal. Available in 22 and 55 minute ver-
        sions.
        In Hebrew with English sub-titles. Looks at the Israeli
        soldier during peace time and war. Shows Theodore Bikel,
        Larry Adler and Geula Gil entertaining Israeli troops.

1531   THE ISRAEL ARMY
        1959-60 / ? / sound / b&w / 16 mm
        Soriano and Moskovitsch. Location: Keren Hayesod, Jerusalem.
        Looks at the Israeli Army in 1959.

1532   ISRAEL DEFENSE FORCES (ZAHAL)
        1959 / 16 min / sound / b&w / 16 mm
        Berkey Pathe Humphries. Location: Prime Minister's Office,
        Information Dept., Jerusalem.
        Available in English and Hebrew soundtracks. Looks at
        various scenes of Israeli military life. Shows women
        soldiers on manoeuvres, military parades, the Four-Day
        March to Jerusalem, and the 1959 Independence Day
        celebration and military parade.

1533   THE ISRAELI AIR FORCE
        (c. 1974) / 23 min / sound / b&w / 16 mm
        NBC. Distributed by Alden Films, and Anti-Defamation
        League of B'nai B'rith. Location: Gratz College.
        Listed in some catalogs as: ISRAEL AIR FORCE. Looks
        at Israeli Air Force training and personnel. Includes
        interview with General Mordecai Hod, Commander of the Air
        Force, and an Air Force graduation celebration.
        Originally broadcast on the NBC series FIRST TUESDAY.

1534   JET PILOTS (TAYASEI SILON)
        1958 / 13 min / sound / b&w / 35 mm
        Israel Film Studios, Herzliyah.
        Available in English and Hebrew soundtracks. Profiles
        jet pilots in the Israeli Air Force.

1535   OFFICER'S COURSE (KURS KTZINIM)
        1963 / 19 min / sound / b&w / 16 mm
        Ministry of Defense. Israel Film Studios.
        Israeli Army information film. Examines officer training
        programs.

1536   SHIELD OF ISRAEL
        (n.d.) / 15 min / sound / b&w / 16 mm
        Producer unknown. Location: Abraham F. Rad Jewish Film
        Archive.
        Reviews the state of the Israeli Army, Parachutists,
        Navy, Air Force and Women's Auxiliary Forces.

1537   THIS WEEK (REDIFFUSION TV)
        1965 / 22 min / sound / b&w / 16 mm
        Producer unknown. Location: Abraham F. Rad Jewish Film
        Archive.
        British television production. Includes a report by
        journalist James Cameron on the state of the Israeli army
        in 1965.

1538   YOUTH LEADERS EMERGE
        (c. 1970?) / 15 min / sound / b&w / 16 mm
        Ministry for Foreign Affairs, Dept. for International
        Cooperation and Ministry of Defense. Locations: Abraham
        F. Rad Jewish Film Archive / Jewish Agency Film Archive,
        Jerusalem.
        Looks at training provided for officers in the Israeli
        Army.

ISRAEL - TRAVELOGS - DATE OF PRODUCTION UNKNOWN

1539   ADVENTURE THROUGH TIME
        (n.d.) / 25 min / sound / color / 16 mm
        Dudley Productions. Credits: Script - Herman Boxer,
        Photographer - Ed Drews. Location: Jewish Agency Film

Archive, Jerusalem.
General subject travelog. Includes scenes of Tel Aviv,
Haifa, Eilat, Beersheva, Nazareth, and Jerusalem. Shows
modern and historical Israel.

1540   ...AND THEY MET IN GALILEE
(n.d.) / 28 min / sound / color / 16 mm
Stephen L. Sharff, Tribune Films, Inc. Distributed by Alden
Films. Locations: Abraham F. Rad Jewish Film Archive /
Jewish Agency Film Archive, Jerusalem / Ministry of Tourism,
Jerusalem.
General travelog of Israel as seen through the eyes of
an American boy and an Israeli girl. Includes scenes of
Haifa, Galilee, Acre, Safed, Mount Tavor, Nazareth,
Tiberias, and Capernaum.

1541   BENEATH THE BELLS OF BETHLEHEM
(n.d.) / 20 min / sound / b&w / 16 mm
Producer unknown. Distributed by the Embassy of Jordan, and
by the Arab Information Office, Washington.
Listed in some catalogs as: BELLS TO BETHLEHEM.
General travelog of Bethlehem, probably made before 1967.

1542   BON VOYAGE
(c. 1960?) / 24 min / sound / color / 16 mm
Producer unknown. Distributed by the Israeli Tourist
Office, and by Alden Films. Locations: Consulate General of
Israel / Gratz College.
Musical travelog of Israel including scenes of Mount
Hermon, the coral reefs at Eilat, and Bethlehem.

1543   CAMPING IN ISRAEL
(c. 1960?) / 15 min / sound / color / 16 mm
Producer unknown. Location: Abraham F. Rad Jewish Film
Archive.
Travelog of Israel. Shows how it is possible to see
the countryside while camping.

1544   FOLLOW THE SUN TO ISRAEL
(c. 1960?) / 17 min / sound / color / 16 mm
I.G.T.C. Lazar Dienar. Location: Ministry of Tourism,
Jerusalem.
Available in English and French soundtracks. Follows an
American couple during a February vacation in Israel.
Shows the warm weather, vacation sites at Herzliyah-on-
Sea, Nazareth, Tiberias, Galilee and the Red Sea.

1545   FROM SINAI TO THE TEMPLE MOUNT
(n.d.) / ? / sound / 16 mm
Don Rav.
General travelog of Israel made by an Israeli film-maker.

1546   GHANA GOVERNMENT DELEGATION VISITS ISRAEL
(n.d.) / 20 min / sound / b&w / 16 mm

Berkey Pathe Humphries for the Israel Ministry for Foreign
Affairs. Location: Jewish Agency Film Archive, Jerusalem.
General travelog of Israel. Shows industrial, economic,
and agricultural production. Follows the Ghana
Delegation as it tours the country.

1547   THE HOLY LAND
        (n.d.) / ? / sound / color / 35 mm
        Modern Learning Aids.
        Describes the history, social customs, politics and eco-
        nomics of Israel. Packet also includes a book and record.

1548   ISRAEL - ADVENTURE THROUGH TIME
        (n.d.) / 27 min / sound / color / 16 mm
        Producer unknown. Location: Abraham F. Rad Jewish Film
        Archive.
        General travelog showing a blend of historical sites and
        modern life in Israel.

1549   ISRAEL - ANCIENT AND MODERN
        (c. 1960?) / 8 min / sound / color / 16 mm
        British Pathe. Location: Abraham F. Rad Jewish Film
        Archive.
        General travelog of Israel intended to promote tourism.

1550   ISRAEL HOLIDAY
        (n.d.) / 30 min / sound / color / 16 mm
        I.G.T.C. Location: Ministry of Tourism, Jerusalem.
        General travelog. Shows hotels, bars and shops in
        Israel. Intended to show modern accommodations and pro-
        mote tourism.

1551   ISRAEL JOURNEY
        (n.d.) / 28 min / sound / color / 16 mm
        Richard S. Milbauer. Location: Abraham F. Rad Jewish Film
        Archive / Jewish Agency Film Archive, Jerusalem / Jewish
        National Fund, Jerusalem.
        General travelog of Israel showing Tel Aviv, Acre,
        Galilee, Peki'in, Safed, Yisrael Valley, Tiberias, Haifa,
        Negev and Jerusalem.

1552   JEWISH HISTORICAL SITES (ATARIM YEHUDI'YIM)
        (n.d.) / 23 min / sound / color / 16 or 35 mm
        Producer unknown. Location: Prime Minister's Office,
        Information Dept., Jerusalem.
        Travelog of Israel showing sites of Jewish historical
        interest.

1553   LAND OF A THOUSAND FACES
        (n.d.) / 15 min / sound / color / 16 mm
        Baruch Dienar. Location: Ministry of Tourism, Jerusalem.
        Available in English, French, Spanish, Italian, German,
        Swedish, Danish, and Dutch soundtracks. General travelog

of Israel stressing the variety of peoples and places found there. Shows seaside resorts, accommodations for tourists, historical and religious sites and the people of Israel.

1554   LOVING YOUNG COMPANY
(n.d.) / 16 min / sound / color / 16 mm
Producer unknown. Distributed by Alden Films. Location: Gratz College.
Intended for junior-senior high school audiences. Follows a group of Jewish youth from around the world during a summer in Israel. Includes scenes of fruit picking on a kibbutz, hiking in the Negev, the Western Wall, an archeological excavation and the Weizman Institute.

1555   MAY IT BE
(n.d.) / 25 min / sound / color / 16 mm
Producer unknown. Distributed by Alden Films.
Hershel Bernardi guides a group of American tourists through Israel. Includes scenes of the Western Wall, Masada, a youth Aliyah village, a Russian immigrant settlement, Beersheba and the Galilee. Promotional film for immigration and fund-raising purposes. Stresses the need to promote Zionism in America.

1556   PICTORIAL REPORT
(n.d.) / 15 min / sound / b&w / 16 mm
Berkey Pathe Humphries. Locations: Abraham F. Rad Jewish Film Archive / Jewish Agency Film Archive, Jerusalem.
Report of work being done to promote tourism in Israel. Includes interviews with Mayor Teddy Kollek of Jerusalem and Levi Eshkol, Minister of Finance. Shows building of new hotels, promotion of arts and crafts and general information on tourism.

1557   RETURN TO ISRAEL
(n.d.) / 22 min / sound / color / 16 mm
I.G.T.C. Location: Ministry of Tourism, Jerusalem.
Travelog of Israel. Looks at changes that have taken place over a period of years. Shows accommodations for tourists and holiday sites around the country. To promote tourism.

1558   SAM SNEAD IN ISRAEL
(n.d.) / 31 min / sound / color / 16 mm
I.G.T.C. Location: Ministry of Tourism, Jerusalem.
Follows golfer Sam Snead's tour of Israel. Included are scenes of Caesarea, Nazareth, Tiberias, Capernaum, Tabga, Acre, and Haifa. Includes information on sports in Israel.

1559   SHALOM YASSU
(n.d.) / 30 min / sound / color / 16 mm

Swissair. Location: Ministry of Tourism, Jerusalem.
General travelog of Israel and Switzerland as seen by an
artist painting both countries.

1560 THIS IS OUR LAND
(n.d.) / 18 min / sound / color / 16 mm
Producer unknown. Location: Abraham F. Rad Jewish Film
Archive.
General travelog of Israel. Includes scenes of Galilee,
Eilat, Lake Kinneret and the Dead Sea. Discusses pro-
jects underway in afforestation, land clearance and new
settlements supported by the Jewish National Fund.

1561 THIS IS THE WAY WE LEARN TO LIVE
(n.d.) / 10 min / sound / color / 16 mm
Stephen Scharff. Location: Central Zionist Archives,
Jerusalem.
General travelog of Israel as seen by a group of youth
Aliyah immigrants from a variety of countries during a
two week tour.

1562 TIME FOR SURVIVAL
(n.d.) / 25 min / sound / color / 16 mm
American Red Magen David for Israel. Distributed by Alden
Films.
Travelog made up of slides of Israel and Magen David
Adom. Stresses the desire for peace in Israel.

1563 THE TIMELESS FAMILY
(n.d.) / 60 min / sound / color / 16 mm
CBS-TV.
Profiles the Museum of the Diaspora in Israel.

1564 A TOUCH OF SUMMER
(n.d.) / 45 min / sound / color / 16 mm
Los Angeles Board of Jewish Education. Distributed by Alden
Films. Location: Gratz College.
Follows a group of teenagers on a summer trip to Israel.
Shows planning for the trip, working on a kibbutz, an
outdoor Shacharit prayer service, a morning excursion to
Masada and a meeting with David Ben-Gurion.

1565 A TRIP TO ISRAEL
(c. 1971?) / 27 min / sound / color / 16 mm
Olympic Airways. Distributed by Association-Sterling Films.
Travelog of Israel. Covers the history of great civili-
zations of the region and shows scenes of Galilee, the
Negev, Jerusalem, Nazareth, Tel Aviv, Eilat, Acre,
Caesarea, and Haifa. To promote tourism.

1566 VACATION FUN IN ISRAEL
(n.d.) / 11 min / sound / color / 16 mm
Producer unknown. Distributed by Alden Films.
General travelog of Israel to promote tourism.

1567   WONDERFUL ISRAEL
       (n.d.) / 20 min / sound / color / 16 mm
       I.G.T.C.   Location: Ministry of Tourism, Jerusalem.
       Shows tourist sites of interest to Christian audiences.
       Includes scenes of Nazareth, Cana, and Capernaum.
       Includes information on hotels and other tourist accom-
       modations.

1568   THE WORLD OF TWA - ISRAEL
       (c. 1971?) / 28 min / sound / color / 16 mm
       TWA Airlines.   Distributed by Association-Sterling Films.
       General travelog of Israel.   Includes scenes of Tel Aviv,
       Haifa, Elath, Avdat, Beersheba, Nazareth and Jerusalem.
       To promote tourism.

ISRAEL - TRAVELOGS   -   PRE-1948 (PALESTINE)

1569   BRONISLAV HUBERMAN IN PALESTINE (HUBERMAN
       BE'ERETZ YISRAEL - 1938)
       1938 / 12 min / silent / b&w / 16 mm
       Ida Ivkin.   Location: Gurit Kadman, Tel Aviv.
       Shows the tour of musician Bronislav Huberman with
       Toscanini in Palestine.   Includes scenes of Haifa, the
       Dead Sea, Jerusalem and Ein Harod.

1570   THE HOLY LAND
       1917 / 4 min / silent / b&w / 16 mm
       Thomas A. Edison.   Released by K.E.S.E. Conquest Pictures.
       George Kleine Collection.   Location: Library of Congress
       (FLA 1548)   *
       In fair condition considering age.   Shot during WWI.
       Shows Gethsemane and the Russian monastery, the Mount of
       Olives, Wailing Wall, market day at the pool of Gihon,
       the Damascus Gate of Jerusalem, Christians carrying a
       cross to Calvary, and scenes of Bethlehem.

1571   HOLY LAND IN PROGRESS
       1947 / ? / sound / b&w / 16 mm
       Producer unknown.   Location: U. of Washington, Seattle.
       Stresses the modernization and industrialization of Arab
       Palestine.   Shot before the creation of Israel.

1572   HULEH VALLEY
       1933 / 20 min / silent / b&w / 35 mm
       Producer unknown.   Location: Abraham F. Rad Jewish Film
       Archive.
       Early film of the Jewish settlements around the Huleh
       Lake area.   Shows Arab residents fishing on the lake,
       canoes made of rushes, women weaving rushes, and
       marketing activities.   New Jewish settlements and
       meetings of Arabs and Jews are shown.

1573 A JOURNEY TO PALESTINE - 1911
1911 / 870 ft. / silent / b&w / 35 mm
Murray Rosenberg. Location: Central Zionist Archives.
Early travelog of Israel. Includes scenes of the
Western Wall, Bezalel School, Jaffa Gate with the "German
Emperor's Marble Fountain" in Jerusalem, a procession
with the scrolls of law led by Rabbi Meir Ba'al Hanes,
and the Holy Sepulchre during Easter. Also shows promi-
nent personalities of the period.

1574 LAND OF PROMISE (CHAYYIM CHADASHIM)
1934 / 45 min / sound / b&w / 16 mm
Palestine Production Co. Jewish National Fund. Locations:
Abraham F. Rad Jewish Film Archive / Israel Film Archives,
Haifa / Keren Hayesod, Jerusalem.
Supposedly the first sound film produced in Palestine.
Includes scenes of early Jewish immigration, agriculture
and industrial achievements, cooperative settlements,
Jerusalem and Tel Aviv.

1575 LIBERANDOS VISIT HOLY LAND
1943 / 22 min / silent / b&w / 16 mm
U.S. Signal Corps. Location: National Archives (18 CS
252-1-3) No other information available.

1576 PALESTINE
1934 / 20 min / silent / b&w / 16 mm
Producer unknown. Location: Abraham F. Rad Jewish Film
Archive.
Shows travelers on a trip from London to Palestine.

1577 PALESTINE
1934 / 38 min / silent / b&w / 16 mm
Producer unknown. (Ideal Traveltalks series) Location:
Abraham F. Rad Jewish Film Archive.
Early travelog of Palestine. Shows Jerusalem, a
Samaritan Passover celebration, and Jewish schools and
collective settlements.

1578 PALESTINE
1937 / 15 min / silent / b&w / 16 mm
Producer unknown. Location: Abraham F. Rad Jewish Film
Archive.
Shows life in Palestine during the British Mandate
period. Includes scenes of the Hebrew University and
Jewish agricultural settlements.

1579 (STREET SCENE AT JAFFA)
June 1903 / 40 seconds / silent / b&w / 16 mm
Thomas Edison. Library of Congress Paper Print Collection.
Location: Library of Congress (FLA 3532) *
In fair condition considering age. Early Edison film
made by A.C. Abadie. Shows a crowd of men and women tra-

veling through a busy Jaffa city street with camels and
donkeys. For documentary and historical purposes only.

1580   (TOURISTS EMBARKING AT JAFFA)
        June 17, 1903 / 1:26 min / silent / b&w / 16 mm
        Thomas Edison. Library of Congress Paper Print Collection.
        Location: Library of Congress (FLA 4909) *
        In good condition. Early Edison film made by A.C.
        Abadie. Shows European tourists being helped out of a
        small boat by an Arab wearing a "Cook's Tours" shirt.
        For historical and documentary purposes.

ISRAEL - TRAVELOGS - PRODUCED BETWEEN 1948-1959

1581   ADVENTURE IN ISRAEL
        1953 / 10 min / sound / b&w / 16 mm
        Producer unknown. Credits: Hosts - George and Jerilyn
        Jessel. Locations: Abraham F. Rad Jewish Film Archive /
        Jewish Agency Film Archive, Jerusalem / Keren Hayesod,
        Jerusalem.
            Travelog of Israel. Produced for purposes of fund
        raising in the U.S. Includes scenes of Tel Aviv,
        Jerusalem, Judean Hills and Beersheva. Shows tent camps
        and stresses need for funds for the young Jewish state.

1582   DAYS TO REMEMBER
        1954 / 15 min / sound / color / 16 mm
        Keren Hayesod. Made by Affiliated Films. Released in the
        U.S. by United Israel Appeal. (NUC FiA 54-1203) Credits:
        Producer - Irving Jacoby, Narrator - William O. Douglas.
        Locations: Abraham F. Rad Jewish Film Archive / Jewish
        Agency Film Archive, Jerusalem / Keren Hayesod, Jerusalem.
            William O. Douglas, Associate Justice of the U.S. Supreme
        Court, discusses progress of Israel in industry, agri-
        culture, sports and in the army. Shot during the 70th
        anniversary celebration of Zichron Yaakov.

1583   THE FACE OF THE LAND
        1959 / 27 min / sound / b&w / 16 mm
        Warner Brothers. United Jewish Appeal. (NUC FiA 64-577)
        Locations: Abraham F. Rad Jewish Film Archive / Jewish
        Agency Film Archive, Jerusalem.
            Rabbi Herbert A. Friedman looks at life in Israel.
        Includes interviews with farmers, factory workers, doc-
        tors, government officials and people on the street.
        Looks at the Israeli attitute towards work and life in
        Israel.

1584   THE HOLY LAND
        1959 / 10 min / sound or silent / color or b&w / 16 mm
        Castle Films. (NUC FiA 59-571)
            General travelog of Israel. Shows sites of significance

302

to Christian audiences. Includes scenes of the Church of
the Nativity, Wailing Wall, and of Tel Aviv and
Bethlehem.

1585   THE HOLY LAND: BACKGROUND FOR HISTORY AND RELIGION
1954 / 11 min / sound / color or b&w / 16 mm
Coronet Instructional Films. Distributed by Modern Film
Rentals. Credits: Educational Collaborator - Robert M.
Perry. Locations: Kent State U. / Library of Congress (FAA
3959) / Syracuse U. / U. of Arizona / U. of Illinois / U. of
Michigan. *
       Intended for junior high school to college audiences.
       Routine travelog. Covers historical and religious sites
       in Israel. Includes scenes of the Dead Sea, Jerusalem,
       Jericho, the Jordan River, Nazareth, Galilee and Acre.
       Shows geography of Israel and explains how the region is
       important to Jews, Christians and Muslims. More suited
       to younger audiences as an introductory history.

1586   ISRAEL
1952 / 9 min / sound / b&w / 16 mm
Dudley Pictures, Corp. Released by Republic Pictures Corp.
(This World of Ours series) (NUC Fi 52-2168) Credits:
Producer - Carl Dudley, Photographer - Edwin E. Olsen.
Trucolor. Locations: Library of Congress (FAA 4114) / U. of
Illinois. *
       Travelog of Israel. Stresses the historic continuity of
       Jews in the area. Looks at Jerusalem, Nazareth, Tel
       Aviv, a kibbutz in the Jordan Valley, Jewish immigrants,
       and a collective farm. Narration, geared towards a reli-
       giously oriented audience, uses Old and New Testament
       passages.

1587   ISRAEL, AN ADVENTURE
1958 / 28 min / sound / color or b&w / 16 mm
Israel Government Tourist Office. Distributed by Alden
Films. (NUC FiA 59-668) Locations: Abraham F. Rad Jewish
Film Archive / Gratz College / Israel Government Tourist
Office / Ministry of Tourism, Jerusalem.
       General travelog of Israel. Includes scenes of Galilee,
       Acre, the Negev, Haifa, Jerusalem and Tel Aviv. Includes
       a performance by the Inbal dancers of a Yemeni wedding
       dance. To promote tourism.

1588   ISRAEL - LAND OF CONTRASTS
1955 / 14 min / sound / b&w / 16 mm
Producer unknown. Location: Abraham F. Rad Jewish Film
Archive.
       Available in English and French soundtracks. Contrasts
       modern and traditional ways of life found in Israel.
       Examples include a new housing complex and a Bedouin camp
       and new agricultural equipment compared to a wooden
       plough.

303

1589   THE LAND OF THE BOOK
1959 / 30 min / sound / b&w / 16 mm
Jewish Theological Seminary of America and NBC. Made by
NBC. Released by National Academy for Adult Jewish Studies.
(Eternal Light, television series) (NUC FiA 64-1123)
Credits: Script - Irve Tunick, Narrator - Ralph Bellamy.
Travelog of Israel using the Bible as a guide book.
Includes scenes of the Plains of Armageddon, River
Jordan, Mt. Tabor, Mt. Zion, the Sea of Galilee,
Jerusalem, Carmel, Caesarea, Haifa, Tel Aviv, Beersheba,
the Negev and Acre.

1590   LETTER FROM RONNY
1955 / 16 min / sound / color / 16 mm
Samuel Elfert. Distributed by Alden Films. (This is Israel
series) Location: Abraham F. Rad Jewish Film Archive /
Jewish Agency Film Archive, Jerusalem.
Follows Ronny, a young Jewish immigrant from Iraq, on a
tour of Israel. Shows Ronny's participation in Scout
activities, scenes of the countryside, historic landmarks
and archeological sites.

1591   A LONG JOURNEY IN A SMALL COUNTRY
1965-66 / 14 min / sound / color / 16 mm
Yoram Gross Films. Locations: Abraham F. Rad Jewish Film
Archive / Jewish Agency Film Archive, Jerusalem / Keren
Hayesod, Jerusalem.
Available in English, Hebrew, French, Spanish and German
soundtracks. Shows the development town of Carmiel,
children on a kibbutz, a trade school for new immigrants
and the city of Eilat.

1592   OF THE BEATEN TRACK IN ISRAEL
1953 / 28 min / sound / color / 16 mm
Stephen Sharff. I.G.T.C. Distributed by Alden Films.
Locations: Abraham F. Rad Jewish Film Archive / Ministry of
Tourism, Jerusalem.
General travelog of Israel as seen through the eyes of
an American and an Israeli boy. Includes scenes of Mt.
Zion, the Biblical Zoo, Ein Karem, Jaffa, Caesarea,
Ashkelon, King Solomon's Mines, Ein Gedi and Beersheba.

1593   RENDEZVOUS IN ISRAEL
(c. 1950?) / 20 min / sound / b&w / 16 mm
Producer unknown. Location: Abraham F. Rad Jewish Film
Archive.
General travelog of Israel as seen through the eyes of
two old friends visiting after the creation of the Jewish
state. Looks at traditional and modern aspects of life
in Israel.

1594   SO YOU WANT TO SEE ISRAEL
1951 / 20 min / sound / b&w / 16 mm

United Israel Appeal. Made by International Films. (NUC FiA 54-1213) Credits: Narrator - Hal Linker. Locations: Abraham F. Rad Jewish Film Archive / Jewish Agency Film Archive, Jerusalem / Keren Hayesod, Jerusalem.
General travelog of Israel showing industry, towns and Yemenite Jewish immigrants.

1595 THREE GIRLS
1957-58 / 20 min / sound / color / 16 mm
Lazar Dunner. Locations: Abraham F. Rad Jewish Film Archive / Jewish Agency Film Archive, Jerusalem / Keren Hayesod, . Jerusalem.
Follows three girls on a holiday in Israel. Includes scenes of Tel Aviv, Jerusalem, the Maccabiah and a farm.

1596 TWO STEPS IN ISRAEL (SHNEI TZE'ADIM BEYISRAEL)
1955 / 13 min / sound / b&w / 16 mm
Berkey Pathe Humphries for the Israel Defense Forces. Credits: Director-Writer - Natan Gross, Photography - Hayim Schreiber. Locations: Jewish Agency, Tel Aviv / Ministry of Education and Culture, Jerusalem.
Available in English and Hebrew soundtracks. Looks at traditional and modern aspects of life in Israel. Includes scenes of landscapes, religious life, settlements, and antiquities.

ISRAEL - TRAVELOGS - PRODUCED BETWEEN 1960-1969

1597 CAMPING (MACHNA'UT-KAMPING)
1967 / 17 min / sound / color / 16 mm
Y. Zaretski. Distributed by Alden Films. Location: Prime Minister's Office, Information Dept., Jerusalem.
Available in English, Hebrew, French, Dutch, Italian, Swedish and German soundtracks. Looks at camping opportunities and recreational sites in Israel.

1598 DESTINATION SUN
1964 / 22 min / sound / color / 16 mm
I.G.T.C. Location: Jewish National Fund, Jerusalem.
Available in English and French soundtracks. Intended to promote tourism in Israel. Looks at hotels and tourist accommodations and beaches and resort areas. Profiles night life in Israel, discusses transportation and buses and describes the services of the Government Tourist Information Offices.

1599 THE FOUR SEAS (ARBA'AT HAYAMIM)
1962 / 26 min / sound / color / 16 mm
Berkey Pathe Humphries. Credits: Director-Writer-Photographer - M. Veredlevsky, B. Koretsky. Locations: Ministry of Tourism, Jerusalem / Prime Minister's Office, Information Dept., Jerusalem.

Available in English, French, Spanish, Italian, Swedish, and Dutch soundtracks. Looks at the four seas found near Israel: the Mediterranean, Lake Kinneret, the Dead Sea and the Red Sea. Follows three tourists as they visit these areas.

1600   HERE IS ISRAEL
        1964 / 14 min / sound / color / 16 mm
        Lazar Dunner and Harold Steinberg. Locations: Abraham F. Rad Jewish Film Archive / Jewish Agency Film Archive, Jerusalem / Keren Hayesod, Jerusalem.
        Available in English and German soundtracks. Looks at agriculture, industry, education, the army and the towns and cities which make up Israel.

1601   THE HOLY LAND
        1962 / 19 min / sound / color / 16 mm
        Producer unknown. Distributed by International Film Bureau. Locations: Middle East Institute / U. of Illinois.
        Historical travelog of Israel showing sites of interest to Christians. Outlines the history of the area during the Crusades and under the Turks and British. Covers the contemporary uneasy peace. Includes scenes of Bethlehem, Calvary, the Church of the Nativity, the Shephard's Fields, Mt. Tabor, Nazareth, the Jordan Valley, the Judean wilderness, the Mount of Temptation, the road from Jerusalem to Jericho, Galilee, Tiberias and Jerusalem.

1602   HONEY ON THEIR FEET (DVASH BARAGLAYIM)
        1963 / 13 min / sound / color / 16 or 35 mm
        Y. Ephrati. Location: Prime Minister's Office, Film Dept., Tel Aviv.
        Available in English and French soundtracks or with German sub-titles. Looks at the annual four day march to Jerusalem in 1963.

1603   ISRAEL - COLOR AND STYLE
        1962 / 14 min / sound / color / 16 mm
        Producer unknown. Distributed by Alden Films. Location: Gratz College.
        Shot on the 24th anniversary of Israel. Looks at a mixture of old and new in Israel. Includes scenes of atomic reactors, traffic, Old Jerusalem, the Annual March, kibbutz life, and cultural activities. Looks at family reunions at Lod Airport as travelers and immigrants are greeted by their loved ones.

1604   ISRAEL - LAND OF A THOUSAND FACES
        1964 / 13 min / sound / color / 16 or 35 mm
        Producer unknown. Location: Abraham F. Rad Jewish Film Archive.
        Available in English, Hebrew and French soundtracks. Possibly the same film as no. 1553. General travelog of Israel showing traditional and modern scenes.

1605   ISRAEL - LAND OF PROMISE
        1966 / 20 min / sound / color / 16 mm
        Associated Film Services. (NUC FiA 67-1725) Credits:
        Writer - Lola Sadlo, Consultant - Mrs. David Newman.
        Eastman color. Locations: Abraham F. Rad Jewish Film
        Archive / Brigham Young U.
            Intended for elementary to high school audiences.
            Examines the geography, economy, religion, government,
            education, and history of Israel. Discusses the problems
            faced by Israel in the 1960's.

1606   ISRAEL: MAKING A LAND PRODUCTIVE
        1967 / 17 min / sound / color / 16 mm
        ABC. Jules Power Productions. Released by McGraw-Hill.
        (Middle Eastern World series) (NUC FiA 67-1653) Locations:
        Kent State U. / Syracuse U. / U. of Illinois.
            Intended for elementary to senior high school audiences.
            Looks at economic and social development in Israel.
            Profiles advances in agriculture and cultivation of land
            and increased productivity to support mass immigration of
            Jews from other countries. Describes how the Arab-
            Israeli conflict must be settled to provide more resour-
            ces and further economic growth.

1607   ISRAEL NOW
        1969 / 20 min / sound / color / 35 mm
        Anthony Gilkison Association, Ltd. Distributed by Columbia
        Pictures. Rated G. Location: Library of Congress (FGC
        6422) *
            General travelog of Israel. Includes scenes of Acre,
            Masada, Haifa, Eilat and Jerusalem. Shows life on an
            agricultural kibbutz, a Bedouin wedding feast, nightclub
            life, tourist beach resorts and favorite tourist spots in
            Jerusalem. To promote tourism.

1608   ISRAEL OF LIGHTS AND COLOURS
        1964 / 13 min / sound / color / 16 or 35 mm
        Producer unknown. Location: Abraham F. Rad Jewish Film
        Archive.
            Uses a musical soundtrack. Covers a colorful cross sec-
            tion of Israeli life.

1609   ISRAEL, THE STORYTELLER (YISRAEL HAMESAPPEREST)
        1969 / 22 min / sound / color / 16 or 35 mm
        Baruch Dienar. Location: Prime Minister's Office,
        Information Dept., Jerusalem.
            Looks at life in Israel after the Six-Day War. Shows life
            in towns, kibbutzim, and in Old and new Jerusalem.
            Discusses the economy, industry and development.

1610   THE LAND OF THE BIBLE (EL PAIS DE LA BIBLIA)
        (DAS LAND DER BIBEL)
        1966 / 20 min / sound / color / 16 mm

20th Century-Fox. Credits: Producer - Edmund Reek, Director
- Jack Muth, Spanish version Narrator - Carlos Montalban.
Cinemascope. Locations: Israel Film Studios, Herzliyah /
Jewish Agency Film Archive, Jerusalem.
Available in English, Spanish and German soundtracks.
General travelog looks at cities throughout Israel.
Includes scenes of the Huleh Valley, Solomon's Mines,
Nazareth, Acre, Jerusalem, Tel Aviv, Beersheva, the Dead
Sea, and the Samual A. Eliot Youth Village. Also looks
at kibbutz life, an agricultural school and the annual
Independence Day celebration.

1611 LAND OF THE SABRAS (ERETZ HATZABOR)
1964 / 28 min / sound / color / 16 mm
George Pessis Films. Location: Prime Minister's Office,
Information Dept., Jerusalem.
Available in English and French soundtracks. Follows a
young girl through Israel in her search for a loved one.

1612 THE LAND SPEAKS OUT
1969 / 12 min / sound / color / 16 or 35 mm
Producer unknown. Distributed by Alden Films. Locations:
Abraham F. Rad Jewish Film Archive / Gratz College.
Available in English, Hebrew, French, Spanish, Italian
and Danish soundtracks. Looks at tourist spots in
Israel. Shows archeological digs, recreational activities, and national parks in Israel. Discusses unique
features of each site for the tourist.

1613 THE MANY FACES OF ISRAEL
1964 / 13 min / sound / color / 16 or 35 mm
Baruch Dienar Films. Location: Prime Minister's Office,
Information Dept., Jerusalem.
Available in English, Hebrew, French, Spanish, German,
Italian, Portuguese, Swedish, Danish and Dutch
soundtracks. General travelog of Israel portraying a
variety of life styles and sites.

1614 MERON
1965 / 18 min / sound / 16 mm
Israel Film Studios, Herzliyah.
Shows the festival of Lag Ba'Omer at Meron. On the 33rd
day of Omer, fires are lit in memory of the failed
rebellion of Bar Kockba.

1615 NEWSREEL FOR TOURIST (YARCHON LETAYARIM)
1968-69 / 16 min / sound / b&w / 16 mm
Berkey Pathe Humphries. Location: Prime Minister's Office,
Information Dept., Jerusalem.
Contains selections from bi-weekly newsreels produced for
English-speaking tourists by Berkey Pathe Humphries in
Herzliyah.

1616　PALESTINE ON THE MARCH
1967 / 45 min / sound / color / 16 mm
Jewish National Fund.
Documents the Adloyada Carnival in Israel.

1617　THE POPE IN THE HOLY LAND OF ISRAEL
1964 / 10 min / sound / b&w / 16 mm
Berkey Pathe Humphries, Israel Motion Picture Studios.
Distributed by Alden Films. Locations: Abraham F. Rad
Jewish Film Archive / Ministry of Tourism, Jerusalem.
Available in English, French and Spanish soundtracks.
Follows the 1964 visit of the Pope to Nazareth, Galilee,
Mt. Zion and Jerusalem.

1618　THE POPE'S VISIT TO ISRAEL (BIKKUR HA'APIFOR BE'YISRAEL)
1965 / 13 min / sound / b&w / 16 mm
Berkey Pathe Humphries. Locations: Abraham F. Rad Jewish
Film Archive / Prime Minister's Office, Information Dept.,
Jerusalem.
Available in English, French, Spanish and Portuguese
soundtracks. Documents Pope Paul VI's visit to Israel.

1619　THE SAND CURTAIN
1966-67 / 45 min / sound / b&w / 35 mm
Israel Motion Picture Studios, Herzliyah. Locations:
Abraham F. Rad Jewish Film Archive / Keren Hayesod,
Jerusalem.
Examination of conditions in Israel in 1966-67 by
reporter Drew Pearson.

1620　SPEAKING OF ISRAEL
1969 / 28 min / sound / color / 16 mm
Baruch Dienar. Distributed by Alden Films. (LC 72-702955)
Locations: Abraham F. Rad Jewish Film Archive / Gratz
College / Israel Tourism Office.
Available in English, Spanish and French soundtracks.
Looks at life in Israel as seen by Israelis. Includes
scenes of Tel Aviv, Haifa and the Negev Desert. Profiles
several archeological sites, and cultural and scientific
life.

1621　STREAMS IN THE DESERT (NACHALIM BAMIDBAR)
1965 / 24 min / sound / color / 16 mm
P. Terez. Locations: Abraham F. Rad Jewish Film Archive /
Prime Minister's Office, Information Dept., Jerusalem.
Film on Israel intended to promote tourism.

1622　THIS IS ISRAEL
1963 / 12 min / sound / color or b&w / 16 mm
Sim Productions. Released by Weston Woods Studios.
Distributed by Alden Films. (Picture Book Parade series)
(NUC FiA 64-279) Credits: Producers - Sonny Fox, Morton
Schindel. Locations: Abraham F. Rad Jewish Film Archive /

Kent State U. / Library of Congress (FAA 5748) / Ministry of
Education and Culture, Jerusalem / Ministry of Tourism,
Jerusalem / New York Public Donnell Film Library.
Available in English and Hebrew soundtracks. Shows
various historical sites in Israel, based on a book by M.
Sasek. Covers a variety of people and cities, including
Tel Aviv, Haifa, Jerusalem, Beersheba, and Eilat.

1623   TO ISRAEL BY SEA
        1961 / 20 min / sound / color / 16 mm
        American Israeli Shipping Co.   Released to adult organiza-
        tions by Sterling Movies.   (NUC FiA 62-1676)
            To promote tourist travel to Israel by boat.   Looks at
            the luxury accommodations abroad ships bound for Israel.
            Shows a stop over in Greece and tours Greek classical
            ruins.   Includes scenes touring modern Tel Aviv and
            historical religious sites in Israel.

1624   VIEWS OF NATURE RESERVES (MAROT BISHAMUROT)
        1966 / 13 min / sound / color / 16 or 35 mm
        Roll Films, Ltd.   Location: Prime Minister's Office,
        Information Dept., Jerusalem.
            Available in English, Hebrew, French and Arabic
            soundtracks.   Examines plant and animal life in Israel
            throughout the four seasons.   Includes scenes of the
            Negev, life on the coast, and in the Galilee.

1625   VOYAGE TO SABRA LAND
        1964 / 15 min / sound / color / 16 mm
        I.G.T.C.   Locations: Abraham F. Rad Jewish Film Archive /
        Ministry of Tourism, Jerusalem.
            Available in English, French, Spanish, German, Swedish,
            Danish and Dutch soundtracks.   Follows two young people
            who meet while traveling to Israel.   Includes scenes of
            the Galilee, the Negev, and Eilat.   Looks at historical
            sites and beaches.

ISRAEL - TRAVELOGS - PRODUCED BETWEEN 1970-1979

1626   DAYS THAT CHANGE LIVES
        (c. 1978?) / 28 min / sound / color / 16 mm
        Hadassah.   Location: Hadassah Film Library.
            Shows various scenes of Israeli life including a Kinnus,
            Erev Shabbat at a Bayit, the march on Yom Ha'atzma'ut,
            Tisha b'Av at the Western Wall, and dawn at Ketura.
            Shows Jewish youth from other countries visiting Israel.
            Produced for Jewish audiences.

1627   GET WITH IT!
        1970 / 18 min / sound / color / 16 mm
        N. Zervanizer for the Information Dept. of the Ministry of
        Foreign Affairs.   Distributed by Alden Films.   Locations:

310

Abraham F. Rad Jewish Film Archive / Gratz College /
Ministry of Foreign Affairs, Jerusalem.
Lively travelog of Israel aimed at visitors in their
teens and 20's. Uses a rock music background. Shows an
Israeli production of "Hair", discos, folk dancing, kib-
butz life, the Hebrew University, and the Billy Rose Art
Garden. Includes scenes of Jerusalem and Eilat.

1628   ISRAEL - IMPRESSIONS OF A DAY
1975 / 13 min / sound / color / 16 or 35 mm
Producer unknown. Location: Abraham F. Rad Jewish Film
Archive.
Available in English and Hebrew soundtracks. Listed in
some catalogs as: A DAY IN ISRAEL. Follows a
day-long tour of the people and landscape of Israel.

1629   ISRAEL: THE LAND AND THE PEOPLE
1970 / 13 min / sound / color or b&w / 16 mm
Coronet Instructional Films. (LC 73-706806) Credits:
Writer - Joseph E. Spencer. Locations: Brigham Young U. /
Kent State U. / Library of Congress (FBA 9391) / Middle East
Institute / Syracuse U. / U. of Illinois / U. of Kansas.   *
Intended for general audiences. Looks at development and
use of resources in Israel. Profiles farming techniques
and land reclamation efforts, the citrus industry and
mineral mining in the Dead Sea area. Looks at cotton,
diamond and candy production. Covers industry, transportation and tourism. Discusses immigration of Jews from
other countries, and the significance of Jerusalem for
Jews, Christians and Muslims. Moderately interesting
over-view of life in Israel.

1630   ISRAEL: A PROFILE
1970 / 28 min / sound / b&w / 16 mm
Anti-Defamation League of B'nai B'rith. (LC 76-707442)
Credits: Moderators   David Schoenbrun, Theodore H. White.
Location: U. of Wisconsin.
Author Theodore H. White and news commentator David
Schoenbrun discuss the historical and religious signifi-
cance of Israel to Americans and to Jews everywhere.
Looks at unrest in the Middle East and the role of the
U.S., England, France and the Soviet Union in Middle
Eastern affairs.

1631   NOAH'S PARK
1976 / 26 min / sound / color / 16 mm
Kronsey Productions. Distributed by Phoenix Films, and by
Alden Films. Locations: Gratz College / Kent State U.
Intended for general audiences. Looks at the national
Biblical Wildlife Preserve in Israel, a preserve
established to restock animals that inhabited the area
since Biblical times. Biblical passages are quoted to
describe the animals found in the preserve. Stresses
cooperation between Arabs and Jews in the project.

311

1632   SHALOM ISRAEL
        1971 / 10 min / sound / color / 16 mm
        Coordinated Photography. (LC 72-700346) Credits:
        Producer-Photographer-Editor - Joseph R. Golberg.
        Uses a musical soundtrack to complement this general mon-
        tage of scenes from Israeli life.

1633   THREE DAY MARCH
        1970 / 11 min / sound / color / 16 mm
        Producer unknown. Location: Abraham F. Rad Jewish Film
        Archive.
        Looks at Israeli citizens, Israeli Defense Forces and
        visitors from other countries participating in the tradi-
        tional annual march to Jerusalem.

1634   TREE OF LIFE
        1974 / 55 min / sound / color / 16 mm
        United Jewish Appeal. Made by John Ferno. Distributed by
        Alden Films. (LC 75-700487) Location: Abraham F. Rad
        Jewish Film Archive.
        Available in 26 and 55 minute versions. Impressionistic
        portrait of Israel narrated by Sir Lawrence Olivier.
        Examines Israel's national character and spirit.
        Discusses the will to survive and to achieve a normal way
        of life in Israel.

1635   WE, THE JEWISH PEOPLE
        1972 / 27 min / sound / color / 16 mm
        Producer unknown. Distributed by Alden Films. Location:
        Abraham F. Rad Jewish Film Archive.
        Looks at the Jewish population of Israel, from native
        born sabras to newly arrived Russian immigrants.
        Includes scenes of Beersheva, Rehovoth, Ashkelon,
        Jerusalem and Tel Aviv. Shows the Hebrew, Bar Ilan and
        Tel Aviv Universities.

ISRAEL - TRAVELOGS - BY REGION

1636   AERIAL VIEWS OF NEGEV, NAHAL DAVID AND NAHAL ZIN
        (n.d.) / 20 min / silent / color / 16 mm
        Producer unknown. Location: Abraham F. Rad Jewish Film
        Archive.
        Looks at the southern desert region of the Negev and the
        agricultural settlements in that area.

1637   BEIT SHEAN
        (n.d.) / 28 min / sound / color / 16 mm
        Producer unknown. Distributed by Alden Films. Location:
        Abraham F. Rad Jewish Film Archive.
        Listed in some catalogs as: BEIT SHEAN: SYMBOL OF
        LIFE. Narrated by Gary Moore. Looks at the Beit Shean
        Valley along the banks of the Jordan River from the Sea

of Galilee to the Dead Sea. Examines kibbutz life, the
need for security and the effort needed to cultivate the
valley.

1638   BETWEEN BEERSHEVA AND EILAT (MITZPE RAMON)
1958 / 15 min / sound / b&w / 16 mm
Berkey Pathe Humphries for the Histadrut. Locations:
Histadrut - General Federation of Jewish Labor, Tel Aviv /
Jewish Agency, Jerusalem / Natan Gross.
        Looks at natural resources of the southern Negev.
Profiles progress in the first year of settlement Mitzpe
Ramon on the Beersheva-Eilat road.

1639   THE BLESSING OF MOUNT GILBOA
1964 / 7 min / sound / color / 16 mm
Newsreel. Locations: Abraham F. Rad Jewish Film Archive /
Jewish National Fund, Jerusalem.
        Available in English and Spanish soundtracks. Newsreel
of climbers of Biblical Mt. Gilboa.

1640   BUS TO SINAI
(c. 1968?) / 54 min / sound / color / 16 mm
Producer unknown. Distributed by Alden Films. Location:
National Jewish Welfare Board, New York.
        Travelog of Israel. Including a five day bus tour of the
Sinai, Mt. Sinai, scenes from the 1967 War, the Suez
Canal, Bedouins, and archeological data on the Exodus.

1641   A CAMP IN THE ARAVA (MACHANE BE'ARAVA)
1953 / 13 min / sound / b&w / 16 or 35 mm
Berkey Pathe Humphries for the Histadrut. Credits:
Director-Writers - Natan Gross, Yona Zaretski. Locations:
Histadrut - General Federation of Jewish Labor, Tel Aviv /
Jewish Agency, Jerusalem / Ministry of Education and
Culture, Jerusalem / Natan Gross, Givata'im.
        Available in English, Hebrew and French soundtracks.
Shows road construction in the Negev. Looks at the
building of a road from Sdom to Kurnub.

1642   CAMP IN THE DESERT
1953 / 30 min / sound / b&w / 16 mm
Producer unknown. Location: Abraham F. Rad Jewish Film
Archive.
        Looks at the building of a road from Sdom to Kurnub in
the Negev. May be a longer version of no. 1641.

1643   THE CHALLENGE OF THE NEGEV
1950-51 / 18 min / sound / b&w / 16 mm
Producer unknown. Location: Abraham F. Rad Jewish Film
Archive.
        Profiles settlement programs in the Negev desert region.

1644   GLORIOUS GALILEE
1962 / 20 min / sound / color / 16 mm

313

Lazar Dunner. Locations: Abraham F. Rad Jewish Film Archive / Jewish Agency Film Archive, Jerusalem / Jewish National Fund, Jerusalem / Keren Hayesod, Jerusalem.
Available in English, Hebrew, French, Spanish and German soundtracks. Profiles land reclamation and settlement in the Galilee area. Shows ancient and modern Safed and Acre, the Biranit region and Tiberias.

1645   HISTORIC GALILEE
1954 / 13 min / sound / b&w / 16 mm
Producer unknown. Location: Kent State U.
Intended for junior-senior high school audiences. Looks at sites in Israel which were important during the time of Jesus. Shows Galilee, Cana, Capernaum and Mt. Tabor.

1646   HOLIDAY IN THE NORTH (CHUFSHA BATZAFON)
1965 / 13 min / sound / color / 16 or 35 mm
Yoram Gross Films. Location: Prime Minister's Office, Information Dept., Jerusalem.
Available in English, Hebrew, and French soundtracks or with German sub-titles. Looks at holiday opportunities in northern Israel. Includes scenes of Acre, Nahariyah, Rosh Hanikrah, Achziv, Shavei, Zion and the surrounding area.

1647   IN LAKHISH
(c. 1964) / 20 min / sound / b&w / 16 mm
Jewish Agency for Israel. Credits: Narrator - Reuven Morgan, Director - Isaac Yeshurun. Locations: Abraham F. Rad Jewish Film Archive / Library of Congress (FBA 4911-12)
*
Listed in some catalogs as: IN LACHISH. Also available in an 84 minute version. Looks at the villages and agricultural settlements in the Lakhish region populated by immigrants gathered by the Agricultural Dept. of the Jewish Agency. Shows routine life of the villagers, and the new settlement of Kiryat Gut.

1648   LIFE ON THE DEAD SEA (CHAYY'IM BE'YAM HAMAVET)
1961 / 15 min / sound / color / 16 or 35 mm
Berkey Pathe Humphries. Location: Prime Minister's Office, Information Dept., Jerusalem.
Available in English, Hebrew and Arabic soundtracks. Covers the Dead Sea area from early geological times to the present. Examines the history of the area, Jewish rebellions in different historical periods, and present day exploitation of mineral resources.

1649   LIGHT IN GALILEE
(n.d.) / 16 min / sound / color / 16 mm
Akiva Barkin. Locations: Histadrut - General Federation of Jewish Labor, Tel Aviv / Ministry of Education and Culture, Jerusalem / Nehora, Jerusalem.

314

Available in English and Hebrew soundtracks. Shows
Jewish historical sites in the Galilee in northern
Israel. Includes scenes of Safed, Meron, Tiberias, and
Bet Shearim. Profiles scholars of the Kabbalah and
Halachah and includes interviews with Rabbi Shimon Bar
Yochai and Rabbi Josef Karo. Looks at folk chants which
are sung each year in Tiberias and Meron.

1650   MODI'IN
       (n.d.) / 7 min / sound / b&w / 16 mm
       Producer unknown. Location: Abraham F. Rad Jewish Film
       Archive.
          Available in English and Spanish soundtracks. Examines
       the Biranit region of Israel. Looks specifically at the
       building and dedication ceremonies at Modi'in.

1651   THE NEGEV
       (n.d.) / 17 min / sound / color / 16 or 35 mm
       Israel Film Studios Ltd. Location: Abraham F. Rad Jewish
       Film Archive.
          Discusses development and settlement programs in the
       Negev Desert region of southern Israel.

1652   THE NEGEV - BEERSHEBA TO AVDAT
       1969 / 4 min / silent / color / super 8 mm film loop in
       cartridge. Eye Gate House. (LC 74-703722) (Living in
       Israel series)
          Short travelog of the Negev region.

1653   THE NEGEV - MITZPEH RAMON TO EILAT
       1969 / 4 min / silent / color / super 8 mm film loop in
       cartridge. Eye Gate House. (LC 74-703723) (Living in
       Israel series)
          Shows modern technologies at work in the development of
       the desert Negev region.

1654   OLD NEW LAND
       (n.d.) / 11 min / sound / b&w / 16 mm
       Producer unknown. Location: Abraham F. Rad Jewish Film
       Archive.
          Looks at the settlement at Ein Hod and profiles the para-
       military Nachal settlers in the Negev.

1655   OPERATION GALILEE
       1964 / 14 min / sound / color / 16 mm
       Newsreel. Locations: Abraham F. Rad Jewish Film Archive /
       Jewish National Fund, Jerusalem.
          Available in English, Hebrew, French, Spanish and German
       soundtracks. Looks at development projects and Jewish
       settlements in the northern Galilee.

1656   PROFILES OF GALILEE
       (n.d.) / 15 min / sound / color / 16 mm

Itzhak Krimolowski. Distributed by Alden Films. Locations: Abraham F. Rad Jewish Film Archive / Jewish Agency Film Archive, Jerusalem / Ministry of Tourism, Jerusalem. Available in English and Spanish soundtracks. Profiles painters Gutman, Rubin, Shmit and Castel and shows the Galilee landscapes each has painted.

1657   PROFILES OF THE NEGEV DESERT
        (n.d.) / 15 min / sound / color / 16 mm
        Yitzhak Kreymolowski. Locations: Abraham F. Rad Jewish Film Archive / Jewish Agency Film Archive, Jerusalem / Ministry of Tourism, Jerusalem.
        Available in English, French and Spanish soundtracks. Looks at agricultural and scientific programs used in the development of the Negev. Includes information on solar energy use, mineral resources and a profile of Eilat.

1658   RECLAMATION OF THE NEGEV
        1976 / 13 min / sound / color / 16 mm
        Environment Protective Service of Israel. Distributed by Alden Films. Location: Gratz College.
        For intermediate to adult audiences. Discusses desalinization and solar energy projects in the Negev.

1659   REGION OF TANACH
        (n.d.) / 28 min / sound / color / 16 mm
        Producer unknown. Distributed by Alden Films.
        Looks at the history of the Moshav, or cooperative farming settlement. An alternative to kibbutz life, each farmer maintains a private parcel of land in addition to communal areas jointly cultivated. Looks at moshav services and the varied immigrant populations found in these settlements.

1660   REGIONAL RURAL PLANNING
        (n.d.) / 15 min / sound / color / 16 mm
        Environmental Protection Service of Israel. Location: Gratz College.
        Traces the history of the Lachish region from early times to the period of Jewish settlement. Attributes high productivity of the area to early planning programs.

1661   RENDEZ-VOUS IN GALILEE
        (n.d.) / 32 min / sound / color / 16 mm
        Producer unknown. Location: Jewish Agency Film Archive, Jerusalem.
        Travelog. Includes scenes of Acre, Haifa, Beth She'arim, the New Hebrew University, and the Jerusalem Ballet Performance of "The Ceremony of a Yemenite Marriage".

1662   ROVING REPORT: DAN TO BEERSHEVA
        (n.d.) / 17 min / sound / b&w / 16 mm
        I.T.N., London. Location: Ministry of Tourism, Jerusalem.

Follows a British reporter who had not been in Israel
since independence as he visits Galilee, the Hatzor excavations, Safed, where he interviews artist Castel, Haifa,
Caesarea, Lydda and Beersheva.

1663   SINAI
1969 / 22 min / sound / color / 16 or 35 mm
Roll Films Ltd., Israel Film service. Locations: Abraham F.
Rad Jewish Film Archive / Jewish Agency, Jerusalem / Prime
Minister's Office, Information Dept., Jerusalem.
Colorful, general travelog. Shows the Sinai desert and
Bedouins of the area. Available in English, Hebrew,
French and Spanish soundtracks.

1664   SONG OF THE NEGEV
1950 / 30 min / sound / b&w / 16 mm
United Palestine Appeal. Made by Jewish Agency for
Palestine. (NUC FiA 54-1212) Location: Abraham F. Rad
Jewish Film Archive.
Available in English, Hebrew and German soundtracks.
Listed in some catalogs as: EIN BRERA. Looks at
Ein Brera in the Negev, and the role that settlement
played in the fight for Israeli statehood.

1665   THIS IS ISRAEL: THE NEGEV
(n.d.) / 11 min / sound / b&w / 16 mm
Israel Motion Picture Studio Production. (Rony Collection,
no. 149) Credits: Director - Adam Goldberg, Narrator -
Melvin Elliott. Location: Library of Congress (FAB 1368)
No other information available.

1666   TIMELESS SAND
1961 / 18 min / sound / color / 16 mm
Newsreel. Locations: Abraham F. Rad Jewish Film Archive /
Jewish National Fund, Jerusalem.
Available in English, Hebrew, French, Spanish and German
soundtracks. Compares the role of man and nature in the
Negev desert region of Israel.

1667   VALLEY IN THE WILDERNESS
1968 / 18 min / sound / color / 16 mm
Newsreel. Location: Jewish National Fund, Jerusalem.
Available in English, Hebrew, French, Spanish and German
soundtracks. Looks at land reclamation in the Arara area
in the desert rift between the Dead and Red Seas.

1668   THE WILDERNESS OF ZIN
1959 / 25 min / sound / color / 16 mm
Producer unknown. Distributed by Alden Films. Location:
Penn. State U.
Israeli and American archeologists trace the history of
the Negev Desert region. Examines evidence of earlier
civilizations. Traces Jewish history in the area.

317

1669 ACRE
(c. 1968?) / ? / sound / 16 mm
Berkey Pathe Humphries. Location: Jewish Agency Film
Archive, Jerusalem.
Looks at history and modern life in the city of Acre.

1670 ACRE, OLD-NEW CITY
1954 / 15 min / sound / b&w / 16 or 35 mm
Keren Hayesod Productions. Released in the U.S. by United
Israel Appeal. (NUC FiA 54-1196) Credits:
Producer-Writer-Director - Michael Elkins, Photographer -
Anthony Heller. Locations: Abraham F. Rad Jewish Film
Archive / Jewish Agency Film Archive, Jerusalem / Keren
Hayesod, Jerusalem / Ministry of Education and Culture,
Jerusalem.
Travelog of the city of Acre as seen through the eyes
of a young teacher living there. Shows historic and
modern aspects of the city.

1671 ASSIGNMENT TEL AVIV
1947 / 20 min / sound / color / 16 mm
Paul V. Falkenberg for Keren Hayesod. United Israel Appeal.
(NUC FiA 54-1197) Technicolor. Locations: Abraham F. Rad
Jewish Film Archive / Jewish Agency Film Archive, Jerusalem
/ Keren Hayesod, Jerusalem.
Follows journalist Quentin Reynolds on a tour of Tel
Aviv. Looks at the port, bus station, industries, the
zoo, education, social welfare and leisure activities in
the city. Contrasts older city of Jaffa with modern Tel
Aviv.

1672 CAESAREA
1956 / 5 min / sound / color / 16 or 35 mm
Israel Film Studios Ltd., Herzliyah. Locations: Abraham F.
Rad Jewish Film Archive / Jewish Agency Film Archive,
Jerusalem / Ministry of Education and Culture, Jerusalem /
Prime Minister's Office, Information Dept., Jerusalem.
Available in English and Hebrew soundtracks. Looks at
the historic city of Caesarea and at the nearby kibbutz
of Sdot Yam. Includes scenes of the port and ruins in
Caesarea.

1673 CAESAREA
1962 / 15 min / sound / color / 16 or 35 mm
J. Pessis. Locations: Abraham F. Rad Jewish Film Archive /
Prime Minister's Office, Information Dept., Jerusalem.
Available in English, French and Spanish soundtracks.
Profiles projects to restore the ancient ruins in
Caesarea and enhance the area as a tourist resort.

1674 A CITY CALLED EILAT
1962 / 26 min / sound / color / 16 mm

318

Keren Hayesod, Jerusalem. Made by Lazar Dunner. Released in the U.S. by United Israel Appeal. (NUC FiA 64-570) Credits: Director-Photographer - Edgar Hirshbein, Narrator - Alexander Scourby. Locations: Abraham F. Rad Jewish Film Archive / Jewish Agency Film Archive, Jerusalem / Keren Hayesod, Jerusalem.

Profiles the city of Eilat. Shows the city as a tourist resort and as a working town with copper works, King Solomon's mines and a harbor. Looks at the inhabitants of the city and their daily activities.

1675　CITY FAMILY - HAIFA
1969 / 4 min / silent / color / super 8 mm film loop in cartridge. Eye Gate House. (LC 74-703709)
Short film which profiles a typical Israeli family living in Haifa.

1676　DAUGHTER OF THE SEA (BAT HAYAM)
1954 / 13 min / sound / b&w / 16 mm
Berkey Pathe Humphries for the Bat Yam Municipality. Credits: Director-Writer - Natan Gross.
Available in English and Hebrew soundtracks. Looks at development, industry and activities in the city of Bat Yam.

1677　A DAY AND A JUBILEE
1964 / 13 min / sound / b&w / 16 or 35 mm
Producer unknown. Location: Abraham F. Rad Jewish Film Archive.
Available in English and Hebrew soundtracks. Profiles Kvutsat Kinneret.

1678　DEVELOPMENT OF EILAT COAST (PITU'ACH CHOF EILAT)
1968 / 12 min / sound / color / 16 or 35 mm
A. Gavrieli and Y. Ravin. Location: Prime Minister's Office, Information Dept., Jerusalem.
Available in English and Hebrew soundtracks. Examines the coastal area of Eilat, the development of the area as a tourist and resort center, and the importance of the city of Eilat as a port.

1679　EILAT
1955-56 / 10 min / sound / b&w / 16 mm
Producer unknown. Location: Abraham F. Rad Jewish Film Archive.
Available in English and Spanish soundtracks. Looks at problems in health care, employment and integration faced by early settlers in Eilat.

1680　EILAT ON THE RED SEA
1966 / 15 min / sound / color / 16 mm
Eilat Tourist Bureau. Made by Yona Zarecki Ltd, Tel Aviv. (LC 79-701605) Locations: Abraham F. Rad Jewish Film

Archive / Jewish Agency Film Archive, Jerusalem / Library of
Congress (FBA 5838) / Ministry of Education and Culture,
Jerusalem / Ministry of Tourism, Jerusalem. *
To promote tourism to Israel and Eilat in particular.
Looks at opportunities for skin diving, swimming, and
touring in Eilat. Shows hotels and scenes of the city,
port and mines nearby.

1681   EIN HOD
1958-59 / 15 min / sound / color / 16 mm
Joseph Navon, Cinegram Ste Geneve. Locations: Abraham F.
Rad Jewish Film Archive / Israel Film Studios, Herzliyah /
Jewish Agency Film Archive, Jerusalem.
Looks at the artist village of Ein Hod. Shows the inha-
bitants of the area and their work.

1682   THE END OF YESTERDAY (SOF ETMOL)
1964 / 25 min / sound / 35 mm
Baruch Dienar. Israel Film Studios, Herzliyah.
Available in English, Hebrew, Spanish and German
soundtracks. Looks at the new town of Upper Nazareth
built above historical Nazareth.

1683   FISHERMAN IN JAFFA (DAYAGIM BE'YAFFO)
1962 / 10 min / sound / b&w / 16 or 35 mm
Berkey Pathe Humphries. Locations: Histadrut - General
Federation of Jewish Labor, Tel Aviv / Ministry of
Education and Culture, Jerusalem / Prime Minister's Office,
Information Dept., Jerusalem.
Available in English, Hebrew, French and Spanish
soundtracks. Shows Jaffa, the oldest port in Israel.
Profiles the ancient fishing industry in Jaffa. Shows
fishermen working and relaxing in coffee shops near the
port.

1684   GATEWAY TO ISRAEL
1956 / 10 min / sound / b&w / 16 mm
Samuel Elfert, Contemporary Films. Israel Office of
Information. (NUC FiA 64-829) (This is Israel series)
Locations: Abraham F. Rad Jewish Film Archive / Jewish
Agency Film Archive, Jerusalem.
Looks at the port of Haifa. Stresses the importance of
the port and shows the diversity of people who work on
the docks. Shows maintenance of ships and fire drills.

1685   HAIFA
1957 / 10 min / sound / b&w / 35 mm
Israel Film Studios, Herzliyah.
Available in English and German soundtracks. Profiles
the port and city of Haifa.

1686   HAIFA PORT (NEMAL HAIFA)
1956 / 13 min / sound / b&w / 16 or 35 mm

Berkey Pathe Humphries. Locations: Jewish Agency, Jerusalem
/ Prime Minister's Office, Information Dept., Jerusalem.
Available in English and Hebrew soundtracks. Looks at
Haifa, Israel's largest port.

1687   HAIL CAESAREA
(n.d.) / 14 min / sound / color / 16 mm
George Pessis. Distributed by Alden Films. Locations:
Abraham F. Rad Jewish Film Archive / Ministry of Tourism,
Jerusalem.
Available in English, French and Spanish soundtracks. A
light-hearted travelog of the ancient city of Caesarea.
Pontius Pilate and a Roman colleague compare historic
Caesarea to the modern city. Includes scenes of the
breakwater, city walls, Roman aquaduct, Crusader-period
buildings, and the modern golf club.

1688   HEY, DARGHA LE'EILAT (SOUTHWARD TO EILAT)
1945-55 / 13 min / sound / b&w / 16 mm
Berkey Pathe Humphries for the Histadrut. Locations: Jewish
Agency Film Archive, Jerusalem / Keren Hayesod, Jerusalem /
Natan Gross, Givata'im.
Profiles the city and port of Eilat. Describes the
importance of the city to Israel in fishing, industry and
shipping.

1689   A HILL IN JUDEA
(n.d.) / 20 min / sound / color / 16 mm
Producer unknown. Location: Abraham F. Rad Jewish Film
Archive.
Looks at the development city of Neveh Ilan in the Judean
Hills. Shows the life of children growing up there.

1690   HISTORIC NAZARETH
1954 / 13 min / sound / b&w / 16 mm
Producer unknown. Location: Kent State U.
For junior-senior high school audiences. Traces scenes
in the city of Nazareth mentioned in the New Testament.
Shows places where Mary and Joseph were said to have
lived, the synogogue where Jesus studied and the fountain
which Mary used.

1691   AN ISLAND IN THE DESERT
1963 / 15 min / sound / color / 16 mm
Lazar Dunner. Jewish National Fund. Distributed by Alden
Films. Locations: Jewish Agency Film Archive, Jerusalem /
Jewish National Fund, Jerusalem.
Available in English, Hebrew, French, Spanish and German
soundtracks. Should not be confused with the feature
film of the same name. Looks at the "island" of settlers
in the Neoth Hakikar area, south of the Dead Sea. Shows
their efforts in agriculture and cattle raising.

1692   ISRAEL 1969
        1969 / 10 min / silent / color / 16 mm
        Producer unknown. Location: Abraham F. Rad Jewish Film
        Archive.
        Looks at the ancient and modern resort of Caesarea.
        Shows Roman ruins and the new golf course.

1693   ISRAEL TODAY
        1960 / 28 min / sound / color / 16 mm
        Martin Murray. (NUC FiA 61-217)
        Looks at the city of Tel Aviv. Includes scenes of busy
        city streets, apartment houses, office buildings and
        daily activities of the people of Tel Aviv.

1694   IT BEGAN HERE IN THE SAND DUNES (KAN BACHOLOT ZE HITCHIL
        1965 / 2240 ft. / sound / 16 or 35 mm
        Roll Films. Israel Film Studios, Herzliyah.
        Available in English, Hebrew, Spanish and French
        soundtracks. Profiles the city of Holon.

1695   JAFFA
        1970 / 13 min / sound / color / 16 mm
        Israel Information Service, Jerusalem. Released in the U.S.
        by Alden Films. (LC 72-702956)
        Intended for junior high school to college audiences.
        Looks at Jaffa on the Mediterranean. Compares the old
        city and narrow streets to the current artists' colony
        where painters and craftspeople work.

1696   JAFFA, SIGHTS AND SOUNDS IN OLD JAFFA (YAFFO, MAROT
        U'TZLILIM BEYAFFO HA'ATIKA)
        1967 / 14 min / sound / color / 16 or 35 mm
        Orav Films. Baruch Dienar. Locations: Abraham F. Rad
        Jewish Film Archive / Histadrut - General Federation of
        Jewish Labor, Tel Aviv / Prime Minister's Office,
        Information Dept., Jerusalem.
        Available in English, Hebrew, German and French
        soundtracks. Listed in some catalogs as: JAFFA -
        SIGHTS AND SOUNDS IN THE OLD CITY. Shows the old
        city of Jaffa and the current artists' colony and tourist
        center the city has become.

1697   MELON BOY OF TEL AVIV
        1973 / 17 min / sound / color / 16 mm
        Perspective Films. (LC 74-700137) Locations: Gratz
        College / Syracuse U.
        For elementary to junior high school audiences. Looks at
        the role of young Israelis in society. Shows a young
        melon boy selling his produce on the street from his
        wagon. In contrast is the modern city with its traffic
        and department stores. The melon boy dreams about sandy
        beaches.

1698   THE ORIGINAL DWELLING PLACE (BEERSHEBA)
        (c. 1977) / 45 min / sound / color / 16 mm
        Anti-Defamation League of B'nai B'rith. Distributed by
        Alden Films. (Dateline Israel series)
        Looks at the ancient and modern city of Beersheba.
        Interviews Jews from around the world on why they
        immigrated to Israel and settled in Beersheba. Looks at
        how their lives have changed since immigration.

1699   THE PORT OF HAIFA
        1969 / 4 min / silent / color / super 8mm film loop in
        cartridge. Eye Gate House. (LC 74-703719) (Living in
        Israel series)
        Short film looking at the activities of the port city
        of Haifa.

1700   PROMISED PEOPLE
        (n.d.) / 15 min / sound / color / 16 mm
        Producer unknown. Distributed by Alden Films.
        Profiles the settlement of Kiryat Gat. Originally deve-
        loped as an agricultural center for immigating Jews, the
        town has developed more industry, schools and auxiliary
        services.

1701   RAMAT HAGOLAN
        1975 / 24 min / sound / color / 16 mm
        Producer unknown. Location: Abraham F. Rad Jewish Film
        Archive.
        Interviews the settlers of Ramat Hagolan. Includes
        discussion on the area and future of the settlement.

1702   ROMAN REVERIE
        (n.d.) / 13 min / sound / b&w / 16 mm
        Producer unknown. Location: Abraham F. Rad Jewish Film
        Archive.
        Humorous travelog of Tiberias. A tourist dreams his
        masseur is a Roman centurion. Both take a chariot tour
        of the sites of the ancient city.

1703   SAFED, A STORY IN BLUE
        1967 / 12 min / sound / color / 16 or 35 mm
        Roll Films Ltd. Location: Prime Minister's Office,
        Information Dept., Jerusalem.
        Available in English, Hebrew and French soundtracks.
        Profiles the historic city of Safed. Looks at the dif-
        ference in the city from weekdays to Shabbat.

1704   SAINT CATHERINE'S MONASTERY
        (n.d.) / 5 min / silent / b&w / 16 mm
        Producer unknown. Location: Abraham F. Rad Jewish Film
        Archive.
        Shows the monastery of Saint Katerina in the Sinai
        Desert and the remaining Greek Orthodox monks who tend
        the monastery.

1705   THE SYMPHONY OF A CITY - HAIFA
        1955-56 / 15 min / sound / b&w / 16 or 35 mm
        Israel Motion Picture Studios. Locations: Abraham F. Rad
        Jewish Film Archive / Jewish Agency Film Archive, Jerusalem
        / Keren Hayesod, Jerusalem.
        Uses a musical soundtrack to follow activities in the
        city of Haifa for a day.

1706   TEL AVIV IN COLOR
        (n.d.) / 4 min / sound / color / 16 mm
        Producer unknown. Location: Abraham F. Rad Jewish Film
        Archive.
        Available in English and Hebrew soundtracks. Short film
        documenting Tel Aviv in the 1930's. Shows the port,
        building construction, the Tel Aviv Gymnasium and the
        Town Hall.

1707   TEL AVIV MARCHES ON
        1962 / 30 min / sound / color / 16 mm
        Israel Film Studios, Herzliyah.
        Looks at the city of Tel Aviv in 1948.

1708   TEL AVIV, MY TOWN
        1959-60 / 13 min / sound / b&w / 16 mm
        Michael Grunblat. Berkey Pathe Humphries. Locations:
        Jewish Agency Film Archive, Jerusalem / Keren Hayesod,
        Jerusalem.
        Shows daily activities and night life in Tel Aviv.

1709   TEL AVIV PLANS AND BUILDS
        (n.d.) / 15 min / silent / b&w / 35 mm
        Producer unknown. Location: Abraham F. Rad Jewish Film
        Archive.
        Looks at building and construction in Tel Aviv around
        1950. Shows kindergartens and schools, the Municipal
        High School, maternity homes, the wholesale fruit market,
        roads, bridges, parks and gardens. Includes aerial views
        of the city. Good documentation of the city.

1710   TIBERIAS: LAND OF THE EMPERORS
        1969 / 14 min / sound / color / 16 mm
        Producer unknown. Distributed by Alden Films. Locations:
        Abraham F. Rad Jewish Film Archive / Gratz College.
        Listed in some catalogs as: TIBERIAS: RESORT OF
        EMPERORS. Examines historical significance of the city.
        Built by Herod as a tribute to the Roman emperor
        Tiberias, the area is now a major resort. Includes sce-
        nes showing the beauty of the city and surrounding area.

1711   THE WALLS OF ACRE
        (n.d.) / 20 min / sound / color / 16 mm
        Norman Lourie. Location: Ministry of Tourism, Jerusalem.
        Looks at the city of Acre from Crusader and Turkish times
        to the present. Shows the fishing industry and port.

1712   WE BUILT US A TOWN
        1965 / 15 min / sound / b&w / 16 mm
        Producer unknown. Location: Abraham F. Rad Jewish Film
        Archive.
        Profiles the city of Holon and describes typical daily
        activities of the inhabitants.

1713   WE REMEMBER
        1965 / 9 min / sound / color / 16 mm
        Producer unknown. Location: Jewish National Fund,
        Jerusalem.
        Available in English, Hebrew, French, Spanish and German
        soundtracks. Shows the Martyr's Forest in the Judean
        hills.

1714   THE WESTERN WALL
        (n.d.) / 30 min / sound / b&w / 16 mm
        Producer unknown. Location: Abraham F. Rad Jewish Film
        Archive.
        Shows religious celebrations at the Western Wall, Israel
        Army paratroopers swearing allegiance and excavations in
        the area of the wall.

1715   ZOHAR BE'AFOR (BRILLIANCE IN GREY)
        (n.d.) / 10 min / sound / b&w / 16 mm
        Nehora Co. Location: Histadrut - General Federation of
        Jewish Labor, Tel Aviv.
        Uses a background of Arab music to complement scenes of
        factories and workers in the port city of Haifa.

ISRAEL   -   WATER AND LAND USE

1716   THE BLESSED WATERS
        (c. 1955?) / 11 min / sound / b&w / 16 mm
        Producer unknown. Location: Abraham F. Rad Jewish Film
        Archive.
        Profiles the Huleh Drainage Project during the 1950's.
        Shows the draining of the swamp and marsh areas for agri-
        cultural purposes.

1717   DESERT LAKES
        1968 / 7 min / sound / color / 16 mm
        Jewish National Fund.
        Available in English, Hebrew, French, Spanish and German
        soundtracks. Shows water storage equipment and dams in
        the Dvir-Adoraim region.

1718   THE DESERT SHALL REJOICE
        1954 / 18 min / sound / color / 16 mm
        Producer unknown. Location: Abraham F. Rad Jewish Film
        Archive.
        Looks at Jewish National Fund supported programs in land
        reclamation. Describes the Huleh and Sde Boker projects.

325

1719   DREW PEARSON REPORTS ON RECLAMATION OF DESERT
        IN ISRAEL
        1957 / 16 min / sound / b&w / 16 or 35 mm
        Orb Films. Released by Orb Films and United Israel Appeal.
        (NUC FiA 64-575) Credits: Producer-Director - Baruch
        Dienar, Photographer - Rolf N. Kneller. Location: Abraham
        F. Rad Jewish Film Archive.
            Listed in some catalogs as: DREW PEARSON REPORTS
            ON DESERTS IN ISRAEL. Looks at reclamation
            projects in the Negev desert. Shows how new acreage is
            made available for farming and pasturage.

1720   EVERY DROP COUNTS
        1975 / 15 min / sound / color / 16 mm
        Environmental Protection Service of Israel. Distributed by
        Alden Films. Location: Gratz College.
            Looks at water conservation projects in Israel. Includes
            scenes of automated irrigation, sewage treatment and
            recycling, and the national water carrier.

1721   FLOODS
        1951 / 10 min / silent / b&w / 16 mm
        Producer unknown. Location: Abraham F. Rad Jewish Film
        Archive.
            Looks at flooding in Israel created by unseasonably heavy
            rains.

1722   FORESTS
        (n.d.) / 5 min / silent / b&w / 16 mm
        Producer unknown. Location: Abraham F. Rad Jewish Film
        Archive.
            Short film showing forests in Israel.

1723   FORESTS ARE BORN
        (n.d.) / 20 min / sound / color / 16 mm
        Jewish National Fund.
            Available in English, Hebrew and Spanish soundtracks.
            Looks at afforestation projects in Israel supported by
            the Jewish National Fund.

1724   HAPPY VALLEY
        1961 / 20 min / sound / color / 16 mm
        Jewish National Fund.
            Available in English, Hebrew, French, Spanish and German
            soundtracks. Examines the project to drain the Huleh
            swamp region.

1725   HARVEST FROM THE WATERS
        1954 / 14 min / sound / color / 16 mm
        Keren Hayesod. Made by Ya'acov Marx, American Film
        Producers, New York. Released by United Israel Appeal.
        (NUC FiA 54-1205) Credits: Director-Writer - Michael
        Elkins. Locations: Abraham F. Rad Jewish Film Archive /

326

Jewish Agency Film Archive, Jerusalem / Keren Hayesod, Jerusalem / Ministry of Education and Culture, Jerusalem. Profiles the fishing industry in Israel. Shows cooperative fishing settlements, deep sea fishing, seeding of fish in Galilee ponds for later harvesting, and training of young fishermen in navigation.

1726   HOPE FROM THE HULEH
(n.d.) / 17 min / sound / color / 16 mm
Producer unknown. Location: Abraham F. Rad Jewish Film Archive.
Looks at the Jewish National Fund supported project for draining the Huleh swamp for agricultural use.

1727   HULEH
(n.d.) / 11 min / silent / color / 16 mm
Producer unknown. Location: Abraham F. Rad Jewish Film Archive.
Looks at programs to drain the Huleh swamp area. Includes information on medical advantages of draining the swamp.

1728   THE HULEH STORY
1958 / 13 min / sound / b&w / 16 mm
Producer unknown. Location: Abraham F. Rad Jewish Film Archive.
Profiles efforts to drain the Huleh swamp and use the area for agricultural purposes.

1729   THE HULEH VALLEY (EMEK HACHULAH)
1954 / 13 min / sound / b&w / 16 or 35 mm
Berkey Pathe Humphries for Histadrut. Credits: Director - Nathan Gross, Writer - H. Hefer. Locations: Abraham F. Rad Jewish Film Archive / Jewish Agency, Jerusalem / Ministry of Education and Culture, Jerusalem / Prime Minister's Office, Information Dept., Jerusalem.
Available in English, Hebrew, French, Spanish and German soundtracks. Examines development plans for the Huleh Valley. Shows nature preserves, drainage of the swamp area, and plans for fields and new settlements.

1730   ISRAEL'S NATIONAL WATER CARRIER
(n.d.) / 18 min / sound / color / 16 mm
Producer unknown. Distributed by Alden Films. Location: Gratz College.
Profiles the national water carrier, a system of tunnels, canals and pipes which take fresh water from the Kinneret in Galilee in northern Israel 100 miles south to the Negev desert region.

1731   ISRAEL'S QUEST FOR WATER
(n.d.) / 22 min / sound / b&w / 16 mm
Producer unknown. Distributed by Alden Films. Location:

Abraham F. Rad Jewish Film Archive.
Looks at how water diverted from the Jordan River is used
for irrigation.

1732   ISRAEL'S WATER SHORTAGE
(n.d.) / 30 min / sound / b&w / 16 mm
Producer unknown. Location: Abraham F. Rad Jewish Film
Archive.
Discusses the significance of the National Water Carrier.
Shows how fresh water is shipped from Galilee to the
Negev Desert.

1733   KEREN KAYEMET DRAINS THE HULEH
(n.d.) / 15 min / sound / color / 16 mm
Lazar Dunner. Locations: Abraham F. Rad Jewish Film Archive
/ Jewish Agency Film Archive, Jerusalem.
Looks at the Huleh swamp drainage project and describes
its significance in providing more agricultural land to
feed a growing population.

1734   MAN AGAINST MOUNTAIN
(n.d.) / 20 min / sound / b&w / 16 mm
Producer unknown. Location: Abraham F. Rad Jewish Film
Archive.
Looks at projects to cultivate land in semi-mountainous
areas of Israel.

1735   MASTERS OF THE DESERT
1967 / 30 min / sound / b&w / 16 mm
British Broadcasting Corp., London. Released in the U.S. by
Time-Life Films. (LC 76-711242) (Horizon series)
Credits: Producer - Peter Cantor, Narrator - Fyfe Robertson.
Describes water conservation projects studied by a Hebrew
University professor. Looks at irrigation of crops from
stored rain water.

1736   MAYIM CHAYIM (THE THIRSTY LAND)
1953 / 10 min / sound / b&w / 16 mm
Berkey Pathe Humphries for Histadrut. Locations: Histadrut
- General Federation of Jewish Labor, Tel Aviv / Jewish
Agency Film Archive, Jerusalem / Ministry of Education and
Culture, Jerusalem / Natan Gross, Givata'im.
Available in English and Hebrew soundtracks. Examines
water conservation projects in Jerusalem and in the
Negev. Shows how water is collected and diverted to
needed areas. Shows the Yarkon-Negev pipeline.

1737   NATIONAL WATER CARRIER (MOVIL HAMAYIM HA'ARTZI)
1964 / 9 min / sound / color / 16 or 35 mm
Credits: Writer - D. Perlov, Photographers - A. Gavrieli, A.
Kenbel, M. Ya'acovolovitz, Y. Ne'eman, A. Solomon, N. Leon,
Y. Shaul, D. Gurfinkel. Locations: Short version: Prime
Minister's Office, Information Dept., Jerusalem. Long

version: Histadrut - General Federation of Jewish Labor,
Jerusalem / Israel Film Studios, Herzliyah / Ministry of
Education and Culture, Jerusalem / Prime Minister's Office,
Information Dept., Jerusalem.
> Available in two versions. The shorter 9 minute version
> is available in English and Hebrew soundtracks. The
> longer 22 minute version is available in English, French,
> Hebrew, Spanish and Arabic soundtracks. Both look at
> construction from 1961-64 of the National Water Carrier,
> a project to bring water to the southern Negev desert
> region from rivers in northern Galilee.

1738   THE SHIKMA RESERVOIR (AGAN SHIKMA)
        1967 / 15 min / sound / color / 16 mm
        O. Kapeluk. Locations: Abraham F. Rad Jewish Film Archive /
        Prime Minister's Office, Information Dept., Jerusalem.
> Profiles water storage for later agricultural use in the
> Shikma Reservoir.

1739   THE THIRSTY LAND
        1953 / 15 min / sound / b&w / 16 mm
        Producer unknown. Location: Abraham F. Rad Jewish Film
        Archive.
> Probably the same film as no. 1736. Looks at water use
> problems in Jerusalem and throughout Israel. Examines
> water collection projects and diverting of water to the
> Negev. Shows the Yarkon-Negev pipeline.

1740   TU BISHVAT
        (n.d.) / 14 min / sound / color / 16 mm
        Y. Brandstaedter. Distributed by Alden Films. Location:
        Jewish Agency Film Archive, Jerusalem.
> Listed in some catalogs as: TU B'SHVAT. Shows the
> festival of the planting of trees in the Jordan Valley
> and the Galilee. Includes scenes of dancing.

1741   WATER PROBLEMS IN ISRAEL
        1964 / 23 min / sound / b&w / 16 mm
        Israel Film Studios, Herzliyah. Location: Prime Minister's
        Office, Information Dept., Jerusalem.
> Available in English, Hebrew, French and Spanish
> soundtracks. Describes the water shortage problem in
> Israel. Looks at the need for water in industry, agri-
> culture and for the population in central and southern
> Israel. Discusses the political implications of piping
> water from Lake Kinneret to the Negev.

1742   WATER RESOURCE PLANNING - THE TECHNION, HAIFA
        1969 / 4 min / silent / color / super 8 mm film loop in
        cartridge. Eye Gate House. (LC 74-703721) (Living in
        Israel series)
> Short silent film looking at water planning projects.

1743   YE SHALL PLANT TREES
        1967 / 18 min / sound / color / 16 mm
        Jewish National Fund, Jerusalem.
        Available in English, Hebrew, French, Spanish and German
        soundtracks. Profiles afforestation projects in Israel
        supported by the Jewish National Fund.

ISRAEL - AGRICULTURE

1744   AGRICULTURAL INPUTS
        1972 / 18 min / sound / color / 16 mm
        Producer unknown. Location: Abraham F. Rad Jewish Film
        Archive.
        Available in English and Spanish soundtracks. Looks at
        development of agriculture and industry in Israel.

1745   AGRICULTURE IN ISRAEL
        (n.d.) / 25 min / silent / b&w / 16 mm
        Producer unknown. Location: Abraham F. Rad Jewish Film
        Archive.
        General survey of agricultural development in Israel.

1746   BETTER METHODS OF COTTON PICKING
        (n.d.) / 14 min / sound / b&w / 16 mm
        Israel Institute of Productivity, Tel Aviv.
        Available in English, Hebrew, French and Spanish
        soundtracks. Demonstrates to Israeli pickers the most
        productive method for plucking cotton. A training, edu-
        cational film.

1747   COTTON (KUTNA)
        1957 / 13 min / sound / b&w / 16 or 35 mm
        Institute of Work and Productivity. Locations: Abraham F.
        Rad Jewish Film Archive / Israel Film Studios.
        Available in English, Hebrew, French and Spanish
        soundtracks. Provides information on cotton production
        in Israel.

1748   COUNTRY OF THE GOLDEN FRUIT
        (n.d.) / 20 min / sound / color / 16 mm
        Jewish National Fund, Jerusalem.
        Profiles the citrus industry in Israel. Also includes
        segments on Biblical and archeological sites, agri-
        cultural settlements and new Jewish immigrants.

1749   FRONTLINE 1952
        1952 / 10 min / sound / b&w / 16 mm
        Producer unknown. Credits: Narrator - Eddie Cantor.
        Locations: Jewish Agency Film Archive, Jerusalem / Keren
        Hayesod, Jerusalem.
        Fund raising film. Describes the shortage of food in
        Israel and asks for donations to help provide economic
        stability in the new state.

1750 GREEN FIELDS
      1975 / 20 min / sound / color / 16 mm
      Producer unknown. Distributed by Alden Films. Locations:
      Abraham F. Rad Jewish Film Archive / Gratz College.
      Intended for high school to adult audiences. Looks at
      agricultural innovations introduced to the West Bank area
      after its occupation by Israel in 1967. Shows Israeli
      advisors with Arab farmers in the West Bank working with
      crops, livestock, and in the olive industry. Intended to
      show assistance of Israel to West Bank Arab farmers under
      Israeli administration.

1751 HARVEST IN GALILEE
      (n.d.) / 8 min / sound / b&w / 16 mm
      Keren Hayesod. Locations: Abraham F. Rad Jewish Film
      Archive / Ministry of Education and Culture, Jerusalem.
      Shows harvest time in the upper Galilee complete with
      workers singing as they return home from the harvest.

1752 HARVEST IN THE NEGEV
      (n.d.) / 2 min / silent / b&w / 16 mm
      Producer unknown. Location: Abraham F. Rad Jewish Film
      Archive.
      Short film showing harvest time in the Negev.

1753 ISRAEL, LAND OF MIRACLES
      (n.d.) / 25 min / sound / b&w / 16 mm
      Lars-Eric Kjellgren for Sveriges Radio. Locations: Abraham
      F. Rad Jewish Film Archive / Jewish Agency Film Archive,
      Jerusalem.
      Looks at use of agricultural land in Israel. Shows land
      made available for crops after draining the Huleh Valley
      swamp areas. Discusses the various crops sown in Israel.

1754 LACHISH
      1964 / ? / sound / 16 or 35 mm
      Jewish Agency. Locations: Israel Film Studios, Herzliyah /
      Jewish Agency, Jerusalem.
      Available in English, Hebrew, French and Spanish
      soundtracks. Profiles the Lachish region agricultural
      development program.

1755 MECHANIZED FRUIT HARVESTING
      (n.d.) / 24 min / sound / color / 16 mm
      Israel Institute of Productivity and Israel Agricultural
      Engineering Institute.
      Available in English and Hebrew soundtracks. Examines
      various available methods for harvesting citrus fruits,
      apples, olives, almonds and dates by machine or with the
      use of mechanical aids.

1756 SCENES OF NATURAL RESERVE (MAROT BISHMUROT)
      1966 / 13 min / sound / color / 16 mm

331

Producer unknown. Distributed by Alden Films. Locations:
Abraham F. Rad Jewish Film Archive / Gratz College.
Listed in some catalogs as: SCENES OF NATURE RESERVES.
Shows variety of flora and fauna found in Israel
including 3000 types of flowers. Looks at turtles,
gazelles and eagles, among other animals. General film
for all age levels.

ISRAEL - INDUSTRY, SCIENCE AND LABOR

1757 CHALLENGE AND RESPONSE
      1973 / 22 min / sound / color / 16 mm
      Producer unknown. Location: Abraham F. Rad Jewish Film
      Archive.
      Available in English, French, Spanish, German and Hebrew
      soundtracks. Traces industrial development in Israel.

1758 THE COPPER STONE (EVEN HANECHOSHET)
      1959-60 / 12 min / sound / color / 16 or 35 mm
      Berkey Pathe Humphries for Film Service, Information Office.
      Credits: Director-Writer - Natan Gross. Locations:
      Histadrut - General Federation of Jewish Labor, Tel Aviv /
      Natan Gross, Givata'im / Prime Minister's Office,
      Information Dept., Jerusalem.
      Available in English, Hebrew and Arabic soundtracks.
      Shows the copper mines at Timna. Traces the stages of
      producing copper from mining to final export.

1759 DAY OF PRODUCTIVITY (YOM PIRYON)
      (n.d.) / 11 min / sound / 35 mm
      Ministry of Productivity. Location: Israel Film Studios,
      Herzliyah.
      Available in English, Hebrew and French soundtracks.
      Looks at improvement in early industrial productivity in
      Israel.

1760 DIAMOND IN THE ROUGH
      1964 / ? / sound / 16 mm
      United Carbon. Location: Israel Film Studios, Herzliyah.
      Profiles the petro-chemical industry in Israel.

1761 DREW PEARSON REPORTS ON SCIENCE IN ISRAEL
      1957 / 15 min / sound / b&w / 16 or 35 mm
      Orb Films. Released by Orb Films and United Israel Appeal.
      (NUC FiA 64-573) Credits: Producer - Baruch Dienar,
      Photographer - Rolf N. Kneller. Location: Abraham F. Rad
      Jewish Film Archive.
      Listed in some catalogs as: DREW PEARSON REPORTING ON
      SCIENCE IN ISRAEL. Looks at atomic science, medicine,
      and other fields of science in Israel. Discusses how
      Jewish refugees from Germany after WWII who worked on
      scientific projects in the U.S. are now working in
      Israel.

1762   FIFTEENTH CONGRESS OF INTERNATIONAL UNION OF LOCAL
        AUTHORITIES
        (n.d.) / 10 min / sound / b&w / 16 mm
        Producer unknown. Locations: Abraham F. Rad Jewish Film
        Archive / Jewish Agency Film Archive, Jerusalem.
            Shows the Congress of the International Union of Local
            Authorities held in Israel. Includes speeches by Mayor
            Brandt of Berlin, mayor of Tel Aviv, President Ben-Zvi,
            Moshe Shapira and Ben-Gurion.

1763   ISRAEL METAL INDUSTRIES
        1971 / 13 min / sound / color / 16 mm
        Producer unknown. Location: Abraham F. Rad Jewish Film
        Archive.
            Profiles the metal industry in Israel and shows the
            International Metal Industries Convention in Tel Aviv in
            1970.

1764   LIFE FROM THE DEAD SEA
        (n.d.) / 14 min / sound / color / 16 mm
        Producer unknown. Distributed by Alden Films.
            Shows exploitation of mineral resources from the Dead
            Sea, the lowest land area on earth. Describes how
            minerals are extracted and processed.

1765   ON NEW RAILS (AL PASSIM CHADASHIM)
        1966 / 11 min / sound / b&w / 16 or 35 mm
        Yosef Hirshnazon Film Producers and Distributors.
        Locations: Histadrut - General Federation of Jewish Labor,
        Tel Aviv / Prime Minister's Office, Information Dept.,
        Jerusalem.
            Available in English and Hebrew soundtracks. Profiles
            the railway system in Israel. Shows modernization of the
            old rails and wooden sleepers to accommodate passengers
            and cargo.

1766   PHOSPHATES
        1957 / 16 min / sound / b&w / 16 mm
        Phosphate Company. Location: Israel Film Studios,
        Herzliyah.
            Available in English and Hebrew soundtracks. Examines
            phosphate mining and processing in the Dead Sea region.

1767   PRINTING AND PUBLISHING
        1972 / 14 min / sound / color / 16 or 35 mm
        Producer unknown. Location: Abraham F. Rad Jewish Film
        Archive.
            Available in English and Hebrew soundtracks. Traces the
            history of printing in Israel from ancient manual pro-
            cesses to present industrialization of the industry.

1768   RHYTHM OF TOMORROW (BEKETZEV HAMACHAR)
        1965 / 12 min / sound / color / 16 or 35 mm

333

Producer unknown. Distributed by Alden Films. Location: Abraham F. Rad Jewish Film Archive.
Available in English, French and Hebrew soundtracks.
Looks at new technologically based professions such as aeronautics in Israel.

1769   THE RISING LINE
1965 / 12 min / sound / color / 16 or 35 mm
Yoram Gross Films. Locations: Histadrut - General Federation of Jewish Labor, Tel Aviv / Prime Minister's Office, Information Dept., Jerusalem.
Available with English sub-titles. Looks at industrial development in Israel from 1955 to 1965. Shows the number of workers has increased. Discusses growth in productivity and improvement in quality of products. Describes future developments in industry.

1770   SCIENCE IN ISRAEL
(n.d.) / 15 min / sound / b&w / 16 mm
Baruch Dienar, Orb Films. Locations: Jewish Agency Film Archive, Jerusalem / Keren Hayesod, Jerusalem.
Possibly a shorter version of no. 1761. Reporter Drew Pearson interviews Ben-Gurion and others concerning science in Israel. Includes scenes of Hadassah Hospital, Tel Hashomen, Agricultural Institute, Malaria Research Station, Weizmann Institute, and looks at researchers working on solar energy and desalinization projects.

1771   THE STORY OF PHOSPHATES
1957 / 16 min / sound / b&w / 16 mm
Phosphate Company. Location: Abraham F. Rad Jewish Film Archive.
Follows production of phosphates extracted from the Dead Sea. Explains how phosphates are used and their significance as one of Israel's resources.

1772   TEXTILE INDUSTRY
1972 / 13 min / sound / color / 16 or 35 mm
Producer unknown. Location: Abraham F. Rad Jewish Film Archive.
Available in English, Hebrew and French soundtracks.
Describes the textile industry in Israel today.

1773   TEXTILES
1964 / 27 min / sound / color / 16 mm
Institute of Productivity. Location: Israel Film Studios, Herzliyah.
Available in English, French and Spanish soundtracks.
General information film on the textile industry in Israel.

1774   A TIME TO BUILD
1972 / 14 min / sound / color / 16 mm

United Jewish Appeal. Distributed by Alden Films.
Locations: Abraham F. Rad Jewish Film Archive / Gratz
College.
Fund raising film. Shows problems faced by the Israeli
building industry. Describes need for housing, aggra-
vated by heavy immigration from the Soviet Union and
other countries. Explains how much money must be put
into the military leaving little for housing. Requests
funds for housing to assist current overcrowded conditions.

1775   WHAT ISRAEL MAKES (PRODUCES)
1957 / 9 min / sound / b&w / 35 mm
Koretsky. Copyright held by Masholav Ben-Dor. Location:
Israel Film Studios, Herzliyah.
Profiles the chemical fertilizer industry in Israel.

1776   A WORK DAY - INDUSTRY
1956-57 / 17 min / sound / b&w / 16 mm
Berkey Pathe Humphries. Credits: Writer-Narrator - Michael
Elkins, Editor - Nelly Bogor. Locations: Jewish Agency Film
Archive, Jerusalem / Keren Hayesod, Jerusalem.
General overview of Israel's light and heavy industry.
Describes research related to industry.

1777   ZIM
1963 / ? / sound / color / 35 mm
Israel Motion Picture Studios. Location: Israel Film
Studios, Herzliyah.
Available in English and Hebrew soundtracks. Profiles
Zim, the Israel National Shipping Company.

ISRAEL - MEDICINE

1778   ALIYAH
1973 / 10 min / sound / color / 16 mm
Marvin Stark Research Foundation in cooperation with Motion
Picture Section, University of California Medical Center.
(LC 73-700854)
Looks at an American mobile dental clinic in a converted
bus providing dental care to Arab and Jewish children in
Israel. Profiles the American students and faculty as
they offer dental services.

1779   BEYOND THE DIVIDING LINE (ME'EVER LAMECHITZA)
1968 / 12 min / sound / b&w / 16 or 35 mm
Berkey Pathe Humphries. Location: Prime Minister's Office,
Information Dept., Jerusalem.
Available in English and Hebrew soundtracks. Follows
effort to rehabilitate paralyzed children and help them
re-enter society.

1780 A BOOK, AN EGG AND A BELL
(n.d.) / 28 min / sound / color / 16 mm
Hazel Greenwald. Locations: Abraham F. Rad Jewish Film
Archive / Central Zionist Archive, Jerusalem.
Hadassah film focusing on the dedication ceremony for
the new Hadassah medical center. Includes profiles of a
doctor fighting cancer, a medical student researching
trachoma and a Hadassah member campaigning for funds.

1781 CANCER (SARTAN)
1966 / 29 min / sound / color / 16 mm
Y. Yeshuron. Location: Israel Film Studios, Herzliyah.
Available in English and Hebrew soundtracks. Intended
for Israeli audiences. Provides information concerning
anti-cancer campaigns in Israel.

1782 THE ESSENCE OF IT ALL
(n.d.) / 27 min / sound / 16 mm
Hadassah. Location: Central Zionist Archive, Jerusalem.
Shows patients and staff of the Hadassah Medical Center.
An information and promotional film.

1783 FIFTY MIRACLE MINUTES
(n.d.) / 28 min / sound / color / 16 mm
Hadassah. Location: Hadassah Film Library.
Documents the transfer of the Hadassah-Hebrew University
Medical Center to Ein Karem.

1784 FORTRESS OF HEALING
(n.d.) / 15 min / sound / color / 16 mm
Hadassah. Location: Central Zionist Archive, Jerusalem.
Shows the construction of the Hadassah Medical Center.

1785 48 HOURS A DAY
1949 / 30 min / sound / b&w / 16 mm
Hazel Greenwald for Hadassah. (NUC FiA 62-914) Locations:
Central Zionist Archive, Jerusalem / Library of Congress
(FBA 412) *
The Israeli War of Independence as seen through the eyes
of a Hadassah Emergency Hospital nurse in Jerusalem. War
footage and hospital scenes combine to show the fight for
survival of individuals and the birth of the Israeli
state.

1786 A GIFT OF LIFE
1974 / 15 min / sound / color / 16 mm
American Red Magen David for Israel. Distributed (free) by
Alden Films.
Looks at services of the American Red Magen David in providing health care and a new blood center for Israelis
struck by accident, illness or war.

1787 THE GREAT ROAD
1952 / 12 min / sound / color / 16 mm

Hadassah. Locations: Abraham F. Rad Jewish Film Archive /
Central Zionist Archive, Jerusalem.
Documents the 1952 groundbreaking ceremony for the
Hadassah University Medical School. Tours the
surrounding area.

1788   HADASSAH NEWSREEL SERIES
(n.d.) / see below / sound / b&w / 16 mm
Hadassah. Location: Abraham F. Rad Jewish Film Archive /
Central Zionist Archive, Jerusalem.
A series of short newsreels profiling Hadassah and
related topics. 1. Religious ceremonies marking the
opening of Hadassah-Hebrew University Medical Center (6
min). 2. Short profile of the Hadassah-Hebrew
University Medical Center in Ein Kerem, entitled VISION
INTO REALITY (5 min). 3. Vocational education and the
Hadassah Medical Center (10 min). 4. A program dealing
with youth Aliyah (18 min). 5. Youth Aliyah's 30th anniversary celebration (5 min).

1789   HANDS OF HEALING
1951 / 23 min / sound / color / 16 mm
Hadassah. Credits: Producer-Photographer - Hazel Greenwald.
Locations: Abraham F. Rad Jewish Film Archive / Central
Zionist Archive, Jerusalem / Library of Congress (FBA 482)
*
Hadassah information and fund raising film. An American
Jew tours Hadassah facilities. Compares care received by
Jews in the Yemen and in Israel. Looks at the Safed
Hospital, the medical center on Mt. Scopus and describes
Hadassah medical services.

1790   HANNAH MEANS GRACE
1958 / 28 min / sound / color / 16 mm
Hadassah. Credits: Writer - Jay E. Raeben, Director -
Michael Brandt, Producer - Hazel Greenwald. Location:
Library of Congress (FCA 2742) *
Shows how Hadassah helps disabled children in Israel.
Follows Hannah, a disabled girl, as she is convinced by
Hadassah to seek medical aid. She visits specialists in
Tel Aviv and receives surgery and rehabilitation therapy.
Basic information-promotional Hadassah film.

1791   HEALTH FOR VICTORY
1942 / 28 min / sound / b&w / 16 mm
Hadassah. Location: Central Zionist Archive, Jerusalem.
Shows the services and presence of Hadassah in Palestine
during WWII. Includes scenes of Mt. Scopus, Dr. Chaim
Yassky, Henrietta Szold, Dr. Yehuda Magnes, the Straus
Health Center and the Children's Village.

1792   THE HEART OF HADASSAH, RESEARCH
(c. 1963) / 18 min / sound / b&w / 16 mm

337

Hadassah. Locations: Abraham F. Rad Jewish Film Archive /
Central Zionist Archive, Jerusalem / Library of Congress
(FBA 495) *
Looks at advancements in medical research at Hadassah
facilities. Includes segments on early detection and
treatment of leprosy, the effect of lens color on balance
and mood, the relationship between stress and heart
attacks, and the effect of B12 deficiency on pregnant
women. More in-depth content than most Hadassah fund-
raising films, this shows the value of Hadassah research.

1793   IF I FORGET THEE
(n.d.) / 28 min / sound / color / 16 mm
Hadassah. Locations: Abraham F. Rad Jewish Film Archive /
Hadassah Film Library.
Listed in some catalogs as 17 minutes. Documents the
re-dedication ceremony of the Mt. Scopus Hospital. Tells
the history of the Hadassah Hospital on Mt. Scopus in
1940's Palestine, the moving of the facility after the
1948 War and the final reopening years later.

1794   MAN AND HEAT (HA'ADAM VEHACHOM)
1964 / 14 min / sound / color / 16 or 35 mm
Yoram Gross Films. Locations: Abraham F. Rad Jewish Film
Archive / Prime Minister's Office, Information Dept.,
Jerusalem.
Available in English and Hebrew soundtracks. Animated
film showing Israelis how to combat the hot climate.
Stresses the importance of correct' drinking habits and
rest in hot weather.

1795   OUT OF THE DARKNESS
(n.d.) / 30 min / sound / b&w / 16 mm
Hadassah. Location: Abraham F. Rad Jewish Film Archive.
Surveys various health services in Israel administered by
Hadassah.

1796   SHIELD OF LIFE
(n.d.) / 15 min / sound / color / 16 mm
Producer unknown. Distributed (free) by Alden Films.
Profiles activities and services of the Israel Red Cross.
Shows a beach rescue, a bloodmobile, helicopter lift of
an emergency patient, and a POW exchange.

1797   A SIMPLE CASE
1966 / 27 min / sound / color / 16 mm
Hadassah, the Women's Zionist Organization of America. Made
by Brighton Films. (NUC FiA 67-610)
Shows health care received by one patient and his family
at the Hadassah-Hebrew University Medical Center in
Jerusalem.

1798   SOME UNFINISHED BUSINESS
(n.d.) / 45 min / sound / color / 16 mm

Hadassah. Location: Abraham F. Rad Jewish Film Archive. Shows the construction, facilities and student body at the Hadassah-Hebrew University Medical Center at Ein Keren. Includes scenes of Dr. Albert Sabin and the Mt. Scopus Medical Center.

1799 THE TEAM
(n.d.) / 28 min / sound / color / 16 mm
American Red Magen David for Israel. Distributed (free) by Alden Films.
Available in English or Hebrew soundtracks. Profiles the work of the Magen David Adom, or Israel Red Cross. Follows ambulance driver Meir and his assistant Yaakov as they provide medical services during a busy day.

ISRAEL - PRIMARY AND VOCATIONAL EDUCATION

1800 AGAINST ILLITERACY
1966 / 16 min / sound / b&w / 16 or 35 mm
Producer unknown. Location: Abraham F. Rad Jewish Film Archive.
Available in English, French and Hebrew soundtracks. Profiles the efforts of a volunteer in the "Language Corps" to fight illiteracy in Israel.

1801 THE BEGINNING OF A STORY
(n.d.) / 27 min / sound / color / 16 mm
Producer unknown. Distributed by Alden Films.
Looks at Boy's Town in Jerusalem, a high school to train and integrate Sephardic or Oriental Jews from the Katamon district in Jerusalem. Shows 1200 boys from 34 countries receiving vocational training.

1802 BEKETZEV HAMACHAR (THE RHYTHM OF TOMORROW)
1965 / 13 min / sound / color / 16 or 35 mm
Israel Motion Picture Studios. Locations: Histadrut - General Federation of Jewish Labor, Tel Aviv / Prime Minister's Office, Information Dept., Jerusalem.
Available in English, Hebrew and French soundtracks. Profiles the Air Force Technical School. An award winning film showing flight training and related technical education.

1803 BIG LITTLE THINGS (YE'UL PSHUTO KEMASHMA'O)
(n.d.) / 11 min / sound / b&w / 16 mm
Israel Institute of Productivity, Tel Aviv.
Available in English, Hebrew, French and Spanish soundtracks. Looks at improved work methods and habits which have led to increased productivity in industry, agriculture, construction, services, and in offices. An instructional, training film showing how improved work methods save time, money and effort.

1804   BI'UR HABA'ARUT (FIGHTING ILLITERACY)
        1966 / 16 min / sound / b&w / 16 or 35 mm
        Israel Motion Picture Studios, Herzliyah. Locations:
        Histadrut - General Federal of Jewish Labor, Tel Aviv /
        Israel Film Studios, Herzliyah / Natan Gross, Givata'im /
        Prime Minister's Office, Information Dept., Jerusalem.
            Available in Hebrew with English or French sub-titles.
            Follows women soldiers who have volunteered to fight
            illiteracy in two settlements in Galilee. Shows Hebrew
            lessons being given to adults.

1805   EDUCATION IS FOR LIFE
        (n.d.) / 10 min / sound / color / 16 mm
        Producer unknown. Distributed by Alden Films. Location:
        Abraham F. Rad Jewish Film Archive.
            Looks at United Jewish Appeal supported educational
            programs in Israel. Stresses importance of education for
            the future of Israel.

1806   ELIAHU'S HOUSE
        1957 / 28 min / sound / b&w / 16 mm
        Women's American ORT. Made by Stephen L. Sharff
        Productions. Distributed by Alden Films. (LC 79-700013)
            Shows a family of Egyptian Jews who immigrate to Rome to
            start a new life. Profiles the work of ORT, the
            Organization for Rehabilitation through Training. Shows
            the father and son receiving vocational training in
            Israel.

1807   FIRST MILLION
        (n.d.) / 27 min / sound / color / 16 mm
        Producer unknown. Distributed by Alden Films.
            One million children, one third of Israel's population
            (at the time this film was produced), are school children.
            Shows how education and training will help them to
            realize their potential and fulfil the needs of Israel
            for skilled workers in the future. Shows how education
            and social agencies are working for this goal.

1808   GREEN HORIZONS
        1958 / 26 min / sound / color / 16 mm
        National Committee for Labor Israel. Made by Joel J. Breit.
        (NUC FiA 59-289)
            Looks at the youth of Israel and the importance of their
            education. Shows programs for vocational training
            offered by Histadrut - General Federation of Jewish Labor
            in Tel Aviv and Beersheba. Includes scenes of the Green
            Village, a working instructional farm, and university
            education. Stresses how young people make heroic sacri-
            fices for the defense and future of Israel.

1809   HERO
        (n.d.) / 30 min / sound / color / 16 mm

340

Harold Mayer. Distributed by Women's ORT, New York.
Profiles the work of the ORT Center in Netanya, Israel.
Looks at services and goals of the Organization for
Rehabilitation through Training.

1810   MOST PRECIOUS RESOURCE
       (n.d.) / 29 min / sound / color / 16 mm
       Producer unknown. Distributed by Alden Films. Location:
       Abraham F. Rad Jewish Film Archive.
       Shows the role of ORT, Organization for Rehabilitation
       through Training, in building Israel's industrial and
       skilled manpower resources. Show the Aron Syngalowski
       Center, the largest vocational high school in the Middle
       East. Includes scenes of training on a kibbutz, the John
       F. Kennedy Apprenticeship Center and the Maritime Center
       in Ashdod where Jewish seamen are trained.

1811   POWER OF A PEBBLE
       (n.d.) / 20 min / sound / color / 16 mm
       Hadassah. Location: Hadassah Film Library.
       Describes the history and services of the Hadassah Israel
       Education Service.

1812   THERE IS HOPE FOR THY CHILDREN
       (n.d.) / 13 min / sound / color / 16 mm
       Producer unknown. Location: Abraham F. Rad Jewish Film
       Archive.
       Profiles educational opportunities for children from
       around the world in Youth Aliyah villages in Israel.
       Shows educational programs for immigrant Jewish children
       from many countries.

1813   TO THE SEA (EL HAYAM)
       1962 / 14 min / sound / b&w / 16 or 35 mm
       Berkey Pathe Humphries. Locations: Abraham F. Rad Jewish
       Film Archive / Histadrut - General Federation of Jewish
       Labor, Tel Aviv / Ministry of Education and Culture,
       Jerusalem / Prime Minister's Office, Information Dept.,
       Jerusalem.
       Available in English, Hebrew and Arabic soundtracks.
       Outlines educational opportunities for sailors and seamen
       in Israel. Stresses importance of the sea to Israel and
       the need to maintain naval schools to train seamen.

1814   TRAINING FOR TOMORROW
       (n.d.) / 30 min / sound / color / 16 mm
       Youth Aliyah with the cooperation of the Information Dept.
       of the World Zionist Organization. Locations: Abraham F.
       Rad Jewish Film Archive / Jewish Agency Film Archive,
       Jerusalem.
       Available in English and Spanish soundtracks. Examines
       Youth Aliyah programs for Jewish youth immigrating to
       Israel. Describes educational programs available.

341

1815   YOSEF
1954 / 26 min / sound / color / 16 mm
Hadassah. (NUC FiA 65-290) Credits: Producer-Director
Stephen L. Sharff, Writer - Millard Lampell, Narrator -
William Redfield. Eastman color. Locations: Abraham F. Rad
Jewish Film Archive / Library of Congress (FCA 3827)
Follows a Jewish immigrant boy from Baghdad as he
receives technical training in a Youth Aliyah vocational
program. Shows a Youth Aliyah village and stresses the
importance of education and training of immigrants to
Israel's changing economy.

ISRAEL -   HIGHER EDUCATION

1816   CITADEL
1957 / 33 min / sound / b&w / 16 m
Producer unknown. Location: Abraham F. Rad Jewish Film
Archive.
Shows students at the Hebrew University in temporary
facilities after 1948 waiting for the new Givat Ram campus to be completed.

1817   A CITY CALLED TECHNION
1962 / 14 min / sound / color / 16 mm
American Technion Society. (NUC FiA 64-564) Credits:
Producer-Editor - Lazar Dunner, Director-Writer - David C.
Gross, Photographer - Edgar Hirshbein.
Profiles the Technion, Israel Institute of Technology.
Looks at academic progress, research projects and the
growth of the physical facilities of the Technion.

1818   A DAY AT THE COLLEGE (YOM BAMIDRASHA)
1966 / 9 min / sound / color / 16 mm
Midrashat No'am. Location: Israel Film Studios, Herzliyah.
Short information film on No'am College.

1819   DEDICATION OF NUCLEAR PHYSICS INSTITUTE AT THE
WEIZMANN INSTITUTE (CHANUKAT HAMACHON LEPHYSIKA
GARINIT)
May, 1958 / 3 min / sound / color / 16 mm
Berkey Pathe Humphries. Location: Weizmann Archives,
Rehovot.
Short film documenting the May 5, 1958 dedication of
the Nuclear Physics Institute at the Weizmann Institute
in Rehovot, Israel.

1820   DEDICATION OF THE HEBREW UNIVERSITY LIBRARY ON
MOUNT SCOPUS
(n.d.) / 10 min / sound / 35 mm
Producer unknown. Location: Abraham F. Rad Jewish Film
Archive.
Short newsreel film documenting the dedication of the
Hebrew University Library on Mount Scopus.

342

1821   DR. CHAIM WEIZMANN MEMORIAL DAY (AZKARAT
        DR. CHAIM WEIZMANN)
        Nov. 1962 / ? / sound / 16 mm
        Israel Motion Picture Studios, Herzliyah. Location:
        Weizmann Archives, Rehovot.
            Includes scenes of conferral of honorary fellowships at
            the Chaim Weizmann Memorial Assembly at the Weizmann
            Institute, Rehovot. Shows dedication of the Levine
            Institute of Applied Sciences and the laying of the cor-
            nerstone of the Feinberg Graduate School.

1822   DR. CHAIM WEIZMANN'S MEMORIAL DAY (YAD WEIZMANN)
        February 11, 1955 / ? / sound / b&w / 35 mm
        Berkey Pathe Humphries. Location: Weizmann Archives,
        Rehovot.
            Shows the ceremonies at Dr. Chaim Weizmann's Memorial Day
            at the Weizmann Institute in Rehovot.

1823   DR. FRIEDMAN
        1962 / 13 min / sound / 16 mm
        Producer unknown. Location: Israel Film Studios, Herzliyah.
            Short review of universities in Israel.

1824   EVENTS OF THE CHAIM WEIZMANN WEEK (ME'ORA'OT SHEKARU
        BEMESHECH SHAVU'A WEIZMANN BEYACHASSEI TZIBBUR)
        1962 / 40 min / sound / 16 mm
        Israel Motion Picture Studios, Herzliyah. Location:
        Weizmann Archives, Rehovot.
            Looks at events of Chaim Weizmann week at the Weizmann
            Institute in Rehovot.

1825   FOUR DAYS ON GIVAT RAM
        1968 / 20 min / sound / b&w / 16 mm
        Benhamin Korechi. Location: Jewish Agency Film Archive,
        Jerusalem.
            Looks at the celebration of Independence Day and the
            Tenth Anniversary of the Hebrew University. Uses flash-
            backs to the opening ceremony of April 24-27th, 1958.
            Tours the main faculties and buildings.

1826   THE HEBREW UNIVERSITY
        (n.d.) / 22 min / silent / b&w / 16 mm
        Producer unknown. Location: Abraham F. Rad Jewish Film
        Archive.
            Traces major events in the history of the Hebrew
            University including the opening ceremony of 1925, the
            opening of the Einstein Institute, the National Library,
            the British High Commissioner's visit to the Mt. Scopus
            campus, the UNSCOP members on Mt. Scopus and a 1934 con-
            cert in the university amphitheater.

1827   THE HIGHEST COMMANDMENT
        1961 / 14 min / sound / color / 16 mm

American Friends of the Hebrew University. Made by Lazar Dunner. (NUC FiA 64-868) Credits: Narrator - Melvyn Douglas. Location: Abraham F. Rad Jewish Film Archive. Stresses the importance of the Hebrew University to the development of Israel's economy and future. Shows the central campus at Givat Ram and agricultural campus at Rehovot. Shows students and faculty doing field work throughout Israel.

1828   ISRAEL NUCLEAR REVELATIONS (GILUI GARINI YISRA'ELI)
February 6, 1954 / ? / sound / b&w / 16 mm
CBS Television. Location: Weizmann Archive, Rehovot.
Profiles the Israel Nuclear Institute at the Weizmann Institute in Rehovot.

1829   MAE BOYAR SCHOOL OF HIGHER EDUCATION (MAE BOYAR BEIT SEFER GAVOHA)
1965 / 15 min / sound / 16 mm
Ministry of Education. Location: Israel Film Studios, Herzliya.
Shows the laying of the cornerstone ceremonies at the Mae Boyar School.

1830   THE OPENING OF THE HEBREW UNIVERSITY ON MOUNT SCOPUS
1925 / 10 min / silent / b&w / 16 mm
Producer unknown. Location: Jewish Agency Film Archive, Jerusalem.
Shows the opening ceremony of the Mount Scopus Hebrew University on April 1, 1925 with Rav Kook, Bialik and others. Also contains scenes of Jerusalem including the Jaffa Gate, souks, Western Wall, and Mount Scopus. Shows Lord Balfour and Chaim Weizmann arriving in Tel Aviv, and Dizengoff, Ussishkin, Mikve Israel and Rishon-le Zion.

1831   RECHOVOT
1962 / 28 min / sound / 16 mm
Y. Harel. Location: Israel Film Studios, Herzliyah.
Available in English and Hebrew soundtracks. Profiles the Weizmann Institute in Rechovot.

1832   STUDENT DAY
1970 / 19 min / sound / color / 16 mm
Micha Shagrir. Locations: Jewish Agency, Jerusalem / Micha Shagrir.
Shows the "Student Day" at the Hebrew University. Includes student pranks and expression of political opinions of students.

1833   TECHNION
1955 / 13 min / sound / color / 16 mm
Producer unknown. Location: Abraham F. Rad Jewish Film Archive.
Describes importance of the Haifa Technion to Israel's future.

1834   THESE NAMES LIVE ON
       1963 / 20 min / sound / color / 16 mm
       Canadian Friends of the Hebrew University, Montreal. Made
       by Crawley Films. (NUC FiA 64-483) Location: Abraham F.
       Rad Jewish Film Archive.
           Fund-raising film to encourage Canadian audiences to sup-
           port higher education in Israel. Discusses the loss of
           the Hebrew University Jerusalem campus after the Israeli
           War of Independence and the need to fund the relocated
           university. Describes work in desert cultivation, medi-
           cine, teaching and scientific research at the Hebrew
           University. Shows the current campus, classrooms and
           students.

1835   TIME, SPACE AND THE HEBREW UNIVERSITY
       (n.d.) / 83 min / sound / b&w / 16 mm
       Producer unknown. Location: Abraham F. Rad Jewish Film
       Archive.
           The Hebrew University is shown continuing in temporary
           quarters in Jerusalem while the new Givat Ram campus is
           under construction.

1836   TO BE A STUDENT IN ISRAEL
       (n.d.) / 17 min / sound / color / 16 mm
       Producer unknown. Distributed by Alden Films.
           Profiles higher education in Israel. Shows typical stu-
           dent activities, student life and educational oppor-
           tunities in Israel.

1837   UNIVERSITY
       1960 / 9 min / sound / color / 35 mm
       Koretzky. Israel Film Studios, Herzliyah.
           Follows activities over four days at the Hebrew
           University of Jerusalem on the Givat Ram campus.

ISRAEL - THE ARTS - GENERAL

1838   HOLLYWOOD IN JERUSALEM
       (c. 1975) / ? / sound / color / 16 mm
       Producer unknown.
           An International Year of the Child film about a Jewish
           and a Bedouin boy who meet in Jerusalem. A feature
           length film produced for children by a teenage film crew.

1839   ISRAEL: THE REALITY
       (c. 1974?) / 28 min / sound / b&w / 16 mm
       CBS. Distributed by the Anti-Defamation League of B'nai
       B'rith.
           Edited version of the 60 minute CBS television program
           based on the photographic exhibit at the Jewish Museum in
           New York. Contains the work of three photographers, a
           Christian doctor, a German Jewish immigrant to Palestine

345

in the 1930's and a Jewish LIFE magazine photographer,
documenting life in Israel. Photographer Cornell Capa is
the narrator.

1840   ISRAEL THEATRE IN 1967 (HATE'ATRON BE'YISRAEL BE 1967)
1967 / 26 min / sound / color / 16 or 35 mm
Roll Films, Ltd. Credits: Director - D. Perlov, Writer - M.
Natan. Location: Prime Minister's Office, Information
Dept., Jerusalem.
Available in English with French and German sub-titles.
Profiles the Israel Repertory Theatre in 1967. Shows
production of classical, modern, and children's plays, as
well as musicals and original compositions. Traces
theater in Israel and attitudes of different groups to
the theater. Shows scenes from "Dybbuk" with Hannah
Rovina.

1841   ISRAELI FASHIONS 1969
1969 / 7 min / sound / color / 16 mm
Producer unknown. Location: Abraham F. Rad Jewish Film
Archive.
Follows models throughout Israel as they are photographed
for a VOGUE magazine feature. Uses musical soundtrack.

1842   JEWELRY
1972 / 12 min / sound / color / 16 or 35 mm
Producer unknown. Distributed by Alden Films. Locations:
Abraham F. Rad Jewish Film Archive / Gratz College.
Available in English, Hebrew and German soundtracks.
Looks at modern jewelry production in Israel. Shows
jewelry being designed in studios and displayed in
markets in Jaffa. Listed in some catalogs as:
JEWELLERY.

1843   MOVEMENTS
1970 / 25 min / sound / color / 16 mm
Producer unknown. Distributed by Alden Films. Locations:
Abraham F. Rad Jewish Film Archive / Gratz College.
Listed in some catalogs as: MOVEMENT. Shows modern
trends in Israeli art, architecture, dance, theater and
cinema. Shows radical experimentation in various media.
For adult groups, contains some nude models.

1844   PART OF THEM IS ME
(n.d.) / 28 min / sound / color / 16 mm
Hadassah. Location: Hadassah Film Library.
Shows the Youth Aliyah Culture Mobile, a traveling, educational program of music, art and drama for children.

ISRAEL - TRADITIONAL AND FOLK DANCE

1845   (ARABIAN JEWISH DANCE)
June 1903 / 1 min / silent / b&w / 16 mm

346

Thomas Edison. Library of Congress Paper Print Collection.
Location: Library of Congress (FLA 4475) *
In fair condition considering age. Shows about half a
dozen men dancing in a circle to the music of a flute. A
line dance begins on the street while pedestrians look
on. For documentary purposes.

1846 ATL SKAPA TRADITION
1968 / 29 min / sound / b&w / 16 mm
Swedish Broadcasting Corp.
Looks at Jewish music and dance traditions from around
the world. Shows how the state of Israel is integrating
these traditions into a new national unity. Shows per-
formances of songs and dances from Morocco, Tunisia,
Kurdistan, and the Yemen. Includes new folk songs using
traditional themes and Biblical passages.

1847 DALIA DANCES
1957 / 7 min / sound / b&w / 16 mm
Lotan, Kibbutz Artzi. Israel Film Studios, Herzliyah.
Available in English and Hebrew soundtracks. Shows the
festival of dance at Kibbutz Dalia.

1848 DANCES OF THE YEMENITE JEWS
(n.d.) / 18 min / sound / color / 16 mm
Producer unknown. Location: Abraham F. Rad Jewish Film
Archive.
Available in English and Hebrew soundtracks. Shows
Yemenite Jews from three areas performing traditional
dances soon after their arrival in Israel. Also includes
dances performed by Jews from the Atlas Mountains and
from Libya.

1849 FOLK DANCES OF YEMENITE JEWS
1950 / 15 min / sound / color / 16 mm
G. Kadman and E. Gerson-Kiwi for Israelia Films, Herzliyah.
In Hebrew with English sub-titles. Documents a receiving
center for immigrants in 1950, where Jews from Southern
Arabia, Haban from the Hadhramaut, Yarim from the Yemen
and Damar of the Yemen arrive. Intended to preserve original dance movements, songs, music and costumes for
study. Shows immigrants playing on a copper plate to
produce a rhythm for one dance. Yemenite girls dance to
a drum built in the immigrant's camps after arrival.

1850 OMER DANCING IN RAMAT YOCHANAN
(n.d.) / 7 min / sound / color / 16 mm
Producer unknown. Location: Abraham F. Rad Jewish Film
Archive.
Shows traditional folk dancing which marks the agri-
cultural ceremony of the cutting of the "omer".

1851 A THOUSAND FLOWERS WILL SUDDENLY BLOOM
1970 / 25 min / sound / color / 16 mm

347

Yehuda Tarma, Israel. Distributed by Alden Films. (LC 72-702954)
Shows different Jewish ethnic groups in national costume performing traditional folk dances at the annual folk dance festival held in the natural amphitheater at Kibbutz Dahlia.

1852 TRADITIONAL FOLKDANCES OF VARIOUS COMMUNITIES IN ISRAEL - I
1951 / 15 min / sound / color / 16 mm
Gurit Kadman.
Documents folk dances of Jews from the Hadramaut, Southern Arabia, and of two groups of Yemeni Jews.

1853 TRADITIONAL FOLKDANCES OF VARIOUS COMMUNITIES IN ISRAEL - II
1954 / 15 min / sound / color / 16 mm
Gurit Kadman.
Documents folk dances of Jews from Kurdistan and the Hadramaut, Southern Arabia. Includes a wedding ceremony.

1854 TRADITIONAL FOLKDANCES OF VARIOUS COMMUNITIES IN ISRAEL - III
1962-63 / 9 min / sound / color / 16 mm
Gurit Kadman.
Documents folk dances of Jews from the Atlas Mountains in Moroccco, from Libya and Cochin, India.

1855 TRADITIONAL FOLKDANCES OF VARIOUS COMMUNITIES IN ISRAEL - IV
1963 / 9 min / sound / color / 16 mm
Gurit Kadman.
Documents folk dances of Arabs from Wadi Ara, a sword dance by Druze from Western Galilee, and shows mass dancing of 2600 dancers at the Folkdance Festival at Beit Berl in 1963.

1856 TRADITIONAL FOLKDANCES OF VARIOUS COMMUNITIES IN ISRAEL - V
1965 / 28 min / sound / color / 16 mm
Gurit Kadman.
Documents wedding ceremony of Jews from Djerba, Tunis, filmed in Ashkelon, and shows folkdances of Jews from Azerbaijan and Kurdistan. Filmed in Lachish.

1857 YEMENITE DANCERS
1973 / ? / sound / color / 16 mm
Sunni Bloland. Location: U. of California Extension Media Center.
Documents traditional costumes, jewelry and folkdances of Yemenite Jews as filmed at a wedding in Israel in 1951 and at a folk festival in 1973. Includes a description of why the group left Yemen and immigrated to Israel.

348

Discusses how Yemenite Jewish dance has been influenced
by African, Indian and Arab dances.

ISRAEL - MODERN DANCE AND BALLET

1858   BAL-ANAT (MIDDLE EAST)
        (c. 1977) / ? / sound / 16 mm
        Dance Film Association, New York. No other information
        available.

1859   BALLET TWO
        1964 / 15 min / sound / 16 mm
        Arik Dichner. Israel Film Studios, Herzliyah.
        Short film about ballet in Israel.

1860   BALLET THREE (A)
        1964 / 21 min / sound / 16 mm
        Arik Dichner. Israel Film Studios, Herzliyah.
        Shows ballet performance in Israel.

1861   BALLET THREE (B)
        1964 / 19 min / sound / 16 mm
        Arik Dichner. Israel Film Studios, Herzliyah.
        Shows continuation of ballet performance in no. 1860.

1862   BALLET THREE (C)
        1964 / 19 min / sound / 16 mm
        Arik Dichner. Israel Film Studios, Herzliyah.
        A continuation of no. 1861.

1863   BALLET FOUR
        1965 / 40 min / sound / 16 mm
        Arik Dichner. Israel Film Studios, Herzliyah.
        Another in the series of ballet performances filmed in
        Israel.

1864   DAUGHTERS OF GARDEN
        1964 / 22 min / sound / 16 mm
        Arik Dichner. Israel Film Studios, Herzliyah.
        Filmed ballet performance from Israel.

1865   MASECHOT (MASKS)
        1966 / 16 min / sound / 16 mm
        Arik Dichner. Israel Film Studios, Herzliyah.
        A filmed ballet performance.

1866   OHEL HAMAROT (TENT OF MIRRORS)
        1966 / 26 min / sound / 16 mm
        Arik Dichner. Israel Film Studios, Herzliyah.
        A filmed ballet performance.

1867   RODINA
        1965 / 20 min / sound / 16 mm

Arik Dichner.   Israel Film Studios, Herzliyah.
A filmed ballet performance.

1868   SARAGOSA
965 / 16 min / sound / 16 mm
Arik Dichner.   Israel Film Studios, Herzliyah.
A filmed dance performance.

1869   TEHILLIM (PSALMS)
1966 / 25 min / sound / 16 mm
Arik Dichner.   Israel Film Studios, Herzliyah.
A filmed ballet performance.

1870   TZAYADIM (HUNTERS)
1965 / 22 min / sound / 16 mm
Arik Dichner.   Israel Film Studios, Herzliyah.
A filmed dance performance.

ISRAEL - PAINTING

1871   AGAM AND ...
(c. 1979?) / 30 min / sound / color / 16 mm
Warren Forma.   Produced for the Guggenheim Museum.
Shows the work of the modern Israeli artist Yaakov Agam.

1872   AGAM - LIGHT AND FORM
(c. 1974?) / 30 min / sound / color / 16 mm and 3/4"
videocassette.   Frank McKevitt.   Distributed by Alden Films.
Location: Gratz College.
Documents the retrospective exhibition in the Tel Aviv
Museum in 1973 of Yaakov Agam's "Kinetic Art" works.
Shows the ultra avant garde pieces and explores their
structure.

1873   BEZALEL
1969 / 12 min / sound / color / 16 or 35 mm
Shesh Ushva Omanut Film Studios.   Locations: Jewish Agency,
Jerusalem /   Prime Minister's Office, Information Dept.,
Jerusalem.
Available in English, Hebrew, Spanish and French
soundtracks.   Traces the history of art in Israel.   Shows
Bezalel, the first school of art in Jerusalem, and its
founder, artist Boris Shatz.   Shows works of art and
artists from the period of the Bezalel school.

1874   CASTEL - THE QUEST FOR ETERNITY
(n.d.) / 22 min / sound / color / 16 mm
Producer unknown.   Distributed by Alden Films.   Location:
Gratz College.
Filmed essay on Moshe Castel and his art.   Shows transformation of earlier traditional subjects into more
ancient themes as more modern techniques are adopted by
the artist.

350

1875   ISRAEL FILM MAGAZINE 1971
        1971 / 15 min / sound / color / 16 mm
        World Zionist Organization. Location: Jewish Agency,
        Jerusalem.
            Profiles the painter Yossl Bergner and shows his studio.
            Also includes scenes of Oriental Jewish folk dances
            filmed at the Mt. Scopus Amphitheater, and the 1971 three
            day march to Jerusalem.

1876   MARC CHAGALL
        1964 / 25 min / sound / color / 16 mm
        McGraw-Hill. Credits: Narrator - Vincent Price.
        Locations: New York Public Donnell Film Library / U. of
        Michigan.
            Shows Marc Chagall's work, tracing pieces from inspira-
            tion to completion. Explores Chagall's work in painting,
            sculpture and stained glass.

1877   RUBIN - PALETTE OF A POET
        1968 / 13 min / sound / color / 16 mm
        Yona Zarecki. Israel Film Studios, Herzliyah. Distributed
        by Alden Films. Location: Gratz College.
            Listed in some catalogs as 20 minutes in length. Docu-
            ments the work of Re'uven Rubin, an Israeli painter who
            has depicted the changing face of Israel over a fifty
            year period.

1878   SHALOM OF SAFED - THE INNOCENT EYE OF A MAN OF GALILEE
        1967 / 28 min / sound / color / 16 mm
        Daniel Doron and Arnold Eagle. (LC 76-702864) Distributed
        by Alden Films. Location: New York Public Donnell Film
        Library.
            Profiles 70 year old Shalom of Safed, a self-taught
            painter who uses ancient and medieval Jewish art as a
            source of subjects and style for his work.

ISRAEL - MUSIC

1879   BANU AL KANFEI NESHARIM (WE CAME ON WINGS OF EAGLES)
        1956 / 4 min / sound / b&w / 16 or 35 mm
        Berkey Pathe Humphries. Locations: Jewish Agency, Jerusalem
        / Prime Minister's Office, Information Dept., Jerusalem.
            One of a series of instructional films for learning
            Hebrew songs. Sub-titled in Hebrew and English.

1880   DAVID MELECH YISRAEL (DAVID, KING OF ISRAEL)
        1956 / 4 min / sound / b&w / 16 or 35 mm
        Berkey Pathe Humphries. Locations: Jewish Agency, Jerusalem
        / Keren Hayesod, Jerusalem / Prime Minister's Office,
        Information Dept., Jerusalem.
            Another in the series of instructional films for learning
            Hebrew songs. Sub-titled in Hebrew and English.

351

1881 THE EARTH SINGS
1951 / 15 min / sound / b&w / 16 mm
Montage Films, Israel. Distributed by Brandon Films. (NUC
FiA 53-378) Credits: Producer - Jules L. Rips,
Director-Photographers - Sidney Lubow, Ed Spiegel, Louis
Stoumen, Arthur Swerdloff.
Contains seven Hebrew folk songs accompanied by scenes of
people and places in Israel.

1882 GOZALI RACHELI (MY LITTLE BIRD, RACHEL)
1956 / 5 min / sound / b&w / 16 or 35 mm
Berkey Pathe Humphries. Locations: Jewish Agency, Jerusalem
/ Prime Minister's Office, Information Dept., Jerusalem.
One of a series of instructional films for learning
Hebrew songs. Sub-titles in Hebrew and English.

1883 GREEN VOICES
(n.d.) / 22 min / sound / color / 16 mm
Producer unknown. Location: Abraham F. Rad Jewish Film
Archive.
Singers from kibbutzim perform musical selections against
a backdrop of kibbutz life.

1884 HARVEST SONG
(n.d.) / ? / sound / 35 mm
Keren Hayesod. Israel Film Studios, Herzliyah.
Available in English, Hebrew, French and Spanish
soundtracks. Contains songs from Israel.

1885 HAZORIM BEDIMA (THOSE WHO SOW IN TEARS)
1956 / 5 min / sound / b&w / 16 or 35 mm
Berkey Pathe Humphries. Locations: Jewish Agency, Jerusalem
/ Prime Minister's Office, Information Dept., Jerusalem.
Another in the series of instructional films for learning
Hebrew songs. Sub-titled in English and Hebrew.

1886 HEBREW SONGS
1957 / ? / sound / b&w / 35 mm
Israel Film Studios, Herzliyah.
Available in English and Hebrew soundtracks. Contains a
performance of a program of Hebrew songs.

1887 ISRAEL IN SONG AND DANCE (YISRA'EL BESHIR UVMACHOL)
(n.d.) / 18 min / sound / color / 16 or 35 mm
Producer unknown. Location: Prime Minister's Office,
Information Dept., Jerusalem.
Looks at people and places in Israel through song and
dance.

1888 MELODIES OF ACRE (MANGINOT ACCO)
1963 / 17 min / sound / b&w / 16 mm
W. Van Leer. Israel Motion Picture Studios, Herzliyah.
Locations: Abraham F. Rad Jewish Film Archive / Israel Film

Archive, Haifa / Israel Film Studios, Herzliyah / Prime
Minister's Office, Information Dept., Jerusalem.
Available in English, Hebrew and Arabic soundtracks.
Presents popular Arab folk songs played on the lute and
mandolin in the city of Acre at the Tzavta Club.

1889   MUSICAL INSTRUMENTS OUT OF PLANTS
1964 / 15 min / sound / color / 16 mm
Producer unknown. Location: Abraham F. Rad Jewish Film
Archive.
Children at Kibbutz Maoz Haim make musical instruments
out of plants grown in the area and perform a concert on
these instruments.

1890   SHIR HABOTZRIM (SONG OF THE GRAPE PICKERS)
1956 / 6 min / sound / b&w / 16 or 35 mm
Berkey Pathe Humphries. Locations: Jewish Agency, Jerusalem
/ Prime Minister's Office, Information Dept., Jerusalem.
Another in the series of instructional films for learning
Hebrew songs. Sub-titled in Hebrew and English.

1891   SONGS OF ISRAEL
1952-53 / 8 min / sound / b&w / 16 mm
Israel Motion Picture Studios, Herzliyah. Credits: Director
- Michael Elkins. Locations: Abraham F. Rad Jewish Film
Archive / Keren Hayesod, Jerusalem.
A performance of songs of Israel.

1892   USHE 'AVTEM MAYIM BESASSON (THOU SHALT DRAW WATER IN JOY)
1956 / 5 min / sound / b&w / 16 or 35 mm
Berkey Pathe Humphries. Locations: Jewish Agency, Jerusalem
/ Prime Minister's Office, Information Dept., Jerusalem.
Another in the series of instructional films for learning
Hebrew songs. Sub-titled in English and Hebrew.

ISRAEL - TRADITIONAL ARTS AND CRAFTS

1893   ARTS AND CRAFTS
1970 / 13 min / sound / color / 16 or 35 mm
Producer unknown. Location: Abraham F. Rad Jewish Film
Archive.
Available in English and Hebrew soundtracks. Shows tra-
ditional arts and crafts of various ethnic communities in
Israel. Discusses the adaptation of the machine in these
traditional crafts.

1894   POTTERS OF HEBRON
1975 / 55 min / sound / color / 16 mm
Robert Haber. Distributed by Phoenix Films. Locations:
New York Public Donnell Film Library / U. of Illinois.
Intended for high school to adult audiences. Documents a
family of Arab potters in Hebron, southeast of Jerusalem.

Shows the five day process of making zirs, or traditional earthenware water jars. Discusses the possibility that this is a dying art as a result of mechanized pottery production.

JORDAN - ARCHEOLOGY

1895 ANCIENT PETRA
1953 / 10 min / sound / color / 16 mm
Encyclopaedia Britannica Films. (NUC Fi 54-82) Credits:
Producers - E.S. Keller, F.W. Keller. Kodachrome.
Locations: Library of Congress (FAA 3260) / Syracuse U. / U.
of Nebraska. *
      Tours the ancient city of Petra. Originally the site of
      a spring in a hidden valley used by the Edomites and
      Nabateans, the area was later used as a warehouse and
      way-station for the caravan trade. Shows Egyptian and
      Greek influence in the buildings carved out of solid pink
      sandstone. Intended for junior high school to adult
      audiences.

1896 JORDAN AND THE WONDERS OF PETRA
1972 / 16 min / sound / color / 16 mm
BFA Educational Media.
      Intended for elementary to high school audiences.
      Profiles archeological sites in Jordan and the ancient
      ruined city of Petra. Shows Greek and Egyptian
      influence in buildings carved out of mountains of red
      sandstone. Contrasts these remains with modern Jordan.

1897 JORDAN: CROSSROADS OF CIVILIZATION
1963 / 20 min / sound / color / 16 mm
American Friends of the Middle East. Location: Permanent
Mission of Jordan to the United Nations.
      Outlines the history of Jordan. Examines several
      archeological sites.

JORDAN - HISTORY

1898 HUSSEIN, KING OF JORDAN, SIGNS PEACE PACT WITH EGYPT
June, 1967 / 1:20 min / sound / b&w / 35 mm
Universal News. (Universal News, Vol. 40, issue 46, story
1) Location: National Archives (40-46-1)
      Short newsreel documenting the signing of a Jordanian-
      Egyptian peace pact.

1899 JORDAN CRISIS - MARTIAL LAW
April, 1957 / 1 min / sound / b&w / 35 mm
Universal News. Location: National Archives (30-35-1)
      Brief newsreel. Documents the imposition of martial law
      in Jordan in 1957.

1900   JORDAN - KING HUSSEIN TIGHTENS GRIP ON NATION
        April, 1957 / 1 min / sound / b&w / 35 mm
        Universal News. Location: National Archives (30-36-1)
        Brief newsreel documenting events of 1957 in Jordan.

1901   KING HUSSEIN OF JORDAN WELCOMED BY PRESIDENT NASSER
        1957 / 7 min / sound / b&w / 35 mm
        Universal News. Location: National Archives (7609x12,11)
        Newsreel footage. Shows meeting between King Hussein of
        Jordan and Gamal Abdul Nasser of Egypt.

1902   KING HUSSEIN OF JORDAN WELCOMES VISITING KING FAISEL
        1958 / 1 min / sound / b&w / 35 mm
        Universal News. Location: National Archives (31-56-1)
        Brief newsreel showing King Hussein of Jordan meeting
        with King Faisel.

1903   KING HUSSEIN WELCOMES KING SAUD
        1957 / 3 min / sound / b&w / 35 mm
        Universal News. Location: National Archives (7646x9)
        Brief newsreel showing the meeting between King Hussein
        and King Saud of Saudi Arabia.

1904   KING HUSSEIN'S SPEECH AT THE UN
        1960 / 15 min / sound / b&w / 16 mm
        Producer unknown. Location: Abraham F. Rad Jewish Film
        Archive.
        Contains the 1960 speech of King Hussein at the United
        Nations General Assembly.

1905   THE SCORCHED EARTH
        (n.d.) / 18 min / sound / b&w / 16 mm
        Producer unknown. Location: Embassy of Jordan. No other
        information available.

1906   YOUNG KING OF JORDAN CROWNED
        May, 1953 / 2 min / sound / b&w / 35 mm
        Universal News. Location: National Archives (26-463-5)
        Brief newsreel. Shows coronation ceremonies of King
        Hussein I of Jordan.

JORDAN - INTERVIEWS

1907   HIS MAJESTY, HUSSEIN I, KING OF JORDAN
        April 13, 1969 / 28 min / sound / b&w / 16 mm
        NBC Television. (Meet the Press, television series)
        Location: Library of Congress (FRA 5055-56) No other infor-
        mation available.

1908   HUSSEIN I
        April 19, 1964 / 28 min / sound / b&w / 16 mm
        NBC Television. (Meet the Press, television series)

356

Location: Library of Congress (FRA 7505-07)
The oldest of several Meet the Press interviews between
King Hussein of Jordan and a panel of American journalists. Covers current topics of interest to the television audience.

1909   KING HUSSEIN OF JORDAN
May 4, 1975 / 30 min / sound / color / 3/4" videocassette
NBC Television. (Meet the Press, television series)
Credits: Moderator - Lawrence Spivak, Journalists - Richard
Valeriani, Rowland Evans, Barry Schweid, Stanley Karnow.
Location: Library of Congress (VBA 2008)   *
Taped on the 22nd anniversary of King Hussein's reign in
Jordan. Good assessment of Jordanian policy in 1975.
Topics covered include the effect of the Vietnam War on
the Middle East, U.S.-Israeli relations, the Palestinian
question, the P.L.O. and the possibility of a Palestinian
state. Also covers the question of the territory cap-
tured by Israel in 1967, the influence of the Soviet
Union on the Middle East, the partition of Jerusalem, and
Jordan's role in a negotiated Middle East peace. A good
interview and presentation of the Arab point of view.

1910   SWORD OR PLOWSHARE: A CONVERSATION WITH HIS MAJESTY
KING HUSSEIN
1969 / 30 min / sound / color / 16 mm
CBS News. (CBS News Religious Special, television series)
Credits: Writer-Producer - Pamela Ilott. Location: Library
of Congress (FBB 2496)   *
Listed in some catalogs as: CONVERSATION WITH
KING HUSSEIN. This is part 1 of a CBS telecast. Part
2 is an interview with Golda Meir of Israel. Slow moving
interview with King Hussein taped in Amman, Jordan.
Outlines possibility of peace in the Middle East.
Hussein discusses the Palestinian and Jordanian peoples,
his place as a leader of these groups, the history of
Arab nationalism after WWI, the period of western colonization of the Middle East, and the beginning of Zionism.
Describes unresolved tensions from the 1967 War, and how
2/3 of Jordan's population is now Palestinian refugees.
Gives reasons why Christian and Muslim Arabs cannot give
up their rights to Jerusalem.

JORDAN   -   TRAVELOGS AND REGIONAL STUDIES

1911   AHLAN WA SAHLAN (WELCOME)
(c. 1960?) / 20 min / sound / color / 16 mm
Permanent Mission of Jordan to the United Nations.
Distributed by the American Friends of the Middle East.
General film showing the tourist attractions of Jordan.
Describes accommodations for tourists.

1912   ARABIAN CHILDREN
        1954 / 15 min / sound / color / 16 mm
        Encyclopaedia Britannica Films. Distributed by Iowa Films.
        (Arab Experience series) (NUC Fi 55-92) Credits: Producer
        - Donald G. Hoffman, Educational Collaborator - Clarence W.
        Sorensen. Locations: Library of Congress (FBA 68) /
        Syracuse U. / U. of Illinois / U. of Iowa / U. of Nebraska.
        Intended for elementary to junior high school audiences.
        Describes life of a farming family in Saahab, Jordan.
        Focuses on the events of a typical day and on the
        children of the family. Shows them helping with sheep
        herds, working in the fields and in the house, going to
        school and visiting friends in their village.

1913   THE BADIA AWAKENS
        1976 / 20 min / sound / color / 16 mm
        Vision Habitat. Distributed by United Nations Films.
        Available in English, Arabic, French and Spanish
        soundtracks. Focuses on the population of Amman,
        Jordan, swollen in 30 years by Palestinian refugees from
        a city of 20,000 to 750,000. Shows how new settlements
        outside Amman have been constructed to relieve housing
        pressure in the city. Looks at a relocated truck driver
        with a new home. Describes access to medical facilities
        and social services. Looks briefly at industry and land
        reclamation in Jordan.

1914   JORDAN
        1976 / 19 min / sound / color / 16 mm
        Jordanian Ministry of Culture and Information. Distributed
        by Jordan Information Bureau, and by Middle East Institute.
        Made at Universal Studios.
        General travelog of Jordan. Includes scenes of Amman,
        the capital, transportation, shipping, industry, agri-
        culture in the Jordan Valley, education, crafts, telecom-
        munications and historic and archeological sites such as
        Petra and Jerash. Includes an interview with King
        Hussein. Pleasant introduction to Jordan stressing its
        modernity and acheivements.

1915   JORDAN
        1977 / 30 min / sound / color / 16 mm
        Embassy of Jordan.
        Contrasts ancient civilization and sites in Jordan with
        modern Amman. Describes advances in industry, education,
        and social programs. Looks at the position of Jordan in
        world politics.

1916   THE JORDAN IMAGE
        (n.d.) / 22 min / sound / color / 16 mm
        Producer unknown. Locations: Arab Information Center - San
        Francisco / Jordan Information Bureau.
        General travelog. Contrasts ancient sites in Jordan to
        modern life.

1917   JORDAN - LAND OF LAWRENCE, PART 1
        (n.d.) / ? / sound / color / 16 mm
        Producer unknown.
        General travelog of Jordan. Includes scenes of a
        muezzin's call to prayer in the morning, Amman, the capi-
        tal, and Biblical sites in Jordan.

1918   JORDAN - LAND OF LAWRENCE, PART 2
        (n.d.) / ? / sound / color / 16 mm
        Producer unknown.
        Follows the routes used by T.E. Lawrence (Lawrence of
        Arabia) in Jordan during the WWI campaign against the
        Turks. Includes a profile on the Jordanian royal family.

1919   JORDAN: LAND OF OPPORTUNITY
        (n.d.) / 15 min / sound / color / 16 mm
        Producer unknown. Location: Jordan Information Bureau.
        Looks at business opportunities in Jordan.

1920   JORDAN OF TODAY
        (n.d.) / 15 min / sound / color / 16 mm
        Producer unknown. Location: Arab Information Center - San
        Francisco.
        General travelog of Jordan showing modern cities and
        ancient archeological sites.

1921   THIRSTY LAND
        1968 / 29 min / sound / color / 16 mm
        Food and Agriculture Organization of the United Nations.
        Distributed by United Nations Films.
        Profiles U.N. projects in Jordan. Looks at drilling
        wells for water in desert areas, settlement of Howaytat
        Bedouins at El Jafr, reconstruction of the Hejaz railway,
        and efforts to stop soil erosion and improve water
        resource management with tree planting projects.

1922   WELCOME TO JORDAN
        (n.d.) / 30 min / sound / color / 16 mm
        Embassy of Jordan.
        Listed in some sources as 20 minutes in length. Presents
        religious and historical sites in Jordan prior to the
        1967 War. Includes scenes of Jerusalem, Bethlehem,
        Jerash, Petra, Qumran and Aqaba. Shows Amman, the capi-
        tal of Jordan, and King Hussein's famous Arabian hor-
        seguard and desert patrols.

JORDAN - THE JORDAN RIVER AND JORDAN RIVER VALLEY

1923   BRIDGE ON THE JORDAN
        (n.d.) / ? / sound / 16 mm
        Formerly distributed by the Embassy of Libya. No other
        information available.

                                359

1924   THE JORDAN RIVER
        1970 / 14 min / sound / color / 16 or 35 mm
        Producer unknown. Location: Abraham F. Rad Jewish Film
        Archive.
            Available in English, French and Hebrew soundtracks.
            Intended for Jewish audiences. Looks at the religious,
            historical and economic importance of the Jordan River
            throughout history.

1925   THE JORDAN RIVER SYSTEM
        1969 / 4 min / silent / color / super 8 mm film loop in
        cartridge. (Living in Israel series) (LC 74-703711)
            Brief silent film. Examines the Israeli water systems
            which connect with the Jordan River.

1926   JORDAN VALLEY
        1950 / 19 min / sound / b&w / 16 mm
        Associated British Pathe, London. Distributed by
        International Film Bureau. (NUC FiA 56-743)
            Intended for junior high school to adult audiences. Tra-
            ces the River Jordan from its origins 35 miles from the
            Mediterranean to its end in the Dead Sea. Includes sce-
            nes of points on the river such as Mt. Hermon, Dan,
            Galilee and Capernaum. Profiles the people of Jordan who
            live in the Jordan River Valley.

1927   (TOURISTS TAKING WATER FROM THE RIVER JORDAN)
        June 1903 / 37 seconds / silent / b&w / 16 mm
        Thomas Edison. Library of Congress Paper Print Collection.
        Location: Library of Congress (FLA 3453) *
            A large party of tourists can be seen on the banks of the
            Jordan River. Two European women in a boat tied to the
            bank are handing up bottles of water dipped from the
            river. One of the short films made by A.C. Abadie for
            Thomas Edison. In fair to poor condition considering
            age. For historic and documentary purposes.

KUWAIT

KUWAIT - SOCIOLOGY AND ETHNOLOGY

1928 FALCONRY
(n.d.) / 20 min / sound / color / 16 mm
Embassy of Kuwait.
Shows the traditional sport of falconry still practised
in Kuwait today. Looks at falcons and the way in which
they are used to kill game birds.

1929 SADDLING CAMELS AMONG BEDOUINS
1956 / 4 min / silent / b&w / 16 mm
Encyclopaedia Cinematographica. Distributed by Pennsylvania
State University.
Shows Arab Bedouins of Kuwait saddling a bactrian camel
and a dromedary, or two and one-humped camels.

1930 SHIP BUILDING (ARABS, ARABIA, AL-KUWAIT)
1956, released 1959 / 5 min / silent / b&w / 16 mm
Encyclopaedia Cinematographica. Distributed by Pennsylvania
State University. (Ency. Cinematographica, no. E 228)
Another in the series of silent ethnographic films
depicting a single action. Shows traditional ship
building methods used in Kuwait.

1931 UTILIZATION OF THE SHEEP AMONG BEDOUINS (ARABIA,
AL-KUWAIT)
1956, released 1959 / 7 min / silent / b&w / 16 mm
Encyclopaedia Cinematographica. Distributed by Pennsylvania
State University. (Ency. Cinematographica, no. E 226)
Another in the series of silent ethnographic films
focusing on a single activity. Looks at the ways in
which sheep are used by Bedouins in Kuwait.

KUWAIT - TRAVELOGS AND REGIONAL STUDIES

1932 CITY PLANNING
(n.d.) / 20 min / sound / color / 16 mm
Embassy of Kuwait.
Shows development of Kuwait from a desert area, formerly
a British protectorate, to a modern state. Shows urban
development in the Gulf country.

1933 CLOSE-UP ON KUWAIT
(n.d.) / 25 min / sound / color / 16 mm
Producer unknown. Distributed by Middle East Institute.
General introduction to Kuwait. Profiles advances in

experimental agriculture, free education and medical services. Shows increased oil production will finance these
social programs. MEI print is experiencing some wear.

1934   A DAY IN KUWAIT
       1978 / 30 min / sound / color / 16 mm
       Embassy of Kuwait.
       General introduction to Kuwait.

1935   FOCUS ON KUWAIT
       1953 / 10 min / sound / b&w / 16 mm
       Gaumont-British Picture Corp., London.   Released in the U.S.
       by British Information Services, 1955.   (NUC FiA 56-1017)
       Credits: Director - A.S. Graham, Writer-Editor - Lewis
       Linzee, Photographers - Peter Sargent, John Page, Martyn
       Wilson.
       British production.   Shows contrasts between ancient and
       modern Kuwait.   Profiles traditional life and customs.
       Describes current development and urbanization financed
       by newly acquired oil resources.

1936   IMAGES OF KUWAIT
       (c. 1977?) / 15 min / sound / b&w / 16 mm
       Akkad International.   Ministry of Guidance of Kuwait.
       Distributed by the Embassy of Kuwait.
       General introduction to Kuwait shown in part through
       paintings by Kuwaiti artists.   Portrays Kuwait as a
       progressive, modern state with well developed social
       welfare programs.   Plays down the role of traditional
       society and customs.

1937   KUWAIT: PAST AND PRESENT
       (n.d.) / 20 min / sound / b&w / 16 mm
       Embassy of Kuwait.
       General introduction showing the contrast between modern
       and traditional aspects of life in Kuwait.

1938   KUWAIT TODAY
       (n.d.) / 30 min / sound / color / 16 mm
       Embassy of Kuwait.   Also distributed by the League of Arab
       States.
       Profiles the transition of Kuwait from a traditional
       desert culture to a modern welfare state within a few
       decades.   Discusses changes brought about by the
       exploitation of oil including free education, medical
       care and housing for Kuwaitis.

1939   LOOK AT LIFE: PIPE-LINE OF PLENTY
       (n.d.) / 15 min / sound / color / 16 mm
       Embassy of Kuwait.   Also distributed by the League of Arab
       States.
       General promotional film dealing with Kuwait.   Shows the
       life style of Kuwaitis financed by oil revenues includes

362

free education, medical care and housing and no taxes. Stresses the area is a "consumer's ultimate dream".

1940   NEW DAWN
(n.d.) / 15 min / sound / b&w / 16 mm
Embassy of Kuwait. No other information available.

1941   NEW GENERATION
(n.d.) / 20 min / sound / 16 mm
Embassy of Kuwait.
Shows the effect and benefits of oil revenues for the new generation of Kuwaitis. Shows opportunities through free education, medical attention and housing for citizens of this formerly quiet, desert region.

1942   PUBLIC GARDENS
(n.d.) / 12 min / sound / b&w / 16 mm
Embassy of Kuwait. No other information available.

1943   SHUAIBAH INDUSTRIAL AREA
(n.d.) / 30 min / sound / color / 16 mm
Embassy of Kuwait.
Shows development of the Shuaibah Industrial Area of Kuwait. Describes its relationship to oil exploitation.

KUWAIT - OIL

1944   AHMADI CARGO
1963 / 17 min / sound / color / 16 mm
Embassy of Kuwait.
Profiles the oil industry in Kuwait. Shows drilling, production, storage and handling of oil.

1945   MADE-MADE ISLAND
(n.d.) / 32 min / sound / color / 16 mm
Embassy of Kuwait.
Shows shipments of oil departing from Mina Al Ahmadi in Kuwait.

1946   MIRROR OF OIL
(n.d.) / 20 min / sound / color / 16 mm
Producer unknown. Distributed by the Arab Information Office, Washington.
Profiles the oil industry in Kuwait.

1947   THEY CHOSE THE SEA
(c. 1970) / 25 min / sound / color / 16 mm
Jack Howells Productions Ltd. Distributed by British Petroleum Company.
A promotional film for British Petroleum. Looks at the life of seamen who operate oil tankers. Follows the tanker "British Queen" from Finnart, Scotland to Kuwait

363

and back through the Suez Canal. Shows the seamen on
shore in Kuwait. Intended to recruit young seamen for
British Petroleum ships.

KUWAIT - AGRICULTURE

1948   AGRICULTURE
       (n.d.) / 20 min / sound / color / 16 mm
       Embassy of Kuwait.
       General film showing traditional agriculture and animal
       husbandry in Kuwait. Looks at sheep and goat herds and
       production of maize, wheats, dates and vegetables.

1949   TREE IN THE DESERT
       (n.d.) / 20 min / sound / color / 16 mm
       Producer unknown. Distributed by the Arab Information
       Office, Washington.
       General profile of agriculture in Kuwait.

KUWAIT - EDUCATION, MEDICINE

1950   ASPECTS OF EDUCATION
       (n.d.) / 20 min / sound / b&w / 16 mm
       Embassy of Kuwait.
       General survey of educational programs and opportunities
       in Kuwait.

1951   EDUCATION IN KUWAIT
       (n.d.) / 20 min / sound / color / 16 mm
       Embassy of Kuwait.
       Shows various levels of education available in Kuwait.
       Profiles the free educational system.

1952   A GIRL'S SECONDARY SCHOOL
       (n.d.) / 10 min / sound / b&w / 16 mm
       Embassy of Kuwait.
       Profiles women's educational opportunities in Kuwait.
       Shows a girl's secondary school and describes oppor-
       tunities for free education for girls.

1953   KINDERGARTENS
       (n.d.) / 10 min / sound / b&w / 16 mm
       Embassy of Kuwait.
       Looks at pre-school education and child care facilities
       available in Kuwait.

1954   MEDICAL SERVICES IN KUWAIT
       (n.d.) / 12 min / sound / b&w / 16 mm
       Embassy of Kuwait.
       Profiles medical services available free to citizens of
       Kuwait. Explains how programs are financed by oil reve-
       nues.

364

1955   PUBLIC HEALTH
       (n.d.) / 10 min / sound / b&w / 16 mm
       Embassy of Kuwait.
       Looks at the advancements in health care available in
       Kuwait compared to services of ten years earlier (date of
       this film unknown). Explains the role of the Public
       Health facilities and examines health care problems in
       Kuwait. Describes free medical services.

1956   STAGE OF HOPE
       (n.d.) / 15 min / sound / color / 16 mm
       Embassy of Kuwait.
       Uses an Arabic music soundtrack. Looks at vocational and
       recreational training of the handicapped in Kuwait.

1957   THIS IS KUWAIT: EDUCATION, PART 1
       (n.d.) / 30 min / sound / color / 16 mm
       Embassy of Kuwait.
       General introduction to educational programs in Kuwait.

LEBANON - HISTORY

1958 ANCIENT PHOENICIA AND HER CONTRIBUTIONS
1968 / 14 min / sound / color / 16 mm
Atlantis Productions. J. Michael Hagopian. (NUC FiA
68-652) Locations: Library of Congress (FBA 9489) /
Syracuse U. / U. of Illinois / U. of Nebraska. *
Profiles contributions of the ancient Phoenicians, especially in navigation and trade. Gives legend of
Phoenicians coming from mythical Atlantis. Tours ancient
cities of Tyre, Sidon, and Baalbek. Shows terracing of
mountains for agriculture but stresses sea-going nature
of Phoenicians who spread the alphabet throughout the
ancient world. Contains some historic inaccuracies.
Stresses Phoenician rather than Arab background of modern
Lebanese. For junior-senior high school audiences. A
confused production.

1959 ITALY, LEBANON AND SOUTH AFRICA
July 9, 1976 / 60 min / sound / color / 3/4" videocassette
CBS News. (CBS News Special Report, television series)
Credits: Correspondent - Charles Collingwood, Executive
Producer - Leslie Midgley, Producers - Bernard Birnbaum, Hal
Haley, Director - Ken Sable. Location: Library of Congress
(VBA 1285) *
CBS News presentation dealing with troubled areas.
Spends about 15 minutes on the Lebanese civil war. Shows
breakdown between Lebanese Christians and Muslims due to
the politicization of Lebanese over the mass of
Palestinian refugees residing in Lebanon. Looks at
fighting, attempts to negotiate cease-fires, and the role
of the Syrian peace-keeping forces in Lebanon. Shows
limitation of the U.S. in negotiating a settlement due to
complexity of problems involved. The Palestinian problem
is shown to be the root of the Lebanese civil war but
this programs offers little in the way of solutions for
either. Confused presentation of a complex subject.
Does little to help the viewer understand the issues
involved.

1960 SUMMER INCIDENT
1959 / 27 min / sound / color / 16 mm
U.S. Dept. of the Navy. (NUC FiE 60-307) Location: U.S.
National Audiovisual Center. (Navy order no. MN 8982)
Looks at the role of the Navy and Marine Corps. in exe-
cuting U.S. foreign policy during the Lebanese crisis in
the late 1950's. Describes U.S. capabilities in crisis
and small war situations.

1961   THE TWENTY THIRD CEASE-FIRE
       1976 / 52 min / sound / color / 16 mm
       Anne Papillaut, Jean Francois Dars, Marc Kravetz and Mare
       Mourani. Distributed by Icarus Films.
       Attempts to represent the Lebanese civil war not as a
       religious conflict but as a class struggle between the
       wealthy minority and impoverished majority. Traces one
       cease fire in 1976. Includes interviews with right-wing
       Christian militiamen, the late Kamal Jumblat and striking
       fishermen in Saida. Presents a montage of destruction,
       refugees and war.

LEBANON - SOCIOLOGY AND ETHNOLOGY

1962   ARAB VILLAGE
       1957 / 11 min / sound / b&w / 16 mm
       Larry Dawson Productions. Released by Young America Films,
       Inc. New York. Created by Orville Goldner and Harold B.
       Allen with the cooperation of the Near East Foundation.
       (NUC FiA 57-280) Locations: Library of Congress (FAA 3268)
       / Syracuse U. *
       Uses a contemporary Arabic music soundtrack. Profiles
       the village of El Marj in Lebanon. Shows traditional
       life centered around wheat farming, winnowing and irriga-
       tion. Shows a villager who has developed a new irriga-
       tion system to increase wheat production after attending
       vocational education programs outside the village. Looks
       at establishment of a cooperative health center in the
       village. Discusses the importance of water, fertilizer
       and technology for village development. Intended as
       training film for agricultural extension volunteers and
       as a sociological study. Comments on "primitive" life in
       the village.

1963   CHANGING WORLD OF LEBANON
       1967 / 24 min / sound / color / 16 mm
       Lem Bailey Productions. Released by AV-ED Films. (LC
       70-701189) Credits: Producer - Earl B. Brink,
       Director-Writer - Lem Bailey.
       General film presenting the beauties of Lebanon. Shows
       traditional villages with terraced hillsides and modern,
       urban Beirut. Profiles the American University of
       Beirut, Bedouins, and the Baalbek International Festival.
       Includes scenes of native dance, music and costumes.

1964   MY VILLAGE
       (c. 1960?) / 45 min / sound / color / 16 mm
       Producer unknown. Distributed by Nu-Arts Films.
       Profiles traditional life in a small Lebanese village.

1965   NUTRITION SURVEY: REPUBLIC OF LEBANON
       1963 / 21 min / sound / color / 16 mm

367

U.S. Public Health Service. (NUC FiE 63-290) (Health
Service order no. M 516)
   Documents a nutritional survey of the Lebanese population
   in 1961. Includes an appraisal of the health of the
   people, food availability, dietary patterns and food
   technology.

1966   YOUTH ACTIVITIES IN THE LEBANON
       (n.d.) / 20 min / sound / color / 16 mm
       Embassy of Lebanon. Distributed by the Lebanon Tourist and
       Information Office.
          Describes activities for young people in Lebanon.
          General introduction to modern Lebanese life.

LEBANON   -   TRAVELOGS AND REGIONAL STUDIES

1967   BUSINESS IN LEBANON
       (n.d.) / 12 min / sound / b&w / 16 mm
       Producer unknown. Distributed by Lebanon Tourist and
       Information Office.
          General introduction to the active and prosperous busi-
          ness and economic life of Lebanon. Produced before the
          civil war.

1968   THE CULTURE OF LEBANON
       1971 / 12 min / sound / color / 16 mm
       Embassy of Lebanon. Distributed by Lebanon Tourist and
       Information Office, New York.
          General travelog. Describes the beauty, culture and
          history of Lebanon.

1969   A LAND CALLED LEBANON
       (n.d.) / 20 min / sound / color / 16 mm
       Producer unknown. Distributed by Lebanon Tourist and
       Information Office.
          General introduction to Lebanon intended to encourage
          tourism. Shows a montage of people and famous places in
          Lebanon.

1970   LAND OF BEAUTY
       (c. 1960) / 45 min / sound / color / 16 mm
       Producer unknown. Distributed by Nu-Art Films.
          General travelog of Lebanon showing its natural beauty.
          To promote tourism and for general information.

1971   LEBANON AT THE CROSSROADS OF TIME
       (n.d.) / ? / sound / 16 mm
       Producer unknown. Distributed by Lebanon Tourist and
       Information Office. No other information available.

1972   LEBANON, A LOVE STORY
       (n.d.) / 20 min / sound / color / 16 mm

Embassy of Lebanon.   Distributed by the Lebanon Tourist and
Information Office.
Shows scenes of people, famous places and history of
Lebanon. To promote tourism and for general information.
Produced before the Lebanese civil war.

1973   LETTER FROM LEBANON
(n.d.) / 12 min / sound / color / 16 mm
Embassy of Lebanon. Distributed by Lebanon Tourist and
Information Office. No other information available.

1974   (PANORAMIC VIEW OF BEYROUTH, SYRIA - NOW LEBANON)
June 1903 / 1:20 minutes / silent / b&w / 16 mm
Thomas Edison. Library of Congress Paper Print Collection.
Location: Library of Congress (FLA 4797) *
A crowd of men and some women and children are shown in
an amusement park area. Children play on ferris wheels,
swings and carrousels. Large city buildings of Beirut
are seen behind the park. In good condition considering
age. For historic and documentary purposes. Some of the
film shot by A.C. Abadie for Thomas Edison.

1975   THE SILENT WITNESS
(n.d.) / 20 min / sound / color / 16 mm
Embassy of Lebanon. Distributed by Lebanon Tourist and
Information Center.
Listed in some catalogs as 12 minutes in length.
Contains scenes of the Lebanese countryside.

1976   SUMMER IN LEBANON
1961 / 45 min / sound / b&w / 16 mm
British Broadcasting Corp. and Beta Film. Made by Denis
Mitchell. Released by Global Television Services, London.
(NUC FiA 66-1770) Credits: Photographer - Ibrahim Chamat,
Editor - Horst Rossberger. Location: Indiana U.
Photographic essay of Lebanon. Shows the coast,
interior, urban and rural areas and profiles occupations
of typical Lebanese.

1977   THIS IS LEBANON
1961 / 25 min / sound / b&w or color / 16 mm
United Artists in cooperation with Middle East Airlines,
Beirut. Distributed by the Embassy of Lebanon. (NUC FiA
62-1416)
General travelog of Lebanon. Shows scenes of the
countryside and native Lebanese dances. To promote
tourism.

LEBANON   -   EDUCATION

1978   AMERICAN UNIVERSITY OF BEIRUT
(c. 1960) / 28 min / sound / color / 16 mm

369

Embassy of Lebanon.
Documents the history of the American University of
Beirut and its role in contemporary Lebanese education.

1979 THE LONELY VOYAGE OF SAMIR SALOUM
1967 / 27 min / sound / color / 16 mm
United Nations. Distributed by United Nations Films.
Follows education and training of Lebanese airplane pilot
Samir Saloum at the Air Safety Center in Beirut.
Describes how the Center is supported by the United
Nations International Civil Aviation Organization. Shows
training on a flight simulator and Samir's handling of
emergency training.

1980 SOUTH OF THE CLOUDS
(n.d.) / 35 min / sound / color / 16 mm
Producer unknown.
Follows Najila, a Muslim woman, during her education and
"transformation" at a Christian college in Beirut.

1981 STORY OF MERJ
(c. 1963) / 30 min / sound / b&w / 16 mm
Near East Foundation and the American Friends of the Middle
East.
Depicts the work of the Near East Foundation in Lebanon.

LIBYA

LIBYA - HISTORY

1982   ITALIAN LIBYA
        1937 / 10 min / sound / b&w / 16 mm
        20th Century-Fox Film Corp. Released for educational pur-
        poses by Teaching Film Custodians, 1939. (Magic Carpet
        series) (NUC FiA 52-4526) Credits: Producer - Truman
        Talley, Narrator - Lowell Thomas, Editor - Lew Lehr.
            Documents Libya during the Italian occupation. Shows
            everyday life of Libyans, local industries, farming,
            desert scenes and the ruins at Leptis Magna. Includes
            scenes of Tripoli.

1983   THE KING AND THE PEOPLE
        (n.d.) / 30 min / sound / sepia tone / 16 mm
        Formerly distributed by the Embassy of Libya. No other
        information available.

1984   WALLS THAT SPEAK (LIBYA)
        1969 / 30 min / sound / color / 16 mm
        BBC-TV, London. Released in the U.S. by Time-Life Films.
        (The Glory That Remain, series no. 13) (LC 78-714491)
        Location: U. of Illinois.
            Host Robert Erskine views the ruined Roman outpost of
            Leptis Magna on the Libyan coast. Shows the temples,
            forum, amphitheaters and bath built during the four
            hundred year history of the city.

LIBYA - TRAVELOGS AND REGIONAL STUDIES

1985   DESERT TRIPOLI
        1932 / 9 min / sound / b&w / 16 mm
        Fox Film Corp. Released for educational purposes by
        Teaching Film Custodians, 1939. (NUC FiA 52-4611)
            General travelog of Libya. Includes scenes of the Roman
            ruins at Leptis Magna, life in Tripoli, Arabs bargaining
            for camels in a market, the desert, irrigation systems,
            girls spinning and weaving and students studying at a
            mosque school and a synogogue.

1986   OASIS
        1965 / 11 min / sound / color or b&w / 16 mm
        Encyclopaedia Britannica. (NUC FiA 65-1168) Credits:
        Educational Collaborator - Arvin W. Hahn. Locations: Kent
        State U. / Iowa Films / Iowa State U. / Syracuse U. / U. of
        Illinois / U. of Nebraska.

Intended for elementary to high school audiences. Shows
the isolation of a Libyan oasis. Describes how limited
natural resources are used to provide food, clothing and
shelter. Looks at cultivation and irrigation of the date
palm, tending animal herds and farming small garden plots.
Shows how motor transportation has increased contact with
the world outside the oasis.

1987   OASIS IN THE SAHARA
1969 / 16 min / sound / color / 16 mm
Institut fur Film und Bild, Munich. Released by Films, Inc.
(Man and His World series) Locations: Iowa Films / Iowa
State U. / Kent State U. / Library of Congress ((FBB 1943) /
Middle East Institute / U. of Illinois / U. of Iowa / U. of
Michigan / U. of Minnesota / U. of Nebraska. *
Intended for junior-senior high school audiences.
Portrays the awesome forces of wind, water and heat in
the Libyan desert. Profiles the Ghadames Oasis, south of
Tunisia near the Algerian border. Shows the inhabitants
living under harsh conditions in a traditional oasis
settlement. Looks at traditional professions including
basket and sandal making and date cultivation. A weekly
bus from the coastal cities is the only contact between
the outside world and the oasis dwellers.

1988   TRIPOLI FAIR
(n.d.) / 30 min / sound / color / 16 mm
Formerly distributed by the Embassy of Libya.
General travelog of Libya. To promote tourism and for
general information.

1989   WELCOME TO LIBYA
(n.d.) / 30 min / sound / color / 16 mm
Formerly distributed by the Embassy of Libya.
General travelog of Libya. To promote tourism and for
general information. No longer available.

LIBYA - AGRICULTURE

1990   THE GREEN SAHARA
1972 / 11 min / sound / color / 16 mm
ABC. Released by Xerox Films. Formerly distributed by the
Embassy of Libya. (LC 75-700246) Credits: Narrator -
Lowell Thomas. Location: U. of Illinois.
Intended for senior high school to adult audiences.
Looks at advances in agriculture in Libya and programs to
contain the Sahara desert. Profiles projects to tap the
vast Great Lake underneath the Sahara. Describes the
history of Libya and the struggle of the people to sur-
vive under harsh conditions. Profiles life in a Libyan
oasis.

1991   SAHARA HARVEST
        (n.d.) / 16 min / sound / 16 mm
        Formerly distributed by the Embassy of Libya.
        Depicts advances in technology and agriculture used to
        grow crops in areas of the Libyan Sahara.

LIBYA   -   INDUSTRY, DEVELOPMENT AND OIL

1992   CHALLENGE IN THE DESERT
        (c. 1960) / 16 min / sound / color or b&w / 16 mm
        United Nations Dept. of Public Information.   Distributed by
        Contemporary Films.   (NUC FiA 57-1128)
            Profiles assistance given by the United Nations to help
            develop the economy and technology of Libya.

1993   DAWN OF THE NEW LIBYA
        (n.d.) / 27 min / sound / b&w / 16 mm
        Formerly distributed by the Embassy of Libya.   Locations:
        Arab Information Office, Washington / Middle East Institute.
            Shows progress made by Libya during its first 15 years of
            independence in education, health programs, agriculture,
            housing, manufacturing, technology, industry, oil produc-
            tion and animal husbandry.   Listed in some catalogs as 30
            minutes in length.

1994   EXPLORING LIBYA
        1962 / 30 min / sound / color / 16 or 35 mm
        California Texas Oil Corp.   Made by Bechtel Corp.
        Distributed by Sterling Movies.   (Caltex International
        Public Relations series) (NUC FiA 66-1524)   Credits:
        Producer - Richard Finnie.
            General overview of the history and people of Libya.
            Profiles oil exploitation in Libya and describes how oil
            revenues could be the basis of the country's economy.

1995   JACKPOT IN LIBYA
        1966 / 28 min / sound / b&w / 16 mm
        CBS News.   Sponsored by Prudential Insurance Co.   (The
        Twentieth Century, television series) (LC 72-701890)
        Credits: Producer - Isaac Kleinerman, Director - James
        Faichney, Narrator - Earl Luby, Reporter - Walter Cronkite,
        Photographer - Youseff Masraff.   Locations: Library of
        Congress (FBA 6132) / Middle East Institute.
            Profiles the effect of oil revenues on life in Libya.
            Looks at advances in education, irrigation, and in the
            oil industry itself.

1996   LIBYA AHEAD
        1962 / 28 min / sound / color / 16 mm
        Ohio Oil Company.   Made by Wilding Films.   Formerly distri-
        buted by the Embassy of Libya.   (NUC FiA 62-158)   Location:
        Middle East Institute.

373

Available in English and Arabic soundtracks. Shows the
oil industry in Libya. Looks at social and economic
advances made possible by oil revenues.

1997   LIBYAN INDUSTRY
(n.d.) / 30 min / sound / color / 16 mm
Formerly distributed by the Embassy of Libya. Location:
Arab Information Office, Washington.
    Profiles advances in industry in Libya.

1998   LIBYAN OIL
1972 / 3 min / silent / color / super 8 mm film loop in
cartridge. Institut fur Film und Bild, Munich. Edited and
released in the U.S. by Films Incorporated. (Man and His
World series) (LC 72701557)
    Profiles the oil industry in Libya. Includes scenes of
    drilling and a refinery at Marsa el Brega.

1999   OIL IN LIBYA
1969 / 15 min / sound / color / 16 mm
Institut fur Film und Bild, Munich. Distributed by Films,
Incorporated. (Man and His World series) (NUC 75-705488)
Locations: Kent State U. / Library of Congress (FBB 1958) /
Penn. State U. / U. of Illinois / U. of Minnesota / U. of
Utah.
    Intended for general audiences and for classroom use.
    Looks at the influence of the oil industry on Libyan
    life. Overview of Libya includes scenes of Marsa el
    Brega, Tripoli, Benghazi and Sebha. Outlines contrasts
    between traditional and modern life and between desert
    and cultivated areas.

2000   REBIRTH OF LIBYA
(n.d.) / 24 min / sound / color / 16 mm
Producer unknown. Distributed by Audience Planners, Inc.
New York.
    Intended for senior high school to adult audiences.
    Profiles the rebirth of Libya as a result of oil wealth.
    Shows programs for irrigation of desert regions and deve-
    loping the economy. Also shows ancient ruins.

LIBYA - THE ARTS, SPORTS

2001   LIBYAN FOLKLORE DANCE
(n.d.) / 10 min / sound / color / 16 mm
Formerly distributed by the Embassy of Libya.
    Documents traditional Libyan folk dances.

2002   LIBYAN HORSES
(n.d.) / 16 min / sound / color / 16 mm
Formerly distributed by the Embassy of Libya.
    A promotional film showing Arabian horses in Libya.

MOROCCO - HISTORY

2003 DEATH TRY ON SULTAN FAILS
1960 / 4 min / sound / b&w / 16 mm
Filmrite Associates. Released by Official Films. (Greatest
Headlines of the Century series) (NUC Fi 62-1909) Credits:
Producer - Sherm Grinberg, Narrator - Tom Hudson, Writers -
Allan Luries, Ray Parker. Location: Library of Congress
(FAA 3723) *
Excellent newreel made up of library footage. Documents
the September 12, 1953 attempt on Mohammed ben Arafa's
life in Rabat, Morocco. Traces overthrow by the French
of Sultan Sidi Mohammed ben Youssef following his refusal
to initiate French programs opposed by the Moroccan independence movement. Follows the placement of Mohammed ben
Arafa in power. Includes information on nationalists'
attempt to run down Ben Arafa with a car and blow him up
with a hand grenade. Shows Moroccan street riots.

2004 MOROCCAN OUTPOST
1951 / 17 min / sound / b&w / 16 mm
March of Time, Inc. Released by McGraw-Hill. A Forum Film.
(McGraw-Hill Textfilms series) (NUC FiA 52-2589)
Intended for senior high school to adult audiences.
Looks at Morocco in the French colonial period.
Describes poverty, illiteracy, and political situation in
Morocco which supposedly justifies the French presence.

2005 OUR STAKE IN TROUBLED MOROCCO
1953 / 27 min / sound / b&w / 16 mm
March of Time, Inc. (NUC Fi 53-176) Locations: Iowa Films
/ Iowa State U. / Library of Congress (FCA 970)
Intended for college and adult audiences. Looks at the
importance of French colonial Morocco to the U.S. as a
strategic location for air bases. Shows growing nationa-
list feeling in the Arab world has influenced the
Moroccan independence struggle, despite efforts by the
French to stress the advantages of colonial status.

MOROCCO - INTERVIEWS

2006 HASSAN II, KING OF MOROCCO
March 31, 1963 / 30 min / sound / b&w / 16 mm
NBC Television. (Meet the Press, television series)
Credits: Correspondents - Ned Brooks, Lawrence Spivak,
Marquis Childs, Benjamin Bradley, Al Able. Location:

Library of Congress (FBA 9351 / FRA 7372-74) *
On a state visit to the U.S., Hassan II of Morocco speaks
with reporters concerning U.S.- Moroccan relations, use of
Moroccan military bases vacated by the U.S., state
socialism, the concept of the "Great Maghreb" or unified
North Africa, the Common Market, if monarchy is still a
viable governmental form in the Middle East, reform in
Morocco, the status of Bahai's in Morocco, Soviet aid,
and the French bureaucratic legacy. Hassan II speaks in
French with an intepreter. He is very careful about his
comments and makes no major statements. However, this is
one of the few interviews concerning Morocco available.

2007   REPORT FROM AFRICA - MOROCCO, LIBERIA AND SIX AFRICAN
        LEADERS
        1957 / 13 min / sound / b&w / 16 mm
        CBS Television. (See It Now, television series)
            Includes interviews with six African leaders. Discusses
            political and social problems of Morocco and Africa at
            that time.

MOROCCO   -   SOCIOLOGY AND ETHNOLOGY

2008   BAKING BALL-SHAPED BREAD (AIT HADDIDOU, NORTH AFRICA,
        HIGH ATLAS)
        1970 / 8 min / silent / 16 mm
        Encyclopaedia Cinematographica. Distributed by Pennsylvania
        State University. (Ency. Cinematographica, no. E 1761)
            Another in the series of silent ethnographic films
            focusing on a traditional activity. Looks at women
            baking bread in Morocco's Atlas Mountains.

2009   BAKING FLAT BREAD (AIT HADDIDOU, NORTH AFRICA,
        HIGH ATLAS)
        1970 / 5 min / silent / b&w / 16 mm
        Encyclopaedia Cinematographica. Distributed by Pennsylvania
        State University. (Ency. Cinematographica, no. E 1760)
            Another in the series of silent ethnographic films.
            Shows women baking traditional flat bread in the Atlas
            Mountains of Morocco.

2010   BUILDING A WALL OF A HOUSE OUT OF A STAMPED LOAM
        WITH THE PLANKING TECHNIQUE (AIT HADDIDOU, NORTH
        AFRICA, HIGH ATLAS)
        1970 / 11 min / silent / b&w / 16 mm
        Encyclopaedia Cinematographica. Distributed by Pennsylvania
        State University. (Ency. Cinematographica, no. E 1772)
            Another in the series of silent ethnographic films.
            Shows building techniques used for a dwelling in the
            Atlas Mountains of Morocco.

2011   BURNING EARTHENWARE IN A SHAFT FURNACE (AIT HADDIDOU,
        NORTH AFRICA, HIGH ATLAS)

1970 / 13 min / silent / b&w / 16 mm
Encyclopaedia Cinematographica. Distributed by Pennsylvania
State University. (Ency. Cinematographica, no. E 1771)
Another in the series of silent ethnographic films.
Shows pottery furnace techniques used in the Atlas
Mountains of Morocco.

2012   CHURNING COW MILK IN A SHEEP HIDE (AIT HADDIDOU,
NORTH AFRICA, HIGH ATLAS)
1970 / 7 min / silent / b&w / 16 mm
Encyclopaedia Cinematographica. Distributed by Pennsylvania
State University. (Ency. Cinematographica, no. 1757)
Another in the series of silent ethnographic films.
Shows simple hand churning methods used by tribes in the
High Atlas mountains of Morocco.

2013   CUTTING BOARDS WITH A CROSSCUT SAW (AIT HADDIDOU,
NORTH AFRICA, HIGH ATLAS)
1970 / 8 min / silent / b&w / 16 mm
Encylopaedia Cinematographica. Distributed by Pennsylvania
State University. (Ency. Cinematographica, no. E 1762)
Another in the series of silent ethnographic films.
Shows board making techniques used by the Ait Haddidou
tribe of Morocco.

2014   DYEING A CLOTH WITH THE "PLANGI" TECHNIQUE (AIT
HADDIDOU, NORTH AFRICA, HIGH ATLAS)
1970 / 12 min / silent / b&w / 16 mm
Encyclopaedia Cinematographica. Distributed by Pennsylvania
State University. (Ency. Cinematographica, no. E 1759)
Another in the series of silent ethnographic films.
Shows dyeing methods used by the Ait Haddidou of Morocco.

2015   THE EDGE OF THE WEST
(c. 1960) / 60 min / sound / color / 16 mm
Producer unknown. Location: Abraham F. Rad Jewish Film
Archive.
Describes the Jewish community in Morocco before it
dispersed in the 1960's. Follows the migration of some
Moroccan Jews to Israel.

2016   GRINDING CORN IN A HAND-MILL (AIT HADDIDOU, NORTH
AFRICA, HIGH ATLAS)
1970 / 7 min / silent / b&w / 16 mm
Encyclopaedia Cinematographica. Distributed by Pennsylvania
State University. (Ency. Cinematographica, no. E 1773)
Another in the series of silent ethnographic films.
Looks at traditional corn grinding techniques used by the
Ait Haddidou of Morocco.

2017   JEWS OF MOROCCO
(n.d.) / 15 min / sound / color / 16 mm
Producer unknown. Distributed by Alden Films. Locations:

Abraham F. Rad Jewish Film Archive / Gratz College.
Looks at Moroccan Jewish life in Casablanca and in
smaller villages. Describes how American Jews provided
food, medicine and education to the community in the
1940's. Looks at the move of the Jewish community to
Israel in the late 1950's. Uses little narration.

2018   A LIGHT FOR LALLA MIMOUNA
       1964 / 28 min / sound / b&w / 16 mm
       United Nations. Distributed by United Nations Films.
       Available in English and Arabic soundtracks. Portrays
       improvements in the village of Lalla Mimouna in Morocco
       as seen through the eyes of Abdel Kader Maiz, a village
       merchant. Shows clearing of cactus to provide arable
       land and introduction of electricity to the village.

2019   MELLAH
       1955 / 30 min / sound / b&w / 16 mm
       Women's American ORT. Made by Stephen L. Sharff
       Productions. Distributed by Alden Films. (LC 72-700014)
       Made by a Jewish production team. Profiles the Mellah,
       or Jewish quarter of Casablanca. Describes the poverty
       there. Follows a boy on his way to school to find a
       better life through education. Stresses role of educa-
       tion in advancement for Jewish communities. Intended to
       show the services of ORT in Jewish education.

2020   MOULAY IDRISS
       (c. 1960) / 10 min / sound / b&w / 16 mm
       Producer unknown. Distributed by Film Images / Radim Films.
       Looks at Holy Week celebrated in Moulay Idriss, Morocco.
       Once a year Muslim pilgrims unable to make the pilgrimage
       to Mecca participate in eight days of prayers and festi-
       vities.

2021   ONCE...AGADIR
       (n.d.) / 27 min / sound / color / 16 mm
       National Film Board of Canada.
       Made by a Moroccan film-maker. Personal memorial state-
       ment to the Moroccan city of Agadir, severely damaged by
       an earthquake.

2022   POTTERY BY CHASING TECHNIQUE (RIFFIANS, NORTH AFRICA,
       MOROCCO)
       1953 / 6 min / silent / b&w / 16 mm
       Encyclopaedia Cinematographica. Distributed by Pennsylvania
       State University. (Ency. Cinematographica, no. 142)
       Another in the series of silent ethnographic films.
       Looks at traditional pottery making techniques used by
       Moroccan tribes.

2023   POTTERY: CHASING AND COILING TECHNIQUE, THROWING
       WHEEL (AIT HADDIDOU, NORTH AFRICA, HIGH ATLAS)

1970 / 6 min / silent / b&w / 16 mm
Encyclopaedia Cinematographica. Distributed by Pennsylvania
State University. (Ency. Cinematographica, no. E 1770)
Another in the series of silent ethnographic films.
Looks at hand and wheel pottery construction methods used
by the Ait Haddidou of Morocco.

2024 PREPARING AND DRINKING TEA (AIT HADDIDOU, NORTH
AFRICA, HIGH ATLAS)
1970 / 7 min / silent / b&w / 16 mm
Encyclopaedia Cinematographica. Distributed by Pennsylvania
State University. (Ency. Cinematographica, no. E 1756)
Another in the series of silent ethnographic films.
Looks at tea preparation by the Ait Haddidou of Morocco.

2025 TYING A TURBAN (BENI MGUILD, NORTH AFRICA, MIDDLE ATLAS)
1964, released 1966 / 2 min / silent / b&w / 16 mm
Encyclopaedia Cinematographica. Distributed by Pennsylvania
State University. (Ency. Cinematographica, no. E 1092)
Another in the series of silent ethnographic films.
Looks at turban winding techniques used by men of the
Beni Mguild of Morocco.

MOROCCO - NOMADS AND TRIBES

2026 BLUE MEN OF MOROCCO - TRIBAL LIFE ON THE SAHARA
1955 / 28 min / sound / color / 16 or 35 mm
Walt Disney Productions. Released by Walt Disney Films.
(People and Places series) (NUC FiA 64-42) Credits: Writers
- Ralph Wright, Winston Hibler, Harrison Negley, Director -
Ralph Wright. Locations: Boston U. / Brigham Young U. /
Iowa Films / Library of Congress (FEA-149-52) / Syracuse U.
/ U. of Illinois / U. of Iowa / U. of Michigan / U. of South
Carolina / U. of Utah / U. of Washington / U. of Wisconsin.
*
Disney ethnographic film dealing with the Tuareg of
Morocco. Gives general history of North African civili-
zation, camel-based nomadic culture and desert con-
ditions. Looks at roles of men and women, daily cooking,
herding, and marketing routines. Follows a group of
Tuareg men on a caravan across the Sahara to market.
Includes some extraordinary footage marred at times by a
cute narration and typical Disney comical touches. For
general television and theater audiences. Useful for
elementary to high school instruction.

2027 A DAY AMONG THE BERBERS
1952 / 14 min / sound / b&w / 16 or 35 mm
Centre cinematographique marocain, Casablanca, Morocco.
Distributed by Film Images / Radim Films. (NUC FiA 52-4301)
Looks at a day in the life of Berbers in Morocco. Shows
daily routines, handicraft production, trading for goods,
and dancing at night.

379

2028   DESERT NOMADS: FRENCH MOROCCO
        1949 / 22 min / sound / b&w / 16 mm
        United World Films. Produced by Louis de Rochemont
        Associates. (The Earth and Its Peoples series) (NUC FiA
        52-350) Credits: Director - John Ferno, Educational
        Consultants - Clyde F. Kohn, W.A. Atwood, Photographer -
        Richard Leacock. Locations: Arizona State U. / Boston U. /
        Florida State U. / Indiana U. / Library of Congress (FBA
        316) / Penn. State U. / U. of Arizona / U. of California
        Extension Media Center / U. of Colorado / U. of Connecticut
        / U. of Michigan / U. of Minnesota / U. of North Carolina /
        U. of Utah / U. of Washington / U. of Wisconsin / Washington
        State U.
            Looks at Moroccan nomads south of the Atlas Mountains.
            Shows how they migrate to find pasturage for their herds.
            Looks at an oasis market where nomads trade for agri-
            cultural products.

2029   DESERT OASIS
        1968 / 4 min / silent / color / 8 mm film loop
        Walt Disney Productions. Released by International
        Communication Films. Distributed by Doubleday Media.
        (North Africa series) (LC 76-703198)
            Excerpt from the 1958 film: BLUE MEN OF MOROCCO -
            TRIBAL LIFE ON THE SAHARA, no. 2026. This clip
            looks at nomadic Tuareg at an oasis. Stresses the impor-
            tance of water for nomads and their herds.

2030   EQUESTRIAN GAMES "FANTASIA" (BENI MGUILD, NORTH AFRICA,
        MIDDLE ATLAS)
        1964, released 1966 / 5 min / silent / b&w / 16 mm
        Encyclopaedia Cinematographica. Distributed by Pennsylvania
        State University. (Ency. Cinematographica, no. E 1096)
            Another in the series of silent ethnographic films.
            Shows nomads on horseback in Morocco.

2031   NEW WAYS FOR OLD MOROCCO
        1950 / 20 min / sound / b&w / 16 or 35 mm
        Les Actualites francaises, Paris. Released in the U.S. by
        A.F. Films. Distributed by Radim Films. (NUC FiA 52-673)
            Looks at Berber tribesmen who agreed in 1929 to colla-
            borate and discontinue raids on each other's property.
            Shows the Seghouchen of Mt. Tichoukt and the Sidi Said of
            the valley. Describes how annual migrations for
            pasturage previously had ended up as raids on settled
            valley areas. Looks at cultivated land, homes, markets
            and schools made possible as a result of this cooperative
            venture.

2032   NOMAD FAMILY MEALS
        1968 / 4 min / silent / color / super or regular 8 mm loop
        Walt Disney Productions. Released by International
        Communication Films. Distributed by Doubleday Media. (North

380

Africa series) (LC 73-703201)
Excerpt from the 1958 film: BLUE MEN OF MOROCCO -
TRIBAL LIFE IN THE SAHARA, no. 2026. Shows
preparation of meals among the Tuareg.

2033   NOMADIC LIFE IN THE MOROCCAN ATLAS
(n.d.) / 4 min / silent / color / 8 mm
Producer unknown. Distributed by A.I.M.
Short silent ethnographic clip showing Moroccan nomad
life.

2034   NOMADS CROSS THE SAHARA
1968 / 4 min / silent / color / regular or super 8 mm loop
Walt Disney Productions. Released by International
Communication Films. Distributed by Doubleday Media.
(North Africa series) (LC 77-703202)
Excerpt from the 1958 film: BLUE MEN OF MOROCCO -
TRIBAL LIFE IN THE SAHARA, no. 2026. Listed in
some catalogs as: NOMADS ACROSS THE SAHARA. Looks
at desert conditions and transportation of goods by camel
across the Sahara desert.

2035   SAHARA FANTASIA: A DESERT FESTIVAL
1969 / 10 min / sound / color / 16 mm
Ideal. Distributed by International Film Foundation.
Locations: Indiana U. / U. of Arizona.
Looks at the four day annual festival or moussem held in
Tan Tan in southern Morocco. Shows nomads gathering in
the town for the religious festival.

2036   SEWING AND ERECTING A TENT (BENI MGUILD, NORTH AFRICA,
MIDDLE ATLAS)
1964, released 1966 / 10 min / silent / b&w / 16 mm
Encyclopaedia Cinematographica. Distributed by Pennsylvania
State University. (Ency. Cinematographica, no. E 1095)
Another in the series of silent ethnographic films.
Looks at traditional tent making methods used by the Beni
Mguild tribe of Morocco.

MOROCCO   -   WOMEN AND CHILDREN

2037   MOROCCO: CHAOUI FACES HIS FUTURE
1967 / 20 min / sound / color or b&w / 16 mm
United World Films. (NUC FiA 67-1761) Credits: Consultant -
Helen B. Warrin. Locations: Library of Congress (FBA 6313)
/ Syracuse U. / U. of Illinois / U. of Nebraska.
Intended for junior-senior high school audiences.
Profiles Chaoui, a teenage boy in the village of Tazarte
in Morocco. Shows how Chaoui must choose between a tra-
ditional farming life and attending high school in
Marrakech. Looks at agriculture, Islam, traditional
customs, village life and the role of education in
Morocco.

2038   MOROCCO: CHAOUI MAKES A CHOICE
        1967 / 18 min / sound / color / 16 mm
        United World Films. Made by Show Associates. (NUC FiA
        67-500)
            Continues with the problems of Chaoui, a Moroccan Berber
            teenager, as he decides his future. Looks at the role of
            education in preparing Moroccans for national life and
            the alternative of being a traditional village farmer or
            herdsman.

2039   PUTTING ON A WOMAN'S ATTIRE (BENI MGUILD, NORTH
        AFRICA, MIDDLE ATLAS)
        1964, released 1966 / 5 min / silent / b&w / 16 mm
        Encyclopaedia Cinematographica. Distributed by Pennsylvania
        State University. (Ency. Cinematographica, no. E 1093)
            Another in the series of silent ethnographic films.
            Looks at traditional women's clothing worn by the Beni
            Mguild of Morocco.

2040   SAINTS AND SPIRITS
        1977 / 26 min / sound / color / 16 mm
        Center for Middle Eastern Studies, University of Texas at
        Austin. Granada Television. Distributed by the General
        Libraries Film Library, U. of Texas at Austin and by Icarus
        Films. Credits: Writer-Associate Producer - Elizabeth
        Fernea, Producer-Director - Melissa Llewelyn-Davies, Islamic
        Consultant - Abdelaziz Abbassi. Locations: U. of North
        Carolina / U. of Texas at Austin. *
            Made from footage shot for the film: SOME WOMEN OF
            MARRAKECH, no. 2041. Studies popular religious activity
            in Morocco centering on Aisha bint Muhammad, a local
            religious figure. Shows Aisha bint Muhammad renewing
            contact with a spirit through a ritual celebration in
            Marrakech, the annual pilgrimage and festival or moussem
            at the shrine of a saint in the High Atlas Mountains, and
            the veneration of a new saint's shrine in a village on
            the plains. An aspect of women and popular Islam in
            Morocco seldom seen. An excellent film although slow in
            parts. Recommended.

2041   SOME WOMEN OF MARRAKECH
        1976 / 55 min / sound / color / 16 mm
        Granada Television, London. Distributed by ICF. Location:
        U. of Texas at Austin.
            Examines the role and status of women in Morocco.
            Describes the strong influence of traditional male-
            dominated society and Islam on urban women. Topics
            discussed include work, segregation, polygamy and reli-
            gion. Includes scenes of a marriage, women's bath,
            dancing and folk religious practises. One of few films
            dealing with North African women.

2042   TWO ARAB BOYS OF TANGIER, MOROCCO
        1959 / 18 min / sound / color / 16 mm

Frith Films, Hollywood. (NUC FiA 59-1093) Location: U. of Illinois.
Follows two teenage boys through the streets of Tangier. Shows them at school, on a trip to the country and the Atlantic coast, and on a visit to a camel farm. Includes scenes of pilgrims leaving for the pilgrimage to Mecca.

2043 WASHING A WOOLLEN BURNOUS (AIT HADDIDOU, NORTH AFRICA, HIGH ATLAS)
1970 / 9 min / silent / b&w / 16 mm
Encyclopaedia Cinematographica. Distributed by Pennsylvania State University. (Ency. Cinematographica, no. E 1758)
Another in the series of silent ethnographic films. Shows women washing wool garments.

2044 WHERE THE BRIDES DO THE CHOOSING
1968 / 25 min / sound / color / 16 mm
BBC-TV, London and Odyssey Productions. Released in the U.S. by Time-Life Films. (Africa series, no. 1) (LC 79-714380) Credits: Narrator - Lowell Thomas.
Looks at mate selection patterns of Moroccan women in the Atlas Mountains. Shows women selecting husbands from available men of the tribe, and rejected suitors entertaining themselves in the evening.

MOROCCO - TRAVELOGS AND REGIONAL STUDIES

2045 AM AMERICAN LOOKS AT MOROCCO
1954 / 29 min / sound / color / 16 mm
Alfred T. Palmer Productions. (Americans Look at the World series) (NUC Fi 55-198) Credits: Producer-Director - Alfred T. Palmer, Writers - George Hausemann, Lawrence A. Williams, Narrator - Phillip E. Walker. Kodachrome.
Location: Library of Congress (FCA 76) *
An American engineer on a construction job in Morocco discusses American stereotypes of Morocco and how they differ from reality. Shows modern Casablanca and Fez, traditional street scenes, craftsmen, handicrafts, irrigation, cultivation methods, and women producing clothing and crafts from wool and hides. Semi-humorous narration is patronizing at times but well meant. Intended to create good will between Americans and Morocco. Looks at popular travelog subjects and avoids politics. Dated but interesting film for juvenile to junior high school audiences.

2046 BAZAAR IN MARRAKECH
1970 / 4 min / silent / color / super 8 mm film loop
Ealing Corporation. (Africa series) (LC 73-706778)
Brief look at the famous bazaar at Marrakech, Morocco. Shows people, crafts and goods found at the bazaar.

2047　BIRDS-EYE VIEW (MOROCCO NORTH)
(c. 1975) / ? / sound / color / 16 mm
Abdelaziz Ramdani and Jean-Paul Joauen. Les Films de la
Fontaine. Distributed by the Moroccan Tourist Office, New
York.
Travelog of northern Morocco seen from the air. Looks at
geography, climate and population centers of the north.

2048　A BIRD'S-EYE VIEW (MOROCCO SOUTH)
1975 / 20 min / sound / color / 16 mm
Abdelaziz Ramdani and Jean-Paul Joauen. Les Films de la
Fontaine. Credits: Writer - Jean-Pierre Chambon. Location:
Moroccan Tourist Office, New York. *
Delightful travelog of southern Morocco filmed from a
helicopter. Excellent scenes of the landscape show irrigation projects, ancient ruins, new buildings, Ksar
es-Skou, Eifoud and its palm groves, Saharan sand dunes,
Rissani, Tinerhir and the Atlas Mountain range. Mansur
Hadabi, Ouarzazate, Tifoultout and Zagora in the
southeast are also shown. One of the few films which
show the impressive natural beauty of Morocco.

2049　COUNTRY OF ISLAM
1957 / 16 min / sound / color or b&w / 16 mm
Churchill-Wexler Film Productions. (Peoples of Other Lands
series, no. 4) (NUC FiA 58-3532) Credits: Photographer -
Gunther V. Fritsch. Kodachrome. Locations: Kent State U. /
New York Public Donnell Film Library / Syracuse U. / U. of
Illinois.
Intended for junior-senior high school audiences.
Follows a Moroccan village boy on his first trip to the
city to attend school. Looks at the role of Islam and
modernization in Moroccan life. Stresses need for educa-
tion to meet demands of modern life in Morocco.

2050　FLIGHT TO NORTH AFRICA
1951 / 30 min / sound / color / 16 mm
Air France. Made by Andre de la Varre. (NUC FiA 56-101)
Travelog of Morocco to promote tourism and air travel.
Includes scenes of Casablanca, Marrakech, Fez and the
famous Casbah. Shows mixture of tradititonal and modern
patterns in Moroccan life.

2051　FORTY YEARS OF EVOLUTION IN MOROCCO
(c. 1960) / 20 min / sound / b&w / 16 mm
French American Cultural Service.
Newsreel of Morocco.

2052　GLIMPSES OF MOROCCO AND ALGIERS
1951 / 8 min / sound / color / 35 mm
Loew's Inc. An MGM Picture. (James A. FitzPatricks's
Traveltalks series) Credits: Producer-Narrator - James A.
FitzPatrick, Photographer - Howard P. Nelson. Location:

Library of Congress (FEA 478) *
Theatrically released travelog of Morocco with a patronizing narration ridiculing traditional Moroccan life.
Includes scenes of Algiers, the Casbah, Casablanca, Rabat
and Marrakech. Discusses "spiritual development" under
French occupation. Good example of a negative stereotype
image distributed in the form of entertainment.

2053   HOW TO GET ALONG IN FRENCH MOROCCO
       1953 / 23 min / sound / b&w / 16 mm
       Office of Information and Education, Dept. of Defense. Made
       by the Dept. of the Army. (LC 79-703886) (A.F.I.F.
       series, no. 35) Location: Library of Congress (FBA 5749) *
       An Army information film intended for American soldiers
       in Morocco. Mixes anti-communist lectures with a basic
       course in avoiding potentially dangerous cultural mista-
       kes while in Morocco. Gives geographic, historic and
       social background of Morocco. Shows Casablanca and
       Rabat. Shows traditional tourist sites along with help-
       ful hints such as: don't stare at or touch women, don't
       go near sacred religious sites, and don't get involved in
       French-Moroccan nationalist disputes. Explains American
       forces are in Morocco to contain communism and discusses
       Morocco's role in NATO. Very interesting, uninten-
       tionally humorous film.

2054   IN MOROCCO
       1939 / 11 min / sound / b&w / 16 mm
       Columbia Pictures Corp. Released for educational purposes
       by Teaching Film Custodians, 1941. (Columbia Tour series)
       (NUC FiA 52-4660) Credits: Producer - Andre de la Varre,
       Narrator - Milton Cross.
       Intended for high school audiences. Looks at mixture of
       modern and traditional influences on Morocco. Includes
       scenes of Rabat, Fez and Marrakech. Shows handicrafts,
       ruins and people. Discusses role of Islam and a brief
       history of North African culture.

2055   LIFE IN MOROCCO
       1957 / 11 min / sound / color / 16 mm
       Pat Dowling Pictures. Distributed by BFA. (NUC Fi 57-63)
       Credits: Producer - Pat Dowling, Writer - Thomas Stanton,
       Narrator - Robert Shield, Photographer - George Hausmann.
       Eastman color. Locations: Library of Congress (FAA 4172) /
       Syracuse U. / U. of Illinois / U. of Texas at Austin.
       General travelog of Morocco. Shows traditional han-
       dicrafts, agriculture and nomads and modern urban life.

2056   MARRAKESH
       1968 / 3 min / silent / color / regular or super 8 mm loop
       Walt Disney Productions. Released by International
       Communication Films. Distributed by Doubleday Media.
       (North Africa series) (LC 70-703200)

385

Excerpt from the 1958 film: BLUE MEN OF MOROCCO - TRIBAL LIFE ON THE SAHARA, no. 2026. Includes scenes of the city of Marrakech.

2057   MOROCCAN HIGHWAYS
1962 / 8 min / sound / color / 35 mm
Paramount Pictures Corp. Made by Hamilton Wright Productions. (NUC Fi 68-1617) Credits: Director - Richard Wright, Narrators - Richard McNamara, Maria Piazzai, Photographer - Giulio Rufini. Location: Library of Congress (FEA 1694)
Travelog of Morocco showing the strong influence on Spanish culture. Includes scenes of the Rif country, Tetuan, Meknes, Rez and Rabat.

2058   MOROCCO
1972 / 10 min / sound / color / 16 mm
Picnic Films. Made by Nicholas Serras. (LC 73-701117) Locations: Library of Congress (FAB 475) / New York Public Donnell Film Library. *
Modern impressionistic film of Morocco. Includes scenes of ruins, crafts, mosques, landscapes and people at work and play. Well filmed and edited. Visually pleasing introduction to Morocco. Lack of narration may limit use of film for classroom purposes. For high school to adult audiences. Recommended.

2059   MOROCCO FOR ALL SEASONS
1976 / 26 min / sound / color / 16 mm
Weleb Productions.
Available in English, Arabic, French and Portuguese soundtracks. Shows tourist attractions of Morocco. To promote tourism.

2060   MOROCCO: LAND OF CIVILIZATION AND PROGRESS
(n.d.) / 15 min / sound / 16 mm
Embassy of Morocco.
General introduction to life and culture in Morocco.

2061   MOROCCO MARCHES ON
1956 / 13 min / sound / b&w / 16 or 35 mm
Telenews Productions. Released by McGraw-Hill. (NUC Fi 56-214) Credits: Producer - Robert W. Schofield, Director-Writer - Leona Carney, Narrator - John Cannon, Editor - Vincent Gramaglia. Location: Library of Congress (FBA 1108)
Looks at technical, social and economic advancement in Morocco in the late 1950's. Discusses government projects in transportation, port expansion, hydro-electric power, industry and development of natural resources.

2062   MOROCCO MOVES FORWARD
(c. 1960?) / 20 min / sound / b&w / 16 mm

Producer unknown. Formerly distributed by the French
American Cultural Service.
Looks at traditional arts and crafts in Morocco.
Contrasts traditional arts to recent modernization in
housing, agriculture and industry.

2063   MOROCCO TODAY
1956 / 27 min / sound / b&w / 16 or 35 mm
Telenews Productions. Released by McGraw-Hill. (NUC Fi
56-215) Credits: Producer - Robert W. Schofield,
Director-Writer - Leona Carney, Narrator - John Cannon,
Music - Edward Craig, Editor - Pat De Rosa. Locations: Kent
State U. / Library of Congress (FCA 819)
Intended for senior high school to adult general audiences. Shows social, economic and industrial progress in
Morocco in the late 1950's. Profiles phosphate mining
and citrus industries, education, medicine, law and
government. Looks at use of natural resources and projects for irrigation and hydro-electric power.

2064   THE MOSLEMS AND THE WEST - MOROCCAN OUTPOST
1951 / 17 min / sound / b&w / 35 mm
Time, Inc. (March of Time, vol. 17, no. 4, series)
Location: National Archives (200MT17.4) No other information available.

2065   SAHARA MARKET TOWNS
1968 / 3 min / silent / color / standard or super 8 mm loop
Walt Disney Productions. Released by International
Communication Films. Distributed by Doubleday. (North
Africa series) (LC 70-703203)
Excerpt from the 1958 film: BLUE MEN OF MOROCCO -
TRIBAL LIFE ON THE SAHARA, no. 2026. Shows typical
activities in an oasis market place including sale of
camels, food and clothing.

2066   THE SAND AND THE SEA
1978 / 20 min / sound / color / 16 mm
J.P. Jaouen. Moroccan National Office of Tourism. (Les
Films de la Fontaine series) Location: Morocco Tourist
Office, New York. *
Intended for junior high school to adult audiences. Very
well produced general introduction to Morocco. Follows
Morocco's Atlantic coast. Shows scenes of nomadic areas,
folkdance, Nixis, a Roman city, and the Casbah. Modern
Morocco is represented by the port of Casablanca and in
metropolitan street scenes. Profiles the fishing and
shipping industries and shows Essaouira, where dyes are
produced. El Jadida and Safi, producers of phosphates
and shipping centers were sites where Portuguese fought
for possession of Morocco. Shows potters, resorts at
Agadir, and a variety of tourist areas and accommodations
for travelers. Intended as an informational film and to
promote tourism. Still useful for classroom purposes.

2067   UNDER MOROCCAN SKIES
        1934 / 10 min / sound / b&w / 16 mm
        Fox Film Corp. Released for educational purposes by
        Teaching Film Custodians, 1939. (Magic Carpet series) (NUC
        FiA 52-4562)
            Intended for elementary to senior high school audiences.
            Theatrically produced travelog showing Spanish Morocco.
            Includes scenes of Muslims praying, Moroccan Arab
            leaders, the cavalry, silversmiths and a wedding cere-
            mony.

MOROCCO - AGRICULTURE, MEDICINE

2068   LA FUGUE DE MAHMOUD
        1952 / 36 min / sound / b&w / 16 mm
        U.S. Economc Cooperation Administration. Made by Films du
        compasse, Paris. (NUC FiE 53-591)
            Presents the story of Mahmoud, a Berber boy in French
            Morocco, who becomes a tractor mechanic in Casablanca.
            He returns to his village to help mechanize village agri-
            culture. Produced for overseas use.

2069   OPEN YOUR EYES
        1974 / 16 min / sound / color / 16 mm
        Actua-Films, Geneva for World Health Organization. Released
        by UNICEF. Distributed by Association Films, and by Iowa
        Films. Locations: Iowa State U. / U. of Illinois / U. of
        Texas at Austin.
            Intended for senior high school to adult audiences.
            Looks at World Health Organization programs to fight
            trachoma and other eye diseases in Morocco. Follows
            efforts to save the sight of a Moroccan villager. Shows
            his son's participation in an anti-trachoma campaign.

2070   TRADITIONAL AGRICULTURE IN THE MOROCCAN ATLAS
        (n.d.) / 4 min / sound / color / 16 mm
        Producer unknown. Distributed by A.I.M. Oakmont,
        Pennsylvania. (Animal, Vegetable and Mineral series) No
        other information available.

MOROCCO - THE ARTS, CRAFTS

2071   BALLET OF THE ATLAS
        1952 / 10 min / sound / b&w / 16 or 35 mm
        Centre cinematographique marocain, Casablanca. Released in
        the U.S. by A.F. Films. Distributed by Film Images/Radim
        Films. (NUC FiA 52-4146)
            Companion film to: SUITE OF BERBER DANCES, no. 2072.
            Shows performance of traditional folk dances by two
            Berber tribes of Morocco. Men and women dance together
            in a rural mountain area dance while men and women dance
            separately in dances from the south.

388

2072   SUITE OF BERBER DANCES
        1952 / 10 min / sound / b&w / 16 or 35 mm
        Centre cinematographique marocain, Casablanca. Released in
        the U.S. by A.F. Films. Distributed by Film Images/Radim
        Films. Credits: Director - Serge Debecove. Location: New
        York Public Donnell Film Library.
        Shows three traditional Berber dances. Includes a
        sophisticated city dance by men, a war dance from the
        foothills of the Atlas Mountains near Tasqueens, and a
        desert dance by a nomad girl of the western Sahara.

2073   A THOUSAND AND ONE HANDS
        1972 / 75 min / sound / color / 16 mm
        Souhel Ben Barka. Distributed by Tricontinental Films, and
        by Icarus Films.
        In French with English sub-titles. Possibly a feature
        film. Looks at the production and sale of colorful
        Berber carpets. Shows how much time and labor is spent
        on producing the carpets while the profit from their sale
        goes to rug exporters not the workers producing them.
        Looks at the socio-economic state of modern Morocco and
        comments on the traditional structure of North African
        society and economics.

2074   WEAVING A TENT SQUARE ON A HORIZONTAL HAND-LOOM (BENI
        MGUILD, NORTH AFRICA, MIDDLE ATLAS)
        1964, released 1966 / 14 min / silent / b&w / 16 mm
        Encyclopaedia Cinematographica. Distributed by Pennsylvania
        State University. (Ency. Cinematographica, no. E 1094)
        Another in the series of silent ethnographic films
        focusing on one traditional activity. Shows weaving on a
        horizontal loom.

2075   DHOFAR: GUERILLA WAR ON THE ARABIAN GULF
        1976 / 40 min / color / 16 mm
        James Vaughn.   Impact Films.   Distributed by Icarus Films.   *
        Listed in some catalogs as 58 minutes in length under the
        title: DOFAR: GUERILLA WAR ON THE ARABIAN GULF.
        From the viewpoint of the separationists in Dhofar.
        Looks at advantages in the secession of Dhofar from the
        Sultanate of Oman.   Accuses the Sultan of withholding oil
        wealth from the people of Oman.   Describes positive
        programs of the Popular Front including liberation of
        women from traditional roles, medical and health care
        programs, and introduction of improved farming tech-
        niques.   Shows how the secessionists have been driven
        into South Yemen by combined British, Iranian and Omani
        forces but vows they will return in the future.   A lef-
        tist viewpoint of a seldom filmed area.

2076   THE FISHERMEN OF OMAN: THE DAY OF THE FISHERMAN
        1975 / 28 min / sound / color / 16 mm
        Mardela International.   Made by Robert Strickland/Film Maker
        Films.   (LC 75-703011)
            An Omani fisherman compares and contrasts traditional and
            modern fishing methods and equipment.   Looks at role of
            modernization in the fishing industry in the Sultanate of
            Oman.   Available in English and Arabic soundtracks.

2077   THE FISHERMEN OF OMAN: REPORT FROM MONTEREY
        1973 / 22 min / sound / color / 16 mm
        Mardela International.   (LC 74-702642)
            Available in English and Arabic soundtracks.   Follows
            eight fishermen from the Sultanate of Oman on a tour of
            the fishing industry in Monterey, California.   Looks at
            modern fishing techniques and equipment used in the U.S.
            and possible application by Omani fishermen.

2078   THE HOUR OF LIBERATION HAS STRUCK
        1974 / 62 min / sound / color / 16 mm
        San Francisco Newsreel.   Third World Newsreel.
            Documents the struggle in Dhofar by the People's Front
            for the Liberation of Oman.   Stresses the backward nature
            of the ruling family of Oman which until a few years ago
            outlawed the wearing of eyeglasses and shoes.   Shows how
            the current Sultan, though somewhat more progressive, is
            not using oil wealth to develop Oman or improve living
            conditions in oil-rich Dhofar province.   Follows a 15
            year old woman unit commander in the PFLO.   Shows
            programs of the organization in attempting to gain

390

control of Oman and institute a leftist, anti-colonial
government. Winner at the 1974 Cannes Film Festival.

2079   THE SULTANATE OF OMAN
1976 / 58 min / sound / color / 16 mm
Gordian Deffarge, M. Claude Troeller. Distributed by Icarus
Films. *
Sub-titled in English. Looks at the conflict between the
traditional Omani ruling family, multi-national business
interests, the Dhofar guerilla fighters and the people of
Oman. Describes primitive conditions of the country
until 1970 when Sultan Qaboos assumed power. Contrasts
arbitrary edicts of the former Sultan, such as no
building of roads or wearing of western clothes, with the
more modern, liberal current Sultan. Stresses British
advisors have suggested liberal policies for Oman as a
counter to leftist guerillas in Dhofar province. Shows
how liberalized business policies have led to a flood of
non-Omani business people causing housing shortages and
inflation. Also profiles positive aspects of education,
women's rights and abolition of slavery under the current
Sultan. Very interesting film. Explains many forces at
work in Omani culture and politics. Intended for college
to adult audiences. Recommended.

PAKISTAN

PAKISTAN - HISTORY

2080 ANTIQUITIES OF PAKISTAN
1953 / 12 min / sound / b&w / 16 mm
Pakistan Pictures. Formerly distributed by the Embassy of
Pakistan. Credits: Writer - Sir Mortimer Wheeler,
Photographer - Mohammad Afzal. Location: Library of
Congress (FAA 2607) *
Traces the long and illustrious history of the area now
called Pakistan and Bangladesh. Traces early Indian
civilizations at Mohengodaro, pre-Mughal Persian monuments, Mughal art and architecture in Lahore, Buddhist
shrines in Taxila and a variety of arts and crafts from
all periods of Pakistan's history. For high school to
college audiences. Includes many unidentified names of
places and peoples. Best for students with some fami-
liarity of Pakistan. Includes beautiful examples of art
and architecture.

2081 A LAND DIVIDED
1972 / 15 min / sound / b&w / 16 mm
Hearst Metrotone News. (Screen News Digest, vol. 14, no. 5)
(LC 72-702748)
Newsreel covering tensions which led to the division of
Bangladesh from Pakistan. Discusses the creation of
Bangladesh out of East Pakistan, the role of India in
Pakistani politics, the Kashmir dispute and status of
Pakistan as a Muslim nation.

2082 MOHAMMAD AYUB KHAN
July 16, 1961 / 30 min / sound / b&w / 16 mm
NBC Television. (Meet the Press, television series)
Location: Library of Congress (FRA 7166)
Includes an interview by members of the U.S. press with
Mohammad Ayub Khan, President of Pakistan from 1959-60,
1963-64, and 1967-71.

2083 PAKISTAN
1953 / 26 min / sound / b&w / 16 mm
March of Time. Distributed by Iowa Films. Location: Iowa
State U.
News report on the newly independent Muslim state of
Pakistan. Looks at differences between Indian Muslims
and Hindus which led to the formation of Pakistan.
Discusses problems in agriculture and industry faced by
the new nation.

2084   PAKISTAN: MOUND OF THE DEAD
        1972 / 27 min / sound / color / 16 mm
        Centron. (People and Places of Antiquity series)
        Locations: Syracuse U. / U. of Illinois.
            Looks at excavations of the ancient civilization which
            flourished for 1000 years at Mohenjo Daro. Shows
            advanced state of building, drainage, and urban organiza-
            tion. Shows foreign influence in art and objects traded
            with the Sumerians in Iraq. Discusses reasons for the
            disappearance of this civilization. Intended for inter-
            mediate to adult audiences.

2085   PRESIDENT MEETS THE PEOPLE
        (c. 1960) / 30 min / sound / color / 16 mm
        Embassy of Pakistan.
            Listed in some catalogs as 20 minutes in length. Follows
            President Ayub Khan's tour of Pakistan in which he
            describes his philosophy of democracy and goals for the
            future of Pakistan.

2086   PROGRESS REPORT ON PAKISTAN
        1953 / 28 min / sound / b&w / 16 mm
        March of Time. Time, Inc. (NUC Fi 53-192) Location:
        Library of Congress (FCA 1062)
            Supreme Court Justice William O. Douglas and Pakistani
            Ambassador Mohammed Ali discuss the progress of Pakistan
            in its first five years. Topics covered include the
            importance of the Khyber Pass, industrial and construc-
            tion programs, the Kashmir dispute with India, and
            programs for modernization.

2087   PROMISE OF PAKISTAN
        1950 / 17 min / sound / b&w / 16 mm
        March of Time. Released by McGraw-Hill. A Forum Film.
        (NUC FiA 52-2565)
            Looks at natural resources of Pakistan, the dispute with
            India over Kashmir and potential for future progress.
            Includes a statement by Prime Minister Ali Khan.

2088   QUAID-E-AZAM
        (n.d.) / ? / sound / 16 mm
        Embassy of Pakistan. No other information available.

2089   SIR MUHAMMAD ZAFRULLA KHAN
        May 19, 1963 / 30 min / sound / b&w / 16 mm
        NBC Television. (Meet the Press, television series)
        Location: Library of Congress (FRA 7384-86)
            Interview by members of the U.S. press with United
            Nations General Assembly President Muhammad Zafrulla Khan
            of Pakistan.

2090   SOUTH ASIA AND INDIA TODAY
        1960 / 21 min / sound / b&w / 16 mm

Dept. of Defense. Office of Information and Education.
Made by Norwood Studios. (World Affairs Films, no. 11)
Credits: Consultants - G. Lewis Jones, Jr. Asst. Sec. of
State for Near East and South Asian Affairs, Ernest K.
Lindley. Location: Library of Congress (FBA 9248)   *
U.S. Dept. of Defense film on Afghanistan, Nepal,
Pakistan, India and Ceylon. Looks at these developing
countries and the threat of "shortcuts offered by com-
munist doctrine". Shows closeness of the Soviet Union to
Southwest Asia, military commitments of the SEATO and
CENTO treaty organizations, U.S. military facilities in
Turkey, Saudi Arabia and Pakistan, and arms and economic
aid to South Asia by both the U.S. and the Soviet Union.
Of limited use for classroom purposes due to dated infor-
mation and cold war presentation. Of use for historic
purposes.

2091   TROUBLE IN PAKISTAN
1953 / 18 min / sound / b&w / 16 mm
Revue Productions, Inc. Distributed by Embassy of Pakistan.
Location: Library of Congress (FBA 120) No other information available.

PAKISTAN - SOCIOLOGY AND ETHNOLOGY

2092   ALI AND HIS BABY CAMEL
1953 / 11 min / sound / color or b&w / 16 or super 8 mm
Atlantis Production. Distributed by Doubleday. (Children
of Our World series) (NUC FiA 55-761) Credits:
Producer-Director-Photographer - J. Michael Hagopian.
    For elementary school audiences. Follows a 10 year old
    boy in West Pakistan as he cares for his baby camel.
    Shows role of camel in a desert environment, camel
    markets, and the use of camels for transportation, food
    and clothing.

2093   CELEBRATIONS ON THE OCCASION OF THE INSTALLATION OF A
CHIEFTAIN (MARMA, EAST PAKISTAN, CHITTAGONG HILL TRACTS)
1955, released 1960 / 21 min / silent / color / 16 mm
Encyclopaedia Cinematographica. Distributed by Pennsylvania
State University. (Ency. Cinematographica, no. E 302)
    Another in the series of silent ethnographic films
    portraying a single traditional activity. Shows celebra-
    tions for a new local leader in East Pakistan.

2094   DINNER IN PAKISTAN
1966 / 4 min / silent / color / super or standard 8 mm loop
Wayne Mitchell and Compass Films. Released by International
Communication Films. (South Asia series) (LC 72-700538)
Credits: Writer-Photographer - Wayne Mitchell.
    Looks at cooking and eating customs of urban families in
    Pakistan and South Asia.

2095   DRIVING OF CATTLE TO AN ALPINE PASTURE AND SACRIFICES
        (KALASH, NORTH-WEST PAKISTAN, CHITRAL)
        1956, released 1959 / 20 min / silent / b&w / 16 mm
        Encyclopaedia Cinematographica. Distributed by Pennsylvania
        State University. (Ency. Cinematographica, no. E 210)
            Another in the series of silent ethnographic films
            focusing on a traditional activity. Looks at change in
            pasturage for cattle in Chitral.

2096   THE LAND OF DUST
        1958 / 23 min / sound / color / 16 mm
        Conservative Baptist Foreign Mission Society. Made by Films
        Afield. (NUC FiA 61-933)
            Looks at obstacles to Christian missionary work in
            Pakistan. Discusses problems with weather, illiteracy
            and the strong belief of Pakistani Muslims in Islam.

2097   PAKISTAN: THE PEOPLE
        1968 / 9 min / sound / color / 16 or 8 mm
        Alpha Corp. of America. (Asia: Lands and People series)
        Credits: Educational Consultant - Elizabeth Eiselen.
        Location: Library of Congress (FAA 7668) *
            Intended for elementary school audiences. Good general
            introduction to Pakistan before East Pakistan split to
            form Bangladesh. Includes repetition for young audien-
            ces. Looks at importance of religion, various occupa-
            tions in East and West Pakistan, language, geography,
            literacy, and problems in agriculture and population.

2098   PEOPLE'S FESTIVAL
        (n.d.) / 20 min / sound / b&w / 16 mm
        Embassy of Pakistan. No other information available.

2099   PUNJABI VILLAGE
        1967 / 33 min / sound / b&w / 16 mm
        Atlantis Productions. (LC 79-704658) Credits:
        Director-Writer-Photographer - Richard Ashworth. Locations:
        Boston U. / U. of Arizona / U. of Washington.
            Filmed during the Cambridge Asian Expedition. Looks at
            typical life of a West Pakistani village. Shows wheat
            farming techniques, modernization, education, religion
            and social activities in the village. Discusses problem
            with population and food shortages.

2100   RURAL LIFE IN PAKISTAN
        (c. 1955?) / 10 min / sound / b&w / 16 or 35 mm
        Pakistan Pictures. Formerly distributed by the Pakistan
        Embassy.
            Profiles life in various provinces of Pakistan. Shows
            grain producing areas in the Punjab, nomadic tribes of
            the north-eastern frontier, rice, sugar and fruit produc-
            tion in Bengal, and the East Bengal fishing industry.

395

2101   SIGN LANGUAGE (SINDHI, WEST PAKISTAN)
        1961, released 1964 / 5 min / silent / b&w / 16 mm
        Encyclopaedia Cinematographica. Distributed by Pennsylvania
        State University. (Ency. Cinematographica, no. E 653)
        Another in the series of silent ethnographic films
        showing one traditional activity.

2102   WOMEN OF PAKISTAN
        (c. 1960?) / 20 min / sound / color / 16 mm
        Embassy of Pakistan.
        Looks at colorful traditional costumes of Pakistani
        women. Profiles the work of the Women's National Guard
        of Pakistan.

2103   WRESTLING MATCHES (JAT, WEST PAKISTAN)
        1961, released 1963 / 4 min / silent / b&w / 16 mm
        Encyclopaedia Cinematographica. Distributed by Pennsylvania
        State University. (Ency. Cinematographica, no. E 548)
        Another in the series of silent ethnographic films
        depicting traditional activities. Shows a local
        wrestling match among tribesmen in West Pakistan.

PAKISTAN - TRAVELOGS AND REGIONAL STUDIES

2104   ASSIGNMENT PAKISTAN
        1961 / 9 min / sound / color / 35 mm
        Twentieth Century - Fox Film Corp. (Movietone Adventure
        series) (NUC Fi 67-1451) Credits: Producer - Edmund Reek,
        Director - Jack Kuhne. Cinemascope. Location: Library of
        Congress (FEA 76) *
        Theatrically released travelog. Shows spots of interest
        to tourists in Pakistan. Includes scenes of the Khyber
        Pass, Peshawar, Lahore, Karachi and East Pakistan.
        Discusses Islam, agriculture, crafts, hydro-electric
        power and the history of Pakistan according to Kipling.
        Library of Congress print is experiencing color
        deterioration.

2105   CHRISTIAN CHURCHES IN PAKISTAN
        (n.d.) / ? / sound / b&w / 16 mm
        Embassy of Pakistan.
        Travelog. Shows Christian churches in predominantly
        Muslim Pakistan.

2106   INDIA AND PAKISTAN: LANDS AND PEOPLES
        1956 / 13 min / sound / color or b&w / 16 mm
        Coronet Instructional Films. (NUC Fi 56-219) Credits:
        Educational Collaborator - Joseph E. Spencer. Locations:
        Brigham Young U. / Kent State U. / Library of Congress (FBA
        557) / U. of Illinois / U. of Kansas / U. of Nebraska.
        Intended for junior-senior high school audiences. Looks
        at life in the northern highlands, Indus Valley, north

Indian plain and the Deccan Plateau of India and
Pakistan. Profiles agriculture, natural resources,
industry, education and housing. Contrasts rural and
urban life.

2107   INDIA (PAKISTAN AND THE UNION OF INDIA)
       1951 / 18 min / sound / b&w / 16 mm
       Encyclopaedia Britannica Films. (NUC Fi 52-1169) Credits:
       Educational Collaborator - Clarence W. Sorensen. Locations:
       Kent State U. / Library of Congress (FBA 559) / U. of Kansas
       / U. of Nebraska / U. of Texas at Austin.
          Intended for junior-senior high school audiences. Traces
          the influence of tradition, religion, land and climate on
          the peoples of India and Pakistan. Looks at complex
          religious, national and linguistic problems of the sub-
          continent and the isolation of villages from urban areas.
          Describes progress in education, industry, and law.

2108   INVITATION TO PAKISTAN
       1962 / 15 min / sound / color / 16 mm
       U.S. Information Agency. Made by Hearst Metrotone News.
       Released for educational use through U.S. Office of
       Education. (NUC FiE 63-282)
          Filmed record of Jacqueline Kennedy's 1962 tour of
          Pakistan with her sister, Lee Radziwill. Includes scenes
          of Karachi, Lahore, the Khyber Pass and Shalimar Gardens.

2109   JOURNEY AMONG FRIENDS
       (n.d.) / 20 min / sound / b&w / 16 mm
       Embassy of Pakistan. No other information available.

2110   JOURNEY FOR PEACE WITH HONOR
       (n.d.) / 10 min / sound / b&w / 16 mm
       Embassy of Pakistan. No other information available.

2111   MARKETS IN PAKISTAN
       1966 / 4 min / silent / color / standard or super 8 mm loop
       Wayne Mitchell and Compass Films. Released by International
       Communication Films. (South Asia series) (LC 78-700550)
          Looks at traditional commerce in Pakistan. Shows an open
          air market and the variety of products sold.

2112   NORTHWEST FRONTIER PROVINCE OF PAKISTAN
       1953 / 20 min / sound / color / 16 mm
       Henry Arian. Released by Kinesis, Inc. (NUC FiA 55-364)
          Looks at semi-nomadic peoples of the north-west frontier
          province in Pakistan. Discusses problems of the
          Pakistani state, disputes with India and the role of the
          British in the creation of Pakistan.

2113   PAKISTAN
       1955 / 14 min / sound / color or b&w / 16 mm
       Encyclopaedia Britannica Films. (NUC Fi 55-118) Credits:

Producer - Milan Herzog, Educational Collaborator - Clarence
W. Sorensen. Locations: Library of Congress (FBA 1205 / U.
of Illinois.
Looks at the new state of Pakistan. Explains Islam is
the force which unifies the two part nation. Includes
scenes of the Punjab, Karachi, village life, and rice and
jute farmers.

2114   PAKISTAN
1974 / 12 min / sound / color / 16 mm
Authentic Pictures. Released by McGraw-Hill. (LC
75-700410) No other information available.

2115   PAKISTAN CAMEOS
(c. 1960?) / 15 min / sound / color / 16 mm
Embassy of Pakistan.
Travelog of Pakistan. Includes scenes of the Lahore
Horse and Cattle Show, Khyber Pass, a Baluchi holiday
celebration, the Seventh Annual National Games, and the
Chittagong Hill Tracts.

2116   PAKISTAN - ITS LAND AND PEOPLE
1955 / 17 min / sound / b&w / 16 mm
Edward Levonian. Released by McGraw-Hill. (Lands and Their
Peoples series) (NUC Fi 55-250) Credits:
Director-Photographers - J. Michael Hagopian, Edward
Levonian. Locations: Kent State U. / Library of Congress
(FBA 1206) / U. of Nebraska. *
Dated general introduction to Pakistan intended for
high school audiences. Outlines physical separation of
east and west Pakistan by India. Looks at trade, communications, and Muslim and Hindu religious communities.
Examines differences in climate and crops produced in
various provinces. Shows local arts and crafts.
Stresses unity of Pakistani people despite differences in
language, culture and religion. Of marginal use for
classroom teaching due to major political changes in the
area.

2117   PAKISTAN LOOKS AHEAD
(n.d.) / 26 min / sound / b&w / 16 mm
Embassy of Pakistan. No other information available.

2118   PAKISTAN PANORAMA
(c. 1960?) / 30 min / sound / color / 16 mm
Afzal Khan. Embassy of Pakistan.
Listed in some catalogs as: WHERE EAST MEETS WEST.
General apolitical travelog of Pakistan. Discusses the
transition to western technology. Includes scenes of
various provinces in Pakistan.

2119   PAKISTAN: A TWO-PART NATION
1970 / 19 min / sound / color / 16 mm

McGraw-Hill Book Co. Made by Authentic Pictures. (The
Oriental World series) (LC 74-709267) Credits: Advisors -
Dorothy W. Drummond, Robert R. Drummond, Clyde F. Kohn.
Locations: Library of Congress (FAB 1346/FBB 0310) / U. of
Illinois. *
   Uses a musical background and no narration. Presents a
   montage of images contrasting West and East Pakistan,
   later called Bangladesh. Shows lack or excess of water
   resources, developed and traditional agriculture and
   industry. Shows scenes of villages, cities, mosques and
   craftsmen at work. Intended for high school to adult
   audiences. If used for classroom instruction, should
   include information on the creation of Bangladesh as a
   separate state.

2120 SEE PAKISTAN
      1963 / 15 min / sound / color / 16 mm
      Pakistan Pictures. Distributed by the Embassy of Pakistan,
      and by the American Friends of the Middle East.
         General travelog of West Pakistan. Includes scenes of
         Karachi, the Indus Valley, the Khyber Pass and the
         northern frontier. Looks at people and customs in these
         areas.

2121 SYMPHONY OF THE SEASONS
      (n.d.) / 35 min / sound / 16 mm
      Embassy of Pakistan.
         To promote tourism. General travelog of Pakistan.
         Includes scenes of spring in the Sind, harvest time in
         the Punjab, and fall and winter in the north-west
         frontier province.

2122 THIS IS PAKISTAN
      1954 / 24 min / sound / color or b&w / 16 mm
      Hal Linker. Released by Hollywood Film Enterprises. (NUC
      FiA 56-838) Eastman Kodachrome.
         General introduction to Pakistan. Includes scenes of
         Lahore, Karachi, Peshawar, the Khyber Pass, Dacca and the
         Chittagong Hill Tracts. Shows transportation, the jute
         and cotton industries and the people of Pakistan.

PAKISTAN - REGIONAL STUDIES

2123 BALUCHISTAN
      (n.d.) / ? / sound / 16 mm
      Embassy of Pakistan.
         Profiles the area of Baluchistan. Includes information
         on the fishing industry along the Makran coast, mining
         minerals in the north, oil and gas drilling, road
         building, and drilling for water. Contrasts desert and
         fertile valley regions. Shows Quetta, capital of the
         province, a local educational and urban center.

2124   CHITRAL
(n.d.) / 15 min / sound / 16 mm
Embassy of Pakistan. No other information available.

2125   CHITTAGONG HILL TRACT
(n.d.) / 10 min / sound / color / 16 mm
Embassy of Pakistan.
General introduction to the Chittagong Hill Tract region
of Pakistan. Profiles geography, agriculture and the
people.

2126   CITY OF LAHORE
(n.d.) / 20 min / sound / b&w / 16 mm
Embassy of Pakistan. No other information available.

2127   DACCA
(c. 1955?) / 20 min / sound / b&w / 16 or 35 mm
Pakistan Pictures. Embassy of Pakistan.
Profiles Dacca, the center of Islamic culture in East
Bengal. Looks at jute industry and history of the area
through Arabic manuscripts and artifacts. Tours the old
fort at Dacca.

2128   EAST OF KHYBER
1955 / 20 min / sound / b&w / 16 or 35 mm
Pakistan Pictures. Formerly distributed by Embassy of
Pakistan.
Profiles tribesmen of the Swat around the Khyber Pass.
Looks at attitudes, customs, a Kathak dance and a
wedding. Contrasts nomadic and sedentary ways of life
around the area of Peshawar.

2129   (EAST PAKISTAN COOPERATIVES)
(n.d.) / 24 min / sound / 16 mm
Agencies for Voluntary Action Programs (Peace Corps.)
Location: National Archives (RG 362-26) No other information available.

2130   ENCHANTING VALLEY
(n.d.) / 18 min / sound / 16 mm
Embassy of Pakistan. No other information available.

2131   GANDHARA
(n.d.) / 20 min / sound / 16 mm
Embassy of Pakistan. No other information available.

2132   HILL TRACTS OF PAKISTAN
(c. 1960?) / 15 min / sound / b&w / 16 mm
Embassy of Pakistan.
Profiles the people of the Chittagong Hill Tracts of East
Pakistan. Looks at activities, customs, music and dance.

2133   INDUS VALLEY ROAD
(n.d.) / 20 min / sound / 16 mm
Embassy of Pakistan. No other information available.

2134   KARAKURUM HIGHWAY
        (c. 1978) / 20 min / sound / color / 16 or 35 mm
        Embassy of Pakistan. Location: Library of Congress. No
        other information available.

2135   LAND OF THE INDUS
        (n.d.) / 30 min / sound / 16 mm
        Embassy of Pakistan.
            Profiles various peoples along the Indus River in
            Pakistan from the Kalash in the Hindu Kush to Pushtoon in
            the Chitralli River area. Traces the river from the
            Punjab to Sind.

2136   MOUNTAIN PARADISE
        (n.d.) / 10 min / sound / 16 mm
        Embassy of Pakistan. No other information available.

2137   NORTHERN REGION OF PAKISTAN
        (n.d.) / 20 min / sound / 16 mm
        Embassy of Pakistan.
            General travelog of Pakistan. Includes scenes of Hunza,
            Chitral and Gilgit. Shows lakes, forts, mountains,
            valleys and rivers of the region.

2138   PLEDGE REDEEMED
        (c. 1960) / 20 min / sound / b&w / 16 mm
        Embassy of Pakistan.
            Looks at rehabilitation of refugees in the Korangi Colony
            of Pakistan. Shows progress of Pakistan in land reform.
            Discusses administrative and constitutional reform
            following independence from India.

2139   RENDEVOUS KARACHI
        (n.d.) / 20 min / sound / color / 16 mm
        Embassy of Pakistan.
            General travelog of the city of Karachi.

2140   RIVER INDUS
        1963 / 30 min / sound / color / 16 mm
        Embassy of Pakistan. Distributed by the American Friends of
        the Middle East.
            Traces the Indus River from the Kashmir Mountains down
            through farmland, villages and cities in West Pakistan.

2141   SONS OF THE RIVER
        (n.d.) / 30 min / sound / 16 mm
        Embassy of Pakistan. No other information available.

2142   STORY OF THE INDUS RIVER
        (n.d.) / 25 min / sound / 16 mm
        Embassy of Pakistan.
            Profiles areas of Pakistan along the Indus River.
            Shows the ancient civilization at Mohenjodaro, the 17th

century Shah Jehan Mosque at Thatta, the city of Islamabad, and modern urban areas. Includes scenes of people living in houseboats on the river, using the Quran to teach reading, a wedding ceremony, and arts and crafts. Profiles the fishing industry along the river.

PAKISTAN - WATER AND LAND USE

2143   HABITAT: PAKISTAN
        1976 / 24 min / sound / color / 16 mm
        Vision Habitat. United Nations Films.
        Profiles urban problems in Pakistan caused by exodus of villagers to the cities. Looks at ways to improve village life including better dam and irrigation projects and technical assistance to farmers. Describes Agroville project to help farmers raise poultry, build roads and houses and increase rice and sugar cane cultivation.

2144   HOT DRY LAND OF PAKISTAN
        1966 / 4 min / silent / color / standard or super 8 mm
        Wayne Mitchell and Compass Films. Released by International Communication Films. (South Asia series) (LC 76-700539)
        Looks at desert climate in West Pakistan and the adaptation of housing to suit the harsh climate.

2145   A LAND OF WATER: EAST PAKISTAN
        1963 / 4 min / silent / color / 8 mm
        International Communications Foundation. (South Asia: India series) (NUC FiA 63-1495) Credits: Writer - L. Van Mourick, Photographer - Frank Chow.
        Excerpt from: HILL TRACTS OF CHITTAGONG. Shows flooded rice paddies and waterways of East Pakistan, later Bangladesh.

2146   LIFE IN DESERT AREAS: WEST PAKISTAN
        1963 / 4 min / silent / color / 8 mm
        International Communications Foundation. (South Asia: India series) (NUC FiA 63-1496)
        Excerpt from the film: THE INDUS RIVER. Looks at the provincial capital of Quetta. Shows development and adaptation of tribesmen to desert areas of West Pakistan.

2147   PAKISTAN: THE LAND
        1968 / 9 min / sound / color / 16 and super 8 mm
        Alpha Corp. of America. (Asia: Lands and Peoples series) (NUC FiA 68-2971) Credits: Educational Consultant - Elizabeth Eiselen. Location: Library of Congress (FAA 7667)
        *
        Intended for elementary to junior high school audiences. Describes Pakistan as a nation of over 100 million people in an agriculturally based society. Contrasts desert West Pakistan with flooded East Pakistan. Briefly looks

at history and geography. A dated but fairly good introduction to Pakistan showing uneven distribution of
natural resources.

2148   PAKISTAN: LAND OF PROMISE
        (c. 1976?) / 15 min / sound / color / 16 mm
        Agency for International Development. U.S. Dept. of State.
        Distributed by Association Films.
        Looks at efforts to provide food for Pakistan's 72
        million people by increasing production using western
        technology. Profiles the Indus Basin Development Program
        and Tarbela Dam, intended to irrigate arid western
        Pakistan. Shows foreign assistance in rebuilding roads,
        houses and schools destroyed by flooding and war.
        Describes efforts to reduce 5000 per day birth rate by
        20%.

2149   SURVIVAL AGAINST SALINITY
        (c. 1960?) / 30 min / sound / b&w / 16 mm
        Embassy of Pakistan.
        Describes problem of irrigation and salt build up in arid
        regions of West Pakistan.

PAKISTAN   -   AGRICULTURE

2150   COTTON - IMPORTANT PRODUCT OF WEST PAKISTAN
        (c. 1966) / 4 min / silent / color / 8 mm
        International Communications Foundation. (South Asia
        series) (NUC FiA 68-2474) Credits: Producer - Wayne
        Mitchell.
        Profiles the cotton industry in West Pakistan. Discusses
        irrigation and traditional labor intensive methods used
        to transform raw cotton into a finished product.

2151   GOLDEN FIBRE
        (c. 1960?) / 15 min / sound / b&w / 16 mm
        Embassy of Pakistan.
        Profiles Pakistan's jute industry. Looks at cultivation,
        manufacture and export of this major crop.

2152   HARVEST OF THE SEA
        (c. 1950?) / 10 min / sound / color / 16 mm
        Embassy of Pakistan.
        Profiles the fishing industry of East and West Pakistan.

2153   MOUNTAIN FARMING (DARD, NORTH-WEST PAKISTAN, GILGIT
        DISTRICT)
        1955, released 1959 / 6 min / silent / b&w / 16 mm
        Encyclopaedia Cinematographica. Distributed by Pennsylvania
        State U. (Ency. Cinematographica, no. E 211)
        Another in the series of silent ethnographic films
        depicting a single activity. Looks at traditional
        farming methods used in mountainous areas of Pakistan.

2154   THE PROMISE OF PAKISTAN
        1964 / 28 min / sound / color / 16 or 35 mm
        California Texas Oil Corp. Made by Rayant Pictures.
        (Caltex International Public Relations series) (NUC FiA
        66-1529) Credits: Producer-Director - John Durst, Music -
        Steve Race, Editor - Nicholas Gurney.
             Profiles the increase of mechanization in agriculture and
             industry following construction of dams in the Indus
             Valley of Pakistan.

2155   A SIMPLE CUP OF TEA
        1966 / 28 min / sound / b&w / 16 mm
        U.S. Dept. of Agriculture. (LC 72-700548) National
        Audio-Visual Center.
             Follows agricultural advisor Ben Ferguson on a tour of
             East Pakistan, later Bangladesh. Describes innovations
             introduced in agriculture.

PAKISTAN - INDUSTRIALIZATION, DEVELOPMENT, EDUCATION

2156   HUMAN WELFARE
        (c. 1960?) / 20 min / sound / b&w / 16 mm
        Embassy of Pakistan.
             Looks at educational and social programs introduced by
             the government of Pakistan.

2157   INDUSTRIAL BEGINNINGS IN WEST PAKISTAN
        1972 / 17 min / sound / color / 16 mm
        Institut fur Film und Bild, Munich. Released in the U.S. by
        Films Incorporated. (Man and His World series) (LC
        71-715386)
             Looks at replacement of labor intensive domestic
             industries with large scale heavy industry in West
             Pakistan. Describes technical training programs and
             resulting improvements in transportation, building and
             manufacturing. Intended for junior-senior high school
             audiences.

2158   INTERNATIONAL CONGRESS ON ALLAMA IQBAL
        (n.d.) / ? / sound / 16 mm
        Embassy of Pakistan. No other information available.

2159   PAKISTAN INDUSTRIALIZES
        1972 / 3 min / silent / color / super 8 mm loop
        Institut fur Film und Bild, Munich. Released in the U.S. by
        Films, Incorporated. (Man and His World series) (LC
        72-701552)
             Looks at introduction of modern industrial techniques to
             Pakistan. Shows training programs and new plants and
             factories.

2160   THE PAKISTANI
        1969 / 17 min / sound / color / 16 mm

Public Media, Inc. Institut fur Film und Bild, Munich.
Released by Films, Incorporated. (Man and His World series)
(LC 73-705490)
   Looks at efforts by the government of Pakistan to introduce mechanized methods of production. Examines labor
   intensive traditional methods currently used in stone-
   cutting and carpet making.

2161   PLANNED PROGRESS OF PAKISTAN
       1956 / 31 min / sound / b&w / 16 mm
       Government of Pakistan. Released by the Pakistan Mission to
       the United Nations. (NUC FiA 64-1388)
          Shows development programs in industry, building and
          manufacturing. Profiles acheivements of Pakistan since
          independence.

2162   ROAD TO PROSPERITY
       1963 / 31 min / sound / b&w / 16 mm
       Embassy of Pakistan.
          Looks at effect of modernization on life in Pakistan.

2163   THREE YEARS OF PROGRESS
       (c. 1961) / 17 min / sound / b&w / 16 mm
       Embassy of Pakistan.
          Profiles development and technical progress in Pakistan
          from 1958 to 1961.

2164   TOWARDS FULFILLMENT
       (c. 1960) / 25 min / sound / b&w / 16 mm
       Embassy of Pakistan.
          Profiles economic development in Pakistan from 1959-1960.

2165   TRIAL BY EFFORT
       (c. 1960) / 20 min / sound / b&w / 16 mm
       Embassy of Pakistan.
          Looks at economic development in East and West Pakistan.

2166   WHEELS OF POWER
       (c. 1960) / 25 min / sound / b&w / 16 mm
       Embassy of Pakistan.
          Traces progress of the first 5 Year Plan in Pakistan.
          Describes goals of the second 5 Year Plan.

PAKISTAN - THE ARTS

2167   ARCHITECTURE OF PAKISTAN
       (n.d.) / 28 min / sound / 16 mm
       Embassy of Pakistan.
          Overview of cultural influences on the region of Pakistan
          from the sixth century B.C. to the present. Looks at the
          combination of traditional and modern designs in
          Pakistani architecture. Shows Gandhara, Sultanate and
          Mughul period structures.

405

2168   HANDICRAFTS OF PAKISTAN
       (n.d.) / 18 min / sound / color / 16 mm
       Embassy of Pakistan.
       Looks at traditional arts and crafts in Pakistan.
       Discusses cultural and aesthetic values held throughout
       the centuries by craftsmen.

2169   HANDICRAFTS OF PAKISTAN
       1966 / 4 min / silent / color / super or standard 8 mm loop
       Wayne Mitchell and Compass Films. Released by International
       Communication Films. (South Asia series) (LC 70-700540)
       Looks at handicraft production in Pakistan and stresses
       the importance of crafts to the economy. Includes
       examples of carved wood, ivory inlay, woven baskets,
       objects in brass and silver, textiles, and felt mats.

2170   MAKING ROCK PAINTING (DARD, NORTH-WEST PAKISTAN,
       GILGIT DISTRICT)
       1955, released 1959 / 3 min / silent / b&w / 16 mm
       Encyclopaedia Cinematographica. Distributed by Pennsylvania
       State University. (Ency. Cinematographica, no. E 212)
       Another in the series of silent ethnographic films on a
       single subject. Shows rock paintings from the north-west
       province of Pakistan.

2171   MEN'S DANCE - DHANDYO (JAT, WEST PAKISTAN)
       1961, released 1963 / 3 min / silent / b&w / 16 mm
       Encyclopaedia Cinematographica. Distributed by Pennsylvania
       State University. (Ency. Cinematographica, no. E 547)
       Another in the series of silent ethnographic films.
       Shows traditional folk dances of West Pakistan among the
       Jat.

2172   PAINTING IN PAKISTAN
       (c. 1953) / 17 min / sound / b&w / 16 mm
       Pakistan Pictures. Embassy of Pakistan. Location: Library
       of Congress (FBA 9379) *
       Intended for high school to adult audiences. Unfor-
       tunately in black and white. Looks at detailed Mughul
       miniatures from the British Museum, Victoria and Albert
       Museum, Bodleian Library and Royal Asiatic Society in
       Great Britain. Also profiles several modern Pakistani
       artists including Abdul Rahman Chagtai, Faizi Ramin,
       Zainul Abd ad-Din, Zubaida Aud, a woman artist of the
       Dacca Art School, and Shafi al-Din Hamid, who works in
       water scenes and woodcuts. More a film on art appre-
       ciation than technique. Good introduction to medieval
       and modern art in Pakistan.

2173   SADEQUAIN
       (n.d.) / 20 min / sound / 16 mm
       Embassy of Pakistan.
       Looks at the life and work of contemporary Pakistani
       artist Sadequain.

2174   SHAMANISTIC DANCE (DARD, NORTH-WEST PAKISTAN, GILGIT
        DISTRICT)
        1955, released 1959 / 4 min / silent / b&w / 16 mm
        Encyclopaedia Cinematographica. Distributed by Pennsylvania
        State University. (Ency. Cinematographica, no. E 213)
        Another in the series of silent ethnographic films
        looking at traditional activities. Documents a tradi-
        tional dance of the Dard of north Pakistan.

2175   THREADLINES PAKISTAN
        (n.d.) / 45 min / sound / 16 mm
        Embassy of Pakistan.
        Looks at the ancient art of weaving in Pakistan.
        Includes examples of woven cotton, wheat straw braiding,
        blanket weaving, wax painting on silk (batik), woven goat
        hair and wool tapestries, hand-blocked patterns on cloth,
        patchwork, applique designs and embroidered fleece mats.

PAKISTAN - MUSIC AND DANCE

2176   DANCES OF NAI KIRAN
        (c. 1960) / 25 min / sound / b&w / 16 mm
        Embassy of Pakistan. Distributed by the American Friends
        of the Middle East.
        Shows performance of folk dances from various regions of
        Pakistan.

2177   FOLK DANCES AND MUSIC OF PAKISTAN
        (c. 1960) / 15 min / sound / b&w / 16 mm
        Embassy of Pakistan.
        Follows a professional dance troupe as it tours. Shows
        performance of traditional Pakistani dances.

2178   FOLK MUSIC OF WEST PAKISTAN
        1968 / 20 min / sound / color / 35 mm
        Directorate of Press Cell. Information Dept. Government of
        West Pakistan. Credits: Director - Ali Ahmed Brohi.
        Location: Library of Congress (FEA 4606-07) *
        General introduction to folk instruments of Pakistan.
        Shows natural daily sounds are reflected in traditional
        instruments such as the reed pipe, drum, flute and three
        stringed lute.

2179   FOLK SONGS AND DANCES OF PAKISTAN
        1954 / 20 min / sound / b&w / 16 or 35 mm
        Pakistan Pictures. Distributed by the Institut fur den
        Wissenschaftlichen Film, Gottingen, Federal Republic of
        Germany, and by Sterling Films. Locations: Embassy of
        Pakistan / Library of Congress (FBA 9378) / Purdue / U. of
        Illinois. *
        Performance of dances from the North-West Frontier,
        Punjab and East Bengal. Includes Pattan tribesmen in

407

twirling dances, women dance to the story of Princess
Sami in the Punjab, the Gida dance at harvest time and
others. Records well performed folk dances but film
quality and sound are very poor. For research pur
poses.

2180   MUSIC AND DANCES OF PAKISTAN
        (n.d.) / 30 min / sound / 16 mm
        Embassy of Pakistan.
        Different forms of Pakistani music and dance are intro-
        duced. Includes lilting jaltrung or water music and dan-
        ces of Baluchistan, Kathak and the Bhangra.

2181   POPULAR DANCES OF PAKISTAN
        (c. 1960) / 17 min / sound / color / 16 mm
        Embassy of Pakistan.
        Shows performance of popular Pakistani folk dances.

PAKISTAN - THE MILITARY

2182   PAKISTAN AIR FORCE
        (c. 1960) / 35 min / sound / color / 16 mm
        Embassy of Pakistan.
        Looks at training of Pakistani Air Force officers.

2183   PAKISTAN NAVY
        (c. 1960) / 35 min / sound / color / 16 mm
        Embassy of Pakistan.
        Looks at training of Pakistani naval recruits. Follows
        naval exercises.

QATAR

2184   FIRE AT DUKHAN
        1954 / 13 min / sound / color / 16 mm
        Producer unknown.
        Shows efforts to extinguish an oil-well fire at Dukhan on
        the Persian Gulf.

2185   FLAME IN THE DESERT
        (n.d.) / 35 min / sound / color / 16 mm
        Qatar Ministry of Information. Made by World Wide Pictures.
        Distributed by the League of Arab States.
        Looks at the state of Qatar. Shows economic and social
        development achieved after statehood and the discovery of
        oil. Profiles advances in education, medical care and
        housing in Qatar.

2186   JOURNEY FROM THE EAST
        (c. 1970) / 25 min / sound / color / 16 mm
        Jack Howells Productions. Distributed by British Petroleum
        Company.
        Follows the path of oil from a well in Qatar to a refi-
        nery in Britain and users in Norway. Shows the process
        of drilling, shipping and storing oil in the chain of
        supply. Promotional, educational film from British
        Petroleum.

2187   QATAR
        (c. 1959) / 35 min / sound / color / 16 or 35 mm
        Film Centre for Qatar Petroleum Company, Ltd. Credits:
        Producer - J.B. Holmes, Director-Writer - Rod Baxter.
        Looks at changes in the traditional sheikhdom of Qatar
        since the discovery of oil. Discusses pre-oil major
        industries including fishing and pearl diving. Stresses
        lack of water is a major problem for Qatar. Shows how
        the oil industry has brought new jobs and technologies to
        the remote nation. Profiles the expanding city of Doha.

SAUDI ARABIA - HISTORY

2188 CHARLES DOUGHTY: ARABIA 1877
1976 / 49 min / sound / color / 16 mm and videocassette
BBC, TV and Time-Life Films.
Looks at two years Charles Doughty spent in Arabia in
the late 19th century. One of the first Europeans to
travel extensively in Arabia, Doughty later published
Travels in Arabia Deserta concerning his experiences.
Shot on location. Recreates episodes from Doughty's
journals.

2189 DEATH OF A KING: WHAT CHANGES FOR THE ARAB WORLD
March 25, 1975 / 30 min / sound / color / 3/4" videocassette
CBS News. (CBS News Special Report, television program)
Credits: Correspondents - Charles Collingwood, Bill
McLaughlin, Marvin Kalb. Executive Producer - Leslie
Midgley, Producers - Bernard Birnbaum, Hall Haley.
Location: Library of Congress (VBA 1137) *
Broadcast the same day King Faisal of Saudi Arabia was
assassinated. Involves mostly speculation as to the
reason behind his death and what questions this raises
for the future of Saudi Arabia. Describes Faisal as the
person who determined how oil money was to be used.
Shows tribal customs have been maintained despite growing
western technological presence in Arabia. Discusses
Faisal's views on Jerusalem and the Palestinians.
Includes some good library footage of interviews with
Faisal. Overall a hastily prepared summary of Faisal's
life with little substance.

2190 FORBIDDEN DESERT
1957 / 60 min / sound / color / 35 mm
Warner Brothers. Credits: Producer - Cedric Francis,
Writer-Director - Jackson Winter. Location: Library of
Congress (FGA 3559, 3563) *
Uses actors in costume to recreate the travels of Swiss
traveler J.L. Burckhardt in Arabia and the Middle East
in the early 1800's. Uses long narrations from
Burkhardt's journals to recount his experiences at the
ruined city of Palmyra, in Damascus, in Jerash with the
Bedouins, Wadi Musa and Egypt. Re-enacts his first view
through a hidden gorge of the lost city of Petra carved
out of living rock. Well produced recreation. This
might interest junior-senior high school audiences in
reading the original journals. Well photographed if a

little theatrical. Library of Congress print has some
color deterioration.

2191 LOST KINGDOMS OF ARABIA
1960 / 30 min / sound / b&w / 16 mm
Insight, Inc. ABC Films, Inc. (Expedition!, television
series) (NUC Fi 68-170) Credits: Narrator - John D. Craig,
Producer - V. Fae Thomas, Writer - P.T. Furst, Music - Robert
Ernst, Photographer - William Terry. Location: Library of
Congress (FCA 2468) *
   Follows the American Foundation for the Study of Man
   expedition to find the lost kingdom of Qataban. Dr.
   Wendell Philips follows a spice route from Makulla to
   Shibam and Wadi Beihan or Timna, the excavation site.
   Shows bronze figures from around 150 B.C., artifacts and
   structures of the city. Describes problems for the expe-
   dition occasioned by the Yemen/Aden border conflict.
   Plays up danger and tribal animosity to the expedition to
   make archeology seem as adventurous as possible. Good
   record of how archeologists work and record their fin-
   dings.

SAUDI ARABIA - INTERVIEWS

2192 PRINCE SAUD AL-FAISAL
September 28, 1975 / 30 min / sound / color / 3/4"
videocassette. NBC Television. (Meet the Press, television
series) Credits: Discussants - Edwin Newman, Bill Monroe,
Roland Evans, Harry B. Ellis, Michael J. Berlin. Location:
Library of Congress (VBA 2029) *
   Interview with Saud al-Faisal, Foreign Minister of Saudi
   Arabia and son of the late King Faisal. Topics discussed
   include Saudi Arabia as a moderating force in the Middle
   East, oil price increases, Palestinian rights and the
   recognition of Israel, modernization of Saudi Arabia,
   especially in the military, Arabian aid to developing
   countries and the situation in the Middle East. Not a
   dynamic speaker, Saud presents general Saudi policy with
   no surprises. Intended for television audiences.

2193 SHEIK AHMED ZAKI YAMANI
December 9, 1973 / 30 min / sound / color / 2" videotape
NBC Television. (Meet the Press, television series)
Location: Library of Congress (VDA 0339) No other infor-
mation available.

SAUDI ARABIA - SOCIOLOGY AND ETHNOLOGY

2194 ARABIA
1928 / 9 min / silent / b&w / 16 mm
Pathe Exchange, Inc. Location: Library of Congress (FAA

411

3269) *
In very good shape considering age. Shows general scenes
of Arabia. Shows women spinning, weaving, gathering
water and milling wheat. Shows men eating and playing
musical instruments. Examines importance of camels and
sheep as food and clothing for nomads. Stresses war-like
nature of tribes. Includes good footage of individuals.
For library footage purposes.

2195   ARABIAN BAZAAR
1953 / 10 min / sound / color / 16 mm
F.W. von Keller. Released by Encyclopaedia Britannica
Films. (NUC FiA 53-946) Credits: Educational Collaborator
- Richard Hartshorne, Photographer - Jack Cardiff.
Locations: Library of Congress (FAA 3270) / Syracuse U. / U.
of Nebraska. *
Intended for junior-senior high school audiences.
Presents the difficulty and loneliness of life in the
desert. Shows a market scene, magicians, women dancing,
a fortune teller and other entertainments of the oasis or
village bazaar. Has poor narration with some inaccuracies and terrible choice of music.

2196   BEDOUINS OF ARABIA
1969 / 20 min / ssound / color / 16 mm
Institut fur Film und Bild, Munich. Public Media, Inc.
Released by Films, Incorporated. (Man and His World series)
(LC 76-704755) Locations: Florida State U. / Kent State U.
/ Library of Congress (FBB 2764) / Middle East Institute /
Penn. State U. / U. of Illinois / U. of Iowa / U. of
Michigan / U. of Minnesota / U. of Nebraska. *
Edited version of the film: THE EMPTY QUARTER, no. 2198.
Intended for general audiences. Looks at traditional
nomadic life among the Bedouins of Arabia. Shows herds
watered at an oasis, preparation of meals, breaking camp
and the search for pasturage for sheep and camels.
Entertainments include conversation, dancing and a camel
race. Says little about women. Mentions many nomads are
now working as laborers in port cities and in oil fields.

2197   DRESSING AND INSCRIBING A TOMBSTONE
1966 / 7 min / silent / color / 16 mm
Encyclopaedia Cinematographica. Distributed by Pennsylvania
State University.
Another in the series of silent ethnographic films
showing a single traditional activity. Profiles a stone
mason in the Hadhramaut as he inscribes a block of red
sandstone with an iron needle.

2198   EMPTY QUARTER
1966 / 48 min / sound / color / 16 mm
Public Media, Inc. Released by Films, Incorporated.
Distributed by International Television Trading Corp. (LC

412

74-706561)   Credits: Director - Richard Taylor, Photographer
- Mustafu Hammuri. Locations: Middle East Institute / New
York Public Donnell Film Library.
Re-enacts experiences of British traveler Wilfred
Thesiger in the Empty Quarter, the Rub al-Khali desert of
southeast Arabia. Describes nomadic Bedouin values and
customs. Shows how post-WWII exploitation of oil effects
the Bedouin. Listed in some catalogs as released in
1969.

SAUDI ARABIA   -   THE HAJJ, PILGRIMAGE TO MECCA

2199   THE HAJJ
        1960 / 25 min / sound / color / 16 mm
        Producer unknown. Distributed by Farm Film Foundation and
        by the Middle East Institute.
            Documents the pilgrimage to Mecca, one of the five reli-
            gious obligations for Muslims. Shows ceremonies con-
            nected with the pilgrimage. Gives historical background
            and information on Islam.

2200   JOURNEY TO MECCA
        (c. 1942?) / 16 min / sound / b&w / 16 or 35 mm
        Marcel Ichac. Distributed by Radim Films. (NUC FiA 52-696)
        Location: U. of Michigan.
            Listed in catalogs as released in 1942, 1948, and 1950.
            For high school to college audiences. Describes the
            significance of the annual pilgrimage to Mecca. Shows
            rituals associated with the hajj. Describes how the
            annual event brings together Muslims from across the
            world. One of the earlier filmed versions of the hajj.
            Includes some misleading statements about Islam.

2201   MECCA: THE FORBIDDEN CITY
        (c. 1960) / 52 min / sound / color / 16 mm
        Abol Rezai, Iranfilm.
            Listed in some catalogs as: FORBIDDEN CITY. Describes
            the hajj or pilgrimage to Mecca for Shi'i as well as
            Sunni Muslims. Shows various rituals associated with the
            hajj. Includes historical background, information on
            Islam, and the social context of the event. Supposedly
            one of the better films on the hajj.

2202   PILGRIMAGE TO MECCA
        1957 / 25 min / silent / color / 16 mm
        Safouh Naamani. Made by W.A. Palmer Films. (LC 76-701954)
        Location: Library of Congress (FCA 1017)
            Documents the 1954 pilgrimage or hajj to Mecca. Includes
            scenes of Arab world leaders performing the hajj, a reli-
            gious obligation in Islam. Another version 40 minutes in
            length is located at Library of Congress (FCA 4271) with
            LC no. 70-701955.

SAUDI ARABIA - DEVELOPMENT AND TECHNOLOGY

2203   ARABIA MOVES AHEAD
       1963 / 20 min / sound / color / 16 mm
       Embassy of Saudi Arabia. Distributed by the American
       Friends of the Middle East.
       General presentation covering development in Saudi
       Arabia.

2204   THE CHALLENGE
       (n.d.) / 26 min / sound / color / 16 mm
       Producer unknown. Distributed by the Farm Film Foundation.
       Shows the challenge faced by Saudi Arabia to use its oil
       resources and revenues wisely.

2205   COMMUNICATION MATTERS
       (n.d.) / 17 min / sound / color / 16 mm
       Producer unknown. Distributed by Farm Film Foundation.
       Looks at improvement in communications in Saudi Arabia as
       a result of oil wealth and revenues.

2206   DEVELOPMENT AND PROSPERITY
       (n.d.) / 16 min / sound / color / 16 mm
       Producer unknown. Distributed by Farm Film Foundation.
       Listed in some catalogs as: STORY OF DEVELOPMENT
       AND PROSPERITY. Looks at advances in education, medicine
       and agriculture in Saudi Arabia made possible by oil
       revenues.

2207   THE FUTURE IS THEIRS
       (n.d.) / 17 min / sound / color / 16 mm
       Producer unknown. Distributed by Farm Film Foundation.
       Looks at advances in education and technology in Saudi
       Arabia made possible by exploitation of oil resources.

2208   KINGDOM OF SAUDI ARABIA
       (n.d.) / 45 min / sound / color / 16 mm
       Producer unknown. Distributed by the Arab Information
       Center, San Francisco.
       Not to be confused with an 80 slide program of the same
       name. Looks at general development in Saudi Arabia as a
       result of oil.

2209   MESSAGE FROM RIYADH
       (n.d.) / 30 min / sound / color / 16 mm
       Embassy of Saudi Arabia. Distributed by Farm Film
       Foundation and by Middle East Institute.
       Listed in some catalogs as 20 minutes in length.
       Contrasts traditional and modern transportation and com-
       munications in Saudi Arabia. Shows modernization
       resulting from oil exploitation and revenues.

2210   THE MIRACLE
       (n.d.) / 26 min / sound / color / 16 mm

Producer unknown. Distributed by Farm Film Foundation.
Looks at "miracles" of modernization made possible in
Saudi Arabia as a result of exploitation of oil resources.

2211   MIYAH - STORY OF WATER
1951 / 45 min / sound / color / 16 mm
Arabian American Oil Company. Distributed by Middle East
Institute. Location: Library of Congress (FCA 3058)   *
Available in English and Arabic soundtracks. Looks at
all aspects of water in Saudi Arabia. Uses animation to
show where water is trapped below ground. Describes how
wells are drilled and water is transported and used. An
interesting subject, well presented. For high school to
adult audiences. Library of Congress print has Arabic
language soundtrack.

2212   THE NEW FACE OF SAUDI ARABIA
(n.d.) / 20 min / sound / color / 16 mm
Embassy of Saudi Arabia. Distributed by Farm Film
Foundation.
Listed in some catalogs as: NEW FACES OF SAUDI ARABIA.
No other information available.

2213   SAUDI ARABIA
(n.d.) / 45 min / sound / color / 16 mm
Embassy of Saudi Arabia. No other information available.

2214   SAUDI ARABIA: THE OIL REVOLUTION
1975 / 25 min / sound / color / 16 mm
Anthony Thomas. Made by Yorkshire Television. Distributed
by Learning Corp. of America. (The Arab Experience series)
(LC 76-700281) Locations: Boston U. / Kent State U. /
Oklahoma State U. / Syracuse U. / U. of Minnesota / U. of
Missouri.
Intended for junior high school to adult audiences.
Shows the major paradox of life in Saudi Arabia.
Contrasts traditional culture and values with adaptation
of western technology especially in the oil industry.
Looks at modernization and development in education, land
reclamation, women's rights and the military. Discusses
stress placed on traditional society by these innova-
tions.

2215   SKYLIFT TO JEDDAH
1977 / 9 min / sound / color / 16 mm
Sikorsky Aircraft.
Shows use of Sikorsky helicopters to unload cargo ships
in the crowded harbor of Jeddah.

SAUDI ARABIA - THE OIL INDUSTRY

2216   AROUND THE CLOCK
1969 / 20 min / sound / color / 16 mm

ARAMCO.
Shows a typical 24 hour day in Aramco oil operations in
Saudi Arabia. Stresses the importance of engineers,
technicians and equipment in drilling for crude oil.

2217 DESERT HORIZONS
1957 / 29 min / sound / color or b&w / 16 mm
ARAMCO, Arabian American Oil Company. Distributed by
American Friends of the Middle East, and by Middle East
Institute.
Looks at early exploration for oil by Aramco in Saudi
Arabia. Outlines early history of Saudi Arabia and shows
how oil has become a mainstay of the economy. Describes
recruitment and training of Aramco employees.

2218 THE EXPLORERS
1962 / 21 min / sound / color / 16 mm
ARAMCO, Arabian American Oil Company. Made by Mediterranean
East, Inc. (NUC FiA 63-487)
Available in English and Arabic soundtracks. Uses animation and live action to describe oil exploration and
exploitation in Saudi Arabia by Aramco. Shows how oil is
formed and how geologists determine where oil may be
found. Looks at exploration in the Rub al-Khali or Empty
Quarter, the south-eastern desert of Arabia.

2219 HASSAN DISCOVERS THE WORLD OF OIL
1957 / 20 min / sound / color / 16 mm
Arabian American Oil Company. Made by Studio Alliance with
Byron, Inc. (NUC FiA 58-782) Location: Library of Congress
(FBA 489) *
Available in English and Arabic soundtracks. Follows
Hassan al-Zahid, a worker on the pipeline of a Saudi oil
field. Describes the way in which oil is found, drilled
and transported. Compares 19th century American life
before the internal combustion engine to the current
mechanized, oil-consuming economy. Rather patronizing
narration. Presents a disturbing image of the U.S. as
exploiting natural resources of foreign countries while
marketing U.S. products. Intended to explain and promote
Aramco.

2220 NEW FRONTIERS
(c. 1960) / 20 min / sound / color / 16 mm
Producer unknown. Distributed by Nu-Art Films.
Looks at impact of oil on the peoples and economies of
the Arabian peninsula.

2221 SCIENCE OF OIL
1962 / 20 min / sound / color / 16 or 35 mm
Arabian American Oil Co. Made by Mediterranean East, Inc.
(NUC FiA 63-517)
Available in English and Arabic soundtracks. Looks at

the use of science and technology in the oil industry.
Profiles research laboratories of Aramco at Dhahran and
describes how oil is found, drilled, refined and
transported.

2222 TOUR OF ARAMCO
1959 / 20 min / sound / color / 16 mm
Arabian American Oil Co. Location: Library of Congress (FBA
1572)
Available in English and Arabic soundtracks. No other
information available.

SAUDI ARABIA - AGRICULTURE, MEDICINE

2223 THE FLY
1969 / 25 min / sound / color / 16 mm
Aramco.
Follows a Saudi farmer who becomes ill on his way to
market in Qatif. A doctor describes how common house
flies can spread disease. Discusses ways in which to
combat fly-spread diseases. Intended for overseas
distribution.

2224 GREEN DESERT
(n.d.) / 20 min / sound / color / 16 mm
Producer unknown. Distributed by Farm Film Foundation.
Describes programs of the Saudi government to modernize
irrigation, improve pest control, provide soil and water
management and increase cultivation and livestock herds.
Discusses implication of settling nomadic families for
the economy.

2225 HEALING SWORD
(n.d.) / 20 min / sound / color / 16 mm
Producer unknown. Distributed by the Farm Film Foundation
and by Middle East Institute.
Profiles expanding health and medical facilities in Saudi
Arabia. Looks at government mobile health units working
with nomadic families.

2226 MALARIA
1969 / 15 min / sound / color / 16 mm
Aramco.
A team supervisor in a malaria control unit describes his
work to a Saudi village boy. Discusses the source of
malaria, how malaria-spreading mosquitos can be
controlled and programs to combat malaria.

2227 TRACHOMA
1969 / 15 min / sound / color / 16 mm
Aramco.
A Saudi sword-maker learns about trachoma when he notices

417

his vision failing. Discusses the symptoms of trachoma,
how it can be treated, and how the spread of the eye
disease can be controlled.

SAUDI ARABIA - EDUCATION

2228 IN A TWINKLING OF AN EYE
(n.d.) / 25 min / sound / color / 16 mm
Producer unknown. Distributed by Farm Film Foundation and
by Middle East Institute.
Listed in some catalogs as: TWINKLING OF AN EYE.
Looks at advances in Saudi Arabian education. Discusses
the importance of vocational education programs.

2229 KNOWLEDGE IS LIGHT
1969 / 22 min / sound / color / 16 mm
Aramco.
Profiles Aramco's industrial and technical training
programs for Saudi employees. Shows college and special
development assignments outside of Arabia. Includes
information on supervisory training.

2230 WE CAME TO LEARN
(n.d.) / 25 min / sound / color / 16 mm
Producer unknown. Distributed by Farm Film Foundation.
Follows three students at the University of Riyadh.
Shows their courses in geology, medicine and chemistry.
Describes higher education in Saudi Arabia and shows gra-
duates entering the professions.

2231 THE WISEMEN
(n.d.) / 15 min / sound / color / 16 mm
Embassy of Saudi Arabia. Distributed by the Farm Film
Foundation.
Profiles all levels of education in Saudi Arabia. Looks
at teacher training programs, adult literacy classes,
university and professional training courses and training
for the blind and deaf.

418

MUSLIM SPAIN - HISTORY

2232 AL ANDALUS
1974 / 34 min / sound / color / 16 mm
Dimensions Visual Productions. Made by Robert Frerck.
Distributed by the League of Arab States and by the Middle
East Institute. (LC 75-703647) Locations: Brigham Young
U. / Penn. State U. / U. of Illinois / U. of North Carolina
/ U. of Wisconsin.
    Intended for high school to adult audiences. Outlines
    Spanish history from the 8th century Islamic invasion to
    the expulsion of Arabs and Jews in 1492. Shows the poli-
    tics, history and culture of the Moorish kingdoms of
    Spain over a 700 year period. Examines Arab contributions
    to art, architecture and scholarship in Spain.

2233 ALHAMBRA
1952 / 19 min / sound / color / 16 mm
Producer unknown. Location: U. of Utah.
    Tours the Alhambra palace, the most famous example of
    Muslim architecture in Spain.

2234 CITADELS OF THE MEDITERRANEAN
1934 / 10 min / sound / b&w / 16 mm
Metro-Goldwyn-Mayer. Released for educational purposes by
Teaching Film Custodians, 1939. (James A. FitzPatrick's
Traveltalks series) (NUC FiA 52-4986)
    Travelog of the Mediterranean area. Includes scenes of
    Gibraltar, the Alhambra and Athens.

2235 MOSLEMS IN SPAIN
1977 / 40 min / sound / color / 16 mm
Pilgrim Films Production. Location: Syracuse U.
    Describes the struggle between Muslims and Christians for
    control of the Iberian Peninsula over a 781 year period.
    Outlines Arab contributions to Spanish culture in art and
    architecture. Shows an annual recreation of the
    Christian reconquest of Spain by the citizens of Alcoy.
    Intended for junior high school to adult audiences.

2236 MYSTIC ALHAMBRA
1954 / 14 min / sound / color / 16 mm
Producer unknown. Location: Oregon State Continuing
Education.
    Tours the Alhambra palace in Spain.

2237   SPAIN: THE LAND AND THE LEGEND
        1978 / 26 or 58 min / sound / color / 16 mm
        Al Waller. Reader's Digest. Distributed by Pyramid Films.
        (James Michener's World series) Location: Penn. State U.
        Describes Spain before, during and after the Islamic
        period. Discusses the Arab invasion and Moorish era.
        Shows examples of Muslim architecture including the
        Alhambra and Great Mosque of Cordoba. Has romanticized
        narration.

2238   SUNLIGHT AND SHADOW - THE GOLDEN AGE OF SPANISH JEWRY
        (c. 1979) / 60 min / sound / color / 16 mm
        Producer unknown. Location: Eternal Light Film Library,
        Jewish Theological Seminary, New York.
        Dr. Gerson D. Cohen describes the golden age of Spanish
        Jewry in medieval Islamic Spain. Discusses Jewish
        contributions to art and scholarship in Moorish Spain.

SUDAN - HISTORY

2239 ACTION SUDAN: THE CHURCH AND THE PEACE
1974 / 26 min / sound / color / 16 mm
Interchurch Committee for World Development and Relief,
Canada, and Church World Service. Made by Religious
Television Associates, Toronto. (LC 75-701430) Credits:
Producer - Des McCalmont, Director-Writer - Peter
Flemington, Narrator - Roy Bonisteel.
Looks at the civil war in the Sudan brought to an end in
1972. Discusses the role of the Sudanese, African and
World Church councils in helping to bring about a peace
settlement.

2240 THE FORGOTTEN KINGDOM: SUDAN
1969 / 30 min / sound / color / 16 mm
BBC-TV, London. Released in the U.S. by Time-Life Films,
1971. (The Glory That Remains series, no. 12)
(LC 75-710766) Credits: Producer - Geoffrey Baines,
Writer-Narrator - Robert Erskine. Location: U. of Illinois.
Looks at the ancient civilization of Kush, isolated even
in antiquity by the Sudanese desert and Nile cataracts.

2241 THE NEW SUDAN
(c. 1960) / 28 min / sound / color / 16 mm
Embassy of the Sudan.
Shows development in the Sudan since independence in
1956.

2242 SUDAN DISPUTE
1948 / 20 min / sound / b&w / 16 mm
J. Arthur Rank Organisation. Released in the U.S. by
British Information Services, 1952. (This Modern Age,
series no 8) (NUC FiA 52-4342) Credits: Sponsor - British
Foreign Office, Producer - Sergei Nolbandov, Associate
Producer-Literary Editor - J.L. Hodson.
Looks at fifty years of administration in the Sudan.

SUDAN - SOCIOLOGY AND ETHNOLOGY

2243 THE GALLANT ARMY
(c. 1960) / 27 min / sound / color / 16 mm
Embassy of the Sudan.
Shows training of the Sudanese armed forces.

2244   THE NUER, PART 1
        1970 / 38 min / sound / color / 16 mm
        Hillary Harris and George Breidenback. Released by
        McGraw-Hill. Locations: Brigham Young U. / New York Public
        Donnell Film Library / U. of California - Berkeley / U. of
        California Extension Media Center.
            An anthropological study of the Nuer or Nilotes of
            Ethiopia and the Sudan.

2245   THE NUER, PART 2
        1971 / 37 min / sound / color / 16 mm
        McGraw-Hill. Location: Brigham Young U.
            Traces relationships and events in the lives of the Nuer
            or Nilotic peoples of Sudan and the Ethiopian frontier.

2246   NURSING A MIRACLE
        1973 / 20 min / sound / color / 16 mm
        Office of the United Nations High Commissioner for Refugees.
        United Nations Films.
            Looks at resettlement of Sudanese refugees at the end of
            the Sudanese civil war.

2247   RESETTLEMENT OF ILLEGAL SQUATTERS IN PORT SUDAN
        TOWN
        1976 / 12 min / sound / color / 16 mm
        Vision Habitat. United Nations Films.
            Available in English, Arabic, French and Spanish
            soundtracks. Profiles the 7000 Sudanese who migrate to
            Port Sudan each year looking for a better life. Shows
            programs to supply squatters with building materials in
            order to build adequate housing for themselves on the
            outskirts of the city. Discusses problem of water and
            services for the growing population of Port Sudan.

2248   SUDAN FOLKLORE
        (n.d.) / 40 min / sound / b&w / 16 mm
        Embassy of the Sudan. No other information available.

SUDAN   -   TRAVELOGS AND REGIONAL STUDIES

2249   DOWN SOUTH UP THE NILE
        1969 / 26 min / sound / color / 16 mm
        KEG Productions, Toronto. Released in the U.S. by A-V
        Explorations. (Audubon Wildlife Theatre series) (LC
        72-710201) Credits: Producers - G.S. Kedey, R. Ellis, D.
        Gibson, Consultant - G. Knerer.
            Produced in cooperation with the National Audubon Society
            and the Canadian Audubon Society.   Examines the Egyptian
            vulture, its habits and habitat in East Africa.

2250   LAND IS GREEN
        (c. 1960) / 15 min / sound / b&w / 16 mm
        Embassy of the Sudan.

Listed in some catalogs as 28 minutes in length. General
travelog of the Sudan.

2251   THE NILE
(c. 1973?) / 2 programs, 60 min each / sound / color
KCET, Los Angeles. (Cousteau Odyssey, television series)
Credits: Executive Producer - Jacques Yves Cousteau,
Writer-Narrator - Theodore Strauss. *
    Jacques Cousteau and his late son follow the Nile River
    on its path through the Sudan. Looks at ways in which
    man attempts to change the Nile. Stresses the total
    dependence of man on the Nile for life and food.

2252   NILE RIVER BASIN AND THE PEOPLE OF THE UPPER RIVER
1950 / 17 min / sound / color or b&w / 16 mm
Academy Films. Distributed by Association Films. (NUC FiA
53-138) Credits: Producer - James A. Larsen, Photographer -
J. Michael Hagopian. Locations: Syracuse U. / U. of
Illinois.
    Looks at the Upper Nile River as it passes through Uganda
    and the Sudan. Shows the people who live along the
    river. Describes how they use the river for water, irri-
    gation, transportation and communication. Uses animation
    to outline the Nile's tributaries, drainage and navigable
    areas.

2253   NILE RIVER BASIN: UGANDA AND SUDAN
(n.d.) / 17 min / sound / b&w / 16 mm
Academy Films.
    Possibly the same film as no. 2252. Looks at the Nile
    River as it passes through Uganda and the Sudan.

2254   NILE RIVER JOURNEY
1972 / 3 min / silent / color / super 8 mm film loop
Institut fur Film und Bild, Munich. Edited and released in
the U.S. by Films, Incorporated. (Man and His World series)
(LC 72-701555)
    Follows a Nile River passenger boat on its run from
    Malakal to Juba.

2255   RIVER JOURNEY ON THE UPPER NILE
1969 / 18 min / sound / color / 16 mm
Public Media, Inc. Released by Films, Incorporated. (Man
and His World series) (LC 79-705462) Locations: Kent
State U. / Library of Congress (FBB 1968) / Penn. State U. /
U. of Illinois / U. of Michigan / U. of Minnesota / U. of
Nebraska.
    Edited version of an Institut fur Film und Bild film.
    Profiles the Sudd, a marsh area flooded by the Nile, lying
    between Juba and Malakal. Looks at problems the region
    experiences such as flooding, rainwater trapped in marsh
    areas while farmland is unirrigated, lack of water in the
    dry season, and lack of advanced equipment for agri-

culture, transportation and communications. Looks at
priority given to education and training programs for
Sudanese farmers.

2256 SAFARI OF THE SUDAN
(c. 1960) / 28 min / sound / color / 16 mm
Embassy of the Sudan.
General travelog of the Sudan. Includes information on
big game hunting.

2257 THE VILLAGE THAT VANISHED BENEATH THE NILE
1969 / 31 min / sound / b&w / 16 mm
Food and Agriculture Organization of the United Nations.
United Nations Films.
Shows the ancient town of Wadi Halfa will be submerged
as a result of the Aswan High Dam project. Shows the
villagers being resettled at Khashm el Girba. Discusses
the resettlement program, its effect on the villagers and
efforts made by the World Food Programme to assist them
until new crops can be harvested. States one tenth of
the population has refused to leave their land despite
inevitable rising water levels.

2258 WELCOME TO PORT SUDAN
(n.d.) / 20 min / sound / color / 16 mm
Producer unknown. Location: Arab Information Office,
Washington. No other information available.

SUDAN - AGRICULTURE

2259 COTTON GROWING AND SPINNING
1967 / 6 min / sound / color / 16 mm
International Film Foundation. Location: Syracuse U.
Intended for junior high school to adult audiences.
Profiles the Dogon people of the Sudan. Shows ecomony of
the Dogon is based on cotton. Outlines cotton growing
and processing techniques. No narration.

2260 THE DISTANT HORIZONS
(c. 1960) / 15 min / sound / color or b&w / 16 mm
Embassy of the Sudan.
Listed in some catalogs as 28 minutes in length. Looks
at land reform and the development project at Gezira.

2261 MECHANIZED FARMING IN THE SUDAN
(n.d.) / 25 min / sound / 16 mm
Embassy of the Sudan.
Looks at new techniques and equipment being introduced in
the Sudan to increase agricultural production.

2262 THEY PLANTED A STONE
1953 / 27 min / sound / b&w / 16 mm

British Central Office of Information. Made by World Wide
Pictures, London. Released in the U.S. by British
Information Services, 1954. (NUC FiA 55-877rev) Credits:
Producer - James Carr, Writer-Director Robin Carruthers,
Commentators - Gordon Davies, John Akar.
Looks at the project to use Nile River water to irrigate
the Sudanese desert for the Gezira cotton project. Shows
the work of the Sudanese and British governments in
construction of new dams. Describes how the standard of
living has improved in the Sudan as a result of the project.

2263   VISIT IN THE DESERT
1965 / 10 min / sound / b&w / 16 mm
World Health Organization. United Nations Films.
Available in English and French soundtracks. Shows the
work of the World Health Organization in combatting com-
municable eye diseases in a control project in Atbara,
Sudan. Shows treatment of trachoma and conjunctivitis.
Profiles a volunteer who is trained to use antibiotics
and provide education programs in the village.

2264   THE WHITE GOLD
(c. 1960?) / 28 min / sound / color / 16 mm
Embassy of the Sudan.
Follows the cycle of cotton production in the Sudan from
cultivation, harvest and processing to the market.

2265 AL-AZEM PALACE
(n.d.) / 20 min / sound / b&w / 16 mm
Producer unknown. Location: Arab Information Office,
Washington.
Tours the al-Azem palace in Syria.

2266 ANCIENT BAALBEK AND PALMYRA
1953 / 10 min / sound / color / 16 mm
Encyclopaedia Britannica Films. Credits: Producers -
E.S. Keller, F.W. Keller, Photographer - Jack Cardiff.
Kodachrome. Locations: Library of Congress (FAA 3258) /
Syracuse U. / U. of Nebraska / U. of Wisconsin.
Tours ruins of two cities of ancient Syria and shows the
people living there today. Describes the importance of
the cities as caravan centers.

2267 EVERYDAY LIFE IN A SYRIAN VILLAGE
1976 / 90 min / sound / b&w / 16 mm
Producer unknown.
An ethnographic film showing traditional life and
conditions in a Syrian village.

2268 FARID ZEINEDDINE
December 16, 1956 / 30 min / sound / b&w / 35 mm
NBC Television. (Meet The Press, television series)
Location: Library of Congress (FLA 6015)
Interview with Farid Zeineddine, Syrian Ambassador to the
United Nations and later Syrian ambassador to the U.S.
until declared persona non grata on August 14, 1958.

2269 FOOD PROCESSING IN SYRIA
1969 / 36 min / sound / color / 16 mm
Food and Agriculture Organization of the United Nations.
United Nations Films.
Looks improved food storage and processing techniques
introduced by the Syrian government and the UN Food and
Agriculture Organization. Discusses new methods for producing tomato puree, dried apricot paste, drying raisins
and olive oil extraction. Discusses automation in food
processing, hygiene, quality control and marketing of
food exports.

2270 MOVIETONE NEWS
1957 / 6 min / sound / b&w / 35 mm
Twentieth Century-Fox Film Corp. (Movietone News, vol. 40,
no. 71) Location: National Archives (200MN40.71)

Theatrical newreel. Looks at Soviet-supplied arms in
Syria. Discusses the Middle East situation in 1957.

2271   REPORT FROM SYRIA
        (n.d.) / 28 min / sound / color / 16 mm
        Producer unknown. Location: League of Arab States.
        Shows the Syrian Jewish community as a normal and
        prosperous group coexisting well within Syrian society.
        Produced as a counter to allegations of exploitation of
        the Jewish community in Syria. Describes the rela-
        tionship between the Jewish community and the Arab state
        in which it resides.

2272   SYRIA
        (n.d.) / ? / sound / color / 16 mm
        Producer unknown. (Port of Call series) No other infor-
        mation available.

2273   (TOURISTS RETURNING ON DONKEYS FROM MIZPAH, SYRIA)
        June 1903 / 1:10 min / silent / b&w / 16 mm
        Thomas Edison. Library of Congress Paper Print Collection.
        Location: Library of Congress (FLA 4911) *
        In fair condition considering age. Shows European
        tourists on donkeys led by Syrians passing in front of a
        stone wall on a country road. About 20 tourists are
        shown. Another in the series of films by A.C. Abadie for
        Thomas Edison. For historical purposes.

TUNISIA

TUNISIA - HISTORY, INTERVIEWS

2274   HABIB BOURGUIBA
May 7, 1961 / 30 min / sound / b&w / 16 mm
NBC Television. (Meet the Press, television series)
Location: Library of Congress (FRA 7143-44)
Television interview with Habib Bourguiba, president of
Tunisia, during a visit to the U.S.

2275   HABIB BOURGUIBA
May 18, 1968 / 30 min / sound / b&w / 16 mm
NBC Television. (Meet the Press, television series)
Location: Library of Congress (FRA 3434-35)
Panel interview with President Habib Bourguiba of Tunisia
during a visit to the U.S.

2276   LORD JULIUS
1958 / 20 min / sound / color / 16 mm
Embassy of Tunisia. Distributed by Tunisian National
Tourism Office.
Available in English and French soundtracks. Uses
mosaics from the Bardo Museum in Tunis and museums in
Sousse and Sfax to recreate the life of a wealthy Roman
landlord of Carthage. Creates feeling for life at the
height of Roman power in North Africa.

2277   PRESIDENT HABIB BOURGUIBA OF TUNISIA
1965 / 30 min / sound / b&w / 16 mm
CBS News. (Face the Nation, television series) (NUC Fi
68-209) Credits: Producers - Prentiss Childs, Ellen Wadley,
Director - Robert Vitarelli, Commentators - George Herman,
Martin Agronsky, Winston Burdett. Location: Library of
Congress (FBA 5197)
Interview with President Habib Bourguiba of Tunisia.
Topics covered include possibilities for a peaceful solu-
tion to the Arab-Israeli conflict, the role of Nasser as
leader of the Arab states, and the relationship between
Egypt and other North African countries.

2278   TUNISIAN VICTORY
1943 / 76 min / sound / b&w / 16 mm
British Ministry of Information and U.S. Office of War
Information. Produced by British Army Film Unit and U.S.
Army Signal Corps. Released in the U.S. by British
Information Services, 1944. (NUC FiA 52-884) Credits:
Producer-Directors - Hugh Stewart, Frank Capra, Roy

Boulting, John Huston, Anthony Veiller. Narration - J.L. Hodson, Anthony Veiller. Location: Library of Congress (FEB 0025-32) / National Archives (111M1012)
Looks at the Tunisian North African campaign during WWII. Covers the period from the American-British landing to the surrender of Axis forces.

TUNISIA - SOCIOLOGY AND ETHNOLOGY

2279   BABAA AOUSSOU
        (n.d.) / 12 min / sound / color / 16 mm
        Tunisian National Tourism Office.
        Shows a mid-summer festival held in Sousse. Describes how the festival has become a national celebration due to Presidential recognition. Includes scenes of parades, giant carnival figures, music and crowds of people celebrating. To promote tourism.

2280   BERBER VILLAGES OF SOUTHERN TUNISIA
        1971 / 30 min / sound / color / 16 mm
        Producer unknown. Distributed by Radim Films, and by Films, Incorporated. Location: Middle East Institute.
        Looks at architectural patterns in village farms and dwellings in the Matmata mountains of Tunisia. Shows the adaptation of nomadic Berbers to the environment. Includes scenes of underground dwellings.

2281   CHANGING TUNISIA
        (n.d.) / 22 min / sound / color / 16 mm
        Center of Mass Communication of Columbia University.
        Examines the people of Tunisia and their changing culture.

2282   THE GOLDEN CHAIN
        (c. 1960?) / 20 min / sound / color / 16 mm
        Embassy of Tunisia.
        Available in English and French soundtracks. Profiles the life of a Tunisian fisherman.

2283   MANTANZA
        (n.d.) / 20 min / sound / color / 16 mm
        Tunisian National Tourism Office.
        Shows traditional techniques used to fish tuna off the Isle of Zembra and the Cap Bon region of Tunisia.

TUNISIA - WOMEN AND CHILDREN

2284   A GRAIN OF SAND
        (c. 1970) / ? / sound / 16 mm
        UNICEF. Distributed by Association Instructional Materials.
        Shows the daily routine and way of life of a young boy in Tunisia.

2285   GROWING UP IN TUNIS
        (c. 1970?) / 14 min / sound / color / 16 mm
        Producer unknown. Distributed by Universal Education and
        Visual Arts.
            Profiles the life of teenagers in Tunisia. Describes how
            they must balance their North African heritage with
            European cultural influences.

2286   WOMANPOWER: EQUALITY AND DEVELOPMENT
        1975 / 28 min / sound / color / 16 mm
        United Nations Films.
            Produced for the International Women's Year in 1975.
            Shows the international women's forum convened by the UN.
            In a visit to Tunisia, women are shown holding jobs,
            receiving family planning information and legal services
            as a result of reforms in the Personal Status Code of
            1956. Discusses how national programs are needed to
            insure integration of women in the development of
            countries aided by the UN.

2287   WOMEN UP IN ARMS
        1965 / 29 min / sound / b&w / 16 mm
        U.N. Distributed by United Nations Films, and by
        McGraw-Hill. (International Zone series) Credits:
        Narrator - Alistair Cooke. Location: Purdue U. / U. of
        Washington.
            Looks at social change and emancipation of women in
            Tunisia through three generations of women in one family.
            Shows a non-speaking grandmother. Her daughter is reluc-
            tant to put aside traditional ways and despite her
            husband's urgings she rejects western values. The grand-
            daughter is shown attending a coeducational school and
            personifies the new Tunisian woman.

TUNISIA - TRAVELOGS AND REGIONAL STUDIES

2288   CAMEL FIGHTS
        (n.d.) / 20 min / sound / color / 16 mm
        Tunisian National Tourism Office.
            General introduction to Tunisia and to camels. Shows a
            camel fight at the coliseum of El Djem. Bets are placed
            while camels fight, crowds shout and musicians play.

2289   DJERBA AND THE SOUTH
        (n.d.) / 27 min / sound / color / 16 mm
        Tunisian National Tourism Office.
            General travelog of southern Tunisia. Includes scenes of
            the Jewish community of Hara Sghira and the ancient syno-
            gogue of La Ghriba. Shows the seaside oases of Zarzis,
            Gabes, the Sahara, Ksar Haddada, crater dwellings at
            Matmata and the dry salt lake of Chott Djerid.

2290   FACES OF TUNISIA
        (n.d.) / 20 min / sound / color / 16 mm
        Tunisian National Tourism Office.
           To promote tourism. Shows a couple on vacation in
           Tunisia. Includes scenes of resorts in the north,
           historical sites of Carthage and Kairowan, souks for
           shopping, Berber villages in the South, Matmata, the
           oases of Douz and the dry salt lake of Chott Djerid.

2291   JOURNEY IN TUNISIA
        1941 / 10 min / sound / color / 16 mm
        Columbia Pictures Corp. Released for educational purposes
        by Teaching Film Custodians, 1946. (De La Varre Travelogue
        series) (NUC FiA 52-4676) Credits: Producer - Andre De La
        Varre.
           A dated travelog showing Tunisia and the city of Tunis.
           Discusses a blend of European, North African and eastern
           influences found in the nation.

2292   JOURNEY THROUGH THE CENTER OF TUNISIA
        (n.d.) / 27 min / sound / color / 16 mm
        Tunisian National Tourism Office.
           Travelog of central Tunisia. Includes scenes of the city
           of Mahdia, mosques of Kairowan, mosaics, crafts, and a
           religious festival. Shows both inland areas and the sea
           coast. To promote tourism. Discusses tourist accom-
           modations.

2293   A MAGIC CARPET OVER TUNISIA
        (n.d.) / 28 min / sound / color / 16 mm
        Tunisian National Tourism Office.
           Travelog of Tunisia seen from a helicopter. Includes
           scenes of Berber villages, the coastline, Roman ruins at
           Sbeitla, Carthage, Dougga, and El Djem, the mosques of
           Kairoan, the resort of Sousse, Monastir, Sidi Bou Said,
           Hammamet, Bizerte and Tunis. In the south, this shows
           the Atlas Mountains, island of Djerba, crater houses at
           Matmata and a desert oases. To promote tourism.

2294   NEW TEMPO IN TUNISIA
        1956 / 27 min / sound / b&w / 16 or 35 mm
        Telenews Productions. Released by McGraw-Hill. (NUC Fi
        56-216) Credits: Producer - Robert W. Schofield,
        Director-Writer - Leona Carney, Narrator - John Cannon.
        Location: Library of Congress (FCA 917)
           General introduction to Tunisia. Describes the
           geography and government. Outlines social, educational,
           and economic advances made during the post-war period.
           Looks at mineral mining and expansion of industry as well
           as famous historic sites at Tunis, Kairouan, Sfax, Dougga
           and Djerba.

2295   THE THREE SHELLS
        (c. 1960) / 20 min / sound / color / 16 mm

431

Embassy of Tunisia.
Available in English and French soundtracks. Shows a
traditional Tunisian wedding dance, seaside resorts and
the island of Djerba. To promote tourism.

2296   TUNISIA, ELEGANCE AND BEAUTY
(n.d.) / 20 min / sound / color / 16 mm
Tunisian National Tourism Office.
Shows the Miss Europe Contest held in Tunisia.
Contestants are shown touring Tunis, visiting historic
sites and meeting Bedouin women.

2297   TUNISIA '57
(c. 1960?) / 20 min / sound / color / 16 mm
Embassy of Tunisia. Distributed by the American Friends of
the Middle East.
Shows famous tourist sites in Tunisia. To promote
tourism.

2298   TUNISIA GREETS YOU
(n.d.) / 25 min / sound / b&w / 16 mm
Embassy of Tunisia.
General introduction to Tunisia. Includes information on
history, agriculture, industry, education, women's
rights, sports and foreign relations.

2299   TUNISIA STEPS FORWARD
1956 / 13 min / sound / b&w / 16 or 35 mm
Telenews Productions. Released by McGraw-Hill. (NUC Fi
56-217) Credits: Producer - Robert W. Schofield,
Director-Writer - Leona Carney, Narrator - John Cannon.
Location: Library of Congress (FBA 1552)
General social and economic introduction to Tunisia.
Shows cultivation of dates, oil processing at Sfax,
breeding of Arabian horses and donkeys on a government
farm and soil conservation measures. Looks at construction of housing, hospitals and schools. Includes scenes
of Tunis and Sousse.

2300   TUNISIA: YESTERDAY AND TODAY
(n.d.) / 30 min / sound / color / 16 mm
Embassy of Tunisia. Locations: Middle East Institute /
Tunisian National Tourist Office.
Travelog of Tunisia. Shows ancient and modern aspects
of Tunisian life and culture. Looks at the Punic-
Carthagenian, Roman-Christian, Arab and Muslim eras in
Tunisian history. Gives information on the society, eco-
nomy, and agriculture of Tunisia. Includes information
for tourists.

2301   TUNISIAN CONCORD
(c. 1960?) / 20 min / sound / b&w / 16 mm
Producer unknown. Distributed by the French American

432

Cultural Service.
Travelog of Tunisia including scenes of Carthage,
Kairouan and Nabeul.

2302   WELCOME TO TUNISIA
25 min / sound / color / 16 mm
Tunisian National Tourist Office / Embassy of Tunisia.
Listed in some catalogs as 35 minutes in length. Looks
at history, politics, economy, education, religion, arts
and crafts, and tourist attractions of Tunisia. Includes
scenes of Tunis, ruins of Carthage, Dougga, Sbeitla, El
Djem, the mosques of Kairouan, the resort area of
Hammamet, Sousse, Monastir, Sidi Bou Said and Djerba.
General introduction to Tunisia.

2303   YOUR VACATION IN TUNISIA
(n.d.) / 20 min / sound / color / 16 mm
Tunisian National Tourist Office.
Without narration. Shows tourist accommodations and
sites in Djerba, Tunisia. Includes scenes of traditional
dances, shopping in the souks or markets, Berber villages, the Cathedral of St. Louis, traditional Tunisian
architecture and resort areas. To promote tourism.

2304   ZAA, THE LITTLE WHITE CAMEL
1962 / 25 min / sound / color / 16 mm
Yannick Bellon, France. Released in the U.S. by Radim Films
for Focus on 16 mm. (NUC FiA 65-1870) Location: Embassy of
Tunisia.
For juvenile audiences. Follows the adventures of a
small white camel as it strays from the oases where it
was born. Shows the landscape and people of southern
Tunisia. Introduces life of southern Tunisian Arabs.

TUNISIA - TRAVELOGS - BY CITY

2305   KAIROUAN
(n.d.) / 15 min / sound / color / 16 mm
Tunisian National Tourism Office.
Studies Kairouan, a holy city in Tunisia. Shows the
Grand Mosque of Sidi Okba, a restored 9th century
building, and other important sites in the city.

2306   (KAIROWAN, ALGIERS)
(c. 1905) / 5 min / silent / b&w / 35 mm
Calaquin Collection. AFI Collection. Location: Library of
Congress Paper Print Collection (FEA 5267, 2nd copy FEA
5268) *
Early silent film. Shows scenes of a mosque, part of the
city from a minaret, street scenes, a cobra and snake
handler, women spinning and weaving a carpet, plowing a
field with camels, camels being used to draw water from a

433

well, shephards, a procession with musicians and flag
bearer, and street performers dancing with short rifles.
Good source of library footage for documentary use.

2307   KEEP YESTERDAY
        1970 / 28 min / sound / color / 16 mm
        United Nations Films.
             Available in English and Arabic soundtracks. Looks at
             the work of the Tunisian government, UNESCO, and UNDP to
             protect the ancient ruins of Carthage from suburban
             expansion of the city of Tunis. Describes plans to save
             the oldest parts of the city, a center for handicraft
             manufacture and trade.

2308   SAHARA FESTIVAL
        (n.d.) / 13 min / sound / color / 16 mm
        Tunisian National Tourism Office.
             Profiles the oases of Douz, the gateway to the Sahara.
             Shows traditional festivals, a wedding celebration, camel
             races, a camel fight and dog races.

2309   TEMPEST OVER TUNIS
        1939 / 11 min / sound / b&w / 16 mm
        20th Century-Fox Film Corp. Released for educational pur-
        poses by Teaching Film Custodians, 1941. (Magic Carpet
        series) (NUC FiA 52-4539) Credits: Producer - Truman
        Talley, Narrator - Lowell Thomas, Editor - Lew Lehr.
             Intended for high school audiences. Originally a
             theatrically produced travelog of Tunisia. Includes sce-
             nes of Kairouan, the Jewish community at Djerba, Arabs at
             prayer, street scenes, the bazaar, the rug industry and
             craftspeople and merchants. Describes the importance of
             Tunisia in terms of U.S. military interests and as the
             home of the Barbary Pirates.

2310   TUNIS
        (c. 1915) / 3 min / silent / b&w / 28 mm
        Located in the Gatewood W. Dunston Film Collection, Library
        of Congress (FLA 402, 28mm Positive)
             Early silent footage of Tunis.

2311   TUNIS, CAPITAL OF TUNISIA
        1970 / 3 min / silent / color / super 8 mm film loop
        Doubleday Multimedia. (North Africa series) (LC 78-708019)
             Short film showing traditional and modern aspects of
             life in Tunis. Includes scenes of mosques, a political
             parade, street scenes, university graduates and a
             parliamentary session.

2312   TUNIS SOUKS
        (n.d.) / 11 min / silent / b&w / 16 mm
        Producer unknown. U.S. Govt. Film Collection. Location:
        Library of Congress (FAA 426) No other information
        available.

TURKEY

TURKEY - ARCHEOLOGY

2313 ANCIENT SARDIS
1969 / 28 min / sound / color / 16 mm
Charles Lyman. (LC 77-701764)
Looks at ten years of archeological research at the
ancient city of Sardis in Turkey. Discusses methods
used and results of the excavation of huge burial mounds.
Shows work on reconstruction of monumental buildings.

2314 GOREME
1968 / 13 min / sound / color / 16 mm
Producer unknown. Distributed by Radim Films.
Shows bizarre volcanic landscape of Goreme in Turkey.
Tours grottos and cells where Christian monks lived.

2315 GOREME - COLOURS IN THE DARK
(c. 1963) / 10 min / sound / color / 16 mm
S. Eyuboglu. University of Istanbul. Released in the U.S.
by International Communications Foundation. (Art History of
Asia Minor, Cultural Film series, no. 4) (NUC FiA 66-944
rev) Location: Turkish Tourism Office. *
Also available in a silent, 5 minute 8 mm version.
Intended for junior-senior high school audiences. Shows
the strange volcanic landscape of Goreme in Cappadocia.
Looks at Christian churches and shrines carved into the
volcanic rock. Examines rock walls covered with religious paintings or layers of paintings made over many
years. Narration is a little overdone but the landscape
itself is fascinating. Listed in some catalogs as:
COLOURS IN THE DARK.

2316 HITTITE SUN, PARTS 1 AND 2
1963 / 2 films, 4 min each / silent / b&w / 8 mm
University of Istanbul. Released in the U.S. by
International Communications Foundation. Distributed by
Doubleday. (Art History of Asia Minor series) (NUC FiA
66-946)
Traces the ancient Hittite civilization in central Turkey
through art and artifacts.

2317 NEMRUT DAG (THRONE OF THE GODS)
1977 / 10 min / sound / color / 16 mm
Marc Mopty. Compaine Cinematographie Belge. Location:
Turkish Tourism Office. *
Belgian film sub-titled in English. Excellently filmed
view of the ancient site of Nemrut Dag. Shows the monu-

435

mental landscape, mountains and ancient, mammoth stone
heads. Narration is more poetic than informative.

2318   ROMAN MOSAICS IN ANATOLIA
        1959 / 10 min / sound / color / 16 mm
        Y. Ipsiroglu. Istanbul University. (Cultural Film series,
        no. 3) Location: Turkish Tourism Office. *
        Intended for junior high school to adult audiences.
        Shows beautiful floor mosaics from 4th century Antioch.
        Includes geometric forms and mosaics of birds, beasts and
        people. Profiles the present city including views of
        crafts, street scenes, and shops. Relates people and
        typical activities found in the mosaics to scenes of
        everyday life in contemporary Antioch. Well produced.

2319   ROMAN MOSAICS IN ANATOLIA
        1963 / 4 min / silent / color / 8 mm
        University of Istanbul. Released in the U.S. by
        International Communications Foundation. (NUC FiA 66-945)
        Possibly a shorter version of no. 2318. Contrasts life
        in modern Antioch with scenes found in ancient Roman
        mosaics from historic Antioch.

2320   STORY OF THE HITTITES
        (n.d.) / 25 min / sound / b&w / 16 mm
        Turkish Embassy / Turkish Tourism and Information Office.
        Looks at ancient Hittite civilization through art and
        artifacts. Includes archeological sites at the village
        of Bogaz, the Hittite Museum in Ankara, the Aldcahoyuk,
        and samples of later Seljuk arts and crafts. Traces
        modern use of Hittite symbols in the arts.

2321   3,000 YEARS UNDER THE SEA
        1960 / 30 min / sound / b&w / 16 mm
        Insight, Inc. Released by ABC Television. (Expedition!,
        television series) (NUC Fi 68-279) Credits: Producer - V.
        Fae Thomas, Writer - P.T. Furst, Music - Robert Ernst,
        Photographer - Stanton A. Waterman. Location: Library of
        Congress (FCA 2480)
        Profiles an American expedition off the coast of Turkey
        examining the oldest supposed shipwreck. Shows 2000 year
        old pottery recovered from the site as well as tools and
        ingots from the Bronze Age.

2322   TURKEY: CROSSROADS OF THE ANCIENT WORLD
        1973 / 27 min / sound / color / 16 mm
        Centron. Chatsworth Films. (People and Places of
        Antiquity) (LC 77-703108) Credits: Narrator - Anthony
        Quayle. Locations: Syracuse U. / U. of Illinois / U. of
        Texas at Austin.
        Listed in some catalogs as: CROSSROADS OF THE ANCIENT
        WORLD and as 52 minutes in length. Intended for junior-
        senior high school audiences. Looks at Asia Minor from

pre-historic times to the present. Traces major civilizations of the area including the Hittites, Assyrians,
Persians, Greeks, Romans, Byzantines, Arabs, Turks and
Mongols. Stresses Turkey has been a crossroads for
eastern and western influences throughout the centuries.

TURKEY - ANCIENT TO MODERN HISTORY

2323   THE FALL OF CONSTANTINOPLE
        1970 / 34 min / sound / color / 16 mm
        BBC-TV, London. Released in the U.S. by Time-Life Films.
        (LC 74-714474)
            Intended for high school to adult audiences. Traces
            history of the city of Constantinople, or Istanbul, from
            its founding by Constantine until its surrender to the
            Turks in the mid-15th century. Shows examples of
            frescoes, manuscripts and jewelry of the Byzantine
            empire.

2324   TALE OF A CITY
        (c. 1955?) / 20 min / sound / color / 16 mm
        Turkish Maritime Lines. Location: Turkish Tourism Office.*
            Intended for elementary to junior high school audiences.
            Tells the story of the city of Byzantium or
            Constantinople. Founded by Constantine and captured by
            the Turks in the 15th century, the city is today cosmopo-
            litan Istanbul. Shows major tourist attractions of the
            city including Aya Sophia Mosque, the Blue Mosque, the
            city walls, archeological museum objects, a carpet shop,
            Topkapi, the Haram, and villas on the Bosphorus.
            Presentation is a little dated but of fair quality.
            Turkish Maritime Lines advertises itself.

2325   TURKEY - EMERGENCE OF A MODERN NATION
        1963 / 17 min / sound / color / 16 mm
        Encyclopaedia Britannica Films. (NUC FiA 63-635) Credits:
        Producer - Clifford J. Kamen, Educational Collaborator -
        Sydney N. Fisher. Locations: Boston U. / Brigham Young U. /
        Indiana U. / Library of Congress (FBA 4041) / Syracuse U. /
        U. of Arizona / U. of Illinois / U. of Iowa / U. of
        Minnesota / U. of Missouri / U. of Wisconsin. *
            Looks at the history of Turkey from ancient times to the
            present. Focuses on developments since the Republic of
            Turkey was founded in 1923. Shows Greek, Roman,
            Byzantine and Muslim influences on the area. Discusses
            Turkey's commitment to NATO and modernization. Library
            of Congress print experiencing color deterioration.

2326   TURKEY - YESTERDAY'S TOMORROW
        1966 / 95 min / silent / color / 16 mm
        Douglas Productions. (NUC FiA 68-622)
            Filmed on location. Looks at the history of Asia Minor

437

from ancient to modern times. Shows art and culture of
Turkey emphasizing the period since the founding of the
Republic.

TURKEY - OTTOMAN TO MODERN HISTORY

2327   A SICK MAN RECOVERS
       (n.d.) / 12 min / sound / b&w / 16 mm
       Pictura Films Corps.
           Looks at the history of Turkey from the Ottoman period to
           the present.

2328   TURKEY
       1947 / 19 min / sound / b&w / 16 mm
       March of Time. A Forum Film. Released by McGraw-Hill.
       (March of Time, television series) (NUC FiA 52-2615)
       Location: Library of Congress (FBA 1587)   *
           Looks at the historic interest of Russia in Turkey.
           Intended to change U.S. public opinion in favor of aid to
           Turkey to counter Soviet influence. Traces history of
           Turkey from WWI to the present. Defines Turkey as a
           buffer between the Soviet Union and the Middle East.
           Describes work of Ataturk, Ismet Inonu and the
           Republicans.

2329   TURKEY: A STRATEGIC LAND AND ITS PEOPLE
       1959 / 11 min / sound / color or b&w / 16 mm
       Coronet Instructional Films. (NUC FiA 59-441) Credits:
       Educational Collaborator - Norman J.G. Pounds. Locations:
       Kent State U. / Library of Congress (FAA 4816) / Syracuse U.
       / U. of Kansas / U. of Nebraska. *
           Intended for junior-senior high school audiences. Looks
           at the position of Turkey between the east and west.
           Profiles Ottoman and Republic Turkey and examines the
           economy, mineral resources, agriculture, and construction
           industries. Narration is a bit patronizing.

TURKEY - ATATURK TO CONTEMPORARY HISTORY

2330   AMERICAN MILITARY MISSION TO TURKEY AND ARMENIA
       1919, revised version 1936 / 23 min / silent / b&w / 35 mm
       U.S. Signal Corps. (Historical Film, no. 1226) Location:
       National Archives (111H1226) No other information available.

2331   EARTHQUAKES: LESSON OF A DISASTER
       1971 / 13 min / sound / color / 16 mm
       Encyclopaedia Britannica. Distributed by Orient Film
       Association. Location: Syracuse U. / U. of California
       Extension Media Center.
           Intended for junior-senior high school audiences. Com-
           pares two major earthquakes in Turkey and California.

Criticizes pre-earthquake planning and detection and
post-quake emergency measures. Discusses measures that
should be taken in high risk earthquake zones.

2332   GRECO-TURK WAR OVER
1961 / 4 min / sound / b&w / 16 mm
Filmrite Associates. Released by Official Films. (Greatest
Headlines of the Century) (NUC Fi 62-1924) Credits:
Producer - Sherm Grinberg, Narrator - Tom Hudson, Writer -
Allan Lurie. Location: Library of Congress (FAA 3764) *
Describes post-WWI treaties which were to give Greece
control of several Turkish cities for a period of five
years. In 1921, Mustafa Kemal sets up a new government
and by 1922 captures Smyrna. Kemal, later called
Ataturk, becomes president of the Republic of Turkey.
Short recreation of events using newsreel footage.
Useful for classroom instruction.

2333   STATE VISIT TO TURKEY BY QUEEN ELIZABETH II
(n.d.) / 15 min / sound / color / 16 mm
Turkish Embassy.
Shows visit of Queen Elizabeth II of England to Turkey.

2334   TURKEY BECOMES A REPUBLIC, OCTOBER 29, 1923
1960 / 4 min / sound / b&w / 16 mm
Official Films, Inc. Made by Richard B. Morros, Inc. in
association with Hearst Metrotone News, Inc. (Almanac
Newsreel series) Location: Library of Congress (FAA 3179)
*
In rapid presentation, shows Mustafa Kemal's consolidation of Turkey following WWI, the founding of the
Turkish Republic, and introduction of western forms in
the calendar, writing system and weights and measures.
Looks at Turkey as a member of CENTO, NATO and as a
UN participant in the Korean Conflict. Shows a 1959
reception for President Eisenhower in Turkey. Much
information in a short time.

2335   TURKEY: KEY TO THE MIDDLE EAST
1950 / 20 min / sound / b&w / 16 mm
J. Arthur Rank Organisation. Released in the U.S. by
British Information Services, 1952. (This Modern Age
series, no. 41) (NUC FiA 52-4322) Credits: Producer
-Sergei Nolbandov, Assoc. Producer-Literary Editor - J.L.
Hodson.
Looks at Turkey since the reforms of Ataturk. Discusses
its present place in world affairs and in relation to
U.S. military interests. Intended for senior high school
to adult audiences. Poorly produced.

2336   TURKEY: MODERN REFORMS
1967 / 16 min / sound / color / 16 mm
ABC, TV. Jules Power Productions. Released by McGraw-Hill.

(Middle East World series) (NUC FiA 67-1696) Locations:
Kent State U. / Syracuse U. / U. of Illinois.
Intended for junior high school to college audiences.
Looks at the strategic position of Turkey as a bridge
between Europe and Asia. Discusses the transformation of
Turkey from an agriculturally based society to a par-
tially industrialized one. Looks at modernization pro-
jects and problems facing Turkey.

2337   TURKEY - A NATION IN TRANSITION
1962 / 27 min / sound / color / 16 mm
Julien Bryan. International Film Foundation. (NUC FiA
63-11) Credits: Producer - Julien Bryan, Writer - Leroy
Leatherman, Consultant - Lewis Thomas. Locations: Arizona
State U. / Boston U. / Brigham Young U. / Florida State U. /
Indiana U. / Kent State U. / Library of Congress (FCA 5469)
/ New York U. / Penn. State U. / Purdue / Syracuse U. / U.
of Illinois / U. of Michigan / U. of Minnesota / U. of
Nebraska / U. of Texas at Austin / U. of Utah / U. of
Washington. *
Uses animation to present history of Turkey and the
Middle East. Includes scenes of farming, village life,
crafts, the silk industry, transportation, mineral wealth
and water usage. Shows folk dance, puppet theater and
miniatures in an outline of the arts. Discusses the
reforms of Ataturk and the results of modernization,
literacy and health programs. Slightly outdated, but a
well presented view of Turkish life and culture.
Intended for junior high school to college audiences.
One of the better general films on Turkey.

2338   TURKEY - REBIRTH OF A NATION
1963 / 17 min / sound / color or b&w / 16 mm
Dudley Pictures Corp. Made by Carl Dudley. Released by
United World Films. (Today's People in Our Changing World)
(NUC FiA 67-5888) Location: U. of Kansas.
General overview of Turkey. Shows modernization and
reform from the time of Ataturk. Includes scenes of
Ankara and Goreme. Profiles agriculture and industry in Turkey.

TURKEY - BIOGRAPHIES OF ATATURK

2339   ATATURK
1971 / 29 min / sound / 16 mm
Sterling Films. SIM Productions. (LC 70-713677)
Location: U. of Utah.
Intended for high school to adult audiences. Uses still
photographs and steel engravings to outline history of
the Ottoman empire and the Turkish War for Independence.
Describes the role of Ataturk in forming modern Turkey.

2340   ATATURK, FATHER OF MODERN TURKEY
1955 / 26 min / sound / b&w / 16 mm

440

CBS, TV. Distributed by McGraw-Hill. (Twentieth Century, television series) Locations: Arizona State U. / Kent State U. / Oklahoma State U. / Oregon State System of Higher Education (Corvallis) / Syracuse U. / Turkish Embassy / U. of Colorado / U. of Florida / U. of Kansas / U. of Michigan / U. of Minnesota / U. of New Hampshire / U. of South Carolina / U. of Washington.

Listed in some catalogs as released in 1960. Follows the career of Mustapha Kemal Ataturk. Shows the consolidation of Turkey following WWI, declaration of a Republic of Turkey in 1923 and efforts made at modernizing and westernizing the new nation. Uses old film clips and newsreels. Looks at position of Turkey in NATO. Listed in some catalogs as: ATATURK: INCREDIBLE TURK.

2341   ATATURK: FATHER OF THE TURKS
(n.d.) / 46 min / sound / color / 16 mm
Time-Life Films. Location: U. of Kansas.

Profiles the life of Mustapha Kemal Ataturk. Traces his efforts to consolidate, westernize and modernize Turkish government and life. Includes film clips and photographs of Ataturk and the Turkish War of Independence.

2342   ATATURK: FIFTY YEARS FORWARD
(n.d.) / 25 min / sound / color / 16 mm
Henry Sandoz. Produced by NATO for the Govt. of Turkey.
Locations: Turkish Embassy / Turkish Tourism Office.   *

Intended for general to adult audiences. One of the better films on Turkey. Uses minimal narration. Shows scenes of interiors of Ottoman palaces. Discusses Allied plan to divide Turkey following WWI and Mustapha Kemal's efforts to find Turkey's "natural boundaries" and form the Turkish Republic. Includes scenes from the Ankara Museum Hittite collection and looks at Roman and Greek city sites. Shows Byzantine ruins, chapels in Cappadocia at Goreme, Aya Sophia and later Muslim sites including the Blue Mosque and Topkapi Saray. Includes a performance of the Janissary army band. Looks at Turkey's position in the European Economic Market and NATO. Well photographed.

2343   ATATURK, FOUNDER OF MODERN TURKEY
1971 / 35 min / color / sound / 16 mm
BBC, TV. Distributed by Time-Life Films.

Uses film clips and photographs to outline the life and accomplishments of Mustapha Kemal Ataturk. Includes comments by Arnold Toynbee concerning the work of Ataturk. Intended for high school to college audiences.

2344   ATATURK, OF A MAN AND A NATION
(n.d.) / 30 min / sound / b&w / 16 mm
CBS, TV. McGraw-Hill. Distributed by American Friends of

the Middle East. Locations: Middle East Institute /
Syracuse U.
Looks at the life of Mustapha Kemal Ataturk and focuses
on reforms in religion, education and politics he
introduced. Shows development in Turkey through the
1950's.

2345 ATATURK: THE RISE OF THE TURKISH REPUBLIC
1970 / 26 min / sound / b&w / 16 mm
Sim Productions. Made by Morton Schindel. (LC 70-713677)
Credits: Director-Writer - Marianna Norris, Consultant -
Talat Halman. Location: Library of Congress (FBB 0579) /
Turkish Embassy. *
Intended for junior high school to adult audiences.
Traces the life of Mustapha Kemal Ataturk and the modern
state of Turkey formed from the remains of the Ottoman
empire. Shows the Ataturk Museum and University of
Istanbul. Outlines reforms in government, the army,
women's rights, education and literacy, and the pro-
fessions. An idealistic presentation of 20th century
Turkey. Fairly well produced.

2346 THE INCREDIBLE TURK
1959 / 27 min / sound / b&w / 16 or 35 mm
Prudential Insurance Co. of America. Made by CBS. (The
Twentieth Century, television series) (NUC FiA 59-363)
Credits: Narrator - Walter Cronkite. Locations: Library of
Congress (FCA 1448) / Turkish Tourism Office. *
Originally broadcast on television, later intended for
junior-senior high school use. Uses old film footage to
show entrance of the Ottoman empire on the side of
Germany in WWI. Shows the division of the empire after
the war, consolidation of Turkey by Ataturk, and creation
of the Republic of Turkey. Outlines reforms made in
writing, women's rights, government and education. Also
looks at Ataturk's ruthless treatment of opposition.
Follows Ataturk's work in modernizing agriculture,
industry and society. Dated but good presentation of
Ataturk. Library of Congress print is damaged.

TURKEY - VILLAGE LIFE

2347 BAKING FLAT CAKES (TURKMEN, MIDDLE EAST,
SOUTH ANATOLIA)
1965, released 1968 / 11 min / silent / b&w / 16 mm
Encyclopaedia Cinematographica. Distributed by Pennsylvania
State University. (Ency. Cinematographica, no. E 1230)
Another in the series of silent ethnographic films
showing a typical traditional activity. Shows women
baking bread.

2348 THE CHILDREN'S FOUNTAIN
(n.d.) / 13 min / sound / color / 16 mm

UNICEF. United Nations Films.
Follows the progress of a Turkish nurse working in a
rural health program.

2349 FAMILIES OF THE WORLD: TURKEY
1976 / 20 min / sound / color / 16 mm
UNICEF. Locations: U. of Illinois / U. of Missouri.
Profiles the life of an extended family in a Turkish
village. Shows men farming while women spin and
embroider cloth to be sold in Istanbul for cash. Shows
the limited standard of living of the villagers.

2350 THE FAMILY: TURKEY
(n.d.) / 28 min / sound / color / 16 mm
UNICEF. United Nations Films.
Available in English, Finnish and Italian soundtracks.
Looks at Turkish village life. Shows the family farming,
producing crafts for sale, praying and eating together.
Shows work of UNICEF in providing health care for the
villagers. May be the same as no. 2349.

2351 HERDING, WATERING, AND MILKING SHEEP AND GOATS
(CRIMEAN TATARS, MIDDLE EAST, CENTRAL ANATOLIA)
1972 / 13 min / silent / color / 16 mm
E.J. Klay. Encyclopaedia Cinematographica. Distributed by
Pennsylvania State University. (Ency. Cinematographica, no.
2029)
Another in the series of silent ethnographic films
showing a traditional activity. Shows shephards tending
and milking their flocks.

2352 MAKING BUTTER (WESTSIBIRIAN TATARS, MIDDLE EAST,
CENTRAL ANATOLIA)
1972 / 8 min / silent / color / 16 mm
E.J. Klay. Encyclopaedia Cinematographica. Distributed by
Pennsylvania State University. (Ency. Cinematographica, no.
E 2031)
Another in the series of silent ethnographic films. This
shows Tatar women making butter.

2353 MAKING WHEAT GROATS "BULGUR" (TURKS, MIDDLE EAST,
CENTRAL ANATOLIA)
1971, released 1973 / 26 min / silent / color / 16 mm
E.J. Klay. Encyclopaedia Cinematographica. Distributed by
Pennsylvania State University. (Ency. Cinematographica, no.
E 1921)
Another in the series of silent ethnographic films.
Shows Turkish women cooking bulgar.

2354 MILKING AND WATERING SHEEP (WESTSIBIRIAN
TATARS, MIDDLE EAST, CENTRAL ANATOLIA)
1972 / 9 min / silent / color / 16 mm
E.J. Klay. Encyclopaedia Cinematographica. Distributed by

443

Pennsylvania State University. (Ency. Cinematographica, no.
E 2030)
  Another in the series of silent ethnographic films.
  Shephards are shown tending and milking their flocks.

2355   PROCESSING BARLEY (WESTSIBIRIAN TATARS, MIDDLE EAST,
       CENTRAL ANATOLIA)
       1972 / 11 min / silent / color / 16 mm
       E.J. Klay. Encyclopaedia Cinematographica. Distributed by
       Pennsylvania State University. (Ency. Cinematographica, no.
       E 2032)
         Another in the series of silent ethnographic films
         showing a traditional activity. Shows how barley is
         processed among the Tatars.

2356   TURKEY
       1976 / 30 min / sound / color / 16 mm
       UNICEF, Japanese Broadcasting Company and the New York State
       Education Dept. (Families of the World series) Location:
       Kent State U.
         Intended for intermediate to junior high school audien-
         ces. Looks at village life in Turkey. May be the same
         film as no. 2349.

2357   THE TURKISH QUESTION
       1963 / 53 min / sound / b&w / 16 mm
       National Educational Television and Westinghouse
       Broadcasting Co. (Intertel series) (NUC FiA 64-802)
       Location: Library of Congress (FDA 272)
         Looks at the problems of Turkey as seen in the village of
         Sida. Shows rural population with high illiteracy and
         problems in adjusting to modern, industrial society.

2358   WEDDING CEREMONIES (WESTSIBIRIAN TATARS, MIDDLE EAST,
       CENTRAL ANATOLIA)
       1972 / 15 min / silent / color / 16 mm
       E.J. Klay. Encyclopaedia Cinematographica. Distributed by
       Pennsylvania State University. (Ency. Cinematographica, no.
       E 2033)
         In a central Anatolian village, people line the streets
         as a wedding party passes. Shows the groom in a cart
         pulled by a tractor. No footage of the ceremony is
         shown.

2359   WORKING WITH THE BODY AND "KARASABAN" (CRIMEAN
       TATARS, MIDDLE EAST, CENTRAL ANATOLIA)
       1971, released 1973 / 6 min / silent / color / 16 mm
       E.J. Klay. Encyclopaedia Cinematographica. Distributed by
       Pennsylvania State University. (Ency. Cinematographica, no.
       E 1923)
         Another in the series of silent ethnographic films
         showing traditional activities.

TURKEY - THE ARMENIANS

2360   THE ARMENIAN CASE
        1975 / 45 min / sound / color / 16 mm
        Atlantis Productions, Inc. Sponsored by the United Armenian
        Commemorative Committee of California. Credits:
        Writer-Producer-Director - J. Michael Hagopian. Location:
        Library of Congress (FCA 8263-64) *
        An emotional film which advocates the creation of an
        Armenian national homeland and asks for reparations from
        the Turkish government for their part in the genocide of
        the Armenian people in 1918. Uses photographs, film
        clips and interviews with Armenians and Armenian-
        Americans to outline the history and culture of the
        Armenians from 100 A.D. to the present. Due to economic
        and assimilation fears on the part of Abdul Hamit in
        1915, the Armenian people were deported or killed by the
        million. Shows failure of the world community to protest
        or stop this action. Well produced, effective statement.

2361   THE FORGOTTEN GENOCIDE
        1975 / 28 min / sound / color / 16 mm
        Atlantis Productions. Credits: Producer-Director-Writer -
        J. Michael Hagopian. Location: Library of Congress (FBB
        5011) *
        Excellent, bitter study of the history of the Armenian
        people. Highlights Armenian achievements in literature,
        art and culture. Includes interviews with Armenians and
        Armenian-Americans. Describes the Ottoman Turkish
        attempt to destroy the Armenian people, the massacres and
        subsequent cover-ups by the Turkish government. Well
        produced.

2362   WHERE ARE MY PEOPLE
        1966 / 28 min / sound / color / 16 mm
        Atlantis Productions. (NUC FiA 67-692) Credits: Producer -
        J. Michael Hagopian.
        Intended for senior high school to adult audiences.
        Another in the series of three films by Hagopian con-
        cerning the massacre of Armenians during WWI by the
        Ottoman government. Profiles the significance of
        Armenian culture and contributions in the arts.

TURKEY - TRAVELOGS - DATE OF PRODUCTION UNKNOWN

2363   GO MOCAMP
        (n.d.) / 20 min / sound / color / 16 mm
        BP Film. Location: Turkish Tourism and Information Office.
        General travelog of Turkey. Includes scenes of Istanbul,
        the Galata Bridge, the Blue Mosque, the enclosed bazaar,
        the BP Mocamp around Istanbul, Turkish cuisine, camp
        life, villages, fruit harvests, the Kumluk Mocamp, Bursa,

Mt. Uludag, the thermal springs at Bursa, the BP Mocamp
in Kusadasi, Ephesus, Bodrum, Gokova, the Mersin
Kizlalesi, Alanya, Silifke, and the volcanic Goreme
valley.

2364   HUNDRED FACES OF TURKEY
(n.d.) / 15 min / sound / color / 16 mm
Claude Renglet. Location: Turkish Tourism Office.   *
General travelog of Turkey without narration. Shows a
variety of scenes of Turkish life including the national
sport of greased wrestling, street scenes, transportation, Cappadocian churches, folk dancing, Hittite
ruins, modern Ankara, arts and crafts and the Mevlevi
order of dervishes. Well filmed.

2365   MAGIC LAND OF TURKEY
(n.d.) / 12 min / sound / color or b&w / 16 mm
Carl Dudley Films. (This World of Ours series) Location:
Turkish Tourism Office.   *
General travelog of Turkey. Somewhat dated, probably
produced in the mid 1950's. Includes scenes of Istanbul,
Aya Sophia, the Blue Mosque, University of Istanbul,
craftsmen, ruins at Ephesus, Seljuk and Ottoman ruins,
the Turkish landscape and agriculture. Profiles
democracy in Turkey and shows the Ataturk monument.
Intended for junior high school audiences. Better
general travelogs are available.

2366   MYSTERIOUS CAPPADOCIA
(n.d.) / 15 min / sound / color / 16 mm
Belga Films. Location: Turkish Tourism Office.   *
Intended for junior high school to adult audiences. Well
photographed travelog of Cappadocia. Shows Konya, famous
sites of the city, craftsmen, rug-weavers and profiles
agriculture. Examines the volcanic landscape of Goreme.
Shows houses and monasteries carved from volcanic rock.

2367   NEW DAWN OVER TURKEY
(n.d.) / 26 min / sound / 16 mm
Producer unknown. Location: Turkish Embassy. No other
information available.

2368   TURKEY: CROSSROAD OF CIVILIZATION
(n.d.) / 15 min / sound / color / 16 mm
Belga Films. Location: Turkish Tourism Office.   *
Intended for junior high school to adult audiences.
Includes scenes of Istanbul, Ankara and Cappadocia.
Describes reforms instituted by Ataturk. Shows Christian
churches and monks' cells found in Goreme. Examines
breathtaking salt and mineral springs at Pamukkale, ruins
of the city of Ephesus, including a 27,000 seat stadium,
and remnants of Ionian civilization. Visually pleasing
travelog. Good general introduction.

446

2369   TURKEY: NEW HORIZONS
        (n.d.) / 13 min / sound / color / 16 mm
        Pan American Airways. Location: Turkish Embassy. No other
        information available.

2370   TURKEY, OLD AND NEW
        (n.d.) / 20 min / silent / b&w / 16 mm
        Bray Studios, Inc. (NUC FiA 55-446)
            General travelog. Probably produced in the early 1950's.
            Includes scenes of Istanbul, the royal mosques, the old
            quarter of the city, the Seraglio, the Baghdad Kiosk and
            marble villas along the Bosphorus.

2371   TURKISH PANORAMA
        (n.d.) / 30 min? / sound / 16 mm
        Producer unknown. Location: Turkish Embassy. No other
        information available.

TURKEY - TRAVELOGS - PRODUCED BEFORE 1959

2372   INTRODUCING TURKEY
        1956 / 21 min / sound / b&w / 16 or 35 mm
        North Atlantic Treaty Organization. Made by Europa
        Telefilm, Rome. Released in the U.S. by the U.S. Dept. of
        State. (The Atlantic Community series) (NUC FiE 56-280)
            General introduction to Turkey. Describes geography,
            history, economy and customs of the nation. Looks at the
            role of Turkey in NATO.

2373   NEW TURKEY
        1938 / 22 min / silent / b&w / 16 mm
        Eastman Kodak Co., Teaching Films Division. Released by
        Encyclopaedia Britannica Films. (NUC FiA 55-106) Location:
        Library of Congress (FAA 5107-08)
            Looks at the modernization of Turkey since the founding
            of the Republic. Shows Ankara, the capital, and scenes
            of Istanbul including Istanbul University. Contrasts old
            and new forms in housing, agriculture and industry.

2374   TURKEY
        1938 / 11 min / silent or sound / b&w / 16 mm
        Eastman Classroom Films. Location: Library of Congress (FAA
        4814-15) *
            Possibly a shorter version of no. 2373. General travelog
            of Turkey including scenes of Ankara and Istanbul. Looks
            at reforms in Republican Turkey and shows progress in
            housing, industry, education and agriculture. Library of
            Congress print in good condition considering age.

2375   TURKEY AT WORK AND PLAY
        (c. 1957?) / 22 min / sound / color / 16 mm
        Producer unknown. Location: Turkish Embassy / Turkish

Tourism and Information Office.
Contrasts industry in Turkey with sites popular to
tourists. Profiles a large steel mill, agriculture, and
a modern farming community and shows dancing, singing,
and tourist facilities. Intended to promote tourism.

2376   THE TURKEY OF ATATURK
        1958 / 40 min / sound / color / 16 mm
        Thomas E. Benner. (NUC FiA 59-537) *
        Intended for senior high school to adult audiences.
        Contrasts traditional and modern, village and urban
        Turkey. Includes scenes of Istanbul, the countryside,
        and Bursa. Looks at education, agriculture and the
        national culture of Turkey. Focused more on entertain-
        ment than instruction. Technically well made but with
        dull narration.

2377   TURKEY'S 100 MILLION
        1947 / 18 min / sound / b&w / 16 or 35 mm
        Time, Inc. Twentieth Century-Fox. (March of Time, vol. 13,
        no. 13) Locations: Library of Congress (FBB 3120) /
        National Archives (200MT.13.13) *
        Dated general travelog of Turkey. Stresses role of
        Turkey in holding back Soviet influence in the Middle
        East. Looks at U.S. aid to Turkey and its strategic
        importance. Profiles city of Istanbul, Turkish govern-
        mental system, Ankara, and the reforms of Ataturk.
        Discusses the lack of modern equipment in agriculture in
        contrast to modern methods used in education. Looks at
        University of Ankara, rights of women and drain on the
        economy as a result of maintaining the army. Intended to
        form public opinion in favor of supporting arms and eco-
        nomic aid to Turkey.

TURKEY - TRAVELOGS - PRODUCED BETWEEN 1960-1969

2378   ANKARA AND CENTRAL TURKEY
        1962 / 11 min / sound / color / 16 mm
        International Film Bureau. Locations: Boston U. / Syracuse
        U. / U. of Illinois.
        Looks at traditional and modern Ankara, capital of
        Turkey. Shows transportation, ancient ruins, modern
        office buildings and homes, agriculture, folk dancing,
        and a parade. Discusses the history and geography of
        Turkey in general terms.

2379   ASSIGNMENT TURKEY
        1960 / 9 min / sound / color / 35 mm
        Twentieth Century-Fox Film Corp. (Movietone Adventure
        series) (NUC Fi 67-1452) Credits: Producer - Edmund Reek,
        Director - Jack Kuhne, Writer - Joe Wills. Cinemascope.
        Location: Library of Congress (FEA 1326) *

Theatrically released travelog. Includes scenes of
Istanbul, the Blue Mosque, Aya Sophia, Sulaymaniyye Mosque
and the Istanbul Hilton. Shows the May 19th youth and
sports day festivities, the Bosphorus ferry, arts and
crafts and ruins at Ephesus. Shows the Ottoman military
band. Library of Congress print experiencing color
deterioration. Not a very good narration. Better travelogs are available covering the same sites.

2380   THE GOLDEN CRESCENT
       1963 / 28 min / sound / color / 16 mm
       California Texas Oil Corp. Released by Sterling Movies.
       (Caltex International Public Relations series) (NUC FiA
       64-912) Locations: Middle East Institute / Embassy of
       Turkey.
          Contrasts traditional and modern Turkey. Includes scenes
       of Istanbul, the capital city of Ankara, and rural
       Anatolia. Shows craftsmen, mosques, churches, and
       industry in Turkey.

2381   ISTANBUL AND IZMIR
       1961 / 11 min / sound / color / 16 mm
       International Film Bureau. Location: U. of Illinois.
          Intended for junior-senior high school audiences.
       Contrasts ancient and modern Turkey. Includes infor-
       mation on geography and history. Shows Istanbul, Izmir
       and western Turkey.

2382   PROSPECT OF TURKEY
       1967 / 32 min / sound / color / 16 mm
       North Atlantic Treaty Organization. Released by National
       Audiovisual Center. (LC 74-705440) Locations: Turkish
       Embassy / Turkish Tourism and Information Office.
          Looks at the economy and geography of Turkey and shows
       sites of interest to tourists. Discusses the role of
       Turkey in countering Soviet influence, Turkey's role in
       NATO, and the Turkish army.

2383   TURKEY - THE BRIDGE
       1967 / 19 min / sound / color / 16 mm
       BP (North America) Ltd. Released in the U.S. by Radim
       Films. (NUC FiA 67-5059) Locations: Turkish Embassy /
       Turkish Tourism and Information Office.
          Looks at the long history of the area now called Turkey.
       Shows how Turkey has been used for the last 3000 years as
       a bridge between Asia and Europe.

2384   TURKEY - A MIDDLE EAST BRIDGELAND
       1961 / 18 min / sound / color or b&w / 16 mm
       Dudley Pictures. Made by Carl Dudley. Released by United
       World Films. (Your World Neighbors series) (NUC FiA
       67-5887) Credits: Educational Consultants - Clyde F. Kohn,
       Walter A. Wittich. Location: U. of Illinois.

Intended for elementary to high school audiences.
Follows an American boy who lives with a Turkish family
for a summer. Profiles history, geography, culture,
natural resources and industry in Turkey. Stresses
recent developments and modernization in Turkey.

2385   YOUR HOLIDAY IN TURKEY
        1967 / 25 min / sound / color / 16 mm
        Producer unknown. Location: Turkish Tourism and Information
        Office. *
            Listed in some catalogs as: HOLIDAY IN TURKEY.
            General travelog of Turkey. Includes scenes of Istanbul,
            the Galata Bridge, the Blue Mosque, Aya Sophia,
            Sulaimaniyah Mosque, University of Istanbul, Topkapi
            palace and gardens, the Bosphorus and the villas along
            its banks, the Istanbul Youth Festival, the tomb of
            Mehmet I and the city of Bursa. Shows summer and winter
            resort areas. Stresses comfort and modern accommodations
            available for tourists. To promote tourism.

TURKEY - TRAVELOGS - 1970-1979

2386   PORTSIDE IN TURKEY
        1973 / 4 min / sound / color / 16 mm
        John Tames, Canada. (LC 74-703748)
            Brief travelog of Turkey.

2387   TURKEY HAS SOME SURPRISES FOR YOU
        1973 / 28 min / sound / color / 16 mm
        Turkish Government Tourist Office. Made by Communetics.
        Released by Association-Sterling and Modern Talking Picture
        Service. (LC 73-702205) Credits: Producer-Writer - John
        Savage. Locations: Turkish Embassy / Turkish Tourism and
        Information Office. *
            Intended for senior high school to adult audiences.
            Upbeat promotional film to encourage tourism. Includes
            well photographed footage of resorts on the Aegean, folk
            dance troupes, the ruins at Ephesus, Greek and Roman
            sculpture, ruins from civilizations going back 9000
            years, a caravanserai, modern Izmir, Pergamum in western
            Turkey, Cappadocia with its Christian churches and lunar
            landscape, and the ruins of Troy. Profiles the city of
            Istanbul. Shows Aya Sophia, Sultan Ahmet Mosque, Topkapi
            palace and street scenes. Stresses low prices for
            tourists, no pollution and lots of entertainment. The
            best of the tourists films on Turkey.

2388   TURKIYE
        1977 / 16 min / sound / color / 16 mm
        Claude Lelouch. Distributed by Pyramid Films. Locations:
        Syracuse U. / Turkish Embassy / Turkish Tourism and
        Information Office. *

Intended for general to adult audiences. This montage without narration captures the essence of ancient and modern Turkey. Includes short film clips of men praying in a mosque, street scenes, dervishes, archeological sites, hot mineral springs, the Haram at Topkapi, a highway cloverleaf, harvest time, Cappadocia, filming of a costume epic and folk dancing. Less useful for instructional purposes as no scenes are identified. Nevertheless, one of the most visually attractive films on Turkey. Recommended.

TURKEY - REGIONAL STUDIES - BY CITY

2389 BURSA
(n.d.) / 30 min / sound / color / 16 mm
Producer unknown. Location: Turkish Tourism Office. *
Intended for junior-high school audiences. Shows scenes of Bursa including folk dancing, trellised streets, ruins from the period when Bursa was capital of the Ottoman empire, farms, Uludag outside Bursa, and modern areas of the city. Shows craftsmen, farmers and workers who make the city a busy economic center. Well presented travelog.

2390 EYE ON ISTANBUL
1973 / 24 min / sound / color / 16 mm
Gunther Less. Vision Association, Inc. Locations: Turkish Embassy / Turkish Tourism and Information Office. *
Intended for junior high school to adult audiences. Looks at ancient and modern Istanbul. Includes scenes of folk dancing, fish sellers, Topkapi, the 3000 shops of the covered bazaar, Trabzon folk dancers and a wedding dance. Does not contain a great deal of factual information.

2391 FABULOUS ISTANBUL
1973 / 28 min / sound / color / 16 mm
John Savage. Communetics, Inc. Locations: Turkish Embassy / Turkish Tourism and Information Office. *
Travelog of old Istanbul. Shows some of the 500 mosques of the city, the Bosporus, Aya Sophia, the Blue Mosque, the Topkapi palace and museum, the Janissary band, Turkish food, coffee and folk dance. Good profile of the city to promote tourism.

2392 ISTANBUL BRIDGE
1972 / 16 min / sound / b&w / 16 mm
E.L. Johnston, Texas.
Looks at the old floating bridge spanning the Golden Horn, connecting old and new Istanbul. Includes scenes of mosques. Contrasts traditional and modern scenes of the city.

2393   ISTANBUL, MAGIC CITY
        (c. 1958) / 30 min / sound / color / 16 mm
        Jan Boon for the Ministry of Press, Broadcasting and
        Tourism. Locations: Turkish Embassy / Turkish Tourism and
        Information Office.
        A study of the city of Istanbul, built on seven hills
        over a thousand year period. Shows the Galata Bridge
        linking Europe and Asia, the Blue Mosque, Aya Sophia,
        Istanbul University, and different styles of architecture
        found in the city. Shows street scenes, craftsmen and
        the annual youth festival held in honor of Ataturk.

2394   LET'S TALK TURKEY
        (n.d.) / 10 min / sound / b&w / 16 mm
        Bray Studios. (NUC FiA 55-445)
        Not to be confused with a film by the same name con-
        cerning turkeys and poultry farming. Shows street scenes
        of Istanbul including mosques and the bazaar.

2395   SOUVENIR OF ISTANBUL
        (n.d.) / 15 min / sound / color / 16 mm
        Belga Film for Turkish Air Lines. Location: Turkish Tourism
        and Information Office.
        A travelog of the city. Includes scenes of the Galata
        Bridge, the Sultan Ahmed Mosque, Blue Mosque, Topkapi
        palace and museum, Rumeli Hisar, passing of ships through
        the Bosphorus, the covered bazaar, old houses of
        Istanbul, Pierloti, Halic, Eyup Sultan Mosque and
        Buyukada.

2396   TREASURES OF ISTANBUL
        1960 / 9 min / sound / color / 35 mm
        Universal-International. Location: Library of Congress (FEA
        1425) No other information available.

TURKEY - THE ARMED FORCES AND NATO

2397   JETS OVER TURKEY
        1954 / 16 min / sound / b&w / 16 mm
        U.S. Information Agency. Released for public use through
        the U.S. Foreign Operations Administration. (NUC FiE 55-49)
        Profiles U.S.-assisted programs for training Turkish jet
        pilots at the Balekesir Air Base in Turkey.

2398   NATO
        1966 / 20 min / sound / b&w / 16 mm
        Europa Telefilm. U.S. Dept. of State. Locations: Turkish
        Embassy / Turkish Tourism and Information Office.
        Shows general scenes of Istanbul including the Galata
        Bridge, Topkapi palace and museum, and the Anit Kabir or
        Ataturk Mausoleum in Ankara. Discusses the strategic
        geographic position of Turkey near the Soviet Union and

shows Turkish NATO headquarters. Traces the Turkish
soldier from the Ottoman empire to the present time.

2399   TURKEY
1949 / 19 min / sound / b&w / 35 mm
Signal Corps. (Orientation film, no. 49)   Location:
National Archives (11OF49)   No other information available.

2400   TURKEY
1952 / 17 min / sound / b&w / 16 or 35 mm
U.S. Dept. of Defense.   Made by the U.S. Dept. of the Army.
(NUC FiE 53-651)
        Intended for U.S. Army personnel.   Explains importance of
        Turkey to NATO.   Describes the political, social, econo-
        mic and industrial significance of Turkey.

2401   TURKISH TROOPS IN WARTIME
1912 or 1913 / 5 min / silent / b&w / 16 mm
Eclipse, France.   Released in the U.S. by George Kleine.
Location: Library of Congress (FLA 1882)   No other information available.

TURKEY   -   AGRICULTURE

2402   CUTTING WHEAT WITH SCYTHES (TURKS, MIDDLE EAST
CENTRAL ANATOLIA)
1972 / 5 min / silent / b&w / 16 mm
E.J. Klay.   Encyclopaedia Cinematographica.   Distributed by
Pennsylvania State University.   (Ency. Cinematographica, no.
E 2028)
        Another in the series of silent ethnographic films.
        Shows traditional harvesting methods used in Anatolia.

2403   REPAIRING A THRESHING FLOAT (TURKS, MIDDLE EAST,
CENTRAL ANATOLIA)
1971, released 1973 / 8 min / silent / color / 16 mm
E.J. Klay.   Encyclopaedia Cinematographica.   Distributed by
Pennsylvania State University.   (Ency. Cinematographica, no.
E 1922)
        Another in the series of silent ethnographic films.
        Shows farmers repairing agricultural equipment.

2404   STONE KNAPPING IN MODERN TURKEY
1974 / 12 min / sound / b&w / 16 mm
Jacques Bordaz and Louis Alpers Bordaz.   Released by
Psychological Cinema Register, Pennsylvania State
University.   (Films in Behavioral Sciences series)   (LC
75-700200)   Locations: Kent State U. / Penn. State U.
        Looks at the ancient art of manufacturing flint blades in
        Turkey.   Shows how blades are formed and used in wheat
        threshing equipment.   Unnarrated.

2405   THRESHING WHEAT WITH A THRESHING FLOAT (MIDDLE EAST,
        ANATOLIA)
        1969, released 1971 / 22 min / silent / b&w / 16 mm
        Encyclopaedia Cinematographica. Distributed by Pennsylvania
        State University. (Ency. Cinematographica, no. E 1779)
            Another in the series of silent ethnographic films. This
            shows traditional threshing methods and equipment used in
            Turkey.

2406   THE TURKISH EXPERIMENT
        1974 / 29 min / sound / color / 16 mm
        Food and Agriculture Organization of the United Nations.
        Distributed by United Nations Films.
            Available in English and French soundtracks. Looks at
            the introduction of new technologies in Turkey to aid
            village farmers. Shows UN/FAO World Food Programme
            assistance in building roads, irrigation canals, and soil
            conservation and afforestation projects. Shows moder-
            nized fruit plantations and beekeeping operations.
            Discusses Turkish cooperatives.

2407   TURKISH HARVEST
        1952 / 22 min / sound / b&w / 16 mm
        E.S. Economic Cooperation Administration. Made by Clarke
        and Hornsby Film Productions, London. (NUC FiE 53-588)
            Produced for overseas use. Follows a Turkish boy as he
            receives training in an agricultural school. He returns
            to his village to show others the advantages of modern
            farm equipment and methods.

TURKEY - ECONOMICS, INDUSTRY, EDUCATION

2408   EDUCATION IN TURKEY
        (n.d.) / 16 min / sound / b&w / 16 mm
        Producer unknown. Location: Turkish Embassy. No other
        information available.

2409   TURKEY
        1962 / 27 min / sound / color / 16 mm
        Julien Bryan. International Film Foundation. Location: New
        York Public Donnell Film Library.
            Looks at economic and social problems of present day
            Turkey. Compares Turkey to other developing countries
            around the world.

2410   ZONGULDAK COAL
        1959 / 23 min / sound / color / 16 mm
        Paul Weir Co., Chicago. Made and released by Cameras
        International. (NUC FiA 61-848)
            Looks at the technological growth of Turkey's coal and
            steel industry near the Black Sea. Discusses the social
            implications of this industry.

454

2411 AKDENIZ FESTIVALI
(n.d.) / 15 min / sound / color / 16 mm
Producer unknown. Location: Turkish Tourism Office. *
Without narration. Shows the Akdeniz Festival of international folk dancing. Shows folk dance troupes from around the world and Turkish dancers, interspersed with scenes of modern and ancient Bursa. Of interest to folk dancers, costumers and general audiences.

2412 DEVE GURESI (CAMEL WRESTLING)
(n.d.) / 15 min / sound / color / 16 mm
Turizm ve Tanitma Bakanligi. Location: Turkish Tourism and Information Office.
Shows the sport of camel wrestling. Includes scenes of preparation of the camels, Mehter groups and marches, the audience, and folk dancers accompanied by drum and flute.

2413 INTERNATIONAL BOSPHORUS RALLY
(n.d.) / 30 min / sound / color / 16 mm
Producer unknown. Location: Turkish Embassy. No other information available.

2414 (TOPKAPI PALACE FASHION SHOW)
1962 / 25 min / silent / color / 16 mm
Producer unknown. Location: Turkish Tourism Office.
Of interest to fashion and textile students. Shows a modern Turkish fashion show set against the background of the Topkapi Palace and Museum. Includes examples of embroidery and metalwork from the museum, scenes of Istanbul life, and armor and jewels from the museum intercut with women modeling modern fashions. A specialized film, of poor technical quality.

UNITED ARAB EMIRATES

2415 ABU DHABI
1967 / 22 min / sound / color / 16 mm
British Petroleum Co. Locations: Middle East Institute / U.
of Kansas.
Listed in some catalogs as: ABU DHABI: LAND OF THE
GAZELLE. Looks at life in Abu Dhabi, one of the seven
Trucial States. Shows traditional life in the nation.
Discusses effect of influx of oil wealth and problems
associated with modernization and expansion of the eco-
nomy.

2416 ADMA
(c. 1970) / 36 min / sound / color / 16 mm
World Wide Pictures, Ltd. Distributed by British Petroleum.
Looks at British Petroleum oil exploration and floating
drilling platforms in the Persian Gulf area. Profiles
the Adma Enterprise, a special platform built in a shi-
pyard on the Kiel Canal and towed to the Persian Gulf.
Shows the petroleum industry operations on Das Island.

2417 AL KHALIJ - THE GULF
1974 / 29 min / sound / color / 16 mm
Caltex Petroleum Co. Made by Rayant Pictures, Ltd.
Released by Association-Sterling Films. (Caltex
International Public Relations series) (LC 74-702436)
Location: Middle East Institute. *
General introduction to Bahrain, Qatar, Oman and the
United Arab Emirates. Looks at the effect of oil
exploitation and rapid modernization on these traditional
societies. Profiles changes in agriculture, transportation, commerce and daily life since oil. Includes scenes of mosques, the desert, camel races on television,
the bazaars and geography of the countries. Offers a
non-political overview for tourists and students.

2418 BEDOUIN SETTLEMENTS
1976 / 10 min / sound / color / 16 m
Vision Habitat. Distributed by United Nations Films.
Looks at changes in nomadic life in the United Arab
Emirates since the discovery of oil. Shows projects by
the Ministry of Housing and Planning to settle nomads.
Describes programs which provide water and services to
settled nomads.

2419 BEHIND THE VEIL
1972 / 50 min / sound / color / 16 mm

456

Eve Arnold. Impact Films. Location: New York Public
Donnell Film Library.
Documents the marriage of the Crown Prince of Dubai.
Shows elaborate preparations and festivities of the
wedding including traditional dances and camel races.
Patronizing narration presents the event in a negative
manner.

2420   THE CALCULATED RISK
(c. 1970) / 28 min / sound / color / 16 mm
World Wide Pictures, Ltd. Distributed by British Petroleum.
Shows the risk involved in searching for areas for oil
exploration, raising capital, and drilling wells. Looks
at the Umm Shaif underwater oil field 60 miles off Abu
Dhabi. Describes the great risk of investments by
British Petroleum to find oil. Intended to promote
British Petroleum and describe one of their projects.

2421   FAREWELL ARABIA
1968 / 53 min / sound / b&w / 16 mm
National Educational Television and Radio Center. Made by
Rediffusion, London. Released by Indiana University
Audio-Visual Center. (Intertel series) (NUC FiA 68-1834)
Credits: Director - Randal Beattie, Editor - David Gill.
Looks at changes and modernization experienced in Abu
Dhabi since exploitation of oil resources. Shows the
struggles in the sheikhdom to maintain traditional
culture while introducing modern technologies and
industries.

2422   PRELUDE TO A NEW AGE
(n.d.) / 35 min / sound / color / 16 mm
Abu Dhabi Petroleum Co., Ltd. Distributed by the League of
Arab States.
Looks at oil exploitation in Abu Dhabi. Profiles the
training of Arab personnel in technical aspects of the
oil industry.

2423   STATION 307
(c. 1954) / 20 min / sound / b&w / 16 mm
Jacques Cousteau. Distributed by British Petroleum.
Jacques Cousteau, on the research ship Calypso, surveys
the Persian Gulf ocean bed in 1954. Divers take samples
and study undersea life while looking for oil.

2424   UNITED ARAB EMIRATES - A NEW OIL NATION
1976 / 14 min / sound / color / 16 mm
Russell Wulff Productions. Released by Oxford Films.
Distributed by Paramount Communications. Location: U. of
Illinois.
Intended for intermediate to junior high school audien-
ces. Looks at changes in the United Arab Emirates since
the discovery of oil. Shows goverment programs to house

and provide services for immigrants working in the oil
industry. Discusses social, economic and agricultural
changes in the Emirates since oil.

2425   COMMUNISTS FOR 1000 YEARS
        1973 / 30 min / sound / color / 16 mm
        Gordian Troeller and M. Claude Deffarge.   Distributed by
        Icarus Films.   *
            With English narration.   Profiles the isolated Carmathian
            sect in South Yemen.   Shows the traditional egalitarian
            social structure with common property and sexual
            equality.   Discusses the policy of the present Marxist
            government to convert the Carmathians to Marxist ideology
            to gain support for annexing North Yemen.   Includes
            interviews with two villagers who describe their way of
            life, philosophy and political beliefs.   Shows women
            bringing water, terraced farming, livestock and com-
            munally worked fields.   Very interesting study of a
            remote people.   Shows the great gulf between urban and
            village Yemenis.

2426   DRESSING PILLAR DRUMS: RAISING OF A PILLAR (ARABIA,
        HADHRAMAUT)
        1966, released 1967 / 10 min / silent / color / 16 mm
        Encyclopaedia Cinematographica.   Distributed by Pennsylvania
        State University.   (Ency. Cinematographica, no. E 1182)
            Another in the series of silent ethnographic films.
            Shows traditional techniques used to raise a pillar.

2427   EXPLODING A BLOCK OF STONE (ARABIA, HADHRAMAUT)
        1966, released 1967 / 5 min / silent / color / 16 mm
        Encyclopaedia Cinematographica.   Distributed by Pennsylvania
        State University.   (Ency. Cinematographica, no. E 1180)
            Another in the series of silent ethnographic films.
            Shows traditional methods used in the south Arabian
            peninsula for quarrying stone.

2428   FAMILIES OF THE WORLD: YEMEN
        1976 / 19 min / sound / color / 16 mm
        UNICEF.   Locations: Kent State U. / Syracuse U. / U. of
        Illinois / U. of Missouri.
            Looks at a traditional extended family in the Arab
            Republic of Yemen, one of the 25 "least developed"
            countries in the world.   Shows how women carry in all
            water and describes family organization and functions of
            different family members.   Predicts change in traditional
            social patterns as a result of modernization and contact
            with other countries and philosophies.

2429   FORGING A HOE BLADE (MODERN TECHNIQUE) (ARABIA,
        HADHRAMAUT)

1966, released 1968 / 11 min / silent / color / 16 mm
Encyclopaedia Cinematographica. Distributed by Pennsylvania
State University. (Ency. Cinematographica, no. E 1315)
Another in the series of silent ethnographic films.
Shows modern methods for forging blades.

2430   FORGING A HOE BLADE (TRADITIONAL TECHNIQUE) (ARABIA,
        HADHRAMAUT)
        1966, released 1967 / 10 min / silent / b&w / 16 mm
        Encyclopaedia Cinematographica. Distributed by Pennsylvania
        State University. (Ency. Cinematographica, no. E 1195)
        Another in the series of silent ethnographic films.
        Shows traditional blade forging techniques used in the
        southern Arabian peninsula.

2431   FORGING AN AX BLADE (ARABIA, HADHRAMAUT)
        1966, released 1967 / 7 min / silent / b&w / 16 mm
        Encyclopaedia Cinematographica. Distributed by Pennsylvania
        State University. (Ency. Cinematographica, no. 1194)
        Another in the series of silent ethnographic films.   This
        shows techniques used to forge an ax blade in the
        southern Arabian peninsula.

2432   FORMING A CLAY CENSER (ARABIA, HADHRAMAUT)
        1966, released 1967 / 6 min / silent / color / 16 mm
        Encyclopaedia Cinematographica. Distributed by Pennsylvania
        State University. (Ency. Cinematographica, no. E 1185)
        Another in the series of silent ethnographic films.
        Shows traditional pottery making techniques and designs
        used in making a clay censer.

2433   FORMING A CLAY WATERPIPE (ARABIA, HADHRAMAUT)
        1966, released 1967 / 4 min / silent / color / 16 mm
        Encyclopaedia Cinematographica. Distributed by Pennsylvania
        State University. (Ency. Cinematographica, no. E 1187)
        Another in the series of silent ethnographic films.
        Shows traditional pottery forming techniques and designs
        used to make a clay waterpipe in the southern Arabian
        peninsula.

2434   FORMING AND PAINTING A CLAY VESSEL (ARABIA,
        HADHRAMAUT)
        1966, released 1967 / 10 min / silent / color / 16 mm
        Encyclopaedia Cinematographica. Distributed by Pennsylvania
        State University. (Ency. Cinematographica, no. E 1186)
        Another in the series of silent ethnographic films.
        Shows pottery making techniques, colors and pigments used
        in producing traditional clay vessels in the southern
        Arabian peninsula.

2435   IRRIGATION CULTIVATING (HADHRAMI, ARABIA,
        HADHRAMAUT)
        1960, released 1962 / 5 min / silent / b&w / 16 mm

Encyclopaedia Cinematographica. Distributed by Pennsylvania
State University. (Ency. Cinematographica, no. E 428)
Another in the series of silent ethnographic films.
Looks at traditional irrigation techniques used in the
southern Arabian peninsula.

2436   MAKING A COFFEE MORTAR (ARABIA, HADHRAMAUT)
       1966, released 1967 / 10 min / silent / b&w / 16 mm
       Encyclopaedia Cinematographica. Distributed by Pennsylvania
       State University. (Ency. Cinematographica, no. E 1198)
       Another in the series of silent ethnographic films.
       Shows how a coffee mortar, for preparation of coffee
       beans, is made in the southern Arabian peninsula.

2437   MAKING A FUNNEL (ARABIA, HADHRAMAUT)
       1966, released 1967 / 18 min / silent / b&w / 16 mm
       Encyclopaedia Cinematographica. Distributed by Pennsylvania
       State University. (Ency. Cinematographica, no. E 1192)
       Another in the series of silent ethnographic films.
       Shows traditional design and techniques used in making a
       funnel in the southern Arabian peninsula.

2438   MAKING A HOOK-SHAPED SICKLE (ARABIA, HADHRAMAUT)
       1966, released 1967 / 9 min / silent / b&w / 16 mm
       Encyclopaedia Cinematographica. Distributed by Pennsylvania
       State University. (Ency. Cinematographica, no. 1193)
       Another in the series of silent ethnographic films. This
       looks at tool-making techniques.

2439   MAKING A PIN OUT OF SHEET-IRON (ARABIA, HADHRAMAUT)
       1966, released 1967 / 4 min / silent / b&w / 16 mm
       Encyclopaedia Cinematographica. Distributed by Pennsylvania
       State University. (Ency. Cinematographica, no. E 1189)
       Another in the series of silent ethnographic films.
       Shows traditional metal working techniques.

2440   MAKING A STONE HANDMILL (ARABIA, HADHRAMAUT)
       1966, released 1967 / 18 min / silent / color / 16 mm
       Encyclopaedia Cinematographica. Distributed by Pennsylvania
       State University. (Ency. Cinematographica, no. E 1181)
       Another in the series of silent ethnographic films.
       Looks at traditional stone working techniques.

2441   MAKING A WATER BUCKET (ARABIA, HADHRAMAUT)
       1966, released 1967 / 11 min / silent / color / 16 mm
       Encyclopaedia Cinematographica. Distributed by Pennsylvania
       State University. (Ency. Cinematographica, no. E 1199)
       Another in the series of silent ethnographic films.
       Looks at traditional methods used to produce water
       buckets.

2442   MAKING A WINDOW (ARABIA, HADHRAMAUT)
       1966, released 1967 / 29 min / silent / color / 16 mm

Encyclopaedia Cinematographica. Distributed by Pennsylvania
State University. (Ency. Cinematographica, no. E 1197)
Another in the series of silent ethnographic films.
Looks at traditional building techniques.

2443   MAKING AN ORNAMENTAL NAIL (ARABIA, HADHRAMAUT)
1966, released 1967 / 9 min / silent / b&w / 16 mm
Encyclopaedia Cinematographica. Distributed by Pennsylvania
State University. (Ency. Cinematographica, no. E 1190)
Another in the series of silent ethnographic films.
Looks at traditional metal-work methods and designs.

2444   MAKING BRICKS, CONSTRUCTING A WALL (ARABIA,
HADHRAMAUT)
1966, released 1967 / 16 min / silent / color / 16 mm
Encyclopaedia Cinematographica. Distributed by Pennsylvania
State University. (Ency. Cinematographica, no. E 1188)
Another in the series of silent ethnographic films.
Shows traditional construction techniques used in Yemen.

2445   MAKING FIRETONGS (ARABIA, HADHRAMAUT)
1966, released 1967 / 6 min / silent / b&w / 16 mm
Encyclopaedia Cinematographica. Distributed by Pennsylvania
State University. (Ency. Cinematographica, no. E 1191)
Another in the series of silent ethnographic films.
Looks at traditional tool construction techniques.

2446   MEDICAL TREATMENT, "BURNING" WITH HEATED IRON
(ARABIA, HADHRAMAUT)
1966, released 1967 / 3 min / silent / color / 16 mm
Encyclopaedia Cinematographica. Distributed by Pennsylvania
State University. (Ency. Cinematographica, no. 1201)
Another in the series of silent ethnographic films.
Shows traditional medicine in Yemen.

2447   MOON TEMPLE OF SHEBA
1960 / 30 min / sound / b&w / 16 mm
Insight, Inc. Released by ABC Television. (Expedition!,
television series) (NUC Fi 68-182) Credits: Producer - V.
Fae Thomas, Writer - P.T. Furst, Photographers - George
Farrier, Wallace Wade. Location: Library of Congress (FCA
2472)
Follows the archeological expedition of American Wendell
Phillips at Marib in the Dhofar region of Yemen.
Explains the group was forced to leave due to political
problems in the Yemen.

2448   NEW LIFE FOR THE BEDOUINS
1976 / 14 min / sound / color / 16 mm
Vision Habitat. Distributed by United Nations Films.
Available in English, Arabic and French soundtracks.
Looks at a traditional Bedouin family in the People's
Democratic Republic of Yemen. Shows the government is

attempting to improve their standard of living by
transporting water, creating settlements, and providing
medical service. Describes education programs for
Bedouin children.

2449   PREPARATION OF CLAY: FORMING AN IBEX
(ARABIA, HADRAMAUT)
1966, released 1967 / 8 min / silent / color / 16 mm
Encyclopaedia Cinematographica. Distributed by Pennsylvania
State University. (Ency. Cinematographica, no. E 1184)
Another in the series of silent ethnographic films.
Shows traditional clay working techniques and designs.

2450   SEWING A TREE TRUNK (ARABIA, HADHRAMAUT)
1966, released 1967 / 7 min / silent / b&w / 16 mm
Encyclopaedia Cinematographica. Distributed by Pennsylvania
State University. (Ency. Cinematographica, no. E 1196)
Another in the series of silent ethnographic films.

2451   SHIBAM
1970 / 14 min / sound / b&w / 16 mm
International TV Trading Corp. Released by Contemporary
Films/McGraw-Hill. (LC 72-706708) Credits:
Producer-Director-Writer - Walter Jacob, Collaborator -
Hanna Weber.
Looks at the small city of Shibam in the southern Arabian
peninsula. Profiles the traditional architecture of the
city and looks at its people.

2452   SILVER WORKING (ARABIA, HADHRAMAUT)
1966, released 1968 / 44 min / silent / b&w / 16 mm
Encyclopaedia Cinematographica. Distributed by Pennsylvania
State University. (Ency. Cinematographica, no. E 1346)
Another in the series of silent ethnographic films.
Examines traditional silver working techniques and
designs.

2453   SMOKING A WATERPIPE (ARABIA, HADHRAMAUT)
1964, released 1967 / 4 min / silent / b&w / 16 mm
Encyclopaedia Cinematographica. Distributed by Pennsylvania
State University. (Ency. Cinematographica, no. E 1200)
Another in the series of silent ethnographic films.
Looks at traditional pipes smoked in the southern Arabian
peninsula.

2454   SOCIAL DANCE OF MEN AND WOMEN (AL MANAHIL,
ARABIA, HADHRAMAUT)
1960, released 1962 / 3 min / silent / b&w / 16 mm
Encyclopaedia Cinematographica. Distributed by Pennsylvania
State University. (Ency. Cinematographica, no. E 429)
Listed in some catalogs as: GESELLIGER TANZ
DER FRAUEN UND MANNER. Produced by the Institut
fur den Wissenschaftlichen Film, Gottingen, West Germany.

Shows men and women dancing together at the village well
of al-Manahil in Southern Yemen.

2455   TEENAGERS OF THE WORLD: YEMEN
(n.d.) / 27 min / sound / color / 16 mm
United Nations Children's Fund. Distributed by United
Nations Films.
Available in English, French and Italian soundtracks.
Looks at problems facing teenagers in the Yemen.
Explains Yemen is an underdeveloped country, dependent on
foreign aid and imported food with a shortage of skilled
manpower. Shows the male-dominated work force and
efforts of women to work as nurses, midwives, teachers
and office workers. Profiles UNICEF training programs.

2456   TRADITIONAL ARCHITECTURE IN YEMEN
1976 / 19 min / sound / color / 16 mm
Vision Habitat. Distributed by United Nations Films.
Available in English, Arabic, French and Spanish
soundtracks. Documents the architectural style found in
the Yemen Arab Republic. Shows groups of men
constructing a house using packed mud bricks and stone.
Traditional decoration of houses, gypsum frames and
stained glass windows made by local craftsmen are shown.
Discusses why the buildings are so well suited to the
climate and society of Yemen.

2457   WE FOUND A VALLEY
(c. 1970) / 32 min / sound / color / 16 mm
Greenpark Productions. Distributed by British Petroleum Co.
Looks at risks involved and engineering achievements of
the British Petroleum Company in its Little Aden refinery
in southern Arabia. Examines the impact of the project
on the remote region.

2458   YEMEN
1976 / 19 min / sound / color / 16 mm
United Nations. (Families of the World series) Location:
Kent State U.
Intended for intermediate to junior high school audiences. Looks at traditional and modern roles for teenagers
in Yemen today. Shows a boy taking advantage of educational opportunities and a modern girl who wishes to be a
teacher. May be the same film as no. 2428.

2459   YEMEN: THE ARAB'S OWN WAR
1963 / 28 min / sound / b&w / 16 mm
CBS News. (Eyewitness, television series) (NUC Fi 67-2238)
Credits: Producer - Leslie Midgley, Director - Russ Bensley,
Reporters - Charles Collingwood, Winston Burdett, Cameraman
- Joseph Falletta. Location: Library of Congress (FCA 2579)
Looks at the civil war between royalists and republicans
in Yemen following the death of the King in 1962.

Discusses intervention by Egypt and Saudi Arabia in the
conflict. Describes effect of the war on people in towns
and villages in the Yemen.

2460   YEMEN - AN EMERGING ARAB REPUBLIC
1976 / 14 min / sound / color / 16 mm
Russell Wulff Productions. Released by Oxford Films.
Distributed by Paramount Communications. Location: U. of
Illinois.
Intended for intermediate to high school audiences.
Looks at the traditional, under-developed Yemen Arab
Republic. Contrasts village bazaars, rural life, caravan
trails and village agriculture to modern educational,
medical and technological development programs sponsored
by the U.S. and China. Discusses changes in the society
of Yemen but does not cover political developments.

TITLE AND SERIES INDEX

A

ABC Presents Dean Pike   211
Abou Simbel   667
Abraham and Isaac   396
Absorption   1307
Abu Dhabi   2415
    Abu Dhabi: Land of the Gazelle - See: Abu Dhabi   2415
Acre   1669
Acre, Old-New City   1670
Action Sudan: The Church and the Peace   2239
Addis Ababa - Pan African Center   882
Adma   2416
Adullam   1482
Adventure in Israel   1581
Adventure Through Time   1539
Advocates, Parts 1 and 2   310
Aerial Views of Negev, Nahal David and Nahal Zin   1636
Afghan Nomads: The Maldar   535
Afghan Treasure: Bamiyan   575
Afghan Village   544
Afghan Women   567
Afghanistan   576
Afghanistan: Emerging From Isolation   577
Afghanistan: Heart of Asia, Part 1   588
Afghanistan: Heart of Asia, Part 2   589
AFGHANISTAN: THE LAND AND THE PEOPLE (series)
    #1   Primitive Agriculture: The Bamian Valley   597
    #2   Highland Village: The Bamian Valley   552
    #4   Kabul: The Capital   583
    #5   Annual Jeshan Celebration   531
    #6   Buzkashi: The National Game   537
    #7   Kabul Family: A Day at Elementary School   602
    #8   Livestock Market: Kabul   585
    #10   Transportation: The Salang Pass and Kabul   587
    #11   Herat Tile Makers: Charikar Grape Harvest   551
    #12   The Rug Makers of Mazar-i-Sharif   608
    #14   Women of Afghanistan   574
    #15   Kuchi Herders   540
Afghanistan: Land of Beauty and Hospitality   578
Afghanistan Moves Ahead   591
Afghanistan: Wheat Cycle   592
Africa   192
AFRICA (series)
    -   Addis Ababa: Pan African Center   882
    -   Bazaar in Marrakech   2046
    -   Continent of Africa   197

467

468

470

473

C

475

479

482

483

487

H

Habib Bourguiba (1961)   2274
Habib Bourguiba (1968)   2275
Habitat: Pakistan   2143
Hadassah Newsreel Series   1788
Hadassim   1388
Hagit - A 17 Year Old on a Kibbutz   1445
Haifa   1685
Haifa Port (Nemal Haifa)   1686
Hail Caesarea   1687
Haile Selassie   867
The Hajj   2199
         Ha-Kibbutz - See: The Kibbutz (Ha-Kibbutz)   1453
Half the World   998
Handicrafts of Pakistan (n.d.)   2168
Handicrafts of Pakistan (1966)   2169
Hands of Healing   1789
Hannah Means Grace   1790
Hanukkah   258
Happy Valley   1724
Harvest From the Waters   1725
Harvest in Galilee   1751
Harvest in the Negev   1752
Harvest of the Sea   2152
         Harvest of the Seasons - See: The Ascent of Man: Part 2.
         Harvest of the Seasons   25
Harvest Song   1884
Harvesting and Threshing Barley (Fellahin, North Africa, Upper
         Egypt)   838
Hasht Behest Palace of Isfahan   1025
Hassan Discovers the World of Oil   2219
Hassan II, King of Morocco   2006
Hazorim Bedima (Those Who Sow in Tears)   1885
Head Start for Omar   451
Healing Hands of Medico   92
Healing Sword   2225
Health for Victory   1791
The Heart of a Nation of Soldiers (Lev Ha'am Im Cha'yalav)   1528
The Heart of Hadassah, Research   1792
Hebrew Songs   1886
The Hebrew University   1826
The Height of 40,000 Feet (Hagovah 40,000 Regel)   1529
Helmand Valley   590
Henrietta Szold   1299
Herat Tile Makers: Charikar Grape Harvest   551
(Herd of Sheep on the Road to Jerusalem)   478
Herding, Watering and Milking Sheep and Goats (Crimean Tatars,
         Middle East, Central Anatolia)   2351
Here Is Israel   1600
The Heretic King   690
Heritage   1446
HERITAGE (series)
         - Charles Malik, Parts 1,2,3 and 4   69
Hero   1809

489

490

493

496

L

503

Movietone News (1957)   2270
Movietone News (1963)   730
Mud Horse   770
Muhammad Kamil 'Abd al-Rahim   746
Museum of Anthropology   921
Music and Dances of Pakistan   2180
Musical Instruments Out of Plants   1889
MUSICAL WORLD JOURNEY (series)
  - Jerusalem, The Holy City   467
Muslim Festivals in India   917
Mussolini vs. Selassie   864
My Brother and I   1370
My Village   1964
Mysteries of the Great Pyramid   665
Mysterious Cappadocia   2366
The Mystery of Nefertiti   666
Mystery of the Mounds   637
Mystic Alhambra   2236
Myth of the Pharaohs   697

N

The Nachal Are Coming   1499
Nachal: Fighting Pioneer Unit   1500
Nagui the Artist   852
Naim and Jabar   573
Napalm Victims   358
Nasser vs. Ben-Gurion   335
NATIONAL ARCHIVES. BUREAU OF MINES (series)
  #113   Through Oil Lands of Europe and Africa, Part 1   134
  #115   Through Oil Lands of Europe and Africa, Part 3   135
NATIONAL ARCHIVES. BUREAU OF PUBLIC RELATIONS (series)
  #1042   (Middle East Conferences)   76
NATIONAL ARCHIVES. COMBAT FILM REPORT (series)
  #403   Axis Saboteurs - North Africa   174
  #320a   Bombers Over North Africa   175
NATIONAL ARCHIVES. FILM BULLETIN (series)
  #51   Allied Offensive in North Africa   172
  #61   How the British Handle Ammunition in the Middle East   52
NATIONAL ARCHIVES. HISTORICAL FILM (series)
  #1226   American Military Mission to Turkey and Armenia   2330
NATIONAL ARCHIVES. MISC. FILMS (series)
  #451   British War Reviews   49
  #483   Operations in Mesopotamia, 1914 to 1918   61
  #503   War Nears End in Abyssinia   866
  #797   Around the World on the U.S. Army Transport Cableship
        "Dellwood"   776
  #1001   At the Front in North Africa with the U.S. Army   173
NATIONAL ARCHIVES. ORIENTATION FILMS (series)
  #49   Turkey (1949)   2399
NATIONAL GEOGRAPHIC SPECIAL (television series)
  - Ethiopia: The Hidden Empire   856

516

523

526

528

Laila ABOU SAIF
19 Gamal-al-Din
Abou al-Mahassen
Garden City, Cairo, Egypt
tel: 30014

ABRAHAM F. RAD CONTEMPORARY
JEWISH FILM ARCHIVE.
Institute of Contemporary
Jewry. Hebrew University of
Jerusalem.
Wolffsohn Building
Hebrew University
Mount Scopus, Jerusalem
Phone: (02)882513

ACI FILMS
35 W. 45th Street
New York, New York   10036
(212) 582-1918

AETNA LIFE AND CASUALTY FILM
LIBRARY
Public Relations and
Advertising
151 Farmington Ave.
Hartford, Connecticut   06115

A.I.M.
Associated Instructional Material
2nd and Delaware Avenues
Oakmont, Pennsylvania   15139

ALDEN FILMS
7820 20th Avenue
Brooklyn, New York   11214
(212) 331-1045

AMERICAN FRIENDS OF THE MIDDLE
EAST, INC.
1717 Massachusetts Ave. NW
Washington, D.C.   20036

AMERICAN UNIVERSITY FIELD STAFF
3 Lebanon St.
Hanover, New Hampshire   03755

ANTI-DEFAMATION LEAGUE OF
B'NAI B'RITH
Lewis Tower Bldg.
225 S. 15th St.
Philadelphia, PA   19102
    or
315 Lexington Ave.
New York, New York   10016

ARAB INFORMATION CENTER
League of Arab States
Hartford Bldg.
Dallas, Texas   75201
(214) 748-4623
    or
747 Third Ave.
New York, New York   10017
(212) 838-8700
    or
235 Montgomery St.
Suite 666
San Francisco, CA   94104
    or
1875 Connecticut Ave. NW
Washington, D.C. 20009
(202) 265-3210

ARABIAN AMERICAN OIL CO.
1345 Ave. of the Americas
New York, New York   10019

ARIZONA STATE UNIVERSITY
AV Dept.
Tempe, Arizona   85281
(602) 965-5073

ARTS COUNCIL OF GREAT
BRITAIN
105 Piccadilly
London, W1V OAU England

ASSOCIATED FILM SERVICES
3419 W. Magnolia Blvd.
Burbank, California

531

ASSOCIATION FILMS, INC.
324 Delaware Ave.
Oakmont, PA 15139

ASSOCIATION/STERLING FILMS
866 Third Ave.
New York, New York 10022
(212) 935-4210
    or
512 Burlington Ave.
La Grange, Illinois 60525
(212) 752-4431

ATLANTIS PRODUCTIONS
850 Thousand Oaks Blvd.
Thousand Oaks, CA 91360
    or
1252 La Granada Dr.
Thousand Oaks, CA 91360
(805) 495-2790

AUDIENCE PLANNERS, INC.
1 Rockefeller Plaza
New York, New York 10020

AV-ED FILMS
178 William Ave.
Westminster, MD 21157
    or
Distribution Division
910 N. Citrus Ave.
Hollywood, CA 90038
(213) 466-1344

Ali Shiva AZIZIAN
139 E. 30th St.
New York, New York 10016
(212) 679-2643

BARR FILMS
P.O. Box 5667
Pasadena, CA 91107
(213) 793-6153

BECHTEL CO.
Public Relations Dept.
50 Beale St.
San Francisco, CA 94105
(415) 768-4596

BENJAMIN PRODUCTIONS
170 Bleecker St. 7C
New York, New York 10012

BFA EDUCATIONAL MEDIA
CBS Educational Publishing
2211 Michigan Ave.
Santa Monica, CA 90406
(213) 829-2901

BOISE STATE UNIVERSITY
Educational Media Services
1910 Col. Blvd.
Boise, Idaho 83720
(208) 385-3289

BOSTON UNIVERSITY
Krasker Memorial Film Library
765 Commonwealth Ave.
Boston, MA 02215
(617) 353-3272

BRIGHAM YOUNG UNIVERSITY
Media Marketing, W-STAD
Provo, Utah 84602
(801) 374-1211 ext. 4071

CALIFORNIA NEWSREEL/
RESOLUTION
630 Natoma St.
San Francisco, CA 94103
(415) 621-6196

CALTEX PETROLEUM CORP.
Public Relations Dept.
380 Madison Ave.
New York, New York 10017
(212) 697-2000

CAROUSEL FILMS
1501 Broadway
New York, New York 10036
(212) 660-0187

CATHOLIC FILM CENTER
29 Salem Way
Yonkers, New York 10710

CBS-TV
524 W. 57th St.
New York, New York 10019

CCM FILMS, INC.
866 Third Ave.
New York, New York 10022

CENTRAL ZIONIST ARCHIVES
1 Ibn Gavirol St.
Jerusalem

CENTRON EDUCATIONAL FILMS
1621 W. 9th St.
Lawrence, Kansas 66044
(913) 843-0400

CONCORD FILMS COUNCIL, LTD.
201 Felixstare Road
Ipswich, Suffolk, England

CORNELL UNIVERSITY
Motion Picture Center
Box 41, Roberts Hall
Ithaca, New York 14853
(607) 256-2225

CORONET FILMS
65 E. South Water St.
Chicago, Illinois 60601
(312) 332-7676
(312) 977-4000

CURRENT AFFAIRS FILMS
24 Danbury Road
Wilton, CT 06897

DANCE FILM ASSOCIATION
250 W. 57th St.
New York, New York 10019

DANELI INTERNATIONAL
P.O. Box 3417
Santa Barbara, CA 93105
(805) 687-1319

DIMENSIONS VISUAL PRODUCTIONS
1050 W. Columbia Ave.
Chicago, Illinois 60626

Walt DISNEY PRODUCTIONS
Educational Film Division
500 S. Buena Vista Ave.
Burbank, CA 91503
(213) 841-2000
(800) 423-2555

DOCUMENT ASSOCIATES
211 E. 43rd St.
New York, New York 10017
(212) 682-0730

DOUBLEDAY MULTIMEDIA
1371 Reynolds Ave.
Irvine, CA 92664

EGYPTIAN GOVERNMENT TOURISM
OFFICE
630 5th Ave.
New York, New York 10020

ELUL PRODUCTIONS, LTD.
31 Burla St.
Tel Aviv, Israel

EMBASSY OF AFGHANISTAN
2341 Wyoming Ave. NW
Washington, D.C. 20008
(202) 234-3770

EMBASSY OF THE DEMOCRATIC
AND POPULAR REPUBLIC OF
ALGERIA
2118 Kalorama Rd. NW
Washington, D.C. 20008
(202) 234-7246

EMBASSY OF CYPRUS
2211 R St. NW
Washington, D.C. 20008
(202) 462-5772

EMBASSY OF EGYPT
Cultural and Educational
Bureau
2200 Kalorama Rd. NW
Washington, D.C. 20008
(202) 265-6400
(202) 234-0981

EMBASSY OF ETHIOPIA
2134 Kalorama Rd. NW
Washington, D.C. 20008
(202) 234-2281

EMBASSY OF INDIA
Audio-Visual Section
2107 Massachusetts Ave. NW
Washington, D.C. 20008
(202) 265-5050 ext. 301

EMBASSY OF ISRAEL
1621 22nd St. NW
Washington, D.C. 20008
(202) 483-4100

EMBASSY OF THE HASHEMITE KINGDOM
OF JORDAN
2319 Wyoming Ave. NW
Washington, D.C. 20008
(202) 265-1606

EMBASSY OF KUWAIT
2940 Tilden St. NW
Washington, D.C. 20008
(202) 966-0702

EMBASSY OF LEBANON
2560 28th St. NW
Washington, D.C.
(202) 462-8600

EMBASSY OF MOROCCO
1601 21st St. NW
Washington, D.C. 20009
(202) 462-7979

EMBASSY OF PAKISTAN
2315 Massachusetts Ave. NW
Washington, D.C. 20007
(202) 332-8330

EMBASSY OF THE STATE OF
QATAR
2721 Connecticut Ave. NW
Washington, D.C. 20008
(202) 338-0111

EMBASSY OF SAUDI ARABIA
1520 18th St. NW
Washington, D.C. 20036
(202) 483-2100

EMBASSY OF THE DEMOCRATIC
REPUBLIC OF THE SUDAN
Suite 400
600 New Hampshire Ave. NW
Washington, D.C. 20037
(202) 338-8565
(202) 338-8571

EMBASSY OF THE SYRIAN ARAB
REPUBLIC
Suite 1120
600 New Hampshire Ave. NW
Washington, D.C. 20037
(202) 232-6313

EMBASSY OF TUNISIA
2408 Massachusetts Ave. NW
Washington, D.C. 20008
(202) 234-6644

EMBASSY OF THE REPUBLIC
OF TURKEY
1606 23rd St. NW
Washington, D.C. 20008
(202) 462-3134

EMBASSY OF TURKEY
Office of the Press Counselor
2523 Massachusetts Ave. NW
Washington, D.C. 20008

EMBASSY OF THE UNITED ARAB
EMIRATES
Suite 740
600 New Hampshire Ave. NW
Washington, D.C. 20037
(202) 338-6500

EMBASSY OF THE YEMEN ARAB
REPUBLIC
Suite 860
600 New Hampshire Ave. NW
Washington, D.C. 20037
(202) 965-4760

ENCYCLOPAEDIA BRITANNICA
EDUCATIONAL CORP.
425 North Michigan Ave.
Chicago, Illinois 60611
(312) 321-7320

ENCYCLOPAEDIA CINEMATOGRAPHICA
American Archive
Pennsylvania State Univ.
Audio-Visual Services
17 Willard Bldg.
University Park, PA 16802

ETERNAL LIGHT FILM LIBRARY
Jewish Theological Seminary
155 Fifth Ave.
New York, New York 10010

EYE GATE HOUSE, INC.
146-01 Archer Ave.
Jamaica, New York 11435

FARM FILM FOUNDATION
Suite 424 - Southern Bldg.
1425 H St. NW
Washington, D.C. 20005
(202) 628-1321

FILMS FOR THE HUMANITIES
P.O. Box 2053
Princeton, New Jersey 08540
(201) 329-6912

FILMS INCORPORATED
1144 Wilmette Ave.
Wilmette, Illinois 60091
    or
440 Park Ave. South
New York, New York 10003
(212) 889-7910

FLORIDA STATE UNIVERSITY
Instructional Media Service
Tallahassee, Florida 32306
(904) 644-2820

FOGG MUSEUM FILMS
Films for the Humanities, Inc.
P.O. Box 2053
Princeton, New Jersey 08540
(201) 329-6912

GRAHAM ASSOCIATES, INC.
1150 17th St. NW
Washington, D.C. 20036
(202) 833-9657

GRATZ COLLEGE
Division of Community Services
Audio-Visual Media Dept.
10th St. and Tabor Rd.
Philadelphia, PA 19141

GREAT PLAINS NATL. ITV LIBRARY
Box 80669
Lincoln, Nebraska 68501

Natan GROSS
14 Herzog St.
Givata'im, Israel

HADASSAH FILM LIBRARY
470 Park Ave. South
New York, New York 10016
    or
National Program Film Dept.
50 W. 58th St.
New York, New York 10019

HEARST METROTONE NEWS
450 W. 56th St.
New York, New York 10019

Robert S. HIRSCHFIELD
Hunter College
695 Park Ave.
New York, New York

HISTADRUT - GENERAL
FEDERATION OF JEWISH LABOR
12 Shenkin St.
Tel Aviv, Israel

HORUSFILM / NAGUI RIAD
17 Emad el Din St.
P.O. Box 2016
Cairo, Egypt

HUNGARIAN ACADEMY OF
SCIENCES
Folk Music Research Group
Roosevelter 9
Budapest V, Hungary

ICARUS FILMS
Middle East and North
African Film Library
200 Park Ave. South #1319
New York, New York 10003
(212) 674-3375

IDAHO STATE UNIVERSITY
Audio-Visual Services
Campus Box 8064
Pocatello, Idaho 83209
(208) 236-3212

IMPACT FILMS
144 Bleecker St.
New York, New York 10012

INDIANA UNIVERSITY
AV Center
Bloomington, Indiana 47401
(812) 337-8087

INSTITUTIONAL CINEMA, INC.
915 Broadway
New York, New York 10010
(212) 673-3990
    or
10 First Street
Saugerties, New York 12477
(914) 246-2848

535

INTERNATIONAL FILM BUREAU
332 S. Michigan Ave.
Chicago, Illinois 60604
(312) 427-4545

INTERNATIONAL FILM FOUNDATION
Room 916, 475 Fifth Ave.
New York, New York 10017
(212) 685-4998
(212) 580-1111

INTERNATIONAL FILMS, INC.
1610 E. Elizabeth St.
Pasadena, CA 91104

INTERNATIONAL LABOR ORGANIZATION
4 Route des Morillons
1211 Geneva 22, Switzerland

IOWA STATE UNIVERSITY
Media Resource Center
121 Pearson Hall
Ames, Iowa 50010
(515) 249-8022

ISRAEL FILM ARCHIVES
142 Rothschild Centre
Hanasi Ave.
Haifa, Israel

ISRAEL FILM SERVICE
P.O. Box 78853
Jerusalem

ISRAEL FILM SERVICES
14 Hillel St.
Jerusalem

ISRAEL FILM STUDIOS, LTD.
Hakessem St.
Herzliyah, Israel

ISRAEL GOVERNMENT TOURIST BUREAU
488 Madison Ave.
New York, New York 10022

ISRAEL INSTITUTE OF PRODUCTIVITY
4 Henrietta Szold
Citrus House
Tel Aviv, Israel

JABOTINSKY INSTITUTE IN ISRAEL
38 King George St.
Tel Aviv, Israel

JERUSALEM FILM CORP.
2315 Kenoak Rd.
Baltimore, Maryland 21208

JEWISH AGENCY FILM ARCHIVE
Beit Shalom
20 Achad Ha'Am St.
Jerusalem

JEWISH MEDIA SERVICE
65 William St.
Wellesley, MA 02181

JEWISH MEDIA SERVICE, JWB
15 E. 26th St.
New York, New York 10010
(212) 532-4949

JEWISH NATIONAL FUND
Hakeren Kakayemet Leyisrael
King George St.
Jerusalem
or
42 W. 69th St.
New York, New York 10021

E.L. JOHNSTON
1200 Dissonnet
Houston, Texas 77005

JORDAN INFORMATION BUREAU
Suite 1004
1701 K St. NW
Washington, D.C. 20006
(202) 659-3322

JWB LECTURE BUREAU
15 E. 32nd St.
New York, New York 10010

Gurith KADMAN
5 Shalag St.
Tel Aviv, Israel

KANSAS STATE UNIVERSITY
South Asia Center Media
Collection
Manhattan, Kansas 66506
(913) 532-5738

KENT STATE UNIVERSITY
Audio-Visual Services
Kent, Ohio 44242
(216) 672-3456

KEREN HAYESOD
King George St.
Jerusalem

LEAGUE OF ARAB STATES
Arab Information Center
747 Third Ave.
New York, New York 10017
(212) 838-8700

LEARNING CORP. OF AMERICA
1350 Ave. of the Americas
New York, New York 10019
(212) 397-9353

LEBANON TOURIST AND
INFORMATION OFFICE
405 Park Ave.
New York, New York 10022
(212) 421-2201

LIBRARY OF CONGRESS
Motion Picture, Broadcasting
and Recorded Sound Division
Washington, D.C. 20540

LOS ANGELES PUBLIC LIBRARY
630 W. 5th St.
Los Angeles, CA 90071

MACMILLAN FILMS
34 Macquesten Parkway S.
Mount Vernon, New York 10550
(914) 664-5051
(800) 431-1994

MARLIN MOTION PICTURES, LTD.
47 Lakeshore Rd. E
Mississaugua, Ontario
L5G 1C9 Canada

McGRAW-HILL FILMS
110 Fifteenth St.
Del Mar, CA 92014
    or
1221 Ave. of the Americas
New York, New York 10020
(212) 997-2183
    or
for local representative call:
(714) 453-5000

Frank McKEVITT
Visual Scope TV
708 Third Ave.
New York, New York

MICHIGAN DEPT. OF EDUCATION
State Library Service
735 E. Michigan Ave.
Box 3007
Lansing, Michigan 48909

MIDDLE EAST INSTITUTE
1761 N St. NW
Washington, D.C. 20036
(202) 785-1141

MINISTRY FOR FOREIGN
AFFAIRS (ISRAEL)
Hakirya, Romema
Jerusalem

MINISTRY OF EDUCATION AND
CULTURE (ISRAEL)
Shivtei Yisrael 34
Jerusalem

MINISTRY OF TOURISM (ISRAEL)
24 King George St.
Jerusalem

MINNESOTA LIBRARY FILM
CIRCUIT
Office of Public Libraries
301 Hanover Bldg.
480 Cedar St.
St. Paul, Minnesota 55101

MODERN FILM RENTALS
1145 N. McCadden Place
Hollywood, CA 90028

MODERN TALKING PICTURE
SERVICE
5000 Park St. N
St. Petersburg, Florida 33709
(813) 541-7571
    or
2323 New Hyde Park Rd.
New Hyde Park, New York 11040
(516) 437-6300
    or
1687 Elmhurst Rd.
Elk Grove Village, IL 60007

Arthur MOKIN PRODUCTIONS
17 W. 60th St.
New York, New York 10023

537

MOROCCAN TOURISM AND
INFORMATION OFFICE
597 Fifth Ave.
New York, New York
(212) 421-5771

NATIONAL ARCHIVES OF THE
UNITED STATES
National Archives and
Records Service
General Services Admin.
Washington, D.C. 20408

NATIONAL ASSOCIATION OF
ARAB AMERICANS
1028 Connecticut Ave. NW
Washington, D.C. 20036

NATIONAL COUNCIL OF CHURCHES
475 Riverside Dr.
New York, New York 10027

NATIONAL COUNCIL ON JEWISH
AUDIO-VISUAL MATERIALS
The American Association for
Jewish Education and the
Commission on Jewish Life and
Culture
15 E. 84th St.
New York, New York 10028

NATIONAL FILM BOARD OF CANADA
1251 Ave. of the Americas
New York, New York 10020
(212) 586-2400

NATIONAL GALLERY OF ART
Extension Services
Washington, D.C. 20565

NATIONAL GEOGRAPHIC SOCIETY
17th and M Streets NW
Washington, D.C. 20036
(202) 857-7095

NATIONAL JEWISH COMMUNITY
RELATIONS ADVISORY COUNCIL
55 W. 42nd St.
New York, New York 10036

NATIONAL JEWISH WELFARE BOARD
15 E. 26th St.
New York, New York 10010

NBC EDUCATIONAL ENTERPRISES
30 Rockefeller Plaza
New York, New York 10020
(212) 247-8300

NEHORA
Heichal Shlomo
P.O. Box 274
Jerusalem

NEW JERSEY STATE MUSEUM
Film Loan Service
205 W. State St.
Trenton, New Jersey 08625

NEW JEWISH MEDIA PROJECT
36 W. 37th St.
New York, New York

NEW YORK UNIVERSITY FILM
LIBRARY
26 Washington Place
New York, New York 10003
(212) 598-2250

NEW YORKER FILMS
43 W. 61st St.
New York, New York 10023
(212) 247-6110

OKLAHOMA STATE UNIVERSITY
A-V Center
Stillwater, Oklahoma 74074
(405) 624-7212 ext. 6241

OREGON STATE CONTINUING
EDUCATION FILM LIBRARY
1633 S.W. Park Ave.
P.O. Box 1491
Portland, Oregon 97207

PALESTINE INFORMATION OFFICE
1326 18th St. NW
Washington, D.C.

PALESTINE LIBERATION
ORGANIZATION
103 Park Ave., Room 701
New York, New York 10017
(212) 686-3530

PARAMOUNT COMMUNICATIONS
5451 Marathon St.
Hollywood, CA   90038
(213) 468-5000
     or
6912 Tujunga Blvd.
N. Hollywood, CA   91605
(213) 506-1402
     or
5904 Joymont
Jackson, MI   49201

PENNSYLVANIA STATE UNIVERSITY
AV Service
6 Willard Bldg.
University Park, PA   16802
(814) 865-6316

Margaret PENNAR
305 E. 40th St. (9T)
New York, New York   10016
(212) 986-6537

PHOENIX FILMS
470 Park Ave. South
New York, New York   10016
(212) 684-5910

PICTURA FILMS
DISTRIBUTION CORP.
43 W. 16th St.
New York, New York   10011

PRIME MINISTER'S OFFICE
(Israel) Information Dept.
Film Service
P.O. Box 2090
Jerusalem

PUBLIC BROADCASTING SERVICE
475 L'Enfant Plaza SW
Washington, D.C.   20024

PURDUE UNIVERSITY
AV Center
Stewart Center
W. Lafayette, Indiana   47907
(317) 749-6188

PYRAMID FILM AND VIDEO
Box 1048
Santa Monica, CA   90406
(800) 421-2304

MAURICE RABINOFF AND ASSOC.
102-25 67th Drive
Forest Hills, New York   11375

RADIM FILMS
220 42nd St.
New York, New York   10036
     or
17 W. 60th St.
New York, New York   10023
(212) 279-6653

RAI / TEXTURE FILMS, INC.
1600 Broadway
New York, New York   10019
(212) 586-6960

RMI FILM PRODUCTIONS
4916 Main St.
Kansas City, Missouri   64112
     or
701 Westport Rd.
Kansas City, Missouri   64111

Sol RUBIN
P.O. Box 40
New York, New York   10038

SAN FRANCISCO NEWSREEL
630 Natoma
San Francisco, CA   94103

SCHLOAT PRODUCTIONS
150 White Plains Rd.
Tarrytown, New York   10591

SOCIAL STUDIES SCHOOL SERVICE
P.O. Box 802
Culver City, CA   90230

STATE AV CENTER
223 South Main
Wichita, Kansas   67202

STERLING EDUCATIONAL FILMS
P.O. Box 8497
Universal City, CA   91608
     or
241 E. 34th St.
New York, New York   10016

SUNRISE FILMS
115 E. 9th Ave.
New York, New York 10003
(212) 592-0415

SYRACUSE UNIVERSITY
FILM RENTAL LIBRARY
1455 E. Colvin St.
Syracuse, New York 13210
(315) 479-6631

TELEMA - FIRST TIER FILMS, INC.
45 W. 45th St.
New York, New York 10033
(212) 489-9820

TEXTURE FILMS
1600 Broadway
New York, New York 10019
(212) 586-6960

THIRD WORLD NEWSREEL
160 Fifth Ave.
New York, New York 10010
(212) 243-2310

TIME-LIFE MULTIMEDIA
DISTRIBUTION CENTER
100 Eisenhower Drive
P.O. Box 644
Paramus, New Jersey 07652
(201) 843-4545
    or
EXECUTIVE OFFICES
Time and Life Bldg.
New York, New York 10020
(212) 556-4554

TOMLIN FILMS, INC.
P.O. Box 27
Sloatsburg, New York 10974
(212) 697-0003

TRC PRODUCTIONS, INC.
Suite 412
4711 Golf Rd.
Skokie, Illinois 60076
(312) 677-8440

TRICONTINENTAL FILM SERVICE
333 Sixth Ave.
New York, New York 10014
(212) 989-3330
    or
P.O. Box 4430
Berkeley, CA 94704
(415) 548-3204
    or
1034 Lake St.
Oak Park, Illinois 60301
(312) 386-5909

TUNISIAN NATIONAL TOURIST OFFICE
630 Fifth Ave., Suite 863
New York, New York 10020
(212) 582-3670

TURKISH TOURISM AND
INFORMATION OFFICE
821 U.N. Plaza
500 Fifth Ave.
New York, New York 10036
(212) 687-2194

UNICEF
331 E. 38th St.
New York, New York 10016

UNITED JEWISH APPEAL
Film Department
515 Park Ave.
New York, New York

UNITED METHODIST FILM SERVICE
1525 McGavock St.
Nashville, Tennessee 37203

UNITED NATIONS FILMS
United Nations Radio and Visual
Services Director
Office of Public Information
New York, New York 10017

UNITED WORLD FILMS
221 Park Ave. South
New York, New York

UNIVERSAL EDUCATION AND VISUAL
ARTS
100 Universal City Plaza
Universal City, CA 91608
(213) 985-4321 ext. 2016

540

UNIVERSITY OF ARIZONA FILM
LIBRARY
Audio-Visual Services, Radio
and TV Bureau
Tucson, Arizona   85721
(602) 884-3852

UNIVERSITY OF CALIFORNIA
EXTENSION MEDIA CENTER
2223 Fulton St.
Berkeley, CA   94720
(415) 642-0462

UNIVERSITY OF CALIFORNIA AT
LOS ANGELES
Instructional Media Library
Royce Hall 8
405 Hilgard Ave.
Los Angeles, CA   90024
(213) 825-0755

UNIVERSITY OF COLORADO
Bureau of AV Instruction
3rd Floor, Stadium 364
Boulder, Colorado   80309
(303) 492-7341

UNIVERSITY OF CONNECTICUT
Center for Instructional Media
and Technology
Storrs, Connecticut   06268
(203) 486-2530

UNIVERSITY OF IDAHO
Audio Visual and Photo Center
Moscow, Idaho   83843
(208) 885-6411

UNIVERSITY OF ILLINOIS
Visual Aids Service
1325 South Oak St.
Champaign, Illinois   61820
(217) 333-1360

UNIVERSITY OF IOWA
Audio-Visual Center
C-5 East Hall
Iowa City, Iowa   52242
(319) 353-5885

UNIVERSITY OF KANSAS
Audio-Visual Center
746 Massachusetts Ave.
Lawrence, Kansas   66044
(913) 864-3352

UNIVERSITY OF MAINE
Instructional Systems Center
16 Shibles Hall
Orono, Maine   04473
(207) 581-7541

UNIVERSITY OF MICHIGAN
Media Resources Center
416 Fourth St.
Ann Arbor, Michigan   48103
(313) 764-5360

UNIVERSITY OF MINNESOTA
University Media Resources
3300 University Ave. S.E.
540 Rarig Center
Minneapolis, Minnesota   55414
(612) 373-3810

UNIVERSITY OF MISSOURI
Academic Support Center
505 E. Stewart Rd.
Columbia, Missouri   65211
(314) 882-3601

UNIVERSITY OF NEBRASKA
Instructional Media Center
Lincoln, Nebraska   68588
(402) 472-1911

UNIVERSITY OF NORTH CAROLINA
Bureau of AV Education
P.O. Box 2228
Chapel Hill, N. C. 27514
(919) 933-1108

UNIVERSITY OF SOUTH CAROLINA
Audio Visual Services
Columbia, S.C.   29208
(803) 777-2858

UNIVERSITY OF SOUTHERN CALIFORNIA
Film Distribution Center
Division of Cinema
University Park
Los Angeles, CA   90007

UNIVERSITY OF TEXAS
Visual Instruction Bureau
Drawer W - University Station
Austin, Texas 78712
(512) 471-3573

UNIVERSITY OF TEXAS AT AUSTIN
Center for Middle Eastern Studies
Austin, Texas 78712
(512) 471-3881

UNIVERSITY OF UTAH
Educational Media Center
207 Milton Bennion Hall
Salt Lake city, Utah 84112
(801) 581-6112

UNIVERSITY OF WASHINGTON
Instructional Media Services
23 Kane Hall DG-10
Seattle, Washington 98195
(206) 543-9909

UNIVERSITY OF WISCONSIN
Bureau of AV Instruction
Box 2093
1327 University Ave.
Madison, Wisconsin 53701
(608) 262-1644

UNRWA FILMS
c/o ASSOCIATION-STERLING FILMS
512 Burlington Ave. 94566
La Grange, Illinois 60525

VIEWFINDERS, INC.
2550 Green Bay Rd.
Box 1665
Evanston, Illinois 60204
(312) 869-0600

WALT DISNEY PRODUCTIONS
Educational Film Division
500 S. Buena Vista Ave.
Burbank, CA 91503
(213) 841-2000
(800) 423-2555

WASHINGTON STATE UNIVERSITY
Instruction Media Services
Pullman, Washington 99164
(509) 335-4535

WHEELOCK EDUCATIONAL RESOURCES
P.O. Box 451
Hanover, New Hampshire 03755
(603) 448-3924

WNET (FILM) / CHANNEL 13
356 W. 58th St.
New York, New York 10019

WOMBAT
77 Tarrytown Rd.
White Plains, New York 10607
  or
Little Lake, Glendale Rd.
P.O. Box 70
Ossining, New York 10562

WOMEN'S ORT
1250 Broadway
New York, New York

WORKER'S LEAGUE
540 W. 29th St.
New York, New York 10011

WORLD WIDE PICTURES
1201 Hennepin Ave.
Minneapolis, Minnesota 55403

Arthur ZEGART
30 Smith Ave. South
Nyack, New York 10960

ZIPPORAH FILMS
54 Lewis Wharf
Boston, Massachusetts 02110

DATE DUE